Microsoft® SharePoint® Server 2010 Bible

Steven Mann

WILEY

Wiley Publishing, Inc.

Microsoft® SharePoint® Server 2010 Bible

Published by
Wiley Publishing, Inc.
10475 Crosspoint Boulevard
Indianapolis, IN 46256
www.wiley.com

Copyright © 2010 by Wiley Publishing, Inc., Indianapolis, Indiana

Published simultaneously in Canada

ISBN: 978-0-470-64383-9

Manufactured in the United States of America

10 9 8 7 6 5 4 3 2 1

For general information on our other products and services or to obtain technical support, please contact our Customer Care Department within the U.S. at (877) 762-2974, outside the U.S. at (317) 572-3993 or fax (317) 572-4002.

Library of Congress Control Number: 2010935565

Wiley also publishes its books in a variety of electronic formats. Some content that appears in print may not be available in electronic books.

Acknowledgments

Appreciation is extended to Ramu Pulipati and Samir Patel from RDA Corporation for generating the downloadable content for this publication. Their examples and code extend the concepts within their related chapters and help dive deeper than what is possible in text and figures.

Special thanks to Richard Phillips, one of my previous customers, who continually challenged me to produce solutions within SharePoint and InfoPath that didn't seem possible. Rich kept my skills sharpened and assisted in expanding my knowledge and capabilities.

I'd also like to thank my family and friends for their support and patience as I've worked on this book. I became committed to the revision of the SharePoint 2007 Bible to produce the SharePoint 2010 version from day one and spent countless hours every night to produce a quality publication. Thank you for standing by me during this time.

Thank you to everyone at Wiley that made this book a reality. I would like to thank Aaron Black, my acquisitions editor, and Beth Taylor, the project editor, for being patient with me and helping me along the process.

About the Author

Steve Mann is a Principal Architect for RDA Corporation and has over 16 years of professional experience. He has been focused on collaboration and business intelligence solutions utilizing Microsoft technologies for the past 7 years. Steve managed the internal BI Practice Group at RDA for several years and is still an active participant. He is also heavily involved within RDA's Collaboration/Search Practice Group.

Steve enjoys vacationing with his family along the east coast including locations such as Orlando, Florida; Williamsburg, Virginia; Ocean City, Maryland; Sea Isle City, New Jersey; and New York City and usually hits three or four locations each year.

Credits

Acquisitions Editor
Aaron Black

Executive Editor
Jody Lefevere

Project Editor
Beth Taylor

Technical Editor
Jeffery Charikofsky

Copy Editor
Beth Taylor

Editorial Director
Robyn Siesky

Editorial Manager
Rosemarie Graham

Business Manager
Amy Knies

Senior Marketing Manager
Sandy Smith

Vice President and Executive Group Publisher
Richard Swadley

Vice President and Executive Publisher
Barry Pruett

Project Coordinator
Katie Crocker

Graphics and Production Specialists
Carl Byers
Andrea Hornberger

Quality Control Technician
Melanie Hoffman

Proofreading and Indexing
Christine Sabooni
BIM Indexing & Proofreading Services

Media Development Project Manager
Laura Moss

Media Development Assistant Project Manager
Jenny Swisher

Media Development Associate Producer
Josh Frank

Contents

Contents

Contents

Part II: Configuring SharePoint Server   165

Chapter 6: Using Personalization Features 167

Contents

Contents

Contents

Contents

Contents

Contents

Contents

Contents

Contents

Contents

Introduction

Welcome to the SharePoint Bible for SharePoint Server 2010. I am excited about this release of the SharePoint technologies as it further improves upon all of the great capabilities and features that MOSS 2007 brought to the table. Web content management, records management, workflow, and business intelligence as well as scenarios for collaboration, searching, Internet publishing, document lifecycle management, and reporting are all available on the SharePoint Server 2010 platform. But such a wide range of capabilities can also make it hard to define how you want to install, configure and use SharePoint for your needs.

Although the word has been dropped from the product title with the last release, SharePoint is still a portal product. A portal that is the window to the workings of your company. As with any other window, what you see through it will vary whether it be an outdated, untidy, difficult to enter room (or stagnant, poorly organized, hard to use data) or a vibrant, active, well-informed community (or dynamic, informative, well-organized, easy to use data). The first vision will result in a portal that is not used and will be replaced in an organization sooner or later. The second vision is what SharePoint is all about and our goal in writing this book is to help you find that vision for your organization.

SharePoint is also a technology platform that can be configured and customized to play a number of roles in your organization. For Microsoft, SharePoint has been a fast growing product in terms of revenue and number of seats sold since the initial release in 2001, which means that there is a good chance that SharePoint is available as a toolset for you to use as an information worker, systems architect or developer. Once you have established that you have SharePoint at your fingertips, you know that you have an extensible platform with which you can wow your audience and achieve many objectives.

In this book, I have tried to not only provide a reference for the SharePoint components but also implementation examples for how you might want to use SharePoint. Whether you are deploying SharePoint in a small or large organization or as an Internet, intranet or extranet deployment, we hope that you will find the answers to your questions as well as be inspired by examples of what SharePoint can do for you within these pages. The book's companion Web site has additional information. Go to www.wiley.com/go/sharepointserver2010bible.

I would like to thank RDA Corporation for thinking it was a good idea to get people ramped up on MOSS 2007 back in 2006. I have been working with SharePoint every day since that time and became an expert over the past 3-4 years. With the new 2010 products and platforms coming out, I quickly spent idle time and personal time ramping up on the new features and integration points. The support of our internal practice groups was instrumental in building new environments to explore SharePoint 2010 and Office 2010.

Part I

Getting Started With SharePoint

Introducing SharePoint Products and Technologies

Microsoft SharePoint products and technologies are server applications that facilitate collaboration, provide comprehensive content management, implement business processes, and provide access to information that is essential to organizational goals and processes. They provide an integrated platform to plan, deploy, and manage intranet, extranet, and Internet applications.

Some applications appeal to particular groups of users. For example, SAP, Excel, and Lotus 123 are targeted at CFOs, accountants, and bookkeepers. PowerPoint has always been an essential tool for sales people and professional speakers on many topics.

SharePoint, in contrast, is a set of technologies that has applicability to everyone in an organization. For example: CEOs can use SharePoint KPIs (Key Performance Indicators) and dashboards to see the health of their business or divisions at a glance. Accountants can use Excel services to publish live financial data to a Web page. Knowledge managers and librarians can use SharePoint's document management features to make information discoverable and accessible, while the legal team can breathe easier knowing that their corporate records management policies are being followed. And finally, the thousands of workers in an organization can use Search to find people and information quickly and to discover valuable relationships and information that they may not have realized existed by using the knowledge network and a well-organized portal taxonomy.

This chapter describes Microsoft SharePoint Server 2010, provides a high-level feature comparison between the previous 2007 and new 2010 product versions, and helps the reader choose between SharePoint Foundation and SharePoint Server.

IN THIS CHAPTER

Exploring SharePoint Server 2010

Comparing product versions

Choosing between SharePoint Foundation and SharePoint Server 2010

Exploring SharePoint Server 2010

SharePoint Server 2010, or SPS 2010, is the fourth release of Microsoft's portal offering. You may have heard that Microsoft products hit their stride in the third release. Having worked with SharePoint since the first release (SharePoint Portal Server 2001), we believe that Microsoft has stayed true to form, releasing a robust, mature, and feature-rich portal platform in this version.

You can find many definitions of portal in the marketplace, but because this book is focused on Microsoft's portal offering, I will share the Microsoft definition with you:

A *portal* is a central Web site that can be used to organize and distribute company information. The portal components in SPS 2010 provide technology to facilitate connections between people within the organization who have the required skills, knowledge, and project experience. Some of the portal-specific features provided in SPS are

- **User profiles:** Each user has a set of attributes, such as a phone number or workgroup, which constitutes a user profile. Users can control which attributes in their user profile can be viewed by others. In addition, user profiles can be used when creating audiences to control content viewing.

- **Audiences:** An audience is a group of users defined based on their user profiles. Portal content can be targeted to specific audiences.

- **Content targeting:** The portal content that appears is customized depending on the group membership or SharePoint audience of the person accessing the portal. This increases productivity by ensuring that users get information that is relevant to them.

- **My Site:** Each user can have his or her own personal site named My Site. This site allows users to store their own content and can serve as a central starting point when they are looking for information. Content in My Site can be designated as private or public to control whether other users have access to the content.

- **Enhanced notification services:** Basic notifications can be sent by e-mail to inform users about changed items in lists or document libraries. Users participating in a workflow automatically receive e-mail notifications related to the workflow. SPS adds the ability to be notified when the results of a search query change.

- **Enterprise search:** Enterprise content such as documents, PDF files, SQL databases, Exchange e-mail files, Lotus Notes, and other types of content can all be crawled by the portal server and exposed by using a search query from any page in the portal.

SPS 2010 improves organizational effectiveness by providing an extensive set of technologies and features that address a diverse set of business-critical needs that are often classified in the following categories:

- **Portals:** Including, but not limited to:
  - **Knowledge:** Collections of organizational knowledge and information
  - **Enterprise:** Aggregation points for enterprise applications and data

- **Business intelligence:** Utilizes OLAP (On Line Analytical Processing) and other analytic techniques to provide a dashboard view of trends and data comparisons that shorten the time needed to make decisions

- **Intranet/extranet:** Internal and externally facing portals and Web sites

- **Partner:** Provides a business partner–facing Web presence

- **Sales and marketing:** Web site focused on sales and marketing materials

- **Enterprise search:** Indexing of many types of enterprise documents and data, providing users the ability to issue one query with results returned by relevance regardless of location and format of content

- **Content management:** Web-content organization, publishing, and editing capabilities

- **Document management:** Version control, security, check- in/check-out, indexing, and archival capabilities

- **Policy and records management:** Regulatory and compliance management using a rules disposition engine and records vault with auditing capabilities

- **Collaboration:** Working with teams or projects in geographically dispersed locations using document libraries, lists, blogs, wikis, discussions, and real-time collaborative tools

- **Process automation:** Adding business rules, approvals, and forms to business process

Many of these scenarios are possible with the out-of-the-box configuration, and others are developed as composite applications or third-party solutions that use SPS 2010 as a set of backend services and functionality.

SharePoint 2007 continues to integrate well with Microsoft's products. By exposing collaborative Web-based functionality in Microsoft Office applications, end users can take advantage of advanced features with minimal training in the context of what they are working on. Microsoft Office XP has basic integration with SharePoint, Office 2003 provided many integration enhancements, and Office 2010 provides the most comprehensive and deepest integration with the platform.

Cross-Reference

The integration between SPS 2010 and Office 2010 is discussed in detail in Chapter 13. The integration points include how Office 2010 applications make using SPS easier and how SPS 2010 can publish Office 2010 content. ■

Comparing Microsoft Office SharePoint Server 2007 and SPS 2010

Microsoft Office SharePoint Server 2007 added popular new functionality such as RSS subscriptions, blogs, and wikis, as well as combed the features that were previously provided by Content Management Server 2003 (CMS) and provided a new and improved platform from Microsoft SharePoint Portal Server 2003. MOSS 2007 was the mature portal solution version.

SharePoint Server 2010 builds on the MOSS 2007 paradigm but provides a complete makeover in the process. Eighty percent of the functionality is the same, but it just looks different. That combined with enhanced features, tighter integration with Office and external data, and improved services make SharePoint 2010 an even more mature and extensible portal solution.

Table 1.1 shows the main differences between MOSS 2007 and SPS 2010. This table does not list every feature available in SharePoint but instead lists the most popular improved features and compares and contrasts the differences between the 2007 and the 2010 products.

TABLE 1.1

Microsoft Office SharePoint Server 2007 and SharePoint 2010 Feature Comparison

Category	Microsoft Office SharePoint Server 2007	SharePoint Server 2010
Content Management and Editing	Publishing Pages	Publishing Pages
	Menu Driven	Site Pages
	SharePoint Designer 2007	Office Ribbon Bar
		Wiki-style Editing
		SharePoint Designer 2010
User Experiences with Lists and Libraries	System Pages	Customizable Display Forms
	Custom Web Pages / Web Parts	Customizable Edit Forms
		Customizable View Forms
		AJAX Support
		Cross-browser Compatibility
		Standards Support
Business Intelligence and SQL Server Integration	Microsoft PerformancePoint Server 2007 (separate server)	Built-In PerformancePoint Services
	KPI Lists	Status Lists
	Reporting Services Integrated Mode	Reporting Services Integrated Mode (with almost fully automated installation process)
		PowerPivot (Analysis Services Integrated Mode)
Office Services	Excel Services	Excel Services
	(InfoPath) Form Services	(InfoPath) Form Services
		Access Services
External Data	Business Data Catalog (BDC)	Business Connectivity Services (BCS)

Category	Microsoft Office SharePoint Server 2007	SharePoint Server 2010
Search	Enterprise Search	Enterprise Search
		FAST Search for SharePoint
Shared Services	Shared Services Provider	Service Applications
Silverlight	Custom or third-party controls required	Built-in Silverlight Web Part
		Silverlight Dialogs
Offline Capabilities	Microsoft Groove	SharePoint Workspace

Choosing between SPS and SharePoint Foundation (SF)

SharePoint Foundation 2010 (SF 2010) is a collection of services for Microsoft Windows Server 2008 that can be used to share information; collaborate with other users via document libraries, blogs, wikis, and discussions; and provide the ability to create lists and Web part pages. In addition to off-the-shelf functionality, SF 2010 is used as a development platform for creating collaboration and information-sharing applications. SF 2010 is very popular and often virulently adopted at the department level in organizations because it is included at no additional charge with the purchase of Windows Server 2008 user licenses.

Comparing SPS and SF 2010

SPS 2010 is built on top of SF 2010, and therefore all SharePoint Foundation features are available in an SPS deployment. Table 1.2 compares the two products from a feature perspective.

TABLE 1.2

SPS 2010 and SF 2010 Feature Matrix

Feature	SharePoint Foundation Server 2010	SharePoint Server 2010
PORTAL		
Social networking		X
Sites and documents roll-up Web part		X
Colleagues and memberships Web parts		X
Web parts	X	X

continued

TABLE 1.2 *(continued)*

Feature	SharePoint Foundation Server 2010	SharePoint Server 2010
PORTAL		
Web part pages	X	X
Enterprise search		X
Content targeting		X
Site directory		X
Automatic categorization		X
News		X
Shared services	X	X
Business intelligence		X
Single sign-on		X
Site and list templates	X	X
Infopath server (Form Services)		X
Excel server		X
Collaboration		
Personal sites		X
Team sites	X	X
Wikis	X	X
Blogs	X	X
Alerts	X	X
Configurable alerts to users and groups	X	X
Discussion boards	X	X
Lists	X	X
Surveys	X	X
Workflow		X
Content review and approval	X	X
Site and list templates	X	X
Usability/Integration		
Outlook calendar	X	X
Save to library from Office applications	X	X
Personal views of Web part pages	X	X
Infopath integration	X	X

Feature	SharePoint Foundation Server 2010	SharePoint Server 2010
Document Management		
Document management sites	X	X
Records management		X
Document libraries	X	X
Document- and folder-level security		X
Content Management		
Page layouts and publishing		X
Web page versioning and approval		X
Design control via master pages		X
Browser-based, in-place content editing		X

Comparing features is useful to help understand and delineate the two products, but business size and requirements are also important additional criteria to consider.

Considering organizational size

Most small businesses (5 to 500 information workers) can benefit from an SFS deployment. If an organization is creating and reviewing documents, tracking contacts, customers, and events, or collaborating with other organizations, they are good candidates for SFS. Perhaps there is the need to quickly create Web sites to communicate with internal employees or external customers. Again, SFS is a great solution for rapid Web site deployments.

Small business owners will want to consider starting with or upgrading to SPS if they will be creating a large number of team sites. For example, many small consulting firms will create a new team site for each project. It doesn't take long to recognize the value of having a site directory structure to help organize those sites by project type or category. In addition to the organizational benefits of a site directory, small businesses may want to perform a companywide search across all sites and other data sources.

Generally, it is not recommended to deploy just SFS in an organization larger than 500 users if the intent is to allow users to create their own team sites for collaboration. If you have ever worked with Lotus Notes or SFS 2003, you know that this type of technology spreads virally with the potential to quickly become unmanageable. The exception to this would be the organization that provisions the team sites and document repositories centrally. In this scenario, SFS can scale and provide valuable functionality for any size organization.

Meeting the requirements

Business requirements can help determine which SharePoint product is appropriate for your organization. The SFS requirements usually center on team-level collaboration and support of easy Web publishing, and SPS requirements are focused on enterprise knowledge management and centralization.

Typical SharePoint Foundation requirements

The following requirements can be met with a standard SharePoint Foundation deployment:

- Template-based Web sites to manage meetings, teams, and project documents
- Blogs and wikis provide RSS aggregation
- Share contact lists, event calendars, and announcements with teams, customers, and partners
- Post documents for review and approval
- Provide self-service site creation for end users
- Provide administration for unused Web sites
- Ability to archive project e-mails
- Document management
- Content notification
- Desire to pilot collaboration and knowledge management software to gain acceptance in the organization

If your business requirements are one or more of the above and your organization falls within the organization size considerations, choosing to deploy SharePoint Foundation is appropriate.

Typical SPS requirements

The common SPS business requirements are enterprise scenarios in which it is important to categorize, find, and administer data across a large department or at the enterprise level. The common SPS requirements are

- Provide enterprise content management
- Records management and compliance solutions
- Use enterprise search to easily find posted content
- Ability to create business intelligence (BI) portals
- Provide business process automation
- Provide single sign-on to multiple internal applications
- Desire to push targeted content to users based on their profile within the company
- Provide personal sites and the ability to locate subject matter experts in the organization

If your requirements align with any of these SPS requirements, you should deploy SPS as your portal and collaboration product.

Note

For most organizations that deploy SharePoint Foundation, I recommend central control of team site creation. SharePoint Foundation does not have a central site directory, nor does it provide cross-site search. Sifting through dozens of sites to find what you are looking for can be a frustrating experience for users and administrators. In general, wait until you have deployed SPS to enable self-service site creation. ■

Summary

The SharePoint products are a powerful set of tools to enable collaboration and publishing for organizations. After reading this chapter, you should be familiar with the feature set provided by both SPS and SF 2010 and be able to decide which SharePoint product works best in your organization.

Installing SharePoint

This chapter guides you through the planning and installation of SharePoint by first presenting the available topology choices and Shared Services decisions you need to make for your environment. SharePoint can be configured in any number of ways to suit the scale, scope, and requirements for your organization, and we help you decide what server and services structure are appropriate for your needs.

Once you have decided the topology for your organization, we then walk you through the installation of the prerequisite components and SharePoint software for both SharePoint Foundation and SharePoint Server installations. After the installation process is complete, this chapter will assist you in configuring SharePoint for first use and create your first SharePoint site.

After you complete the steps in this chapter, you will have a working SharePoint installation and a fully functional portal.

IN THIS CHAPTER
Planning your SharePoint deployment
Installing SharePoint
Configuring your SharePoint environment
Creating your first site

Planning Your SharePoint Deployment

Planning your SharePoint deployment is important so that you not only know what to expect during the installation process but also develop your plan for growth and user support. This section presents the decisions you need to make before starting your SharePoint installation and discusses how your portal will integrate with the authentication and messaging components that may be present in your environment.

Choosing your shared service application roles

Shared service applications provide various services to your farm that are available to all Web applications and site collections. These services include Search and Excel services. In SharePoint 2010, each service application is independent, whereas in MOSS 2007 configuring the Shared Service Provider implemented all shared services as one unit.

Shared service applications in SharePoint Server 2010 SPS can be installed on one SharePoint location while providing services to one or more SharePoint instances, with each installation sharing the same settings and administration model. Before you proceed with installation, decide whether you will provide or host shared services or consume shared services, meaning that you are using the shared services provided by another installation.

Unlike MOSS 2007, Web applications consume any available services on an individual basis. The running of the services is no longer an all-or-nothing deal. Multiple examples of the same service application may be deployed using unique names for each. The new model supports cross-farm service applications as well, although this capability depends on the service application supporting multiple farms.

The shared services provided in SharePoint Server 2010 are detailed in Table 2.1.

TABLE 2.1

Service Applications Provided in SharePoint Server 2010

Shared Service	Description
Access Services	Allows for the rendering and editing of Access databases.
Business Data Connectivity Service	The Business Data Connectivity Service lets you make data in external sources available to your SharePoint application. The definitions of what external data sources to connect to and the processing of those connections is performed by this service application. Not only can SharePoint read from these external sources, but when configured appropriately, changes and additions can be written back to the source system.
Excel Services	Provides server-side calculation and thin rendering of Excel workbooks.
Managed Metadata Service	Manages keywords, social tags, taxonomy hierarchies, and content types across site collections.
PerformancePoint Service Application	Enables the creation of scorecards, dashboards, and analytic reports.
Search Service Application	The operations that run search and indexing are shared services. Content sources are defined at the shared service level, and search is responsible for gathering and processing alerts that are set on each portal.
Secure Store Service	Provides a mechanism for storing secure data which is associated to identities (or groups of identities).

Shared Service	Description
State Service	Provides temporary user session state processing for SharePoint components. InfoPath uses the State Service.
Usage and Health Data Collection Reporting	Processing of user activity and health data is done by shared services. Reports on usage and server health are available from this application.
User Profile Service Application	This service application is used to manage profiles, users, audiences, and organizations. It is also used to set up and configure My Sites.
Visio Graphics Service	Enables the rendering of Visio diagrams within SharePoint.
Web Analytics Service Application	Processes and analyzes Web analytics data and provides insight into SharePoint usage.
Word Conversion Service Application	Manages automated document conversions.

Note

An Enterprise License is required to install and use Access Services, Excel Services, PerformancePoint Services, and Visio Graphics Services. ■

The default sharing behavior is to share both the service application and the service data. However, the service data may be partitioned so that the service application is shared but the service data is unique to the Web application or farm. Conversely, the service applications may be deployed to separate application pools and therefore are isolated instances.

If you can agree with another group in your organization about the shared services configuration and administration, you are a good candidate for sharing these services, either as a consumer or a provider. It is important to agree upon the service level of the shared service administration if you opt to share so that expectations are clear. For example, you may want to implement a service level agreement in the organization that outlines processes and the duration of implementing requests to make changes, such as adding content sources to search or uploading a business data catalog entity.

Defining your SharePoint farm topology

Several factors can help you determine what SharePoint farm topology is appropriate for your organization. These factors include:

- The size of your portal content (number of documents and so on)
- Number of SharePoint users
- Expectations of up time
- Scope of the SharePoint services (whether this installation provides or consumes Shared Services)

Based on these factors, you will choose whether a single-server or a farm installation (small, medium, or large farm) is right for your installation. Each scenario is described in detail in the following sections along with some guidelines to help you pick the right topology. It is important to test your proposed architecture in your environment by simulating the users and load on your network by using your hardware and representative sample data.

Physical architecture key concepts

The planning and deployment process involves a few key concepts and terms:

- **Portal topology:** How servers and services are configured and deployed to provide the engine that runs an organization's portal.
- **Server roles:** Servers can be configured with different services so that they play unique roles within your SharePoint deployment.
  - **Web front end:** Renders Web pages and processes business logic.
  - **Application server:** Provides services to the farm such as indexing, search, Excel calculations, and Project Server.
  - **Database:** Runs the SQL Server databases.
- **Server farm:** A collection of servers that work together to provide your SharePoint services.

Choosing your portal topology

You can choose from four possible portal topologies, or distribution of services and servers, for your SPS 2010 deployment. Only the first two (single server and small server farm) are applicable to SharePoint Foundation deployments. The four topologies are described in the following list:

- A single server installation has all the services including SQL Server and SharePoint residing on a single piece of hardware. The SQL Server installation can either be SQL Server Express, SQL Server 2005 SP3, SQL Server 2008 SP1, or SQL Server 2008 R2.
- A small server farm separates the SQL Server back end from the SharePoint front end. The SQL Server can be either SQL Server 2005 SP3 (or later), SQL Server 2008 SP1, or SQL Server 2008 R2. The SPS front end can be one or two servers, and one or both run all of the SharePoint services and are configured as Web servers managing client requests and application servers providing shared service roles.
- A medium server farm has the Web application server separated from the application server and the SQL Server back end. The SQL Server can be either SQL Server 2005 SP3 (or later), SQL Server 2008 SP1, or SQL Server 2008 R2. The Web server front end can be one or more SPS servers providing Web services and search services. The application server is an SPS installation that provides shared services such as indexing and Excel services, if applicable. This topology is not applicable for SharePoint Foundation.
- A large server farm has a clustered SQL Server back end and several Web server front ends and application servers. The front-end Web servers are two or more SPS installations that support client requests. The two or more application servers have the application services such as search, indexing, and Excel services delegated among the servers. This topology is not applicable for SharePoint Foundation.

These topologies vary in number of servers and distribution of services for performance and ability to withstand hardware failures. They also can be differentiated by the number of users that they are designed to support. The following list provides approximate numbers for each topology:

- **Single server with SQL Express:** Typically < 500 users
- **Single server with SQL Server:** Typically < 5,000 users
- **Small farm:** Typically < 50,000 users
- **Medium farm:** Typically < 100,000 users
- **Large farm:** Typically < 500,000 users

Note

The number of users varies depending on usage profiles, type of data being saved, and the type of hardware and network the system is deployed on. ∎

Table 2.2 details sizing guidelines that help you choose the appropriate configuration for your environment based on the number of users that you support, as well as the pros and cons.

TABLE 2.2

SharePoint Server and Farm Topologies

Topology	Number of Servers Required	Applicable to SharePoint Foundation?	Pros	Cons
Single Server	1	Yes	Simple installation	No redundancy
			Can use SQL Server Express, SQL Server 2005 SP3 (or later), SQL Server 2008 SP1, or SQL Server 2008 R2	
			All being the 64-bit edition	
Small Farm	2–3	Yes	Multiple front ends can provide some protection from failure	Data is not protected for server failure
Medium Farm	3–4	No	Provides capacity for growth to break out services	Data is not protected for server failure
Large Farm	6+	No	Provides the most protection against server failure	Requires more server hardware and server hardware maintenance
			Provides great deal of growth capacity	

Considering Administrator Security Needs

SPS provides many levels of administrator security permissions. By defining your administrator roles before the installation, you establish a strategy for managing your portal throughout its deployment.

The administrative levels that you need to consider are

- **Service Application administrators:** These administrators are responsible for configuring and maintaining the shared service applications. It is possible to give permissions to particular items in shared services, like personalization features such as profiles and audiences, but that granularity should only be necessary in the most distributed environments. This level of administration is not necessary for SharePoint Foundation installations.

- **Central admin:** Central administration permissions are specific to the SharePoint farm. There are both operations and application administrative tasks, such as creating and extending Web applications that your administrators with central admin permissions perform.

- **Site owners:** Site owners are allowed to configure the overall site settings for the site, such as content types and navigation.

Integrating with network infrastructure

As with most Microsoft products, integrating with other network server components enables you to extend SharePoint functionality. The following are some of the network interface points you should consider.

Providing authentication

There are several methods available to provide SharePoint authentication. The goal in choosing the authentication method appropriate for your organization is to only require one logon by the user and to use any existing authentication infrastructure.

Active Directory

Active Directory (AD) is the standard default authentication option for organizations that primarily use a Microsoft server infrastructure. As in previous releases, SharePoint integrates nicely with Active Directory out of the box. The key integration points are

- User authentication
- User and group management
- User profile replication
- Active directory federation for single sign on
- AD directory management Web service

Pluggable authentication

SPS and SharePoint Foundation support non-Windows-based identity management systems via integration with ASP.NET pluggable forms. Forms-based authentication allows integration with systems that implement the membership provider interface and provide a way for non-Active directory organizations to integrate with their authentication provider.

Claims-based authentication

SharePoint 2010 supports claims-based authentication such that identities may be authenticated using the claims assertion model which has been extended in Active Directory to support non-Windows authentication of users within a domain.

Cross-Reference

See Chapter 10 for more information on using pluggable authentication. ■

SQL Server authentication

As with the forms-based authentication method, it is now possible to bypass Windows authentication and authenticate directly with SQL Server. This is useful for environments that don't have any authentication provider available.

Using SQL Server

If you are deploying any of the farm configurations, the back-end database server must be running SQL Server 2005 SP3 (or later), SQL Server 2008 SP1, or SQL Server 2008 R2. If you are installing a single-server scenario, you can either have an SQL Server 2005 SP3 (or later), SQL Server 2008 SP1, or SQL Server 2008 R2 database, or you can use SQL Server Express (installed during SharePoint installation). All SQL Server editions must be 64-bit.

Using Exchange Server

Exchange server is one of the most widely deployed corporate e-mail server platforms in the world. Configuring SharePoint to send e-mail via exchange or using SMTP is straightforward. SharePoint also includes protocol handlers that allow the indexer to crawl Exchange content and make it available in the portal. Other areas of integration include:

- Using public folders for team site e-mail integration
- Accepting incoming e-mail SharePoint through discussion boards, calendars, document libraries, and announcements
- Accessing inboxes, calendars, and to-do lists via Web Parts

Installing Your SharePoint Farm Components

After you have chosen the right product and topology for your organization, you can proceed with installing the necessary prerequisite components and SharePoint. By the end of this section, you should have successfully installed SharePoint.

Installing prerequisite components

Several prerequisites must be installed before proceeding with your SharePoint installation. If any of these components are not installed at the time of the main SharePoint installation, the installation will fail. The SharePoint 2010 Preparation Tool ensures that all requirements are met and installs (and possibly configures if needed) any software or operating system requirements. You do need to meet the base hardware and software requirements before proceeding.

Checking the hardware and software requirements

SharePoint requires a 64-bit, four-core processor computer with 2.5 GHz of speed per core or higher and at least 8GB of RAM. The servers must be running Windows Server 2008 with SP2 or Windows Server 2008 R2. If the server(s) are running Windows 2008 Server without SP2, the preparation tool automatically downloads and applies the service pack for you.

For development purposes, SharePoint may be installed and executed on the 64-bit versions of Windows 7 or Windows Vista.

Note

It is not recommended to install SharePoint on a domain controller for a production environment. Although it is possible, it complicates the installation and maintenance and therefore creates unnecessary difficulty. This is not a supported or encouraged installation procedure. ■

Installing SQL Server

You must install SQL before starting the SharePoint install if you are using any of the farm topologies or have chosen not to use SQL Server Express with your single-server installation.

After you have installed SQL Server 2005/2008, you need to configure the connections by following the steps below on the server that runs your SQL Server:

1. Choose Start ⇨ All Programs ⇨ Microsoft SQL Server 2005 (or 2008) ⇨ Configuration Tools ⇨ SQL Server Surface Area Configuration.

2. In the dialog, click Surface Area Configuration for Services and Connections.

3. Expand your instance of SQL Server, expand Database Engine, and click Remote Connections.

4. Click Local and Remote Connection, select Using both TCP/IP and named pipes, and click OK.

Running the SharePoint 2010 Preparation Tool

The SharePoint 2010 Preparation Tool installs all of the necessary prerequisite software onto the server. Depending on what or what is not already on the server, the preparation tool installs or configures the following items:

- Windows Server 2008 SP2
- Web Server (IIS) role
- Application Server role
- Microsoft .NET Framework version 3.5 SP1
- Microsoft "Geneva" Framework
- Microsoft Sync Framework Runtime v1.0 (x64)
- Microsoft Filter Pack 2.0
- Microsoft Chart Controls for the Microsoft .NET Framework 3.5
- Windows PowerShell 2.0 CTP3
- SQL Server 2008 Native Client
- Microsoft SQL Server 2008 Analysis Services ADOMD.NET
- ADO.NET Data Services v1.5 CTP2

Note

If Windows PowerShell 1.0 was previously installed on the server, you need to uninstall it before Windows PowerShell 2.0 CTP3 can be successfully installed. ■

1. From the product disc, run setup.exe or officeserver.exe from the product download.

2. Under the Install section of the setup splash screen, click on the Install Software Prerequisites link.

   The preparation tool runs and displays a list of software components that will be installed. Click Next.

3. Accept the license terms on the next screen and click Next.

   The preparation tool installs and configures the necessary software.

4. Click Finish on the finished screen when the installation is completed.

Note

The preparation tool uses the Microsoft Download Center, and therefore the server must have Internet access to perform the proper installations. ■

Preparing administrative accounts

You will need one to many administrative accounts based on your chosen topology. If you are installing on a single server, you will need an account that belongs to the administrator group on your server.

If you are installing SharePoint in any of the farm topologies, you will need the following accounts:

- **Installation account:** This account is the one used during the SharePoint installation and is automatically given full rights to all of your SharePoint administrative tasks during the installation. It must be a domain account, a member of the administrator group on the front-end and application servers, a member of the SQL Server Logins (to have access to your SQL Server instance), and a member of the SQL Server Security Administrators and Database Creators roles.

- **Service account:** SharePoint uses this account to connect to the configuration database and as the application identity for the central administration application pool. This account must be a domain user account; SharePoint grants the appropriate SQL permissions during installation (SQL Server Logins, Database Creator, and Security Administrators roles).

- **Search service account:** This is the account under which the search service runs. It must be a member of the administrator group on the computer running the search service and should have read access to all content on the network that will be crawled. SharePoint respects access control lists (ACLs) and returns only search hits to which a user has access.

- **Web application identity account:** This account is the application pool identity for your Web application. This account must be a domain user account.

- **Shared services application service account:** This is the account under which your service applications run. This account must be a domain user account.

You can combine these accounts to use fewer accounts if the less-distributed permission model is appropriate given the security policies for your organization.

Note

SharePoint 2010 automatically synchronizes with your Active Directory password changes once the account is configured. In past versions, managing password changes was a time-consuming process because this synchronization did not exist. ■

Installing SharePoint

The three installation scenarios to choose from are single server installation (applies to both SharePoint Foundation and SPS), a farm installation for SharePoint Foundation, and a farm installation for SPS.

Installing on a single server with SQL Server Express

If you are installing on a single server with SQL Server Express, you can install SharePoint with the Standalone option. Follow these steps:

1. **From the product disc, run setup.exe or officeserver.exe from the product download.**

2. **Enter your product key when prompted and click Continue.** (This step is not necessary if you are installing SharePoint Foundation.)

3. **Review the terms of the Microsoft Software License, select I accept the terms of this agreement, and click Continue.**

4. **Choose the installation you want:** Click on Standalone.

5. **Complete the installation by selecting the Run the SharePoint Products and Configuration Wizard now check box, and then click Close to launch the wizard.**

6. **Click Next on the welcome page of the wizard.**

7. **Click Yes on the page notifying that services might need to be restarted or reset.**

8. **Click Finish.** SharePoint central administration opens.

Installing SharePoint Foundation in a farm configuration

The following installation steps must be done on every front-end server before creating sites and configuring services:

1. **From the SharePoint Foundation 2010 product disc, run setup.exe or officeserver.exe.**

2. **Click on the Install SharePoint Foundation link on the setup splash screen.**

3. **Review the terms of the Microsoft Software License, select I Accept the Terms of This Agreement, and click Continue.**

4. **On the Choose the installation you want screen, click on the Server Farm button.**

5. **Select the Complete option on the Server Type tab and if desired click on the Data Location tab to change the data directory path. Click Install Now.**

6. **Complete the installation by selecting the Run the SharePoint Products and Configuration Wizard now check box and then click Close to launch the wizard.**

The SharePoint Products and Configuration Wizard walks you through the steps necessary to connect to the back-end database.

1. **Click Next on the welcome page of the wizard.**

2. **Click Yes on the page notifying that services might need to be restarted or reset.**

3. **On the connect to a server farm page, select one of the options:**

   - If you are configuring your first front-end server, click Create a new server farm and then click Next.

   - If you have already configured your first front-end server, click Connect to an existing server farm and then click Next.

4. On the Specify Configuration Database page, enter the name of your back-end computer in the database server field:

   - If you are configuring your first front-end server, use the default database name for the configuration database, or type your own name in the database name field.
   - If you have already configured your first front-end server, click retrieve database names, and in the database name field select the database that you used for your configuration database (default name is SharePoint_Config).

5. Enter the service account username in the username field in domain\username format and the password in the password field and click Next.

6. Enter a farm passphrase and confirm the passphrase. Click Next.

7. **If you are configuring your first front-end server, select the Specify port number check box and enter a port number for SharePoint Central Administration on the SharePoint Central Administration Web Application page.** If you leave the specify port number box unchecked, it assigns a random number (which is shown in the port box).

8. **If you are configuring your first front-end server, select whether you want to use NTLM (the default) or Negotiate (Kerberos) authentication.** If you select Kerberos, you must support Kerberos in your environment.

9. **Review your settings on the Completing the SharePoint Products and Technologies Wizard page and click Next. (Click Advanced Settings if you wish to setup accounts from Active Directory.)**

10. **Click Finish.** SharePoint central administration opens.

Installing SPS in a farm configuration

The following installation steps must be done on every SharePoint server before creating sites and configuring services. If you have a topology that has multiple front-end servers, all the front-end servers must have the same SharePoint products installed:

1. From the product disc, run setup.exe or officeserver.exe from the product download.

2. On the setup splash screen, click on the Install SharePoint Server link.

3. Enter your product key when prompted and click Continue.

4. Review the terms of the Microsoft Software License, select I Accept the Terms of this Agreement, and click Continue.

5. Change the file locations if desired on the file location screen.

6. Click Install Now.

7. Complete the installation by selecting the Run the SharePoint Products and Configuration Wizard now check box and then click Close to launch the wizard.

The SharePoint Products and Configuration Wizard walks you through the steps necessary to connect to the back-end database:

1. Click Next on the welcome page of the wizard.

2. Click Yes on the page notifying that services might need to be restarted or reset.

3. On the connect to a server farm page, select one of the options:

   - If you are configuring your first front-end server, click Create a new server farm and then click Next.

   - If you have already configured your first front-end server, click Connect to an existing server farm and then click Next.

4. On the Specify Configuration Database page, enter the name of your back-end computer in the database server field:

   - If you are configuring your first front-end server, use the default database name for the configuration database, or type your own name in the database name field.

   - If you have already configured your first front-end server, click Retrieve Database names, and in the database name field select the database that you used for your configuration database (default name is SharePoint_Config).

5. Enter the service account username in the username field in domain\username format and the password in the password field and click Next.

6. Enter a farm passphrase and confirm the passphrase. Click Next.

7. If you are configuring your first front-end server, select the Specify port number check box and enter a port number for SharePoint Central Administration on the SharePoint Central Administration Web Application page. If you leave the specify port number box unchecked, it assigns a random number (which is shown in the port box).

8. If you are configuring your first front-end server, select whether you want to use NTLM (the default) or Negotiate (Kerberos) authentication. If you select Kerberos, you must support Kerberos in your environment.

9. Review your settings on the Completing the SharePoint Products and Technologies Wizard page and click Next.

10. Click Finish. SharePoint central administration opens.

Central Administration Configuration

The SharePoint installation creates a central administration console that opens when you complete the installation. Central administration is located on the first SharePoint server that you install in your farm and can be accessed by using a Web browser by `http://<servername>:port`, where `<servername>` is the physical server name of your first server and `port` is the port number that was either randomly generated during installation or that you specified. A program entry is added to your Start Menu under the SharePoint 2010 Products heading so you don't need to memorize the URL or port number.

After a successful installation, there are several things to configure at the central administration level for both SPS and SharePoint Foundation installations.

Configuring your SharePoint Farm

When Central Administration is rendered for the first time, the Configure your SharePoint Farm configuration wizard is presented to be launched:

1. Click on the Start the Wizard button.
2. Select a managed service account or create a new one by entering in the information in the account text boxes. Select the services that you wish to run on the server. Click Next.
3. You may create the root site collection now using the next screen or you can click on Skip. The site collection creation is described in the next section of this chapter.

Configuring incoming/outgoing e-mail settings

Outgoing e-mail settings enable SharePoint to send alerts and site notifications by Simple Mail Transfer Protocol (SMTP).

1. Open SharePoint Central Administration and select System Settings.
2. Click Outgoing e-mail settings under the Email and Text Messages (SMS) section.
3. Enter the name or IP address of your e-mail server in the Outbound SMTP server field.
4. Enter the e-mail address that you want to use as the from address in the From address field. This is the address that the mail sent by the server will appear to be from.
5. Enter the reply-to address in the reply-to address field. This is the address used when a user replies to e-mail sent by the server. It is recommended to use a distribution list as the reply-to address so that e-mails get sent to the appropriate user(s), and you can maintain that distribution list to reflect changes in your server administrator organization.
6. Click OK.

Note

Make sure that your SMTP server is configured to accept e-mails from your SharePoint server. Many e-mail servers limit the scope of servers that they accept outgoing mail from to reduce the possibility that unknown servers will relay mail through their services. If the SMTP server is not configured to accept e-mail from the SharePoint server, the e-mails get dropped and are not sent. ■

By configuring incoming e-mail settings, you enable SharePoint sites to accept and archive incoming e-mail to support features like archiving e-mail discussions, saving e-mailed documents, and presenting calendar invites on site calendars. To configure incoming e-mail settings, follow these steps:

1. Open SharePoint Central Administration and select System Settings.

2. Click Incoming E-Mail Settings under the Email and Text Messages (SMS) section.

3. Select Yes under Enable sites on this server to receive e-mail.

4. Select the Automatic settings mode.

5. Enter a display name for the e-mail server in the E-mail server display name text box.

6. Click OK.

Alternating access mapping

Alternate access mapping allows you to set different names for your default, intranet, and extranet portals. The default portal name is returned for most users (although SharePoint maintains the namespace by which the user accessed the portal). Your default name is configured when you install SharePoint and is set to the physical name of your server. To set the name to be a host name all front-end servers will respond to, you need to change the alternate access mapping by following these steps:

1. Open SharePoint Central Administration and select Application Management.

2. Click Alternate access mappings under the Web Applications section.

3. Select the incoming URL that you want to edit and type in the URL that you want to use.

4. Click OK.

5. Click Edit Public URLs and enter the URL that you want to be used to access your site in the default zone field and click Save.

Tip

You will need to make a DNS entry for the host name so that users can resolve the name. There are several ways to get multiple front-end machines to share this name and load-balance the Web traffic. One method is to use DNS round robin, which is to say that you enter the IP address for each of your front-end machines under one name host entry. DNS then rotates through those names, giving each subsequent user request the next IP address entry until it reaches the end of the list and starts again at the top. This method is inexpensive and straightforward but does not have any automation built in to check that each of the servers is up and responding to requests before handing out the request. Therefore, if you have a server down, you need to modify the DNS entry to remove that IP address from the list.

There are both hardware and software products that do load balancing, and they automate checking the status of the target servers to make sure they are available for requests before sending users to the server. You may want to consider making the investment on this hardware if your topology is large enough or if you cannot risk users being delivered to a server that is not responding. ■

Configuring diagnostics logging

Diagnostics logging is important for troubleshooting and includes trace logs, event messages, user-mode error messages, and Customer Experience Improvement Program events.

SharePoint allows you to configure how many log files and what type of events to capture so that you modulate the size and depth of your logged information. The default settings are good for normal mode operations, but you may want to tune them if you have server or application issues. To modify the diagnostic logging settings, follow these steps:

1. Open SharePoint Central Administration and select Monitoring.
2. Click Diagnostic logging under the Reporting section.
3. Select All Categories or use the tree view to select individual categories and sub-catagories (click on the plus sign to expand the categories).
4. Modify the Least critical event to report to the event log drop-down to capture more or less granular event data.
5. Modify the Least critical event to report to the trace log drop-down to capture more or less granular event data.
6. Change the path if you would like to store the log files in a different location.
7. Change the Number of log files field if you want to save more or less log data.
8. Change the Number of minutes to use a log file if you want to increase or decrease the size of each log file.
9. Click OK.

Backing up a SharePoint farm

Backups are a vital component to protecting your SharePoint data and providing a method for recovering from server failure. To back up your SharePoint farm, do the following:

1. Open SharePoint Central Administration and select Backup and Restore from the Quick Launch bar.
2. In the Farm Backup and Restore section, click Perform a Backup.
3. Select the check box next to the Farm option at the top of the page.
4. Click Next.
5. Select Full or Differential in the Type of backup section. Full creates a backup of all the SharePoint farm settings. Differential creates a backup of all SharePoint data that has changed since your last successful full backup. You should do a full backup at least once a week.
6. Enter the file location for the backup files. This path can either be a UNC path or a local file path.
7. Select OK.

Application configuration

The Application Management page provides links to the activities necessary to manage your sites and applications.

Add administrator group to manage Web applications

During the installation, the account used to install SharePoint is by default given broad administrator access for the farm. During the postinstallation configuration, you should grant an administrator group the same level of access that your install account was given so that all administrative tasks are possible for the right group of administrators. To grant this access, follow these steps:

1. Open SharePoint Central Administration and select Application Management.
2. Select Manage Web applications under the Web Applications section.
3. Select the Web application for which you want to grant administrator privileges.
4. Select User Policy from the Ribbon.
5. Click Add Users, select the Zone, click Next, and then add the group or user. Select the Full Control check box.
6. Click Finish.

Turn on self-service site creation

Enabling self-service site creation allows end users with the appropriate permissions to create their own site. By turning on this option, an announcement is added to the top-level Web site, advertising the ability for users to create sites. By default, the setup process automatically turns this on. However, to turn self-service site creation on or off, follow these steps:

1. Open SharePoint Central Administration and select Application Management.
2. Click Configure self-service site creation in the Site Collection section. (You may also reach the same settings from the Security Page under the General Security section.)
3. Select the Web application from which you want to enable self-service site creation from the Web application pull-down menu.
4. Select On (or Off).
5. Select the Require Secondary Contact box if you want to force users to enter at least two contacts when creating a site. Having a secondary contact often prevents sites from becoming orphaned when the primary contact leaves the organization or changes roles.
6. Click OK.

Associating Web applications and SSAs

After you have created a Web application, you need to configure which shared services it should consume. A Service Application can support multiple Web applications. To associate your Web applications with a Service Application, follow these steps:

1. Open SharePoint Central Administration and select Application management from the quick launch.
2. Select Manage Web applications under the Web Applications section.

3. Select the Web application by clicking on the row and then select Service Connections from the Ribbon.

4. Select services that the Web Application should consume.

5. Click OK.

Configuring Excel Services

Excel Services extends the business intelligence capabilities provided with SPS and enables dynamic, easy publishing with Office 2010 Excel spreadsheets. This service is available if you have installed the Enterprise version of SPS. To install and configure Excel Services, follow the steps below:

Cross-Reference

See Chapter 13 for more information on integration with Office 2010 and Chapter 14 for more information on business intelligence. ∎

1. Open SharePoint Central Administration and click on Application Management.

2. Click on Manage service applications under the Service Applications section.

3. Find the Excel Services Application (this is the proxy entry) and click on the link under the entry (this is the application entry).

4. Click Trusted File Locations.

5. Click Add Trusted File Location.

6. **Type the address of the trusted file location in the Address field.** This address can be a SharePoint 2010 site (recommended) or any http Web site or universal naming convention (UNC) path.

7. Click Windows SharePoint Services in the location type if your location is a SharePoint 2007 site, or click http or UNC as appropriate for your source.

8. **Select the trust level for external data sources in Allow External Data.** Levels are as follows:

   - **None:** This setting prevents Excel Calculation Services from processing links to any external data connection.

   - **Trusted data connection libraries only:** This setting allows Excel Calculation Services to process links to trusted data connection libraries but not links to external data sources.

   - **Trusted data connection libraries and embedded:** This setting allows Excel Calculation Services to process links to trusted data connection libraries and to process links to external data sources.

9. Click Ok.

Cross-Reference

Please see Chapter 9 for more information about configuring and using Excel services. ∎

Creating Top-Level Sites

After you have performed your installation and initial SharePoint configuration, you can proceed with creating and configuring your portal or top-level site collection.

Creating a top-level site is the fun part of the installation process because you finally get to see the results of your SharePoint installation efforts. The process is slightly different depending on whether you have installed SharePoint Foundation or SPS, mostly with regard to the site templates and services that are available. For SPS installations you are creating a top-level site that is a portal because it has all the portal services such as search available to it. See Chapter 3 for a complete description of the site templates.

The installation process creates the main Web application. However, the following steps explain the manual process for creating a new one.

To create a Web application, follow these steps:

1. **Open SharePoint Central Administration and select Application Management from the Quick Launch bar.**

2. **Under the Web Application section, click Manage Web Applications.**

3. **Click New on the Ribbon.**

4. **Click Create a New IIS Web site and change the port setting to 80 so that users do not have to specify the port number in the URL.** Port 80 is the standard port expected by Web browsers.

5. **Select NTLM or Negotiate (Kerberos) as the appropriate authentication provider in the Security Configuration section.** NTLM is recommended, but if you choose Kerberos, it must be supported by your environment.

6. **In the Application Pool section, click Create new application pool.**

7. **Type the name of your application pool or use the default name in the Application pool name field.**

8. **Enter your Web application identity account credentials in the username and password field in domain\username format.** For more information about the Web application identity account, see the "Preparing administrative accounts" section in this chapter.

9. **Verify the database information in the Database Name and Authentication section.**

10. **Click Windows authentication in the Database Name and Authentication section.**

11. **Select the service connections for this Web application.**

12. **Click OK.**

13. **Verify that your new Web application has been created on the Application Created page.**

14. **Open a command prompt window (Run As Administrator), type** iisreset, **and then press Enter.**

After your Web application has been created, you can proceed with creating a site collection for it. The site collection creation is part of the configuration wizard; however, to create a site collection follow these steps:

1. **Open SharePoint Central Administration and select Application Management from the Quick Launch bar.**

2. **In the Site Collection section, click Create Site Collection.**

3. **In the Web application drop-down list, select the Web application that you created in the previous steps above.**

4. **Enter a title and description for your site.**

5. **In the Web site address section, click the Create site at this URL option and then choose root in the URL path.**

6. **Enter a username for the site collection administrator in the Primary Site Collection Administrator section.**

7. **Select No Quota in the Quota Template section.** Alternatively, you can create a quota template to limit the size of the site collection by clicking the Manage Quota Templates link in that section and apply it to this site collection.

8. **Select your template for the site collection from the available templates in the template selection section.**

   If you are using SharePoint Foundation, a suggested template for departmental sites is the Team Sites template.

   If you are using SPS, a suggested template for intranet portals is the Team Site template from the Collaboration tab.

9. **Click OK.**

Configuring a Site

Now that you have created your site, you are ready to configure it for first use. The installation process automatically creates three site groups for your site collection. The groups are as follows:

- **Owners:** This group is for users who will manage your site collection. They have access to manage permissions, navigation, and site settings.

- **Members:** The members group is for users who will contribute to your site collection. Because SharePoint has library-, list-, and file-level security, the members will not have access to items from which they have been excluded.

- **Visitors:** Members of the visitors group have read access to your site collection.

Using these site groups helps to keep SharePoint security management centralized and easy to audit. To assign users to these groups so that they can start working with the portal:

1. Use a browser to open the home page of your site.

2. From the top-left corner, click Site Actions and then click Site Settings.

3. In theUsers and Permissions section, click People and Groups in the.

4. Select the site group that you want to add users to from the left navigation bar.

5. Click New on the top navigation bar and click Add users.

6. Add the users that you want to add to the group in domain\username format and separate them with a semicolon if you are adding multiple users.

7. Click OK.

Summary

This chapter discussed choosing the right SharePoint topology for your organization and the planning steps required for a successful SharePoint implementation. After those planning steps, it walked through the necessary prerequisites for installation and then installed SharePoint. The final sections of this chapter talked about the necessary post-installation configuration steps and the creation of your first top-level site. You should now be ready to begin working with your fully operational SharePoint installation.

Using Sites and Pages

A portal is based on the building blocks of sites and publishing page libraries. These key elements make it possible for SharePoint users to collaborate, publish content, and find content. This chapter shows you how to plan the structure of how sites make up your portal and design the navigation of your sites. In addition, we review the functionality provided by SharePoint sites and site templates. We show you step by step how to create your own site templates so that you can reuse site functionality and structure that you have designed for your organizational needs.

Page layouts are a Web content management feature that allows you to design the layout for a page. This layout is stored separately from the content of the page so that you can centrally update page layouts without having to modify each page that is using the layout. I describe this functionality in detail and provide the steps to show you how to customize this powerful functionality.

Designing Your Site Structure

If you start your site development by planning your site structure, the growth of your SharePoint environment will be logical to your users and administrators. A well-planned hierarchy of sites provides the following advantages:

- **Security inheritance:** Sites that are grouped together so that the sub-sites can inherit the site groups from the parent sites lessen the time spent on security administration. If you can manage the membership of the site group on one site and then use those site groups on multiple sites, the membership is more likely to be maintained accurately and consistently than if you are maintaining the groups in multiple sites.

- **Autonomy for teams and divisions:** Creating autonomous branches for unique teams and/or divisions allows them to work independently and add content and columns without affecting other teams and divisions.

- **Logical navigation:** The navigation provided with SharePoint 2010 relies to a great degree on breadcrumbs that show you the entire path from your site to the top level of the portal. By organizing your site structure, this breadcrumb navigation will be more useful to your users.

- **Aggregation of data:** A common requirement for organizations is that content is published in just one location and then displayed in every location pertinent to that content or topic. For example, you can publish a team document that your team members will share, but this content should also be available to be displayed at a division and enterprise level. If your site hierarchy is well constructed, this aggregation of data is possible.

In the following sections, I walk you through the steps necessary to create a well-organized and effective site structure.

Defining site-related terms

Whether you have worked extensively with SharePoint or other portal technology before, several of the site-related terms used to describe sites and their attributes may already mean something to you. These terms are defined in this section in order to eliminate any confusion caused by different interpretations of terminology.

- **Portal:** A portal is a central Web site that can be used to organize and distribute company information. For SharePoint technologies, SPS has the necessary features to aggregate company information and WSS does not (for example, audiences and user profiles and enterprise search).

- **Metadata:** Data used to describe content contained in a library or list. For example, you can add a metadata column to a document library that requires users to provide the document status such as draft, in review, or final when they upload a document.

- **Top-level site:** This site is at the root of your sites. This site has sub-sites but is not a sub-site of another site.

- **Namespace:** This is the name that you use to address your top-level site. This name could be a host name or a fully qualified domain name (FQDN) and should be a persistent name (changed rarely) to help avoid confusing users of the portal and sites by changing URLs too often. For example, if you have a division-level intranet portal for human resources, this name would be `http://hr`, or if you have an extranet portal for your company, the namespace would be `http://extranet.company.com`.

- **Managed Path:** A path under the root site in which additional site collections may be created within the same Web application. For example, /sites/ is a preconfigured managed path (meaning it is created during installation and is considered an out-of-the-box managed path), and therefore you may create a new site collection under `http://<servername>/sites/<new site collection name>`.

- **Site Collection:** A site collection defines a boundary between SharePoint sites. Within a site collection you can share navigation, site groups, content (using the content query Web Part or dataview Web Part), and workflows with other sites in the collection.

Cross-Reference
See Chapter 5 for more information on Web Parts. ∎

- **Taxonomy:** A classification that you use to divide your organization's information into a hierarchical scheme your users can understand.

You can think of top-level sites as sites that require their own namespace. This could be based on your organizational structure, the scope of the namespace (intranet or extranet or Internet), or the purpose of the site (document collaboration site or records management site). Working with the key stakeholders (IT leaders, interested parties from each division, and Internet/extranet publishers) in your company, you must determine which of the following items need to have their own namespace:

- **Divisions:** Can all divisions share the same namespace such as `http://portal` for intranet collaboration? If not, what division-level namespaces do you need?

- **Projects:** Are there any projects or initiatives within your organization that require their own namespace? You should only create portals based on projects if the projects are long term because namespace choices should be persistent.

- **Central portal:** If you have chosen to create smaller portals for your organization, you should create a central portal that can pull all your overall organizational content into one location.

- **Extranet:** If you are planning extranet collaboration with partners and customers, we recommend a separate namespace from your intranet content so that internal users are clear where they are posting content. It is less likely that users will accidentally post internal-only content to the extranet namespace.

- **Team Sites:** Do you want to have a namespace (or managed path) for self-service site creation? If you have teams that will be creating collaboration sites that are not logically related to any of your division, creating a separate namespace (or managed path) for self-service sites is recommended.

- **Specific purpose sites:** Do you need separate namespaces to support specific applications or purposes? Examples of these applications are portals for staging Web content or Excel servers or project servers.

As you make the namespace decisions, keep in mind that these sites need their own URL. If what you or your users want is a friendly name for a site that resolves to a URL that is part of a different namespace, you should use a redirect to support that friendly name. Resolving `http://IT` to a site that is located on `http://portal/IT` is not a namespace but instead a friendly name. See the section "Implementing Your Site Structure" later in this chapter for instructions on how to implement a friendly name redirect.

Defining site collections and site maintenance policies

After you have defined your top-level sites, you need to define the site collections for each top-level site and the maintenance policies that will be applied to them. Site collections isolate content into logical groupings and maintenance policies to help manage their usage and life cycle.

Defining site collections

As defined earlier, site collections are divisions of security, content, and navigation, so your decision to create multiple site collections involves creating more autonomous sites. Your top-level site is a site collection, so you must create more site collections in that namespace. To decide whether you need additional site collections, consider the following factors:

- **Security:** You can use site security groups across a site collection to ease administration. These are the visitors, members, and owners groups created by SharePoint, or any custom groups that you define for the site collection. If a portion of your site has unique security requirements, it is good candidate for a new site collection.

- **Portability/Administration:** Site collections are easy to package up and move (between portals and other top-level sites) and backup/restore at a site level (or sites and sub-sites within the site collection). If you need these capabilities for portions of your top-level site, consider making site collections to match the portions of your site that may need to move.

- **Navigation:** Within a site collection, you can choose to use the global navigation from the parent site or not. However, you do not have this choice if you are in a different site collection. When creating site collections, keep in mind that navigation to other site collections will not be possible using the out-of-the-box navigation.

- **Self-service site creation:** Most site collections are created by the top-level site administrators. However, when you turn on self-service site creation, all sites that users of this feature create will be site collections. The idea behind this is that the self-service user should be an island that is separated from the other self-service users. Self-service sites are great for users that create their own sites for team, project, or community interaction. These sites may or may not be persistent within the organization, but because they are end-user driven as opposed to information-architecture driven, they should be isolated from each other in site collections.

Note

Site collections are created and contained within unique content databases and therefore cannot span across content databases. Portability is dependent on the backup and restore of the respective content databases. ■

Cross-Reference

See Chapter 2 for the steps necessary to turn on self-service site creation. ■

Defining site maintenance policies

Site maintenance policies help you manage the growth and content for your site collections, especially the site collections created by end users that may not have a lot of administrator oversight or visibility. SharePoint provides two tools to manage site collections:

- **Site collection quotas:** You can create one or more quotas that limit the size (measured in MB) of site collections.

- **Site use confirmation and deletion:** To help eliminate sites that might be forgotten or abandoned, SharePoint monitors sites and notifies the site owner when the sites are not used; if this option is selected, SharePoint can also delete the site if no action is taken after notification. Site use and confirmation parameters are defined for each Web application.

Although both tools help you manage SharePoint space utilization, they have different roles in the SharePoint life cycle. The site collection quotas help more with planning the growth of your SharePoint storage, whereas the use confirmation and deletion policy helps you reclaim unused space.

Creating site collection quotas

When created, site collection quotas are applied to site collections. However, you can change the template applied to site collections after the site collections are created by using the central administration console. To start, you define the site quotas for your organization:

1. **List the site quotas that you need.** Site collections vary on uses and content and therefore most likely require different quotas.

2. **For each of the site quotas, determine the warning size and maximum size for the site collection.** The difference between the warning size and the maximum size should be a reasonable number so that the site collection owner has time to react to the warning before the maximum is reached. For example, if your warning size is 80MB and the maximum size is 81MB, the 1MB difference will probably be met and exceeded before the site collection owner has time to take an action from the warning.

To create a site quota template:

1. **Open SharePoint Central Administration and select Application Management from the Quick Launch.**

2. **Click Specify Quota templates under the Site Collections section.**

3. **Select Create a New Quota template and provide a new template name.**

4. **Enter your maximum size in MB and size for when an e-mail warning is sent in MB.**

5. **Click OK.**

6. **Repeat Steps 1 to 5 for all templates that you have defined.**

To apply a site quota to a site collection after it has been created:

1. **Open SharePoint Central Administration and select Application Management from the Quick Launch.**

2. **Click Configure quotas and locks under the Site Collections section.**

3. **Select the site collection to which you would like to apply or modify the quota template from the Site Collection drop-down menu.**

4. Select the desired quota template in the Current quota template drop-down menu.

5. Click OK.

Defining site use confirmation and deletion parameters

Of course, if you are an IT administrator, you hope that users delete their collaboration sites when the sites are no longer necessary. However, this does not always happen because users often think they might need the information later or that others are still possibly accessing the data.

To manage unused sites, SharePoint allows you to create site use confirmation and deletion policies at the Web application level. These policies allow you to define:

- **How often to ask users to confirm that their site is still in use:** This parameter lets you set the number of days after the site is created or confirmed to still be in use to contact the site owner for confirmation. This number should reflect the duration of a typical project life cycle in your organization. The default is 90 days, but that probably is low for most organizations. Setting this to 180 days is a pretty reasonable interval so that users get prompted for a use confirmation two times a year.

- **How often to check for unused sites and send e-mails:** You can set the interval (daily, weekly, or monthly) and hour for when usage processing should take place.

- **Whether to automatically delete sites if use is not confirmed:** You can select whether you want SharePoint to delete sites if they are not confirmed to be in use (site collections are presented with a URL to click if the site owners want to confirm that the site is in use). If you do automatically delete, you tell SharePoint how many notices to send before the deletion. So, if you select to delete after four notices and the notices are processed weekly, the user will have four weeks to confirm that the site is in use. Make sure that the users have plenty of time; otherwise someone could come back from vacation to find his or her inbox filled with site notices and a deleted SharePoint site.

Caution

If you do enable automatic deletion be sure that your outgoing e-mail is enabled and working. The site-deletion process relies on sending messages to site collection owners that provide a URL to click on and confirm site usage. If the e-mail does not send successfully, the user will not have the chance to confirm site usage, and their SharePoint site will probably be deleted erroneously. SharePoint does not actually check the usage statistics for this process, so using the site itself does not prevent this from happening. ■

After you have determined the appropriate parameters for your organization, you can configure the site use confirmation and deletion policies by following these steps:

1. Open SharePoint Central Administration and select Application Management.

2. Click Confirm site use and deletion under the Site Collection section.

3. From the Web Application drop-down menu, select the Web application to which you would like to apply or modify the site use confirmation and deletion settings.

4. Select the Send e-mail notifications to owners of unused site collections check box and enter the number of days after creation or confirmation that you want notifications sent.

5. Select the period (daily, weekly, monthly) and hour that you want notifications to be processed and sent.

6. If appropriate for your organization, select the Automatically delete the site collection if use is not confirmed check box and enter the number of notices that you want to be sent.

7. Click OK.

Using Site Templates

Site templates can help users be more productive by creating sites that are already populated with lists, functionality, and some design elements. The product provides many templates for collaboration, meetings, Web databases, and enterprise functionality. If you design a specific site layout and lists that are helpful to other users, you can publish your own template to the site template gallery as well.

Most site templates can be applied to both sub-sites and site collections. The Enterprise site templates are not available in SharePoint Foundation installations.

The new site templates introduced in SharePoint Server 2010 are

- Assets Web Database
- Basic Search Center
- Business Intelligence Center
- Charitable Contributions Web Database
- Contacts Web Database
- Enterprise Search Center
- Enterprise Wiki
- FAST Search Center
- Group Work Site
- Issues Web Database
- Projects Web Database
- Visio Process Repository

The site templates from MOSS 2007 that no longer exist in SharePoint 2010 are

- Collaboration Portal
- News Site
- Report Center
- Search Center
- Search Center with Tabs
- Site Directory
- Wiki Site

MOSS 2007 Deprecated templates still exist

Even though the removed templates are not available for selection when creating a site or site collection, they still exist for migration and backward-compatibility purposes. This means that SharePoint 2010 still needs to "know" about MOSS 2007 templates. **Although it is recommended to move forward with the new templates**, it is possible to create SharePoint 2010 sites using the old deprecated templates.

For advanced users, the templates are stored inside the webtemp files located in the 14 hive under the TEMPLATES\1033\XML folder. You may use the Name property of the template (for example, SPSNEWS) to create sites programmatically with the WSS object model.

These templates can also be modified so that they appear for user selection although there may be feature dependencies (meaning certain features must be activated for them to appear). Once again it is not recommended to use the MOSS 2007 templates, as future versions of SharePoint may no longer provide support and therefore could increase future migration complexity.

Note
Some of the new templates replace the removed templates (for example, Enterprise Wiki replaces Wiki). ■

Using collaboration templates

Collaboration templates are focused on creating the elements most often used to facilitate team collaboration. As with all the templates, the goal is to provide something for teams to start with so that they are not looking at a blank site and wondering what to do next.

Team site template

The Team site template is the most versatile and most used template, probably because it is the default, top-of-the-list selection. This template hasn't changed from the WSS v3 template and still provides a basic structure for team collaboration. When you select the Team site template, SharePoint creates a site that has a document library, four empty lists, two supporting libraries, and a discussion board. These are

- Shared Documents
- Announcements
- Calendar
- Links
- Site Assets
- Site Pages
- Tasks
- Team Discussion

SharePoint also populates the home page with the shared documents and site image on it, as shown in Figure 3.1.

FIGURE 3.1

SharePoint site created from the Team site template

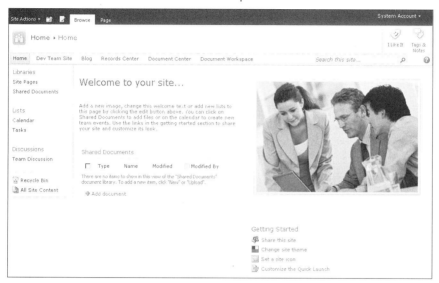

Cross-Reference

For more information about lists, see Chapter 4 and for information about Web Parts, see Chapter 5. ■

Blank site template

The Blank site template creates a blank site. No lists and libraries are created, and the default home page is completely blank. This site is a blank page ready to be populated with your Web Parts of choice. Figure 3.2 shows a site created with the Blank site template.

Enterprise Wiki site

A site created from the Enterprise Wiki site template has a wiki page library created and is intended for quick Web page editing and collaboration by nontechnical users. The Enterprise Wiki option is only available from a Publishing Portal, Publishing Site, or any site/site collection with publishing enabled. However, the underlying wiki style of editing pages can be spread throughout all sites. This means that when you edit a page, you can get the standard rich-text editing capabilities along with other features.

FIGURE 3.2

SharePoint site created from the Blank site template

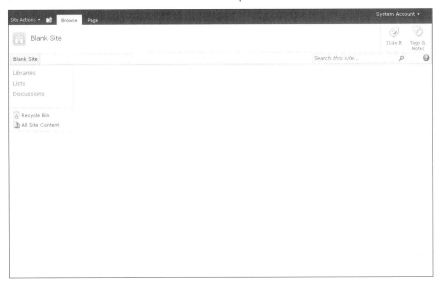

The Team site template has this feature activated, but for other sites all you need to do is activate the Wiki Page Home Page feature at the site level, and you can begin to create pages using the full editing capabilities. See the "Using Site Pages and Site Assets" section at the end of this chapter.

There is also an Enterprise Wiki Site Collection template, which is used to create an entire site collection dedicated to Wiki pages and content.

Tip

An Enterprise Wiki Site Collection can form a great knowledge base within an organization. ■

A site collection created from the Enterprise Wiki site template has a wiki page library created and is intended for quick Web page editing and collaboration by nontechnical users. Wiki pages can be associated to specific categories as well as keep track of user ratings of the page, as shown in Figure 3.3.

Tip

Wiki means "quick" in Hawaiian. ■

This template is very popular for documenting knowledge because everyone that has rights can contribute content and edit contributed content for accuracy. The Wikipedia project that has been in existence on the Internet since 2001 now boasts 1.3 million entries (August 2006) for English language entries.

FIGURE 3.3

SharePoint site created from the Enterprise Wiki site template

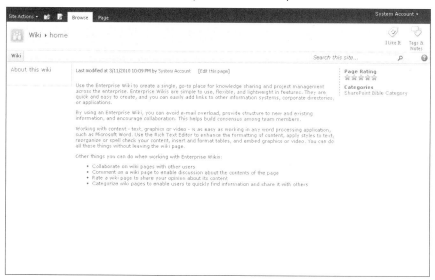

Unlike MOSS 2007, in SharePoint 2010, wiki page editing includes selection of styles, adding any Web Part that is available within the site and saving any site that has the Wiki feature as a template. You cannot, however, save an Enterprise Wiki site collection as a template.

Blog

Another collaboration template in the SharePoint 2010 site gallery is the Blog template. Sites created from the Blog template are ready for you to start adding postings for others to read and comment on. The template creates one library and five lists:

- **Photos:** Image library for storing pictures that you want to share.
- **Categories:** List of categories that you can use to organize your blog. See Chapter 4 to find out more about customizing lists.
- **Comments:** This list stores the comments that are made about a post.
- **Links:** Links list for helpful or related sites.
- **Posts:** The posts list stores the posts made by the author.

The default page is populated with Web Parts that show these lists, as shown in Figure 3.4.

FIGURE 3.4

SharePoint site created from the Blog template

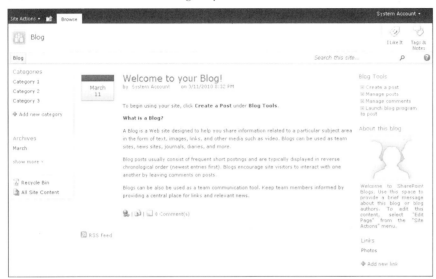

The Blog site template has specialized logic built into it to tie all the lists together (the posts with the comments and categories) so if you want a blog, start with a blog site and add the other site functionality to it. This is different than wikis, where you can add a wiki library to just about any site with very similar functionality. The blogs are more touchy, so use the Blog site template if you need one and customize from there.

Records Center (SPS only)

The Records Center site template creates a site intended to store records that are part of the records management process. Records management is discussed in detail in Chapter 12.

This site template creates six libraries and two lists:

- **Hold Reports (accessed from Site Settings):** This library stores reports on records included in a hold.

- **Holds (accessed from Site Settings):** This list is used to track external actions like litigations, investigations, or audits that require a suspension of record disposition. By listing an item in one or more holds, that item will be suspended until it is no longer managed by holds.

- **Customized Reports:** The site collection library used for analytical reports.

- **Form Templates:** The site collection form template library.

- **Style Library:** The site collection library used to store common styles.

- **Drop Off Library:** The Drop Off Library provides the structure to route incoming records to the appropriate document library.

- **Record Library:** This library stores official documents considered Records.

- **Content Organizer Rules (accessed from Site Actions ⟹ Manage Record Center):** This list stores the rules for records routing.

The Drop Off Library is integral to the functionality of the Records Repository site template and is viewed on the home page of the site, as shown in Figure 3.5. The list allows you to specify the type of record, the associated title and description of that record type, and the location where you want to store records of that type. In addition, you can specify aliases of other record types that also should be stored in the same location.

Documents Center

The Document Center template creates lists and libraries focused on sharing and collaborating on documents. It is a watered-down version of the Records Center but is intended to provide a collaborative repository. The template contains a single document library and a list:

- **Documents:** This document library stores documents that you are sharing with your team. The document center creates this as a version-enabled list, and you can also add other SharePoint features such as workflow to the library. See Chapter 8 for more information on workflows.

- **Tasks:** This list stores the tasks that are assigned to all team members and can support a workflow created on documents in the document library.

This template provides a central location to store and manage documents and is shown in Figure 3.6.

FIGURE 3.5

SharePoint site created from the Records Center template

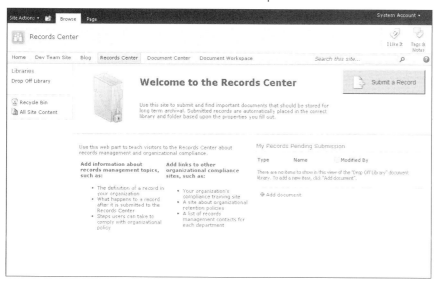

FIGURE 3.6

SharePoint site created from the Document Center template

Document workspace

To actually collaborate and work with team members on documents, a document workspace provides the means. The Document Workspace site template contains a document library, four empty lists, and a discussion board. These are

- Shared Documents
- Announcements
- Calendar
- Links
- Tasks
- Team Discussion

SharePoint also populates the home page with the announcements, shared documents, tasks, links, and even a Members Web Part on it, as shown in Figure 3.7.

FIGURE 3.7

SharePoint site created from the Document Workspace template

Group Work site

To take group collaboration to a new level, SharePoint 2010 provides you with a new collaboration site template. The Group Work site template contains a document library, eight empty lists, and a discussion board. These are

- **Announcements:** This list stores announcement items which can have optional expiration dates.

- **Shared Documents:** This library stores group documents.

- **Group Calendar:** Used to track group events and meetings.

- **Circulations:** Communication vehicle that allows group members to communicate and confirm information.

- **Phone Call Memo:** A tracking list that stores phone call information.

- **Tasks:** A task list to track group tasks.

- **Links:** A links list for group-related links and references.

- **Resources:** List for tracking resources such as projectors, scanners, and so on.

- **Wherabouts:** List for tracking group members throughout the day.

- **Team Discussion:** Discussion board for the group.

SharePoint populates the home page with the announcements, group calendar, links, whereabouts, and a What's New Web Part on it, as shown in Figure 3.8.

FIGURE 3.8

SharePoint site created from the Group Work site template

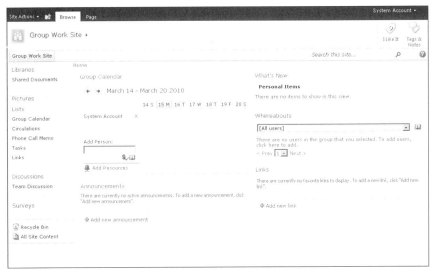

Using publishing templates

The publishing templates are designed to create sites used for Web publishing so that they have the publishing feature turned on and are populated with the Web Parts and lists to support the publishing process.

Publishing site with workflow (SPS only)

The Publishing site template is designed to be a center for publishing pages using the available page layouts. The template creates four libraries:

- **Documents:** Document library for storing documents that might be referenced in pages published on the site.

- **Images:** Image library for storing images that might be used in pages published on the site.

- **Pages:** Page library for storing the published pages on the site.

- **Workflow Tasks:** Custom list that stores the workflow tasks assigned by pages published on the site.

The home page created by the template is a publishing page created with a welcome page layout, but none of the lists or libraries is set to be shown in the Quick Launch bar. Therefore, the initial site creation appears as a blank site as shown in edit mode in Figure 3.9. This page is under publishing control just as other pages created in the page library. The "with Workflow" means that before content can be published as a major version, an approval workflow is initiated. For more information on these publishing features, see the "Using Pages and Page Libraries" section in this chapter.

FIGURE 3.9

SharePoint site created from the Publishing with Workflow site template

Note

Any site with publishing features turned on cannot be saved as a template and used. ■

Publishing site (SPS only)

The publishing site template is designed to be a center for publishing pages using the available page layouts. The template creates four libraries:

- **Documents:** Document library for storing documents that might be referenced in pages published on the site
- **Images:** Image library for storing images that might be used in pages published on the site
- **Pages:** Pages library for storing the published pages on the site
- **Workflow Tasks:** Custom list that stores the workflow tasks assigned by pages published on the site

The home page created by the template is a publishing page created with a welcome page layout, but none of the lists or libraries are set to be shown in the Quick Launch. Therefore, the initial site creation appears as a blank site, as shown in Edit Mode just like the Publishing with Workflow template, shown in Figure 3.9. This page is under publishing control just as other pages created in the page library. For more information on these publishing features, see the "Using Pages and Page Libraries" section in this chapter.

This site template limits the lists and libraries that can be created to only those necessary for publishing. However, you can create a sub-site of any template of a publishing site.

Note
Any site with publishing features turned on cannot be saved as a template and used. ■

Using meeting templates

The meeting templates are designed to enable successful meetings within an organization by providing a workspace for commonly used meeting items. This helps provide meeting organizers and attendees a template for how to prepare and participate in meetings.

Basic meeting workspace

The Basic Meeting template creates a collaborative space for a basic organizational meeting. The template creates four libraries:

- **Agenda:** This list stores the agenda items for your meeting.
- **Attendees:** This list stores the attendee names and information about their attendance.
- **Document library:** This library stores documents that support the agenda and topic of the meeting.
- **Objectives:** This list stores the objectives for your meeting.

No left navigation is provided with this template; however, you can create new pages from the Site Actions menu to create a tab across the top navigation, as shown in Figure 3.10. This allows you to expand your meeting space across topics or meeting dates.

FIGURE 3.10

SharePoint site created from the Basic Meeting template

Blank meeting workspace

The Blank Meeting template is true to its name. The template creates the attendees list that stores the attendee names and information about their attendance and creates a site with a blank home page. This is one of our least favorite site templates because it is literally a blank page that does not help the user think about the purpose and content of the meeting.

If you use the Blank Meeting workspace, you will want to create additional lists and libraries, and this is possible from the Edit Page options in the Site Actions menu, as shown in Figure 3.11. Unlike most SharePoint sites, the Meeting template sites allow you to create lists from the Web Part menu so that they are created and added to the page at the same time. This is fairly useful if you want to create one of the frequently used meeting lists that are available via that menu. However, if you want to create a list or library other than those, you need to click through to the list creation page. To do this, follow these steps:

1. **On the home page, click the Site Actions menu in the top-left corner.**

2. **Select More Options from the menu.**

3. **Select the type of list or library, provide a name, and then click Create.**

FIGURE 3.11

Creating lists from the Add Web Parts tool pane in a Blank Meeting site

Decision meeting workspace

The Decision meeting workspace is intended to help organizers and participants drive decisions when participating in a meeting. The template creates five lists and one document library to support this goal:

- **Agenda:** This list stores the agenda items for your meeting.
- **Attendees:** This list stores the attendee names and information about their attendance.
- **Decisions:** This list stores the decisions that are made in the meeting. This is helpful for documenting the contact information for and status of decisions.
- **Document library:** This library stores documents that support the agenda and topic of the meeting.
- **Objectives:** This list stores the objectives for your meeting.
- **Tasks:** This list is created to support the tasks that are assigned during the meeting. Every member of the meeting site can be assigned tasks, and the list will e-mail the assignment to the owner as a reminder. You can modify the e-mail behavior and workflow for tasks; see Chapter 4 for more information.

The site home page is populated with the Web Parts for these lists and libraries so that all the Decision meeting information is visible to participants at a glance, as shown in Figure 3.12.

FIGURE 3.12

SharePoint site created from the Decision meeting template

Social meeting workspace

The Social Meeting Workspace template is centered on collaborating on the right information for social events. The site template creates one library, three lists, and a discussion board:

- **Picture Library:** This image library stores photos of the event.
- **Attendees:** This list stores the attendees, their responses (accepted, tentative, or declined), their attendance status (required, optional, or organizer), and comments. The attendees are added from the address book.
- **Directions:** The Directions list is a multiline text field used to store directions to the event.
- **Things to Bring:** This list stores the items that were assigned or volunteered and their owners.
- **Discussion Board:** The Discussion Board is designed to store discussion topics and the associated replies.

The site template populates three pages with the Web Parts for these lists and libraries and provides navigation between the pages via the Quick Launch bar on the left of the screen, as shown in Figure 3.13. The home page is designed for the essential event information and the discussion, and photo pages display their associated information.

FIGURE 3.13

SharePoint site created from the Social Meeting Workspace template

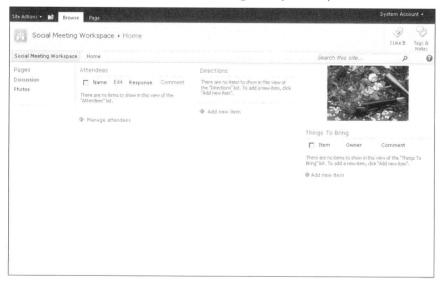

Multipage meeting workspace

The Multipage meeting template creates a meeting collaborative space that has two pages added when the site is created. The template creates three lists:

- **Agenda:** This list stores the agenda items for your meeting.
- **Attendees:** This list stores the attendee names and information about their attendance.
- **Objectives:** This list stores the objectives for your meeting.

You can manage the pages from the Manage Pages option under the Site Actions menu, as shown in Figure 3.14.

Using Enterprise site templates

The Enterprise site templates are primarily designed to deploy the features that are available with SPS, such as search and business intelligence.

Personalization site

Personalization sites are designed to provide a distinct personalization experience that connects your portal to users' My Sites. Use this site to push personalized and targeted information to your users based on who they are and why they visit your portal. You should publish information on personalized sites that can be targeted to the individual user or user role, such as performance indicators or business metrics. The personalization site is designed to help you target that information to your users.

The Personalization site template, shown in Figure 3-15, creates three libraries and one list:

- **Documents:** This document library stores documents that you are sharing with your team. The Document Center creates this as a version-enabled list with workflow approval enabled. See Chapter 8 for more information on workflows.
- **Images:** Image library for storing images that might be used in pages published on the site.
- **Pages:** This library stores the published pages on the site.
- **Workflow Tasks:** Custom list that stores the workflow tasks assigned by pages published on the site.

After your personalization site is developed, register your site as a Personalization site so that it shows up in the My Site navigation bar for all users. For information about registering your personalization site see Chapter 6.

FIGURE 3.14

Managing pages in a multipage site

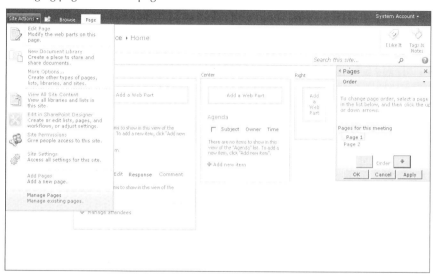

FIGURE 3.15

SharePoint site created from the Personalization template

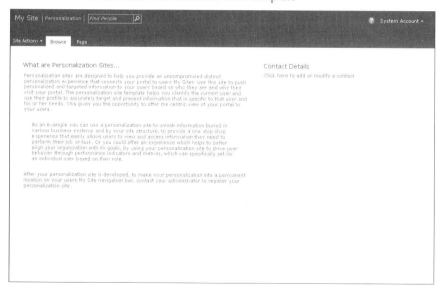

Enterprise Search Center

The Enterprise Search Center template, shown in Figure 3-16, creates a site populated with the Search Web Parts and is dedicated to locating content by using the SharePoint search service. The template creates three libraries and three lists and populates the pages libraries with pages to support simple search, people search, and advanced search.

- **Documents:** This document library stores documents that you are sharing with your team.

- **Images:** This library stores images that might be used in pages published on the site.

- **Pages:** This library stores the published pages on the site.

- **Tabs in Search Pages:** This list stores links to pages on the site and populates the tab navigation control for pages that support the search control. The links should be to pages located in the pages document library.

- **Tabs in Search Results:** This list stores links to pages on the site and populates the tab navigation control for pages that display search results. The links should be to pages that located the pages document library.

- **Workflow Tasks:** This is a custom list that stores the workflow tasks assigned by pages published on the site.

The Enterprise Search Center template is the replacement for the MOSS 2007 Search Center with Tabs template and functions the same way.

FIGURE 3.16

A SharePoint site created from the Enterprise Search Center template

Basic Search Center

The Basic Search Center template creates a page populated with the search Web parts so that you can create a site that is dedicated to finding content via search. The template doesn't create any libraries; however, it does create the Tabs lists which do not appear to provide any functionality in this template.

The Basic Search Center template is the replacement for the MOSS 2007 Search Center template and functions the same way. However, it is recommended to use the Enterprise Search Center template if possible and utilize the tab functionality for additional search scopes.

FAST Search Center

The FAST Search Center template creates pages populated with the search Web parts so that you create a site that is dedicated to finding content via FAST Enterprise search. The template creates three libraries and three lists and populates the pages libraries with pages to support simple search, people search, and advanced search.

- **Documents:** This document library stores documents that you are sharing with your team.
- **Images:** This library stores images that might be used in pages published on the site.
- **Pages:** This library stores the published pages on the site.
- **Tabs in Search Pages:** This list stores links to pages on the site and populates the tab navigation control for pages that support the search control. The links should be to pages located in the pages document library.
- **Tabs in Search Results:** This list stores links to pages on the site and populates the tab navigation control for pages that display search results. The links should be to pages that are located in the pages document library.
- **Workflow Tasks:** This custom list stores the workflow tasks assigned by pages published on the site.

Note

FAST is an optional/add-on component that provides enhanced search capabilities and capacity. It is only available within the Enterprise Edition of SharePoint Server 2010. ■

Using Web Database site templates

A new category of site templates has appeared in SharePoint 2010 named Web Databases. These sites are prebuilt Access database sites that utilize databases to store and track business information for several specific yet common business functions. These include Assets, Charitable Contributions, Contacts, Issues, and Project, as shown in Figure 3.17. Instead of storing the information in lists (which can get very large and impossible to maintain), the data is persisted in an Access database.

These sites are very different in that they are solely based on Access components such as Tables, Forms, Reports, and Queries. Technically, these sites are Access Web Databases running under Access Services. Therefore, you need to be running Access Services to create any Web database site.

Web Databases site templates selection

Each site has a tabbed navigation for various sections within the database. The Report Center tab is used to render the reports defined in the database. The site menu is named Options instead of Site Actions. When clicking on Settings from Options, you don't see the site settings, you see the Access database contents as shown in Figure 3.18. An example of a Web database site is shown in Figure 3.19.

Web Database Access components

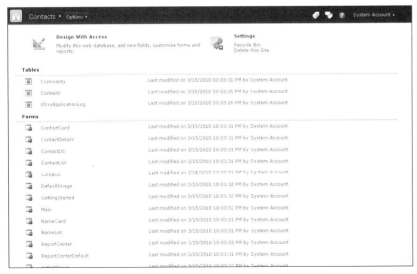

FIGURE 3.19

Assets Web Database site template

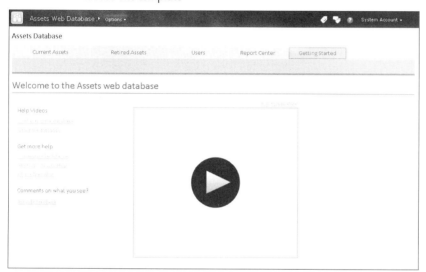

Creating a custom Web database site

Instead of using the Web Database templates, you can create your own Web database site using Access 2010. (You need to have Access Services running on your farm and thus an Enterprise license.) Here are the steps:

1. Launch Access 2010 and click Blank Web Database from the New section under File (when opening Access this screen should appear by default).

2. Enter a name for the database (this is not the site name) on the right. Click the Create button.

3. Create your tables, forms, queries, and reports as necessary. You will want to create a navigation form to present options on the Web site.

4. Once your database is ready to deploy as a Web site, you will need to set the default Web display such that SharePoint knows what to show upon reaching your site. To do this, click on Options under the File menu, select Current Database, and then select a navigation form from the drop-down menu next to Web Display.

5. To publish your Web database, click on the Info option from the File Menu and then click on the Publish to Access Services button.

6. On the right of the screen, enter the SharePoint site collection (for example, root site) URL where you want the site to live. Provide a site name in the Site Name box (you may use spaces here). Click on the Publish to Access Services button.

7. The SharePoint Web database site will be created. You can access the site by using the link that is presented in the confirmation screen.

The most efficient way to make changes to these types of sites is to modify the database directly in Access. You need Access 2010 installed on your local machine. From the Options menu of a Web database site, select Open in Access. SharePoint downloads a local copy for editing as shown in Figure 3.20.

After the local database changes have been made, you can use the File menu to easily sync those changes back to the SharePoint site as shown in Figure 3.21.

Creating a custom site template

If you customize a site that you want to reuse within your portal as a template, you can make a custom site template and place it in the site template gallery so that other users within the site collection can also access it. The site template includes all the lists and libraries and site customizations such as additional Web Part pages, applied themes, and Quick Launch customizations. When you create a site template, you choose whether or not you want to include the site content. As noted in the site template descriptions earlier, you cannot create a site template from wiki sites or sites with publishing enabled. Membership of the site is not included as part of the site template, nor is any personalization or alerts. Web Parts that were imported to the site and Web discussions are not included in a site template.

FIGURE 3.20

Editing the Contacts Web Database in Access 2010

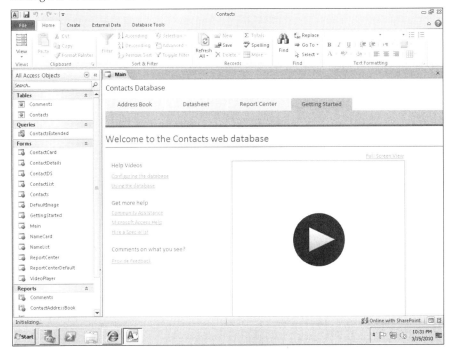

FIGURE 3.21

Syncing local changes with the live Web database site

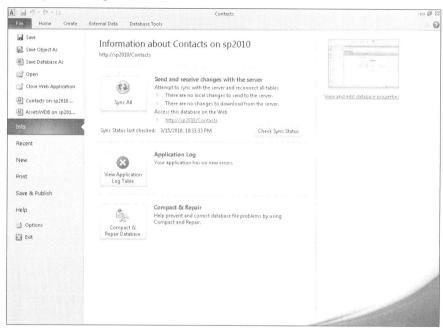

To create a custom site template, you must be an administrator of the site that the template is being created from. Follow these steps:

1. From the Site Actions menu in the top-left corner, select Site Settings.

2. Under Site Actions (yes, it's the same name as the menu), click Save site as template.

3. Enter the filename that you want to use for the site template in the File name box. Site templates now have a .wsp file extension. (Previously in MOSS 2007 they were .stp files.)

4. Enter the title that you want to use for the template in the site template gallery in the Template name box.

5. Enter a description for the site template (optional) in the Template description box.

6. If you want to include content, select the Include Content box.

7. Click OK.

8. From the Site Actions menu of the site collection in the top-left corner, select Site Settings.

9. From the Galleries menu, select Solutions.

10. Right-click your site template file and select Save Target As to save the file to your local machine.

If you have created a template in a sub-site or different site collection, you will need to upload the file created in the previous steps to the site gallery of the site collection that you want to make the template available in. It is only possible to use a custom template on the same server that the template was created from, so this is not a viable method of moving sites between servers.

To save the site to the site template gallery, you must have Add Item permissions for the site template gallery. Follow these steps:

1. Go to the top-level site in the site collection in which you want the template to appear and select Site Settings from the Site Actions menu in the top-left corner.

2. From the Galleries menu, select Solutions.

3. From the Ribbon bar, select the Solutions tab and click on the Upload Solution button.

4. Browse to the file on your machine that you saved previously in Step 10 above and click OK.

5. Click Activate or Close on the Activate Solution dialog that appears.

Note
A solution cannot be deleted from the gallery unless it is deactivated first. ∎

Implementing Your Site Structure

Once you have decided on your portal site structure, you can implement it by creating the root sites necessary to support your individual namespaces. Each root site created on your portal infrastructure requires a unique TCP/IP port (unless you use host headers in conjunction with DNS entries which will enable multiple root sites to be on port 80; see the "Creating Multiple Sites on Port 80" sidebar.). The first site you create will use port 80; because that is what port browsers expect to use, you do not need any further customization so that users can type a friendly URL. For any additional sites, you need to do a domain name server (DNS) entry to support the namespace and friendly name.

Creating your root sites

For each of your root sites, follow these steps:

1. Open SharePoint Central Administration and select Application Management from the Quick Launch bar.

2. Click Manage Web applications under the Web Applications section.

3. **Click Create a new IIS Web site and change the port setting to 80 if it is not already in use so that users will not have to specify the port number in the URL.** Port 80 is the standard port expected by Web browsers. If you are creating additional top- level sites and port 80 is already taken, enter a port that is not in use or let SharePoint pick one for you.

4. **Select the NTLM or Negotiate (Kerberos) as the appropriate authentication provider in the security configuration section.** NTLM is recommended for ease of configuration, but if you choose Kerberos, it must be supported by your environment. Kerberos has performance benefits in large farm environments and may be necessary for certain security implementations depending on the configuration (for example: Reporting Services).

5. Click Create new application pool in the application pool section.

6. Type the name of your application pool or use the default name in the Application pool name field.

7. **Enter your Web application identity account credentials in the username and password field in domain\username format.** For more information about the Web application identity account, see Chapter 2.

8. Verify the database information in the database name and authentication section.

9. Click Windows authentication in the Database Name and Authentication section.

10. Select the service connections for this Web application.

11. Click OK.

12. Verify that your new Web application has been created on the application created page.

13. **Open a command prompt window (Run As Administrator), type** iisreset, **and then press Enter.**

After your Web application has been created, you can proceed with creating a site collection for it. Follow these steps:

1. **Open SharePoint Central Administration and select Application Management from the Quick Launch bar.**

2. In the Site Collection section, click Create Site Collection.

3. In the Web application drop-down menu, select the Web application that you created in the previous steps above.

4. Enter a title and description for your site.

5. In the Web site address section, click the Create site at this URL option and then choose root in the URL path.

6. Enter a username for the site collection administrator in the Primary Site Collection Administrator section.

7. **Select No Quota in the Quota Template section.** Alternatively, you can create a quota template to limit the size of the site collection by clicking the Manage Quota Templates link in that section and apply it to this site collection. For more information on site quotas, see Defining Site Maintenance Policies in this chapter.

8. **Select your template for the site collection from the available templates in the template selection section.**

   If you are using SharePoint Foundation, a suggested template for departmental sites is the Team Sites template.

   If you are using SharePoint Server, a suggested template for intranet portals is the Team Site template from the Collaboration tab.

9. **Click OK.**

Implementing your friendly names

For top-level sites that are not created at port 80, you will want to create friendly names so that users do not have to enter the port number in the URL like `http://<namespace>:<port number>`. You configure the friendly name by setting the default access mapping for the Web application and a domain name system (DNS) entry so that the friendly name is mapped to the appropriate TCP/IP address.

To implement friendly names for each site that is not on port 80, follow these steps:

1. **Open SharePoint Central Administration and select Application Management from the Quick Launch.**

2. **Click Alternate access mappings under the Web Applications section.**

3. **Click Add incoming URLs.**

4. **Select the appropriate Web application from the drop-down menu, enter the friendly name in** `http://<friendlyname>` **format in the New default zone URL protocol, host and port field, and confirm that Default is selected in the zone drop-down menu.**

5. **Click OK.**

6. **Request that the administrator of your DNS servers add a host record that maps the friendly name to the IP address of the front-end server(s).**

Implementing navigation

SharePoint provides two main navigation mechanisms on a given page. On the left side of the page, you see that the Quick Launch bar links to content within the site you are viewing and also links to other sites as tabs along the top portion of the content area, as shown in Figure 3.22.

Creating multiple root sites on port 80

You can create multiple root sites on port 80 within SharePoint 2010. This is accomplished by creating subsequent Web applications using port 80. When this is implemented, you do not need to configure friendly name. The steps to accomplish this are as follows:

1. During the Web application creation process, specify port 80 and enter a host header name on the creation screen.

2. Create a DNS host entry specifying the host header name used in Step 1 as the host name. Use the same IP address as the first host.

3. Create a new site collection using the new Web application.

4. You should now be able to access the new site collection using `http://<host header name>`.

5. If your first Web application did not utilize a host header, you will need to go into IIS and edit the site binding for the initial Web site created on port 80. A binding entry should be listed with a blank host name. Edit that binding and enter the server name or desired root name as the host.

Providing cohesive and consistent navigation is important to the usability of portals. The SharePoint navigation control allows child sites within a site collection to use the navigation of the parent site to keep this navigation consistent.

You can modify the navigation at the parent site level to provide navigation to the key content pieces. That includes the ability to add links to external content as appropriate, trimming the navigation to hide items that are not key, and reordering the navigation items. To modify your navigation, follow these steps:

1. Open the parent site of your site collection and select Modify Site Settings from the Site Actions menu in the top-left corner.

2. Click Navigation from the Look and Feel menu.

3. Select the Show pages check box if desired. This setting is not recommend for larger sites because it can create a navigation list that is too long and cluttered.

4. Use the control in the Navigation and Editing and Sorting section, as shown in Figure 3.23, to add, hide, or move the order of navigation items. The global navigation section shows all items for the top bar navigation. The current navigation section shows items for the left navigation. If you want to add a link, it is added at the same level as the sub-sites.

5. Click OK.

FIGURE 3.22

Navigation provided by SharePoint 2010

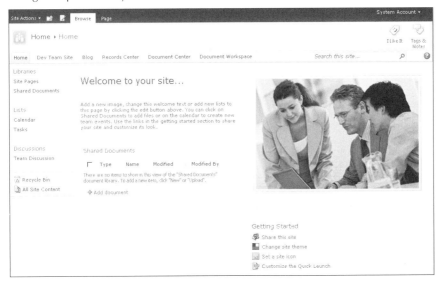

FIGURE 3.23

The SharePoint navigation control

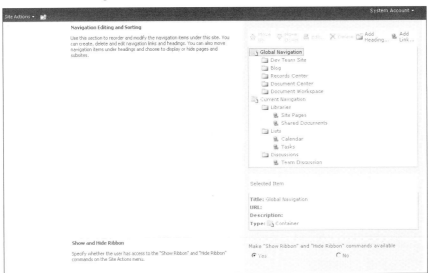

After you have configured your parent site navigation to meet your portal needs, you can configure the sub-sites to use the same navigation. To do this, follow these steps:

1. **Open the sub-site that will inherit the parent navigation and select Modify Site Settings from the Site Actions menu in the top-left corner.**

2. **Click Navigation from the Look and Feel section.**

3. **Select Display the same navigation items as the parent site radio button in the Global Navigation section.**

4. **Select Display the current site, the navigation items below the current site, and the current site's siblings in the Current Navigation section to use the lists and libraries of the current site in the left navigation.**

5. **Use the control in the Navigation and Editing and Sorting section to add, hide, or move the order of left navigation items.**

6. **Click OK.**

Turning on site features

Based on the site template that you choose, SharePoint turns on the site features to support the template. You can change the site features after the site is created if you need additional features. The available site features for both SPS and SharePoint Foundation are

-   **Group Work Lists:** Provides Calendars with added functionality for team and resource scheduling

-   **Team Collaboration Lists:** Provides team collaboration capabilities for a site by making standard lists such as document libraries and issues

-   **Wiki Page Home Page:** Creates the Site Pages and Site Assets libraries and allows the creation of a wiki-based home page as well as subsequent wiki pages within the site

The site features available for SPS sites only are

-   **Content Organizer:** Create metadata-based rules that move content submitted to this site to the correct library or folder.

-   **E-mail Integration with Content Organizer:** Enable a site's content organizer to accept and organize e-mail messages. This feature should be used only in a highly managed store, like a Records Center.

-   **Hold and eDiscovery:** This feature is used to track external actions like litigations, investigations, or audits that require you to suspend the disposition of documents.

-   **Metadata Navigation and Filtering:** Provides each list in the site with a settings page for configuring that list to use metadata tree view hierarchies and filter controls to improve navigation and filtering of the contained items.

-   **Office SharePoint Server Enterprise:** The Office SharePoint Server Enterprise License includes features such as the business data catalog, forms services, and Excel services.

- **Translation Management Library:** Create a translation management library when you want to create documents in multiple languages and manage translation tasks. Translation management libraries include a workflow to manage the translation process and provide sub-folders, file versioning, and check-in/check-out.

- **Office SharePoint Server Publishing:** Office SharePoint Server Publishing.

- **Office SharePoint Server Standard:** Features such as user profiles and search, included in the Office SharePoint Server Standard License.

- **Offline Synchronization for External Lists:** Enables offline synchronization for external lists with Outlook and SharePoint Workspace.

- **PerformancePoint Services Site Features:** Features enabling the PerformancePoint Services list and document library templates.

To activate or deactivate site features, do the following:

1. From the Site Actions menu in the top-left corner, select Site Settings.

2. Click Site features from under the Site Actions section (for site collection features, at the top level site settings, select Site Collection Features under the Site Collection Management section).

3. Select Activate for any features that you want to activate or Deactivate for features you want to disable.

Configuring the site welcome page

Any site with publishing features turned on cannot be saved as a template and used to create additional sites. If you turn on the publishing feature after a site is created, you need to set the welcome page to the correct page that you want to present as the home page of the site. Sites created without the publishing feature turned on create a default.aspx in the root directory of the site (home.aspx under Site Pages if it is a team site or the Wiki Home Page feature is enabled). Sites with the publishing feature turned on create a default.aspx in the pages library of the site. If you want to change which page to use for the welcome page, follow these steps:

1. From the Site Actions menu in the top-left corner, select Site Settings.

2. Click Welcome Page from the Look and Feel menu.

3. Enter the URL of the page that you would like users to first see when they visit the site. The URL must be a page in the current site.

Using Pages and Page Libraries

Page libraries are designed to store publishing pages. The columns of the page library store the content of the page, and the page layout defines how that content is displayed. Page libraries and publishing features are only available in SPS 2010 and not WSS 2010.

The benefits of using page libraries is that you can standardize how you want content to appear and update the page layout to change the appearance for every page that uses that layout. There are several building blocks used in the publishing feature set:

- **Content Types:** Content types are the types of pages available for publishing. They define the collection of information that the page will contain as well as the page policies and workflow. You can associate content types with page libraries to limit the type of content submitted to that page library. For example, if you create a site from the Publishing site template, the Page, Welcome Page, and Article Page content types are associated with that page library.

- **Page layouts:** An Active Server Page is defined for each content type. The page layout defines where each piece of content appears on the page. In addition to the page content, the page layouts can also define Web Part zones, Web Parts, server controls, and Cascading Style Sheets (CSS). The page layout is combined with the master page to render the content in the browser. You can have multiple page layouts for each content type; for example, an article page has a page layout with the image on the left and a page layout with the image on the right. For each page library, you can define which page layouts are available.

- **Page content:** Each page is stored as an item in the pages library, and the content is stored in the columns of that item. The columns are defined by the content types associated with that library.

- **Site columns:** Columns of metadata that are associated with that site. Site columns are different from document library metadata columns in that they are available sitewide and are available for filtering with the content query Web Part. See Chapter 5 for more information about the content query Web Part.

- **Server columns:** Columns of metadata that are defined for all sites on the server. You can choose which server columns are available as site columns.

Modifying page content types

SPS provides three page content types: the Welcome page, the Article page, and the Redirect page. These types have associated columns relevant to their content type, but as you work with the types, you may find the need to modify the columns to fit your needs.

The welcome page content type is intended to work as the home page of a publishing site. The columns associated with this content type are

- **Scheduling columns:** Start date and end date.
- **Contact columns:** Contact name and e-mail address for primary page contact.
- **Audience targeting columns:** Audiences that will see the content on the welcome page.
- **Images:** Images to be included on the page.
- **Page content:** Column for the main page text. This column can hold any HTML content.
- **Links:** Columns to display links on the page.

The article page content type works for publishing news and in-depth articles for your organization. The columns associated with this content type are

- **Scheduling columns:** Start date and end date.
- **Contact columns:** Contact name and e-mail address for primary page contact.
- **Images columns:** Images to be included on the page and image captions.
- **Page content:** Column for the main page text. This column can hold any HTML content.
- **Links:** Columns to display links on the page.
- **Byline column:** The byline column is used to capture/show the author of the page content.

The redirect page content type is used for pages that redirect to another page. This is useful when you want to provide a link to content that is already published in another location and publicize that content and description in your page library.

Adding site and server columns

Before associating a new column with a content type, you need to create the column on either the site or server level. If the column is applicable to numerous sites, you should create the column at the server level so that the definition can be widely used. If the column has limited applicability, create it at the site level.

Creating a site column at the server level

To create a site column at the site collection level, follow these steps:

1. **Open the top-level site for the site collection and select Site Settings from the Site Actions menu in the top-left corner.**
2. **Select Site columns from the Galleries menu.**
3. **Click Create.**
4. **Enter your column name and choose the column type (choice, text, number, HTML, etc.).**
5. **Select Custom Columns in the Put this site column into field.**

6. Select whether or not the field is required.

7. Click OK.

Creating a site column at the site level

To create a site column at the site level, follow these steps:

1. On the site that you want to use the new site column, select Site Settings from the Site Actions menu in the top-left corner.

2. Select Site Columns from the Galleries menu.

3. Click Create.

4. Enter your column name and choose the column type (choice, text, number, HTML, etc.).

5. Select Custom Columns in the Put this site column into field.

6. Select whether or not the field is required.

7. Click OK.

Associating columns with content types

A column can be used in multiple content types. You must own the content type in order to modify it. If you want to modify it with a server column, you can do that from anywhere in the site collection. If you want to modify it with a site column type, the gallery that holds the content type must be in the same site as the column. For information about how to create site content types for your site, see the next section, "Creating a site content type."

To associate a column with a content type, follow these steps for each content type to which you want to add the column:

1. On the site that you want to use the new site column, select Site Settings from the Site Actions menu in the top-left corner.

2. Select Site content types from the Galleries menu.

3. Click the content type that you want to modify (for example, article page).

4. Select Add from existing site columns in the columns section.

5. Select Custom Columns from the Select columns from drop-down menu.

6. Select your column from the available columns and click Add.

7. Select OK.

Creating a site content type

To create a site content type, follow these steps:

1. **On the site that you want to use the new site content type, select Site Settings from the Site Actions menu in the top-left corner.**

2. **Select Site Content Types from the Galleries menu.**

3. **Click Create.**

4. **Enter the site content type name and select the Parent Content Type for your content type.** The new content type will inherit the columns from the parent content type, and you can also add your own columns.

5. **Select Custom Content Types in the Put this site content type into field.**

6. **Select whether or not the field is required.**

7. **Click OK.**

After the column has been associated with the content type, modify the page layout associated with that content type so that the column appears on the new page form.

Modifying page layouts

Page layouts define the layout for a content page by providing the controls by which the content is edited and displayed. There can be multiple page layouts for a single content type, as is the case with both the article page and the welcome page content types. The availability of multiple page layouts for a content type gives users different options for publishing a page. For example, the article page content type has four page layouts:

- **Article page with body only:** A simple layout for an article that includes areas for the title and page content columns.

- **Article page with image on left:** An article page with the article image, if populated, appears on the left side. The page also includes areas for the title, byline, article date, image caption, roll-up image (which shows only in content query views of the article), and page content columns.

- **Article page with image on right:** An article page with the article image, if populated, appears on the right side, as shown in Figure 3.24. The page also includes areas for the title, byline, article date, image caption, roll-up image (which shows only in content query views of the article), and page content columns.

- **Article page with summary links:** This article page includes a Web Part for the author to add a list of hyperlinks, as well as areas for the title, article date, byline, and page content columns. See Figure 3.25.

FIGURE 3.24

Page layout of article page with image on right

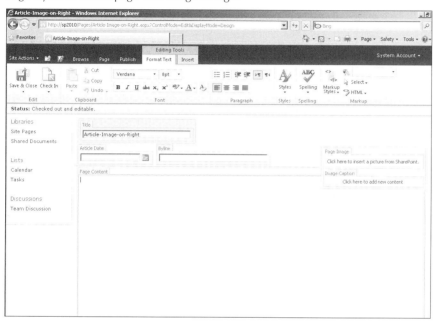

FIGURE 3.25

Page layout of article page with summary links Web Part

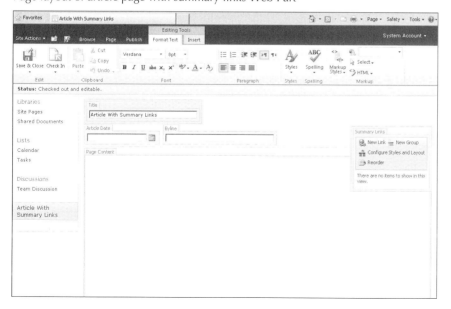

Page layouts are stored in the Master Page Gallery in the top-level site of the site collection. This gallery has the SPS features of versioning and approval turned on to safeguard the master page and page layouts.

You can modify page layouts to include site columns that you have added to the content type or Web Parts that would be helpful. You can also limit the page layouts available for page creation on a per library basis.

After creating a new page on a site, you can easily modify the page layout it uses by selecting the Page tab on the Ribbon and then selecting a layout from the Page Layout visual drop-down menu.

Editing the page layouts using SharePoint Designer

To modify the page layouts, you must have contributor access to the Master Page Gallery. Each layout is under versioning and approval control, so page layouts are not changed until a major version is published and approved.

To modify a page layout to add a site column, follow these steps:

1. **Launch SharePoint Designer and open the top level site of the site collection.** A quicker way to accomplish this in SharePoint 2010 is to simply select Edit in SharePoint Designer from the Site Actions menu.

2. **On the left-hand content list, click on Page Layouts and then select the page layout that you want to modify.**

3. **Click on Edit file in the main settings page that is shown under the Customization section. When prompted to check out the document, click yes.** This is important because SharePoint does not save changes that you make when the document is checked in. You may also get prompted to open in Advanced mode for edit; click Yes.

4. **Click on the Insert menu to display the Insert tab on the Ribbon, as shown in Figure 3.26.**

5. **Move to the end of the page in the designer area and then click on the Web Part Zone button on the Ribbon.** Doing this adds a Web part zone to the bottom of the page, as shown in Figure 3.27.

6. **Save the file and check in the changes.**

7. **Approve the page layout if you have the appropriate permissions.**

FIGURE 3.26

Insert tab on the Ribbon

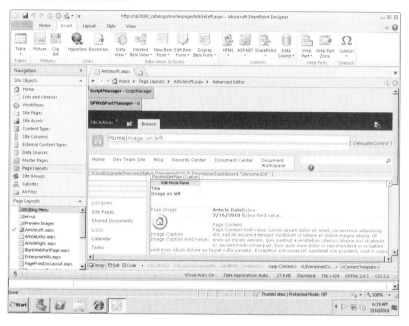

FIGURE 3.27

New Web part zone on page layout

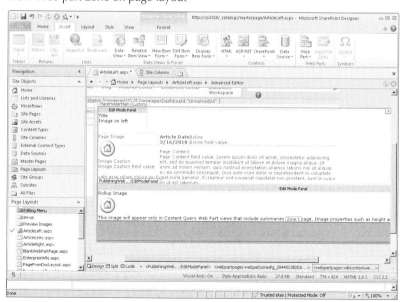

Selecting the page layouts available in a page library

You can modify the page layouts that are available to users creating a new page in a page library. To modify the available page layouts, follow these steps:

1. Select Site Settings from the Site Actions menu in the top-left corner.

2. Select Page layouts and site templates from the Look and Feel menu.

3. In the Page Layouts section, select Pages in this site can only use the following layouts radio button.

4. Select the page layouts that you do not want users to be able to use and click Remove, as shown in Figure 3.28.

5. Click OK when you have all the page layouts that you want selected.

FIGURE 3.28

Selecting the page layouts available for new pages

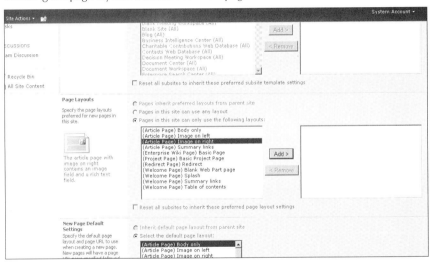

Using Site Pages and Site Assets

Site Pages and Site Assets are two libraries that become part of your site when the Wiki Home Page feature is activated. They exist automatically in a Team Site as the Wiki feature is activated within that template. These two libraries are synonymous with the Pages and Images libraries created within publishing sites. However the modification and utilization of these libraries are slightly different.

Modifying site pages

The creation and editing of site pages is through wiki-style editing; however, many more capabilities are available in these wiki pages over the previous MOSS 2007 wiki pages. These pages have three main Ribbon tabs:

- **Page:** Contains overall page options including saving and setting permissions
- **Format Text:** The text options for content creation and editing
- **Insert:** Options for adding SharePoint objects to your page

Whether or not your site is considered a wiki site, these pages become wiki pages so all of the wiki rules apply. Figure 3.29 displays a new page being created using the formatting tools and wiki entries. Styles may be changed by using the styles menu option. Selecting the Text layout modifies the page layout.

Placing text within double brackets creates a link to a page on the site whether the page has been created or not. Clicking on the link when viewing the page either takes you to the page or creates a new one if it hasn't been created yet. When first entering the double brackets, SharePoint now displays a quick menu to add links to existing items on the site, as shown in Figure 3.29.

FIGURE 3.29

Creating or editing a site page

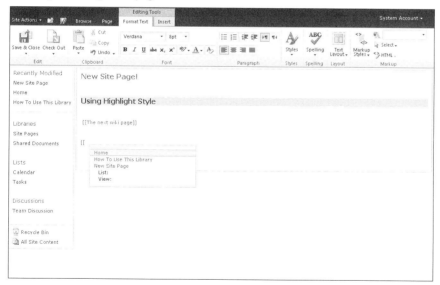

Creating a new site page

If you want to create a new site page, follow these steps:

1. Select New Page from the Site Actions menu in the top-left corner.

2. **Enter a name for the page.** A notification appears, stating that the page will be created in Site Pages. If you do not see this, you may need to activate the Wiki Home Page feature. A blank new page appears.

3. **Add content and then click Save & Close on the Ribbon.**

Editing a site page

Navigate to the site page you wish to edit and then follow these steps:

1. Select Edit Page from the Site Actions menu in the top-left corner.

2. **Edit the content and then click Save & Close on the Ribbon.**

Utilizing site assets

The Site Assets library is similar to the Images library. You may use this to store files that can be used within the site pages. These files are mostly media based and can be images, movies, audio files, and so on.

Adding files to site assets

Within the site in which you want to upload items to be used in the site pages, follow these steps:

1. Select View All Site Content from the Site Actions menu in the top-left corner.

2. Click on the Site Assets library.

3. Click on the Add Document link.

4. Click Browse and select the file you wish to upload from your local machine. Click OK.

The file or files are uploaded to the Site Assets library, as shown in Figure 3.30.

Using site asset items in site pages

Once images or other media files have been uploaded to the Site Assets library, they now can be used within a site page. To facilitate this action, follow these steps:

1. Navigate to the page you wish to add the site asset item.

2. Select Edit Page from the Site Actions menu in the top-left corner.

3. Click on the Insert tab at the page.

4. Click on the Picture button and then select From SharePoint.

5. In the dialog, select Site Assets from the left side and then select the image from the main list, as shown in Figure 3.31. Click Ok.

   The image is placed onto your site page as shown in Figure 3.32.

FIGURE 3.30

Images uploaded to site assets

FIGURE 3.31

Selecting a site asset

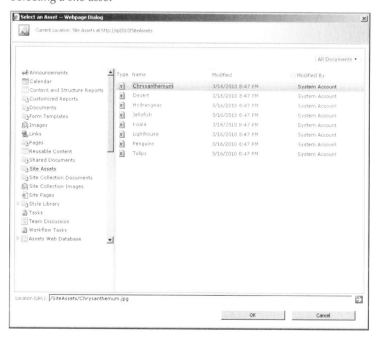

FIGURE 3.32

Image on site page

Summary

This chapter covered the SharePoint site and page library functionality, the site capabilities that SharePoint provides through rich templates, and the ability to create and share site templates of your own. Additionally, it discussed the publishing features that page libraries provide and the steps for customizing site columns, page layouts, and libraries to show the content that is important for your publishing process.

Using Lists and Libraries

L ists and libraries are the cornerstone of the SharePoint collaborative functionality. Lists provide a basic structure to organize data, and libraries provide a basic structure to store documents or other files. SharePoint provides lists and library templates to help with the most common information storage needs, but it also allows us to customize lists and libraries to meet our specific organizational requirements. With the SharePoint platform you can customize views of your list and library information so that you can slice, dice, and present data for each and every user audience.

This chapter covers the list and library functionality, including the List and Library templates SharePoint provides. I walk you through the options for customizing lists and libraries and creating views of list and library information so that they work best for every need and situation. Finally, you use the Web Parts provided for lists and libraries on Web Part pages to show list data in context with other information and connected to other lists.

Implementing SharePoint Lists and Libraries

SharePoint lists and libraries can be created from the list and library templates provided, or created as custom lists according to your needs. The templates that SharePoint provides include some basic functionality to meet the purpose of the lists. You can customize the columns for both lists that are created from templates and custom lists. Document libraries are specialized list types where each item is a file that can also have additional columns, or metadata, associated with that file. Document libraries also have an associated template file that is used as the basis for creating new files to be stored in the document library.

Using the SharePoint list templates

The SharePoint list templates fall into four areas:

- **Blank & Custom:** Templates for creating lists from scratch.
- **Communications:** These list templates focus on connecting site users by providing platforms for sharing contact information, ideas, and announcements.
- **Data:** Lists for accessing external data or conducting a survey.
- **Tracking:** The tracking list templates focus on helping site users manage schedules and activities.

Blank & Custom list templates

Use these list templates to create lists from scratch using the following methods:

- **Custom list:** Creates a blank list with only the system columns
- **Custom list in datasheet view:** Creates a blank list that uses the datasheet as the main view
- **Import Spreadsheet:** Generates a list based on spreadsheet data

Communication list templates

Use these list templates to create lists that store and share community information:

- **Announcements:** The announcement list is designed for adding short news articles for consumption on the local site. The list creates a list to support the article title, body, and expiration date. The Web Part created for the announcement list automatically filters based on expiration date so that only unexpired items are presented.
- **Contacts:** The contacts list template creates a list intended for storing contact information for your external contacts. You can use this list for internal contacts, but you may want to modify extraneous columns that are not applicable for internal contacts such as address fields and Web site.

Cross-Reference

You can synchronize contacts between SharePoint and an SFS-compatible contacts program such as Outlook. See Chapter 13 for more information about integration between Office and SharePoint. ∎

- **Discussion Board:** Discussion boards are intended to provide newsgroup-like discussions. The design is centered around threading for discussion topics and allows you to moderate the approved postings.
- **Links:** Links lists are simple lists that store the URL, friendly name, and description of sites that you want to link to. The friendly name appears in most views and is configured to link to the URL provided. As with any list that uses the hyperlink style column, you must be in the item's edit mode to configure the friendly name field; otherwise, you can only edit the URL field in datasheet edit mode.

Data list templates

The Data list templates allow you to create lists to access external content types or store information based on surveys. The two templates available under this category are:

- **External List:** Views the data of external content types.

- **Survey:** The survey list template creates a framework so that you can create survey questions of different types (ratings, multiple choice, or free text) and allow users to submit one or more responses. The survey functionality also allows you to create branching logic that selects the questions presented based on the answer to a specific question. The survey list template provides a graphical interface to view all submitted responses.

Tracking list templates

These tracking list templates help manage group activity and action.

- **Calendar:** Calendar lists are used for storing event, milestone, or other date-based information.

Note

You can synchronize events between SharePoint and an SFS-compatible calendar program such as Outlook. ■

- **Tasks:** The Tasks list stores task items that are assigned to site users. This list type allows users to easily view their tasks, task assignments, and overdue tasks and is a powerful tool for managing action and progress.

- **Status List Template (SPS only):** The Status list template is designed to create a list that stores key performance indicators created from spreadsheets, Analysis Services databases, SharePoint lists, or manually entered information. This list type supports logic that allows you to set goal and warning values to determine whether each indicator is at a green, yellow, or red level.

  Project Tasks: The project list stores task items assigned to users and is configured to support a Gantt view of the project.

- **Issue Tracking:** The issue tracking list is designed to log and track support issues as they are recorded, assigned, and resolved by site users. This list type has logic included that allows for e-mail to be sent when issues are assigned. In addition, the issue tracking list provides lookups to other related issues in the list.

Note

The issue tracking list has an associated issue tracking workflow to facilitate seamless issue resolution. See Chapter 8 for more information about workflows. ■

Creating a list using a template

To create a list using any of the templates previously discussed in this chapter, follow these steps:

1. Select More Options from the Site Actions menu in the top-left corner of any page on the site on which you would like to create the list.

2. Select the list template that you would like to use.

3. Enter the name and description (optional) for your list and select whether you would like the list displayed on the Quick Launch. (Click on More Options to get to the other settings.)

4. Click Create.

Using the SharePoint library templates

The SharePoint library templates fall into two main areas:

- **Content:** Most libraries are content libraries in which certain types of files or documents are stored.

- **Data:** Libraries to store data connections or reports.

Content library templates

Library templates provide some functionality based on the type of content that they expect to contain in the library. For example, a picture library has functionality for displaying library contents as thumbnails or as a slide show to assist with management of images because it expects to contain items with image formats. By selecting the appropriate document library template to use for your purposes when creating your libraries, you take advantage of this built-in functionality for your content. The following list describes the library templates SharePoint provides:

- **Document Library:** The Document Library template provides a document that can store any type of object that is allowed by the file include list.

- **Form Library:** The Form Library is designed to store XML-based forms such as InfoPath forms. You can upload other document types to a form library, but users that start a new form are presented with the default form that you have configured for that library. In addition, the form library can be configured to extract fields from forms that are saved to the form library, which is an effective and flexible way to extract information that can be aggregated and reported.

    Users who are filling out and saving forms to a form library are required to have a SharePoint-compatible XML editor such as InfoPath. Only one form template can be identified per form library.

- **Wiki Page Library:** The wiki page library is intended to store wiki pages. You can customize the wiki page library to add additional columns, but only wiki pages can be stored in the library.

- **Picture Library:** The picture library is intended to store graphics items. The picture library has built-in functionality to display items as thumbnails and to enable slide shows for all items in the library. In addition, the picture library has a picture editor selector for uploading multiple pictures so that you can link to your most commonly used picture locations and preview the items you are selecting. This library accepts non-picture file types but can display preview images only for graphic extensions that it recognizes, such as .jpg, .bmp, .tif, and .gif.

- **Slide Library (SPS only):** The slide library is designed to store presentation slides so that they can be sorted, managed, and reused. Each slide is available as a thumbnail and can be selected for inclusion in a new presentation directly from the slide library.

Data library templates

- **Report Library (SPS only):** Report libraries are designed for publishing and storing reports that SQL Server Reporting Services publishes.

Cross-Reference

See Chapter 15 for more information on reports and their functionality. ∎

- **Data Connection Library (SPS only):** Data connection libraries are designed to store ODC (Office Data Connection) and UDC (Universal Data Connection) files that enable definition and sharing of common data sources.

Cross-Reference

Please see Chapter 16 on Status Lists for information on creating and sharing ODC files. ∎

Creating a library using a template

To create a library using any of the library templates previously discussed in this chapter, follow these steps:

1. Select Create from the Site Actions menu in the top-left corner of any page on the site on which you would like to create the library.

2. Select the library template that you would like to use.

3. Enter the name and description (optional) for your list and select whether you would like the library displayed on the Quick Launch bar.

4. Click Create.

Creating custom SharePoint lists

If none of the list templates are designed to meet your purposes, you can create custom lists that contain the columns you need. You can create these lists in the standard Web view or in Data view or by importing a spreadsheet that has columns already defined.

Creating custom lists in a Web page

If you choose to create a custom list in a web page, SharePoint creates a list with a title column, and you can add additional columns to suit your design. To create a custom list in standard view, follow these steps:

1. Select More Options from the Site Actions menu in the top-left corner of any page on the site on which you would like to create the custom list.

2. Select List from the Filter By section and then select Custom List from the Blank & Custom category section.

3. Enter the name and description (optional) for your list and select whether you would like the list displayed on the Quick Launch bar. (Click on More Options to get to the other settings.)

4. Click Create.

To add additional columns to your custom list, follow these steps:

1. Open your list and select Create Column from the List tab on the Ribbon.

2. Provide a name for your column and choose the column type.

Cross-Reference

For details on available column types, see the "Implementing Custom Columns" section in this chapter. ■

3. Select whether you want this column to require information, and enter a default value if appropriate.

4. Click OK.

5. Repeat for any additional columns that you want to add.

Creating custom lists in Datasheet view

Creating a list in Datasheet view creates a list with the title column and configures the default view (All Items) as a datasheet view. You can then use the settings menu to add the additional columns that you need.

To create a custom list in datasheet view, follow these steps:

1. Select More Options from the Site Actions menu in the top-left corner of any page on the site on which you would like to create the custom list.

2. Select List from the Filter By section and then select Custom List in Datasheet View from the Blank & Custom category section.

3. Enter the name and description (optional) for your list and select whether you would like the list to appear on the Quick Launch. (Click on More Options to get to the other settings.)

4. Click Create.

To add additional columns to your custom list, follow these steps:

1. Open your list and select Create Column from the List tab on the Ribbon.
2. Provide a name for your column and choose the column type.
3. Select whether you want this column to require information, and enter a default value if appropriate.
4. Click OK.
5. Repeat for any additional columns that you want to add.

Importing spreadsheets to create custom lists

By importing a spreadsheet to create a custom list, you can leverage the existing column definition of the spreadsheet as well as quickly import the data. You must have Excel 2003 or later on the client machine from which you are importing the spreadsheet.

To create a custom list by importing a spreadsheet, follow these steps:

1. Select Create from the Site Actions menu in the top-left corner of any page on the site on which you would like to create the custom list.
2. Select List from the Filter By section and then select Import Spreadsheet from the Blank & Custom category section. Click Create.
3. Enter the name and description (optional) for your list and browse to the location of your spreadsheet. Select the spreadsheet and click Open.
4. Click Import.
5. Select Range of Cells in the Range Type field and then click the – symbol to the right of the Select Range field, as shown in Figure 4.1.

FIGURE 4.1

Using the Range Selector to define your spreadsheet import

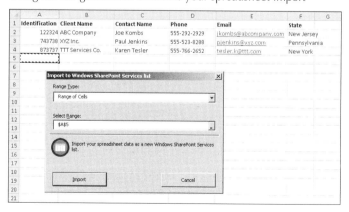

6. Drag the selector circle around the data that you would like to include in your spreadsheet import and click the icon with the red down arrow to the right of your named range, as shown in Figure 4.2.

7. Click Import.

FIGURE 4.2

Selecting the cells to import

After your spreadsheet has been imported, you can change the column types. For example, in our sample import, you might want the State column to be a Choice column. You can follow these steps to change the column type:

1. On the List tab of the Ribbon, click List Settings.

2. Select the column that you want to change.

3. Change the selection in the Type of information in this column field, as shown in Figure 4.3. Changing to a Choice type of column populates the choices from the values that exist in your current data.

4. Click OK.

FIGURE 4.3

Changing the column type for an imported list

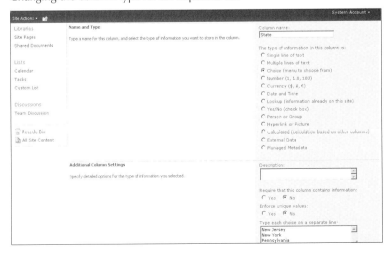

Note

SharePoint selects the first column that is a single line of text to be the primary column or the equivalent of the title column in a new custom list created in a browser. You cannot change the column type or delete this column, but you can change the column order. ∎

Configuring list and library settings

After you have created your list, you can modify the general list settings to configure the name, content approval, and versioning. By modifying the permissions and management settings, you configure the permissions, workflow, and information management policy settings. Finally, you can configure the RSS settings for your list or library by configuring the communications settings.

Configuring general settings

The general settings for a list allow you to configure the name, description, content approval, versioning, audience targeting, high-level permissions, and availability for search for your list. These settings help to tune the general behavior for your list, such as whether items are available for reading and editing by the owner only or by all readers (configured in Advanced Settings).

To configure the Title, Description, and Quick Launch settings for a list or library, follow these steps:

1. Select List Settings or Library Settings from the List tab or the Library tab on the Ribbon.
2. Select Title, description, and navigation in the General Settings section.
3. Edit the name, description, and Quick Launch bar selection as desired and click Save.

Note

If you change the name of the list after it is created, the Web address is not updated to reflect the same name. For example, if I create a list called List1, the Web address will be `http://<servername>/<sitename>/lists/List1`, and if I update the name of the list to be List2, the Web address will remain the same. This provides consistency for list users who have bookmarked the list, but it is often confusing for SharePoint users who look for list names based on the list Web address. ∎

To configure the versioning settings for a list or library, follow these steps:

1. Navigate to the list or library you would like to configure and click List Settings (or Library Settings) from the List (or Library) tab on the Ribbon.
2. Select Versioning settings in the General Settings section.
3. Select whether or not items in the list require content approval in the Content Approval section. Items that have not yet been approved will appear only to the item creator and users who have the right to view draft items as configured in Step 5 of this procedure.
4. Select whether you would like to keep versions. You can keep an infinite number of versions or specify how many versions that you would like to keep and how many drafts you would like to keep for each version. This setting helps manage the size of your list or library.

If your list is a document library, it can track both major and minor versions. Using major and minor versions is useful if you will be collaborating and developing many versions of the document. The minor versions represent work in progress, whereas the major versions represent milestones such as distributed version for review. SharePoint supports up to 511 minor versions for each major version, but you can tune the settings if you want to limit the number of minor versions to less that 511.

The content approval feature creates draft items that are similar to minor versions for both lists and document libraries. For lists that require content approval, the versions that are submitted for approval are considered draft versions. Minor versions are also considered draft items and do not require content approval if that feature is enabled.

Optionally enter the number of major versions to keep as well as the number of major versions in which drafts should be preserved. The drafts selection is only available on libraries.

5. **Select which users should be allowed to see draft items in your list or library.** These users will be able to see the items before they are approved. This option is available only if you require content approval or are creating minor versions.

6. **If your list is a document library, select whether or not you would like to require check out for documents before they are edited.** By enabling this option, you can ensure that multiple users are not editing the same document at the same time. If an item is checked out, other users cannot edit or upload updated versions of that document.

7. Click OK.

The advanced settings for a list are fairly different from those of a document library. Advanced settings for a list allow you to configure whether users can see and/or edit all or only their items, which is not an option with document libraries. Advanced settings for a document library allow you to configure the template for that library as well as the behavior for opening documents and locations to which documents can be sent.

To configure the advanced settings for document library, follow these steps:

1. Select Library Settings from the Library tab on the Ribbon.

2. Select Advanced settings in the General Settings section.

3. **Select whether or not you will allow the management of content types in the Content Types section.**

Cross-Reference
See Chapter 18 for more information about content types. ∎

4. **Provide the URL for the document library template.** This template will be used if a user selects to create a new document in the document library. If you have enabled management of content types, the content type manages the template setting.

5. **Select how you would like documents to open for items that can be opened in both a client application and Web page.** Opening in a client application provides the user with the familiar application interface and menus while leaving the browser open on the team site in another window. Opening in a Web page still enables editing but can be frustrating because if a user closes the document by closing the browser, they also close the team site as well.

6. **Enter a Destination name and URL in the Custom Send To Destination section if you want to provide the capability for users to send copies of documents to other locations.** This feature is typically used in records management scenarios.

Cross-Reference

See Chapter 12 for more information about records management and configuring send to locations. ■

7. **Select whether you will allow folders for your list.** Folders provide excellent ways to organize items in subcategories for your list and are commonly used in document libraries. However, items can only be in one folder or another, so folders cannot be used to assign multiple attributes to an item; using metadata is a better option for multiple attributes.

8. **Select whether you will allow list contents to appear in search results.**

9. **Click OK.**

To configure the advanced settings for a list, follow these steps:

1. **From the List tab on the Ribbon, select List Settings.**

2. **Select Advanced settings in the General Settings section.**

3. **Select whether you will allow the management of content types in the Content Types section.**

Cross-Reference

See Chapter 18 for more information about content types. ■

4. **Configure the item-level security by selecting whether users can read only their own items or all items, and whether users can edit only their own items, all items, or no items.** For users to be able to edit all items, they must also be contributors to the list.

5. **Select whether you would like to enable attachments for the list.** If attachments are enabled, users can attach one or more files to each list item.

6. **Select whether you will allow folders for your list.** Folders provide excellent ways to organize items in subcategories for your list and are commonly used in document libraries. However, items can only be in one folder or another, so folders cannot be used to assign multiple attributes to an item; using metadata is a better option for multiple attributes.

7. **Select whether or not you will allow list contents to appear in search results.**

8. **Click OK.**

To configure the audience targeting settings, follow these steps:

1. Select List Settings or Library Settings from the List or Library tabs on the Ribbon.

2. Select Audience targeting settings in the General Settings section.

3. Select the check box to enable audience targeting if you want Web parts to provide conditional display of your list data based on the audience membership of the user. The audience configuration settings are on the Web Part itself.

4. Click OK.

Adding ratings to your lists

A new feature in SharePoint 2010 lists is the rating of content. You may now allow users to rate items in a list or library and display the average rating to everyone. When this setting is selected, the list or library receives two new columns: Ratings (0-5) and Number of Ratings. The Ratings (0-5) column is automatically added to the default view.

1. Select List Settings or Library Settings from the List or Library tabs on the Ribbon.

2. Select Rating settings in the General Settings section.

3. Select Yes to allow items in the list to be rated.

4. Click OK.

Note

Ratings may not be reflected immediately. They are calculated on a timed basis. ∎

Managing lists and configuring list permissions

The Permissions and Management configuration options for lists and libraries allow you to tune the permissions for your list as well as configure some advanced functionality, such as workflow and information rights management. In addition, you can save your list or library as a template or delete your list or library.

To delete a list or library, follow these steps:

1. Select List Settings or Library Settings from the List tab or the Library tab on the Ribbon.

2. Select Delete this list (or Delete this document library) in the Permissions and Management section.

3. Confirm that you want to send the list to the Recycle Bin.

To save a list or library as a template, follow these steps:

1. Select List Settings or Library Settings from the List tab or the Library tab on the Ribbon.

2. Select Save list as template (or Save document library as a template if you have a document library) in the Permissions and Management section.

3. **Enter the File name, Template name, and Template description and whether you want to include the list content or not.** The template name is the name that will appear on the Create page. The filename and template description appear in the list template gallery. If you choose to include content, a list created from the list template will include your list items.

4. **Click OK.**

To configure permissions for a list or library, follow these steps:

1. **Select List Settings or Library Settings from the List tab or the Library tab on the Ribbon.**

2. **Select Permissions for this list (or Permissions for this document library) in the Permissions and Management section.**

3. **Click on the Stop Inheriting Permissions or Manage Parent.** When a list is created initially, the list inherits permissions from the site in which it is located. If you want to modify the permissions for the list, you can copy the permissions from the parent and discontinue the inheritance. You can then modify the list permissions separately from the site.

   If you choose to discontinue the inheritance of permissions, you still have the option to inherit from the parent site if you want to revert to that model.

4. **Whether you stop inheriting or manage the parent, use the permissions buttons in the Permission Tools tab on the Ribbon to grant, edit, or remove permissions to users and groups.**

Many times users or groups receive permissions from being in other groups, part of Active Directory groups, or having permissions inherited from parent sites. A new feature in SharePoint 2010 is the ability to test the permissions of a user or group.

To check permissions for a list or library, follow these steps:

1. **Select List Settings or Library Settings from the List or Library tabs on the Ribbon.**

2. **Select Permissions for this list (or Permissions for this document library) in the Permissions and Management section.**

3. **Click on the Check Permissions button on the Ribbon.**

4. **Enter a user or group and click the Check Now button.** (Use of the check names or directory buttons are optional.)

5. **Enter a user or group and click the Check Now button.** SharePoint displays the permissions for the user (or group) entered as well as explains how they are receiving those permissions.

6. **You may continue to check more names or click Close when done.**

Cross-Reference

See Chapter 10 for more information on configuring security. ∎

Files that are checked out in a document library that do not have a checked-in version can block productivity of that file, especially if the document owner is not available to check the document back in. The management settings for document libraries allow you to take control of these documents so that they can be checked in and used. To manage checked-out files for a document library, follow these steps:

1. On the Library tab on the Ribbon, click Library Settings.

2. Select Manage files which have no checked-in version in the Permissions and Management section.

3. Select the document that you want to manage and select Take Ownership of Selection from the top of the list.

Note

Taking ownership of checked-out items could result in a loss of changes. ■

To configure workflow settings for a list or library, follow these steps:

1. Select List Settings or Library Settings from the List tab or Library tab on the Ribbon.

2. Select Workflow settings in the Permissions and Management section.

3. Select the workflow template that you want to use for your list. The description to the right of the Select a workflow template field provides details of the intended use of the workflow.

4. Type a name for the workflow in the Type a unique name for this workflow field.

5. Select an existing or create a new task list for storing the workflow items in the Task List section.

6. Select an existing (if already created) or create a new history list for the workflow.

7. Select whether you want the workflow to be initiated when an item is created or edited, or manually launched by a user. If you have turned on versioning, you can also initiate the workflow when a major version is published.

8. Click Next to fill in workflow-specific information if appropriate for your workflow (this is necessary for the out-of-the-box Approval or Collect Feedback workflows) or OK to finish.

Cross-Reference

See Chapter 8 for information on configuring and customizing workflows. ■

Information management policies allow you to set policies for your list. These policies are used to enforce organizational requirements such as who can access the information, how long list items are retained, and to audit the adherence to the policy. Information rights management policies apply even after documents have been downloaded and protect that information. Information management policies can also be applied to content types.

You can select to either apply a site collection information management policy or create a new information policy to apply to your list. To configure information management policies for a list, follow these steps:

1. Select List Settings or Library Settings from the List tab or the Library tab on the Ribbon.

2. Select Information management policy settings in the Permissions and Management section.

3. Select a site collection policy or the option to define a policy.

4. Click OK.

Configuring communication settings for a list

SharePoint provides the capability for users to subscribe to a Really Simple Syndication (RSS) feed for a list and displays RSS items in a Web page format. This allows users to consume new list items in any RSS reader or to view them in an RSS Web Part on a SharePoint Web Part page.

To configure RSS for a list or library, follow these steps:

1. Select List Settings or Library Settings from the List or Library tabs on the Ribbon.

2. Select RSS settings in the Communications section.

3. Select whether you would like to enable RSS for the list or not in the List RSS section.

4. Provide the Title for the RSS feed, Description of the RSS feed, and the URL to the image for the RSS feed in the RSS Channel Information. Additionally, configure whether or not the RSS feed should truncate multiline text fields to 256 characters or not.

   If you are configuring the RSS settings for a document library, configure the Document Options section to select whether to include file enclosures for items in the feed or to link RSS items directly to their files.

5. Select what fields you would like to include in the RSS feed in the Columns section. If you include fields that are marked with an asterisk, they will be matched to standard RSS tags such as Modified to Publish Date and Modified By to Author.

6. Configure the maximum items to include and the maximum days to include in an RSS feed in the Item Limit section.

7. Click OK.

To view the RSS feed for your list or library, follow these steps:

1. Select RSS Feed from the Library or List tabs on the Ribbon.

2. In the RSS feed view, you can subscribe to the feed by clicking on the link, as shown in Figure 4.4, or you can use the URL that is generated to configure an RSS Web Part.

FIGURE 4.4

Viewing an RSS feed for your list

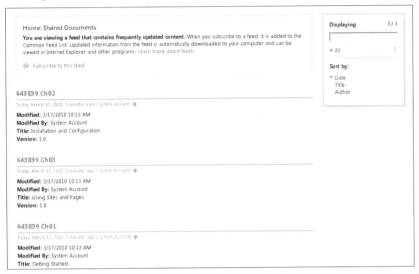

Tip

The RSS feed is cached, meaning that even though you make changes to the RSS settings, you may not see the changes. In order to see the changes you may need to refresh the browser when viewing the RSS feed page. ■

Organizing content using folders

For any list or library, you can create folders in which to organize your items if the folder option is enabled in the advanced settings for your list or library. This feature is most commonly used in document libraries to provide organization for large number of documents. Folders are URL addressable so that you can provide a link to a specific folder in your list or library.

Items can only be stored in one folder, so creating a folder structure that takes that into account is important. However, you can create views that show items across all folders, which provides some flexibility for providing additional ways to find items in addition to the folder structure. See the "Creating Views" section in this chapter for more information about views.

To create a folder in your list or library, select New Folder from the New menu in the top navigation bar of the list or library that you would like to create your folder. If you have created your folder in a document library, you can then view your library in Explorer view by selecting Open with Windows Explorer from the Actions menu.

Once the library is open in Explorer view, you can drag and drop or copy and paste documents into the folder. Alternatively, you can upload documents to your folder by using a Web browser by navigating to the folder and then selecting Upload from the top navigation bar while in that folder. The breadcrumb of your site will show that you are in the folder as shown in Figure 4.5.

FIGURE 4.5

Document Library breadcrumb that indicates you are in a folder

Customizing Lists and Libraries

By customizing lists and libraries, you are able to tailor your lists, whether they are created from a template or as custom lists, to match your needs. You can add columns to track the information that is important to you, create custom lookup lists as centralized references to other lists, and set item-level security to secure each item appropriately.

Implementing custom columns

Custom columns allow you to track the information that is important for you. With list items, the additional columns are customized so that you are tracking the information that is important to the task, announcement, event, or other list type. With documents, columns provide the additional metadata about the document so that it is easy to find, categorize, and track.

With every column, you have the opportunity to suggest default values. Default values provide a suggested entry for a field but can be replaced by whatever the user types. For some column types like choice columns, the first choice option is automatically populated in the default value field so if you would like a different default value or none at all either enter that default value or clear the field. You can also suggest a default value that is a calculated value like [Me] for a single line of text field which will automatically enter the username of the creator of the item in the field. See the section on calculated values below for valid operators.

For each column, you also have the option of making it a required column. This setting will ensure that the user cannot save the item without entering a value. However, this can make bulk updating of data somewhat dicey because if you have a value that you want to fill down in datasheet view (similar to the Excel capability to fill a column), it will not let you do that for the column if another column for that item is required and empty (you are not allowed to leave the row until that column is populated). So, you may want to deselect requiring a value for columns before doing bulk updates.

The following column types are available for use in customizing your SharePoint lists and libraries whether they are custom lists or additional columns added to the list created from a list template.

- **Single line of text:** This column type accepts up to 255 characters of text. This is the column type for the title column of every list and cannot be changed for that title column. The default value (if configured) can be a text value or a calculated value.

- **Multiple lines of text:** A large text box for text longer than 255 characters. This column type can be configured to allow plain text, rich text, or enhanced rich text which supports pictures, tables, and hyperlinks. If you choose either of the rich text options, the text gets stored in SharePoint as raw HTML. If viewed by the display page or edit page, this text is displayed properly. If it is exposed via another method such as the data view Web Part, you will get the HTML markups and it will not render correctly. If you will be exposing the content of a multiple lines of text field in this fashion, it is recommended that you limit uses to plain text.

  In addition, you can configure this column to append edits of the text in this field to previous content stored in the field. This is great for notes columns that contain a running log of notes so that each entry is preserved.

  The ability to set the number of lines for editing allows you to determine how big a text box you will give users to edit. If you enter a large number such as 40 lines of text, you will be using a large portion of the edit item real estate (for a 1024 x 768 screen).

- **Choice (menu to choose from):** This list column allows you to enter the choices that you enter as options. Each choice is entered on a separate line in the Type Each Choice on a Separate Line field, and you can allow whether or not users can enter their own "fill-in" choices.

  Choices can be either offered from a drop-down menu or radio buttons, both of which allow users to select only one option. Alternatively, you can allow multiselect choices by presenting the choices using check boxes. If you allow multiselect, you limit the ability to group by this field because there is an array of choices for multiselect that grows exponentially with each choice option. For example, a list with multiselect of options A, B, or C allows seven options:

  - A
  - B
  - C
  - A, B

- A, C
- B, C
- A, B, C

Because of the unpredictable number combination of options, SharePoint will not group by a multiselect choice field nor allow them to be used as lookup columns.

- **Number (1, 1.0, 100):** The number column is used for columns that contain numbers and provides some value checking to confirm that correct numbers are being entered. Number columns allow you to set a minimum and maximum allowed value and to limit number of decimal places from 0 to 5. You can also configure the column to display number entries as percentages; however, keep in mind that the value will still be the stored value. For example, a value that shows 50 percent will be stored as .5.

- **Currency($, ¥, €):** The currency column is used for columns that contain currency numbers and provides some value checking to confirm that correct numbers are being entered. Currency columns allow you to set a minimum and maximum allowed value and to limit number of decimal places from 0 to5. You also configure the column to display the correct currency format from a wide list of currencies ranging from Albanian to Zimbabwe currency. If the user attempts to enter the currency symbol with the number, the list will reject the entry.

- **Date and Time:** The date and time column supports date entries. You can configure the column to provide a date field only or a date and time field for specific time entries. The default value can be set to be today's date, a specified date, or a calculated value (such as [today]+2) for date values that you will like to suggest.

- **Lookup (information already on this site):** The lookup column allows you to select a column from other lists on the site to use as references for your current list. This allows you to create relationships between lists. The lookup must be to a column of single line of text format or to supported built-in columns which are ID (automatically generated unique ID for each item), content type, copy source (available for form, picture, document, and wiki libraries), and version.

    SharePoint will only show the lookup field that you select and not other related values from the list. For example, if you choose Last Name from the Contact list as a lookup field for your list, SharePoint will just show the last name selected and cannot be configured to show the related First Name for the item as well.

- **Yes/No (check box):** The yes/no column presents a check box for a user to select to indicate "Yes" or deselect to indicate "No."

- **Person or Group:** This column provides functionality so that users can select one or more people or groups from the directory service that supports SharePoint. You can configure this column to allow users to select only people or people and groups.

- **Hyperlink or Picture:** The hyperlink or picture column allows users to enter any linkable entry. When editing the hyperlink field using the edit form, the user is prompted for two fields for the column — a Web address and a description. The description is presented as the friendly name for the column to the viewer but it is delivered to the configured web address.

- **Calculated (calculation based on other columns):** The calculated column type allows you to calculate a value based on other columns in the list. The user is not allowed to edit the calculated value for an item. The calculated column is not allowed as an input for a lookup column. Standard math, comparison, and logical operators are allowed in equations including +, -, /, *, %, ^, >, <, >=, <=, <>, &, OR, NOR, and XOR.

  Examples of types of calculations that are valuable for SharePoint lists are

  - **Text calculation for full name:** Calculation of full name given a first name column and last name column using this formula: [First Name]+' '+[Last Name].

  - **Text calculation of first 15 characters of string:** Calculation of the leftmost 15 characters of a text field using this formula: =LEFT([Single line of text],15) will result in a calculated field as shown in Figure 4.6.

  - **Date calculation of due date:** Calculation of due date for seven days after the create date for an item using this formula: [Created]+7.

  - **Logical calculation of Yes/No:** Calculation that shows yes if a value of the actual sales column has exceeded the value of the sales goal column using this formula: =IF([Actual Sales]>[Sales Goal],"yes","no").

    The resulting column would show values as shown in Figure 4.7.

FIGURE 4.6

Results of a calculated text column that returns the 15 leftmost characters

FIGURE 4.7

Results of logically calculated column for Met Sales Goal

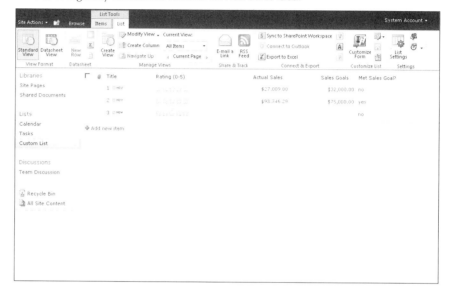

- **Statistical calculation of an average:** Calculation of the average of two columns (Q1 Sales and Q2 Sales) if they do not add to 0 (which would result in an error for the average using the formula: =IF(([Q1 Sales]+[Q2 Sales])<>0,AVERAGE([Q1 Sales],[Q2 Sales],0).

Because you select the type of data that the calculated value returns such as single line of text, number, currency, date, and time or yes/no, SharePoint can accurately display the calculated value.

Tip

Use the list of available columns to add them to your formula. The Silverlight-based dialog is unforgiving, and if there is an error in your formula, you will need to go through the creation steps all over again. ■

- **External data:** This column allows users to select a value from an external content type. You can configure this column to also return other fields from the content type when viewed, although these other columns do not display when the user is editing the column.

Cross-Reference

Please see Chapter 17 for more information on using external content types in lists and defining business data applications. ■

Linking to Lookup Lists

You can select "Title (linked to item)" as the lookup column as well. This creates a field that links through to the lookup list. For a simple lookup list like the one in the "Creating lookup lists" section, this is not very useful because the list only contains values for that particular column. However, if you are referring to a lookup list with a wealth of additional information, you can use the lookup column (linked to item) to create a click-through to the full lookup item. Items that have lookup columns that are linked to the lookup item will most likely (depending on the columns selected in the view) have more than one linked field, one to the item in the current list for viewing and editing and one to the linked item. To help users understand what information that they are linking to, it is helpful to name the column appropriately to give additional guidance.

As an example, I have created a contact list that has a lookup to a customer list with the customer (linked to customer list) as the column. The view of the resulting contact list is shown.

Lookup list with link to edit contact item and link to view and edit of lookup column for customer.

Creating lookup lists

One custom list that is very useful is to create a list of values that are used as lookups for other lists. This list is very helpful if you want to standardize choices to be consistent across multiple lists and only have to update one location. For example, you may create a list of the regions that your company is divided into. You can then use that list as a lookup for the contact list so that your contacts are divided by region and for your document library so that documents are targeted to the correct region and so on. If your company adds a region, you can then update the custom region list with the new value which then becomes available to all lists using the region list as a lookup.

To create a lookup list, follow these steps:

1. Select Create from the Site Actions menu in the top-left corner of any page on the site that you would like to create a lookup list.

2. Select Custom List from the Custom Lists section.

3. Enter the Name and Description (optional) for your lookup list and do not select to have the list displayed on the Quick Launch bar (using the More Options button).

4. Click Create.

5. Enter each lookup value in the Title field of the list.

To use your lookup list as a reference in an existing list or library:

1. Select Create Column from the Settings menu in the top navigation bar of the list or library that you want to use the lookup list.

2. Enter the name of the column that will use the lookup values.

3. Select lookup in the The Type of Information in this Column Is field.

4. Select your lookup list in the Get Information From: field.

5. Select the Title column in the In This Column: field as shown in Figure 4.8.

6. Click OK.

FIGURE 4.8

Creating a column based on a lookup list

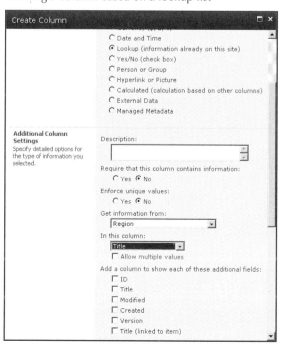

Tip

You may now specify relationship behavior between lists. The two options are Restrict Delete or Cascade Delete and appear when setting up the lookup column. These options determine what happens when you delete an item from a list that is being used as a lookup. Either the deletion is restricted if there are items in the child list linking to that item or the deletion of the item deletes the items in the child list. ∎

Configuring list and library item security

With SharePoint 2010, you can also set item-level security on the contents of your lists and libraries. This allows you to combine items in libraries that make sense for navigation and views while still preserving the security of your items.

To configure security for a list or library item, follow these steps:

1. **Click on the down arrow on the item that you want to manage permissions and select Manage Permissions from the Edit menu, as shown in Figure 4.9.**

2. **On the Edit tab on the Ribbon, click the Stop Inheriting Permissions button to copy permissions from the parent list or library and to discontinue inheritance of permissions.** Items inherit permissions from the parent list until this action has been taken.

3. **Click the Grant Permissions button to add users with permissions to the item.**

   If you want to remove users, select the users in the permissions list that you want to remove and click the Remove User Permissions button from the Edit tab on the Ribbon, as shown in Figure 4.10.

FIGURE 4.9

Managing permissions for a list item

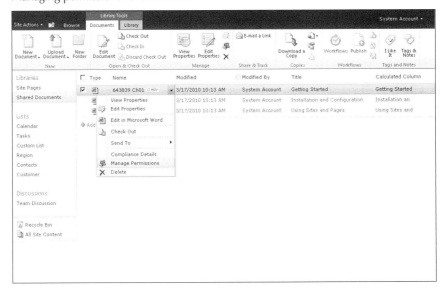

FIGURE 4.10

Removing permissions for users on a document

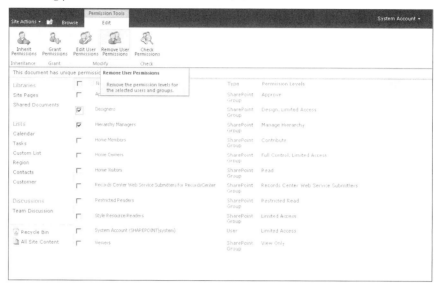

If you want to edit permissions for existing users, select the users in the permissions list that you want to remove and select Edit User Permissions from the Actions menu.

Creating Views

Creating views for your lists and libraries is a critical activity that allows you to present the right information to your users in a format and grouping that is meaningful to their purpose. Views are very flexible tools that allow you to explicitly define the selection, sorting, and presentation of items.

Selecting the view type

Each view creates a new page by which the list data is viewed. There are four view types that you can choose from, and each is detailed below. Once you have selected a view type for your view, you cannot change the view type setting for that view. although you can put a standard view or Gantt view into datasheet mode for quick editing.

- **Standard view:** The standard view is a Web page list view that displays the columns selected in the sort order and groupings as defined for the view.

- **Calendar view:** The calendar view type displays list items in a day, week, or month calendar view.

- **Datasheet view:** The datasheet view type creates a view in an Excel-like grid for bulk editing of data. Users must be using Office 2003 or later to take advantage of the datasheet editing features like the ability to drag and fill a value down a column. Standard and Gantt view types can be put in datasheet mode once created, but only the datasheet view type will open in that mode.

- **Gantt view:** The Gantt style view is intended to display list items over time. When you define a Gantt view, you need to specify a title (such as task name) and the start date and due date columns so that the view can be created using those parameters. The issue list, project task list, and task list have those columns already defined so they are excellent candidates to support a Gantt view, but this view style can also be applied to any custom list columns that you can designate as title, start date, and due date columns. The Gantt view of a list is shown in Figure 4.11.

FIGURE 4.11

Gantt view of a list

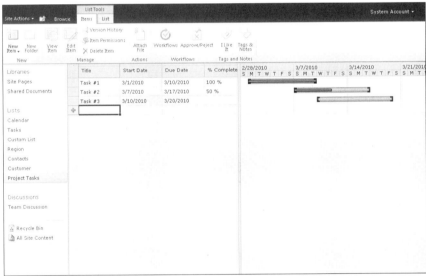

If you choose to create a view based on an existing view instead of picking a view type, the view type of the view you are copying will be used.

Configuring view settings

After you have selected the view type, you configure the view settings to select the item set that you want and to present that item set in a view that is sorted and styled to meet the goals of the view.

- **Public or Private View:** You can create a public view that is visible to all users of the list or a private view that will only show up as an option in your view choices. This selection can only be made at the time of the view creation and cannot be modified after the view has been created.

- **Audience:** If you configure the view to be a public view, you can select whether or not you would like the view to be the default view for the list. If the view is the default view, users will open this view of the list if they select the list without navigating directly to a fully qualified view name.

- **Visible Columns:** The selected columns in the visible columns section will be displayed in the view. You can also modify the position each visible column will have counting from the left side. If you are using a column for a criterion to filter by or group by, you can optimize page utilization by not selecting them as a visible column.

  The visible column selection presents several versions of the primary column (name for a document type and title or first text field for a list) so that you can select the columns that will link to the document or item and edit the document and item. The columns that note (linked to document) or (icon linked to document) will allow users to click on them to open the document or item. The columns that note (linked to document with edit menu) will present the edit menu when the users clicks on the document. And finally, the edit column (linked to edit item) will open the document properties or item in edit mode.

- **Sort Order:** The sort section allows you to choose which columns dictate which items are presented first. If you choose more than one column to sort on, the second column will sort items that have the same first sort column value.

- **Filter Options:** The filter section allows you to enter the criteria so that only items that match your filter criteria are displayed in a view. This allows you to create views for subsets of items that are particular to an audience or purpose.

  You can use more than one filter criteria (up to ten) to select the exact subset of list items that you want. For example, you may want to select all items that have the category column equal to bug and the assigned to column equal to the current user.

  The filter fields accept two variables. The first is [Me] to filter a field by the current user and the second is [Today] to filter by the current date. You can use the [Today] variable in an equation so that it returns everything created in the past week by setting the filter to show items when the "created" column is greater than [Today]-7 as shown in Figure 4.12.

FIGURE 4.12

Creating a filter to show items created in the past week.

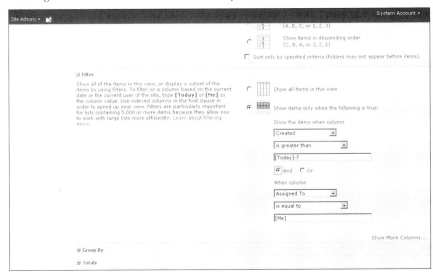

If you have more than one filter criteria, you must select whether the filters are AND so that they are cumulative so that items have to meet all filters or OR so that items have to meet only one of the filter criterion. You can mix AND and OR criteria so that the filter will pull all items that match the AND filters and pull all items that map the OR filter. For example, you can create a view that shows all issues that are assigned to me and are due in the past two weeks OR items that are high priority. In that case, the filter will return items that are high priority that are not assigned to me or due in the past two weeks.

Global query: DO these quotation marks need to appear? – not really – removed – sm.

Issue lists have a default filter set for the column Current equal to YES so that only the most recent version of an issue will appear.

- **Group By:** The group by view allows you to define the columns by which your items will be grouped. If you select a subgroup, the items will be nested under the primary group according to subgroup as shown in Figure 4.13. Multichoice columns are not available to be used for grouping.

  The group by field allows you to configure whether grouping will be showed as expanded and collapsed. This setting applies to all groupings, so if you select that groupings will be collapsed, the group, and subgroups will be collapsed.

- **Totals:** You can configure totals for any of your visible columns. If the column is a text-based column (text, choice, or person/group), you can configure the total as a count of that column as shown in the count of issue ID in Figure 4.13. If you have a number-based column (either number or currency), you can perform statistical operations on that column, as shown in Figure 4.14. Date columns allow you to show counts, average (in datasheet view only), maximum, or minimum totals.

FIGURE 4.13

Grouping and subgrouping view

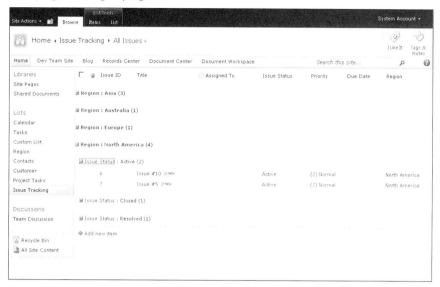

FIGURE 4.14

Statistical total options for a number column

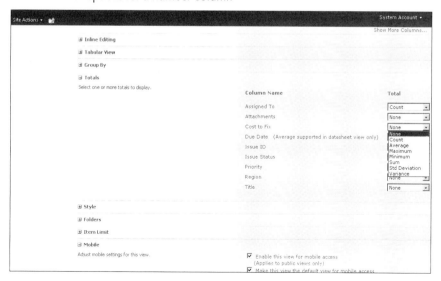

Style: The style setting allows you to pick a style that will delineate the items. The style choices are:

- **Basic Table:** Each item in a separate row in a table with a dividing border.
- **Newsletter:** This style presents the content in a multiline format similar to a news article with a separator line between each item, as shown in Figure 4.15.
- **Newsletter, no lines:** The newsletter no lines style presents the content in a multiline format similar to a news article, with no separator line between each item.
- **Shaded:** The shaded view shows items in a single line and shades every other row.
- **Boxed (lists only):** The boxed style shows items in two columns with a box surrounding each item.
- **Boxed, no labels (lists only):** The boxed style, no labels, shows items in two columns with a box surrounding each item but does not include the column labels for the items.
- **Document Details (document libraries only):** The document details style is a two-column view that shows each document item (including folders) in a box as shown.
- **Preview Pane:** The preview pane style creates a two-column view in which all the task item titles are listed in the left-hand column and the titles are linked to the item. In the right column or preview pane, the columns for the view are listed, and when you hover over an item in the left column, the values for that item are displayed in the right pane, as shown in Figure 4.16.

FIGURE 4.15

List using the newsletter style option

FIGURE 4.16

Preview pane style for a list view

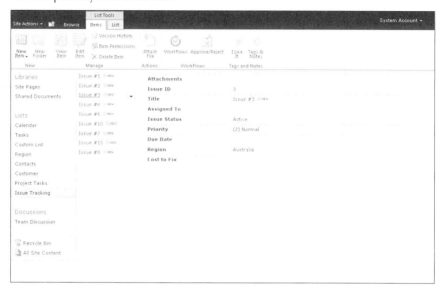

- **Default:** The default style shows each item on its own line with all the columns selected for the view displayed from left to right.

- **Folders:** Select whether or not you would like to show items inside folders in the Folder or Flat: field. This allows you to select whether you want the view to retain your folder structure and only show the qualified items when a user clicks into a folder or whether you want to use the view to show all items regardless of the folder they are stored in.

- **Item Limit:** Specify how many items will be displayed in the Number of items to display field. Additionally, specify if the items will be displayed in batches of that specified size or limited to the number of items you have specified so that the view only returns the specified number of documents sorted according to the view and no more.

- **Mobile:** Specify if you would like to make the view available for mobile view and whether it is the default mobile view or not. This section also provides the Web addresses for both this mobile view and the currently configured default mobile view.

Selecting and modifying views

Views are presented in a drop-down list in the right-hand corner of the list. From this view selector, you can select both public and private views, modify the current view, and create a new view.

Using List Web Parts

The information stored in lists and libraries can be made more powerful when presented in a Web Part page that presents the information in context for a user audience. Once a list or library has been created in your site, it is available as a Web Part that can be added one or many times throughout your site, connected to other Web Parts, and modified to show the information most appropriate for that Web page audience.

Adding a list Web Part

All lists and libraries on your site can be added as Web Parts to pages on your site. This allows you to create pages with multiple Web Parts that provide a consolidated view of the site content and to present the list and library information in a page that adds context to the information either through additional text or other list data that is relevant for the user tasks.

To add a list or library Web Part to your page, follow these steps:

1. On the page that you want to add the list or library Web Part, select Edit Page from the Site Actions menu in the upper-left corner.

2. Select the zone in which you want to add the Web Parts and click Add a Web Part.

3. Select the lists and libraries that you want to add to your page, as shown in Figure 4.17. If you select Web Parts that you want to display in a zone other than the one that you are in, you can drag the list Web Part to that zone after you have added it to the page.

4. Click Add.

FIGURE 4.17

Add Web Parts tool pane

The list and library Web Parts are added to your page with the default look and feel for that type of list as shown in Figure 4.18.

FIGURE 4.18

List Web Part default views

List Web Parts are added with the link to add a new item at the bottom of each list. This is controlled by the toolbar type setting on the Web Part. If you would like to modify whether this link is shown, follow these steps:

1. **On the page with the list Web Part that you would like to modify, select Edit Page from the Site Actions menu in the upper-left corner.**

2. **Select Edit Web Part from the Edit menu on your Web Part.**

3. **Select a toolbar option.** The Summary Toolbar option provides the link to add a new item at the bottom of the list Web Part as shown in the Announcements Web Part in Figure 4.19. The Full Toolbar option will insert the toolbar for the list or library at the top of the list Web Part, as shown in the Shared Documents Web Part in Figure 4.19. The No Toolbar option will just present the list content as shown in the Links Web Part.

4. **Click OK.**

FIGURE 4.19

Toolbar options for list Web Parts

The list and library Web Part title is linked to the default view for that list or library. If you want to change the link for the Web Part title, follow these steps:

1. On the part with the list Web Part that you want to modify, select Edit Page from the Site Actions menu in the upper-left corner.

2. Select Edit Web Part from the Edit menu on your Web Part.

3. Expand the Advanced section of the Web Part settings and enter the new link for the title in the Title URL field.

4. Click OK.

List and library Web Parts are connected to the list data, but if they are deleted from a page, they do not delete the list itself.

Cross-Reference

See Chapter 5 for more information about Web Part settings and configuration. ■

Modifying list Web Part views

You can modify the view of a list or library Web Part once it has been added to your page so that you display the appropriate information for your audience. You can select a view that you have already configured for your list or library or you can modify the view directly in the Web Part. If you choose to use a view that you configured in your list or library, the Web Part will adopt those view settings but will not stay synchronized, so if you make changes to your list and library view, the list Web Part will not reflect those changes unless you select the view again in the Web Part pane.

To modify the view for your list Web Parts, follow these steps:

1. On the page with the list Web Part that you want to modify, select Edit Page from the Site Actions menu in the upper-left corner.

2. Select Edit Web Part from the Edit menu on the Web Part.

3. Click Edit the current view in the List Views section, as shown in Figure 4.20, or select a view that you have already configured in the Selected View drop-down menu.

4. Modify the view settings as appropriate by changing the visible columns, sort order, filter, group by, or other settings. The item limit section determines how many items will show up in the view on your Web Part page.

5. Click OK.

Cross-Reference

For more information on the view settings, see the "Configuring view settings" section of this chapter. ■

FIGURE 4.20

Editing the view for a list Web Part

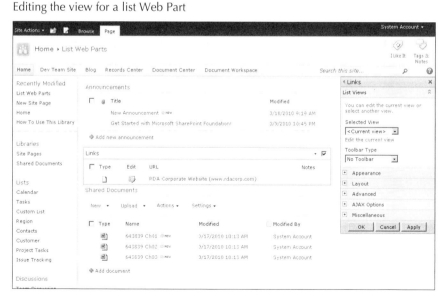

Connecting Web Parts

List Web Parts on a page can be connected so that you can configure a master-slave Web Part relationship. This allows you to configure a Web Part page so that users narrow the information to exactly what they need to see without leaving the page.

To connect list Web Parts, follow these steps:

1. On the page with the list Web Parts that you want to connect, select Edit Page from the Site Actions menu in the upper-left corner.

2. Select Edit Web Part from the Edit menu on the provider Web Part that will provide the row to the consumer Web Part.

3. In the Edit menu for the Web Part, select Connections ⇨ Provide Row To ⇨ <Web Part Name> where Web Part Name is the list Web Part that you want to provide the connection to, as shown in Figure 4.21. The Configure Connection dialog appears.

4. In the Configure Connection dialog box, select the field in the provider list that you will be sending to the consumer list as well as the field in the consumer list that will be used to filter on, as shown in Figure 4.22. If you do not see your column in the drop-down menu, confirm that the column is visible in the Web Part view.

FIGURE 4.21

Configuring the connection between lists

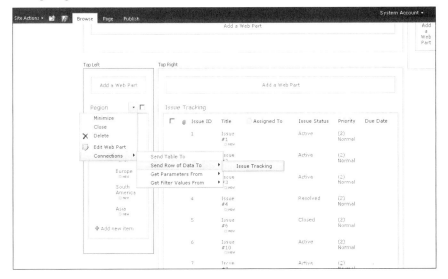

Tip

If your browser is blocking pop-ups, the connection dialog does not appear. You must allow pop-ups for your SharePoint site to use the connection functionality. ■

FIGURE 4.22

Selecting the columns that will be sent and received

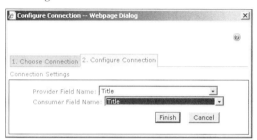

5. Click OK in the Web Part tool pane.

You can connect a list to multiple Web Parts. Once a list is configured to be a master Web Part, a diagonal arrow selector for the list items will appear. If the arrow is darkened, that is the provider row that is being sent to the consumer.

Customizing a List Data Entry Form Using InfoPath 2010

A great new integration point in SharePoint 2010 is with InfoPath forms. You may now use InfoPath to change the user experience in working with lists. Previously, in MOSS 2007, you needed to create a new page and customize data entry that way (either with Web Parts or custom controls). Nonetheless, users could still get to the base list and the SharePoint system interface for that list. Now you can change how the system renders the data entry using InfoPath 2010.

Note

In order to modify the list forms in InfoPath 2010, you must have the InfoPath 2010 Designer application installed locally. ■

To customize a list's data entry form, follow these steps:

1. Navigate to the list you want to modify.

2. On the List tab on the Ribbon, click the Customize Form button that shows the InfoPath icon, as shown in Figure 4.23. InfoPath opens with the default data entry fields, as shown in Figure 4.24.

FIGURE 4.23

Customize Form button on the Ribbon

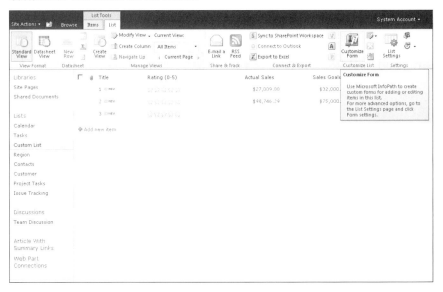

FIGURE 4.24

List data entry form in InfoPath 2010

3. You may now use InfoPath to modify the form. You may drag other fields from the fields box onto the form and format the layout as you like. Figure 4.25 shows an example.

4. Using the one-click publish option saves the changes back to SharePoint. Select File, and then on the Info screen click the Quick-Publish button to save changes back to SharePoint.

5. Click OK on the publishing confirmation message box. Return back to the list and click Add New. The customized form now appears, as shown in Figure 4.26.

Tip

Any new fields you add in the InfoPath Fields box become new columns in the list you are customizing upon publishing the form back to SharePoint.

The list is now using the custom InfoPath form and not the default form. If you need to revert back to the default form, click on the List Settings of the list and then Form settings from the General section. Click the option to use the default SharePoint form and optionally check the box to remove the InfoPath form from the server. ■

FIGURE 4.25

Modified list data entry form in InfoPath 2010

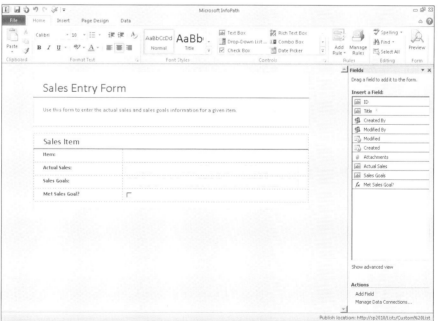

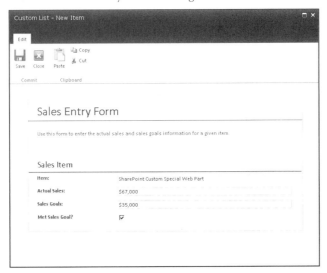

FIGURE 4.26

Modified list data entry form showing in SharePoint

Modifying Form Web Parts

In previous sections, I discuss the modification of views and how lists are presented to users. You can also modify the actual forms that display when editing, viewing, or creating a new item. These are the default system forms but may be customized such that the end-user experience is catered to your business needs. Once again, previously in MOSS 2007, you needed to create new pages and use custom Web Parts, but now you have the ability to modify the actual forms that appear.

In this section, you can use the Modify Form Web Parts button from the List tab on the Ribbon. There are three options: Default New Form, Default Display Form, and Default Edit Form. If you modified the data entry with InfoPath from the previous section, you will also see Item menu options as well, which follow the same concept. The reason you see the Item options, too, is because the list is not using the default forms anymore.

Tip

If you need to revert back to the default form, click on the List Settings of the list and then Form settings from the General section. Click the option to use the default SharePoint form and optionally check the box to remove the InfoPath form from the server. ∎

Default New Form

The New Form displays when a user is entering data into the list. To modify the New Form, follow these steps:

1. Navigate to the list you want to modify.

2. On the List tab on the Ribbon, click on the Modify Form Web Parts button and select Default New Form. You can see a page with the list data entry fields, as shown in Figure 4.27.

3. You may now add additional Web Parts to the page to display with the list. Use the Insert tab on the Ribbon to add text or media to the page. An example is shown in Figure 4.28.

4. Click Stop Editing from the Page tab on the Ribbon to save the changes.

5. Click Add New Item to see the changes, as shown in Figure 4.29.

FIGURE 4.27

Modifying the Default New Form

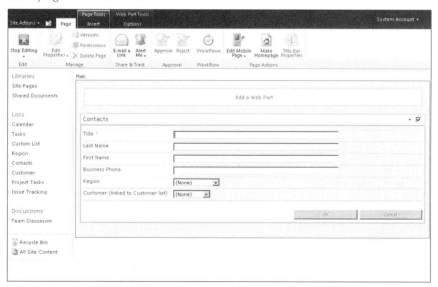

FIGURE 4.28

Adding an image to the Default New Form

FIGURE 4.29

Viewing the modified Default New Form

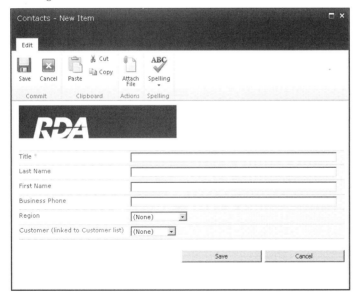

Default Display Form

The Display Form is displayed when viewing an item. It is read only. To modify the Display Form, follow these steps:

1. Navigate to the list you wish to modify.

2. On the List tab on the Ribbon, click the Modify Form Web Parts button and select Default Display Form. You see a page with the list fields.

3. You may now add additional Web Parts to the page to display with the list. Use the Insert tab on the Ribbon to add text or media to the page.

4. On Page tab on the Ribbon, click Stop Editing to save the changes.

5. Select an item in the list and then click View Item on the Ribbon to see the changes.

Default Edit Form

The Edit Form is displayed when a user is editing an item. To modify the Edit Form follow these steps:

1. Navigate to the list you want to modify.

2. On the List tab on the Ribbon, click the Modify Form Web Parts button and select Default Edit Form. You see a page with the list fields.

3. You may now add additional Web Parts to the page to display with the list. Use the Insert tab on the Ribbon to add text or media to the page.

4. On the Page tab on the Ribbon, click Stop Editing to save the changes.

5. Select an item in the list and then click Edit Item on the Ribbon to see the changes.

Tip

To edit the way the overall list is shown, simply navigate to the list and click Edit Page from the Site Actions menu. Insert Web Parts, text, images, video, and so on as needed. ■

Summary

The lists and libraries functionality provided by SharePoint is an extensible platform for storing and sharing information. In this chapter, we covered how to implement lists and libraries, both through using the templates provided by SharePoint and by creating custom lists. We then customized these lists and libraries by configuring their settings and adding custom columns. In addition, we reviewed the functionality provided by views to filter, sort, group by, and otherwise tailor the presentation of list and library information to meet your specific audience(s) requirements. We used list and library Web Parts to show list and library information in context with and/or connected to related information on a Web Part page. Finally, you looked at how we may change the data entry interface with InfoPath 2010 as well as modifying the New, Edit, and Display forms that are presented to the user.

Using and Customizing Web Parts

H ave you ever been involved in a corporate development project and thought to yourself, "Someone must have created functionality like this before?" Wouldn't it be great if there were a consistent framework that allowed developers to create the features and functionality that users need and then make those developed components available in a catalog that could be used for applications across the entire organization? There is an answer to this question, and it's called the SharePoint Web Part.

Web Parts are beneficial to users, developers, and to IT administrators. In addition, .NET is leveraged to develop Web Part applications, so they can be reused on many Web Part pages and SharePoint sites. The Web Part infrastructure lets developers focus on writing code that delivers business value on a platform that has taken care of most of the deployment and hosting concerns. IT administrators also benefit because they can centrally manage which applications are available from a central location and interface. They can approve Web Parts and install them on a SharePoint Web front end where they are available to users immediately via the Web Part Gallery. From there, users can drag and drop the Web Parts on as many pages as they like and configure them for their particular needs.

This chapter explains what a Web Part is in the context of SharePoint Server 2010. You learn how to configure, deploy, and manage out-of-the-box Web Parts and custom third-party Web Parts using the Web Part gallery. This chapter also provides a comprehensive list of available Web Parts with descriptions of their purpose and usage.

IN THIS CHAPTER

Examining Web Parts

Using Web Parts

Understanding Web Part Galleries

Managing Web Parts

Exploring Web Parts

A Web Part is a component-based application that serves as a modular building block for creating and maintaining SharePoint Web Part pages. Web Part applications can range from a simple view of static HTML to complex Web applications integrated with multiple back-end systems. Web Parts empower developers and information workers to manage their own SharePoint-enabled Web pages through the use of drag-and-drop functionality from a Web browser.

Web Parts are also the tools users employ to personalize SharePoint pages. Users can add Web Parts to Web Part pages and share them with other users. Like creating a mosaic by arranging colored tiles, you assemble a complete Web site using out-of-the-box SharePoint Web Parts. These tiles of information can show content local to the site, data from another system, and also content from other Web sites applied in the context of a project or organizational team.

You can develop your own custom Web Parts by using the Web Part framework in SharePoint. For more information, see the Microsoft Developer Network Web site at `http://msdn.microsoft.com/library/default.asp?url=/library/en-us/dnvs05/html/WebParts.asp`.

Web Parts can connect to each other, send requests to other Web Parts, and share data. For example, one Web Part might provide filter criteria to another on the page to change the view of rendered data depending on the list item selected.

SharePoint 2010 provides out-of-the-box (OOB) Web Parts in several categories that address common business scenarios.

The following are the OOB Web Part categories:

- **Lists and Libraries:** Provides views of lists and various types of content libraries
- **Business Data:** Provides views of information from the business data catalog
- **Content Rollup:** Aggregates multiple lists and libraries into one view
- **Dashboard:** Provides views of Key Performance Indicators (KPIs)
- **Default:** Provides integration points for other systems such as RSS
- **Filters:** Allows users to connect and filter data in other Web Parts
- **Miscellaneous:** A set of Web Parts that are generally used in many locations
- **Outlook Web Access:** Allows users to view their Outlook tasks, inbox, and calendar
- **Search:** Provides integration with SharePoint Search
- **Site Directory:** Provides a way to arrange sites in a site directory

Web Parts are designed for developer flexibility. The following components are the building blocks of a Web Part. These components are well documented and standardized so developers can optimize their work toward features instead of having to be concerned about deployments and server configurations.

Web Parts have five major building blocks:

- **ASP.net Server control:** Server Controls are compiled components that perform application logic on the server and then render HTML and script to the browser.

- **Tool Pane (viewable in edit mode on the rendered Web Part page):** Manages the Web Part's properties and settings.

- **DWP.dwp file (Web Part Definition file):** DWP files are XML files that contain metadata about a Web Part. A Web Part can be exported as a DWP file, imported to another site or portal, and then placed within a Web Part zone.

- **Web Part file:** A Web Part file is an XML file that describes the Web Part. The Web Part file also makes your Web Part appear in the Web Part Gallery.

- **Visual Web Part Layout:** The visual Web Part layout is an ASCX file that is used to create Web Parts using user controls.

Using Web Parts

To insert and delete Web Parts in a SharePoint site, you must have either the Add/Remove Personal Web Parts permission or the Add and Customize Pages permission. By default, at least one of these permissions is granted to members of the Designer, Hierarchy Managers, and Home Owner site groups. If you are unable to insert or delete a Web Part or Web Part zone, contact your server administrator. If you add a Web Part in Personal view, remember that no one else will see the modifications that you have made.

Adding a Web Part to a Web Part page

You can quickly add content to a Web Part page by adding one or more Web Parts to a Web Part zone.

Note
Users viewing Web Parts in the browser can customize only those located in a Web Part zone. ∎

Using Web Part zones has several advantages including:

- **Easy customization in the browser:** The content on the page can easily be changed by anyone comfortable working in a browser.

- **Grouping and arranging:** Using Web Part zones gives you greater control over how your Web Parts are arranged on the page. Also, when you include multiple Web Parts in a single Web Part zone, you can either stack them vertically within the zone or arrange them side by side horizontally.

- **Format and appearance:** One of the properties that you can control for all Web Parts in a single Web Part zone is whether they display a title bar only, both a title bar and a border, or neither.

- **Customized Access:** For each Web Part zone, you can control whether users are allowed to add, delete, resize, and move the Web Parts; change their personal Web Part settings; or change Web Part settings for all users.

To add a Web Part to a Web Part zone, follow these steps:

1. **Navigate to the Web Part page on your SharePoint site where you want to add the Web Part(s).** In the Web Part page, click Site Actions and select Edit Page as shown in Figure 5.1.

   Notice that the Web Part zones have frames around them to delineate the limits of the zone, as shown in Figure 5.2. In this sample there are two Web Part zones (Header and Right). The Header Web Part zone already contains a Web Part (Project Tasks). The Right Web Part zone contains no Web Parts.

2. **Click Add a Web Part in the Web Part zone where you want to add the Web Part.**

3. **The Add Web Parts tool pane appears with a list of Web Parts that are available for use, as shown in Figure 5.3.** Select the Web Part you want and click Add. The Add Web Part to: drop-down defaults to the zone you selected in Step 2. Optionally, you may change the zone location by using this drop-down.

FIGURE 5.1

Putting a Web Part page into Edit mode using the Site Actions menu

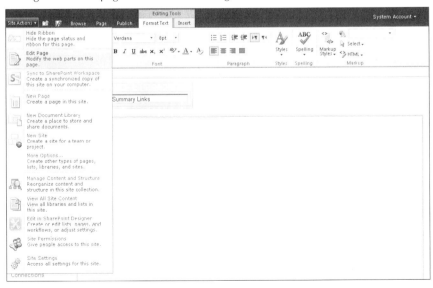

FIGURE 5.2

A Web Part page with multiple zones

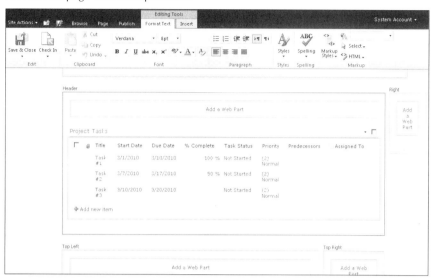

FIGURE 5.3

The Add Web Parts tool pane

Other Web Part Editing Options

After working with SharePoint for a while, you will notice that there are other editing options that help you with configuring your Web Part pages. The following items are tricks that may help you in customizing your Web Part pages:

- While you are in Edit mode, you can move Web Parts within a zone or across zones by clicking the title bar of the Web Part and dragging it to a new location in a Web Part zone.

- You can add the same Web Part multiple times to a Web Part zone. For example, you could have two Announcement Web Parts on the same Web Part page.

- It is often more precise to drag and drop a Web Part to the location within the Web Part zone where you want the Web Part to appear instead of using the Add Web Part button.

- You can customize the appearance of the Web Part by clicking the Edit drop-down menu within the Web Part title bar. You can minimize, close, delete, or modify the Web Part. These options are discussed in more detail later.

Closing or deleting a Web Part from a Web Part page

To remove a Web Part from a page, you can either close the Web Part or delete it. If you close the Web Part, it is no longer visible on the page, but it can be readded to the page from the Closed Web Parts Gallery, as shown in Figure 5.4, or with SharePoint designer. However, these Web Parts are still validated by SharePoint when the page is accessed, so they can slow a page load if, for example, they are accessing outside resources.

FIGURE 5.4

The Closed Web Parts Gallery

If you delete a Web Part, you remove it completely from the page. This cannot be undone; however, in general, when you delete a Web Part from a page, only the Web Part itself is deleted from the page. The associated content and data — in a list or library, for example — is still available, and the Web Part is still available in the gallery and can be added again at any time. Exceptions to this rule include the Content Editor Web Part and any other Web Part that contains static content that was added to the current page only. Such content is permanently deleted if the Web Part is deleted.

Closing a Web Part

You can close a Web Part from a Web Part zone while in Edit mode. Follow these steps to close a Web Part:

1. From the Site Actions menu in the top-left corner, choose Edit Page.
2. Close the Web Part by selecting Close from the edit menu on that Web Part.
3. On the Page tab on the Ribbon, click Save & Close to return the page to View mode.

Deleting a Web Part

To remove a Web Part completely from the Web Part page, you can delete the Web Part from a Web Part zone within Edit mode. Follow these steps to delete a Web Part:

1. From the Site Actions menu in the top-left corner, choose Edit Page.
2. Delete the Web Part by selecting Delete from the edit menu on that Web Part.
3. In the dialog box, click OK to confirm your selection.
4. Select Exit Edit Mode from the top-left corner to return the page to View mode.

Configuring Web Parts

Each Web Part can be configured in Edit mode to modify its appearance on the Web Part page. To modify the Web Part's properties, click the edit drop-down menu within the Web Part and select Modify Shared Web Part. The properties dialog box for the Web Part appears on the right. The Web Part whose properties are being edited will have a dotted orange line around it.

The properties dialog box contains three or more collapsible sections. In general, three of these — Appearance, Layout, and Advanced — appear for every Web Part. You can expand or collapse the sections by clicking on the + and – to the left of the section name.

Note

You may not see these three Web Part properties for three reasons. First, in order to use the Advanced section in the Web Part tool pane, you must have sufficient permissions on that site. Second, a developer can choose which properties to expose or hide. This could be the explanation for finding that some of the common properties are missing from the tool pane. You may also see additional custom properties not listed in the common set. Third, some permission and property settings may disable or hide Web Part properties. ■

Modifying the Appearance settings

The Appearance settings control how a Web Part is presented on a page. The section has the following settings, as shown in Figure 5.5:

- **Title:** Type the text that you want to appear in the Web Part's title bar.

- **Height:** If you want the Web Part always to appear with the same height, regardless of the height of the browser window, select Yes, type a value, and select the unit of measure. Otherwise, select "No. Adjust height to fit zone" radio button option.

- **Width:** If you want the Web Part always to appear with the same width, regardless of the width of the browser window, select Yes, type a value, and select the unit of measure. Otherwise, select No. Adjust width to fit zone radio button option.

- **Chrome State:** You have the option to make the Web Part appear "minimized" when the Web Part first appears (only the title bar will be visible). The user will have to maximize, or expand, the Web Part to see its contents. If you want the Web Part to appear minimized, select Minimized. Otherwise, select Normal. By default, the Chrome State is set to Normal and the entire Web Part appears.

- **Chrome Type:** Choose one of the settings in the drop-down menu to modify the frame surrounding the Web Part.

- **Default:** Inherits the frame style of the surrounding Web Part zone.

  - **None:** Neither the title bar nor the border appears around the Web Part.

  - **Title and Border:** Both the title bar and the border appear around the Web Part.

  - **Title Only:** Only the title bar (but not the border) appears around the Web Part.

  - **Border Only:** Only the border (but not the title bar) appears around the Web Part.

FIGURE 5.5

The Appearance settings on a Web Part

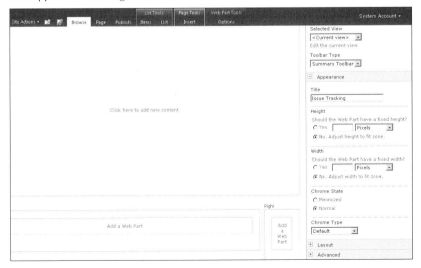

Note

You may not be able to see modifications reflected in the Web Part until you exit Edit mode — even if you click the Apply button. ∎

Modifying the Layout settings

The Layout section controls where the Web Part appears on the page and has the following settings:

- **Hidden:** Specifies whether a Web Part is hidden when a user opens the Web Part page. Check this box to make the Web Part hidden. Select the box if you want to process the Web Part on the server but suppress its display. If this check box is selected, the Web Part is visible only when you are designing the page, and it has "(Hidden)" added to the title. Hiding a Web Part is especially useful if you want to use a Web Part to provide data to another Web Part through a Web Part connection but don't want to display the Web Part to the user. Web Part connections are described in more detail later in this chapter.

- **Direction:** Specifies the direction of the text in the Web Part content. For example, Arabic and Hebrew are right-to-left languages; English and most other European languages are left-to-right languages.

- **Zone:** Specifies the zone in which the Web Part will be displayed. Use the drop-down menu to select the Web Part zone.

- **Zone Index:** Specifies the order in which the Web Part will appear within the Web Part zone. If you enter **1**, the Web Part appears at the top of the Web Part zone. If you enter **2**, the Web Part appears below the first Web Part, and so on.

Modifying the Advanced section

The Advanced section has the following settings:

- **Allow Minimize:** Check this box to allow users to toggle the Web Part between minimized and normal. In general, when you minimize a Web Part, only the Title Bar appears.

- **Allow Close:** Check this box to allow users to close the Web Part. This removes the Web Part from the view completely. Closing a Web Part is not the same as hiding it or deleting it from the page. In the browser, a closed Web Part does not appear on the page; it is stored in the Closed Web Parts Gallery, from where you can reopen it. You might opt to close a Web Part for several reasons. For example:

  - You don't currently want to use a particular Web Part on the page, but you have made customizations to it that you don't want to have to reconfigure if you decide to add it back to the page later.

  - You may have a Web Part that you want on a page only at certain times. To render the Web Part inactive when it is not wanted, you can close it and then open it when you want it again.

- If you are creating a custom Web Part that you want to make available to users of a specific page so that they can include it in their personalized views of the page, but you don't want to make that Web Part available in the larger Web Part Gallery for the whole site, you can add the Web Part to the page in Shared view, configure the Web Part as you want, and then close it.

- If a Web Part that you are creating or customizing is causing the page to function incorrectly, you can close that Web Part until you fix it.

- **Allow Hide:** Specifies whether users can hide the Web Part. This removes the Web Part from the view but still allows it to process on the server.

- **Allow Zone Change:** Specifies whether users can move the Web Part to a different zone within the same page. Users can move Web Parts from zone to zone by modifying the Web Part's Zone or by dragging the Web Part to another zone.

- **Allow Connections:** Specifies whether users can connect the Web Part to another Web Part. Enabling connections between Web Parts allows for one Web Part to interact with another.

- **Allow Editing in Personal View:** Specifies whether the Web Part properties can be modified in Personal view.

- **Export Mode:** Specifies the level of data that is allowed to be exported for this Web Part.

- **Title URL (as appears in SPS):** Specifies the URL of a file that contains additional information about the Web Part. The file is displayed in a separate browser window when you click the Web Part title.

- **Description:** Specifies the ScreenTip that appears when you rest the mouse pointer on the Web Part title or Web Part icon. Also, the value of this property is used when you search for Web Parts with the Search command on the Find Web Parts menu, which appears when you click the title bar of the Web Parts task pane.

- **Help URL:** Specifies the location of a file that contains Help information about the Web Part. The Help information appears in a separate browser window when you click the Help command on the Web Part menu.

- **Help Mode:** Specifies how a browser displays Help content for a Web Part.

  - **Modal:** Opens a separate browser window, if the browser has this capability. A user must close the window before returning to the Web page.

  - **Modeless:** Opens a separate browser window, if the browser has this capability. A user does not have to close the window before returning to the Web page. This is the default value.

  - **Navigate:** Opens the Web page in the current browser window.

Note

Even though ASP.NET Web Parts support this property, default Help topics in Windows SharePoint Services version 4 open only in a separate browser window. ■

- **Catalog Icon Image URL:** Specifies the location of a file that contains an image to be used as the Web Part icon in the Web Part List. The image size must be 16 x 16 pixels.

- **Title Icon Image URL:** Specifies the location of a file that contains an image to be used in the Web Part title bar. The image size must be 16 x 16 pixels.

- **Import Error Message:** Specifies the message that appears if there is a problem importing the Web Part.

Connecting Web Parts

Web Parts can be "connected" to pass data from one Web Part to change the display of another Web Part's data. Typically, you connect Web Parts together so that actions you perform in one Web Part change the contents of another Web Part.

Connecting sets of data from different data sources often requires programming skills. The SharePoint Web Part infrastructure, however, provides a standardized set of interfaces called *connection interfaces* that allow Web Parts to exchange information with each other at runtime. Making data connections between Web Parts is straightforward through menu commands.

By connecting Web Parts, you can significantly enhance the user experience. You can present data from two Web Parts in alternate views, perform related calculations between two Web Parts, and filter a Web Part using values from another Web Part — all on one Web Part Page. For example, the List Web Part that is built into Microsoft Windows SharePoint Services can provide (send) a row of data to any other Web Part that can consume (receive) that row, such as a Web Part that implements a form to display the row. Another example is to use one Web Part to enter data about a mortgage payment (loan amount, interest rate, loan term) and then pass that data through a connection to another Mortgage Calculator Web Part to compute the mortgage and display the monthly payment schedule.

Because the Web Part infrastructure provides a standard set of connection interfaces, connectable Web Parts can be developed by entirely different developers or companies to communicate with one another. A Web Part that supports connection interfaces can be connected by an end user with either Microsoft Office SharePoint Designer or a Web browser. This allows end users to build sophisticated combinations of Web Parts through a simple menu-driven user interface.

There are three components of a Web Part connection:

- **Provider:** The Web Part that provides the data. The data can be lists, rows, cells, or parameter values.

- **Consumer:** The Web Part that acts on the data that it receives.

- **Connection:** The definition of the relationship between the consumer and provider and the definition of the action that will take place on the consumer.

Creating a Web Part connection is a three-step process:

1. **Decide what information or data you want available to Web Parts on the Web Part page.**

   Usually there are views of list data presented by List View Web Parts already available in the Web Part Gallery that displays data within the site. If you create a new list in the site, you will see it appear in the Web Part Gallery and it will be ready for use on your Web Part page. These lists represent data in a tabular format and make it very easy to refresh and modify data, filter data within the list, change the way the data is sorted, and filter the data. By using the view selector in the tool pane, you can easily change the view of a List Web Part to work with just the columns you need.

2. **Add the Web Parts to the Web Part Page.**

3. **Connect the Web Parts to get the results you want.**

   a. From the Site Actions menu in the top-right corner, choose Edit Page.

   b. Select the "Connections" option from the edit Web Part menu on the source Web Part and select the target list from the "Send Row of Data To" list, as shown in Figure 5.6. If you do not see the list that you expect to connect to, make sure it is on the page. Some Web Parts do not support Web Part connections, such as page viewer or content editor Web Parts, and the Provide Row To menu item only shows Web Parts that are compatible.

   c. Follow the wizard as it walks you through the connection steps. In the dialog box, select the field in the provider list that you will be sending to the consumer list as well as the field in the consumer that will be used to filter. If you do not see your column in the drop-down, confirm that the column is visible in the Web Part view. Click OK.

   d. On the Page tab on the Ribbon, click the Save & Close button to return the page to View mode.

More detailed options on Web Part connections are available when you modify a Web Part page with SharePoint designer. See Chapter 20 for more information on SharePoint designer.

Tip

Not only can you make Web Part connections on the same Web Part page, but you can also make connections between Web Parts on two different Web Part pages in the same top-level site by using a Microsoft Windows SharePoint Services–compatible HTML editor, such as Microsoft Office SharePoint Designer 2010. ■

FIGURE 5.6

The Web Part connections menu

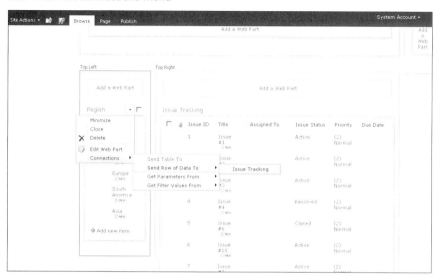

Understanding Web Part Galleries

A Web Part Gallery is an organized central library of Web Parts that you can use to locate a specific Web Part to add to your Web Part page. You can access Web Part galleries when you are in Edit mode in your Web Part page by selecting Browse from the Add Web Parts menu of the Web Parts tool pane. See the "Adding a Web Part to a Web Part page" section earlier in this chapter.

Web Part galleries are actually lists of installed Web Part Definition (.dwp file extension) and Web Part (.Web Part file extension) files. Depending on how your site administrator has configured your site, there are typically three Web Part galleries:

- **Closed Web Parts:** Contains Web Parts assigned to the page but not visible.
- **Site Gallery:** Contains Web Parts that a server administrator has decided are safe and are therefore available to all sites in a collection. The name of this gallery is the name of the collection's top-level root Web site.
- **Server Gallery:** Contains Web Parts that a server administrator has made available to all site collections (sites and subsites) on a single virtual server.

Web Parts in common with SharePoint Foundation

The following Web Parts are available in both SharePoint Foundation and SharePoint Server 2010. The Web Parts that require SharePoint Server 2010 follow this section. Both sections give descriptions of the Web Parts and some examples of how these Web Parts can be used.

Content Editor Web Part

The Content Editor Web Part (as it appears in SPS) is a very versatile and useful Web Part that renders Hypertext Markup Language (HTML) content. We often use this Web Part to present text in an attractive manner. There are three ways to enter content into the Content Editor Web Part once you have put the Web Part into Edit mode:

- **Rich-Text Editor:** The rich-text editor is an easy way for non-HTML users to input content. Using the rich-text editor, you can insert and format text, links, and tables and insert pictures. The editor controls, though lacking the full breadth of Microsoft Word tools, should be familiar to Word users.

- **Source Editor:** The source editor provides an edit window where you can input or edit the HTML for the Web Part.

- **Content Link Field:** If you have HTML in a file, you can point the Content Editor Web Part at that file. This is useful if you want to present the same text on multiple pages so you can upload an HTML file to a location available to all the pages and link the Content Editor Web Part to those files.

Although it is easy to enter and edit content in the rich-text editor, there are times that it is not possible to format the content as neatly as is possible by editing the HTML code. In this case, you can input the content via the rich-text editor and then open the source editor and modify the HTML.

Another approach is to paste into the Content Editor Web Part some standard HTML that you use to encapsulate content so your end users can edit the text once it is there. As an example, here is some HTML that we use to present text in a text box with rounded corners (small graphic files provide the rounded corners and gradient):

```html
<TABLE id=table27 style="BORDER-COLLAPSE: collapse" cellPadding=0
    width="100%" border=0>
<TBODY>
<TR>
<TD vAlign=top width="100%">
<TABLE id=table28 style="BORDER-COLLAPSE: collapse" cellPadding=0
    width="100%" border=0>
<TBODY>
<TR>
<TD width=6><IMG height=19 src="image%20library/tplft-crnr.jpg"
    width=6 border=0></TD>
<TD style="BACKGROUND-POSITION: left top; BACKGROUND-IMAGE:
    url(image%20library/part-grad.jpg); BACKGROUND-REPEAT: repeat-x"
    bgColor=#f7941d> <FONT color=#000000 size=2><B>Content
    Header </B></FONT></TD>
<TD width=6><IMG height=19 src="image%20library/tprt-crnr.jpg"
    width=6 border=0></TD></TR>
<TR>
<TD style="BACKGROUND-POSITION: left top; BACKGROUND-IMAGE:
    url(image%20library/side-lft.jpg); BACKGROUND-REPEAT: repeat-
    y"> 
```

```
<P> </P></TD>
<TD vAlign=top align=middle>
<TABLE height=100 width="100%" border=0>
<TBODY>
<TR>
<TD vAlign=top><SPAN>Content    </SPAN></TD></
   TR></TBODY></TABLE></TD>
<TD style="BACKGROUND-POSITION: right top; BACKGROUND-IMAGE:
   url(image%20library/side-rt.jpg); BACKGROUND-REPEAT: repeat-
   y"> </TD></TR>
<TR>
<TD vAlign=top align=left><IMG height=6 src="image%20library/btmlft-
   crnr.jpg" width=6 border=0></TD>
<TD style="BACKGROUND-POSITION: center top; BACKGROUND-IMAGE:
   url(image%20library/btm.jpg); BACKGROUND-REPEAT: repeat-
   x"> </TD>
<TD vAlign=top align=right><IMG height=6 src="image%20library/btmrt-
   crnr.jpg" width=6 border=0></TD></TR></TBODY></TABLE></TD>
</TR></TBODY></TABLE>
```

The resulting Content Editor Web Part is shown in Figure 5.7, and end users can easily modify the text while leaving the structure in place.

FIGURE 5.7

A Content Editor Web Part with HTML code to frame the text

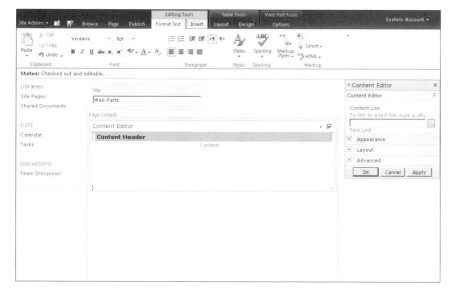

HTML Form Web Part

The HTML Form Web Part is very similar to the Content Editor Web Part in function because it renders HTML code. However, the Form Web Part is designed so that it can be connected to provide data to other Web Parts, whereas the Content Editor Web Part is not connectable.

Image Web Part

This Web Part makes it easy to display image files. In the Image section of the tool pane, you set:

- The path to the image in the image link field
- The alternative text that appears if users cannot see the image in the alternative text field
- The image vertical alignment (top, middle, bottom) and the image horizontal alignment (left, center, right)
- Web Part background color (transparent, pick from palette, or enter RGB in hex)

The Content Editor Web Part can also be used to display images on a page, but the image Web Part is preferable if you are displaying an image only because it does a better job with centering and placement.

Image Viewer

The Image Viewer Web Part displays an image on the Web page.

Silverlight Web Part

The Silverlight Web Part is a built-in Web Part that renders a Silverlight application within SharePoint. Adding this to a page immediately displays an input for the location of the Silverlight application (XAP file – pronounced "zap"). The location is URL-based but can point to a XAP file in a document library if needed.

Site Users

The Site Users Web Part shows all users that have rights to this site and their online status.

Page Viewer Web Part

The Page Viewer Web Part is a useful Web Part to connect to data that is external to the site. You can select whether you want to connect to a Web Page folder or a specific file.

The linked content is isolated from other content on the Web page. It may seem logical to use the Page Viewer Web Part to show content from other SharePoint sites — for example, to show a view of a document library. Unfortunately this results in a poor display because there are two sets of navigation rendered: the navigation of the page where the Page Viewer Web Part is installed and the navigation of the Document Library view. A better solution is to use a Data View or Content Query Web Part to surface data located in other sites.

Displaying a folder with the Page Viewer Web Part is a good way to show content that is located on a file share as shown in Figure 5.8.

FIGURE 5.8

Page Viewer Web Part showing a file share

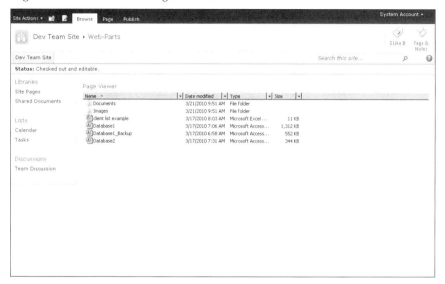

Relevant documents

This Web Part displays documents that are relevant to the current user. The options for configuring this Web Part are in the Data section of the task pane. The settings allow you to select whether to include or display:

- Documents last modified by me
- Documents created by me
- Documents checked out to me
- A link to the containing folder or list
- Maximum number of items shown (between 1 and 10,000)

This can be an effective Web Part to aggregate content for each user, especially if the site collection is small enough so that this Web Part can display documents from multiple sites.

User tasks

This Web Part aggregates and shows tasks that are assigned to the current user. The options for configuring this Web Part are in the data section of the task pane. The settings allow you to decide whether to:

- Display Item Link column
- Set Maximum number of items shown (between 1 and 10,000)

This can be an effective Web Part to aggregate content for each user, especially if the site collection is small enough so that this Web Part can display tasks from multiple sites.

XML Web Part

This Web Part renders Extensible Markup Language (XML) just as the Content Editor Web Part renders HTML. You can enter XML via the XML Editor, link to an XML file, and enter Extensible Stylesheet Language (XSL) via the XSL Editor, or link to an XSL file. The XSL file is used to style, handle, and manipulate your XML data.

As an example of how the XML Web Part renders, here is some sample XML data:

```
<?xml version="1.0" encoding="ISO-8859-1"?>
<catalog>
<name>
<firstname>Simeon</firstname>
<lastname>Cathey</lastname>
<gender>male</gender>
<fullname>Simeon Cathey</fullname>
<telephone>555-1212</telephone>
<pet>cats</pet>
</name>
<name>
<firstname>Wynne</firstname>
<lastname>Leon</lastname>
<gender>female</gender>
<fullname>Wynne Leon</fullname>
<telephone>555-1212</telephone>
<pet>dog</pet>
</name>
<name>
<firstname>Wayne</firstname>
<lastname>Tynes</lastname>
<gender>male</gender>
<fullname>Wayne Tynes</fullname>
<telephone>555-1212</telephone>
<pet>dog</pet>
</name>
</catalog>
```

The code below shows the associated XSL for the XML data. The XSL formats the table, the table headings, and the table heading color and selects which columns of the XML data to show:

```
<?xml version="1.0" encoding="ISO-8859-1"?>
<xsl:stylesheet version="1.0
xmlns:xsl="http://www.w3.org/1999/XSL/Transform">
<xsl:template match="/">
 <html>
 <body>
  <table border="1">
   <tr bgcolor="#9acd32">
```

```
      <th>Fullname</th>
      <th>Number</th>
     </tr>
     <xsl:for-each select="catalog/name">
     <tr>
      <td><xsl:value-of select="fullname"/></td>
      <td><xsl:value-of select="telephone"/></td>
     </tr>
     </xsl:for-each>
    </table>
   </body>
   </html>
  </xsl:template>
  </xsl:stylesheet>
```

The XML Web Part renders the XML and XSL as shown in Figure 5.9.

List View Web Part

The List View Web Part is generated every time you create a list or library on your site so that you can add a Web Part view of that list or library on any of your site pages. The list view varies the columns that are displayed based on the type of list that is added, but all list views have the following edit options:

XML Viewer Web Part rendering of XML data with the applied XSL style sheet

- **Selected View:** The Selected View option lets you pick from any of your existing list views or lets you edit the current view. By editing the view, you can change which columns are displayed and filter the list and also the number of items that are returned. For more information about list views, see Chapter 4.

- **Toolbar Type:** The Toolbar Type gives you the option to choose from a full toolbar, a summary toolbar, and no toolbar. The full toolbar gives you the toolbar for the list so you can perform any action on the list on the Web Part page that you could while in the list. The summary toolbar is a small link at the bottom of the list that allows users to add a new item from the view, and the no toolbar option just shows the list items.

The edit options for the List View Web Part are shown in Figure 5.10.

Data View Web Part

The Data View Web Part allows you to create custom views of data contained in lists, libraries, or databases. This Web Part works for all data within the site collection so you can use it to display content that is not on your site. The Data View Web Part can be connected to other Web Parts on the page.

The Data View Web Parts should be edited using SharePoint Designer. See Chapter 20 for more information on how to use SharePoint Designer to create and customize Data View Web Parts.

FIGURE 5.10

Edit options for the List View Web Part

Web Parts specific to SPS

The Web Parts described in this section are available only on SharePoint Server 2010 installations.

Business Data

The Business Data Web Parts are intended to connect a user to business applications.

Business Data Actions

Displays a list of actions associated with an entity as defined in the Business Data Catalog. For example, you can use a Business Data Actions Web Part to display all the actions that portal users can perform on the Customer entity. Some examples of these actions are sending e-mail to a customer or editing the address of a customer.

Business Data Connectivity Filter

Filters the contents of Web Parts using a list of values from Business Data Connectivity Services.

Business Data Item

Displays the details of an item from the data source of a business application that has been registered in the Business Data Catalog. For example, you can use a Business Data Items Web Part to display the details of a particular customer from a CRM database.

Business Data Item Builder

Creates a Business Data item from parameters in the query string and provides it to other Web Parts. This Web Part is used on Business Data profile pages only.

Business Data List

Displays a list of items from a business application. For example, you can use a Business Data List Web Part to display all of the customers from a CRM database.

Business Data Related List

Displays a list of items related to one or more parent items from a business application. For example, you can use a Business Data Related List Web Part to display all the orders for a particular customer from an order management database.

Chart Web Part

Displays a chart on the page based on data from a list, another Web Part, business data, or Excel Services.

Excel Web Access

Use the Excel Web Access Web Part to interact with an Excel 2010 workbook as a Web page. This Web Part requires the portal to be running Excel Web Services. To configure this Web Part, follow these steps:

1. From the Site Actions menu in the top-left corner, select Edit Page.

2. From the Edit menu on the Excel Web Access Web Part, select Edit Web Part.

3. In the Workbook Display section, enter the path to the workbook in the Workbook field.

4. Enter the range of cells that you want to show in the Named Item field.

5. Enter the number of rows to display and columns to display in their associated fields.

6. Click OK.

Status List

Shows a list of status indicators. Status indicators display important measures for your organization and show how your organization is performing with respect to your goals.

Indicator Details

Displays the details of a single status indicator. Status indicators display an important measure for an organization and may be obtained from other data sources including SharePoint lists, Excel workbooks, and SQL Server 2008 Analysis Services KPIs.

Visio Web Access

Allows the display of Visio Web drawings.

Content Rollup

The Content Rollup Web Parts are intended to consolidate SharePoint information from numerous sites for ease of use.

Categories

This Web Part shows the categories from your site directory. If you put this Web Part on a page that is not located on the same site as your site directory, you must configure the Web Part to find your site directory site. To do this:

1. From the Site Actions menu in the top-left corner, select Edit Page.

2. From the Edit menu on the Categories Web Part, select Edit Web Part.

3. Expand the Miscellaneous section in the Web Part tool pane.

4. Enter the URL in the Web URL field.

5. Click OK.

After this Web Part is configured, the results show in the Sites in Category Web Part if it is added to the page.

Note

The Site Directory template is no longer available in SharePoint 2010 but may be migrated from MOSS 2007. The Categories and Sites in Category Web Parts can only be used for these migrated MOSS 2007 Site Directory sites. The location of the site directory needs to be configured in Central Administration. ■

Content Query Web Part

The Content Query Web Part is used to roll up lists and libraries of similar content from one or more sites in a site collection. You can think of this Web Part as a content aggregator. A simple example would be to use this Web Part to display all documents in your site collection. In this case, you can keep documents located in their own document library in the context of a particular topic and have a rollup view in a single location to aggregate your documents. This can quickly provide another way to navigate your document structure.

To modify the Content Query Web Part, follow these steps:

1. From the Site Actions menu in the top-left corner, select Edit Page.

2. Next, click one of the Add a Web Part buttons in a Web Part zone. The Add Web Parts Web page dialog appears.

3. Select the Web Part category labeled Content Rollup and select the Content Query Web Part, as shown in Figure 5.11.

4. Click the Add button to the right of the tool pane. The page refreshes and shows a new Web Part labeled Content Query Web Part, as shown in Figure 5.12.

FIGURE 5.11

Selecting the Content Query Web Part from the Web Part Gallery

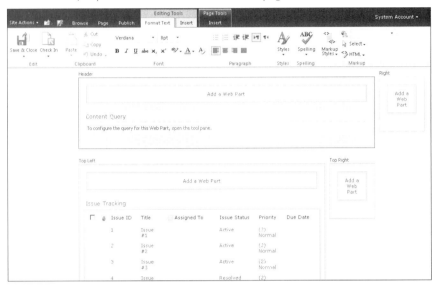

FIGURE 5.12

The Content Query Web Part when first added to a page

5. **To view all of your site collection documents, edit the query of the Web Part.** Select Edit Web Part from the Web Part edit menu.

   The Content Query Web Part has two configurable sections, Query and Presentation, in addition to the default Web Part properties. Expanding the Query section gives you access to the settings needed to customize the location to query as well as the types of content.

6. **In the Source section, choose Show items from all sites in this site collection.** If you know a specific site that you would like to show in the Content Query Web Part, you can limit the query to a specific site or even as granular as a single list.

7. **In the List Type section, choose Document library from the drop-down combo box.** To give you an idea of the many uses for this Web Part, some of the available choices are Announcements, Calendar, Contacts, Converted Forms, and Custom List.

8. **From the Content Type section, select Document Content Types from the Show items of this content type group combo box.**

9. **Select Document from the Show items of this content type combo box.**

10. **If you have audiences defined in your deployment, you can enable audience targeting for this Web Part as a way to show or hide data.** You can also use the Additional Filters section to refine what data is displayed.

11. **Use the presentation section to customize the appearance of the data on the page.** You will likely want to experiment with these settings to familiarize yourself with the different options.

12. **Click OK at the bottom of the Web Part tool pane.** This refreshes the page and applies all of the settings you chose.

Note

In the Additional Filters section, you can filter only on system site or server column properties. You can select from out-of-the-box default list columns or plan ahead and set up site or server list columns before you will be able to select them from the Additional Filters section. For information about site and server columns, see Chapter 3. ■

Memberships

The membership Web Part displays a list of Exchange Distribution lists and SharePoint sites that you are a member of.

The list of Distribution Lists that you belong to is displayed as Mailto links. Clicking one of the links opens your default e-mail program and populates the "To" field with the e-mail address of the distribution list.

The list of SharePoint sites you are a member of appears as links to each of those sites. Clicking any of the links redirects you to that site.

This list helps you keep track of the projects and distribution lists you are interacting with at a glance.

My Links

As you navigate around your SharePoint sites, a My Links link appears at the top of each page. Clicking it allows you to add a link to the current page to your global My Links list. Adding the My Links Web Part to a page allows you to view the list of links you have associated to you in the context of a particular topic or area of a SharePoint site. This can be particularly useful on a page you designate as an aggregator of information you use on a daily basis. Your My Site is a good candidate for this Web Part.

Opening the tool pane for this Web Part shows only the typical default properties.

My SharePoint Sites

Use to display documents you have authored on sites where you are a member and sites of your choice. This Web Part works only on personalized sites (My Sites).

My Workspaces

Displays sites created under your My Site. This Web Part works only on personalized sites (My Sites).

RSS Viewer

Renders the RSS Feed. To configure this Web Part, you must have the URL of the feed to which it is subscribed and configure the number of items that you want to display. You can also choose to show the feed title and description.

SharePoint Documents

Displays the documents a user has authored. This Web Part works only on personalized sites (My Sites).

Site Aggregator

Use to display sites of your choice. The Site Aggregator creates a tab for each site that you enter and then encapsulates that site in the Web Part. This doesn't look very good for high-content sites but otherwise provides an embedded view of sites. To configure this Web Part to show your sites:

1. **From the New Site Tab menu drop-down list of the Web Part, select New Site Tab.**
2. **Enter the Site URL and Site Name in the corresponding fields.**
3. **Click Create.**

When added to a page, the Site Aggregator Web Part is configured to append _layouts/MyInfo.aspx to any URL that you create a tab for. To change this behavior, modify the URL section of the Web Part properties.

Sites in Category

Displays the results of the Categories Web Part. When a category in selected in the Categories Web Part, the sites in that category appear in the Sites in Category Web Part.

Note

The Site Directory template is no longer available in SharePoint 2010 but may be migrated from MOSS 2007. The Categories and Sites in Category Web Parts can only be used for these migrated MOSS 2007 Site Directory sites. The location of the site directory needs to be configured in Central Administration. ■

Table of Contents

Displays the contents of a site and provides a navigational hierarchy based on the site's structure.

Web Analytics Web Part

Displays statistics on the most viewed content or most frequent search queries of a site (or search center).

WSRP Consumer Web Part

Displays portlets from Web sites using WSRP 1.1. For this Web Part to function, WSRP providers must be configured for your site.

Filters

The Filter Web Parts help you filter the contents of the page to a user's exact needs. They help users refine larger amounts of data down to items only relevant to a specific topic or other set of criteria:

- **Choice List Filter:** Filter the contents of Web Parts using a list of values from the Business Data Catalog.

- **Current User Filter:** Filter the contents of Web Parts by using the logged-on user properties of the current page.

- **Date Filter:** Filter the contents of Web Parts by allowing users to enter or pick a date.

- **Filter Actions:** Filter Actions will execute any filters set within the page.

- **Page Field Filter:** Filter the contents of Web Parts using information about the current page.

- **Query String(URL) Filter:** Filter the contents of Web Parts using values passed via the query string.

- **SharePoint List Filter:** Filter the contents of Web Parts by using a list of values from an Office SharePoint Server list.

- **SQL Server Analysis Services Filter:** Filter the contents of Web Parts using a list of values from SQL Server Analysis Services cubes.

- **Text Filter:** Filter the contents of Web Parts by allowing users to enter a text value.

Forms

Form Web Parts are used to render HTML or InfoPath forms within a Web page. Forms are parts of a Web page that are submitted back to the server. I cover the HTML Form Web Part under the SFS section.

InfoPath Form Web Part

A new Web Part in SharePoint 2010 is the InfoPath Form Web Part. This Web Part displays InfoPath forms that have been published to a site, site collection, or Forms Services. This Web Part allows you to generate various interfaces that you can use for end-user input.

Note

Technically, there was an InfoPath Form Web Part in MOSS 2007 but it was a system-based Web Part that was used to render InfoPath forms via Forms Services. SharePoint 2010 opens the door to new possibilities using InfoPath Forms and the InfoPath Form Web Part. ■

Media and Content

These Web Parts enable the rendering of various media such as images and movies. I have covered several of them already in the SFS section.

Media Web Part

Use this Web Part to display movies or add audio files to a Web page.

Picture Library Slideshow

This interesting Web Part cycles through images in a specified image library within the SharePoint site. It displays a slideshow of pictures on a Web page.

Tip

Use the Picture Library Slideshow Web Part as an Ad Rotator. ■

Outlook Web Access

The Outlook Web Access Web Parts allow users to integrate e-mail and calendaring capabilities with the portal. These Web Parts are most often used on personalized sites (such as My Sites) so that users can get a single window into all their most used business information.

My Calendar

Use to display your calendar. This Web Part works with Microsoft Exchange Server 2003 and above. To configure this Web Part to view your calendar:

1. From the Site Actions menu in the top-left corner, select Edit Page.
2. From the Edit menu on the My Calendar Web Part, select Edit Web Part.
3. In the Mail Configuration section in the Web Part tool pane, enter the OWA address of your mail server in the Mail server address field and your username in the Mailbox field.
4. Select whether you would like the Web Part to show a daily or weekly view of your calendar in the View drop-down.
5. Click OK.

My Contacts

Displays your contacts using Outlook Web Access for Microsoft Exchange Server 2007. To configure this Web Part to view your contacts:

1. From the Site Actions menu in the top-left corner, select Edit Page.
2. From the Edit menu on the My Contacts Web Part, select Edit Web Part.
3. In the Mail Configuration section in the Web Part tool pane, enter the OWA address of your mail server in the Mail server address field and your username in the Mailbox field.
4. Select whether you would like the Web Part to show a phone list or two-line view of your contacts in the View drop-down.
5. Click OK.

My Inbox

Displays your inbox using Outlook Web Access for Microsoft Exchange Server 2003 or later. To configure this Web Part to view your inbox:

1. From the Site Actions menu in the top-left corner, select Edit Page.
2. From the Edit menu on the My Inbox Web Part, select Edit Web Part.
3. In the Mail Configuration section in the Web Part tool pane, enter the OWA address of your mail server in the Mail server address field and your username in the Mailbox field.
4. Select whether you would like the Web Part to show a two-line message by sender, by subject, or by conversation view of your inbox in the View drop-down.
5. Click OK.

My Mail Folder

Displays your calendar using Outlook Web Access for Microsoft Exchange Server 2000 or later. Use this Web Part if you cannot use the My Inbox Web Part because of the server version.

My Tasks

Displays your tasks using Outlook Web Access for Microsoft Exchange Server 2003 or later. To configure this Web Part to view your tasks:

1. From the Site Actions menu in the top-left corner, select Edit Page.
2. From the Edit menu on the My Tasks Web Part, select Edit Web Part.
3. In the Mail Configuration section in the Web Part tool pane, enter the OWA address of your mail server in the Mail server address field and your username in the Mailbox field.
4. Select whether you would like the Web Part to show a by-due-date or by-subject view of your tasks in the View drop-down.
5. Click OK.

Search

The Search Web Parts provide all the simple and advanced search components for MOSS. These Web Parts are delivered in this gallery so that users can drag search components on their custom pages.

Advanced Search Box

This Web Part enables users to find documents using various search criteria including words, phrases, scope, language, and document type, as shown in Figure 5.13 You can further restrict your search by specifying the search scope and document properties, such as author, document size, and create date.

FIGURE 5.13

Page showing the Advanced Search Web Part

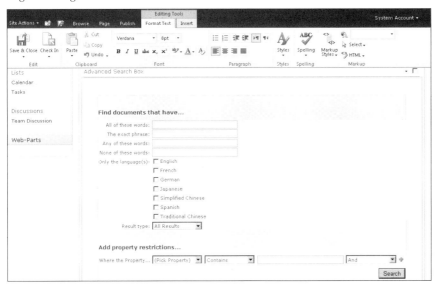

Cross-Reference

SharePoint Search capabilities are explored in detail in Chapter 7. ∎

Federated Results

This displays results from a configured location.

People Refinement Panel

This Web Part provides filtering of people search results. Depending on the actual results, refinement is performed by various profile items including Department, Title, and Responsibilities.

People Search Box

This Web Part provides the same capability that is provided when users click the People tab in Advanced Search. It enables users to search for a person by name. Additional search options include Department, Title, Responsibilities, Skills, and Memberships.

People Search Core Results

Displays the people search results and would typically be on the same page as the People search box. To use the People Search Box and People Search Core Results Web Parts together, follow these steps:

1. From the Site Actions menu in the top-left corner, select Edit Page.

2. In the zone that you want to add the People Search capabilities, select Add a Web Part.

3. Select the People Search Box and click Add

4. Select Add a Web Part again and select the People Search Core Results. Click Add.

5. Select Edit Web Part from the edit menu on the People Search Box Web Part.

6. Expand the Miscellaneous section.

7. Enter the name of the ASPX page that you have added the Web Parts to in the Target Search Results Page URL.

8. Click OK.

To test your Web Parts, exit Edit Mode and search for a person, as shown in Figure 5.14.

FIGURE 5.14

The People Search results Web Part

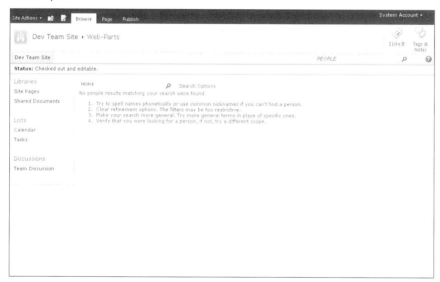

Refinement Panel

This Web Part provides filtering of search results. Depending on the actual results, refinement is performed by various item properties such as document type.

Related Queries

Displays similar queries that other users have used to perform the current query.

Search Box

This Web Part contains the search box found on all portal pages by default. Use this Web Part to enable search on custom portal pages and to place search anywhere you want on the page.

Search Core Results

This Web Part displays the search results generated from the Search Box search. Configuring the Search Box and Results Web Parts are accomplished the same way as configuring the People Search and Results Web Parts — by configuring the Miscellaneous property to point at the page the part is on.

Search High Confidence Results

This Web Part is used to display the special term and high confidence result sets.

Search Paging

This Web Part displays the search paging capability, so a user can scroll through multiple pages of search results.

Search Statistics

Displays search statistics, including number of results and duration of search time.

Search Summary

This displays search summary.

Search Visual Best Bets

This displays best bets for the current search results based on the search query.

Top Federated Results

This displays the top results from a configured location.

Social Collaboration

The social collaboration Web Parts provide information about people and content within sites and My Sites. Some are only available within My Site.

Ask Me About

The Ask Me About Web Part presents topics that a user knows or likes to discuss (My Sites). The keywords are configured in the user profile. You need to have a Note Board Web Part on the same page as the Ask Me About in order for the Web Part to function properly. Clicking on a topic presents a question in the user's Note Board, as shown in Figure 5.15.

FIGURE 5.15

The Ask Me About Web Part and Note Board behavior

Colleagues

In this version of SharePoint, you can have a list of people (colleagues) in your organization who are associated to you in an easy-to-navigate tree structure view. This view also allows you to see their online status and links you to the public view of their SharePoint My Site. You can associate colleagues to you in order to have them show up in your Colleagues Web Part:

- Manually search for users and then add them.

- Let SharePoint automatically suggest colleagues that it determines are associated to you and should be shown in the Colleagues Web Part. SharePoint makes these suggestions based on relationship to you in the organizational structure found in your Active Directory — looking at other members of sites and workspaces you are a member of, people who have worked on the same documents as you, people who have e-mailed you — and by comparing your user profile to others and finding similarities.

After placing the Colleagues Web Part on a page, you need to configure it. Choose from three links:

- The first link shows you a list of suggested colleagues. You can then choose which colleagues will be actively tracked.

- You can also select whether or not to show all of your colleagues or only ones with recent changes.

- The settings link opens the tool pane and allows you to switch the following on or off:

  - Show colleagues without changes

  - Only show colleagues in my workgroup

- Anniversaries

- Profile Property Changes

- Membership Changes

- New Documents

- Out Of Office

- Blog Changes

With the Colleagues Web Part Web Part, viewing at-a-glance events and activities that may affect you and the people you work with is easy.

Contact Details

Displays contact information for the person or people whom are responsible for the content of a site.

In Common With You

This Web Part shows users what they have in common with the person they are viewing within a My Site page (My Sites).

Note Board

The Note Board Web Part allows users to post comments on a page in which everyone can view. It provides similar functionality found on social Web sites, as shown in Figure 5.16.

FIGURE 5.16

Note Board Web Part

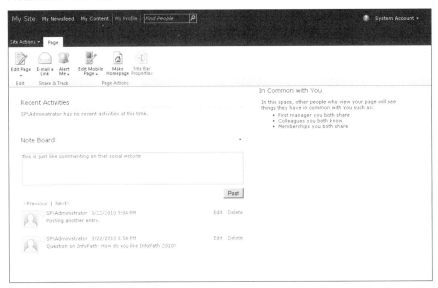

Organization Browser

The Organization Browser Web Part provides an interactive view of the organization based on the imported profiles and reporting structures.

Recent Activities

Displays a listing of recent activities a user performed (My Sites).

Recent Blog Posts

Displays a listing of recent posts a user performed within blog sites (My Sites).

Tag Cloud

Provides a list of the most used keywords based on tags and notes within the SharePoint sites.

What's New

Provides a newsfeed based on a user's colleagues, interests, and activities the user is monitoring (My Sites). The interests and activities are configured within the user profile, as shown in Figure 5.17. Notice the Interest box suggests keywords.

FIGURE 5.17

Profile settings used by the What's New Web Part

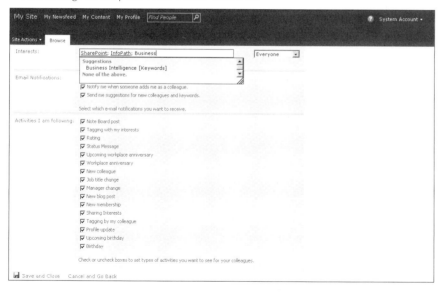

Managing Web Parts

This section covers how to deploy third-party or your own custom Web Parts. This includes steps for installation on a SharePoint Web front end or server farm, as well as making them available within Web Part Galleries to enable user customization and personalization.

Adding Web Parts to the Web Part Galleries

There are two galleries to which you can add your custom Web Part: the Site Gallery or the Server Gallery.

- The Site Gallery lists all of the Web Parts registered for a particular site collection. Using this Web Part Gallery, administrators can control what modular applications are available to specific site collection user populations. Specialized teams may need specific Web Parts that other teams do not. You can add one or more specialty Web Parts to a site collection.

- Large enterprises with many sites may decide to install the same set of Web Parts on many sites. In this case, consider storing these Web Parts in a Server Gallery. You can deploy Web Parts in a Server Gallery by developing a Web Part Package file (.cab). For more information on developing Web Part Package files, see the Windows SharePoint Services Software Development Kit.

Deploying a Web Part to the Server Web Part Gallery

After developing your own or acquiring third-party Web Parts, you will want to deploy to your server so that users within your organization can take advantage of the new features and functionality they possess. After you have a Web Part Package file, to deploy it, follow these steps:

1. Log on at the Windows SharePoint Services server with an account that has administrative rights.

2. Launch the SharePoint 2010 Management Shell from the Start menu (choose Programs ⇨ Microsoft SharePoint 2010 Products).

3. Run the following command:

```
Install-SPWebPartPack -Name name_of_package -LiteralPath path_to_
    Web_part_package_file
```

Doing this installs the Web Parts contained in the CAB file into the virtual server library.

Note

If there are multiple virtual servers on the same machine, install the Web Part Package on all of them using the -GlobalInstall switch in the given command. ∎

Deploying a Web Part to the Site Web Part Gallery

In SharePoint 2010, once a Web Part DLL is registered in the Web.config correctly, SharePoint automatically detects Web Parts from those DLLs. This makes it easy to surface new Web Part applications from the site settings page. The following steps explain how to automatically populate the Web Part Gallery for your site collection:

1. From your SharePoint site, click Site Actions and then Site Settings.

2. In the Site Collection Administration section, click Go to top level site settings (if you are not already at the top level site).

3. In the Galleries section click Web Parts and then click New Document from the Documents tab on the Ribbon.

4. **The list shows all of the Web Parts registered on the server, including your new one.** You may have to do an IISRESET (by typing `IISRESET` from a command line and pressing Enter) on the server if you have recently deployed new Web Parts and they don't appear in the list, and then refresh the page.

5. Select the Web Part you want to add to the gallery and click Populate Gallery.

Removing Web Parts from the gallery

You may find that some Web Parts are not useful or that you do not want to expose them to users. The following steps explain how to remove Web Parts from the Web Part Gallery for your site collection:

1. From your SharePoint site, click Site Actions, Site Settings, and then Modify All Site Settings.

2. In the Site Collection Administration section, click Go to Top-Level Site Settings (if you are not already at the top level site).

3. In the Galleries section click Web Parts and then click the Edit icon next to the Web Part you'd like to remove (or check the check box next to Web Part filename).

4. Click the Delete Item button in the dialog box (or click Delete on the Ribbon).

5. Click OK.

Exporting and importing Web Parts

The following example scenario explains how you can export and then import a Web Part and its settings.

You can add a Web Part to a Web Part page by importing a DWP file you exported from another site or received from another site user. For this to work, you and/or your colleague need to perform the following tasks to the Web Part that has already been configured:

1. Load the Web Part page that contains the already configured Web Part.

2. Click Edit Page from the Site Actions menu on that page.

3. After the page is in Edit Mode, click the down arrow in the title bar of the Web Part you want to transfer, and then choose Export from the drop-down menu.

4. When the File Download dialog box appears, click Save.

   - When the Save As dialog box appears, choose a file location, a filename, and a filename extension of .dwp, and then click the Save button.

   - Send the resulting DWP file to the person who wants to install the Web Part with a configuration identical to yours.

The team member who wants to add the Web Part would then follow this procedure:

1. Browse to the page where you want the preconfigured Web Part to appear.

2. Display the Add Web Parts form in either of two ways:

   - Choose Add Web Parts from the page in Edit mode and select Upload Web part from the Add Web Parts tool pane.

   - From the Insert tab on the Ribbon, click the Web Part button, and select Upload Web part from the Add Web Parts tool pane.

3. Click the Browse button and use the resulting Choose File dialog box to locate the DWP file you received.

4. Click the Upload button.

5. When the Web Part appears under the Imported Web Parts category, set the Add To drop-down list to the Web Part zone you want, and then click Add.

Summary

In this chapter, you learned what Web Parts are and the types of Web Parts available in SFS and SPS. You also learned how to customize your Web pages by adding, configuring, and removing Web Parts as well as how to add a Web Part to the Web Part gallery. Finally, you learned how to manage and administer Web Parts, including how to change their views, behaviors, and availability based on user roles and access rights.

Part II

Configuring
SharePoint Server

Using Personalization Features

Personalization is a key component of SharePoint technologies. By personalizing the information available to portal users, you make the experience easier and more streamlined. In this chapter, I discuss these personalization features and how they can be implemented to improve your portal experience and functionality. In addition, I cover planning and administration responsibilities for each of these personalization features.

This chapter gives you an overview of how information can be designed to surface for the groups, teams, and individuals who will most benefit from it, as well as review how SharePoint 2010 makes it is easy to find the people in the organization who know what you need to know.

Defining Personalization Features and Functions

When you access portal pages and team sites, the SharePoint 2010 platform has the ability to present to users content that they care about and that is useful for their daily activities. With the introduction of Web Part Pages in SharePoint 2003 and additional features included in SharePoint 2010, personalization and customization are provided via a rich feature set in a variety of ways. SharePoint 2010 knows who you are and makes the user experience much richer. In the following section, you will see that by combining the User Profile, Audience, and My Site features together, you will create a powerful social network that will promote efficiency in your organization.

Information Overload

With so many features and options available in SharePoint 2010, information can become unstructured and overwhelming as more information is published and stored. The convenience of publishing to team sites, discussions, blogs, wikis, and document libraries and lists can contribute to increased difficulty for users to find useful information relevant to their roles and responsibilities within an organization. Published information can also be presented and structured in ways that cater to the masses but not necessarily to one's specific needs.

Creating User Profiles

The User Profile features in SharePoint 2010 allow you to connect with and search for people within your organization based on information people publish about themselves. In addition, information already stored in your Active Directory (as well as other LDAP-based identity management systems such as Organization or Manager) can be imported and surfaced within the portal. User profile information is also used by MOSS when a My Site is created. Users can then edit and personalize their My Site, which has two views: the owner's view and the public facing view. User profiles are also integrated with search and indexing services to provide a better search and results experience. And last but not least, you can use many of these profile attributes to define audiences for content targeting throughout your portal environment. More information about these features appears later in this chapter.

You can edit your profile so that you can connect with people who have similar interests or expertise. Start by describing yourself and then identify people that you know. Administrators control which properties are editable and can add more properties if needed. Portal users can edit their profile from their personal view of their My Site. By default, your profile details are shown on the public view of your My Site. You can view and edit your profile in this view as well as the private view to which only you have access. Administrators are the only other users that have access to your Private Document Library.

The public view of the User Profile is visible to all other portal site users when they click your name in the portal site. For example, when you search for a document and see the author name in the search results, clicking on it opens that user's profile.

If you access user profile information programmatically in SharePoint and use it within line-of-business applications, your application can talk directly to the `UserProfileManager` object, which accesses and loads property values of specific users. You can use this information to render user-specific information or present relevant information in your own custom applications.

SharePoint 2010 offers the following types of properties for developers who are building solutions using the User Profile store.

- **Properties can have open or closed choice lists.** Your list can be open, meaning that users can manually add new values, or it can be closed, which means that you cannot add new values, only administrators can. Now you can tie user profile properties to a constrained list of possible values.

- **Properties now support multiple values appropriately called Multivalue Properties.** This improved feature opens up many possibilities and scenarios for connecting users together and to content; for example, you might add multiple areas of expertise to your profile. Your job may require one skill, but adding additional skills to the Multivalue Property called Expertise allows users to identify your skills in other areas as valuable to accomplish team and/or organizational goals not related to your position.

- **Properties can have an assigned Property privacy policy or policies.** Now you can assign privacy policies restricting who can access a particular property. This feature enables you to set policies that define restricted access to Only Me, My Manager, My Workgroup, My Colleagues, or to Everyone. You can also decide if a property is disabled, optional, or required.

- **Properties can also be mapped to other relevant external business data Property items originating from external data sources other than Active Directory.** When you create a new property for a profile instance, you can map the property to an external data source, such as to an entity registered in the Business Data Catalog application. This allows you to tie people to data that already exists in other business applications or databases. In the Microsoft Office SharePoint Portal Server 2003 release, the import of user profiles from the Active Directory services was the only configuration supported out of the box. Customers found it hard to manage the profile database and keep it up to date, especially those who did not have Active Directory deployed. Administrators taking advantage of the profile features were not able to centrally or easily manage the data.

SharePoint 2010 addresses this issue by importing profile information from all of the following external data sources in addition to Active Directory (AD):

- LDAP directory (other than AD)
- Custom Databases
- Enterprise applications (that is, PeopleSoft or SAP)

Note

SharePoint Server 2010 supports the last two types of data sources by connecting to the SharePoint feature called Business Data Connectivity Services. It uses this data to provide additional information that exists outside of the master connection, which augments user profiles imported from Active Directory and LDAP directories. ∎

User Profiles are much more than just a grouping of properties about a person. They can be used for a variety of things within the context of SharePoint 2010, such as implementing My Sites and targeting content. The public view of your profile is where these properties appear to users throughout your organization.

Included in all users' public profile pages are the following sections of information:

- **Profile Properties that are set to public appear on the public profile page.** User Profile Service Application administrators are the only people who can see and edit all user profile properties at the User Profile Service Application level. Site collection administrators can see values of User Profile Service Application level properties in the user information list on the site collection, but cannot edit the actual user profiles and properties. They can edit site level properties that are included in the user information list, but these are not added to user profiles stored in User Profile Services.

- **Relationship information that includes the sites, security group memberships for each person, registered distribution lists, and a section that lists your current associated colleagues.** As you view someone else's public profile, you can also see the colleagues they are associated with.

- **A list of related shared Documents for each person that includes documents stored on all sites where the person is a member.** These documents are organized in a convenient tab view.

- **Policies are available to administrators.** You can gain access to override certain policies as well. The Policies section manages how the profile information in other sections appears and which users have the ability to see it.

These features are presented to reinforce connections and encourage collaboration between people in your organization. When you access other users' public profiles you can quickly see who they are, what they may be working on, and who they typically work with. It also enables you (as an administrator) to make decisions about how information is shared and who can see this information in your organization.

Targeting audiences

Audience targeting is a great way for you to get specific people or groups of people the data relevant to them. After you have defined an audience based on attributes in users' profiles, SharePoint groups, or distribution lists, you can use them throughout the site collection. You could, for example, create an audience for everyone on the marketing team called "Marketing" and another for everyone on the sales team called "Sales," and have Web Parts on a page targeted at each. You might have a Web Part that reports marketing news and another displaying sales trends. After configuring the Web Parts to show for their respective audience, users in each group would see only the content targeted to them. Another good use of this feature is if you'd like to show a list of links to secure areas of the site to only users who have access, You can get very granular in your targeting of content to audiences in SharePoint 2010. You even have the ability to target a specific list item to a defined audience.

You define Audiences in the User Profile Service Application. The settings are accessible by the administrator on the server farm providing the Shared Application Service. There you can manage these three types of audiences:

- **SharePoint group audiences, which are defined by SharePoint groups by associating each with a set of permission levels within a site collection.** Members are then added to groups based on their user accounts. As an administrator you can create SharePoint groups and define their rights, which is a good way to manage access to content and features for large groups of people needing similar access. You can create SharePoint groups during initial server configuration and deployment or any time after your site is created. In this way, you use Audiences that are based on SharePoint groups that target content to users who are members of the selected group(s). You author your Audiences based on SharePoint groups to be very general or as granular as a single user, depending on your particular business needs.

- Global audiences are audiences based on the properties of user profiles, which are managed by your User Profile Service Application administrator. This type of audience targets content to users based on properties in their user profile and can be as simple as targeting a Web Part displaying up-to-the-minute football scores to all users who have selected "Football" from the Favorite Sport option in their profile, to more complex options like displaying training links to people who report to a specific manager that work on the day shift and already have some expertise in engineering.

- Distribution lists and security groups are another option when creating and managing audiences. Distribution lists can be created by different users in an organization, depending on the policies of each organization, whereas security groups are generally managed by your directory administrator.

You must import properties of distribution lists and security groups to be used for audiences from mail servers and directory services, such as Microsoft Exchange Server, Windows security, Lightweight Directory Access Protocol (LDAP), and Active Directory. Each of these properties and distribution lists are imported when user profiles are imported to the system.

These user profile properties and their underlying sources can change frequently. SharePoint 2010 provides the ability to schedule audience compilation to ensure that audiences remain current. The User Profile Service Application administrators can configure the schedule to regularly update and can manually compile audiences from time to time if needed. The Audience Compilation settings and scheduling features are part of the User Profile Service Application.

Note

SharePoint 2010 includes a Web service that finds all sites that are targeted to you or any specific user. ∎

Exploring My Site

My Sites are personal SharePoint sites that provide personalized and customized information for you. The server administrator can enable personal sites from within the Shared Service Provider. After enabling this feature, users can access their personal profile and manage their personal information in SharePoint, and also store and share information with the rest of the organization. You can think of My Site as your personal team site or dashboard where you keep track of your colleagues, manage your exchange inbox, and save links to locations useful and important to you.

Your My Site is created the first time you click the My Content link within the My Site site collection. Because your My Site is created based on a team site template, you have the same abilities you find on a typical team site as well as additional features, all of which can have a public view and a private view for storing secure information that you don't want to share. The Profile page of your My Site shows your SharePoint memberships, colleagues, your Web log, and documents to which you have an association.

In your default installation of SharePoint 2010, My Sites are enabled so that everyone in your organization with access to the site collection can have a unique My Site.

A My Site is a site collection composed of three different areas:

- **My Newsfeed:** This is the landing area when you click on My Site. This page displays a What's New Web Part that allows you to track various activities within the portal. An example is shown in Figure 6.1.

- **My Profile:** This area is the public profile page that anyone in the organization can see. This page contains various tabs that dive into specific profile areas. The Content tab displays shared content from your personal site. An example My Profile page is shown in Figure 6.2.

- **My Content:** A unique personal site for storage of private content and shared content, making it easy to collaborate with colleagues. The personal site is an actual private site that only the site owner can access and view. Any shared content from this site will appear in your profile page under the Content tab. An example of the personal site is shown in Figure 6.3.

FIGURE 6.1

My NewsFeed (My Site landing area)

FIGURE 6.2

My Profile

FIGURE 6.3

My Content

Tip

Easily navigate between the My Site areas by using the My Site top link bar. ∎

Each person can access their My Site by clicking the My Site link in the Login drop-down as shown in Figure 6.4. The first time you click the My Content link within the My Site site collection, your unique My Site is created automatically for first use. The My Profile menu item underneath the My Site menu item brings you to the same area but on the My Profile page.

You, the owner or administrator of your My Site, are presented with the Site Actions menu with the following actions available:

- Clicking Create directs you to a page where you choose to add a document library, list, Web Part page, and other content needed for public profiles and My Site.

- Selecting Edit Page from the Site Actions menu opens your My Site in Edit Mode. This gives you the ability to add, edit, or remove the Web Parts (the content) presented on your pages.

- After clicking Site Settings, you are taken to a central page to manage your My Site. Some examples of settings include managing Users and Permissions, Look and Feel, Galleries, and other administrative tasks.

Clicking on My Site brings you to your newsfeed page as shown in Figure 6.2. Your My Site personal site is actually under My Content from the My Site top navigation as shown in Figure 6.3.

FIGURE 6.4

My Site Login Menu option

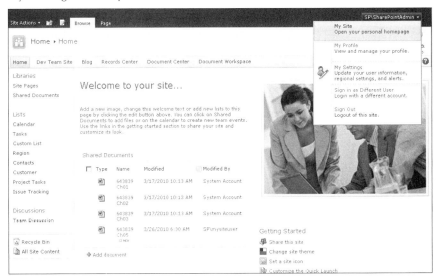

Your My Site personal site is private by default, so only you (or an administrator) can view the home page.

You do not need to plan any policy settings for the home page of your personal site because only you have access to the private site. You are the administrator of your personal site, which allows you to create and edit additional pages, change the default layout, customize the page to personal taste, and change your personal site settings.

Other pages and subsites in your personal site, such as workspaces created, libraries, and lists, can be shared and viewed by other users. In that sense the personal site is not entirely private. Planning considerations for subsites and other shared content are really no different from those of any other site, except that management and decisions are up to each site owner for normal operations.

The public view of each user's My Site is called the My Site Public Page. This page is accessed by clicking any link to a user within a portal site or site collection including links in lists (created by, modified by, and so on) and search results.

Using Personalization sites

Personalization targets information personalized to all members of your organization by using user filter Web Parts and personalized Web Parts. Site collection administrators are responsible for creating each personalization site; but another user with site creation permissions can also create them. Your User Profile Service Application administrators can add links to personalization sites to the My Site left navigation, which can appear for every member of each site or be targeted to specific audiences. You can add links to personalization sites to the top navigation pane and the left pane of the All Site Content page of the main site. Because personalization sites are registered in the User Profile Service Application, personalization sites from all site collections using the same shared service all appear in My Site — that is, as long as you belong to the audience the link was targeted to. Individual users can add links to other personalization sites that have not been registered by an administrator in the User Profile Service Application, but those links only appear on that user's My Site left navigation.

Personalization sites can be branded with either the main site logo or the My Site logo. The default layout for personalization sites is as follows:

- User Filter Web Parts in the top zone

- Your Picture above the Quick Launch

- Quick Launch left navigation, including links to the View All Site Content page and the Recycle Bin for the personalization site

- A Content Editor Web Part in the middle left zone that has some information explaining the purpose and prescribed use of the personalization site

- The Site Actions menu in the top link bar that contains an option to pin the personalization site to the My Site top link bar

Each personalization site uses filter Web Parts that connect Web Parts on the site to each individual person viewing the page, but there are no default Web Parts, and each personalization site uses a different set of Web Parts.

Like any SharePoint site, each personalization site may include subsites such as workspaces and lists and libraries that are relevant to the personalization site.

Navigating personal sites is easy. You can use the top link bar on your My Site personalization sites to go to the personal site or the public profile of My Site. You can also go to any other linked personalization sites. You may also use the breadcrumb navigation to view other parts of the main site.

Your organization probably has its own unique personalization needs. When planning My Sites, you may want to consider several factors:

- The My Site feature is enabled by default in SharePoint 2010, but you may want to disable it.
- You should think about where personal sites are stored and managed and how My Sites will work across multiple User Profile Service Applications.
- You may have profile policy considerations that determine what information is shown on each person's public profile.
- Think about specific personalization sites that are needed for your organization and who will create and own each site.

Designing User Profiles and Memberships

You may want to augment the profiles in the out-of-the-box profile database to suit your needs. Your organization may have specific properties associated with users that, if identified, could be useful in connecting people with similar expertise or skills as well as related job tasks. The complexity of your organizational structure may dictate that you plan ahead when defining or importing profile information — especially because in this version of SharePoint you can import profile information from a variety of sources, including Active directory, other LDAP-based identity management systems, external data defined in the Business Data Catalog, custom sources via the user profile object model, and properties manually created by the administrator and edited by users.

Determining user profile fields

Each user profile contains information about a single user. This profile is a set of name/value pairs that describe the user's personal information and information related to your organization. This information can be listed, searched, and displayed to other users in your organization. Index Server crawls the user profile store to get available user information.

Information about the people in your organization is stored in user profiles within the User Profile Service Application. The User Profile Service Application is managed by the services administrator who has additional permissions not available to User Profile Service Application administrators.

Administrators for User Profile Services import information about people from your directory services, such as the Active Directory service and Lightweight Directory Access Protocol (LDAP). When you plan an initial deployment of SharePoint 2010, you need to plan your User Profile Synchronization connections and directory services, plan which properties of user profiles are used, determine the policies for displaying and editing user profiles, and decide how user profiles are consumed by other personalization features, such as custom applications and personalization sites.

SharePoint 2010 provides a search scope for searching for people specifically. Understanding your organization and what information differentiates people is the first step in determining which profile properties and fields to use.

Before you can personalize the sites and content within your organization, you have to understand what information is useful for people to know about each other, how they work together, and who they are.

Planning for user profiles consists of starting with the default properties of user profiles in SharePoint Server 2010, identifying the connections to directory services (to supplement the default properties with the information about people you already have), and considering additional business data that enables you to connect people to line-of-business applications. The key planning principle is consistency across data sources for all people in your organization. Planning decisions should be written down and be easily referred to when managing your deployment.

User Profile Services enables you to configure and schedule the collection of information about people in your organization across directory services and other business applications so that timely and consistent information is always available to you. Information about people is synchronized across your deployment to all site collections that use the same User Profile Service Application. This information can also be used by personalization features to increase the value and relevance of collaboration features and relationships within your organization.

When you click My Content under the My Site site collection for the first time, your user profile is automatically created for you. During profile creation, SharePoint 2010 attempts to retrieve data from the Active Directory service, which is configured by your server administrator. If your environment doesn't have directory services available such as AD as an import source, you must enter their user profile properties manually. After user profiles are imported or added, you can update profile information by editing each user's profile. Editing user profiles does not change the set of properties displayed in that user profile. You can edit, add, or delete the profile properties on the Manage User Properties page in the People section of the User Profile Service Application administration page.

User profiles and properties are available to administrators from the Profile Service Application administration page. Every site using the same User Profile Service Application receives the same basic set of properties from the user profile store and displays them in the site's user information list. This allows User Profile Service Application administrators to manage profile properties in a central place. Depending upon your particular business needs, site collection administrators cannot add properties to user profiles, but they can add properties to the user information list for certain people. When you plan your user profiles, you'll need to consider several factors:

- **Educate yourself about your existing and planned directory services.** The foundation for your user profiles is derived from the information available in these services. You will need to determine what properties you will designate as your core user profile based on those that are relevant across your organization (or across the User Profile Service Application if your organization has multiple sets of shared services). To make the most of your deployment, it is essential that you include properties that can be used to create audiences for targeting content and finding people, and that can be used when establishing relationships between colleagues and work groups. Review the list of properties in directory services for starters and the default properties provided by SharePoint Server 2010, and then you can modify that list according to these considerations.

- **Review the line-of-business applications you use that have information about people.** Ask yourself whether or not these properties can be mapped to the properties of directory services. It's a good idea to write down these mappings in a spreadsheet or list and note which mappings should have priority if there should be a conflict. Make sure you add the line-of-business applications you'll use to your list of business applications. They must be identified and registered via Business Connectivity Services. You will want to integrate this information into your business intelligence planning.

- **Ask yourself what other, if any, non-people-related business application properties might be useful for people in your organization.** You can use these properties in personalized Web Parts to target business data to audiences.

- **Be conscious of the number of people in your organization and how often information in your directory services changes.** This will help you determine how often to schedule Profile Services to import. The frequency of scheduled imports depends upon the number of records, how extensively you're using personalization features, and when imports will have the least impact on availability and performance. It is important that the administrator of these services knows this information for inclusion in deployment planning.

- **Try to anticipate what profile properties you will need at the site level.** It's possible to manage this centrally, but you may also choose to leave this up to the discretion of each site collection administrator.

SharePoint 2010 contains a default set of properties and policies. Review these properties and the policies that apply to them before you decide what changes you'll make, which properties you'll keep or remove, and what properties to create as additions to the default set.

The properties imported from your directory service and the default properties included with SharePoint 2010 may be supplemented with properties that you create for tracking additional information not available from other sources and that you consider key to people within your organization.

You should plan to add properties at the User Profile Service Application or site collection level depending upon the business needs you identified in earlier planning. Key business needs can often be addressed by creating new properties that associate people with important business processes or skill sets. For your information architecture, consider if there should be a custom profile property that should correspond to each major concept to link people to information related to that concept. These custom properties can be used by the search service to find people or by personalization features in SharePoint 2010 to target content to people. Remember that any property can be hidden but still used to tie people and information together. You can choose to make Profile Properties invisible or visible on public profiles or My Sites. Therefore, they can be useful for search or personalization without being displayed to all users in public profiles or My Sites.

If you spend a lot of time thinking about and identifying many of the concepts related to your organization, you might end up with a very large property list. We recommend you prioritize that list to limit the properties to the most important concepts that will become custom profile properties and make your user profiles more valuable. Don't worry about making the right choice now. You can always identify relevant properties in the course of daily operations and add them later. It's possible that the out-of-box properties in SharePoint 2010 and properties imported from your directory service may be most of what you need, but this exercise is still considered worthwhile in case there are any obvious needs.

When you identify valuable custom properties to add or find default SharePoint 2010 ones valuable, you can define them as property choice lists. Profile Services administrators can suggest values or limit the values for any property by defining the list of suggested or approved choices. The managed list of choices then appears to users in a drop-down list for that property. You can either configure the Property choice list selection to be up to the user, or you may define the list of choices that can be added manually or imported from (or exported to) a comma-delimited file. A defined property choice list is a powerful way to control useful suggested values for a custom property. You can also decide to prevent the inclusion of irrelevant values by completely limiting the choices to your defined list.

If you want, users can select multiple values from property choice lists pertaining to the same property. For example, your custom property choice list can be used to enable employees to choose their relevant technical skills and other relevant skills, all of which appear as values for the property.

Here is an example of using a defined property choice list to make information easier to find and promote collaboration. After adding a custom property for users to define their area of expertise, the User Profile Service Application administrator identifies the top 15 areas of expertise most relevant to users in your organization. Adding these values as your defined property choice list and allowing users to associate themselves to an area of expertise will help users find users with specific expertise easily. If the search administrator maps the same property and the site collection administrator can identify Best Bets associated with keywords for each area of expertise, people can search for common keywords, and experts for each relevant area will appear at the top of search results.

Establishing mapping between profile properties and your directory service

After reviewing the information detailed earlier in this chapter, you are ready to connect to your directory service and map user profile properties to Profile Services. After you have them connected and mapped, you can see the results by using the features in your SharePoint 2010 deployment.

Profile Services is used to connect people-based properties of data sources such as line-of-business applications and directory services (primarily Active Directory and LDAP) with user profiles and properties that enable many of the features of SharePoint Server 2010.

You can access Profile Services from the User Profile Service Application administration pages. From the Import Connections link on the User Profiles and Properties administration page, you can connect directly to Active Directory or LDAP in order to import user profiles from those sources into SharePoint Server 2010. Services administrators select the properties from directory services to import to user profiles.

We will use connecting to AD in this example to help you become familiar with connecting Profile Services to directory services.

User Profile Service Application

The first step in mapping your profile properties to your directory services is ensuring that the proper services are running and navigating to the User Profile Service Application administration page. To achieve this, follow these steps:

1. Navigate to SharePoint 2010 Central Administration, as shown in Figure 6.5.

2. Click on Manage Services on Server under the System Settings section. Verify that both the User Profile Service and User Profile Synchronization Service are started as shown in Figure 6.6. If they are not started, click Start link in the Action column.

3. Click Application Management in the Quick Launch bar and then click on the Manage service applications link under the Service Applications section.

4. Locate the User Profile Service Application, as shown in Figure 6.7 and click on the link.

FIGURE 6.5

Central Administration link on the server Web front end

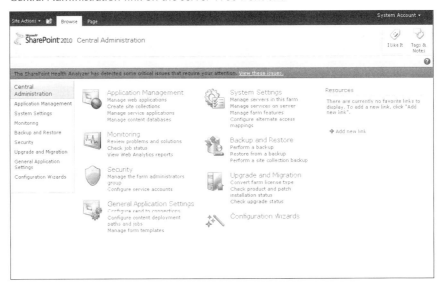

FIGURE 6.6

Services on server

FIGURE 6.7

Service applications

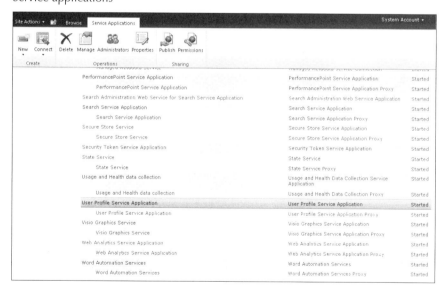

The User Profile Service Application administration page appears as shown in Figure 6.8. Use this page for performing the additional actions in this section.

FIGURE 6.8

User Profile Service Application administration page

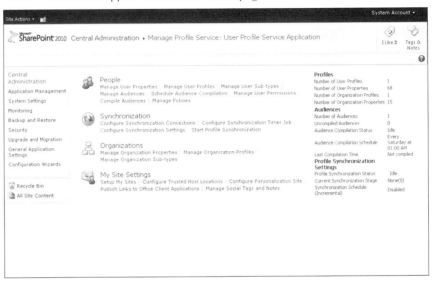

Configure synchronization connections

The next major step in importing profiles is setting up the actual connection. For these steps you must be using a server added to your domain. To create a new synchronization connection, follow these steps:

1. From the User Profile Service Application administration page, click on Configure Synchronization Connections under the Synchronization Connections section.

2. Click Create new connection. The Add new synchronization connection page appears as shown in Figure 6.9.

3. Enter a name for the connection. Leave the Type set to Active Directory.

4. Enter the forest name and domain controller for your Active Directory Services.

5. Enter a service domain account that has access to the Active Directory Services.

6. Scroll down the page and click on the Populate Containers button as shown in Figure 6.10. The Containers window will populate with your Active Directory Structure.

7. Navigate the tree structure and select Users under the Users section. Select any groups that need to be imported.

8. Click OK. The new connection is created and appears under Synchronization Connections as shown in Figure 6.11.

FIGURE 6.9

Add New Synchronization page (top part)

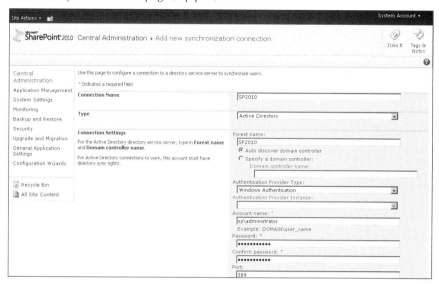

FIGURE 6.10

Add New Synchronization page (bottom part)

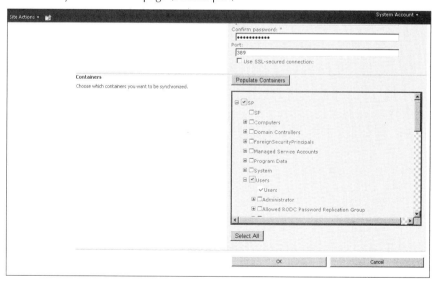

FIGURE 6.11

Synchronization connections

Tip

If the new connection does not appear or if you return to the Synchronization Connections page a few days later and it is no longer there, check to make sure that the Forefront Identity Manager Service and the Forefront Identity Manager Synchronization Service are both started on the Windows Server. Receiving a MOSS MA Not Found error is an indication that both of these services are not started even though they are set to Automatic. ■

Profile synchronization

The profile synchronization uses the synchronization connection to import user profiles into SharePoint 2010. The profile synchronization runs on a daily schedule by default and can be started on demand.

Configure synchronization settings

It is recommended to first run a full import on Users and then run an incremental import on Users and Groups. You switch between these options by configuring the synchronization settings:

1. From the User Profile Service Application administration page, click on Configure Synchronization Settings under the Synchronization Connections section.

2. Switch the Synchronization Entities to Users Only, as shown in Figure 6.12.

3. Click OK.

FIGURE 6.12

Configure synchronization settings

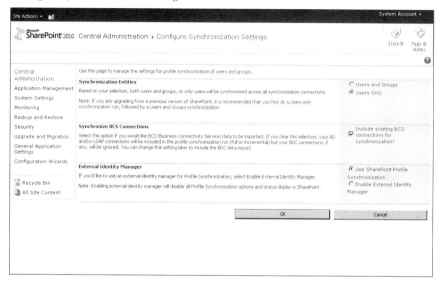

Start profile synchronization

To start the profile synchronization, follow these steps:

1. **From the User Profile Service Application administration page, click on Start Profile Synchronization under the Synchronization Connections section.**

2. **Select Incremental or Full as shown on the Start Profile Synchronization page in Figure 6.13.** The page recommends not running a full import, however. Since this is the first synchronization, it is actually recommended to run a Full import on Users first and then continue running incremental imports on Users and Groups. To switch between the two, use the Configure Synchronization Settings page.

3. **Click OK.**

4. **The synchronization status displays on the User Profile Service Application administration page on the right-hand side, as shown in Figure 6.14.** You may need to refresh the browser to see the updated status.

FIGURE 6.13

Start Profile Synchronization page

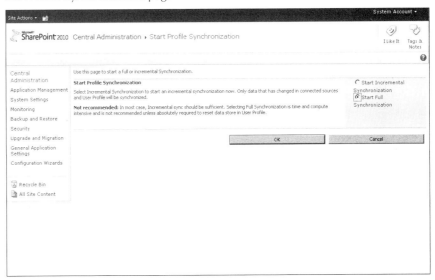

FIGURE 6.14

Profile synchronization status

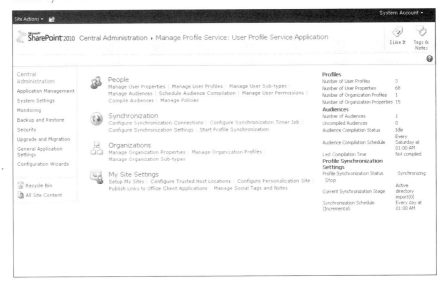

Scheduling profile synchronization

The profile synchronization is automatically scheduled to run daily at 1:00 a.m.; however, you can modify the scheduled times for User Profile Services to import updates to your AD. If your organization experiences regular changes in your directory, you may want to schedule regular imports. Updates to users' profile information will be synchronized during an incremental import. This type of import has little impact to the AD in terms of resource usage. The incremental import is the only type of import that is scheduled. You may no longer schedule a full import.

Note

To perform incremental imports, the service domain account must have the Replicate Changes permission for Active Directory. ■

After you have specified the right schedule for your organizational needs:

1. From the User Profile Service Application administration page, click on Configure Synchronization Timer Job under the Synchronization Connections section.

2. The Edit Timer Job screen appears as shown in Figure 6.15.

3. Change the incremental schedule as necessary.

4. Click OK.

Tip

Changing the timer job returns you to the Timer Job page. Click the browser Back button twice to get back to the User Profile Service Application administration page quickly. ■

FIGURE 6.15

Editing Profile Synchronization Timer Job

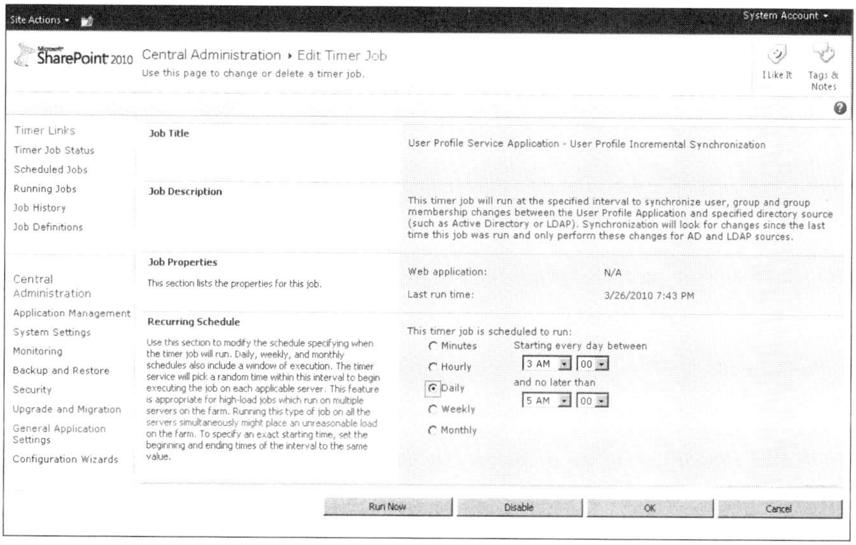

Profile mapping

During the initial import, Profile Services automatically maps as many default SharePoint 2010 Profile Properties to your AD Profile Properties as possible. You can see the number of User Profiles and User Properties mapped on the right-hand side of the User Profile Service Application Administration screen, which is also shown in Figure 6.14.

The steps in this section so far should have successfully connected your Directory Service (AD in this case) to your Profile Services. Next, you will want to make sure that each Directory User Profile property is mapped correctly to your SharePoint 2010 Profile Service. The next section introduces you to creating these mappings by walking through a series of steps. One of the default properties included in the SharePoint 2010 default User Profile is an HTML property called About me. Let's assume that the description of a person in your organization is important for other users to see, but you already control this by managing this property in the Description field of each user's AD entry as shown in Figure 6.16. To override and map the existing AD property to the default SharePoint 2010 property, follow these steps:

FIGURE 6.16

Active Directory user Description profile property

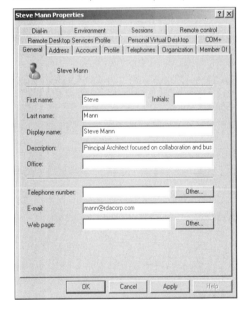

1. Click Manage User Properties in the People section of the User Profile Service Application administration page.

2. Scroll down until you locate the Property Name About me.

3. Hover over About me. This is the SharePoint 2010 property that we are mapping to AD.

4. Click on the drop-down arrow on the right of the menu.

5. Select Edit, as shown in Figure 6.17.

   On this page you are able to manage all of the Profile Property settings. For example, you can edit the Display Name of the property that shows up in the user profile page, User Description that shows up on the page for editable properties, Policy Settings (as it appears in SharePoint 2010), Edit Settings, Display Settings, Search Settings, and Property Import Mappings.

6. Scroll to the bottom of the page and select the drop-down box labeled Data source field to map, as shown in Figure 6.18.

7. Select adminDescription from the list.

8. Click the Add button to add the mapping.

9. Click OK.

FIGURE 6.17

Edit control box menu drop-down for About me property

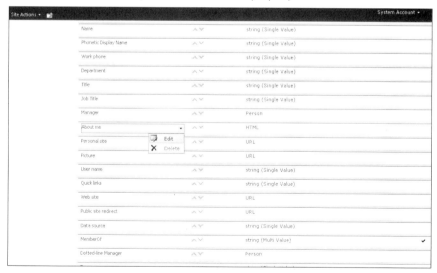

FIGURE 6.18

Drop-down list of properties imported from your AD

Now you've mapped your AD profile property adminDescription to your SharePoint 2010 User Profile property About me.

You can also add business data properties that contain information about people to existing user profiles by connecting to the Business Data Catalog, selecting a relevant entity from a registered business data application, and either mapping that entity to an existing profile property or adding it as a new property. These properties augment the existing profiles imported from directory services.

Note

You cannot create or import entirely new user profiles from the Business Data Catalog. You can add the data only to existing user profiles. ■

You can import the properties from all of these sources into user profiles by connecting to the relevant service or database and mapping the unique identifier for each property in the shared service to the unique identifier of the corresponding property in the business application. These connections can be made regardless of the authentication method used by the business application.

The User Profile Service Application maintains the connections with the relevant business applications and updates the properties of user profiles during regularly scheduled imports from all relevant data sources. Data is not exported, however, so the user profile database cannot overwrite the source databases.

Designing audiences

Your use of the Audience features in SharePoint 2010 is dependent on how you manage and design other administrative features in your organization. When you do your planning for how you use Audience features, you will want to understand and use the following information:

- Understand and plan your organization's AD security and user management
- Design and implement your user profile strategy
- Plan your distribution lists and SharePoint groups
- Plan your deployment of sites and site collections

After becoming intimate with the four points above, you are ready to begin your audience planning. In your initial deployment you should record all distribution lists, SharePoint groups, and the purpose you have identified for creating each site collection. After you have this information identified, you can condense and group that information into a small number of audiences that best represent the important groups of users in your organization.

Some of your needs to target content to specific groups of people may require creating new SharePoint groups with audiences in mind. Each site collection will generally have a focused set of business processes associated with a group of users, and custom SharePoint groups can be used to define an audience as precisely as your planning allows. If you combine those groups with existing SharePoint groups, AD groups, user profile properties, and distribution lists, you should have a list of audiences that meet the needs of the groups of users who are using each site collection. You can use the following audience rules to maximize their value:

- Audiences based on user profile properties include a logical operator that is used to evaluate the property.
- Organization hierarchy is recorded in the user profile and is viewable in the My Site Web Parts.
- User memberships such as distribution lists or AD groups can be used and also appear in My Site.

Audiences can also be created directly from distribution lists and SharePoint groups. These can be used to define an audience without having to build complex rules. With thoughtfully managed groups and distribution lists, you may already have groups of users that can easily be managed as audiences.

One natural starting point when creating new audiences may come from existing teams of users that are already working together. You may also start creating relevant audiences quickly by using existing mature business processes, cross-group projects, and current site structures. These groups of users can sometimes easily be translated into useful audiences. Organizational reporting structure is another fairly straightforward place to get started.

Audience planning may also cause you to think differently about your current distribution lists, user profile properties, SharePoint groups, site structures, and security groups, and possibly identify areas where you can improve them. If during your planning you think of a group of users to whom you want to target content and there are no existing SharePoint groups, distribution lists, or user profile properties to tie them to an audience, it's a good idea to document them and plan for adding or editing those groups, lists, or user properties.

Designing and creating your audiences is half of the equation. After you have your audiences defined, you'll want to make use of them to target content, highlight relevant information to the proper users, and reduce the amount of irrelevant information to users.

In SharePoint 2010, you target content to users in the following ways:

- List item or Web Part
- Using the My Site navigation bar to target personalization sites
- As part of the discovering servers feature
- By targeting Web Parts by audience

Targeting by list item or Web Part

Any Web Part available can be targeted to specific sets of audiences. You can add those audiences to the Target Audiences text box in the Advanced section of the Web Part's tool pane. To change this setting on any of your Web Parts:

1. **Navigate to the page you want to target content to audiences.**
2. **Click Site Actions as shown in Figure 6.19.**
3. **Click Edit Page.**

FIGURE 6.19

Site Actions menu

4. Click the down arrow on the Web Part you would like to modify, as shown in Figure 6.20.

5. Click Edit Web Part.

6. In the tool pane of the Web Part, scroll to the bottom.

7. Expand the Advanced section.

8. Again, scroll to the very bottom of the tool pane.

9. Click the Address book icon in the Target Audiences section.

10. Select SharePoint Groups from the Find drop-down list, as shown in Figure 6.21.

11. Type Management in the Find text box. (Your results will depend on the SharePoint groups in your site collection.)

12. Click the magnifying glass.

13. Select the Audience that appears in the picker results box.

14. Click the Add button, shown in Figure 6.22.

FIGURE 6.20

Edit menu for Web Parts

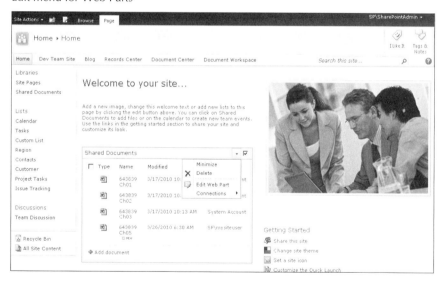

FIGURE 6.21

Audience picker

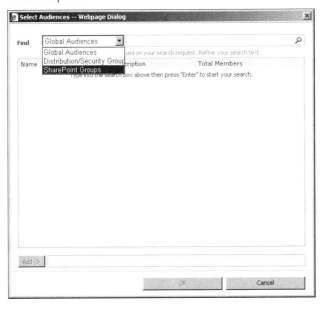

FIGURE 6.22

Audience picker results

15. Click OK.

16. Click OK again in the Web Part tool pane.

17. Click Publish on the Page Editing toolbar.

Now only members of the management group you selected will see that Web Part when they navigate to that page. Other users of the site that are not in that group will not see that content.

You can use Audiences to target content to users in many ways by using different Web Parts available in SharePoint. One of the best Web Parts to use within a site collection for this purpose is the Content Query Web Part.

Many SharePoint site templates, such as team collaboration sites, and pages have the Content Query Web Part available by default. You can target content in these three ways:

- You can group results by filter options or audience. Often this Web Part is used to target content both by Web Part and by list item.

- Display list items from multiple hierarchical levels across a site collection.

- You can target specific list items to specific audiences by using the Content Query Web Part. Even when those list items appear in pages or Web Parts, only the individual list item is targeted to an audience.

Targeting content by using Trusted My Site host locations

In a global deployment that has geographically distributed shared services or other scenarios, some users may have access to more than one My Site host location. In these scenarios, your User Profile Service Application administrator for each User Profile Service Application manages a list of Trusted My Site host locations across all User Profile Service Applications and then targets each location to the audiences of users who need to view them.

Your Trusted My Site host locations are processed in priority order within the list. Each user sees personalized information that is most relevant for the My Site he or she is viewing. Personalization information is available even if individual User Profile Service Applications are unavailable due to geography. During your initial deployment, as in most deployments, there will be only one User Profile Service Application; therefore, you will typically not need to configure this feature. Personalization links that are presented in the My Site top navigation bar can be targeted to audiences as well. User Profile Service Application administrators can add these links. In this way, personalization sites that may be relevant to one group of users and not to another can be targeted to them and placed in context of their daily activities. The User Profile Service Application administrator can target links so that they appear only for users for whom the personalized content in the site is relevant.

Using Web Parts that filter by audience

A group of powerful Web Parts called *filters* can be connected to other Web Parts and provide filter criteria to control what information appears based on certain properties. These available properties vary from filter to filter, but one of the options available is to filter by audience. You can imagine how useful it may be to filter business data by audience so that business intelligence information is relevant to each user or group of users. Tying these features together enables you to provide relatively complex calculations or business analysis in your displayed results.

Managing memberships

Users can have a relationship to other users in your organization depending on how you design your SharePoint 2010 deployment site structure. These relationships appear on the public profile page for each user as well as on each person's personal site, illustrating connections between different people depending on how they use the sites in your organization. The administrators for the User Profile Service Application can also see in Profile Services information about these people and their relationships. This information includes:

- Memberships of distribution list

- Memberships of security groups (including by default groups that are e-mail enabled)

- Site membership (a view of global memberships for each person)

- Colleagues (accomplished by using the In Common With Web Part and My Colleagues Web Part)

Thinking about how relationships between users are identified based on memberships will help you plan your site collection structure. People become members when you add them or a group they are in to the Member group for each site. You should consider having a site for each key business process in your organization and include the relevant people to that process in the Site's Members group.

Distribution lists and security group memberships exist for all but the newest of organizations. If you are not responsible for security in your organization, you will want to connect with the person responsible for security planning and educate them about how SharePoint 2010 uses memberships to ensure people have the correct permission levels to do their jobs. Organizational policies and architecture will also need to be considered in your planning.

Early in your deployment it is recommended that you review and reorganize distribution lists to reflect your planned information architecture. Unused or redundant distribution lists can be discontinued, and new distribution lists can be created to meet additional needs.

Colleagues are automatically identified based on your organization hierarchy imported from your directory services such as AD. Your colleagues include all people within your immediate work group, including your manager, peers, and any employees that report to you directly. No specific planning is needed to make these connections. In some organizations there may be key relationships between people on teams that work on projects together from time to time. You or management may want to add My Colleagues lists for certain cross-teamwork groups. User Profile Service Application and site collection administrators should also encourage managers to make these changes early in the deployment, and encourage them to review the organizational hierarchy in their My Site so they can verify their organizational hierarchy and make changes to directory services if needed.

During the planning phase for people and their relationships, start with planning for membership in sites, SharePoint Groups based on security considerations, distribution lists, your organizational hierarchy, and the roles of individuals and teams of people in your organization. Consider how people currently collaborate, based on common managers or common tasks across workgroups, and then consider ways in which you might improve that collaboration with new distribution lists or groups, or by adding people as colleagues. Think about other functionality that relies on membership in these groups. For example, membership can be used to target content to specific audiences.

Managing Personalization Features

With all of the capabilities and features surrounding personalization in SharePoint 2010, your planning efforts can help make managing the various personalization aspects of your deployment easier and scalable. As users learn how to use these features, they will find new and creative ways to connect and collaborate in the context of their daily activities. It's a good idea to provide a channel for feedback and requests to be collected and reviewed so that they can be taken into consideration during the ongoing information architecture management and planning of your deployment. You may find that these features will enable users to find more optimal ways to work together.

Managing user profiles and properties

User profiles and properties are managed by the User Profile Service Application administrator. After reviewing your directory services, identifying your business data relevant to personalization and the default SharePoint 2010 profile properties, and then comparing each to your collaboration needs, you should have a good idea of the profile properties you will implement. To access the administrative interface for scheduling user profile imports and managing user profiles and profile properties, follow these steps:

1. On the Quick Launch bar of SharePoint 2010 Central Administration, click Application Management.

2. Click on the Manage service applications link under the Service Applications section.

3. Locate the User Profile Service Application, as shown in Figure 6.7, and click on the link.

4. From the User Profile Service Application administration page, click on Configure Synchronization Timer Job under the Synchronization Connections section.

5. The Edit Timer Job screen appears, as shown in Figure 6.15.

6. Change the incremental schedule as necessary.

7. Click OK.

Note

To perform incremental imports, the account must have the Replicate Changes permission for Active Directory provided by Windows Server. ∎

Managing user profile properties is also done by the User Profile Service Application administrator for each User Profile Service Application. There are many default properties in SharePoint 2010, and you're likely find that there are quite a few properties in each user profile recorded in your directory services. After you have completed your first profile import, you should review which properties were mapped and which properties are important to your organization, and compare to your planning efforts earlier in this chapter. There will likely be some changes to the profile properties in the system, so let's take an example and get more familiar with profile property management by following these steps:

1. On the Quick Launch of SharePoint 2010 Central Administration, click Application Management.

2. Click Application Management in the Quick Launch and then click on the Manage service applications link under the Service Applications section.

3. Locate the User Profile Service Application as shown in Figure 6.7 and click on the link.

4. Under the People section, click Manage User Properties (see Figure 6.23).

FIGURE 6.23

View Profile Properties page

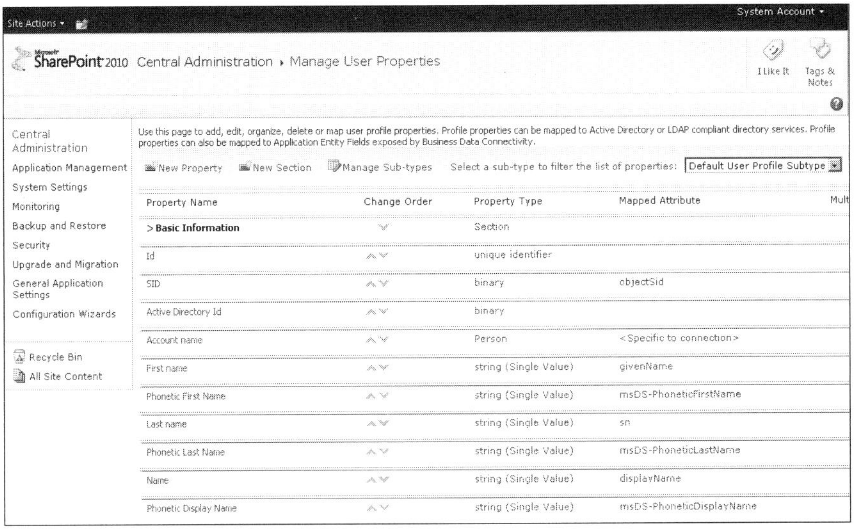

The Manage User Properties page displays the list of default properties in property sections, as shown in Figure 6.15. You can see a mixture of default SharePoint 2010 properties as well as user profile properties imported from your directory services after your first full import. Profile properties are organized by a property type called Section. Each property is assigned to a section, which helps make them easier to manage. On the View Profile Property page you can manage either sections or properties. To get familiar with how to manage the user profile properties, let's use geography as an example. If your organization were composed of offices in several locations across the United States, it could be useful to personalize or target information to each region. For this particular scenario, suppose it would be useful to have users control what location they are associated with.

1. Click New Property from the toolbar.

2. On the Add User Profile Property page, locate the Property Settings section and add the following information:

   - Type **OfficeRegion** in the Name text box.
   - In the Display Name text box, type **Region**.
   - In the Type drop-down list, select string.

3. In the User Description section, type a descriptive explanation of what the property is and why it may be useful, as shown in Figure 6.24.

4. In the Policy Settings section choose Required from the Policy Setting drop-down list and Everyone from the Default Privacy Policy drop-down list.

5. In the Edit settings section, select the Allow Users to Edit Values for This Property radio button.

FIGURE 6.24

Add User Profile Property page

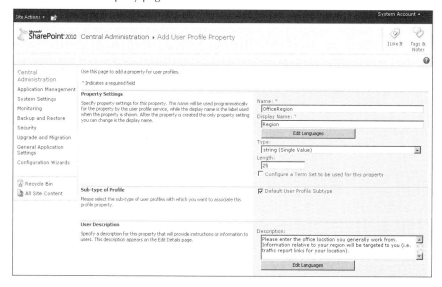

6. **In the Display Settings section, check all three available check boxes:**
   - Show in the profile properties section of the user's profile page
   - Show on the Edit Details page
   - Show updates to the property in newsfeed.

7. **Click OK.**

On the Manage User Profile properties, scroll to the bottom of the page. You will see your new custom property in the Custom Properties section, which is where they appear by default after you create one. Just to the right of the new Region property is a light blue arrow pointing up. Click the blue arrow as many times as needed to move the Region property just above the Contact Information section. This puts the Region property in the Details section of the user profile. Now that you have created this new property, it's time to see what the user experience is like. From the portal site, click My Site from the Login drop-down menu in the top-right corner of the page, and then do the following:

1. **Click My Profile in the top navigation of your My Site.**

2. **Below your picture on the page, click Edit My Profile.**

3. **On the Edit Details page, begin filling out your user profile properties.**

4. **Scroll down to the details section.** Notice the new Region property, as shown in Figure 6.25.

5. **Enter a value.**

6. **Scroll back to the top of the Edit Details page and click Save and Close.**

FIGURE 6.25

Region property on the Edit Details page of your user profile

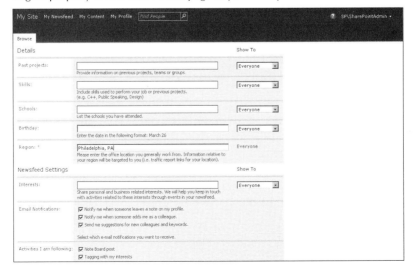

This new property is now available to the User Profile Service Application administrator for use when creating rules for audiences and for content targeting.

Setting Profile Services policies

SharePoint 2010 comes with the capabilities to collect information about people from many diverse sources. To that end, you should carefully review and decide what information is appropriate for the people in your organization to see or have available to them. Information, like employee payroll for example, should not be available to all employees. Sensitive information like this should be available only to certain users and administrators to preserve privacy, while other information can and should be shared freely with other people to encourage collaboration. Each organization may have different requirements depending on the type of business and decisions you make while keeping privacy and relevancy in mind. The decision about what information to share is an important one.

SharePoint 2010 provides a set of policies that are configurable so that your Profile Services administrator can control what information is available to meet the needs of your organization for each profile property. Your policies may vary between User Profile Service Applications, so you should review during the planning phase your collaboration needs across the organization in order to develop your plan for implementing the right set of policies.

The personalization features and properties exposed in user profiles and personal sites come with a default recommended policy. You may want to change the default policies based on the needs of your organization. There are two parts to each policy:

- **Policy Setting:** Some personalization features provide information that is critical for key business processes within an organization. Other information may be inappropriate for sharing across an organization. Some information will be useful for some people to share, but not other people, so that different policies are needed for different people. You can decide to change the policies by feature or property to meet the business needs of your organization. The specific options are

    - **Required:** This feature or property must contain information, and the information is shared based on default access. Forms containing these features or properties cannot be submitted until the required information is provided. For example, the Manager property is often mandatory so that it can be used to provide information for the My Work Group feature and audiences based on an organization's reporting hierarchy.

    - **Optional:** The feature or property is created and its values may or may not be provided automatically. Each person decides whether or not to provide values for the property or leave the property empty. For example, the phone number of a user is often left blank, and each person can decide whether or not to provide a telephone number visible to other people. The My Colleagues feature is optional, but rather than being blank, the list of colleagues including everyone in the current work group is visible by default to people with access, and each person can decide to opt out by removing colleagues from the list or expand the list by adding additional colleagues.

- **Disabled:** The property or feature is not visible to anyone but the User Profile Service Application administrator. It does not show up in personalized sites or Web Parts and cannot be shared.

- **User Override:** Properties with the override option selected allow users to change the default access policies for user profile properties. With this option selected, each person can decide who can see the values he or she entered for the property. If override is not selected, only administrators can change default access settings.

- **Replicable:** Properties and features with the replicable option selected can be replicated to other SharePoint sites, but only if the default access is set to "Everyone" and the User Override option is not selected.

- **Default Privacy Setting:** Visibility policy determines who can see information for a particular personalization feature. Available policies include:

  - **Everyone:** Every person with viewer permissions to the site can see the relevant information.

  - **My Colleagues:** Every person in this person's My Colleagues list can see the information for this person.

  - **My Workgroup:** Every colleague in the person's work group can see the information.

  - **My Manager:** Only the person and their immediate manager can see the information.

  - **Only Me:** Only the person and the site administrator can see the information.

Some organizations allow individual User Profile Service Application administrators to configure policies, and other organizations want to implement a consistent policy across the organization. By setting expectations for policies during initial planning, you can avoid later confusion, surprises, and misunderstandings. Whatever your decision, you should make the policies clear to people in your organization when they begin using SharePoint 2010 so they can expect that certain information about them and their work will be available to others.

Policies can vary depending upon the purpose of the sites in your User Profile Service Application. Consider your information architecture planning and site hierarchy when deciding what policies to use. For example, a site based around collaboration is likely to have a less restrictive set of policies than a site designed as a document repository where interaction is defined by mature business processes.

You will also want to consider who is using your sites. Customer-facing sites will have entirely different policy considerations compared to collaboration sites, and a central portal site for a large organization may have less need to share information than a departmental site. Many of these issues will be handled as part of security planning, but privacy policies and security considerations are sufficiently related that it's a good idea to consider them together.

Policies with fewer restrictions mean that people will be viewing public profiles more frequently, which affects how often you must update user profiles and compile audiences. In organizations with a large number of users, this could affect performance and capacity planning.

Site and User Profile Service Application administrators should record their policy decisions on the People, Profiles, and Policies planning worksheet for every feature and property, and share that information with IT professionals in the organization. Some issues that could affect IT planning include:

- Expected frequency of updating user profile information
- Frequency of compiling audiences
- Effect on performance and capacity of servers running Profile Services
- The effect on security planning

Profile Properties such as preferred name, account name, work phone, department, title, and work e-mail are key methods of enabling collaboration and developing organizational relationships. Many of them are also used by SharePoint 2010 in enabling other features such as colleagues and audiences.

By default in SharePoint 2010, users can't override these properties because it's important to administrators of Profile Services that access to information stay consistent and predictable.

By default, most out-of-the-box properties are visible to everyone having access to the portal, but only people who have been selected as colleagues can view sensitive information such as home phone numbers.

Organizations have different needs. A company with many employees in the field, for example, may find that mobile phone information is important for everyone to see. Other organizations may keep all non-work phone numbers completely private. Organizations focused around small-team collaboration may want to limit more properties to a core group of colleagues.

When managing the policy settings for a property, consider the following factors:

- Consider making a property required if:
  - The properties are used by key people features
  - The properties are associated with key business data for applications in the Business Data Catalog
  - The properties are used in creating audiences
  - Administrators for Profile Services expect consistent and meaningful values for those properties
- Consider disabling a property if:
  - The property will rarely be used.
  - The property will distract from more important properties. You can change the display settings for properties to hide them from users viewing public profiles, the Edit Details page, or the My Colleagues Web Part.

- Consider selecting Optional if you decide to provide default values for properties but you still want users to be able to remove the information, or if you want to allow each user to provide the relevant value for the property.

When planning default access policy, consider the following factors:

- If you want to use the property in search so that people can be found by searches for the property, set the default access policy to Everyone. Properties with more restrictive access will not be used by search.

- If the property is useful across work groups and other divisions in your organization and doesn't contain sensitive information, consider making it visible to everyone.

- If the property is mostly useful for collaboration within an immediate work group or within a particular group of individually selected colleagues, consider making it visible only to colleagues.

- If the property is of a private or sensitive nature, consider making it visible only to the immediate manager, or in some cases only the individual user. What is considered private information can vary from organization to organization.

When deciding whether to allow users to override the policies for properties, consider the following factors:

- Configure key user profile properties that need consistent values and clear administrator control so that users cannot override them. Override should be enabled only when the access to a property is not central to the needs of an organization.

- People should be able to override the access policy for a property if the sensitivity of the information can vary between different users, and the administrator cannot predict a single policy for all users. For example, an employee's hire date might be considered private to one employee and a point of pride to another.

- People should be able to override properties that may be relevant to different groups of people over time by changing the default access policy.

Another thing to consider is what information will be replicated from the User Profile Service Application to user information lists on SharePoint sites. You can limit replication of information by making policies more restrictive, or by limiting the information that is replicated. Only properties can be replicated. Properties with the replicable option selected are replicated to other SharePoint sites, but only if the default access is set to Everyone and the User Override option is not selected. Every site that uses the User Profile Service Application will use the replicable properties in user information lists. Properties set to Everyone that are not replicable can be seen in the public profile, but those properties do not appear in user information lists. If a property is not replicated, the values for the property in the user information lists for SharePoint sites remain, but changes are no longer replicated and must be made by the site collection administrator. When planning the initial deployment of user profiles, decide which properties you want in the user information lists and record those decisions.

Configuring My Site settings

The My Site feature is activated by default at the Web application level. Some organizations may decide to deactivate the feature for the farm or for individual sites. When deciding whether to use My Site, the following factors are important:

- Site purpose
- Web application performance

The most important factor to consider when deciding whether to use the My Site feature is the purpose of your sites. Sites that are designed to enable people to work and share information easily will almost certainly benefit from My Sites. Each person in the organization will be able to easily find people and information related to them.

On the other hand, sites that are not built upon collaboration might not benefit from personal sites. An example is a large document repository that doesn't contain team sites or workspaces, doesn't target content by audience, and isn't a place where people go to find or share organizational information about themselves or their colleagues.

Because My Site is activated at the Web application level, it's usually a good idea to retain the feature if any of the sites on the Web application will benefit from using it. One exception to this is a Web application that is optimizing for other functionality of SharePoint 2010. Although the My Site feature is not particularly resource-intensive, Web applications with a large number of users, a high volume of content, and relatively little need for personalization or collaboration might benefit from deactivating the My Site feature. When you are planning for personalization you should talk to IT administrators in the organization about performance and capacity considerations if this is a concern.

As soon as the My Site feature is activated, any user profiles from an existing installation of Microsoft Windows SharePoint Services are replaced by the public profiles that are part of My Site. A My Site link is added to the top menu bar for all sites in the site collection, along with the My Links menu.

You activate or deactivate the My Site feature from the Manage Web application features link in the SharePoint Web Application Management section of the Application Management tab in Central Administration. You can also limit the ability to create My Sites by removing the right from the authenticated users group for the User Profile Service Application or deleting that group from the Personalization Services Permissions page.

You can turn off My Sites at the site collection or site level by deactivating the Office SharePoint Server Standard feature in Site Settings, but you will also lose the search functionality for the site. This can be a good option for sites such as large document repositories. In that case, the documents on the site can still be crawled so that they appear in searches from other sites in the server farm but without having to support My Sites features that aren't relevant for the site but that are available on other sites in the farm that have kept the features active.

Configuring Trusted My Site host locations

User Profile Service Application administrators for personalization consider the interaction between personalization sites across all site collections in all farms using the User Profile Service Application, and how personalization sites are made available within My Sites. They also make decisions about the presentation of the My Site as a whole. Their considerations include:

- Personalization links
- Trusted My Site host locations
- Personal sites settings

These settings are managed from the User Profiles, Audiences, and Personal Sites sections of the User Profile Service Application.

From the User Services Shared Services administration page, you can add additional trusted personal site locations. This enables User Profile Service Application administrators to select My Site locations from multiple site locations. This is needed in any scenario with more than one User Profile Service Application, such as a global deployment with geographically distributed sets of shared services, where each User Profile Service Application contains a distinct set of users. By listing the trusted personal site locations for all other User Profile Service Applications, you can ensure that My Sites are created in the correct location for each user. This also enables you to replicate user profiles across User Profile Service Applications.

Creating published links to Office clients

Just as personalization sites can appear on the My Site navigation bar based on targeting of the personalization sites on the personalization links list, it is possible to target the links on the Links Published to Office Applications page. This list, available from the User Profiles and My Sites section of the Shared Services Administration page, is used to include links to Office Server sites from Office client applications. Examples of links that show up in client applications include:

- Sites, including team sites, portal sites, and project workspaces
- Data connection libraries
- Document libraries or document repositories

For example, if a personal site directory is added to this list, that location is provided as a choice whenever someone shares a document from an Office client application. This enables users to use the same personal site from multiple client computers. Similarly, data connection libraries added to the list show up in the Microsoft Excel client, and document libraries show up whenever saving documents from any Office client application. By default, links to Office client applications appear for all users in the User Profile Service Application. Those links become much more powerful when they are targeted to users who most need them so that users see only the personal sites, data connection libraries, and document libraries relevant to their own work.

When planning the initial deployment of SharePoint Server 2010, consider each of these kinds of links and plan to add links to cover each kind. Plan to add links to cover sites, data connection libraries, and document libraries for all the site collections by using the User Profile Service Application.

Configuring personalization links

Anyone with permission to create sites within a site collection can select the personalization site template, but not all of these sites will be relevant for all users in the site collection, much less all users within the same User Profile Service Application. Personalization sites that are relevant for users across the User Profile Service Application can be added as links to the My Site left navigation bar. Every person using My Site will see links to all personalization sites that were linked by the User Profile Service Application administrator, regardless of site collection, except for personalization site links targeted to specific audiences.

Personalization sites planned for initial deployment are important enough to add to the My Site link for the people who use the corresponding site collection, but not all people in the User Profile Service Application will consider the same personalization sites to be relevant. My Site links to personalization sites can be targeted to specific audiences so that only relevant people see them. For something like human resources information that applies to everyone in an organization, a My Site link to the personalization site may make sense for everyone. For a personalization site that shows personalized content to the sales team, it makes sense to target the My Site link so that it appears only for members of that team, or for members of the sales site collection.

The decision about what personalization sites will be linked in My Site navigation should be recorded during the site structure planning, along with decisions about targeting to audiences.

Setting personalization services permissions

The User Profile Service Application administrator can control who has personalization service permissions from the User Profile and My Sites section of the Shared Services administration page from within Central Admin. You may decide you want to allow one person or a group of users the ability to manage any or one of the following:

- Create Personal Site
- Use Personal Features
- Manage User Profiles
- Manage Audiences
- Manage Permissions
- Manage Usage Analytics

Most organizations focus on enabling user collaboration and give all information workers the rights to Create Personal Sites, Use Personal Features, and Manage Permissions.

To manage personalization services permissions:

1. On the Quick Launch of SharePoint 2010 Central Administration, click Application Management.

2. Click Application Management in the Quick Launch and then click on the Manage service applications link under the Service Applications section.

3. Locate the User Profile Service Application as shown in Figure 6.7 and click on the link.

4. Click on the Manage User Permissions under the People section of the User Profile Service Application administration page.

5. Enter users or groups in the people picker text box, click the Check Names icon, and then click Add.

6. Select the Create personal site, Use personal features, and Manage permissions check boxes.

7. Click Save.

Note

All authenticated users are automatically given permissions. Use these steps to modify the permissions accordingly. ■

Managing My Sites

It is a good idea to have My Sites inherit a common look that differentiates them from other sites in your organization, while still being consistent with the overall appearance and layout of your portal site. The out-of-the-box templates used for My Sites can be customized just like any other SharePoint site or site template. Before modifying these templates, understand and familiarize yourself with the default layout and out-of-the-box functionality and default and available Web Parts for each site. This helps in planning how users make use of My Sites in concert with the tasks and information relevant in your organization.

You can redesign the layout and appearance of the My Site Public Page as a site collection administrator or a user designated as the designer for the site collection hosting your My Sites. The layout and design you choose or create can be different between User Profile Service Applications even though the same user profile properties are displayed. We suggest you consider maintaining a similar or consistent look and feel for ease of use, but you may find that sites for different purposes necessitate some variation in content and appearance. The default My Site Public Page layout includes:

- The Quick Launch left navigation displays links to shared lists such as Shared Pictures and Shared Documents as well as My Site subsites such as workspaces. These links enable people visiting your public profile to navigate to shared content quickly.

- The "As seen by" drop-down list that is shown to you only when you are viewing your own profile page. This feature allows you to switch between the various views so you can see how your public profile appears to you or other groups of users when they access your profile. The drop-down list is a good way to verify that selected policies are configured and working properly.

- Useful Web Parts populating each of the Web Part zones including Contact Information, Organization Hierarchy, Colleagues, Membership, Links, and Documents.

To ease navigation between these areas, you can use the links on the My Site top link bar to switch between the personal site, the public profile, and newsfeed.

By default, the My Sites host location is created on the server running the User Profile Service Application. Public profiles are created and stored on the Web application that runs the User Profile Service Application, and personal sites are stored on the default Web application for the server. However, you can change the Web application so that My Sites can be stored on the default Web application, the Web application for the User Profile Service Application, or any other Web application. Personalization sites are created on individual site collections that can be on any farm using the same User Profile Service Application. The settings for those sites are controlled by the administrators of those respective sites, by using the same Site Settings pages that are available for any site.

The User Profile Service Application administrator manages the unique settings for personal sites. Personal sites settings appear on the Manage Personal Sites page, which is available from the My Site settings link on the Shared Services Administration page. Manageable settings include the following:

- Personal site services that by default are stored on the (same as My Site host) Web application for the server running the shared service applications, typically using port 80. The public profiles are also stored on the Web application for the User Profile Service Application, using a different port. You can decide to set a different provider for personal site services so that personal sites are stored on a different Web application. This can be a different application on the same server or another server. The Web application must already exist. Existing sites are not migrated and must be moved manually. For large organizations with a large number of people, it may make sense to store personal sites on a separate server. When planning personal sites, User Profile Service Application administrators should talk to IT administrators about the number of users and expected use of personal sites so that the appropriate choice can be implemented during initial deployment.

  If your deployment process involves using a test server before rolling out to a production server, realize that restoring a backup image of the first server to the second server will not update the location of personal site services. You will have to update this property in order to use the personal site services on the second server.

- Personal site location is the Web directory where personal sites are stored and accessed. It's a good idea for this to be memorable, and it shouldn't duplicate directories already used for other purposes. Otherwise, you don't have to plan for this setting.

- Site naming format provides three options to resolve possible conflicts between usernames in multiple domains. If your users are in a single domain, you can format with a simple username. If your users are from multiple domains, it makes sense to use both domain and username in the format. The option to resolve conflicts by formatting the second instance of the same username by including the different domain name should be reserved for after initial deployment, such as when you're adding users from additional domains to a deployment that previously used accounts from a single domain.

- In a multilingual deployment, you can allow users to choose the language of their personal site.

- You can select which users are members of the SharePoint Reader group for personal sites. By default, this Reader group is the same as the site collection containing personal sites, but you can limit access based on specific policies of your organization.

Searching for People

As mentioned earlier in this chapter, SharePoint 2010 enables people to find other people based on their expertise and role in the organization. With careful planning, your deployment will allow easy discovery of other people within teams and around your organization. In addition to creating these relationships through common properties, you can utilize SharePoint Search to find the people you are looking for. By default, the following methods of finding people are enabled:

- **The People search scope:** This is a search scope that limits search results to the public profiles in the user profile store of the User Profile Service Application. Regardless of the search terms used, only people who match those terms appear in search results.

- **The People tab:** In the Search Center the People tab provides options for finding people. You can find people by name or related subject, or by people-related properties such as Title and Department.

- **Advanced search:** Allows you to find people by searching specific user profile property values. Every user profile that matches the value of the selected profile will appear in search results.

- **From values for user profile properties:** You can find people without explicitly searching by clicking values for users to find other users with the same value for the property. These properties can appear in user profiles, user information lists, SharePoint lists, or in general search results.

- **Refined searches:** You can refine search results for a people search to include only results for people with a specific value in their user profiles.

- **People group by social distance:** By default, all searches for people are grouped by social distance. People who work most closely with the person viewing search results are grouped first, followed by people more distant.

Regardless of the search method used, the people search results contain links to the public profiles of each user, including links to contact them by e-mail or other messaging programs like Office Communicator.

You may want to consider supplementing the default people search scope and Search Center tab with customized search scopes and tabs for more specific groups of people. You or the User Profile Service Application administrator should consult the information architecture and site hierarchy to identify key business concepts that might relate to specific groups of people that may be sought out by users across sites. Then you can develop search scopes and people search tabs for those specific groups. You may also use your knowledge of the user profiles you manage to identify other useful groups of people and create additional specific search scopes and search tabs for those groups.

Site collection administrators can get as granular with search as creating site-level search scopes for people who are members of the site collection.

People search planning and configuration also feeds back into user profile planning and management. Planning may reveal individuals or groups of people that you'd like to make easier to find, but properties may not exist that allow these people to be found easily. You can then identify new properties to create and add them to the list of existing and planned properties.

Summary

It's good practice to sketch out a plan for deploying functionality before actually beginning any deployment or configuration changes. It's up to you and your planning team to determine what documents and data come out of your planning phase, but having some kind of worksheet for planning personalization features is a good idea. Your Audiences, User Profiles, and Policies worksheet should contain some if not all of the following information:

- A list of connection sources for user profiles, such as Active Directory, LDAP, and business applications like SAP or Siebel that track people in your organization. Include the location, authentication type, accounts, and any other information needed to connect each source.

- A list of the people features that are available from within user profiles, along with the policy setting, default access policy, and override and replication policies for each feature.

- A list of user profile properties managed by the User Profile Service Application administrator, along with the same policy information used for features. Add columns for each connection source to record the property mappings you want to use.

- A list of portal sites and site collections and a note recording who is planning the user information list properties for each site collection.

- If the User Profile Service Application administrator is planning user properties at the site collection level, record a list of properties and decide if they are best stored in the user profile so that they are available for site collections across the User Profile Service

Application or added later to the user information list for a site collection. The properties in user information lists in a site collection are based on replicated properties of user profiles but are not connected to user profiles. Properties added to the information list are not stored in the user profile. These properties are not imported, so you don't have to worry about planning property mappings.

Careful planning ensures your success in deploying and managing the personalization features in SharePoint 2010. With the combination of user profiles, their policies, audiences, My Sites, and personalization links, you can be sure information workers in your organization have the latest relevant information available.

Searching and Retrieving Content

Search is a key component of easily finding content in a portal or site of any considerable size. When navigation, bookmarks, and guessing let users down, search is the right tool to find what they need. This chapter discusses how to use the search features of SharePoint to find content and to proactively notify users of new content; in addition, it covers the steps necessary to plan, configure, and maintain the search components of SharePoint.

The underlying technology used for SPS 2010 and SFS 2010 search is the same but the functionality provided is very different. SPS 2010 provides enterprise search capabilities, including the ability to index content sources located throughout the organization such as e-mail servers, file shares, and business data, and ability to customize search scopes to provide users the ability to scope their searches appropriately. SFS 2010 provides site collection level search. Because it is not possible to customize content sources, scopes, search schedules, or indexed properties with SFS 2010, this chapter is focused on the SPS 2010 feature set.

Configuring and Maintaining the Search and Indexing Components

Configuring search and indexing correctly is important so that users receive accurate, relevant, and expected results. Configuring search for your organization involves three primary steps:

- **Indexing content:** All the content that you want to make available to users must be defined as content sources and indexed on a regular basis so that the results are available to be returned in searches. Content sources are defined and indexing is scheduled and completed by the Search Service Application (SSA).

- **Configuring the search service:** The Search Service Application requires configuration to determine how content is crawled.

- **Define scopes:** Search scopes allow users to target the slice of content they want to search. If configured appropriately, users should be able to pick a scope for their search that returns a reasonable number of relevant results.

Indexing content

Choosing what content to index and configuring your indexing settings is the primary task for indexing content. SPS can index content from several types of content sources, including these sources for which SharePoint has provided out-of-the-box support:

- **File share content:** SharePoint can index content that is placed on file shares.

- **Exchange server content:** Exchange public folders content is a good potential source for indexing corporate knowledge.

- **Lotus Notes servers:** If your organization uses Lotus Notes, SharePoint can index the Lotus Notes databases. You will need to run the Lotus Notes Index Setup Wizard to configure the Lotus Notes protocol handler before configuring a Lotus Notes content source.

- **SharePoint sites:** SPS searches all the local SharePoint content and can be configured to index content that is not a consumer of the local SSA for cross-organizational content.

- **Business data:** SPS can also index data that has been defined in the Business Connectivity Service.

Cross-Reference
For more information on the Business Connectivity Service, see Chapter 18. ■

- **Web sites:** SPS can index Web site content for cross-platform or cross-product integration.

Planning content sources

Selecting your content sources from the myriad of available corporate repositories of data is an important step in the indexing configuration process. Indexing content can be a resource-intensive task, both for the indexing server and for the server that is responding to the crawler requests for the content.

The SSA is automatically configured with a content scope that searches all the local SharePoint sites, which is defined as all the site collections that are using the SSA. You can choose to index SharePoint content that is external to the SSA, but this will most likely result in content being indexed more than once: first by the local SSA and one or more times by external SSAs that have defined it as a content source. The exception to this would be in the SharePoint sites that you are indexing as part of an SFS farm.

For each set of content that is a potential source for your SSA users, you need to decide what the source is and how often you will do full and incremental updates to the index.

Warning

Keep in mind that for external content, or content that you do not control, requesting too much content or content too often may overload the external source, and that administrator can block you from crawling in the future. ■

For each content source that you identify, determine the following content source options:

- **How deep would you like to crawl?** For SharePoint sites, you can determine whether you want to search for everything under the start address or just the SharePoint site of the start address. For Web content, you need to decide if you will stay on just the first page of the site or the entire server. You can also set custom hop settings for the indexing to follow to limit the number of server hops and depth of the pages. Setting the server hop limit to 2 or more can be overwhelming to your indexing resources because indexing will not only index your starting address, but also any server that is linked from the starting address content (one server hop) and any other servers mentioned in the first server hop (second server hop).

- **What is the crawl schedule?** The crawl schedule can be determined by understanding how often the target content changes and how long it takes to index the content source. Try to plan full crawls for times when the content source has low resource usage and schedule them less frequently if the content does not change frequently. Schedule incremental crawls to update the content between full crawls.

- **Does this content source need to be accessed by an account other than the default content access account?** The default content access account credentials will be presented to gain read access to content sources unless specified by a crawl rule for a specific site. Managing several content access accounts can be a time-consuming procedure, especially if the accounts require password changes on a regular basis. We recommend only defining unique content access accounts if necessary because the default content access account cannot be used.

Implementing content sources

To implement the content sources that you have identified, follow these steps for each content source:

1. Navigate to the administration page for your Search Service Application and select Search settings from the Search section.
2. Select Content sources.
3. Click New Content Source in the top navigation bar.
4. Enter a name for your content source in the Name field, as shown in Figure 7.1.
5. Select the type of content to be crawled.

FIGURE 7.1

Add a new content source

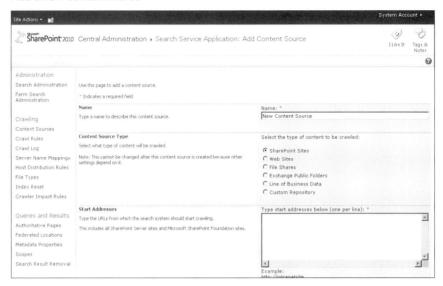

If your content source is a SharePoint server, enter the address of the top-level SharePoint site in the start address box. If you want to include more than one top-level site in your content source, you can add additional start addresses on separate lines. Select whether you want the crawl to crawl everything under the hostname or just the SharePoint site in the Crawl Settings section.

If your content is a Web Site, enter the address of the site in the start address box. If you want to include more than one site in your content source, you can add additional start addresses on separate lines. Select whether you want the crawl to crawl the server, only the first page, or a custom depth of your start addresses in the Crawl Settings section. The custom crawling behavior allows you to set the page depth and server hops. Page depth is how many levels down from the first page the crawler will follow. The number of server hops defines how many servers the crawler is allowed to follow.

If your content is a file share, enter the address of the site in the start address box. If you want to include more than one file share in your content source, you can add additional start addresses on separate lines. Select whether you want to crawl only the start address folder or the folder and its subfolders in the Crawl Settings section.

If your content is an Exchange public folder, enter the address of the site in the start address box. If you want to include more than one public folder in your content source, you can add additional start addresses on separate lines. Select whether you want to crawl only the start address folder or the folder and its subfolders in the Crawl Settings section.

If your content is business data, select which BCS application you would like to crawl or select whether you want to crawl the entire BCS in the Applications section.

6. **Set the schedule for the full crawl and incremental crawls in the Crawl Schedules section.** Any schedules that you have previously configured will be available in the drop-down, or you can select the Create Schedule link to define a new schedule.

7. **Select whether the crawl should immediately start a full crawl of the content source in the Start Full Crawl section.**

8. **Click OK.**

Implementing SSA settings for all sources

There are several SSA search and indexing settings that apply to all content sources, including the default content access account, crawl rules, and file-type inclusions.

The default content access account provides the credentials that are used to gain read access to the content sources for indexing content. You should choose a default content access account that has broad read access to your content sources to simplify the content access account administration process.

Crawl rules are used to limit the content crawls as appropriate to either increase the relevancy of results or to limit resource impact on the sources. You can create crawl rules to include or exclude from a URL or set of URLs. You can also create crawl rules to set broad rules of how the crawler handles whether to just crawl links identified at the source, whether the crawler should crawl URLs with complex characters, and whether SharePoint sites should be crawled as HTTP. Crawl rules also allow you to specify authentication for a particular path to be different from the default crawling account.

File-type inclusions let the crawler know what file extensions to crawl or not crawl. You can add file types to the file-type list that is populated initially with the commonly used file types. If you add a file type, you must have an iFilter that SPS can use to understand and crawl that content type.

To create crawl rules, follow these steps:

1. **Navigate to the administration page for your Search Service Application.**

2. **Select Crawl rules.**

3. **Click New Crawl Rule link on the page under the test area.**

4. **Enter a path in the Path field.** You can use wildcards in the path to designate that the rule should apply to anything that matches, so `http://*.*` would match any hostname.

5. **Select whether you want to include or exclude content with this rule in the Crawl Configuration section.**

6. **Specify whether you want to use a different crawling account from the default crawling account or client certification in the Specify Authentication section, as shown in Figure 7.2.**

7. **Click OK.**

FIGURE 7.2

Specifying a different crawling account using a crawl rule

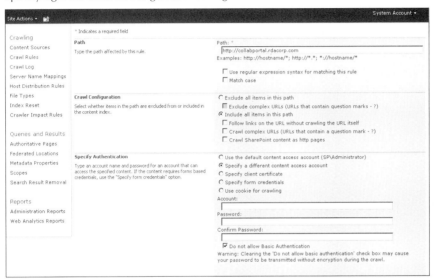

Implementing server name mappings

SharePoint provides the capability to change the display location URL for search item results by using server name mappings. Server name mappings are configured at the SSA level and are applied when search queries are performed.

Server name mappings are useful when you want to replace local addresses for content with addresses on the server or if you want to hide the source of the content. However, you should not use them unless you have access or display problems. To implement server name mappings, follow these steps:

1. Navigate to the administration page for your Search Service Application.

2. Select Server name mappings.

3. Click New Mapping link on the page.

4. **Type an address in the Address in index field.** This is the name that you want the SSA to find and replace.

5. **Type an address in the Address in search results field.** This is the name that you want the SSA to insert in the search results.

6. Click OK.

Configuring Search for your server farm

In addition to configuring your content sources, you need to configure the settings that the crawler uses to reach the content sources. These settings are configured at the farm level. To configure your farm search settings, follow these steps:

1. Navigate to the administration page for your Search Service Application.

2. The System Status section of the administration page contains the farm search settings. Clicking the value of each configurable property allows you to make modifications as follows:

   - **Default content access account:** This account is used to crawl content. This account should not be an administrator such that unwanted content does not appear in search results. Clicking the current account entry allows you to modify the account settings, as shown in Figure 7.3.

   - **Contact Email Address:** This is the e-mail address that the gatherer will use to let other administrators know who to contact in the case of a problem. Clicking on the current e-mail setting entry allows you to modify the e-mail settings, as shown in Figure 7.4.

FIGURE 7.3

Configuring the default content account in server farm settings for search

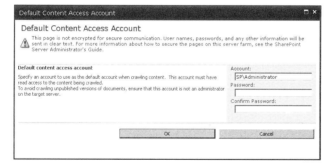

FIGURE 7.4

Configuring the e-mail account in server farm settings for search

- **Proxy Settings:** The proxy settings need to be configured so that the crawler can reach sites that are on the other side of the proxy, if appropriate for your organization. Clicking on the current setting displays a dialog to make the proper proxy modifications, as shown in Figure 7.5.

FIGURE 7.5

Configuring the proxy server in server farm settings for search

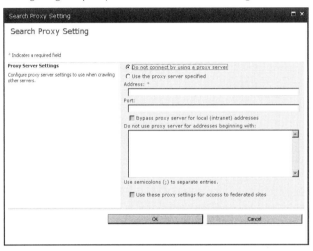

The farm-level search settings also include the settings for the crawler impact rules. These rules determine how many documents that the crawler requests at a time and how frequently the crawler requests documents from a particular site. To configure crawl rules, follow these steps:

1. **Navigate to the administration page for your Search Service Application.**

2. **Select Crawler impact rules from the left-hand Quick Launch bar.**

3. **Click Add Rule in the page.**

4. **Enter the site for which you want this rule to apply.**

5. **Select how many documents you want the crawler to request at a time.** You can configure the crawler to make simultaneous requests of up to 64 documents without waiting between requests, or you can configure the crawler to request one document at a time with a specific waiting time between requests.

6. **Click OK.**

Configuring search scopes

Search scopes can be configured at both the SSA level and the site collection level. SSA search scopes should be broad scopes that are relevant to all users regardless of the site collection. In the out-of-the-box installation, SharePoint creates two SSA-level search scopes: All Sites and People. Additional SSA search scopes could be configured for organizational information that is pertinent to everyone such as a corporate event portal. Site collection search scopes should be specific to the information on that site collection.

Note
SPS provides the ability to create an RSS subscription to search results. However, this subscription will work only for search scopes created at the SSA level. ■

Search scopes are defined by one or more rules. The rules can be based on managed properties and location or content sources and can include rules that exclude content. Your goal in creating search scopes is to create logical divisions of the content so that users understand which scope to pick and get a reasonable number of results returned when they execute their search.

Search scopes are organized in display groups. Search Web Parts use these groups to identify which scopes to show in the search drop-down menu.

Defining search scopes at the SSA

In addition to defining the SSA scopes, the SSA administrator can also create scope rules. To define a scope at the SSA level, follow these steps:

1. Navigate to the administration page for your Search Service Application.

2. Select Scopes from the Queries and Results Quick Launch section.

3. Select New Scope from the page's top navigation bar.

4. Provide a name for your search scope in the Title boxes shown in Figure 7.6.

5. Select whether you want to use the default Search results page or enter a different search results page that you would like to use and click OK.

6. From the View Scopes page, select Edit Properties and Rules from the drop-down menu on the scope title that you just added.

7. Select New Rule.

8. If you want to create a rule based on the Web address properties of the indexed items, select Web Address in the Scope Rule Type and select whether the Web address will be limited by folder, hostname, or domain/subdomain.

   If you select folder, enter the URL of the folder that you want the rule to be based on in the Folder box, as shown in Figure 7.7. For example, `http://server/site/folder`.

   If you select hostname, enter the hostname that you want the rule to be based on in the Hostname box. For example, servername.

FIGURE 7.6

Creating a new shared scope

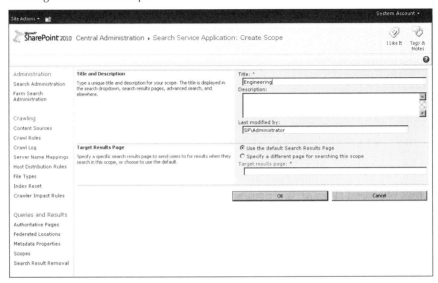

FIGURE 7.7

Creating a scope rule to include content from a Web address

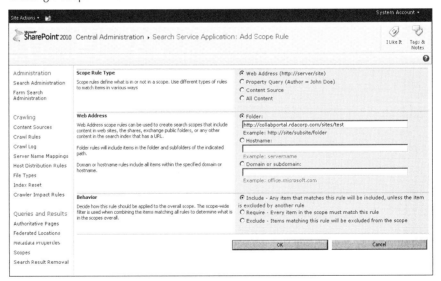

If you select domain or subdomain, enter the domain name that you want the rule to be based on in the Domain or subdomain box. For example, `office.microsoft.com`.

9. **If you want to create a rule based on the properties of the indexed items, select Property Query in the Scope Rule Type section.** Select the property that you want the rule to be based on in the Add property restrictions drop-down menu. Enter the rule value in the = field. For example, Author (is the property) = John Doe (rule value).

10. **If you want to create a rule that is based on a specific content source, select Content Source in the Scope Rule Type section and select the content source from the drop-down menu.**

11. **Select the All Content radio button if you want the scope to return all indexed items.**

12. **Select if you want to include, require, or exclude content based on the rules you enter.** Include rules specify what content will be included unless another rule excludes them. If you choose a required rule, all items returned in the scope must match the rule. Exclude rules specify what content will not be included. This content will not be included even if it matches the other rules.

13. **Click OK.**

14. **Add as many rules as you need to tune your scope to the appropriate content.**

Copying SSA scopes for your site collection

Although it is not possible for a site collection administrator to modify a scope created by the SSA administrator, the site collection administrator can duplicate and subsequently modify a copy of an SSA search scope.

If you want to implement changes to an SSA scope by copying it to your site collection, follow these steps:

1. **Go to the top level site of the site collection for which you want to add the scope and select Site Settings from the Site Actions menu in the top-right corner.**

2. **Select Search Scopes from the Site Collection Administration menu.**

3. **From the pull-down menu on the scope that you want to copy, select Make copy.**

Defining site collection search scopes and scope display groups

SharePoint provides two display groups to organize your site collection search scopes, one for the search drop-down and one for the advanced search page. To create a new display group, follow these steps:

1. Go to the top level site of the site collection for which you want to add the scope and select Site Settings from the Site Actions menu in the top-right corner.

2. Select Search scopes from the Site Collection Administration menu.

3. Select New Display Group from the top navigation bar.

4. Provide a name for your display group in the Title field.

5. If you have already created the scope or scopes that you want to include in this display group, select the scope in the Scopes section, as shown in Figure 7.8.

6. From the View Scopes page, select Edit Properties and Rules from the drop-down menu on the scope title that you just added.

7. Click OK.

FIGURE 7.8

Creating a new display group

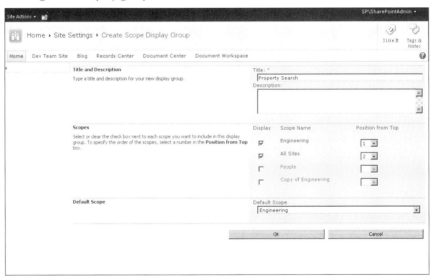

Tip

The scopes text colors give the appearance that they are disabled. You can still click on the check boxes next to them. You may see them jump out of order, depending on the order you click them. This is a result of the defaulting position from top based on your click order. ■

To define a scope for your site collection, follow these steps:

1. Go to the top level site of the site collection for which you want to add the scope and select Site Settings from the Site Actions menu in the top-left corner.

2. Select Search scopes from the Site Collection Administration menu.

3. Select New Scope from the page menu bar.

4. Provide a name for your scope in the Title field.

5. Select whether you want to use the default Search results page or enter a different search results page and click OK.

6. From the View Scopes page, select Edit Properties and Rules from the drop-down menu on the scope title that you just added.

7. Select New rule.

8. If you want to create a rule based on the Web address properties of the indexed items, select Web Address in the Scope Rule Type section and select whether the Web address will be limited by folder, hostname, or domain/subdomain.

   If you select folder, type the URL of the folder that you want the rule to be based on in the Folder box. For example, `http://server/site/folder`.

   If you select hostname, type the hostname that you want the rule to be based on in the Hostname box. For example, servername.

   If you select domain or subdomain, enter the domain name that you want the rule to be based on in the Domain or subdomain box. For example, `office.microsoft.com`.

9. If you want to create a rule based on the managed properties of the indexed items, select Property Query in the Scope Rule Type section. Select the property that you want the rule to be based on in the Add property restrictions drop-down. Enter the rule value in the = field. For example, Author (is the property) = John Doe (rule value). This rule operates by finding exact matches.

10. Select the All Content radio button if you want the scope to return all indexed items.

11. Select if you want to include, require, or exclude content based on the rules you enter.

    Include rules specify what content will be included unless another rule excludes them. If you choose a required rule, all items returned in the scope must match the rule. Exclude rules specify what content will not be included. This content will not be included even if it matches the other rules.

12. Click OK.

13. Add as many rules as you need to tune your scope to the appropriate content.

Tuning Search Results

After you have gathered all the content and made it available to your site collection, you can modify search settings so that it returns the most relevant results for your site users. You do this by configuring relevance settings, defining managed properties to use in search scopes, and configuring keywords. You can use the search usage statistics to view what searches are being executed and then modify all of these settings over time to improve results for your users.

Configuring relevance settings to prioritize content

After you have created search scopes to slice the content sources into manageable pieces for the user, you can further improve the search experience by prioritizing the relevance, and therefore the order in which the content is returned, of results. Relevance settings work in concert with the other factors that determine the results order such as keywords, managed properties, and search engine weighting factors.

You can define sites and pages as either authoritative or nonauthoritative and search will use these definitions to rank the results. SharePoint provides three levels of authoritative pages so that you can rank first, second, and third level authoritative pages or sites as well as define sites that are not authoritative. The resulting ranking options are as follows:

- **Most authoritative:** The highest level of relevance is given automatically to the top level Web applications. You can also choose to highlight key business data and process sites and pages as most authoritative so that they are a priority in search results.

- **Second-level authoritative:** Sites and pages listed as second-level authoritative are returned after most authoritative sites and pages.

- **Third-level authoritative:** You can use the third-level authoritative level to define sites and pages that are relevant but less valuable or reliable than most authoritative or second-level authoritative sites and pages.

- **Nonauthoritative sites:** These sites have the same weighting as third-level authoritative sites but are returned after the authoritative sites. This level can be used for sites that are possible resources but do not offer any guarantees because you do not control the contents.

Manage relevance only for the sites that you (or your users) feel strongly about. This is not a process that needs to be completed for all sites within and external to your organization, because that would be a true administrative feat. Instead, stick to setting and adjusting the relevance for sites based on organization priorities (such as key executive or initiative sites) and user feedback.

To add authoritative sites and pages and nonauthoritative sites, follow these steps:

1. **Navigate to the administration page for your Search Service Application.**

2. **Select Specify authoritative pages under the Queries and Results section of the Quick Launch.**

3. **Enter the URL to your authoritative sites and pages in the most authoritative pages, second-level authoritative pages, or third-level authoritative pages box, one per line.**

4. **Enter any nonauthoritative sites in the Sites to demo box, one per line.** The nonauthoritative sites box will devalue anything starting with the URLs that are listed.

5. **Select whether you want to refresh the ranking now by selecting the Refresh Now box.**

6. **Click OK.**

Using managed properties

Managed properties are gathered during the indexing process and selected by the SSA administrator(s) to be used to customize and hone a search. Managed properties are part of the formula that determines the relevance ranking of search results and can also be used to configure search scopes.

By defining managed properties, you can make sure that the metadata that is important to your organization and content is consistent and used to order search results. The SSA administrator maps managed properties to crawled properties. SPS creates many or most of the useful managed property mappings when it is installed, including:

- Author
- Department
- Division
- Location
- Status
- Title (not job title)

You should add managed properties for key pieces of metadata that the crawler returns and that are important to your organization. Keep in mind that these properties can be used both for search scopes and relevancy ranking. If you want a division-level portal to be able to create search scopes based on the division, you must have division as an SSA managed property. SSA managed properties are not available as search criteria unless specified in their managed property settings.

Note
You can map one or more crawled properties to one managed property to eliminate duplication of properties. For example, you may want to map each appearance of the author in the crawled properties to the author managed properties. ∎

To create a new managed property, follow these steps:

1. Navigate to the administration page for your Search Service Application.

2. Select Metadata Properties under the Queries and Results section of the Quick Launch bar.

3. Select New Managed Property from the page menu bar.

4. Type the name you want to use in the Property name field. This should be a clear and identifiable name such as "author."

5. Select the type of property, for example, text, integer, decimal.

6. Enter the crawled property that you want to match to the managed property. If you want to map multiple crawled properties to the managed property, add the multiple crawl property values and order them in descending order, of which the top value is the most authoritative value, as shown in Figure 7.9. If a document has multiple crawled property values, the managed property returns the crawled property at the top of the list.

7. Select whether you want the managed property to be used in search scopes.

8. Click OK.

FIGURE 7.9

Creating managed properties

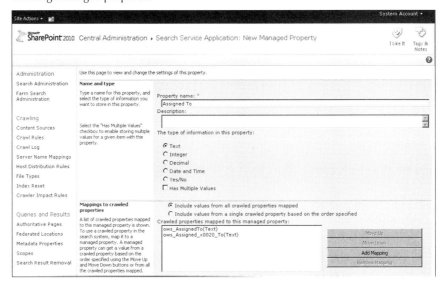

Implementing keywords

Keywords are another tool to ensure that high-priority content is returned for any search executed that includes the keyword or any of its synonyms. Keywords are implemented at the site collection level where the administrator associates the keyword with synonyms, a keyword definition, and best bet URLs. Keywords can return any item that is URL-addressable but most often are associated with documents, sites, and people.

Keywords should be chosen to highlight the key items for the site collection. For example, if you have a site collection for your human resources department, you should provide keywords for the most requested documents and sites. Table 7.1 shows some keyword examples for human resource content.

TABLE 7.1

Sample Keywords for a Human Resources Site Collection

Keyword Phrase	Synonyms	Definition	Best Bet
Expense Reports	Expense policy Submitting expenses Reimbursable expenses Expenses	Form to fill out to submit company reimbursable expenses	Link to expense form Link to document explaining company policy
401K	Retirement account Employee benefits 401K Enrollment IRA Tax-deferred savings	Program for individual retirement savings accounts	Link to enrollment form Link to business data showing year-to-date savings Link to 401K FAQ site Link to 401K provider site Link to employee benefits site Link to employee in charge of 401K program
Vacation Request	Time off Vacation form Vacation calendar	Form for submitting vacation request	Link to vacation request form

Keywords should point to best bets that are fairly static so that they return accurate and available results. For each keyword, identify the contact and start, review, and expiration dates to ensure that the appropriate person is maintaining the keyword. These keyword attributes are configured when you create keywords, as detailed in the following steps:

1. Go to the top level site of the site collection for which you want to add the scope and select Site Settings from the Site Actions menu in the top-left corner.

2. Select Search keywords from the Site Collection Administration menu.

3. Select Add Keyword from the top navigation bar.

4. Type the keyword phrase (one or more words) and synonyms in the Keyword Information section.

5. **Click Add Best Bet to create links to the best bet content.** You will be prompted to enter the URL, Title, and Description for the best bet.

6. Type the definition for the keyword in the Keyword Definition section.

7. Type the contact for the keyword.

8. Type the start date, end date, and review date in the Publishing section, as shown in Figure 7.10

9. Click OK.

FIGURE 7.10

Setting the review date for a keyword

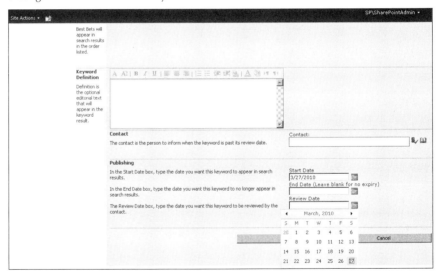

Customizing the Enterprise Search Center

SPS 2010 provides the search components as Web Parts so that you can customize how and where search results are returned. This flexibility allows you to customize the Enterprise Search Center so that results are returned in the most usable format for your organization and users.

The available search Web Parts are

- **Advanced Search Box:** This Web Part enables users to find documents using various search criteria including words, phrases, scope, language, and document type.

- **Federated Results:** This Web Part displays results from a configured location.

- **People Refinement Panel:** This Web Part provides filtering of people search results. Depending on the actual results, refinement is performed by various profile items including Department, Title, and Responsibilities.

- **People Search Box:** This Web Part enables users to search for a person by name, department, title, responsibilities, skills, and memberships.

- **People Search Core Results:** This Web Part displays the people search results and should typically be on the same page as the People Search Box Web Part.

- **Related Queries:** This Web Part displays similar queries that other users have used to perform the current query.

- **Search Box:** This Web Part contains the simple search box found on all portal pages by default.

- **Search Core Results:** This Web Part displays the search results generated from the search box search.

- **Search High Confidence Results:** This Web Part displays the special term and high confidence result sets.

- **Search Paging:** This Web Part displays the search paging capability, so a user can scroll through multiple pages of search results.

- **Search Statistics:** Displays search statistics, including number of results and duration of search time.

- **Search Summary:** Displays search summary.

- **Search Visual Best Bets:** Displays best bets for the current search results based on the search query.

- **Top Federated Results:** Displays the top results from a configured location.

There are many ways that you can customize the Enterprise Search Center to suit your organization. Some of the common Enterprise Search Center customizations are

- Creating a new search tab to search and display results for a unique display group

- Modifying the number of search results displayed on each result page

- Changing the layout of where best bets are returned

As a sample of customizing the Enterprise Search Center, you'll create a new tab to display search results for a display group. To do this, follow these steps:

1. From the Site Actions menu on any page in your Enterprise Search Center site, select Create Page and type a Title for your new page.

2. Click Create.

3. SharePoint creates the page as a Search Results page, as shown in Figure 7.11.

4. Select Add New Tab in the top section of your new page.

5. Type a tab name in the Tab Name field, your page address in the Page field, and Tooltip (optional), as shown in Figure 7.12.

Tip

Unlike MOSS 2007, SharePoint 2010 uses dashes ("-") to compensate for spaces in the page name. In this example the Custom Search page is saved as custom-search.aspx. ■

6. Click OK.

7. Select Edit Web Part from the edit menu on the Search Box Web Part.

8. Expand the Miscellaneous section of the Web Part.

9. Type your page name in the Target search results page URL field, as shown in Figure 7.13.

FIGURE 7.11

New Enterprise Search Center Search Results page

FIGURE 7.12

Creating a new Enterprise Search Center tab

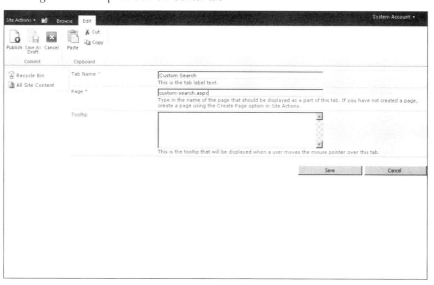

FIGURE 7.13

Modifying the target search results page

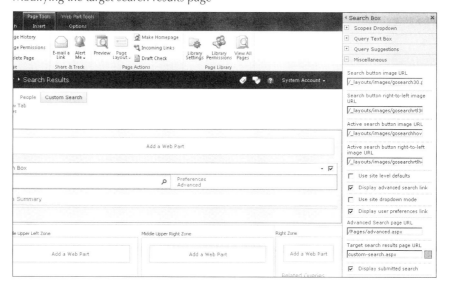

10. Type the name of your display group in the Scope Display Group field, as shown in Figure 7.14.

11. Click OK to close the Search Box Web Part.

12. If you would like to return more than ten results per page, select Edit Web Part from the edit menu on the Search Core Results Web Part.

13. Expand the Results Display/Views section.

14. Type the number of results that you want returned in the Results Per Page field, as shown in Figure 7.15.

15. Click OK to close the Search Core Results Web Part.

Tip

If you want to use a specific scope but do not want to show the scope drop-down in the search box Web Part, you can configure the Web Part to not show the scope drop-down and enter the scope in the additional query terms field in the query text box section of the Web Part. The display group term should be entered as scope: "scope name" where scope name is the name of your scope in the additional query terms field. ■

FIGURE 7.14

Modifying the scope display group in the Search Box Web Part

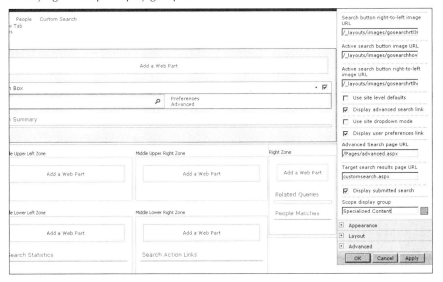

234

FIGURE 7.15

Modifying the number of results returned in the Search Core Results Web Part

Finding Content with Alerts

When users subscribe to alerts anywhere on the portal, the search service processes those alerts. This interdependence means that if search is not working, alerts also are not working; and in addition, the search server performance can be impacted if your portal has a lot of alert subscriptions.

There is a unique additional scenario where search and alerts are combined. Users can subscribe to search-based alerts so that they receive notifications when the results of their search query have changed. This ability can be enabled or disabled at the SSA. Search-based alerts increase the load on the search server that processes the search query each time it processes the search-based alert. If you want to enable or disable this feature, follow these steps:

1. **Navigate to the administration page for your Search Service Application and select Search Administration from the Administration Quick Launch bar.**

2. **Locate the Search Alerts status on the page.**

3. **Click Enable if you want to activate the feature.** If the feature is already activated, it displays this status next to the Enable/Disable link.

4. **Click Disable if you want to deactivate the feature.** If the feature is already deactivated, it displays this status next to the Enable/Disable link.

If you want to review and manage what alerts are active on your sites, follow these steps:

1. Choose Site Settings from the Site Actions menu on the site in which you want to review alerts.

2. Select User alerts from the Site Administration menu.

3. Select a user from the Display alerts for drop-down menu and click Update.

4. If appropriate, select the alerts that you want to delete and click Delete Selected Alerts.

Summary

Search is a key component in a portal deployment. Users search to find content quickly and effectively without using the navigation. In this chapter, we configured the SPS indexing and search services so that it gathered the appropriate content and returned the most relevant results to users. In addition, we reviewed how the Enterprise Search Center can be customized to be usable for your organization.

Alerts and search are closely related because not only does search manage the processing of alert subscription, but also users can subscribe to search results. This chapter reviewed the impact of having these two services tied together.

Workflow and Process Improvement

W orkflow technologies facilitate human processes by attaching business logic to items and documents, while providing context and tracking progress. With the proliferation of digital information and the speed with which that information is propagated, having a way to track and manage the creation, approval, and publishing of information to the right place and at the right time is much easier with workflow technologies. Approvals can continue unimpeded even when the designated approver is out of the office by automatically routing the work item to a supervisor. If a response isn't received within documented guidelines, reminders can automatically be sent out. Workflow technology has the ability to increase customer satisfaction by helping to keep responses within Service Level Agreements (SLAs) and provide an audited method of maintaining compliance.

The SharePoint technologies make it easy to build workflows out of the box with templates that provide support for a broad range of routing and tracking scenarios without IT involvement.

SPS and SF also empower organizations to build a broad range of sophisticated workflow-based solutions that utilize the functionality of the Windows Workflow Foundation (WF) platform. The platform facilitates the integration of workflow into both the SharePoint and Office applications, and when combined with Visual Studio, developers can create an amazing variety of high-value workflow applications.

This chapter discusses the Microsoft Office workflow environment, tools, and platform and how it all comes together in SharePoint. This technology is very cool indeed!

IN THIS CHAPTER

The Microsoft Office workflow environment

Creating basic workflows

Using Office SharePoint Designer

Creating advanced workflow solutions with Visual Studio and InfoPath

The Microsoft Office Workflow Environment

The SharePoint development team chose to focus their workflow development efforts around what SharePoint technologies does best, which is share and collaborate on documents. Therefore, you will notice that most of the document-centric workflow templates take documents through their typical lifecycle. There is also a heavy focus on human workflow items, which are task-driven processes as opposed to just programmatic automation. The other types of workflows can be addressed using WF and Visual Studio, of course, but you can see the document-centric/human-workflow focus throughout the workflow UI in the browser and SharePoint Designer tool.

Windows Workflow Foundation and Windows SharePoint Services are the fundamental technologies that make up the Microsoft Office Workflow Environment. We move up the complexity continuum starting with browser-based workflow creation to more sophisticated options in the Office SharePoint Designer tool, and finally to full programmatic flexibility with the tools available in Visual Studio.

Windows Workflow Foundation

The Windows Workflow Foundation (or WF) is a common workflow technology for Microsoft products, ISVs, and customer solutions. It is a framework to build on; it is not a server or an application per se. Instead, it should be thought of as a foundation for developers to create workflow applications. The key features include:

- A unified model for human and system workflow

- An extensible activity framework

- The ability for workflows to run in any application or server

- A visual designer for graphical and code-based authoring

Workflows are built from activities and they execute using the runtime engine. The runtime services will persist a workflow's state and monitor its execution. These workflows can run in any application or server including desktop applications as well as on a portal server farm. With regard to the runtime services, they can be replaced depending on the type of application.

The WF functionality is included in WinFX and is used in all of the Microsoft Office 2007 workflows.

WF components

Workflow foundation components include the visual design capability in Visual Studio as well as the various components that are included in the .NET 3.5 framework used by developers to create workflow solutions. These components are explained in this section.

- **Visual Designer:** Graphical and code-based development environment that is available in Visual Studio.

- **Base Activity Library:** Out-of-the-box activities and base for custom activities.

- **Sequence:** Activities are executed one at a time in the order specified.

- **If/Else:** Activities are executed in two or more possible paths depending on the condition met.

- **While:** Activities are executed repeatedly as long as the condition is true.

- **Code:** A defined block of code is executed.

- **Listen:** Waits for a set of events, then executes one or more activities when the event fires.

- **InvokeWebService:** Calls a Web Service.

- **Policy:** Defines and executes business rules using a supplied Windows Workflow Foundation rules engine.

  - **Runtime Engine:** Workflow execution and state management.

  - **Runtime Services:** Hosting flexibility and communication.

- **Workflow Runtime:** The runtime is a lightweight and extensible engine for executing activities. It is hosted within any .NET process and allows developers to add workflow to Windows Forms applications, ASP.NET Web sites, or Windows Services.

Windows SharePoint Services

Windows Workflow Foundation and Windows SharePoint Services are standard parts of Windows. The core services utilized for workflow processing in WSS are the Source List, Task List, History List, Reporting and Administration, Workflow, and Web Services. Workflows can be initiated by any of the Office authoring applications, from the Browser UI, Outlook, Access, or programmatically.

WSS acts as a host for the WF runtime engine. The functionality of the runtime engine and the hosting capability provided by WSS are exposed via the WSS object model.

Workflow templates

Workflow templates are installed on the server and contain code that defines a workflow. Templates are associated with any WSS list. Workflows that run on a specific item in SharePoint are called *instances,* and several instances of a workflow template are able to run at the same time on different items.

Association

Workflow templates are made available via *association*. A template is associated when the template has been made available to a document library, content type, or list. You associate a basic workflow with a template in the "Creating Basic Workflows" section. To do this, you can:

- Create a unique name for the workflow

- Select a task list for use with the workflow

- Select a history list

- Configure start options

The association is created outside of the actual workflow. The association information is stored by WSS in an internal workflow association table, and the data is used to set the parameters when the instance is started.

Creating Basic Workflows

Basic workflows can be created directly from an authoring application or a browser. One template is available out of the box in SFS and more are available in SPS. More sophisticated workflows can easily be designed using Office SharePoint Designer without writing code. This section discusses the creation of the most basic workflows as well as how the power user can take advantage of Office SharePoint Designer.

Out-of-the-box workflows in common with SFS

The only workflow template available from the browser out of the box in SFS is the Three-State Workflow. This workflow can be used to manage business processes that require organizations to track items that may have three states (and only three states) such as Active, Resolved, and Closed. Other custom templates can be added and associated with document libraries, lists, and content types.

Workflows that are available on a list or site are called *templates*. Workflows that are running on a SharePoint item are called *workflow instances*. It is possible to have several instances of the same workflow template running against a singe list, each on a separate SharePoint item. It is also possible to have more than one workflow running against a particular SharePoint item at a time.

Configuring Three-State Workflow on an Issue Tracking list

Configuration of the Three-State workflow begins at a basic SharePoint Foundation Services Team Site and a list or library.

1. **From your WSS site home page, click More Options from the Site Actions menu.**

2. **Under Tracking click the Issue Tracking link.** Although you can configure an Issue Tracking workflow on another type of list, this list maps nicely to the features available in the workflow template.

3. **Enter a name for your tracking list as shown in Figure 8.1.** Click on More Options. Enter a description for the list. Selecting Yes for displaying on the Quick Launch bar makes the list show up in your left-hand navigation under Lists, and you have the option of sending e-mail when ownership of an item is assigned or when a change occurs to the item. This feature can be configured later, and users can configure alerts on the list, too.

4. **From your main Issue Tracking list view, click the List tab on the Ribbon, as shown in Figure 8.2, and then click Workflow Settings.**

FIGURE 8.1

Issue Tracking list

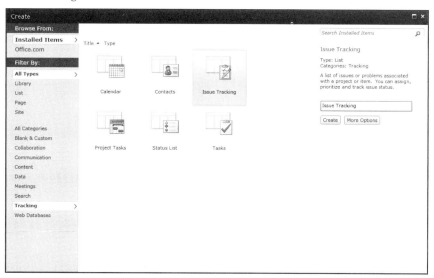

FIGURE 8.2

Workflow Settings on List Tools tab of Ribbon

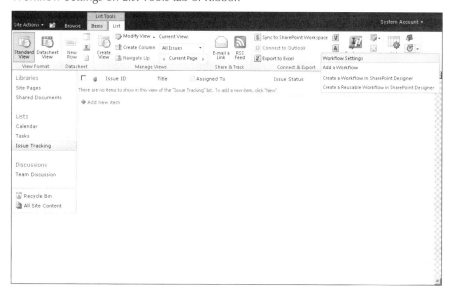

5. **The Workflow settings appear.** Your screen should look similar to Figure 8.3.

6. **Select Issues for the type of item the workflow is configured to run. Click on Add Workflow.** The Three-State workflow is the only workflow available for SFS installations while an SPS installation will contain others. The Add a Workflow page is shown in Figure 8.4.

7. **Give your workflow a unique name.**

8. **Select the Task List you want to use to monitor the workflow tasks.** You can use an existing list or have SharePoint create a new one for this workflow. Do the same for the History List.

9. **Under Start Options you can choose to allow the workflow to be started manually, when a new item is created, or when an item is changed.** The manual start is selected by default and places the option to start the workflow on the drop-down menu for list items.

   The Three-State Workflow can only start when items are created and not when they are changed. Therefore, that option is disabled.

10. **Click Next to continue configuring the workflow options.**

Workflow Settings page

FIGURE 8.4

Add a Workflow page

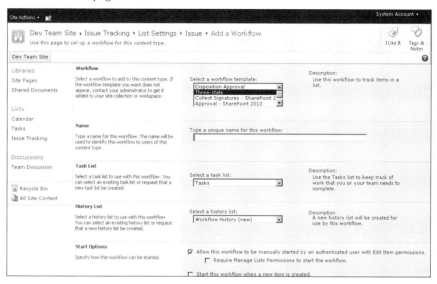

Customize the Three-State workflow — settings and options

To customize workflow settings and options we configure the field whose state we will set at the outset of the workflow called the Choice field. The options are

- Issue Status
  - Active
  - Resolved
  - Closed
- Priority
  - (1) High
  - (2) Normal
  - (3) Low
- Category
  - (1) Category1
  - (2) Category2
  - (3) Category3

Each of the choices has three states that can be configured. The item updates automatically as it moves through the stages of the workflow. Follow these steps:

1. **Specify what you want to happen when a workflow is initiated.** Depending on your earlier choices, you will have a new task created in an existing task list or a new list that was created by the workflow. Under the Task Details section the first option is to configure Task Title with a custom message. This text will be the first part of the subject text of your new task. You can select any field from the Issue Tracking list items as the text to append to your custom message.

2. **The Task Description can be customized in a similar way.** The custom message can be the first part of the description with a field from the Issue Tracking list appended to it, as in the task view in Figure 8.5.

3. **Check the Insert link to List item check box to include a link.**

Note

If your links don't work in the e-mails that are sent from the server, you may need to configure Alternate Access Mappings. See Chapter 2 for detailed information on configuring additional access mappings. ■

4. **For Task Due Date, you can select from one of the following Issue Tracking list fields:**

   - Due Date
   - Modified
   - Created

5. **Select the field that drives who the task will be assigned to.** The most common option would be who was "Assigned To" or a custom assignee, but in some cases you may want to assign the task to whoever modified or created the item, and "Modified by" and "Created by" are available field options.

6. **Configure the E-mail Message Details if you want by selecting the Send e-mail message check box.** The e-mail can be sent to people that are defined as field variables, such as "Assigned To" or to some custom e-mail address. The same is true for the Subject and Body fields as well.

7. **Specify what happens when a workflow changes to its middle state.** Again, this state was defined earlier in the process. If you accepted the default, the middle state would be Resolved and the final state would be Closed. For example, a user enters an issue because SharePoint search is not working on a particular site. Once that issue is entered, an e-mail is sent to a first-level SharePoint technician. If the technician sets the issue to "Resolved" (the middle state), a workflow item can be created for someone in documentation to ensure that the issue is written up as a knowledge base article for future issues of a similar nature.

   Again, the task title, description, due date, whom it is assigned to, and the e-mail message sent out can all be customized using text and fields from the Issue Tracking list item.

FIGURE 8.5

Issue Tracking task list view

SharePoint Server out-of-the-box workflows

The following workflow templates are available directly from the browser interface after install:

- **Approval:** This workflow routes a document or item to a group of people for approval. By default, the Approval workflow is associated with the Document content type, and it is thus automatically available in document libraries. A version of the Approval workflow is also associated by default with Pages libraries in a Publishing site, and it can be used to manage the approval process for the publication of Web pages.

- **Collect Feedback:** This workflow routes a document or item to a group of people for feedback. Reviewers can provide feedback, which is then compiled and sent to the person who initiated the workflow when the workflow has completed. By default, the Collect Feedback workflow is associated with the Document content type and it is thus automatically available to document libraries.

- **Collect Signatures:** This workflow routes a Microsoft Office document to a group of people to collect their digital signatures. This workflow must be started from within the relevant 2010 Office release client program. Participants must also complete their signature tasks by adding their digital signature to the document in the relevant 2010 Office release client program. By default, the Collect Signatures workflow is associated with the Document content type and it is thus automatically available to document libraries. However, the Collect Signatures workflow will appear for a document in the library only if that document contains one or more Microsoft Office Signature Lines.

- **Disposition Approval:** This workflow, which supports records management processes, manages document expiration and retention by allowing participants to decide whether to retain or delete expired documents.

Using Office SharePoint Designer

Although Microsoft Office SharePoint Designer does much more than provide a way to add additional workflow functionality to applications, this section focuses on workflows. The Office SharePoint Designer includes a Workflow View and Workflow Editor, as shown in Figures 8.6 and 8.7, to assist with the creation of workflows. It includes the basic workflow building blocks such as Document workflows, send mail, and update list item, as well as providing an interface to deploy custom developed workflows.

FIGURE 8.6

Workflow view

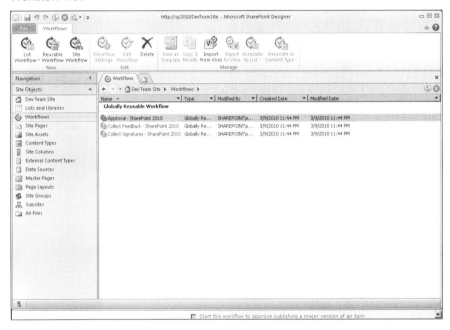

FIGURE 8.7

Workflow Editor

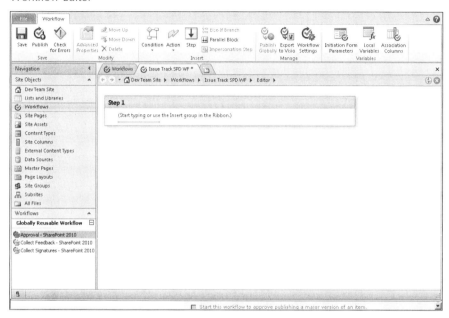

For the nondevelopers, SharePoint Designer provides the tools to create and deploy reasonably sophisticated workflows without writing code. This may become a very heavily used capability in organizations that want to manage human workflow activities.

Workflows developed in SharePoint Designer are authored directly against a specific list or document library in SharePoint. The activities available are predefined and the workflow is not compiled as an assembly. The workflow is stored as source files and then compiled the first time it runs. On each site, the workflows are stored in a separate document library that has a folder for each workflow authored. The folder contains:

- The markup file
- The rules file
- Any ASPX forms

Table 8.1 compares and contrasts the feature sets when developing workflows in SharePoint Designer versus Visual Studio.

TABLE 8.1

Creating and Customizing Workflows:
Visual Studio 2010 versus SharePoint Designer 2010

	Visual Studio 2010	SharePoint Designer 2010
Authoring	Code is authored in the Visual Studio Designer and saved as a template that can be associated with multiple lists, sites, and content types.	Easy-to-use wizard-type of interface for authoring workflows. A workflow can be bound to a specific list or created as a reusable workflow.
Custom activity and condition creation	Yes	No — limited to predefined set of activities and conditions (although custom activities for SharePoint Designer workflows may be created using Visual Studio or downloaded from CodePlex).
Generation of workflow markup file	Yes	Yes
Types	State Machine, Sequential	Sequential
Code-behind	Yes	No
Completed workflow	The workflow markup file and code-behind files are compiled into the workflow assembly and deployed to the server.	The workflow markup, rules, and files are stored uncompiled in a document library on the site and are compiled on demand.
Deployment	The workflow assembly and definition are packaged as a SharePoint Feature and deployed on the site.	Deployment is handed automatically to the appropriate list.
Dynamic data gathering and workflow modification	Workflow applications can use almost any forms technology including InfoPath and ASP.NET forms — it is possible to modify an active/running workflow.	ASP.NET forms are automatically generated and can then be customized — it is not possible to modify an active/running workflow.
Debugging	Yes	No

The basic steps you follow when designing workflows using SharePoint Designer are

- Collect and assemble the actions and conditions that will become the workflow sequence
- Generate any required forms (InfoPath, ASP.Net, or Data Form Web Parts) for the initiation of the workflows
- Customize the forms

As you can see from the Workflow Designer UI, all SharePoint Designer workflows must be attached to a particular list, and it is an event in that list that starts the workflow.

Using the Workflow Editor

To see the options available in the Workflow Editor, follow these steps:

1. **Go to any team site in SharePoint.** From the Site Actions menu select Edit in SharePoint Designer.

   I go through these steps with an example in mind, and you can replace these entries with your own scenario. Assume you have an HR team site and you want to send candidates that apply to developer positions to a development manager for review, and you want to send candidates for a sales position to the sales department manager. I call this new workflow New Candidate.

   For this example, I have already created a document library called New Candidates on my HR site as well as a Candidate Type column that includes Developer and Sales Manager as selection options. If you want to follow this example, create these items prior to beginning this section. You can also just follow along with your own example relevant to your business.

Note

Running SharePoint Designer on a client requires the installation of Windows Workflow Foundation client side code which is included in the .NET Framework. SharePoint Designer checks the client the first time you load it and point to a SharePoint site. It then prompts with a link for the installation of the correct version of the .NET Framework. ∎

2. From the Workflow tab on the Ribbon, click on List Workflow and select New Candidates.

3. **Give your workflow a name.** This name identifies your workflow to the people who use it.

4. **Click OK.** The Workflow Editor opens.

5. **Click on the Workflow Settings tab on the Ribbon.** The Workflow Settings screen appears, as shown in Figure 8.8.

6. **Under Settings on the right-hand side, you see the Task List and History List options.** This is similar to the SharePoint workflow settings that you reviewed in the Three-State workflow configuration. Leave these as the defaults.

7. **Under Start Options I leave the default selected for Allow This Workflow to be Manually Started from an Item.** This allows a workflow to be launched from the document drop-down menu. I select the Automatically start this workflow when a new item is created check box so that new resumes saved always kick off a new review process. I leave Automatically start this workflow whenever an item is changed unchecked because I don't need to start a review for simple edits or metadata changes.

8. **Click Edit Workflow from the left-hand side or from the Ribbon.**

   The Workflow Editor screen allows you to design steps in our workflow. Steps are simply a way to group a set of related conditions and actions. The conditions and actions in the step are evaluated and processed at one time. For this simple example, you have one step to evaluate. Is this a Developer or Sales Manager's resume? If it is a Developer's resume, send to the designated reviewer; likewise if it is a Sales Managers resume, it should be sent to the designated reviewer for those candidates.

FIGURE 8.8

Workflow Settings

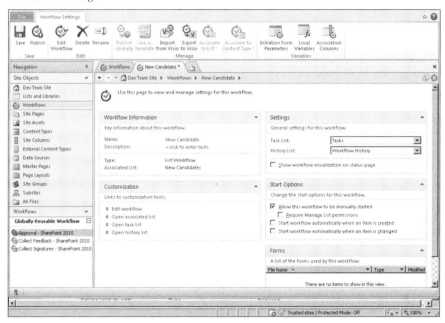

For more complicated multistep workflows, you simply want to create a design that logically follows the actions in the previous step.

9. **Name the step Route Resume because that is the primary function of this single-step workflow.** Click on Step 1 to edit the step name.

10. **Add a condition.** Click the Conditions button on the Ribbon and select If current item field equals value A line is added to the conditions row with underlined values that indicate these can be configured.

11. **Click field and select Candidate Type.** Click value and select Developer.

12. **Click the Actions button from the Ribbon and select Send an Email.**

13. **Click the underlined This Message link to configure the e-mail message.**

14. **Click on the These Users link. Add an e-mail user to the To: field, a subject line for the e-mail, and the body.** Any text that has been captured in a list item field can be added as a variable to the message body by clicking the Add lookup to Body button.

Other Workflow Actions

Add a Comment: Adds a comment to the item.

Add Time to Date: Provides the ability to add a time increment in minutes, hours, days, months, or years and then output that new amount to a variable that could be used in an e-mail, field, and so on.

Assign a Form to a Group: Adding this action provides the ability to assign a custom form to a group of users. Clicking "a custom form" in the action loads the Custom Task Wizard. Values that are submitted using the form are stored in the Tasks list. The workflow remains paused until all of the survey forms are completed. A practical example for this action would be collecting feedback on potential new hires at a company. To complete the task a user would review a resume, click Edit this task, and answer several survey questions about the candidate. The task list could have a custom view that counts the number of Hire and No Hires and displays those totals in a view.

Assign a To-do Item: This action adds a to-do item to the Tasks list for each user that is specified. Until all items are completed, the workflow remains paused.

Extract String Actions: There are several actions to perform string manipulations in order to create dynamic strings. The output is set to a workflow variable.

Check In Item: This action allows any item in a list to be checked in with a custom comment.

Check Out Item: With this action any list item can be checked out based on conditions being satisfied in the workflow. Filling in the field and value tells the code which item to check out.

Collect Data from a User: The action definition launches a Custom Task Wizard to help define the data to be collected from a user and includes custom form fields. Values submitted by the user are stored in the Tasks list and can be referenced later in the workflow. The workflow remains paused until the task is completed.

Copy List Item: Allows the user to specify a list item to copy to another list by defining the list, field, and value in the source.

Create List Item: Creates a new list item by defining which list and the values of the fields in the list. The Create New List Item UI also allows you to append a unique identifier to the end of the filename to deal with list items of the same name; otherwise, the item can be overwritten.

Declare Record: Declares item as a record.

Delete Drafts: Removes minor versions of the item.

Delete Item: Provides for the selection of a list and item for deletion when the condition is met.

Delete Previous Versions: Removes all previous versions of the item (both major and minor).

Discard Check Out Item: This option is used to terminate a Check Out on an item without initiating a Check In.

Do Calculation: This action is useful when you want to take the values of two list items and perform a calculation that outputs to a variable.

Find Interval Between Dates: Calculates minutes, hours, or days between two dates and outputs the result to a workflow variable.

continued

continued

Log to History List: A custom message related to a workflow action can be logged to the workflow history list using this action.

Lookup Manager of User: Retrieves the manager of the specified user (must be configured in user profiles).

Pause For Duration: This action pauses the workflow for a period of days, hours, and minutes specified.

Pause Until Date: An action that pauses the workflow until the date specified.

Send an Email: Send an e-mail with defined To, CC, Subject, Body, and variables.

Send Document to Repository: Copies or moves a document to a specified document repository.

Send Document Set to Repository: Copies or moves a document set to a specified document repository.

Set Content Approval Status: This action sets the content approval status to Approved, Rejected, or Pending, and adds comments to go with the approval.

Set Content Approval Status for Document Set: This action sets the content approval status for the document set to Approved, Rejected, or Pending, and adds comments to go with the approval.

Set Field in Current Item: Changes the value of the field to the setting in the action.

Set Time Portion of Date/Time Field: This action configures the time portion of the specified Date/Time Field.

Set Workflow Status: Enables the modification of the workflow status to Approved, Cancelled, or Rejected.

Set Workflow Variable: Allows the configuration of a workflow variable.

Start Document Set Approval Process: This action will kick off an approval workflow for the document set.

Stop Workflow: This action stops the workflow and posts a custom message to the workflow history log.

Undeclare Record: Undeclares item as a record.

Update List Item: An action that updates any of the fields in a list item to the values specified.

Wait For Change in Document Check-out Status: Pauses a workflow until the check-out status is checked-in, checked-out, discarded, or unlocked by document editor.

Wait For Field Change in Current Item: Pauses a workflow until a specified field equals the value entered.

15. To add the logic for a Sales Manager candidate, click Add 'Else If' Conditional Branch. Your step screen should look similar to Figure 8.9.

16. Click Finish. You should see a Processing New Candidate dialog box, and then you are returned to the SharePoint designer workspace. A Workflows folder now appears on the left side of the workspace. You can expand the folder to see the workflows you have created on this site.

FIGURE 8.9

Workflow Designer Route Resume step

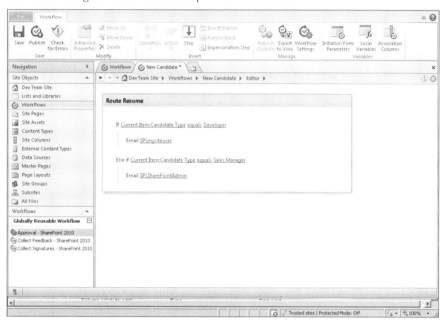

Adding Custom Activities and Conditions

Developers can add activities and conditions to the SharePoint Designer Safe List. To do this:

1. Develop the activity or condition.

2. Compile the activity or condition as a strong-named assembly.

3. Deploy to the global assembly cache.

4. Add the activity or condition to the action safe list in the web.config file.

5. Add rules and parameters for the sentence that represents the activity or condition in the user interface to the WSS.Actions file. The WSS.Actions file is a markup specifying the appearance and performance of the activity or condition.

Testing the New Candidate workflow

These steps will test the new workflow you created:

1. Go to the HR site and click the New Candidates document library.

2. Click Upload and upload a sample document.

3. Select the Candidate Type to be Developer.

4. An e-mail should be sent to the contact you configured.

5. Run a similar test for Sales Manager to confirm that your conditional branch is working properly.

Creating Advanced Workflow Solutions with Visual Studio and InfoPath

The Visual Studio Workflow Designer provides a project system for developing workflow solutions. It allows you to quickly define a workflow graphically by dragging activities from the Toolbox onto the design surface and provides code-beside for business logic, a mechanism for compiling workflows, and integrated workflow and code debugging.

InfoPath provides a rich-forms development environment that integrates nicely with Visual Studio. This chapter walks you through a detailed tutorial that introduces you to how these capabilities all come together to develop advanced workflow solutions.

Tutorial: Build a custom workflow

This tutorial guides a beginner-to-intermediate–level developer through creating a workflow in Visual Studio for SharePoint and using InfoPath to control the state of the workflow. You use Visual Studio to facilitate the action of sharing data between InfoPath forms. The workflow is attached to a Wiki document library, and when a new Wiki page is created, the workflow assigns a task to a user to moderate the Wiki content. This user is assigned according to the information entered into the initialization form you create with InfoPath. The assigned user receives an e-mail containing the normal task-assigned information as well as the Wiki page content that you will append to the e-mail body. The user then must verify in the second InfoPath form that he or she has completed moderating the Wiki before the task will be set to complete and the workflow set to finish. In order to create custom workflows with this level of control, you must use Visual Studio to pass the information between the forms and also to modify the e-mail sent out when creating a task to include the Wiki content.

Prepare your environment

On the Client: Install InfoPath 2010 and Office 2010. On the Server: Install Visual Studio 2010

Wiki site and list creation

Create the Enterprise Wiki site and list to use for the example.

1. From your portal or a team site, click View All Site Content above the left navigation.

2. Click Create, and under the Libraries heading click Wiki Page Library.

3. Call it something such as WF Wiki, enter a description if you want, and click Create. Your new Wiki site appears as in Figure 8.10.

4. A SharePoint Wiki is simply a set of pages in a document library, and you assign your workflow actions to this library. Your document library is located at `http://(Yourservername)/(Yourwikisitename)/forms/allpages.aspx`. Using my example, it was created at `http://mossdev/WF%20Wiki/Forms/AllPages.aspx`.

FIGURE 8.10

New Wiki site

Create the Visual Studio project

To create a Visual Studio project, follow these steps:

1. Open VS 2010 and choose File ➪ New ➪ Project.

2. In the New Project dialog box, under Visual C#, select SharePoint, then 2010, and then Sequential Workflow, as shown in Figure 8.11.

3. Name your project Wikiworkflow, or another name that will help you identify it later, and enter a location for the files and a name for the Solution. Keep the Create directory for solution box selected and click OK.

4. The SharePoint Configuration wizard runs after you click OK. Accept the defaults on the first screen and click Next.

5. Change the name so it just states Wikiworkflow. Click Next.

6. Select the WF Wiki library from the first drop-down on the next screen as shown in Figure 8.12. Click Next.

7. Click Finish. The solution is created and defaults to the graphical workflow designer tool.

FIGURE 8.11

New Project dialog box

FIGURE 8.12

SharePoint Customization Wizard

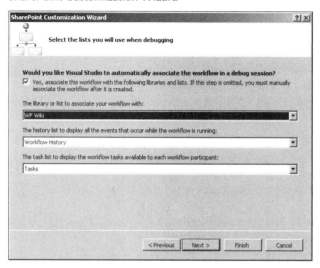

InfoPath Form #1 creation — Workflow Association and Instantiation Form

You will create two InfoPath forms for this workflow example. You need one form to kick off the workflow, which will assign the user to the task of viewing the links created in the Wiki and then searching for duplicate content. The second form is a moderation form that will list all of the Wiki links for the user, along with links to the corresponding created page.

1. Open Microsoft InfoPath Designer 2010.

2. Choose File ⮑ New, and choose Blank.

3. Click on the Design Form button on the right.

4. Click the Insert tab on the Ribbon.

5. Create a simple two-column table with five rows by clicking Custom table and selecting Layout Table. Enter 2 for Number of columns and 5 for Number of rows.

6. Type text for the Assigned To and Comments fields in the cells.

7. Merge the left and right columns in the third table row and drag it.

8. Click on the Home tab on the Ribbon and locate the Controls section. Click on the cell to the right of Assigned To and then click the Text Box control. Click in the merged cell and then click the Text Box control.

9. Click in one of the bottom cells and then select the Button control, as shown in Figure 8.13.

10. To name your controls, right-click on them and select the Properties menu item to open the properties dialog box, as shown in Figure 8.14. Name these text boxes AssignedTo and Comments.

FIGURE 8.13

InfoPath form layout

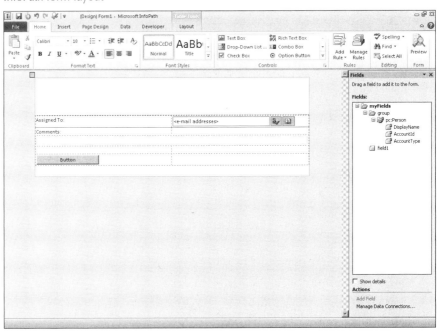

FIGURE 8.14

Text Box Properties

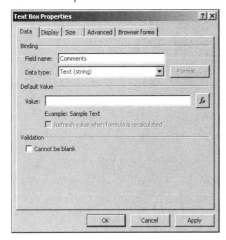

11. To make the Comments text box a Multi-line text box, click the Display tab and select the Multi-line check box.

12. Right-click the button and select Button Properties to open the Button Properties dialog box. Change the Label to OK. Click OK.

13. The button should still be selected. Click the Add Rules button from the Properties tab on the Ribbon under the Control Tools contextual tab.

14. Select When This Button Is Clicked and then select Submit Data, as shown in Figure 8.15.

15. Click the Add button to open the Data Connection Wizard. Accept the default selection to create a new connection for submitting data and click Next.

16. Select To the hosting environment, such as an ASP.NET page or a hosting application, and click Next.

17. Give a descriptive name to your data connection and click Finish. Then click OK on the Rule Details (Action) dialog box. The Rules pane appears.

18. Click Add in the Rule pane.

19. Select Close this form from the Add drop-down menu, then click OK. Your rule should now look like Figure 8.16.

FIGURE 8.15

Add Rule Menu for Button

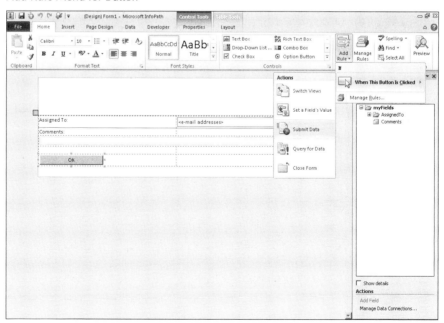

20. **You need to change some properties of your form to prepare it to work properly with SharePoint.** Click File ➪ Info and the click on the Form Options button. In the Form Options dialog box, click Security and Trust in the left category list. Uncheck Automatically determine security level and select the Domain option as shown in Figure 8.17, and then click OK to close the dialog box.

FIGURE 8.16

Rule with Submit and Close actions

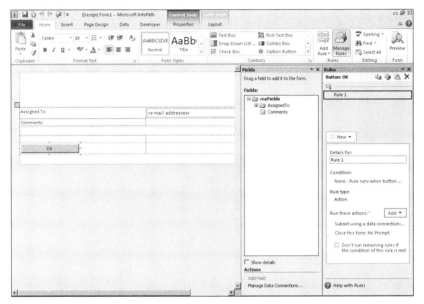

FIGURE 8.17

Form options — Security and Trust

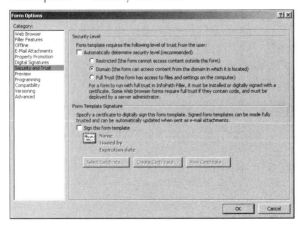

Note

Most likely the Domain security level is already selected, but it is a good idea to disable the automatic determination such that the form can be published properly. ■

21.   **From the File ⇨ Info page click the Design Checker button.** The Design Checker pane opens.

22.   **Click the Change Settings link at the bottom of the Design Checker pane.** The Form Options dialog box appears again and defaults to Compatibility.

23.   **In the Form Options dialog box, under Compatibility, ensure that the Form Type is set to Web Form Browser as shown in Figure 8.18.**

FIGURE 8.18

Form options — Compatibility

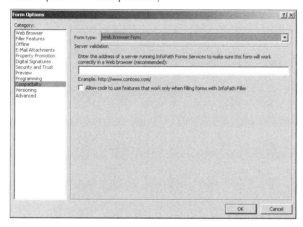

Note

While in the Form Options the first time we could have easily selected Compatibility instead of going to the Design Checker. However, if there are any Web browser conflicts, they appear in the Design Checker window pane. ■

24.   **Enter the URL of the SharePoint server on which you are deploying the workflow to verify that the form will work.** Click OK and the connection progresses. If no errors are reported, you are in good shape to continue.

25.   **Give your data a unique name.** Your main data source is called myFields by default. Double-click myFields in the Fields window pane and change the Name to **WikiInit** as shown in Figure 8.19. Click OK to save the changes.

FIGURE 8.19

Main data naming

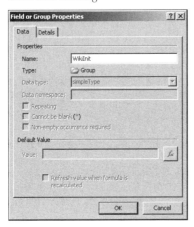

26. Save this form on your drive where you can easily open it again.

27. Publish the InfoPath form by clicking the Network Location button on the File ⇨ Publish page.

28. Click the Browse button, browse to where you created your VS 2010 workflow project, and pick the same directory as workflow1.cs. Name the file **wikiInit.xsn**. Now the wizard should look something like Figure 8.20.

FIGURE 8.20

Publishing Wizard

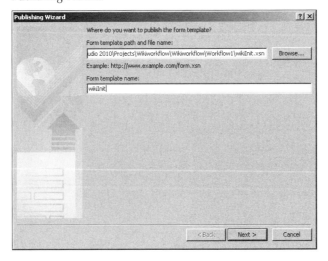

29. **Click Next.** Remove the alternate path to avoid problems with the form installation and click Next again. A warning dialog box appears as shown in Figure 8.21. Simply click OK to continue publishing the form.

InfoPath security warning dialog box

30. **Click Publish and then click Close to close the wizard.**

    To have the data that is entered into the form passed to your workflow, you need to extract a class from the form and use it in your Visual Studio project.

31. **In the InfoPath form, click File ⇨ Save As and save to a convenient location using WikiInitSource.xsn (or similar).** Close the InfoPath application.

32. **Locate the file you just saved and change the extension from .xsn to .cab. Double-click on the file to show the contents as shown in Figure 8.22. Create a new folder in the same location named WikiInitSource.**

InfoPath source files

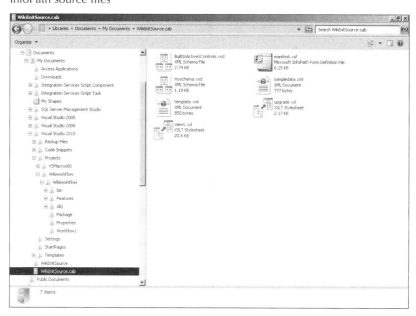

33. Extract these files from the CAB file by dragging them into the WikiInitSource folder.

34. Open a Visual Studio Command Prompt by clicking Start ⟹ All Programs ⟹ Microsoft Visual Studio 2010 ⟹ Visual Studio Tools ⟹ Visual Studio x64 Win64 Command Prompt.

35. **Navigate to where you stored the source files, type dir, and press Enter to list the files.** The screen should look like Figure 8.23.

Tip

A quick way to navigate to the location of the source files is to copy the path from Windows Explorer and then type "cd " in the command prompt (note the space) followed by right-clicking and selecting Paste from the mouse menu. ■

FIGURE 8.23

Visual Studio Command Prompt

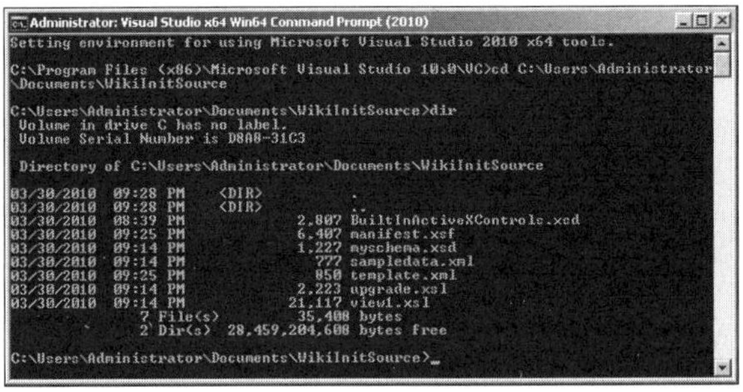

36. **Create a class out of the myschemea.xsd file to include in your Visual Studio solution. Type xsd myschema.xsd /c and press Enter.** This creates a C# file at this location. Type **dir** to ensure that `myschema.cs` was created.

Note

Some control types may not be compatible with the XSD Visual Studio utility and therefore the class may not be created. ■

37. **To rename the** `myschema.cs` **file so that it maps to your solution, type** rename myschema.cs wikiInit.cs.

38. **If the Wikiworkflow Visual Studio solution isn't open, open it now.** In the Solution Explorer pane, right-click Wikiworkflow and select Add ⟹ Existing Item. Browse to your source files directory and add the wikiInit.cs file. Your Visual Studio solution window should be similar to Figure 8.24.

39. **Add the Namespace to the wikiInit.cs class.** Open the Workflow1.cs class (right-click on select View Code) and copy the namespace declaration. Open the wikiInit.cs class and paste the namespace declaration at the top after the using statement and add a curly bracket on the next line as shown in Figure 8.25. Add the closing bracket at the bottom of the class.

FIGURE 8.24

Wikiworkflow Solution — Visual Studio

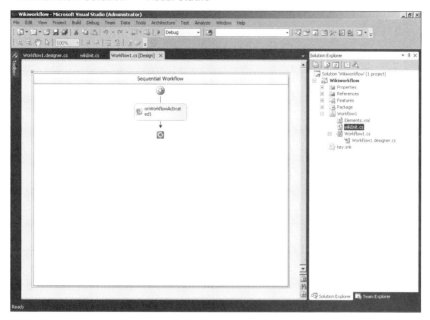

FIGURE 8.25

Adding Namespace to the WikiInit class

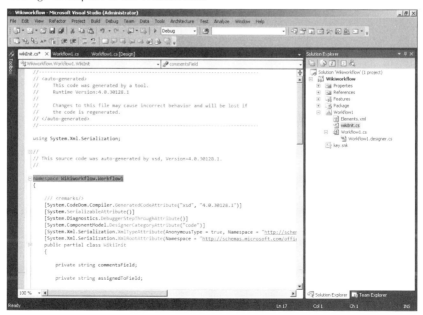

InfoPath Form #2 creation — Workflow Form

In these steps we will create the second InfoPath form and repeat some of the steps followed during the creation of form #1.

1. You will now create Form #2. Open InfoPath.

2. Select File ⇨ New, and choose Blank. Click on the Design Form button on the right.

3. Click the Insert ribbon menu.

4. Create a simple two-column table with five rows by clicking Custom table and selecting Layout Table. Enter 2 for Number of columns and 5 for Number of rows.

5. You need only three controls for this form: text box for comments, "complete" check box, and your Submit button. Type **Comments** in the first cell to label the field. Next, add the text box for comments, a check box control, and button control to the form.

6. Rename the Comments control to Comments and the check box control to isComplete and the button to Submit using the procedures outlined previously. Now your form should look like Figure 8.26.

7. Repeat Steps 21 to 30 in the previous section again for this form. When you get to Step 25, name your data source **ModerateWiki**. When you get to Step 28, name the form **wikiInit2.xsn** so you do not overwrite the first form. After completing those steps, begin again at Step number 8 here.

8. To pass the comment field from the initialization form to this form, you need to add a data source in which to pass the value. Open Notepad.

FIGURE 8.26

Form #2

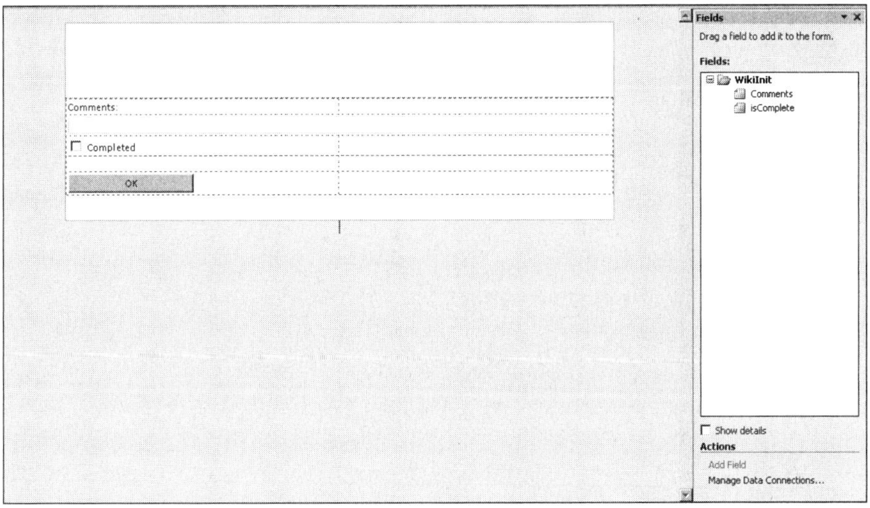

9. Type <z:row xmlns:z="#RowsetSchema" ows_comments="" />, **which should look like Figure 8.27.** Be careful here not to copy and paste this row from Word because the quotes may change and cause an error when processing the XML code. You should just type this row into Notepad.

FIGURE 8.27

Notepad text

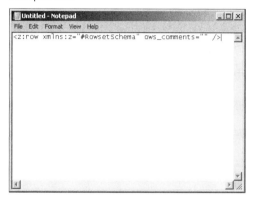

10. The `ows_comments` **attribute corresponds with the Comments field in the form.** You could associate other values in this file by preceding the InfoPath forms control names with ows_. Save this file as `ItemMetadata.xml`. Be sure the case is exactly the same as documented for the filename and save where you can easily retrieve it.

11. **Add this file to your InfoPath schema. Go back to InfoPath, and in the Data ribbon click Data Connections.**

12. **Click Add, and for Create a new connection to, select Receive data, as shown in Figure 8.28.**

13. **Click Next, select XML document, click Next, browse to the location of your `ItemMetadata.xml` file, select it, and then click Next.** If you see an error here about expecting quotes, go back to Step 7 and retype the quotes in Notepad. Word formats into something the code doesn't recognize.

14. **Leave Include the data as a resource file in the form template or template part selected and click Next.**

15. **Leave the name as ItemMetadata, select Automatically retrieve data when form is opened, and click Finish and then Close to get back to the form.**

16. **You have to bind your comment control so the data is populated.** Right-click the comments text box and select Text Box Properties to open the properties window. Click the formula button beside the Default Value text box to open the Insert Formula dialog box. Click Insert Field or Group, and select the ItemMetadata data source from the drop-down box, as shown in Figure 8.29.

FIGURE 8.28

Data Connection Wizard

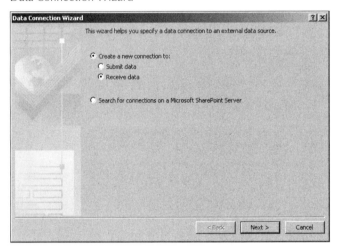

FIGURE 8.29

Select a Field or Group dialog box

17. Select :ows_comments from the available fields (it should be the only one) and click OK.

18. **Click OK to close the Insert Formula dialog box, and click OK to close the Text Box Properties dialog box.** Save the form and click File ⇨ Publish to a network location as you did for the first form. Again, to make sure that you don't have problems with the Access path, save it with a new name again even though you named it earlier. Save the form this time with the name ModerateWiki.xsn and click Next.

19. Delete the Access Path and then click Next again.

20. Click OK to continue publishing the template, click Publish, and then Close.

21. Repeat Steps 31 to 38 in the previous InfoPath form section.

22. Close InfoPath to begin the Visual Studio Section.

Visual Studio Code Authoring/Programming

After all of those steps, it may be valuable to walk through the workflow logic again.

Visual Studio should still be opened to your project. If not, open the project you created earlier. You already have the onWorkflowActivated1 control in the Visual Studio Designer. To view the code behind the workflow, right-click the Workflow1.cs [Design] page and choose View Code. You will see the screen in Figure 8.30.

1. Go back to the Designer and double-click the onWorkflowActivated1 control, which generates the onWorkflowActivivated1_Invoked event handler in the code and will open it for editing.

2. Click the onWorkflowActivated1 control. The Properties pane shows the properties of this workflow step. (If the Properties pane does not appear, right-click the onWorkflowActivated control and select Properties.)You don't have to change anything in the properties, but you should note the properties that are available to you. Notice the CorrelationToken, and expand the WorkflowProperties item and notice the two child properties: Name and Path. The workflowProperties that the path is associated with are the same as in this section of code:

```
public Microsoft.SharePoint.Workflow.SPWorkflowActivationProperties
   workflowProperties =
       new Microsoft.SharePoint.Workflow.
   SPWorkflowActivationProperties();
```

3. **Drag on the first activitiy.** Click View ➪ Toolbox and find CreateTask in the Toolbox under the SharePoint Workflow section and drag it on to the designer. Place it directly under the onWorkflowActivated1 activity.

4. **Double-click the** createTask1 **control to create the code to handle that event.** Go back to the Designer tab. There are a few properties that need to be set at this point. Make sure that the focus is on the createTask1 control, and have a look at the Properties pane as shown in Figure 8.31.

FIGURE 8.30

Workflow code

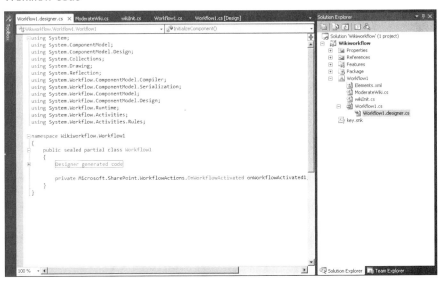

FIGURE 8.31

The createTask Properties pane

5. Place your cursor into the field next to the `CorrelationToken` property. Type taskToken.

6. Expand CorrelationToken by clicking the plus sign, click OwnerActivityName, and set Workflow1 as the activity name.

   There are two ways to bind your tasked and task properties. You can do it via code, or you can allow Visual studio to bind them. Let's do it both ways, starting with code.

7. Add the line

```
public Guid taskId = default(System.Guid);
```

   into the code, anywhere outside of any method is fine. Your code should now look like this:

```
using System;
using System.ComponentModel;
using System.ComponentModel.Design;
using System.Collections;
using System.Drawing;
using System.Workflow.ComponentModel.Compiler;
using System.Workflow.ComponentModel.Serialization;
using System.Workflow.ComponentModel;
using System.Workflow.ComponentModel.Design;
using System.Workflow.Runtime;
using System.Workflow.Activities;
using System.Workflow.Activities.Rules;
using System.Xml.Serialization;
using System.Xml;
using Microsoft.SharePoint;
using Microsoft.SharePoint.Workflow;
using Microsoft.SharePoint.WorkflowActions;
using Microsoft.Office.Workflow.Utility;
namespace WikiWorkflow
{
  public sealed partial class Workflow1:
   SequentialWorkflowActivity
  {
        public Workflow1()
        {
              InitializeComponent();
        }

    public Guid taskId = default(System.Guid);
    public Guid workflowId = default(System.Guid);
    public SPWorkflowActivationProperties workflowProperties =
      new SPWorkflowActivationProperties();

    private void onWorkflowActivated1_Invoked(object sender,
    ExternalDataEventArgs e)
```

```
    {

    }

    private void createTask1_MethodInvoking(object sender,
        EventArgs e)
    {

    }

    }

}
```

You don't need all of the `using` statements, so feel free to refactor to get rid of the unused ones at any time.

8. **Back in the designer, you can now bind to the** `taskId`. Click the `TaskId` property on the Properties pane for `createTask1`, and then click the ellipse that appears (...). This opens the binding dialog box. Select taskId as shown in Figure 8.32.

FIGURE 8.32

Bind TaskId to an activity's property

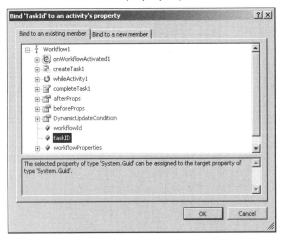

9. **Click OK.** In the Properties pane, expand the TaskId node. You will notice that the path is now set to taskId.

10. **The other method of binding is to let Visual Studio handle the work.** You use this method to bind the TaskProperties node. Click the `TaskProperties` property and

then click the ellipse to open the binding dialog box. This time, click the "Bind to a new member" tab.

11. Click the Create Field radio button and change the member name to taskProps, as shown in Figure 8.33, and click OK.

FIGURE 8.33

Bind TaskProperties to an activity's property

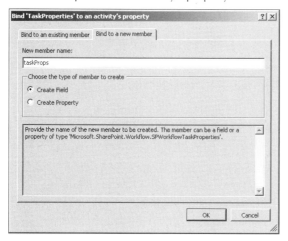

12. Expand the `TaskProperties` node and notice that the path is now set to `task-Props`. Go to the code view and notice that the following line was added to the code:

```
public Microsoft.SharePoint.Workflow.SPWorkflowTaskProperties
    taskProps = new Microsoft.SharePoint.Workflow.
    SPWorkflowTaskProperties();
```

13. Now you need to loop and wait until the task is set to complete. Go back to the Design tab and Find the While control in the Toolbox under the Windows Workflow 3.0 category. Drag it under the `createTask1` activity.

14. In the `Conditions` property, choose Code Condition from the drop-down menu. Expand the node, and beside Condition type **notFinished** and press Enter. The `not-Finished` method is generated in the code.

15. Add an activity into the `while` loop to tell the loop when to break and move forward. Find the `OnTaskChanged` control under the SharePoint Workflow category and drop it into the `while` loop.

16. Set the `CorrelationToken` property to `taskToken`. Bind the `TaskId` to the existing `taskId` and bind the `BeforeProperties` and `AfterProperties` to new members, leaving the radio button on the default of Create Property for both. Your list of existing properties now looks like Figure 8.34.

FIGURE 8.34

Before and after properties

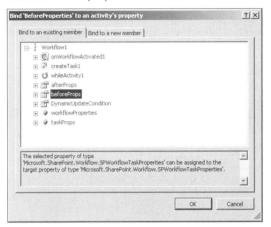

17. **Click OK.** In the Properties pane, under Handlers, click Invoked, type **onTaskChanged**, and press Enter to generate the `onTaskChanged` method in the code.

18. **Add the last item to the designer.** Find CompleteTask in the Toolbox and drop it under the `While` activity. Bind the `CorrelationToken` property to `taskToken`, the `TaskId` to the existing `taskId`, and double-click the `completeTask1` control you just dragged onto the form to create the event handler in the code. Your designer should now look like Figure 8.35.

FIGURE 8.35

Designer

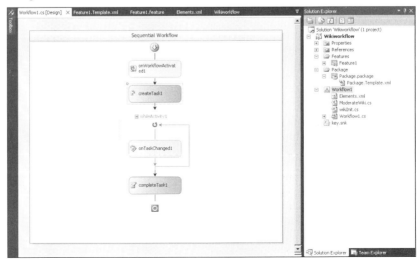

Your code, without all of the using statements at the top, should look like:

```
namespace Wikiworkflow.Workflow1
{
    public sealed partial class Workflow1:
    SequentialWorkflowActivity
      {
            public Workflow1()
              {
                InitializeComponent();
              }

  public Guid taskId = default(System.Guid);
  public Guid workflowId = default(System.Guid);
  public Microsoft.SharePoint.Workflow.
SPWorkflowActivationProperties workflowProperties = new
Microsoft.SharePoint.Workflow.SPWorkflowActivationProperties();

  private void onWorkflowActivated1_Invoked(object sender,
    ExternalDataEventArgs e)
  {

  }

  private void createTask1_MethodInvoking(object sender,
    EventArgs e)
  {

  }

  public Microsoft.SharePoint.Workflow.SPWorkflowTaskProperties
    taskProps = new Microsoft.SharePoint.Workflow.
    SPWorkflowTaskProperties();

  private void notFinished(object sender, ConditionalEventArgs e)
  {

  }

  public static DependencyProperty afterPropsProperty =
    DependencyProperty.Register("afterProps", typeof(Microsoft.
    SharePoint.Workflow.SPWorkflowTaskProperties),
    typeof(Wikiworkflow.Workflow1));

[DesignerSerializationVisibilityAttribute(DesignerSerialization
  Visibility.Visible)]
[BrowsableAttribute(true)]
```

```
[CategoryAttribute("Misc")]
    public Microsoft.SharePoint.Workflow.SPWorkflowTaskProperties
      afterProps
    {
      get
{
return ((Microsoft.SharePoint.Workflow.SPWorkflowTaskProperties)
    (base.GetValue(Wikiworkflow.Workflow1.afterPropsProperty)));
}
      set
{
base.SetValue(Wikiworkflow.Workflow1.afterPropsProperty, value);
}
    }

    public static DependencyProperty beforePropsProperty =
      DependencyProperty.Register("beforeProps", typeof(Microsoft.
      SharePoint.Workflow.SPWorkflowTaskProperties),
      typeof(Wikiworkflow.Workflow1));

[DesignerSerializationVisibilityAttribute(DesignerSerialization
   Visibility.Visible)]
[BrowsableAttribute(true)]
[CategoryAttribute("Misc")]
    public Microsoft.SharePoint.Workflow.SPWorkflowTaskProperties
      beforeProps
    {
      get
{
return ((Microsoft.SharePoint.Workflow.SPWorkflowTaskProperties)
    (base.GetValue(Wikiworkflow.Workflow1.beforePropsProperty)));
}
      set
{
base.SetValue(Wikiworkflow.Workflow1.beforePropsProperty, value);
}
    }

    private void onTaskChanged(object sender, ExternalDataEventArgs e)
    {

    }

    private void completeTask1_MethodInvoking(object sender,
      EventArgs e)
    {

    }
```

```
    }
  }

}
```

19. Find the `onWorkflowActivated1_Invoked` method, and just above it, declare some properties:

```
private string assignedTo = default(String);
private string comments = default(String);
```

Tip

The designer places code all over the place in the code behind. You may want to move all of the public variable declarations to the top of the class for readability. You may also want to create regions in the code to group similar functions such as the MethodInvoking event handlers. ■

20. **These should look familiar.** They represent the InfoPath controls you added to your first form. You need to set these properties with the data passed into the workflow in the workflowProperties code. In order to access the workflow properties though, you need to parse the XML string passed in. This is where you use the `WikiInit.cs` file you added to the solution.

You first need to add the following using statements to the top of the code page:

```
using System.Xml;
using System.Xml.Serialization;
```

Inside the `onWorkflowActivated1_Invoked` method, add the following code between the brackets:

```
private void onWorkflowActivated1_Invoked(object sender,
   ExternalDataEventArgs e)
{
  workflowId = workflowProperties.WorkflowId;

  XmlSerializer serializer = new XmlSerializer(typeof
    (WikiInit));
  XmlTextReader reader = new XmlTextReader(new System.IO.
    StringReader(workflowProperties.InitiationData));
  WikiInit wikiInit = (WikiInit)serializer.Deserialize(reader);

  assignedTo = wikiInit.AssignedTo;
  comments = wikiInit.Comments;

}
```

Basically what you are doing is reading in the data passed in from the first InfoPath form into our workflow when the workflow is initialized.

21. The `createTask1_MethodInvoking` method is called just before the task is actu-
    ally created, so you should set some properties on the task here, by adding the code
    between the brackets below:

```
private void createTask1_MethodInvoking(object sender, EventArgs e)
  {
    taskId = Guid.NewGuid();
    taskProps.Title = "Moderate Wiki please.";
    taskProps.AssignedTo = assignee;
    taskProps.Description = comments;
    taskProps.ExtendedProperties["comments"] = comments;

    // just for fun, lets add the wiki content to the email
       thats going out to the
    // assignee - note - this will only work for wiki items
    SPListItem item = workflowProperties.Item;
    if (item["Wiki Content"] != null)
      taskProps.EmailBody += item["Wiki Content"];


  }
```

22. Recall in the second InfoPath form, you added a check box called isComplete. You
    have to add that corresponding flag to your code, so directly at the top of the class
    in the declarations section add the following:

```
private bool isComplete;
```

All of the declarations within the class placed together at the top should now look similar to
the following:

```
public Guid workflowId = default(System.Guid);
public Guid taskID = default(System.Guid);
public SPWorkflowActivationProperties workflowProperties = new
     SPWorkflowActivationProperties();
public SPWorkflowTaskProperties taskProps = new Microsoft.
     SharePoint.Workflow.SPWorkflowTaskProperties();
public static DependencyProperty afterPropsProperty =
     DependencyProperty.Register("afterProps", typeof(Microsoft.
     SharePoint.Workflow.SPWorkflowTaskProperties),
   typeof(Wikiworkflow.
     Workflow1.Workflow1));
public static DependencyProperty beforePropsProperty =
     DependencyProperty.Register("beforeProps", typeof(Microsoft.
     SharePoint.Workflow.SPWorkflowTaskProperties),
   typcof(Wikiworkflow.
     Workflow1.Workflow1));
private string assignedTo = default(String);
private string comments = default(String);
private bool isComplete;
```

23. Your `while` loop calls the `notFinished` method and loops until the event passed into the `notFinished` method is set to `false`. Add the code between the brackets below to the notFinished method.

```
private void notFinished(object sender, ConditionalEventArgs e)
{
  e.Result = !isComplete;
}
```

24. Check the check box state in the afterProperties node in the `onTaskChanged` method and set the `isComplete` boolean equal to this condition. Add the code between the brackets to the method.

```
private void onTaskChanged(object sender, ExternalDataEventArgs e)
{
    isComplete = bool.Parse(afterProps.ExtendedProperties
        ["isComplete"].ToString());
}
```

25. Click Build ⇨ Build WikiWorkflow in the top navigation to build your workflow. Hopefully, you will not have errors, and you can move on to the Deploying and Debugging activities.

Deploying

This section details the deployment and debugging of the example, and we can enjoy the fruit of our hard labor.

1. From the Visual Studio solution, double-click on the Elements.xml file located under Workflow1. The Elements.xml file opens as shown in Figure 8.36.

2. In your project directory, find your published forms — not the templates you designed, but the forms you published. Right-click `WikiInit.xsn` and open it in Design mode. Click File ⇨ Info and then the Form Template Properties button. Copy and paste the ID into the `Instantiation_FormURN` and `Association_FormURN`, nodes. Do the same for `ModerateWiki.xsn` and paste that ID into `Task0_FormURN`. You can remove the `Modification_GUID_FormURN` and `Modification_GUID_Name` nodes. Your `workflow.xml` file should look like similar to Figure 8.37.

3. Click Build ⇨ Build Solution in the top navigation to build your solution. This ensures everything compiles properly and that your solution package can be created.

4. Click Build ⇨ Deploy Solution. Visual Studio 2010 automatically adds your solution to the SharePoint farm and deploys.

5. Verify deployment. Open SharePoint 2010 Central Administration. Click on System Settings from the Quick Launch. Click on Manage Farm Solutions under Farm Management. The Wiki Workflow solution will appear as shown in Figure 8.38.

FIGURE 8.36

Elements.xml

FIGURE 8.37

Elements.xml with form IDs

FIGURE 8.38

Solution management

6. **Upload the form templates.** Click General Application settings from the Central Administration Quick Launch. Click on Manage Form Templates under InfoPath Form Services. Click on Upload Form Template and navigate to where you published the forms. Upload WikiInit.xsn and ModerateWiki.xsn.

7. **Activate the form templates.** Back at the Manage Form Templates screen, your uploaded form templates appear. Click each one and select Activate to Site Collection. Select the site collection and click OK.

Activating, Running, and Debugging

1. Open a new browser and navigate to your Wiki site. Select Site Settings from the Site Actions menu. If this is not a site collection, click on the Go to top level site settings link.

2. Under Site Collection Administration, click on Site collection features. Scroll down and activate the Wiki Workflow feature as shown in Figure 8.39.

3. Go to your Wiki site and to the Wiki Pages document library.

4. **Choose Workflow settings from the Library ribbon bar.** Click on Add a Workflow. Choose Wiki Workflow from the workflow list, and give it a unique name, shown in Figure 8.40.

FIGURE 8.39

Activating the Wiki Workflow feature

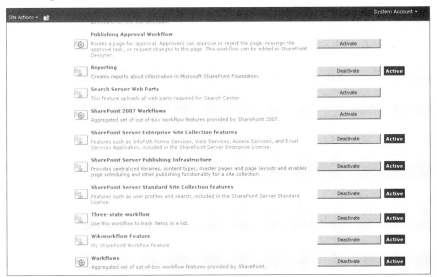

FIGURE 8.40

Adding the Wiki Workflow to the Pages Library

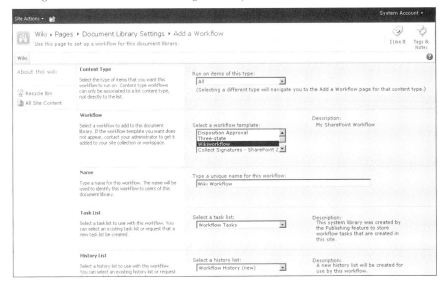

5. **Select a new task list and a new history list, and select Allow this workflow to be manually started by an authenticated user with Edit Items Permissions, Start this workflow when a new item is created, and Start this workflow when an item is changed.** Click Next. Surprise, there's your first form!

6. **Fill out this form with some valid data.** Use a name that you know will resolve with a valid user e-mail address. Click OK.

7. **To debug, go back to Visual Studio and click Debug ➪ Attach to Process.** Find `w3wp.exe` in the list and click Attach.

8. **Give Visual Studio a few seconds before proceeding.** Go to the `Workflow1.cs` code and put a breakpoint on the first line of all four of your methods. The process will now stop at these breakpoints and you can see the values that are passed in.

9. **Go back to the Wiki site.** Open one of the Wiki pages and click Edit. Wrap a few words in [[ ]] tags so SharePoint knows to create a Wiki page. Click OK, and Visual Studio should grab that process because you set it to start on edit of a page.

10. **The line is yellow where the debug process has stopped, and you can step through by pressing F10.** You can run through to the next breakpoint by pressing F5, but I suggest stepping through. Mousing over the variables should give you a popup of the values they hold.

11. **Go check out the task list that was created, and you should see a new task assigned to the assignee you specified, with the title Moderate Workflow please.** Open this task and you'll see the Workflow Form (form #2).

12. **Add some more comments and click Save.** Don't set as complete yet. Step through Visual Studio. You will notice that `OnTaskChanged` was called, but not the `initialize` method or the `create task` method. Open the task again, and you'll see that your comments were saved. This time, check Complete and click OK. The workflow is complete, nice work!

Summary

With SharePoint 2010, there are workflow capabilities targeted at end users, power users, and developers. End users can modify out-of-the-box and custom-developed workflows using only their browsers. Power users can use SharePoint Designer to add sophisticated logic to their workflows, quickly automating business processes and making their workflows available to other team members. Developers still have a common workflow foundation to develop against and a rich set of server tools available to develop complex human workflow applications.

Extending Office Server

T here are many ways to develop functionality to extend the capabilities of your SharePoint server, such as developing Web Parts, authoring workflows, and using the SharePoint object model to perform code-based operations. This chapter covers two methods SharePoint provides to extend the SharePoint functionality by defining features and configuring Excel Services so that you can publish Excel workbooks for HTML access to the data.

The feature capabilities within SharePoint provide a structure so that you can define a number of operations using XML files without writing any additional code. The use of features within SharePoint is so pervasive that many of the more than 100 features defined by SharePoint are implemented using feature definitions such as document libraries, the issue list template, and the report center functionality. Features allow you to target your extended SharePoint functionality for exactly the audience you want through four levels of deployment — the farm, the Web application, a site collection, or a Web site. This chapter discusses both authoring a feature definition and installing and activating your feature.

Excel Services is another way to extend the capabilities of SharePoint by allowing you to publish Excel workbooks, often a cornerstone of corporate knowledge, in a secure manner that allows connections to trusted data, and publishes workbooks in an HTML format without requiring file conversation, while still securing the underlying data and formulas. Excel Calculation Services, which is a component of Excel Services, enables the capability to perform calculations in published worksheets while still in the browser page. This chapter walks through the steps to make Excel Services work for your organization in a flexible yet trusted way. Excel Services require SharePoint Server and are not available SharePoint Foundation deployments.

IN THIS CHAPTER

Developing features for Office Server

Installing and activating feature definitions

Configuring Excel Service settings

Developing Features for Office Server

Features enable you to deploy site functionality at a site, site collection, Web application, or farm level either in a mode where users can see the feature in order to activate or deactivate it or in a mode where it is hidden and always present. In addition to the features that you see as options to activate and deactivate on a site, as shown in Figure 9.1, most of the building blocks of SharePoint are implemented by using features such as document libraries, the issues list, and the records management functionality.

By using features to deploy custom functionality, you are able to:

- Leverage the SharePoint structure for installing features at the site, site collection, Web application, or farm levels

- Leverage the SharePoint structure for activating or deactivating features

- Have SharePoint manage the feature definition across distributed SharePoint servers

Almost anything is possible when thinking about the potential uses for Office Server features because SharePoint has provided for a lot of different functionality options. This can make envisioning the scenarios in which you will use features difficult. Here are some examples to get the creative juices flowing:

FIGURE 9.1

Standard features available for activation and deactivation on a SharePoint site

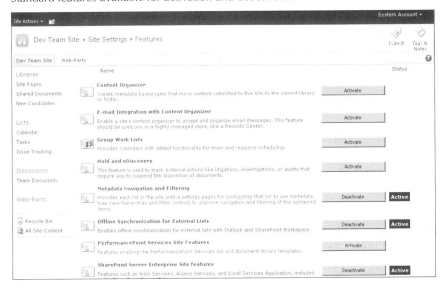

- Associating a workflow with a particular list type and site template

- Adding an additional action for a list or library and customizing the actions menus for that library

- Creating a custom list type with defined fields and making it available for all sites in a farm

- Modifying a site template to include a feature definition for any new instances of that site template

- Replacing a control within existing functionality with a control defined by your feature

Tip

If you want to further familiarize yourself with the possibilities that features present, take a look at the definitions that are used to create the SharePoint out-of-the-box functionality. You will be able to review how Microsoft used features to define lists, add actions, control navigation, and many other things and get a good introduction to feature definition files. In addition, Visual Studio 2010 SharePoint solutions automatically create and maintain these definition files, reducing the previously cumbersome manual configuration. ■

Creating a feature.xml file

The feature.xml file provides a name and ID — as well as defines the properties, including dependences, files, and assemblies — for your feature.

The structure of the feature.xml file is

```
<Feature
<!-- Required Feature Attributes -->
  Id = "Text" <!-- This is the GUID for the feature -->
<!-- You can generate a GUID for your feature by using a GUID
    generator tool like the one provided with Visual Studio -->
  Scope = "Text"
  <!-- Values are Web (web site), Site (site collection),
    WebApplication (web application) or Farm (farm) -->
<!-- Optional Feature Attributes -->
  Title = "Text"  <!-- Feature title up to 255 characters -->
  Version = "Text" > <!-- Version number in 0.0.0.0 format -->
  Creator = "Text" <!-- Name of feature author -->
  Description = "Text" <!-- Description of purpose of the feature -->
  DefaultResourceFile =  "Text"
  <!-- Specifies the path for the resource file to be used for
   resource descriptions. -->
  Hidden = "TRUE" | "FALSE"
  <!-- If set to TRUE, the feature and its status will not be visible
   to users -->
  ReceiverAssembly = "Text"
```

```
<!-- Strong name for receiver assembly in the GAC to use for
  feature events. Requires you to specify receiver class as well.
  -->
ReceiverClass = "Text"
<!-- Class used by the event processor. Requires you to specify
  receiver assembly as well. -->
RequireResources = "TRUE" | "FALSE"
<!-- If set to TRUE, this tag will force SharePoint to check to see
  if a resource file is available for the current culture. If the
  file is not present, the feature will not be available for
  activation in the user interface. -->
ActivateOnDefault = "TRUE" | "FALSE"
<!-- This attribute is not valid for site or web scope features and
  if set to TRUE means the feature is activated during installation
  or web application creation. -->
AlwaysForceInstall = "TRUE" | "FALSE"
<!-- If set to TRUE, the feature is installed by force even if it
  is already installed -->
AutoActivateInCentralAdmin = "TRUE" | "FALSE"
<!-- This attribute is not valid if feature is enabled for the farm
  scope. If set to TRUE, the feature is activated by default in the
  scope -->
  ImageUrl = "Text" <!-- URL for image to be used next to feature
  name in the site features interface -->
  ImageUrlAltText = "Text" <!-- Alternate text to use if the image is
  not loaded -->
  SolutionId = "Text" <!-- Ties the feature to a specific solution
  -->

<!- Child Elements -->
  <ElementManifests> <!-- Specifies manifests and files that make up
    the feature -->
    <ElementFile
          Location="Path">
    <!-- Relative path to the supporting element file, if any -->
    </ElementFile>
    <ElementManifest
          Location="Path">
    <!-- Required attribute that defines path to the manifest file
    -->
    </ElementManifest>
  </ElementManifests>


  <ActivationDependencies> <!--Specifies features that are
    dependencies for this feature -->
    <ActivationDependency
```

```
            FeatureId="GUID">
   <!-- One to many feature dependencies specified by GUID -->
   </ActivationDependency>
   </ActivationDependencies>

   <Properties>
   <!-- Contains property names and values for the feature -->
    <Property
            Key="Text"
            Value="Text">
    </Property>
    <!-- If included, one or more feature properties and the
    associated default value -->
    </Properties>
  </Feature>
```

To generate a GUID, you can use the guidgen.exe tool provided with Visual Studio. To create a new GUID for your feature, follow these steps:

1. Open Visual Studio 2010.

2. Select Tools ⇨ Create GUID from the top menu.

3. Select Registry Format, as shown in Figure 9.2.

4. Click the Copy button and paste the value into your feature.xml file. Delete the { } characters surrounding the GUID value.

FIGURE 9.2

Using the GUID Generator tool to generate a new GUID

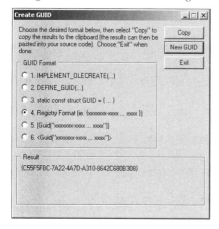

Using the element types

The feature.xml file is the core of the feature deployment, but the element types are where all the fun action is found. Each element type has its own function and can be used within the scopes it is designed for. The four scopes available for features are

- **Farm:** A feature can be applied to all sites within the Web farm.

- **WebApplication:** The Web application means that the feature is available for all sites within that Web application as defined in Central Administration.

- **Site:** The site scope applies the features to all sites within that site collection.

- **Web:** Features scoped for the Web are available to the site on which the feature is installed.

Element types for all scopes

The following element types can be used within a feature deployed for any scope in SharePoint:

- **Control:** The Control element allows you to replace a control with a different control. For example, you can use it to call a different ASCX page for the search control to use on a SharePoint site. Here is some sample code using the control element that is part of the content light-up feature provided with SharePoint out of the box.

  ```
  <Control
      Id="SmallSearchInputBox"
      Sequence="100"
      ControlSrc="~/_controltemplates/searcharea.ascx">
  </Control>
  ```

  This content light-up feature is a farm-level feature that provides some standard interface components such as the search box on SharePoint sites and the custom action link for exporting an event or a contact.

- **Custom Action Group:** The CustomActionGroup element type defines a grouping for custom actions. This tag is not necessary if you are adding or hiding a custom action to a particular list type.

  The structure for the custom action group is shown in this code sample:

```
<CustomActionGroup
  Title="Text"
  <!-- Required attribute that provides the description for the
    action group. -->
  Location="Text"
  <!-- Required attribute that specifies a text string that tells
    SharePoint where to place the action. The text should match the
    name in the LinkSectionTable control on the page. -->
  Description="Text"
  <!-- Optional attribute for a longer description for the action
    group. -->
```

```
Sequence="Integer"
<!-- Optional number for ordering priority for the action group.
 -->
Id="Text">
<!-- Optional value for unique identifier for the element. -->
</CustomActionGroup>
```

- **Custom Action:** The CustomAction element allows you to add actions for your feature. This code, from the content light-up feature, adds a custom control for exporting an event and is not in a custom action group because the custom action is bound to a list type and ID (the Event list).

```
<CustomAction
    Id="ExportEventToolbarButton"
    Location="DisplayFormToolbar"
    Title="$Resources:ContentLightup_EventToolbar_
ExportEventButton;"
    RegistrationType="List"
    RegistrationId="106">
    <UrlAction Url="~site/_vti_bin/owssvr.dll?CS=109&amp;Cmd=Disp
lay&amp;List={ListId}&amp;CacheControl=1&amp;ID={RecurrenceId}&am
p;Using=event.ics"/>
  </CustomAction>
```

The custom action for exporting an event shows up in the location DisplayFormToolbar for the display form for a calendar event, as shown in Figure 9.3.

FIGURE 9.3

Using the custom action code to add an option for exporting an event in the display form

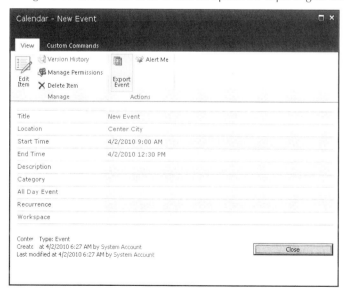

Creating a Custom Action Using SharePoint Designer

If you don't need a custom action to be part of a feature, you can easily create a custom action graphically by using SharePoint Designer. Follow these steps:

1. Either navigate to the list you want to customize and select Edit List (in SharePoint Designer) from the Ribbon, or launch SharePoint Designer, open the site, and navigate to the list.

2. Select Custom Action from the Ribbon. There are five options (in order of appearance):

   - **List Item Menu:** This custom action will appear in the drop-down of an item in a list.
   - **Display Form tab Ribbon:** This action will appear in the ribbon when viewing an item.
   - **Edit Form tab:** This action will appear in the ribbon while editing an item.
   - **New Form tab:** This action will appear in the ribbon while creating a new item.
   - **View tab:** This action will appear in the Item ribbon bar while viewing the list or library and having an item from the list selected.

3. Select the type of action from the drop-down menu.

4. Enter the action details.

5. Click OK. Your custom action will appear where specified.

The structure of the custom action element is shown in the following code sample. Make sure that you follow the CustomAction tag with the UrlAction tag that provides the URL for the action, as shown in the Custom Action Group section.

```
<CustomAction
  Title="Text"
  <!-- Required attribute that provides the action description to the
    user. -->
  Description="Text"
  <!-- Longer description for the action that is shown as a tool-tip
    or sub-description -->
  Id="Text"
  <!-- Optional value for unique identifier for the element. -->
  Location="Text"
  <!-- Optional attribute that specifies where the action will
    appear. If contained in a custom action group, location will
    equal the location of the CustomActionGroup element. The location
    could also be a part of a site settings menu, a toolbar item or
    menu item. -->
  RegistrationType="Text"
  <!-- Option attribute that allows you to create a per-item action.
    Allowable values are ContentType, FileType, List, or ProgID. -->
  RegistrationId="Text"
```

```
  <!-- Option attribute that provides the value for the registration
    type defined above. The value is the identifier of the list,
    content type, document or programmatic ID. -->
  GroupId="Text"
  <!-- Option attribute that identifies the action group such as
   "SiteManagement". If custom action is a subelement of
    CustomActionGroup, the value must match the GroupId of the
    CustomActionGroup. -->
  ContentTypeId="Text"
  <!-- Optional attribute that specifies the content type ID for the
    custom action to associate with. -->
  ImageUrl="Text"
  <!-- Optional attribute for a relative path for the action icon.
    -->
  RequireSiteAdministrator="TRUE" | "FALSE"
  <!-- Optional attribute that if set to TRUE, the action will only
    show for site administrators. -->
  Sequence="Integer"
  <!-- Optional value for ordering the action. -->
  Rights="Text"
  <!-- Optional value that lets you specify for which roles the
    action should appear. -->
  ShowInReadOnlyContentTypes="TRUE" | "FALSE"
  <!-- Optional value that if set to TRUE, the action will only be
    displayed for read-only content types. -->
  ShowInSealedContentTypes="TRUE" | "FALSE"
  <!-- Optional value that is set to TRUE, the action will only be
    displayed for sealed content types. -->
  ControlAssembly="Text"
  <!-- Optional attribute that specifies the assembly for the action.
    -->
  ControlClass="Text"
  <!-- Optional attribute that defines the class for the control
    assembly, if used. -->
  ControlSrc="Text">
  <!-- Optional attribute that specifies source of the control. -->
</CustomAction>
```

- **Hide Custom Action:** This element hides a custom action defined by another custom action. The structure of the HideCustomAction element is shown in this sample code:

```
<HideCustomAction
  HideActionId="Text"
  <!-- Optional value that specifies the ID of the action you want to
    hide. -->
  Location="Text"
  <!-- Optional attribute that specifies the location of the action
    you want to hide. -->
  GroupId="Text"
```

```
<!-- Option attribute that identifies the action group such as
 "SiteManagement".  -->
Id="Text">
<!-- Optional attribute that specifies the ID for this
 HideCustomAction element. -->
</HideCustomAction>
```

Element type for farm, Web application, or site scopes

There is one element that can be applied at the farm, Web application, or site scope levels. The Feature/Site Template Association element associates your feature with a site template and allows you to define features (custom or otherwise) that will be included in new sites created from the template when your feature is activated.

An example of the FeatureSiteTemplateAssociation element is the translation management functionality. When turned on, the code below associates the translation management with four sites.

```
<Elements xmlns="http://schemas.microsoft.com/sharepoint/">
  <FeatureSiteTemplateAssociation Id="29D85C25-170C-4df9-A641-
    12DB0B9D4130" TemplateName="STS#0" />
  <FeatureSiteTemplateAssociation Id="29D85C25-170C-4df9-A641-
    12DB0B9D4130" TemplateName="STS#1" />
  <FeatureSiteTemplateAssociation Id="29D85C25-170C-4df9-A641-
    12DB0B9D4130" TemplateName="BDR#0" />
  <FeatureSiteTemplateAssociation Id="29D85C25-170C-4df9-A641-
    12DB0B9D4130" TemplateName="SPS#0" />
</Elements>
```

The structure of the feature/site template association element is shown in the following code sample:

```
<FeatureSiteTemplateAssociation
 Id="Text"
<!-- Required attribute that provides the GUID for the feature
 (see http://msdn2.microsoft.com/en-us/library/aa544552.aspx). -->
 TemplateName="Text" />
<!-- Required attribute that provides the name of the associated
 site template. -->
 <Property
 <!-- Optional child element to provide properties for the
 association. If included, the property must have key and value
 tags. -->
      Key="IncludeInGlobalNavigation"
      Value="False" />
</FeatureSiteTemplateAssociation>
```

Element types for Web application scope

The DocumentConverter (it refers to XML element tag) element defines a document converter that processes a file and generates a copy of that file in the converted document type format.

The structure of the DocumentConverter element is shown in the following code sample:

```
<DocumentConverter
 Id="Text"
 <!-- Optional attribute for specifying the GUID for the document
   converter. -->
 Name="Text"
 <!-- Optional attribute for naming the document converter. -->
 App="Text"
 <!-- Optional attribute for the document converter executable-->
 From="Text"
 <!-- Optional attribute that specifies the extension of the source
   file. -->
 ConverterUIPage="Text"
 <!-- Optional attribute that specifies the extension of the target
   file. -->
 ConverterSpecificSettingsUI="Text"
 <!-- Optional attribute that provides the .ascx control for the
   converter configuration page. -->
 ConverterSettingsforContentType="Text"/>
 <!-- Optional attribute that specifies the .aspx page where
   administrators can configure the document conversion for each
   site content type. -->
```

Element types for site scope

There are several elements that can be deployed at the site scope level. Some of these items create items once, like content type and list templates, which can be used thereafter by other elements.

- **Content Type:** The ContentType element defines a custom content type that will be created when the feature is activated.

Note

Because activation is an activity that you need to do only once, it is primarily useful for content types out of the box or for deploying an entirely new feature set at the site collection level. ■

The following code provides the structure for the ContentType element:

```
<ContentType
 ID="Text"
 .<!-- Required attribute that provides the ID for the content type.
   -->
 Name="Text"
 <!-- Required attribute provides a name for the content type. -->
 .Description="Text"
   <!-- Optional attribute that provides the longer description for
     the content type. -->
 Group="Text"
 <!-- Optional attribute that specifies to which group the content
   type should belong. -->
```

```
ReadOnly="TRUE" | "FALSE"
<!-- Optional attribute that if set to TRUE, makes the content type
   read-only. -->
Hidden="TRUE" | "FALSE"
<!-- Optional attribute that if set to TRUE, will hide the content
   type so that it is not presented as an option for the New button.
   -->
Sealed="TRUE" | "FALSE"
<!-- Optional attribute that if set to TRUE, makes the content type
   sealed. -->
V2ListTemplateName="Text"
<!-- Optional attribute that associates the content type with a WSS
   2.0 list template. -->
FeatureId="Text">
<!-- Optional attribute that provides the feature ID for the content
   type. -->
<Folder
TargetName="Text"
<!-- Optional attribute for providing relative path for content
   type's resource folder. -->
 />
 <FieldRefs>
 <!-- This section defines column references for your content type.
   -->
        <FieldRef
             ID="Text"
             <!-- Optional attribute that specifies the field ID
   this FieldRef references -->
             Name="Text"
             <!-- Optional attribute that provides a column name
   -->
             Description="Text"
             <!-- Optional attribute that provides long-name
   description for the field. -->
             DisplayName="Text"
             <!-- Optional attribute that provides the column
   display name for use in a form. -->
             Format="Text"
             <!-- Optional attribute that specifies formatting for
   columns. Options can be set to DateOnly, DateTime, ISO8601,
   ISO8601Basic, Dropdown (Choice column), RadioButtons (Choice
   Column), Hyperlink (URL column), Image (URL column). -->
             Required="TRUE" | "FALSE"
             <!-- Optional attribute that specifies whether or
   not the field is required.  -->
             Filterable="TRUE" | "FALSE"
             <!-- Optional attribute that specifies whether or
   not the field can be used for filtering. -->
             FilterableNoRecurrence="TRUE" | "FALSE"
```

```
            <!-- Optional attribute that specifies if the column
is filterable with no recurrences. -->
            Sortable="TRUE" | "FALSE"
            <!-- Optional attribute that specifies whether or
not the field is available for sorting. -->
            Hidden="TRUE" | "FALSE"
            <!-- Optional attribute that specifies whether or not
the field is hidden.  -->
            Node="Text"
            <!-- Optional attribute that specifies the XML node
that contains the field value. -->
            Aggregation="sum" | "count" | "average" | "min" |
"max" | "merge" | "plaintext" | "first" | "last"
            <!-- Optional attribute that provides the action to
take on the XPath expression if returned by Node value. -->
            NumLines="Integer"
            <!-- Optional attribute that limits the number of
viewable lines for text editing.  -->
            PIAttribute="Text"
            <!-- Optional attribute that specifies the attribute
that will be used for document processing instruction. Must be
paired with PITarget. -->
            PITarget="Text"
            <!-- Optional attribute that specifies the document
processing instruction storage location. Must be paired with
PIAttribute. -->
            PrimaryPIAttribute="Text"
            <!-- Optional attribute that specifies the attribute
that will be used for document processing instruction. Must be
paired with PrimaryPITarget and will trump any present
PIAttributed. -->
            PrimaryPITarget="Text"
            <!-- Optional attribute that specifies the document
processing instruction storage location. Must be paired with
PrimaryPIAttribute and will trump any present PIAttribute.-->
            ReadOnly="TRUE" | "FALSE"
            <!-- Optional attribute that specifies whether or
not field is read-only. If ready only, the field will not be
displayed in new or edit forms. -->
            Sealed="TRUE" | "FALSE"
            <!-- Optional attribute that specifies whether or
not the column is sealed. -->
            ShowInDisplayForm="TRUE" | "FALSE"
            <!-- Optional attribute that specifies whether or
not the column will be included on the display form. -->
            ShowInEditForm="TRUE" | "FALSE"
            <!-- Optional attribute that specifies whether or
not the column will be included on the edit form. -->
            ShowInFileDlg-"TRUE" | "FALSE"
```

```
                   <!-- Optional attribute that specifies whether or
     not the column will be included in the file dialog. -->
                   ShowInListSettings="TRUE" | "FALSE"
                   <!-- Optional attribute that specifies whether or not
     the column will be included on the new item form. -->
                   ShowInNewForm="TRUE" | "FALSE"
                   <!-- Optional attribute that specifies whether or
     not the column will be included on the new form. --> >
          </FieldRef>
          <RemoveFieldRef
          <!-- This element removes a field that is present in the
     parent content type from this content type. -->
                   ID="Text">
          <!-- Specifies the field ID of the column that you want to
     remove. -->
       </FieldRefs>
       <XMLDocuments>
          <XMLDocument
          <!-- This optional element defines XML documents to be
     included in the content type. -->
                   NamespaceURL="Text">
                   <!-- Optional value that provides path to the
     namespace for the XML document. -->
          </XMLDocument>
       </XMLDocuments>
     </ContentType>
```

- **Content Type Binding:** The ContentTypeBinding element allows you to define a content type for a list that is defined in the onet.xml schema, because lists defined by the onet.xml schema cannot be modified directly.

  The following structure is used for the ContentTypeBinding element.

```
<ContentTypeBinding
  ContentTypeId="Text"
  <!-- Required attribute that provides content type ID that you want
    to bind to the list. -->
  ListUrl="Text"
  <!-- Required attribute that provides a relative path for the list
    for which you want to bind the content type. -->
 />
```

- **Field Element:** The Field element creates site columns for use in any list.

  Here is an example on how this Field element is used within the report list template to create the fields for storing reports:

```
       <Fields>
           <Field ID="{FA564E0F-0C70-4AB9-B863-0177E6DDD247}"
    Type="Text" Name="Title" ShowInNewForm="FALSE"
    ShowInFileDlg="FALSE" DisplayName="$Resources:core,Title;"
```

```
Sealed="TRUE" SourceID="http://schemas.microsoft.com/sharepoint/
v3" StaticName="Title" />
        <Field ID="{2A16B911-B094-46e6-A7CD-227EEA3EFFDB}"
Name="ReportDescription" StaticName="ReportDescription" Descripti
on="$Resources:spscore,BizAppsFields_ReportDescription_
Description;" DisplayName="$Resources:spscore,BizAppsFields_
ReportDescription_Name;" Group="$Resources:spscore,BizAppsFields_
ReportGroup;" Type="Note" SourceID="http://schemas.microsoft.com/
sharepoint/v3"></Field>
        <Field ID="{90884F35-D2A5-48dc-A39F-7BCBC9781CF6}"
Name="SaveToReportHistory" StaticName="SaveToReportHistory" Descr
iption="$Resources:spscore,BizAppsFields_
ReportSaveToReportHistory_Description;" DisplayName="$Resources:s
pscore,BizAppsFields_ReportSaveToReportHistory_Name;" Group="$Res
ources:spscore,BizAppsFields_ReportGroup;" Type="Boolean"
SourceID="http://schemas.microsoft.com/sharepoint/v3">
            <Default>0</Default>
        </Field>
        <Field ID="{1BE428C8-2C2D-4e02-970B-6663EB1D7080}"
Name="ParentId" StaticName="ParentId" Description="$Resources:sps
core,BizAppsFields_ReportParentID_Description;" DisplayName="$Res
ources:spscore,BizAppsFields_ReportParentID_Name;" Group="_
Hidden" ShowInNewForm="FALSE" ShowInEditForm="FALSE"
ShowInFileDlg="FALSE" Type="Number" SourceID="http://schemas.
microsoft.com/sharepoint/v3"></Field>
        <Field ID="{2E8881DA-0332-4ad9-A565-45B5B8B2702F}"
Name="ReportOwner" StaticName="ReportOwner" Description="$Resourc
es:spscore,BizAppsFields_ReportOwner_Description;" List="UserInfo"
DisplayName="$Resources:spscore,BizAppsFields_ReportOwner_Name;"
Group="$Resources:spscore,BizAppsFields_ReportGroup;" Type="User"
SourceID="http://schemas.microsoft.com/sharepoint/v3"></Field>
        <Field ID="{D8921DA7-C09B-4a06-B644-DFFEBF73C736}"
Name="ReportCategory" StaticName="ReportCategory" Description="$R
esources:spscore,BizAppsFields_ReportCategory_Description;" Displ
ayName="$Resources:spscore,BizAppsFields_ReportCategory_Name;"
Group="$Resources:spscore,BizAppsFields_ReportGroup;"
Type="Choice"  SourceID="http://schemas.microsoft.com/sharepoint/
v3">
            <CHOICES>
                <CHOICE>$Resources:spscore,BizAppsFields_
ReportCategory_Choice1;</CHOICE>
                <CHOICE>$Resources:spscore,BizAppsFields_
ReportCategory_Choice2;</CHOICE>
                <CHOICE>$Resources:spscore,BizAppsFields_
ReportCategory_Choice3;</CHOICE>
            </CHOICES>
        </Field>
        <Field ID="{BF80DF9C-32DC-4257-BCF9-08C2EE6CA1B1}"
Name="ReportStatus" StaticName="ReportStatus" Description="$Resou
```

```
rces:spscore,BizAppsFields_ReportStatus_Description;" DisplayName
="$Resources:spscore,BizAppsFields_ReportStatus_Name;" Group="$Re
sources:spscore,BizAppsFields_ReportGroup;" Type="Choice"
SourceID="http://schemas.microsoft.com/sharepoint/v3">
            <CHOICES>
                <CHOICE>$Resources:spscore,BizAppsFields_
ReportStatus_Final;</CHOICE>
                <CHOICE>$Resources:spscore,BizAppsFields_
ReportStatus_Preliminary;</CHOICE>
                <CHOICE>$Resources:spscore,BizAppsFields_
ReportStatus_PeriodToDate;</CHOICE>
            </CHOICES>
        </Field>
        <Field ID="{27C603F5-4DBE-4522-894A-AE77715DC532}"
Name="ReportHistoryLink" StaticName="ReportHistoryLink" Group="_
Hidden" ReadOnly="TRUE" Type="Computed" DisplayName="$Resources:s
pscore,BizAppsFields_ReportHistory_Name;" SourceID="http://
schemas.microsoft.com/sharepoint/v3">
            <FieldRefs>
                <FieldRef Name="ContentType"/>
                <FieldRef Name="ID"/>
            </FieldRefs>
            <DisplayPattern>
                <IfEqual>
                    <Expr1><Column Name="ContentType"/></Expr1>
                    <Expr2>$Resources:spscore,BizAppsContentTy
pes_Report;</Expr2>
                    <Then>
                        <HTML><![CDATA[<a href="]]></HTML><ListUr
lDir/><HTML><![CDATA[/Forms/rpthist.aspx?FilterField1=ParentId&Fi
lterValue1=]]></HTML><Field Name="ID"/><HTML><![CDATA[&Lis
tId=]]></HTML><List/><HTML><![CDATA[&ID=]]></HTML><ID
/><HTML><![CDATA[">]]></HTML>
                        <HTML>$Resources:spscore,BizAppsFields_
ReportHistory_ViewHistory;</HTML>
                        <HTML><![CDATA[</a>]]></HTML>
                    </Then>
                    <Else />
                </IfEqual>
            </DisplayPattern>
        </Field>
```

This code results in a list showing the fields that you see when you upload a document to a report library, as shown in Figure 9.4.

FIGURE 9.4

Viewing the fields created by the Report list field elements

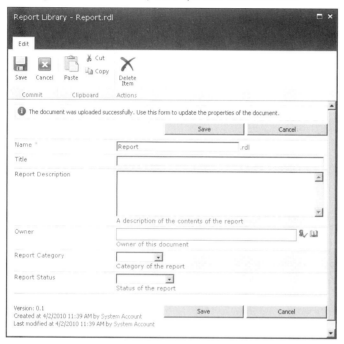

Cross-Reference

For more information on all the functionality provided by report libraries, see Chapter 15. ■

- **List Instance:** The ListInstance element instantiates a list when your feature is activated and can also be applied at the Web scope level.

  The following code sample shows the structure of the ListInstance element:

```
<ListInstance
  Id="Text"
  <!-- Required attribute for unique identifier for the list
    instance. -->
  FeatureId="Text"
  <!-- Required attribute for GUID of the feature with which this
    list instance is associated. -->
```

```
      TemplateType="Integer"
      <!-- Required attribute that provides integer ID for the list
        template to use. -->
      Title="Text"
      <!-- Required attribute that gives list title. -->
      Url="Text"
      <!-- Required attribute that provides relative place to where the
        list should be created. -->
      Description="Text"
      <!-- Optional attribute that provides list description. -->
      OnQuickLaunch="TRUE" | "FALSE"
      <!-- Optional attribute  that specifies whether or not the list
        should be placed on the quick launch.-->
      QuickLaunchUrl="Text"
      <!-- Optional attribute that provides the URL that the Quick Launch
        link should point to. -->
      RootWebOnly="TRUE" | "FALSE">
      <!-- Optional attribute for whether or not the list only exists in
        root web site. -->
      <Data>
            <Rows>
                  <Row>
                    <!-- Provides default data to include when the list
        is instantiated. -->
                        </Row>
            </Rows>
      </Data>
</ListInstance>
```

- **List Template:** The ListTemplate element calls a list defined in the schema.xml file. This feature element can also be applied at the Web scope level.

Note

Because defining a list template is an activity that you need to do only once, it is primarily useful for list templates out of the box or for deploying an entirely new feature set at the site collection level. ∎

The following code sample shows the structure of the ListTemplate element:

```
<ListTemplate
  DisplayName = "Text"
  <!-- Required attribute that provides name of list definition. -->
  BaseType = "0" | "1" | "2" | "3" | "4"
  <!-- Required attribute that provides the default schema for list
    created from this list definition. Base type 1=document library.
    -->
  Name = "Text"
    <!-- Required attribute that provides name reference used to find
    the folder that provides the schema.xml. SharePoint will look in
    the features directory for a name\schema.xml file -->
```

```
Description = "Text"
 <!-- Optional attribute that provides a description. -->
Default = "TRUE" | "FALSE"
   <!-- Optional attribute that specifies whether or not this list
will be included on all new SP lists. -->
 VersioningEnabled = "TRUE" | "FALSE"
 <!-- Optional attribute that if set to TRUE, turns versioning on
the list on. -->
 AllowDeletion = "TRUE" | "FALSE"
 <!-- Optional attribute that specifies whether or not the lists
created through the template can be deleted. -->
 AllowEveryoneViewItems = "TRUE" | "FALSE"
 <!-- Optional attribute -->
 AlwaysIncludeContent = "TRUE" | "FALSE"
 <!-- Optional attribute that when set to TRUE will make list
templates created from this list definition include content when
saved. -->
 CacheSchema = "TRUE" | "FALSE"
 <!-- Optional attribute -->
Catalog = "TRUE" | "FALSE"
 <!-- Optional attribute that when set to TRUE means that list
definition is for a list, site or web part gallery. -->
 Category = "Libraries" | "Communications" | "Tracking" | "Custom
Lists"
 <!-- Optional attribute that specifies which category the lists
created from the template should be associated. -->
 DisableAttachments = "TRUE" | "FALSE"
 <!-- Optional attribute that specifies whether or not lists will
allow attachments. -->
 DisallowContentTypes = "TRUE" | "FALSE"
 <!-- Optional attribute that if TRUE specifies that content types
can be managed. -->
DontSaveInTemplate = "TRUE" | "FALSE"
 <!-- Optional attribute that if set to true, will exclude content
from being saved when a template is being created from the list.
-->
 EditPage = "Text"
 <!-- Optional attribute that provides path to page for modifying
the list settings. -->
 EnableModeration = "TRUE" | "FALSE"
 <!-- Optional attribute that if set to TRUE will create a list
that requires content approval. -->
FeatureId = "Text"
 <!-- Optional attribute that associates a Feature GUID with this
list. -->
 FolderCreation = "TRUE" | "FALSE"
 <!-- Optional attribute that if set to TRUE allows folders to be
created in the list. -->
Hidden = "TRUE" | "FALSE"
```

```
  <!-- Optional attribute that if set to TRUE will hide the list
  template from the create page. -->
HiddenList = "TRUE" | "FALSE"
  <!-- Optional attribute that is set to TRUE if lists created from
  this template will be hidden. -->
Image = "URL"
  <!-- Optional attribute that provides path to icon for the list.
  -->
 NewPage = "Text"
  <!-- Optional attribute that specifies alternative page to be
  used for creating a new list from this template. -->
 NoCrawl = "TRUE" | "FALSE"
  <!-- Optional attribute that if set to TRUE will exclude list
  results from search results. -->
OnQuickLaunch = "TRUE" | "FALSE"
  <!-- Optional attribute that if set to true will add a link to
  the Quick Launch for lists created from the template. -->
SecurityBits = "Text"
  <!-- Optional attribute that allows you to define list security
  for the read, write and schema design roles for all lists other
  than document libraries. -->
Sequence = "Integer"
  <!-- Optional attribute that specifies the order that you want
  the template to appear on the create page. -->
 SetupPath = "Text"
  <!-- Optional attribute that specifies the path to the folder
  containing the list definition file and assumes that the path is
  relative to the templates directory.  -->
 SyncType = "Text"
  <!-- Optional attribute -->
Type = "Integer"
  <!-- Optional attribute that provides a unique identifier for the
  template.  -->
 Unique = "TRUE" | "FALSE">
  <!-- Optional attribute that when set to TRUE, the list template
  can only be used to create lists during site creation. -->
</ListTemplate>
```

- **Module:** The Module element, which can also be applied at the Web scope level, builds a packing list of files to be implemented to support the feature.

  Here is the code the publishing resources features use to include the pages for a publishing site:

```
<Module Name="PageLayouts" Url="_catalogs/masterpage" Path=""
RootWebOnly="TRUE">
    <File Url="WelcomeLinks.aspx" Type="GhostableInLibrary" >
        <Property Name="Title" Value="$Resources:cmscore,PageLay
out_WelcomeLinks_Title;" />
```

```
            <Property Name="MasterPageDescription" Value="$Resources:
cmscore,PageLayout_WelcomeLinks_Description;" />
            <Property Name="ContentType" Value="$Resources:cmscore,co
ntenttype_pagelayout_name;" />
            <Property Name="PublishingPreviewImage"
Value="~SiteCollection/_catalogs/masterpage/$Resources:core,Cult
ure;/Preview Images/WelcomeLinks.png, ~SiteCollection/_catalogs/
masterpage/$Resources:core,Culture;/Preview Images/WelcomeLinks.
png" />
            <Property Name="PublishingAssociatedContentType" Value=";
   #$Resources:cmscore,contenttype_welcomepage_name;;#0x010100C
   568DB52D9D0A14D9B2FDCC96666E9F2007948130EC3DB064584E219954237
   AF390064DEA0F50FC8C147B0B6EA0636C4A7D4;#" />
      </File>
      <File Url="VariationRootPageLayout.aspx"
Type="GhostableInLibrary" >
            <Property Name="Title" Value="$Resources:cmscore,PageLay
out_VariationRootLayout_Title;" />
            <Property Name="ContentType" Value="$Resources:cmscore,co
ntenttype_pagelayout_name;" />
            <Property Name="PublishingAssociatedContentType" Value=";
   #$Resources:cmscore,contenttype_redirectpage_name;;#0x010100C
   568DB52D9D0A14D9B2FDCC96666E9F2007948130EC3DB064584E219954237
   AF3900FD0E870BA06948879DBD5F9813CD8799;#"/>
            <Property Name="PublishingHidden" Value="true" />
      </File>
   </Module>
```

The structure of the Module element is shown in the following code sample:

```
<Module
  Name="Text"
  <!-- Required attribute for name of file set -->
  List="Integer"
  <!-- Optional attribute which specifies the type of list as defined
   in onet.xml -->
  IncludeFolders="Text"
  <!-- Optional attribute that specifies whether or not to include
   sub-folders to contain files -->
  Path="Text"
<!-- Optional attribute that specifies the URL for the file set. -->
  RootWebOnly="TRUE" | "FALSE"
  <!-- Optional attribute that if set to TRUE will only copy the
   files to the root web site of the site collection. -->
  SetupPath="Text"
  <!--  Optional attribute that specifies the location for the
   sources files and is assumed to be located to the element if
   blank. Used to be the path variable. -->
  Url="Text">
```

```
<!-- Optional attribute that provides the URL of the target folder
in which you want the files placed. -->
     <File
             Url="Text"
             <!-- Required attribute that provides the URL for the
target file -->
             Name="Text"
             <!-- Optional attribute that specifies the file name.
-->
              Path="Text"
             <!-- Optional attribute for the source of the file
(URL). -->
             IgnoreIfAlreadyExists="TRUE" | "FALSE"
             <!-- Optional attribute that if set to TRUE will
copy the file even if it already exists. -->
             Type="Text"
             <!-- If present, specifies that you want the file to
be cached on the front-end web server. If your file is stored in
a document library, the value will be GhostableInLibrary. If your
file is stored somewhere other than a document library, the value
is set to Ghostable. -->
             NavBarHome="TRUE" | "FALSE">
             <!-- Optional attribute that if set to TRUE,
indicates that this file is the home page for the top navigation
bar in the site. -->
     </File>
             <AllUsersWebPart>
             <!-- Tag to use if your file is a web part. -->
                 WebPartOrder="Integer"
                 <!-- Required attribute that specifies the
vertical order of the web part in the zone. -->
                 WebPartZoneID="Text">
                 <!-- Required attribute that provides the ID
of the web part zone to insert the web part in. -->
             </AllUsersWebPart>
             <NavBarPage
             <!-- Provides file information to the nav bar so that
it can be linked. -->
                 ID="Integer"
                 <!-- Required attribute that provides the ID
for the page. -->
                 Name="Text"
                 <!-- Required attribute that provides the text
for the page that will show in the nav bar. -->
                 Position="Text">
                 <!-- Optional attribute that provides the
position of the item in the navigational bar. -->
             </NavBarPage>
             <View
```

```
                <!-- Allows you to provide view values for files
that are views. -->
                  Name = "Text"
                  <!-- Required attribute that provides a name
for the view. -->
                  DisplayName = "Text"
                  <!-- Required attribute that provides a
display name for the view. -->
                  Hidden = "TRUE" | "FALSE"
                  <!-- Optional attribute that when set to
TRUE, hides the view. -->
                  Url = "URL"
                  <!-- Optional attribute that provides the
target URL of the view. -->
                  DefaultView = "TRUE" | "FALSE"
                  <!-- Optional attribute that when set to
TRUE, indicates that this is the default view. -->
                  Threaded = "TRUE" | "FALSE"
                  <!-- Optional attribute that if TRUE shows
items as threaded. -->
                  Type = "HTML" | "Chart" | "Pivot"
                  <!-- Optional attribute that renders view as
HTML, Chart or Pivot. -->
                  Scope = "Text"
                  <!-- Optional attribute that sets the limit
for which items are returned. FilesOnly will return files of
current folder, Recursive will show all files in all folders,
RecursiveAll will show all files and all subfolders of all
folders. -->
                  List = "Integer"
                  <!-- Optional attribute that specifies the
type of list as defined in the onet.xml file. -->
                  AggregateView = "TRUE" | "FALSE"
                  <!-- Optional attribute that when set to TRUE
indicates that the view is a merge forms view for a form library.
-->
                  BaseViewID = "Integer"
                  <!-- Optional attribute that specifies the ID
of the base view. -->
                  FailIfEmpty = "TRUE" | "FALSE"
                  <!-- Optional attribute that when set to
TRUE, returns a HTTP error code if no items are returned in the
view. -->
                  FileDialog = "TRUE" | "FALSE"
                  <!-- Optional attribute that when set to TRUE
displays the view in file dialogs. -->
                  FPModified = "TRUE" | "FALSE"
```

```
                      <!-- Optional attribute that when set to TRUE
    indicates that the file has already been modified and cannot be
    modified within SharePoint UI. -->
                         FreeForm = "TRUE" | "FALSE"
                         <!-- Optional attribute that when set to TRUE
    allows alternate field formatting for view columns. -->
                         OrderedView = "TRUE" | "FALSE"
                         <!-- Optional attribute that when set to TRUE
    indicates that the view is ordered. -->
                         Path = "Text"
                         <!-- Optional attribute that provides the
    source path for the view. -->
                         ReadOnly = "TRUE" | "FALSE"
                         <!-- Optional attribute that when set to TRUE
    marks the view as read-only. -->
                         RecurrenceRowset = "TRUE" | "FALSE"
                         <!-- Optional attribute that when set to TRUE
    will show recurring values as individual line items. -->
                         RowLimit = "Integer"
                         <!-- Optional attribute that specifies
    maximum number of rows to return in an HTML view. -->
                         ShowHeaderUI = "TRUE" | "FALSE">
                         <!-- Optional attribute that if set to TRUE
    enables sorting and filtering from column headers. -->
                  </View>
</Module>
```

- **Workflow:** The Workflow element calls a workflow. The following code sample shows the structure of the Workflow element:

```
<Workflow
  Name="Text"
  <!-- Required attribute that provides value that is displayed in
   WSS interface. -->
  Id="Text"
  <!-- Required attribute  that provides workflow GUID. -->
  CodeBesideAssembly="Text"
  <!-- Required attribute for code beside assembly. -->
  CodeBesideClass="Text"
  <!-- Required attribute for workflow class for code beside assembly
   file. -->
  Title="Text"
  <!-- Optional attribute for title of workflow. -->
  Description="Text"
  <!-- Optional attribute for workflow description. -->
  AssociationUrl="Text"
  <!-- Optional attribute for the URL to the association form. -->
  InstantiationUrl="Text"
  <!-- Optional attribute for the URL to the instantiation form. -->
  ModificationUrl="Text"
```

```
<!-- Optional attribute for the URL to the form used to modify the
  workflow.  -->
TaskListContentTypeId="Text" >
<!-- Optional attribute that specifies the content type ID for the
  content type associated with the workflow task list. -->
<AssocationData>
<!-- Optional element that provides XML data to pass to the
  workflow association form. -->
</AssocationData>
<MetaData>
<!-- Optional element that defines additional metadata to associate
  with the workflow. -->
</MetaData>
</Workflow>
```

Element types for Web scope

Like the List Instance, List Template, and Module element types, the Receiver element type is
defined in the site scope section and can be applied at either the site scope or Web scope level. The
Receiver feature element registers an item event receiver.

The structure of a Receiver element is shown in the following code sample:

```
<Receivers
  ListTemplateId = "Text"
  <!-- Optional attribute that specifies the ID of the list template
    that the event applies to. -->
  ListTemplateOwner = "Text">
  <!-- Optional attribute that specifies the GUID of the list
    template owner. -->
</Receivers>
  <Receiver>
        <Assembly></Assembly>
        <!-- The assembly tag must be in the format of Name,
  Version=0.0.0.0, Culture=neutral, PublicKeyToken=xx -->
        <Class></Class>
        <!-- The class tag provides the fully qualified name of the
  class. -->
        <Data></Data>
        <!-- The data element passes parameters to the event
  receiver. -->
        <Name></Name>
        <!-- Event receiver name -->
        <Type></Type>
        <!-- Provides the type of event. -->
        <SequenceNumber></SequenceNumber>
        <!-- Specifies the sequence number used for the event
  registration. -->
  </Receiver>
```

Installing and Activating Feature Definitions

After you create your feature definition and define the necessary feature elements, you need to install the feature so that it is available for activation at the appropriate scope.

Installing the feature

Features are stored at `Program Files\Common Files\Microsoft Shared\web server extensions\14\TEMPLATE\FEATURES`. To install a new feature, create a subdirectory under this feature folder and place your feature.xml file in that folder. The folder can also contain supporting element files and subdirectories. Confirm that you have configured the new directory to inherit permissions from the parent folder so that SharePoint has the appropriate rights to access your feature definition.

After you have added your feature folder in the appropriate directory, follow these steps to use the Stsadm.exe command-line tool (MS use) to install your feature:

1. **Open a command prompt on your SharePoint server.**

2. **Navigate to the** `<system drive>\Program Files\Common Files\Microsoft Shared\web server extensions\14\BIN` **directory.**

3. **Enter the** `stsadm` **command with the filename parameter pointing to your feature subdirectory and XML file as follows:**

    ```
    stsadm -o installfeature -filename <featuresubdirectory>\
    feature.xml <ENTER>
    ```

    This command is shown in Figure 9.5.

FIGURE 9.5

Adding a feature using the `stsadm` command

Using PowerShell to Administrate Features

The use of the stsadm console application is being phased out and replaced by the SharePoint 2010 Management Shell. The SharePoint 2010 Management Shell provides Windows PowerShell command capabilities to administer SharePoint 2010. The equivalent commands discussed in this chapter to administer features are as follows:

- Install-SPFeature FeatureFolderName
- Uninstall-SPFeature FeatureFolderName
- Enable-SPFeature FeatureFolderName -Url http://server/site/subsite
- Disable-SPFeature FeatureFolderName -Url `http://server/site/subsite`

4. When the command line returns that the operation completed successfully, type exit <ENTER> to exit the command line.

You can also uninstall a feature by using the Stsadm.exe command-line tool. To uninstall a feature, follow these steps:

1. Open a command prompt on your SharePoint server.

2. Navigate to the `<system drive>\Program Files\Common Files\Microsoft Shared\web server extensions\14\BIN` directory.

3. Enter the stsadm command with the filename parameter pointing to your feature subdirectory and XML file as follows:

```
        stsadm -o uninstallfeature -filename <featuredirectory>\
   feature.xml -url
```

4. When the command line returns that the operation completed successfully, type exit <ENTER> to exit the command line.

Tip
If you add the BIN folder location to your server PATH environment variable, you can run STSADM from any folder location. ∎

Activating/deactivating features

After a feature has been installed, you can activate it in the scope you want by either using the Stsadm.exe command-line tool or by activating it in the SharePoint site settings user interface if the feature is installed as a visible feature.

To activate a feature using the Stsadm.exe command-line tool, follow these steps:

1. Open a command prompt on your SharePoint server.

2. Navigate to the `<system drive>\Program Files\Common Files\Microsoft Shared\web server extensions\14\BIN` directory.

3. Enter the `stsadm` command with the filename parameter pointing to your feature subdirectory and XML file as follows:

```
stsadm -o activatefeature -filename <featuredirectory>\
feature.xml -url http://Server/Site/Subsite <ENTER>
```

This command is shown in Figure 9.6.

FIGURE 9.6

Activating a feature using the `stsadm` command

4. When the command line returns that the operation completed successfully, type exit <ENTER> to exit the command line.

To activate a visible feature, follow these steps:

1. Navigate to the site in which you want to add the feature.

2. Choose Modify All Site Settings from the Site Actions ⇨ Site Settings menu in the top-right corner of any page in the site.

3. Click Site features from the Site Administration section.

4. Click Activate next to your feature definition, as shown in Figure 9.7.

To deactivate a feature using the Stsadm.exe command-line tool, follow these steps:

1. Open a command prompt on your SharePoint server.

2. Navigate to the `<system drive>\Program Files\Common Files\Microsoft Shared\web server extensions\14\BIN` directory.

3. Enter the `stsadm` command with the filename parameter pointing to your feature subdirectory and XML file as follows:

```
stsadm -o deactivatefeature -filename <featuredirectory>\
feature.xml -url http://Server/Site/Subsite <ENTER>
```

4. When the command line returns that the operation completed successfully, type exit <ENTER> to exit the command line.

Activating a feature using the SharePoint site administration user interface

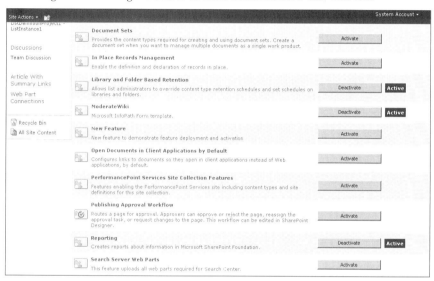

To activate a visible feature, follow these steps:

1. Navigate to the site in which you want to add the feature.

2. Choose Modify All Site Settings from the Site Actions ⇨ Site Settings menu in the top-left corner of any page in the site.

3. Click Site features from the Site Administration menu.

4. Click Deactivate next to your feature definition.

Optimizing Excel Services

Excel Services allows you to reuse your existing corporate spreadsheet assets in SharePoint without having to convert the file format. It also allows you to use and connect your spreadsheet data while protecting and securing the business logic and data contained in your spreadsheets. You must be running SharePoint Server to use Excel Services.

Excel worksheet functionality can extend to external data sources, user-defined functions, and programmatic access to services, so it's important to secure the file locations and data sources that you will be using to support your Excel Services. Doing this enables you to take advantage of the Excel Services functionality without exposing your SharePoint infrastructure to malicious or bad behavior.

This section covers how to configure Excel Services to be secure and usable, and have high performance.

Configuring Excel Services settings

To configure your Excel Services settings and optimize its security and performance, follow these steps:

1. Open the administration page for your Excel Services Application.

2. Select Global Settings.

3. In the Security section, select whether you would like to use Impersonation or the Process account to access workbooks that are not stored on SharePoint. If you select impersonation, Excel Services will use the credentials of the service account.

4. In the Security section, select whether encryption is required between the Excel Services front end and the client computer.

5. Select whether you would like to use the Workbook URL, Round Robin, or Local for the load-balancing scheme, and in the Load Balancing section enter the Retry Interval, which defines how long to wait between attempts to communicate with unresponsive Excel Calculation Services servers. Acceptable responses for the retry interval range from 5 seconds to 24 days (2073600 seconds).

    The load-balancing choices allow you to pick the right method for distributing the load if you have multiple application servers providing Excel Services. The Workbook URL load-balancing option will pass requests for the same workbook URL to the same application server to try to take advantage of caching on the application server. The Round Robin load-balancing option distributes requests to application servers in turn. The Local option is for the scenario when your application server is also your Web front end.

6. Enter the maximum number of sessions allowed for each user in the Session Management section. You can configure Excel Services to not have a session limit by specifying a –1 value or any positive integer for the limit.

7. Configure the memory utilization behavior by entering the Maximum Private Bytes, Memory Cache Threshold, and the Maximum Unused Object Age settings in the Memory Utilization section.

    The Maximum Private Bytes (in MB) sets the maximum amount of memory that the Excel Calculation Services process can command. If you configure this setting to a –1 value, it will use up to 50 percent of the server memory. You can also specify any positive integer as a valid value.

The Memory Cache Threshold is a percentage (1–95 percent) that determines how much of the maximum private bytes can be used for caching inactive objects to improve performance. Excel Calculation Services releases cached objects if the Memory Cache Threshold is exceeded. If you configure this setting to 0, it does not cache inactive objects.

For the Maximum Unused Object Age, set the maximum time in minutes that you want inactive objects to be cached. This setting can be disabled by configuring a −1 value if you do not want to set a maximum time. Otherwise, you can enter a value between 1 minute and 24 days (34560 minutes).

8. **Configure the disk space usage settings in the Workbook Cache section by defining an alternative Workbook Cache Location and Maximum Size of Workbook Cache and by enabling or disabling the caching of unused files.**

The Workbook Cache Location is a local server file directory to use for caching if you do not want to use the system temporary directory setting. Leave blank if you are fine with using the system temporary directory.

The Maximum Size of Workbook Cache setting allows you to limit (in MB) the disk space Excel Calculation Services uses, including space used for files that are not active but were recently used.

You can decide whether to use the Caching of Unused Files. Disabling this feature slows Excel Services performance but also reduces the disk space used.

9. **In the External Data section, configure the timeout for connections to external data sources and service account credentials to be used for accessing external data.**

The Connection Lifetime setting configures the number of sections that a connection to an external data source is kept open. If you disable this feature by configuring the setting as −1, the external data connections close at the end of each query. Other valid settings are 0 seconds to 24 days (2073600 seconds).

The Unattended Service Account settings determine what credentials are used for connecting to external data locations that require authentication.

10. Click OK.

Adding trusted file locations

Trusted file locations are locations that you designate as secure sources for workbooks for Excel Services. They can be SharePoint libraries, file shares, or non-SharePoint Web sites, and you can designate as many trusted file locations as you need to support your structure and the different level of trust. For example, you may allow user-defined functions from one trusted location but not another, and the ability to use external data and user-defined functions in a different trusted location. To add trusted file locations for Excel Services, follow these steps:

1. Open the administration page for your Excel Services Application.

2. Select Trusted file locations.

3. Click Add Trusted File Location in the top navigation bar.

4. Enter the address for your document library, file share, or Web site address in the Address field, as shown in Figure 9.8.

FIGURE 9.8

Entering the address for your trusted file location

5. Select whether the location is a SharePoint site, file share, or Web site address using the Location type radio buttons.

6. **Select whether you would like to trust child libraries or directories by checking the Children trusted box.** This setting can be very helpful if you don't want to granularly manage libraries; however, you need to be confident that the users with the site creation permissions will not create subsites that should not be considered trusted locations.

7. **Enter the appropriate session management settings in the Session Management section:**

   • **Session Timeout:** Values between –1 and 2073600 seconds (no timeout to 24 days). This is the maximum time that an Excel Calculation session can stay active as measured from the end of the request. If you enter a value of 0, the session stays active only for that particular request.

   • **Short Session Timeout:** Values between –1 and 2073600 seconds (no timeout to 24 days). This is the maximum time that an Excel Web Access session can stay open but inactive as measured from the start of the open request. If you enter a value of 0, the session stays active only for that particular request.

   • **Maximum Request Duration:** Values are –1 (no limit) and between 1 and 2073600 seconds (1 second to 24 days). This defines the maximum duration of a single request in a session.

8. Enter the appropriate workbook values in the Workbook Properties section:

   • **Maximum Workbook Size:** Values are 1 to 2000MB. This is the maximum size of the workbook that Excel Calculation Services can open.

   • **Maximum Chart Size:** Any positive integer is a valid value. This is the maximum size of the chart that Excel Calculation Services can open.

9. Enter the calculation behavior in the Calculation Behavior section.

   • **Volatile Function Cache Lifetime:** Valid values are –1 (calculated once per session) and 0 (function is always calculated) and 1 to 2073600 seconds (1 second to 24 days). These values define the maximum time in seconds that a manual or automatic calculation will be cached.

   • **Workbook Calculation Mode:** File, manual, automatic, or automatic except data tables. This setting defines the calculation mode of Excel Calculation Services and overrides the workbook settings unless you select File.

10. Enter the external data settings in the External Data section as shown in Figure 9.9. You will want to configure these settings according to the needs and trust levels of workbook authors. External data allows Excel to process data from a variety of sources, such as databases and ODBC sources, and therefore surfaces sources that many users wouldn't otherwise see. By limiting the ability to use external data defined in trusted data connection libraries and limiting the publishing of DCLs to trusted authors, you can manage external data risk while still allowing a wide range of functionality.

    • **Allow External Data:** Select none, trusted data connection libraries only, and trusted data connection libraries and embedded. Because external data could potentially be harmful, you can select what external data sources are allowed. If you limit the external data to trusted data connection libraries, the spreadsheet must be calling a data connection from a trusted location. The trusted data connection libraries and embedded setting allows external data from DCLs and from custom connection strings that are embedded in the spreadsheet.

    • **Warn on Refresh:** Select this option if you want to display a warning before refreshing the data from external locations.

    • **Stop When Refresh on Open Fails:** Selecting this option stops the open operation on an external file if the file contains a Refresh On Open data connection and the file cannot be refreshed when it is opening and the user does not have open rights to the file.

    • **External Data Cache Lifetime:** Valid values are –1 (never refresh after first query) and 0 to 2073600 seconds (0 seconds to 24 days). These values define the maximum time in seconds that the system can use cached manual or automatic external data query results.

- **Maximum Concurrent Queries Per Session:** Any positive integer is a valid value. This defines the maximum number of concurrent queries that can be executed during a single session.

Configuring the external data settings for your trusted data location

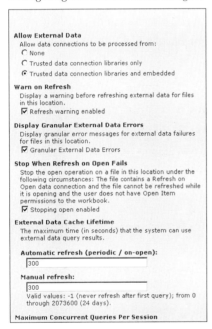

11. Select whether you would like to allow user-defined functions in the User-Defined Functions section.

12. Click OK.

Defining trusted data connection libraries

Data connection files that are stored in data connection libraries provide central access to data sources for users and applications that may not even realize that they are using the data connections. You can configure your Excel Services to use data connections that are stored in data connection libraries instead of data connections embedded in the file. If Excel Services will be opening files that rely on data connection files, you will need to add the location(s) of the data connection library to the trusted data connection library list so that Excel Services can use the data connection.

If you limit the access to external data to only connections in DCLs in workbooks in trusted locations, you need to define the trusted locations that are viable and trusted for your workbook authors to use.

To add a trusted data connection library, follow these steps:

1. Open the administration page for your Excel Services Application.
2. Select Trusted data connection libraries.
3. Select Add Trusted Data Connection Library in the top navigation bar.
4. Enter the address for your data connection library in the Address field, as shown in Figure 9.10.

FIGURE 9.10

Entering the address for your trusted data connection library

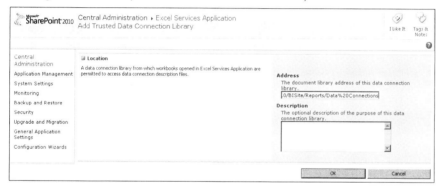

5. Click OK.

Configuring trusted data providers

External databases that are explicitly trusted can be configured as trusted data provided for Excel Services. Excel Services processes data from a data connection if the data is from a trusted provider. This allows you to further control the external data sources that can be used in your Excel Services environment.

1. Open the administration page for your Excel Services Application.
2. Select Trusted data providers.
3. Click Add Trusted Data Provider in the top navigation bar.
4. Add the name for the driver in the Provider ID field, as shown in Figure 9.11.

FIGURE 9.11

Entering a trusted data provider ID

5. Select whether you provider is OLE DB, ODBC, or ODBC DSN in the Provider Type section.

6. Enter a description for your provider.

7. Click OK.

Adding user-defined function assemblies

User-Defined Functions (UDFs) are a way to extend the Excel capabilities to support calculations or data access that is not built into Excel. With UDFs, you can:

- Create custom mathematical functions
- Access data from data sources that do not have Excel data connection support
- Make Web services calls

Because of the flexibility the UDF framework provides, the security ramifications of allowing UDFs must be considered. You should upload only UDF assemblies that have been created by a trusted source.

In addition to uploading the assemblies as outlined in this section, you need to enable workbooks stored in a trusted file location to call user-defined functions. This setting can be enabled for each trusted file location, so for further control of the security opening, you can have just one file location and not allow user-defined functions.

The UDF assembly is a DLL file that needs to be added to your Excel Services UDF library. To add a UDF file to Excel Services, follow these steps.

1. Open the administration page for your Excel Services Application.

2. Select User-defined function assemblies in the Excel Services Settings section.

3. Click Add User-Defined Function Assembly in the top navigation bar.

4. **Enter the path to the UDF in the Assembly field, as shown in Figure 9.12.** This can be a file in the Global Assembly Catalog, on a network server, or local to the SharePoint server.

FIGURE 9.12

Defining the location of your UDF assembly

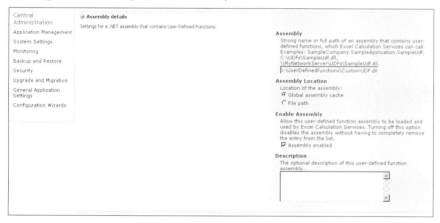

5. In the Assembly Location section, select whether the assembly is stored in a file location or in the Global Assembly Cache.

Tip

The assembly will need to live on each Web front-end server in the farm that is running Excel Services. Therefore, it either needs to be replicated on the file system or added to the GAC of each server. Wrap the assembly into a feature or solution using Visual Studio 2010 to easily manage GAC deployment across multiple servers. ■

6. **Select Assembly enabled if you want the assembly to be available for use.** If you want to add a disabled assembly or disable a current assembly without deleting it, you can deselect the Assembly enabled check box and the assembly remains but is not available for use.

7. **Enter an assembly description so that administrators can identify the purpose of your assembly.**

8. Click OK.

After you have added your UDF, confirm that workbooks that will call the UDF are stored in a trusted file location that allows user-defined functions.

Cross-Reference

For information about how to add trusted file locations, see the "Adding trusted file locations" section of this chapter. ■

Summary

You can define and add features that customize your SharePoint environment by adding action menus, calling events and workflows, instantiating lists, and performing other activities to extend the functionality of your SharePoint environment. You can also extend SharePoint by configuring Excel Services to enable the reuse and publishing of your Excel workbooks.

This chapter delved into the structure and possible operations enabled by feature definitions and feature elements. It also discussed how to develop, install, and activate those features.

Finally, we covered how to configure your SharePoint server to use Excel Services to support publishing workbooks and the supporting data connections.

Securing Office Server

This chapter discusses how to secure Office Server. We have all seen the high-profile cases in the press when hackers steal digital information. Typically, the stories have been about personal information theft that involves credit card and social security numbers. When you consider the type of information that is stored in a collaborative content management environment like SharePoint, unauthorized access could be devastating to an organization.

This chapter provides an overview of the types of threats to be aware of and the available countermeasures to those threats. It is organized into three sections that focus on securing servers, clients, and content.

Securing Servers and Farms

It would be remiss to begin a chapter on securing SharePoint without discussing a critical security component that is often overlooked and taken for granted — the password. As is the case with security in the physical world, most crimes are committed against persons and organizations by people we know. When administration, user, and default passwords stay the same for too long, inevitably someone with that knowledge and a grudge is going to do harm. Having a strict policy of changing passwords on a regular basis and making those passwords strong is still one of the best defenses we have against a potential security breach.

A password weakness can exist at either the Active Directory level or the local machine level, and both can be exploited by malware/viruses or an insider. Additionally, the presence of the single sign-on feature, which is also discussed in this chapter, means a compromise of one password may lead to a compromise of data on other systems.

Note

SharePoint Foundation Services has an Active Directory Mode. This feature is activated when site administrators create new SharePoint FoundationSharePoint accounts and automatically create corresponding accounts in Active Directory. When using this feature, you should consider creating security policies with regard to which users can be site administrators and when new accounts can be created in Active Directory from a SharePoint FoundationSharePoint site. ■

Be sure to enforce a strict password policy for all users on your domain. Your policy should include both complexity requirements as well as password expiration.

You may want to consider implementing a policy to periodically test passwords across the enterprise. There are great tools for this such as THC Hydra, LOphtCrack, and others that can check for blank and simple passwords.

Although this is an important topic, we have to limit the scope of this chapter to focus on configuring SharePoint security, but remember that your system is only as secure as its weakest link.

Internet/extranet portals and sites

Internet and extranet portals and sites are probably the most exposed to security threats by nature of their accessibility on the Internet. This section discusses the following areas:

- Securing your server farm against risks present in an anonymous access environment
- How to secure server-to-server communications when publishing content between internal and external servers and server farms

Securing servers in an anonymous access environment

When anonymous access is enabled on a Web site, anonymous users are able to browse the site, including lists, libraries, folders within lists and libraries, list items, or documents that inherit their permissions from the site. Once anonymous access has been enabled by the server administrator, it allows members of the site's Owners group to grant anonymous access to lists and libraries on a site or to block anonymous access on a site. A word of caution is appropriate with regard to granting anonymous access because it is inherently less secure. Any time you expose a site to unauthenticated users there are more chances for hackers to try to access or deny service to your site.

Granting anonymous access is not recommended in an intranet environment because there are limitations, security risks, and other issues of concern. A better way to grant broad access to content in an intranet is via the Authenticated Users group. When you add this group for access, all authenticated users can access the site, and their actions can be traced back to who was logged in.

Note

Anonymous users are unable to open sites for editing in Microsoft Office SharePoint Designer 2010, and they are not able to view the site or document libraries in My Network Places. ■

Enable anonymous access using central administration

To enable anonymous access using the central administration utility, follow these steps:

1. From the server desktop, click Start ⇨ Programs ⇨ Administrative Tools ⇨ SharePoint 2010 Central Administration.

2. In Central Administration, click Security on the Quick Launch bar.

3. Under General Security, click Authentication providers.

4. Click the zone for which you would like to enable anonymous access.

Note

If you don't see the site/zone you are looking for, you may need to click the Web Application selector and choose the appropriate Web application. ■

5. From the Edit Authentication page, as shown in Figure 10.1, select the check box to enable Anonymous Access and then click Save.

FIGURE 10.1

Edit Authentication page

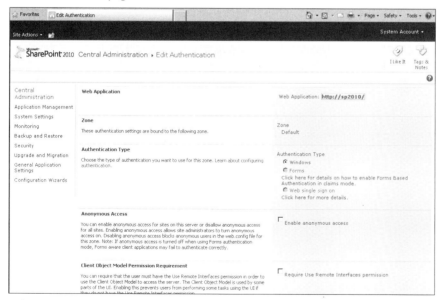

To enable Anonymous Access in the site:

1. From the home page of the SharePoint site to grant the anonymous access, click Site Actions ⇨ Site Permissions.

2. Click on the Anonymous Access button on the Ribbon, as shown in Figure 10.2. The Anonymous Access dialog box appears, as shown in Figure 10.3.

FIGURE 10.2

Anonymous Access under User Permissions

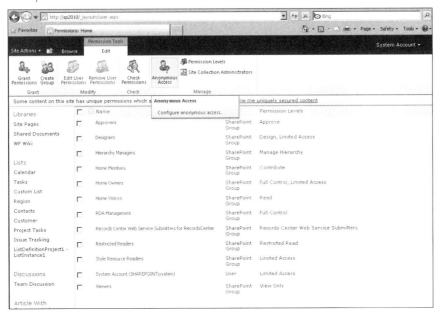

Note

If you don't see the Anonymous Access button on the Ribbon, you may not have enabled it in the Central Administration section. You must enable the option there, not only in IIS. ∎

The Anonymous Access Settings dialog box allows you to specify what parts of your Web site (if any) anonymous users can access. If you select Entire Web site, anonymous users can view all pages in your Web site and view all lists and items which inherit permissions from the Web site. If you select Lists and libraries, anonymous users can view and change items only for those lists and libraries that have enabled permissions for anonymous users.

Note

If you choose Lists and libraries from the dialog box in Figure 10.3, the site must use unique permissions to be accessed. In other words, lists and libraries that have inherited permissions from a site cannot be viewed by anonymous users. ∎

FIGURE 10.3

Anonymous Access dialog box

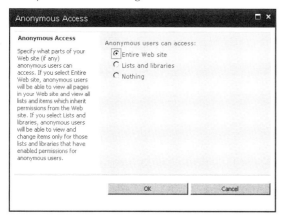

Securing server-to-server communications during content publishing

One of the new scenarios available with SharePoint 2010 is the ability to use features that were previously available only with Microsoft's Content Management Server to create content and then have it published via workflow to an internet or extranet site. Publishing content from one server to another exposes the data to security threats.

Some common threats are

- **Network Eavesdropping:** Using network monitoring software, an attacker could intercept data moving from the Web server to the application server and from the application server to other systems and databases.

- **Unauthorized Access:** Via ports used by SharePoint, an attacker could try to communicate directly with the server.

Most servers are hosted behind a firewall, and we consider a firewall a minimum security requirement. The lines between internet and extranet are easier to cross with a technology like SharePoint, and properly configuring security in these environments is critical.

I suggest the following countermeasures:

- **Network Eavesdropping:** A network attacker may place a packet-sniffing tool on the network to capture your network traffic. Countermeasures to prevent this type of attack can include:

  - **Using secure authentication, such as NTLM-based Windows authentication.** Windows authentication does not send packets over the network.

- **Encrypting SQL Server authentication credentials.** SQL Server credentials can be encrypted automatically by installing a server certificate on the database server.

- **Using SSL to encrypt browser-to-server communications and IPSec to encrypt all IP traffic that flows between two servers.**

- **Unauthorized Access:** Common unauthorized access attacks may include:

  - Port scanning to detect listening services

  - Banner-grabbing that may give away services available on the server as well as the version of software running

  - Password attacks against a default account

Countermeasures to prevent unauthorized access attacks may include:

- Solid firewall policies that will block traffic from any port with exceptions for those your application uses

- IP filtering and IPSec policies that prevent unauthorized hosts from establishing connections

- Disabling any services that are not being used reduces that threat surface for attacks

Encrypting SPS SharePoint application connection strings

The usual location of connection strings is in your web.config or machine.config files. This allows a developer to access the connection strings and application settings easily through the ConfigurationManager in ASP.NET 4.0, which could lead to a security risk if these connection strings are not encrypted.

You are not limited to a specific type of encryption in SharePoint 2010, and you are able to create your own encryption providers. ASP.NET 4.0 has two technologies available for you to use, however: Windows Data Protection API (DPAPI) or RSA. DPAPI uses the SPS SharePoint server machine key to encrypt and decrypt your data, while RSA lets you use public keys.

The easiest way to encrypt your connection strings is using the DPAPI encryption through the command line. Because the key is the server machine key, any intruder to the machine could gain access to this key and use it to decrypt your connection strings. Also, the encrypted data would be usable only on the machine it was encrypted on, with the correct machine key.

RSA encryption allows machine-level and user-level containers for key storage. This enables you to have some control over user access to sensitive information. For example, in a shared hosting environment, you would want to implement RSA encryption on a user level, allowing users to access only their own encrypted connection string data.

Configuring antivirus settings

Because documents don't always end up on a SharePoint site directly from a virus-protected client machine, it is important to configure virus protection on your SharePoint servers. The server-based virus protection products protect the server from viruses, worms, and Trojan horses in all of the major file types.

1. Install the virus software on every Web front-end server in your farm.

2. From the server desktop, click Start ⇨ Programs ⇨ Administrative Tools ⇨ SharePoint 2010 Central Administration.

3. In Central Administration, click Security on the Quick Launch bar.

4. Under General Security, click Manage antivirus settings.

5. From the Antivirus page, shown in Figure 10.4, in the Antivirus Settings section, choose from the following options:

   - Scan documents on upload

   - Scan documents on download

   - Allow users to download infected documents

   - Attempt to clean infected documents

FIGURE 10.4

Antivirus settings

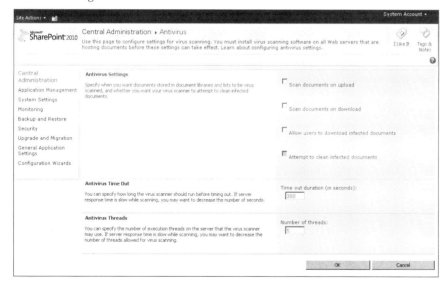

6. Go to the Antivirus Time Out section, and in the Time out duration (in seconds) text box type a value for how long to wait for the virus scanner to time out.

7. Go to the Antivirus Threads section, and in the Number of threads text box enter a value for the number of threads that the virus scanner can use.

Managing blocked file types

Another way to help secure all of your servers is to limit the types of files that can be stored on the machines. By eliminating EXE files and VBA files, for example, you can reduce the threat of worms and Trojan horses on the servers and network. Table 10.1 shows a list of the file types that are blocked by default and their extensions.

TABLE 10.1

File Types Blocked By Default

File Extension	File Type	File Extension	File Type
.ade	Microsoft Access project extension	lts	Internet Document Set file
.adp	Microsoft Access project	.jse	JScript Encoded script file
.app	Application file	.ksh	Korn Shell script file
.asa	ASP declarations file	.lnk	Shortcut
.ashx	ASP.NET Web handler file. Web handlers are software modules that handle raw HTTP requests received by ASP.NET.	.mad	Shortcut
.asmx	ASP.NET Web Services source file	.maf	Shortcut
.asp	Active Server Pages	.mag	Shortcut
.bas	Microsoft Visual Basic class module	.mam	Shortcut
.bat	Batch file	.maq	Shortcut
.cdx	Compound index	.mar	Shortcut
.cer	Certificate file	.mas	Microsoft Access stored procedure
.chm	Compiled HTML Help file	.mat	Shortcut
.class	Java class file	.mau	Shortcut
.cmd	Microsoft Windows NT command script	.mav	Shortcut
.com	Microsoft MS-DOS program	.maw	Shortcut
.config	Configuration file	.mda	Microsoft Access add-in program
.cpl	Control Panel extension	.mdb	Microsoft Access program
.crt	Security certificate	.mde	Microsoft Access MDE database
.csh	Script file	.mdt	Microsoft Access data file
.dll	Windows dynamic-link library	.mdw	Microsoft Access workgroup

File Extension	File Type	File Extension	File Type
.exe	Program	.mdz	Microsoft Access wizard program
.fxp	Microsoft Visual FoxPro compiled program	.msc	Microsoft Common Console document
.hlp	Help file	.msh	Microsoft Agent script helper
.hta	HTML program	.msh1	Microsoft Agent script helper
.htr	Script file	.msh1xml	Microsoft Agent script helper
.htw	HTML document	.vb	Microsoft Visual Basic Scripting Edition file
.ida	Internet Information Services file	.vbe	VBScript Encoded Script file
.idc	Internet database connector file	.vbs	VBScript file
.idq	Internet data query file	.ws	Windows Script file
.ins	Internet Naming Service	.wsc	Windows Script Component
.isp	Internet Communication settings	.wsf	Windows Script file
		.wsh	Windows Script Host Settings File

To change blocked file types, follow these steps:

1. From the Security page in Central Administration, click Define blocked file types from the General Security section.
2. From the Blocked Files Types page, type the file extensions that you want to block on separate lines in the text box, as shown in Figure 10.5.
3. To remove blocked file extensions, delete the extension in the text box.
4. Click OK.

Architect your administrator security

There are many levels of administrator security permissions in SPS. By defining your administrator roles before the installation, you establish a strategy for managing your portal throughout its deployment.

The administrative levels that you need to consider are

- **Shared services administrators:** These administrators are responsible for configuring and maintaining the shared services. It is possible to give permissions to particular items in shared services, like personalization features such as profiles and audiences, but that granularity should be necessary only in the most distributed environments. This level of administration is not necessary for SharePoint Foundation installations.

- **Central admin:** Central administration permissions are specific to the SharePoint farm. There are both operations and application administrative tasks like creating and extending Web applications that your administrators with central admin permissions will perform.

- **Site owners:** Site owners are allowed to configure the overall site settings for the site, such as content types and navigation.

It is recommended that you configure security groups that grant permissions to each of the administrative levels described above.

Blocked file types

Securing Client Communications

Having a secure network and server is not enough to ensure the security of your data. With users working in coffee shops, airports, and hotels, you also need to be sure that their data is encrypted on its way from their clients to the servers in your datacenter. After you have made sure that the packets going from the client to the server are secure, you then need to turn our attention to the authentication mechanism being used to determine who is at the other end of the connection as well as what they will be able to do once connected. Some authentication methods are more secure, while others will perform better across a network. Business and environmental factors must be assessed before selecting the best method for an organization.

In this section we review the various authentication methods available and provide suggestions and guidance to help you select the best way to communicate with the clients in your environment. We wrap the section up with the steps need to successfully configure SSL.

Authentication

A client connecting to SPS or SharePoint Foundation can take the form of a Windows PC saving a document from Word or the same PC uploading a document to a SharePoint Foundation site via a browser. A client may also be a hand-held device accessing SPS via a mobile URL or a Mac PowerBook accessing a site page via a Mac browser. There are many client options for access to SPS and SharePoint Foundation, but only a limited number of supported authentication methods.

The default method is Windows Authentication, but SPS 2010 supports multiple authentication methods as shown in Table 10.2.

TABLE 10.2

Authentication Methods

Authentication Method	Description	Examples
Windows	The standard Windows authentication method that is selected by default.	Anonymous, Basic, Digest, Certificates, Kerberos, NTLM (Windows)
ASP.NET forms	SPS 2010 can support non-Windows-based systems via integration with ASP.NET forms authentication. This authentication allows SPS 2010 to interact with systems where the Membership Provider interface has been implemented.	Lightweight Directory Access Protocol (LDAP), SQL Server or other database systems, any other ASP.NET forms authentication solutions
Web Single Sign-On (SSO)	SPS 2010 supports the storage and mapping of credentials including account names and passwords. SSO provides a way for users to authenticate one time while accessing data from other applications and systems.	Active Directory Federation Services (ADFS), Additional Identity Management Systems

Windows Authentication versus Kerberos

Although the default/recommended authentication method is stated in the product as "Windows Authentication," there are some compelling reasons to choose Kerberos instead. Windows or NTLM is a more familiar challenge-response authentication mechanism and is easier to develop against as well as configure and administrate.

Kerberos is a ticket-based authentication method that authenticates both the client to the server and the server to the client. Kerberos is more secure and has the ability to increase performance but is also a challenge to set up properly.

The reason Kerberos performs better is that it caches information about the client after the client authenticates. NTLM issues its challenge and response for each request, which places additional demands on the servers and network. This issue starts to have more impact in large farm environments.

Kerberos also can delegate the client's credentials from front-end to back-end servers. If you have ever had to log in multiple times when accessing a SharePoint server that is getting data from another server, then you have experienced the pain of *not* having Kerberos delegation.

Basically, Kerberos is a better authentication option, and large environments that have the expertise available should seriously consider selecting it instead of NTLM. See the Knowledge Base article located at http://support.microsoft.com/?kbid=832769 for information on configuring Kerberos authentication.

Forms-based authentication

Another of the exciting features of SPS is forms-based authentication. This is a pluggable feature based on ASP.NET 4.0 that allows your users to authenticate without an NT Login prompt. Instead, you could build a customized signup/login process to obtain information about your users. Forms authentication uses encrypted cookies and authentication tickets.

Scenarios for successful forms-based authentication implementation are broad, but would include

- Allowing anonymous and unauthenticated users access to unrestricted, public areas of your sites — an ecommerce store, for example

- Allowing users to fill out a custom form to create a user profile, where they could then log in and access restricted areas of your site — to view previous orders, for example, or to add new items to the catalog if the user had the appropriate role.

The following steps detail how to configure forms-based authentication:

1. **Open a Visual Studio Command Prompt and run aspnet_regsql**. Doing this opens the ASP.NET SQL Server Setup Wizard, as shown in Figure 10.6.

2. **Select Configure SQL Server for application services and click Next**. Add your connection information, as shown in Figure 10.7, and click Next.

3. **Confirm your settings summary and click Next again to create the database. Click Finish.**

FIGURE 10.6

ASP.NET SQL Server Setup Wizard

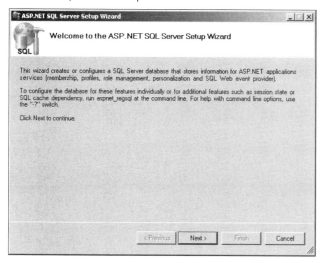

FIGURE 10.7

ASP.NET SQL Server connection

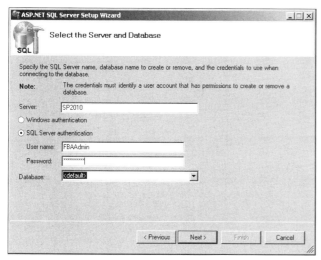

4. **The next step is editing your web.config files — the one in your SharePoint virtual directory folder and also the web.config for SharePoint Central Administration.** You need to add the `<connectionStrings>` node to both of these files, with the credentials you set up for the database in the previous step.

At the bottom directly below the `</appsettings>` node in each web.config file, add the `<connectionStrings>` node:

```
<connectionStrings>
        <remove name="LocalSqlServer" />
        <add name="LocalSqlServer" connectionString="Server=servern
    ame;Database=aspnetdb;uid=username;pwd=pass;"
    providerName="System.Data.SqlClient" />
</connectionStrings>
```

Now add a role and a user to the aspnetdb with which you can log into your site. Open Visual Studio and create a new Web site by following these steps:

1. **Open Microsoft Visual Studio 2010 and choose File ⇨ New ⇨ Web Site.** You can keep the default settings in place. Open the `web.config` created and add your `<connectionStrings>` node from the previous step. Change the `<authentication mode>` (to be consistent with formatting of nodes, ex. `<connectionStrings>`?) node attribute to Forms:

   ```
   <authentication mode="Forms" />
   ```

   Save the file and build your project.

2. **From the Website menu, select ASP.NET Configuration to open the ASP.Net Web Site Administration Tool (Configuration Manager). Click the Security tab.** If Roles are not enabled, click Enable Roles, as shown in Figure 10.8.

3. **When roles are enabled, click Create or Manage roles.** You can see the Create New Role screen, shown in Figure 10.9, and then you can add your new role.

FIGURE 10.8

ASP.Net Web Site Administration Tool

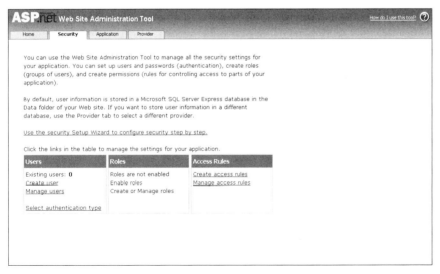

336

4. **Click Back to return to the Security tab.** Click Create User and fill out the fields, as shown in Figure 10.10.

FIGURE 10.9

ASP.Net Web Site Administration — Create New Role

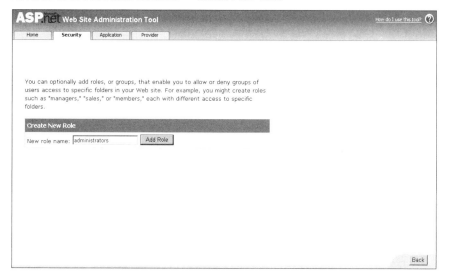

FIGURE 10.10

ASP.Net Web Site Administration — Create User

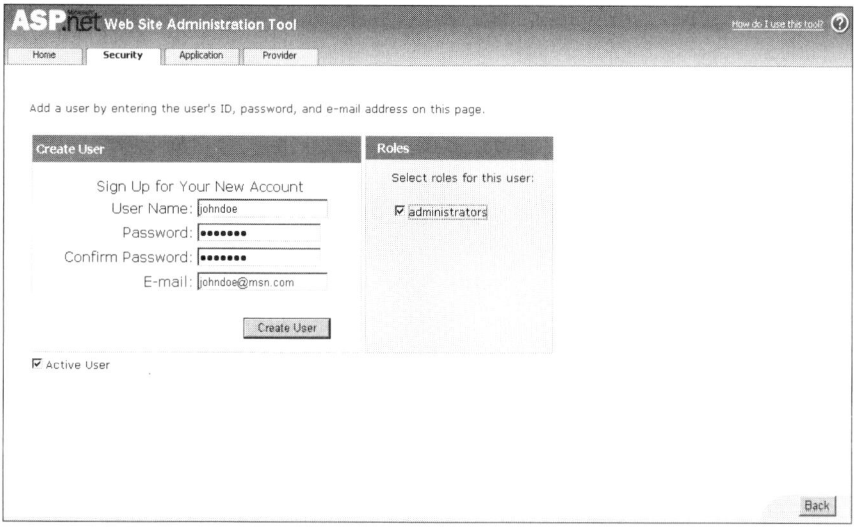

5. **Select the role you created and ensure that the Active User box is selected.** Click Create User. The Security tab should now show one user and one role created, as shown in Figure 10.11.

6. **Choose Central Administration ➪ Application Management ➪ Manage Web Applications**.

FIGURE 10.11

ASP.Net Web Site Administration — Security

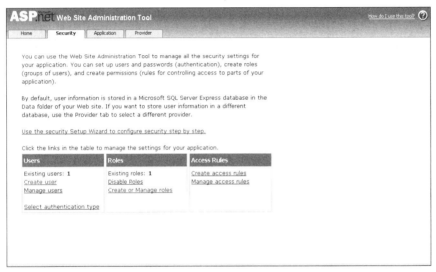

7. **Click the New button on the Ribbon.** The New Web Application screen appears, as shown in Figure 10.12. Fill out the settings as you normally would.

FIGURE 10.12

Create New Web Application screen

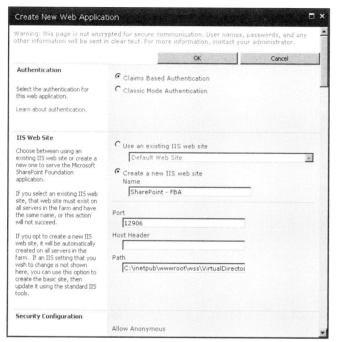

8. **Click on Create Site Collection from the Application Created confirmation dialog, the Create Site Collection dialog appears, as shown in Figure 10.13..** Leave the creation location as root and enter the username of the Primary Site Collection Administrator and Secondary Site Collection Administrator. This will change later.

FIGURE 10.13

Create Site Collection

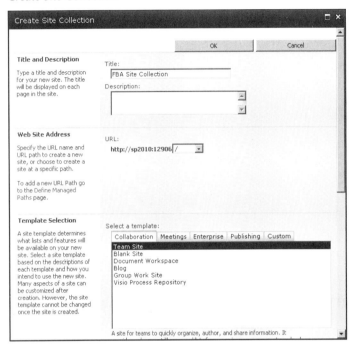

9. **The last step to take is adding the user you created as the Site Collection Administrator in Central Administration.** Navigate to Application Management ➪ Change site collection administrators. Replace the site collection administrator name with the user you created and press Ctrl+K to check that username, as shown in Figure 10.14.

10. Open a new browser and navigate to the root of the site collection you created. A Sign In page appears, as shown in Figure 10.15. Select the Forms Authentication option. Enter your user credentials you created with Visual Studio on the next screen as shown in Figure 10.16.

FIGURE 10.14

Site Collection Administrators page

FIGURE 10.15

Sign In page — Authentication Selection

FIGURE 10.16

Sign In page

Web Single Sign-On using the Secure Store Service

The Single Sign-On (SSO) capabilities provided with SPS allow you to configure stored application passwords for individuals and groups. In SharePoint 2010, this is handled by the Secure Store Service (SSS). The SSS offers smooth, integrated access between applications without continual password prompts to irritate users. Additionally, SSS gives you the capability to provide application access to groups of users that you would not normally give individual access to without having to distribute the username and password information. You can embed application integration within SharePoint and provide seamless information access.

The following components of SPS can leverage SSO capabilities:

- Excel Services
- InfoPath Services
- Business Data Catalog
- Status Lists
- SharePoint Designer DataForm Web Part
- Custom Web Parts

To configure SSO using the Secure Store Service, follow these steps:

1. Launch SharePoint 2010 Central Administration from Start ⇨ Administrative Tools ⇨ SharePoint 2010 Central Administration.

2. Click the Application Management Quick Launch bar and select Manage Service Applications under the Service Applications section.

3. Scroll down and click on the Secure Store Service link to open the SSS Administration page.

4. Click the Generate Key button on the Ribbon, as shown in Figure 10.17. You need to generate a key before proceeding.

FIGURE 10.17

Generate New Key button

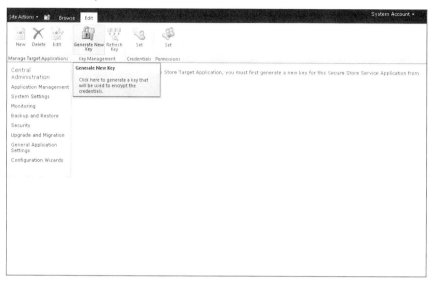

5. Enter a pass phrase in the Generate New Key dialog, as shown in Figure 10.18.

FIGURE 10.18

Generate New Key dialog box

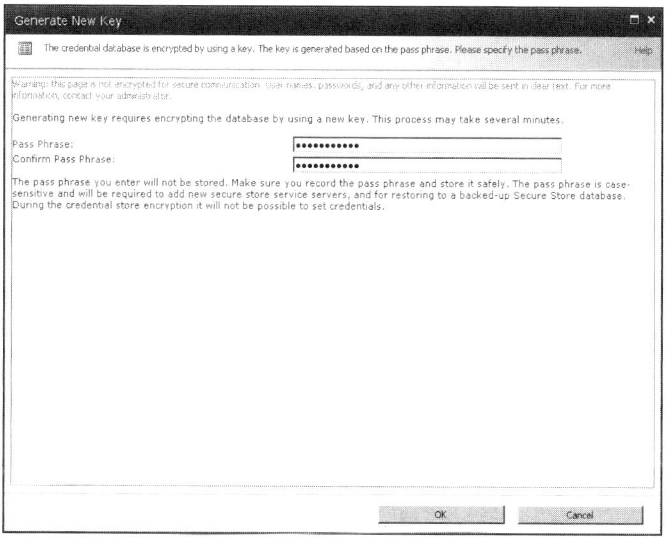

6. Click New on the Ribbon to create a new target application.

7. **Enter your target application details.** An example is shown in Figure 10.19. **Click Next.**

Tip

Select Group if you would like to allow all users to connect with the credentials stored in SSS for the target application. If you would like individual users to have individual credential mappings to the target application, select Individual. ■

FIGURE 10.19

Target application settings

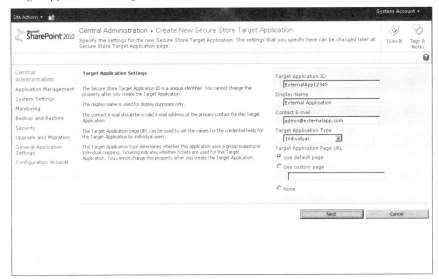

8. Enter the target application fields and field types as shown in Figure 10.20. Click Next.

9. Enter accounts or users that are allowed to administer the target application settings, as shown in Figure 10.21. (This step is not to be confused with administrators of the target application.) This action grants rights to people to change the settings that you are entering now. Click OK.

10. The new target application appears in the main page list. Select the entry by selecting the check box to the left of the name.

11. With the target application selected, click the Set button in the Credentials section of the Ribbon.

FIGURE 10.20

Target application fields

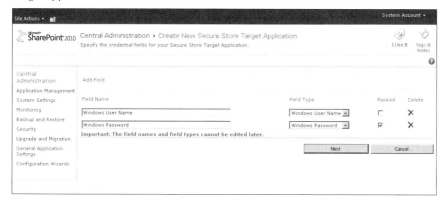

FIGURE 10.21

Target application administrators

12. Enter the account name and the credentials to use in the Set Credentials page, as shown in Figure 10.22.

13. Click OK.

Note

These credentials fade into thin air. There is no way to manage them once they are set. Entering another mapping for a given account will overwrite any existing credentials for that account for the same target application. ∎

FIGURE 10.22

Target application credential mapping

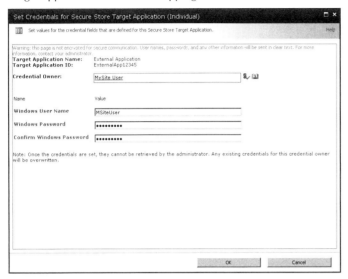

Implementing SSL

I highly recommend implementing Secure Sockets Layer (SSL) to secure the communications between your client and server computers. If you don't use SSL, passwords and other sensitive data are at risk as they are sent from the client to the server because the data packets can be picked up by a network-sniffing type of device.

Configuring SSL

The following is a simple example that would apply for some environments. The intent is for you to be able to apply and substitute the steps for your unique situation. Configuring SSL is generally composed of the following steps:

- Creating a server certificate using the certificate wizard. You can also obtain a certificate from a certification authority or from any publicly trusted authority.

- Assigning an existing certificate.

- Creating alternate access mappings in Central Administration.

Creating a new certificate

To create a new certificate, follow these steps:

1. **Open IIS and select the server from the left-hand tree-view. Double-click on the Server Certificates in the main area as shown in Figure 10.23.**

FIGURE 10.23

IIS server certificates

2. **Click Create Certificate Request from the right-hand Action pane.** The Request Certificate Request wizard opens.

3. **Enter the Distinguished Name Properties, as shown in Figure 10.24.** Enter a common name for your site (this is the name with which users will access the site, and so it needs to be valid). Enter your Organization name and Organizational unit. Enter the geographical information and click Next.

FIGURE 10.24

Certificate distinguished properties

Request Certificate	? X

Distinguished Name Properties

Specify the required information for the certificate. State/province and City/locality must be specified as official names and they cannot contain abbreviations.

Common name:

Organization:

Organizational unit:

City/locality:

State/province:

Country/region: US

Previous	Next	Finish	Cancel

5. Select the Cryptographic Provider and Bit Length on next screen and click Next.

6. Select an output location and filename for your certificate and click Finish.

7. Use the contents of the outputted certificate request file to process a certificate request either with a local certificate authority (if you are accessing this site only on the local network) or with a third-party certificate issuer that processes certificates for Web servers (if you are going to access this site via the Internet).

8. After you have processed your certificate request you can complete the request process. (If this is a third-party certificate, follow the instructions provided by the issuer because you may need to install root certificates.)

9. Open IIS and select the server from the left-hand tree-view. Double-click on the Server Certificates in the main area as shown in Figure 10.23.

10. Select Complete Certificate Request from the right-hand Action pane.

11. Browse to the file location of your processed certificate request, as shown in Figure 10.25, select the file, provide a friendly name, and click OK.

FIGURE 10.25

Complete a certificate request

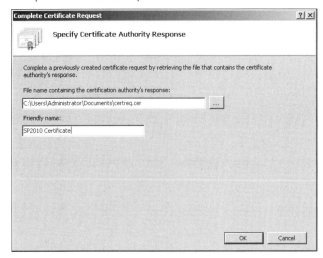

Assigning an existing certificate

To assign an existing certificate, follow these steps:

1. Right-click your Web site in IIS and choose Edit Bindings.

2. Click Add. The Add Site Binding dialog box appears as shown in Figure 10.26.

FIGURE 10.26

Add site binding

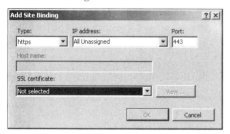

3. Select https, enter a port (443 is the default port number), and select the SSL certificate. Then click OK.

4. Close the Edit Bindings dialog.

5. From the main IIS area, double-click on SSL Settings. The SSL settings appear, as shown in Figure 10.27.

6. Select the Require SSL check box to enable the Require radio button. Select Require once enabled.

7. Click Apply from the right-hand Actions pane.

Creating alternate access mappings

After you have SSL-enabled your IIS site, you need to add an alternate access mapping so that the site can be accessed via https.

1. Go to Applications Management on the Central Administration site and click Configure alternate access mappings under the Web Applications section.

2. From the drop-down menu, select the site to which you need to add the new alternate access mapping.

3. After the proper collection is selected, click Edit Public URLs.

4. Enter the new URL in the appropriate zone:

   - Internal — Use Intranet

   - External — Use Internet or Extranet as appropriate

   Click Save to complete the process.

FIGURE 10.27

SSL settings

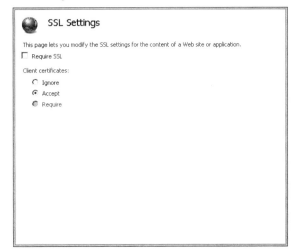

Securing Content

Sites that are grouped together so that the subsites can inherit the site groups from the parent sites lessen the time spent on security administration by taking advantage of security inheritance, a feature that is native to SharePoint. If you can manage the membership of the site group on one site and then use those site groups on multiple sites, the membership is more likely to be maintained, accurately and consistently, than if you are maintaining the groups in multiple sites.

You can use site security groups across a site collection to ease administration. These are the visitors, members, and owner groups SharePoint creates, or any custom groups that you define for the site collection. If a portion of your site has unique security requirements, it is a good candidate for breaking inheritance and changing the permission given to your SharePoint groups, removing one or more entirely from the site or creating and managing new/separate groups.

The following scenarios are examples of how an organization's business needs will translate into security settings and how they are applied to SharePoint sites and features.

Team collaboration

Many organizations deploy SharePoint based on its collaboration merits alone. In a collaborative environment, it is important to determine the correct level of access for users to ensure safe collaboration without breaking some of the valuable features that support the synergistic nature of team collaboration.

SharePoint collaboration sites, or Team Sites, are generally effective for teams of 50 people or smaller. Managing security for a small set of users on an individual basis should not be too daunting;

however, you may still need to allow different levels of access and manage users in groups. For example, you may have a team of engineers that require the ability to create, edit, and delete content. For the engineers, you may want to add them individually to the site members group. For executives, you may want to add an NT security group that already includes the executive team in the active directory to the site visitors group. Now you are managing individual users in a SharePoint group and using an active directory security group to manage visitor site access.

Securing anonymous content

If your organization requires publishing content to anonymous users on the Internet, you may want to have areas on the site that are available only to logged in or authenticated users. While anonymous users will see content published for external viewing, managing and assigning tasks and publishing of content can and should be limited to authenticated users.

Note

If a content manager accidentally links to secured content, anonymous users will be prompted to login. As a best practice, test your Internet-facing site with an anonymous test user. ■

Often companies will have a simple ASP.NET or HTML page as the first page accessed by anonymous users on a public Internet site. SharePoint pages have to load quite a bit of code when first accessed and they make requests to the database for dynamic content, which can also take longer to render. Using a simple page as the first page accessed allows for a fast initial load, and that page can point users to areas that require a login or that then take advantage of SharePoint lists and other functionality.

Enterprise portal/Intranet security

Most organizations' portal taxonomies are based on their departmental structure. Users accessing the portal to perform tasks will require rights related o the department they work in or that are mapped to tasks they are performing. For example, in Human Resources, most content will be read-only content; however, SharePoint lists and workflow can be used to manage vacation requests, benefit change requests, and other HR-related tasks.

Turning site features on and off

One way to limit and control activities on a site is to turn on only the site features that are relevant to your application. In the same way that limiting ports reduces the threat area on your server, reducing the number of available features can have a similar effect from a security perspective.

Based on the site template that you choose, SharePoint turns on the site features to support the template. You can change the site features after the site is created if you need additional features. To activate or deactivate site features, perform the following steps:

1. From the Site Actions menu in the top-left corner, choose Site Settings.
2. Click Site features from the Site Administration section.
3. Select Activate for any features that you want to activate or deactivate for features you want to disable.

Security groups

During site creation, the groups in Table 10.3 are created by default. During subsite creation, your sites inherit the same groups and their associated permissions.

TABLE 10.3

Default Security Groups

Group Name	Group Description
Approvers	Members of this group can edit and approve pages, list items, and documents.
Designers	Members of this group can edit lists, document libraries, and pages in the site. Designers can create master pages and page layouts in the Master Page Gallery and can change the behavior and appearance of each site in the site collection by using master pages and CSS files.
Site Members	Use this group to give people contribute permissions to the SharePoint site: Test Site.
Hierarchy Managers	Members of this group can create sites, lists, list items, and documents.
NT AUTHORITY\authenti-cated users	All users in the Active Directory are members of the authenticated users group by default. Therefore anyone who has an account on the domain is considered an authenticated user.
Quick Deploy Users	Members of this group can schedule Quick Deploy jobs.
Restricted Readers	Members of this group can view pages and documents but cannot view historical versions or review user rights information.
Style Resource Readers	Members of this group are given read permission to the Master Page Gallery and the restricted read permission to the Style Library. By default, all authenticated users are members of this group. To further secure this site, you can remove all authenticated users from this group or add users to this group.
Site Owners	Use this group to give people full control permissions to the SharePoint site: Test Site.
Site Visitors	Use this group to give people read permissions to the SharePoint site: Test Site.
Viewers	Members of this group can view pages, list items, and documents. If the document has a server rendering available, they can view the document using only the server rendering.

You may want to create a new group, manage it separately, and assign it permissions. To do this, you would break inheritance when you create the subsite. You can break inheritance during site creation or after the site has been created. If you break it during site creation, the groups from the parent site will not be added to your subsite.

Note

New groups are created during subsite creation with unique permissions. Those new groups will be added to the list of site collection SharePoint groups. ■

Creating a site with unique permissions

1. From the home page of your site where the subsite will reside, click Site Actions.

2. Click New Site.

3. Select a template, enter a unique title, and assign your site a unique URL in the Web Site Address section, as shown in Figure 10.28

FIGURE 10.28

Create SharePoint site

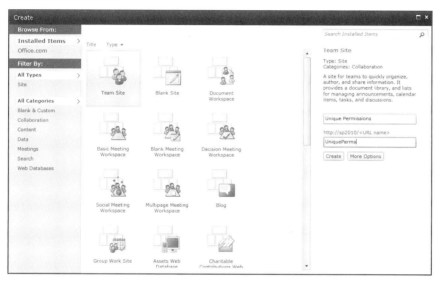

4. Click More Options.

5. Scroll down to the Permissions section and select Use unique permissions, as shown in Figure 10.29.

6. Click Create.

7. On the Set Up Groups for this Site page, you can choose an existing group to manage existing permissions or create new ones; in this example, you can create new ones. In the Visitors to this Site section, click the Create a new group radio button.

    SharePoint automatically suggests group names. Your screen should be similar to Figure 10.30.

8. Click OK.

Tip

By clicking the Add All Authenticated Users button in the "visitors to this site" section, you can give all users in your organization read access to the content stored in this site. ∎

FIGURE 10.29

Create SharePoint site — More Options

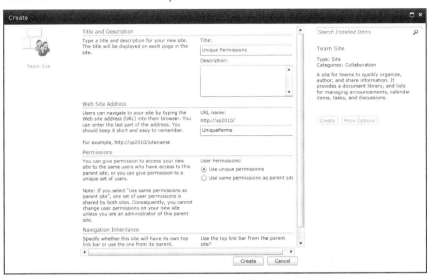

You have now created a site that has unique permissions, and security can be managed separately from your site collection.

Breaking inheritance for an existing site

If you already have a site created that requires permissions managed separately from its parent site, the following steps will break inheritance:

1. From the home page of your site, click Site Actions.

2. Choose Site Settings ⇨ Site Permissions.

3. On the Ribbon, click the Stop Inheriting Permissions button, as shown in Figure 10.31.

4. The dialog box warning you that you are about to create unique permissions for this site appears (see Figure 10.32). Changes made to the parent Web site permissions will no longer affect this Web site. Click OK.

Warning

Although inheritance has been broken, the security groups still exist from the parent site, so users added to or removed from these groups still have the corresponding access that they had previously been granted. ∎

FIGURE 10.30

Set Up Groups for this Site screen

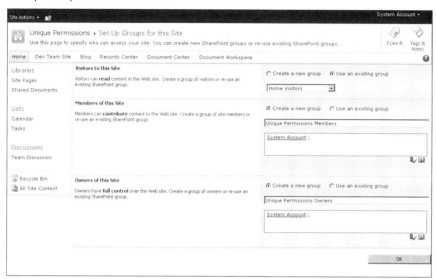

FIGURE 10.31

Stop Inheriting Permissions

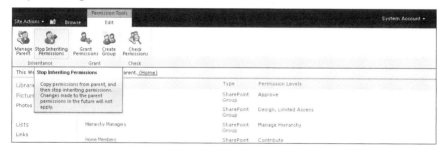

FIGURE 10.32

Breaking inheritance warning

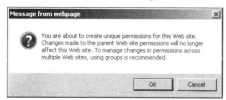

Creating a new permission level

To create a new permission level, follow these steps:

1. From the home page of your site, click Site Actions ➪ Site Permissions.

2. Select Permission Levels from the Ribbon in the Manage section.

3. From the Permissions Levels page, click Add a Permission Level.

4. In the Name and Description section, type View Web Analytics, **as shown in** Figure 10.33.

FIGURE 10.33

Add a Permission Level

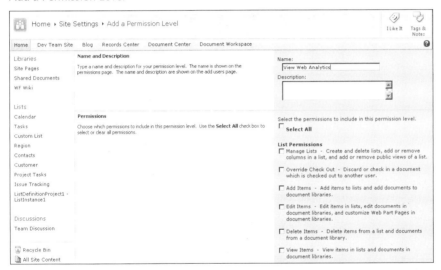

5. In the Permissions section under the Site Permissions heading, select the View Web Analytics Data check box.

Note

By selecting View Web Analytics Data, the other required permission levels are added automatically to be sure the user has proper access to the feature. In this example, View Pages and Open have automatically been checked. ■

6. **Click Create.** This completes a new permission level creation.

Creating a new SharePoint group

If you find you need different rights than those available by default, creating a new permission is a way to customize and fine-tune the security access.

1. From the home page of your site, click Site Actions ⇨ Site Settings.

2. Click Advanced permissions from the Users and Permissions section.

3. In the Permissions list toolbar, click New.

4. Select New Group to create the new group.

5. In the Name and About Me Description section, type Usage Reporters in the Name text box.

6. In the Owner section, add the appropriate user. By default, the user is the user who created the site.

Note
The owner can modify anything about the group. Only one user can be the owner. ■

7. In the Group Settings section, select who can view and edit the membership of the group.

8. In the Membership Requests section, select whether to allow requests to join or leave this group.

Warning
If you select Yes for the auto-accept option, all users requesting access to this group will automatically be added. ■

9. In the Give Group Permissions to this Site section, check the View Usage Reports permission level created earlier. Click Create.

10. To edit the group settings for this group, in the People and Groups list toolbar, click Settings and click Group Settings.

Configuring list and library item security

With SharePoint 2010, you can also set item-level security on the contents of your lists and libraries. Doing this allows you to combine items in libraries that make sense for navigation and views while still preserving the security of your items.

To configure security for a list or library item, follow these steps:

1. Click the down arrow on the item that you want to manage permissions and select Manage Permissions from the Edit menu, as shown in Figure 10.34.

2. Click the Stop Inheriting Permissions button from the Edit tab on the Ribbon to copy permissions from the parent list or library and to discontinue inheritance of permissions. Items inherit permissions from the parent list until this action has been taken.

3. Click the Grant Permissions button to add users with permissions to the item.

If you want to remove users, select the users in the permissions list that you want to remove and click on the Remove User Permissions button from the Edit tab on the Ribbon, as shown in Figure 10.35.

FIGURE 10.34

Managing permissions for a list item

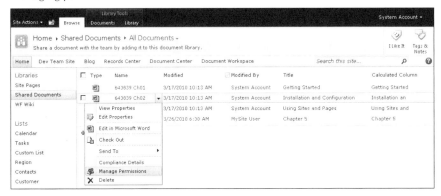

FIGURE 10.35

Removing permissions for users on a document

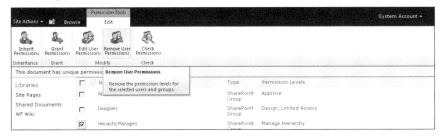

If you want to edit permissions for existing users, select the users in the permissions list that you want to remove and select Edit User Permissions from the Actions menu.

Summary

This chapter discussed securing SharePoint servers, communications between servers, securing clients, and finally the content that lives on your SharePoint servers. It also highlighted security threats and provided countermeasures, as well as guidance on anonymous access and encryption.

Part III

Content Management with SharePoint

Managing Web Content

S harePoint Server 2010 incorporates many features to help you manage the publishing of content to a public-facing Internet site. This chapter covers the features and process of designing and managing Web content, starting with using and modifying the page layout and master page design so that your Web content has a consistent, centrally managed look and feel. We also discuss how to use site columns and content types to define your page elements and how to use the page administrative and approval processes to ensure that page content is approved and scheduled.

After we design our web content, we then use the publishing features provided by SharePoint to post content via staging servers, and configure content variations to support multiple languages for ease of deployment throughout your entire infrastructure.

This chapter will help you gain insight into the architecture of the new SharePoint page model, and then discuss the details of the provisioning and approval process for Web content. I show you how to manage Web sites so that you can view, edit, and delete your sites and pages based on activity. Finally, we cover how to provide for mobile access for the end user.

Designing Web Pages

There are many ways to design, deploy, and manage Web pages. This process can be daunting, especially when you have the challenge of maintaining a custom enterprise portal, which in many cases involves many content authors and must tie into both the internal and external presence of a typical business. Though there may be many solutions and opinions in your organization of how Web publishing should be done, you must still ensure a uniform experience for users at all levels. Providing a consistent look and feel can be challenging, but in our Web-enabled lives, it is completely necessary and useful, given the amount of time we spend sharing and consuming knowledge via Web technologies.

SharePoint Server 2010 simplifies the design process by breaking down the Web pages into modular elements for ease of customization and authoring. This is the result of including the powerful content management features of Microsoft Content Management Server in the SharePoint platform.

Master Pages, Page Layouts, and Field Controls are the primary elements of the publishing infrastructure in SharePoint Server 2010.

- **Master Pages:** Master pages define the site's look and feel. In addition, master pages reveal the global elements of the site, such as the top navigation in a default deployment.
- **Page Layouts:** Page layouts provide the definition of the content on each page, as well as the means by which content is stored and made available to content authors and visitors of the site. Page layouts also contain the policies that determine the published content scope and availability, as well as field controls.
- **Field Controls:** Field controls serve the dual purpose of representing content to site users and enabling users to author and revise the content.

Working with master pages

Master pages encompass controls that are responsible for rendering shared elements across virtually every page in a SharePoint site. The elements of a typical site may include:

- Navigation menus
- Logos
- Search fields
- Text/HTML controls
- Access controls
- Custom controls

Master pages also contain references to cascading style sheets (CSS) that define the look and feel of pages in a site. Most of the pages in a site collection use the same master page to apply a consistent brand, although a single site collection may also utilize multiple master pages for different sites in the site collection. In this case it may be necessary to create a custom master page to apply a unique look and feel for the site and its pages.

The master page gallery provides storage for the master pages at the site collection level. A master page gallery is available upon installation of SharePoint Server 2010 and the creation of a site collection.

The master page gallery is a document library and as such has all the features of a document library, including versioning, page creation, approval, and workflow. Every site in the site collection is linked to its master page gallery. You can access the master page gallery by following these steps:

1. From the Site Actions menu in the top-left corner, choose Site Settings.
2. Within the Galleries section, click the Master pages and page layouts link.

The master page gallery lists all of your master pages and layout pages available to the site collection.

Modifying a master page

Modifying a master page demonstrates how powerful and useful the master page is for Web publishing. In this exercise, you will modify the Global Links area in the top-right portion of an existing master page to include a link to a privacy policy for the site.

1. Open Microsoft Office SharePoint Designer 2010.
2. From File ⟳ Sites click the Open Site button and then type the URL of the site to be edited.
3. In the Folder List, Click Master Pages.

Note
The best practice for modifying master pages at the site collection level is to create a new master page in the master page gallery by copying and pasting the source master page to a new name. ■

Tip
You can also open the master page for editing by opening the Master Page Gallery and then selecting Edit in Microsoft Office SharePoint Designer from the drop-down menu. ■

4. Click the master page file to open the master page, as shown in Figure 11.1.
5. Click Yes when prompted to check out the master page for editing. From the settings page click on Edit File under the Customizations section.
6. Open the master page in Split view so that you can see both the page code and page design, as shown in Figure 11.2.
7. In the Design pane, click the location on the page where you want to insert your privacy link.
8. In the Code pane, add a table cell and the hyperlink to the privacy policy page, as shown in Figure 11.3.
9. Switch to the Design pane and highlight the new table cell. Click on the Apply Style button from the Styles tab on the Ribbon, as shown in Figure 11.4.

FIGURE 11.1

Opening a master page in SharePoint Designer

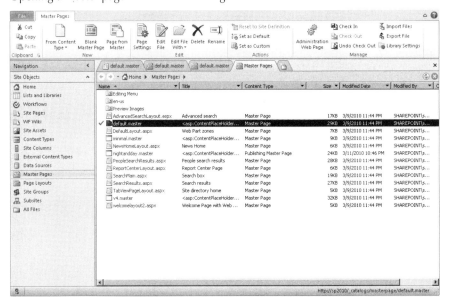

FIGURE 11.2

Using Split view in SharePoint Designer

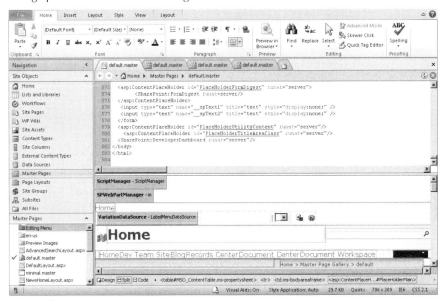

FIGURE 11.3

Adding a table cell and hyperlink to the master page

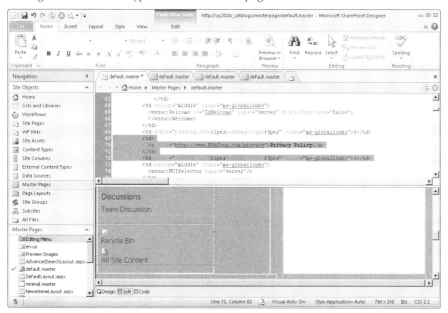

FIGURE 11.4

Applying styles

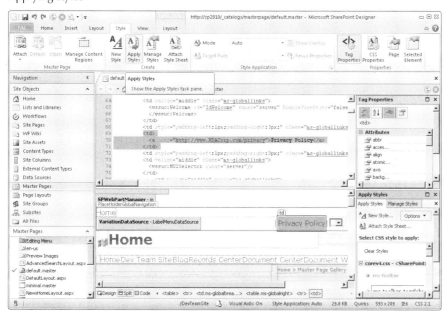

10. Choose the CSS class to be applied to the new cell in the Apply Styles pane.

Note

Since the styles of the surrounding cells in this example are all ms-globallinks, you may want to leave the CSS class alone. The modification of the CSS is to demonstrate the capability. ∎

11. Save the page and then click Yes in the Site Definition Page Warning box.

12. Go back to the list of master pages and right-click the customized page. Select Check In, as shown in Figure 11.5.

FIGURE 11.5

Check In customized master page

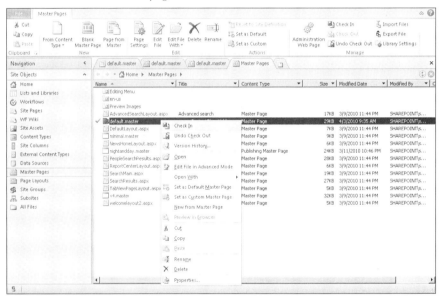

13. **Select Publish as major version.** This page may require content approval. If you are prompted, click Yes to modify the approval status.

    The master page gallery opens with default.aspx under the Pending section.

14. From the item drop-down select Approve/Reject, as shown in Figure 11.6.

15. In the Approve/Reject dialog, select Approved and enter comments within the Comments box as shown in Figure 11.7.

FIGURE 11.6

Changing approval status

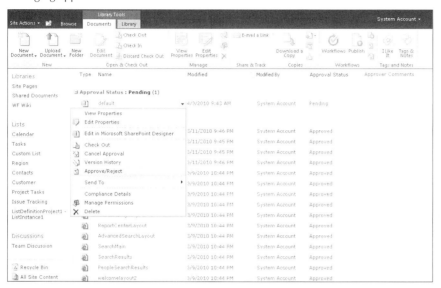

FIGURE 11.7

Approve/Reject Dialog

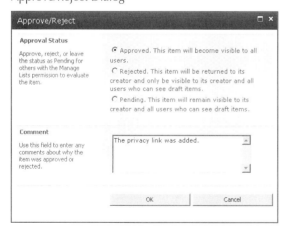

16. **Back in your SharePoint site, refresh the page and review the changes made.** Verify that the link appears throughout the site.

Discovering page layouts

A page layout provides a structured approach for displaying authored content on pages within a portal site by provisioning elements on the page. These may include rich HTML controls that allow authors to add and edit content through a Web browser, or they could be the building blocks of a custom Web Part page, depending on your requirements. The combination of master pages and page layouts further the simple but powerful possibilities of your publishing portal.

When a SharePoint page is opened in a browser, the corresponding layout page is first combined with the master page. The page contents are then rendered into the field controls on the layout page. Because layout pages display content from a content type's stored columns, they must be designed for that specific content type. As with master pages, any changes you make to an existing page layout are immediately reflected on all the Web pages that use the page layout, enabling you to update your page authoring framework without having to revise all pages that were previously published.

Administrators may restrict the ability to format Web page content or to add additional elements including images or hyperlinks to site pages to only a select group of page layout administrators. This may be necessary in a controlled environment where style elements are controlled by a centralized CSS so as to provide a uniform experience for the user.

It is possible for administrators to grant or remove these permissions by using Microsoft Office SharePoint Designer or Microsoft Visual Studio 2005 to edit the tags associated with the field controls on a particular layout page. An example of this is if the page properties for an HTML control are redefined to false, then the associated editing commands in Microsoft Office SharePoint Server are removed.

Managing Content

Because the page layout is applied to the content, the content itself is stored in the columns of the page library. The columns can be site columns or columns defined for just that page library, but only content that is stored in site columns can be added to the page layout.

To manage the content, you can edit the properties of each page in the page library. This can even be done in bulk mode by showing the library in data sheet mode and editing the columns through the data sheet interface. This functionality is very helpful, especially if you want to update a field for several pages like the contact field or scheduling fields.

The separation between content and layout also allows you to modify the page layout that is applied to your page content. You can do this by editing the page and selecting a new page layout in the page settings.

Content types

Content types are reusable definitions of document types. Content types provide definition to documents that share common sets of attributes. These may include many different facets of the content, including:

- Document templates
- Specific metadata
- Document conversion types
- Site columns
- Defined policies
- Workflows

SharePoint document libraries and lists may support multiple content types. Content types relate to page layouts because page layouts use site columns to store the page layout content, and content types define those site columns.

Cross-Reference

For more information about using content types, see Chapter 18. ■

Creating custom page layouts

In this example, you will create a custom page layout for a corporate newsletter. The first step will be to create custom content types to associate with the new page layout. You'll create this content type at the site collection level of your publishing site.

1. Choose Site Actions from the top-left corner on the portal home page.

2. Select Site Settings.

3. Choose Site content types in the Galleries section.

4. Click Create from the Site Content Type Gallery toolbar.

5. Name the new content type Executive Newsletter as shown in Figure 11.8.

6. Choose Publishing Content Types in the Select parent content type from drop-down menu of the Parent Content Type field.

7. Choose Page in the Parent Content Type drop-down menu of the Parent Content Type field.

8. Select the New group radio button and enter Executive Newsletter as a name for the new group. Click OK. The Site Content Type settings page appears.

   Now add columns to the new content type from the Site Columns gallery.

FIGURE 11.8

Creating an Executive Newsletter Site Content Type

9. Click Add from existing site columns from the bottom of the Columns section.

10. Add Article Date, Byline, and Page Content from the Available Columns field. Click OK when warned that the Page Content control must be updated by using a Web browser.

Tip

Change the Select columns from drop-down to Publishing Columns and Page Layout Columns to easily find the existing site columns. ∎

11. Choose No from the Update List and Site Content Types section and click OK.

The page layout template is used to author new executive newsletters. Because new page content is authored within the page layout, all site columns that you want users to fill out for the page must be visible on the page. New page layouts may be created from the site Master Page Gallery or in Microsoft Office SharePoint Designer.

1. Open your portal site in Office SharePoint Designer.

2. Select the Page layouts folder and click on the New Page Layout button.

3. Choose Executive Newsletter from the Content Type Group and Content Type Name drop-down menus, as shown in Figure 11.9.

FIGURE 11.9

Create an Executive News page layout

4. Enter a URL and Title for the new page layout.

5. Click OK.

6. In the Toolbox pane at the left, expand the SharePoint Controls (field) node.

7. Expand the Content Fields node, as shown in Figure 11.10.

FIGURE 11.10

Expanding the page fields for use on your page layout

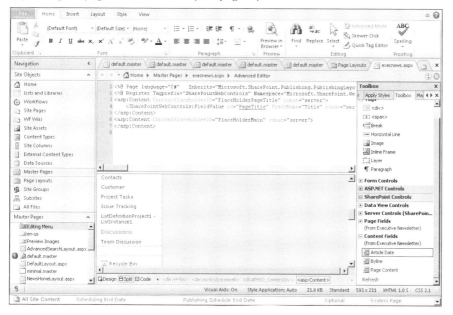

8. Drag the Article Date, Byline, and the Page Content fields into the PlaceHolder Main content placeholder.

9. Drag Rollup Image and Title fields from the Page Fields section onto the page.

10. Save and check in the new page layout.

Creating pages

Now that you have created a new page layout using a custom content type, you can create a new publishing page ready for use on the site. To do this, follow these steps:

1. On the site in which you want to publish your new page, choose New Page from the Site Actions menu.

2. Enter today's date as the Title of the new page. Click OK.

3. From the Page tab on the Ribbon, click the Page Layout button and choose the page layout you created from the Page Layout list, as shown in Figure 11.11.

FIGURE 11.11

Creating a new page using the Executive News page layout

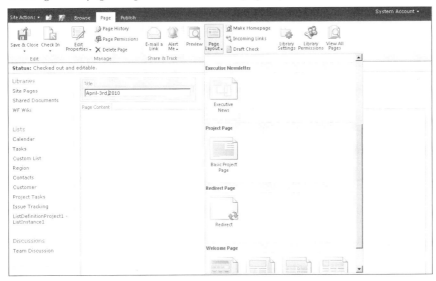

4. Fill out the content fields and click Publish.

You have now created a new Web-based newsletter using your page layout, ready for content authors to update and publish as needed, and consistently branded for your organization.

Note

You may want to return to SharePoint Designer 2010 to modify the page layout depending on how an actual page is rendered on the site. Tweaking the cosmetics can be a back-and-forth process. ■

Associating page layouts with libraries

Upon creation, the top-level site collection can use any page layouts in the Master Pages and Page Layouts gallery. You can specify which page layouts and subsite templates can be used for this site and any subsites from the top level site collection settings page. To do this, follow these steps:

1. **Click Site Actions in the top-left corner of any page in your top-level site collection site.** Choose Site Settings.

2. **Choose Page layouts and site templates from the Look and Feel category.**

3. **Choose from the options below:**

    - **Subsites can use any site template:** Sites created below the top level site may use any site template.

    - **Subsites can only use the following site templates:** Opens a menu for the site administrator to select the appropriate template or templates for use on the site.

    - **Reset all subsites to inherit these preferred subsite template settings:** This check box grants site administrators control over templates for sites.

    - **Pages in this site can use any layout:** All page layouts are available to be used to create pages in the site.

    - **Pages in this site can use only the following layouts:** Opens a menu for the site administrator to select the appropriate layouts for use on the site, as shown in Figure 11.12.

    - **Reset all subsites to inherit these preferred page layout settings:** This check box grants site administrators control over layouts for sites.

4. **Click OK.**

Enabling page scheduling

Page scheduling allows you to set the start date and end date for each published article. Publishing pages do not have scheduling enabled out-of-box. If this is required in your organization, perform the following steps:

1. **On the site that stores your page library (Publishing Site or site with Publishing Features activated), click View All Site Content from the Quick Launch bar navigation.**

2. **Choose the Pages library.**

3. **From the Library tab on the Ribbon, choose Library Settings.**

4. **Choose Versioning settings and enable content approval; verify as well that both major and draft versions are allowed, as shown in Figure 11.13.** These settings must be activated in order to enable item scheduling.

FIGURE 11.12

Selecting a page layout for use on the site

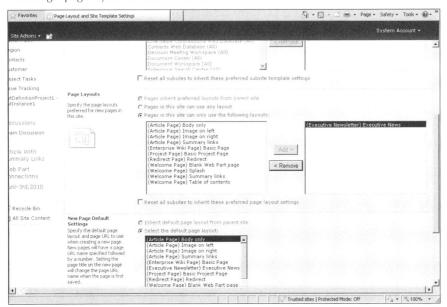

FIGURE 11.13

Configuring versioning settings to support item scheduling

5. Click OK.

6. Choose Manage Item Scheduling.

7. Select Enable scheduling of items in this list, as shown in Figure 11.14.

FIGURE 11.14

Enabling item scheduling

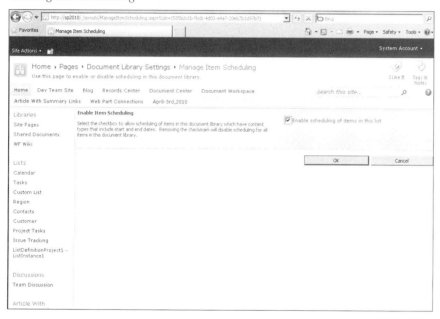

8. Click OK.

You are now able to schedule the publication of pages in this document library. To do this, follow these steps:

1. On the site that stores your page library (Publishing Site or site with Publishing Features activated), click View All Site Content on the Quick Launch bar.

2. Choose the Pages library.

3. On the item that you want to edit the scheduling, choose Edit Properties from the item drop-down menu.

4. Enter the Scheduling Start Date (or choose Immediately) and the Scheduling End Date, as shown in Figure 11.15.

FIGURE 11.15

Setting the page scheduling schedule

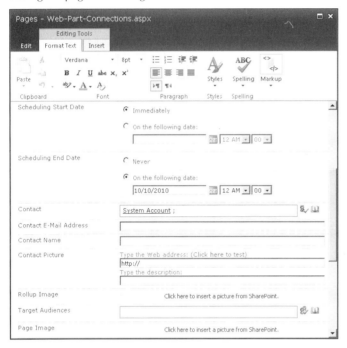

5. Click Save.

Tip

You may implement this scheduling for any list or library — not just Publishing. The Pages library was used as an example, as most publishing content will be contained within this library. For Wiki sites (or sites with the Wiki Home Page feature activated), you may follow the same steps but using the Site Pages library instead. ■

Implementing Web Content Workflow

Web content has three primary workflow options that can be used alone or in concert to control the publication of materials to your Web site. These three options are content approval, staging of content, and using variations to replicate and assign parallel versions of content.

Using the approval workflow

Content publication may be controlled by *content approval*, a permission granted to members of the Approvers site group. These users control the publication of authored content. Document drafts are in the Pending State while they await content approval; upon approval, content becomes available for viewing. Owners of document libraries may enable content approval for a document library and alternately assign approval workflows to the library to expedite the process of approval. You should set content approval so that all users can publish content, but the content should be reviewed by a limited audience for changes and approval before becoming widely available.

There are different versioning settings that determine the document submission process:

- **None:** When versioning has been disabled, changes saved cause the document state to become Pending. The previous version of the document is retained until the content is approved, and the content is still accessible to members of the reader site group. Upon approval, earlier versions are discarded and the new version of the document becomes available to readers. This is true of documents which are uploaded to the document library as well.

- **Major versions only:** A document saved with this setting enabled becomes Pending, and users with read permissions can view the previous major version of the document. After the changes to the document are approved, a new major version of the document is created and the previous version is saved to the document's history list.

Note

If major versioning has been enabled, when a new document is uploaded to the document library it is added to the library in the Pending state. It is unavailable to users with read permissions until it has been approved as a major version. ■

- **Major and minor versions:** With major and minor versioning enabled, changes to a document are saved, and the author has the choice of saving a new minor version of the document as a draft or creating a new major version, both of which change the document's state to Pending. Upon approval, a new major version of the document is created and made available to site users with read permissions. Both major and minor versions of documents are kept in a document's history list in major and minor versioning.

With major and minor versioning enabled, when a new document is uploaded to the document library it may be added to the library in the Draft state as version 0.1, or approval may be immediately requested, which changes the document's state to Pending.

Approval workflows are processes by which a document or item is sent to the appropriate group for review and approval. This lends efficiency to the business process of approval by managing and tracking all the human tasks which comprise the process and then providing a record of the process upon completion.

Cross-Reference
See Chapter 8 for more information on workflows. ■

You may create an approval workflow immediately from a document or item in a list or library if workflows are enabled for that library. The workflow process begins with the selection of the appropriate workflow. Then you define the workflow with a form, which itemizes the content approvers, due dates, and any additional conditions or elements relevant to the approval process.

The approval workflow is included with SharePoint and can be configured using a Web browser. To enable an approval workflow for a publishing pages library, follow these steps:

1. On the site that stores your page library (Publishing Site or site with Publishing Features activated), click View All Site Content on the Quick Launch bar.

2. Choose the Pages library.

3. From the Library tab on the Ribbon, choose Library Settings.

4. Choose Versioning settings and enable content approval.

5. Click OK.

6. In the Permissions and Management category, select Workflow settings.

7. Select the Approval — SharePoint 2010 workflow template from the Workflow field.

8. Give the new workflow a name to identify it to site users.

9. In the Task List field, choose the Workflow Tasks list, as shown in Figure 11.16. A workflow task list is created when publishing features are enabled on the site collection to track the workflow process, although any task list previously created for the site collection appears on the drop-down menu. You may also opt to create a new task list to track the workflow.

10. Select Workflow History (new) from the History List field.

11. Choose from among the Start Options available. Choose the options that are applicable for the task at hand, although selection of these items in conjunction with conflicting conditions causes the previous item to uncheck to ensure the workflow process will be able to run.

    • Allow this workflow to be manually started by an authenticated user with Edit Items Permissions: Users with permissions to edit must manually initiate the workflow process. Alternatively, you can set the workflow to Require Manage Lists Permissions to start the workflow: users must have permissions to manage lists in order to fire the workflow manually. Selecting this supercedes the previous option.

    • Start this workflow to approve publishing a major version of an item: The workflow is automatically started when a major version of the document has been submitted for approval.

- **Start this workflow when a new item is created:** Automatic initiation of the workflow when a new item is created.

- **Start this workflow when an item is changed:** Automatic firing of the workflow process when a document has been revised.

For the purposes of this example choose Allow this workflow to be manually started by an authenticated user with Edit Items Permissions.

FIGURE 11.16

Selecting a task list to track workflow items

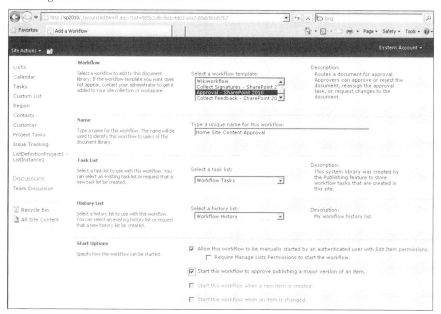

12. Click Next.

13. **On the Customize Workflow page, in the Approvers section, specify the users or groups who require approval.** Enter your alias for this example. Define how tasks will be assigned to the approvers. Choose from the following options.

- **All participants simultaneously (parallel):** Tasks are assigned to all users.

- **One participant at a time (serial):** Tasks are assigned to approvers in order.

Choose the latter option, One participant at a time (serial), for this example.

14. **Expand Groups is selected which will assign a task to each member of the group. Deselect this check box to assign a single task to each group entered.**

15. **If you opted to assign the workflow tasks to the approvers in parallel, you may choose the due date for the content approval process.** If you chose instead to delegate the workflow tasks to the approvers serially, you may now designate how many days are allowed for the users to complete the task. In serial approval, you may also copy additional users to notify them of the task at hand.

16. **You may choose the end the workflow on the first rejection and/or if the document changes while the workflow is running by selecting the checking the check boxes at the bottom of the page (as show in in Figure 11.17).**

FIGURE 11.17

Completing the approval workflow

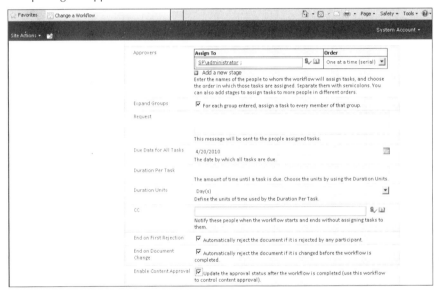

17. **For Post-completion Workflow Activities select the Update the approval status (use this workflow to control content approval) check box if you want to have the content published upon approval.**

18. **Click OK.**

If you want to test your example workflow, return to the Pages library and create a new page. You should receive an e-mail notification that provides a link to the item in the Workflow Tasks list.

Deploying content between servers

SharePoint Server 2010 allows site administrators the ability to deploy content across multiple servers, from one site collection to another. This functionality is typically used for staging content so that users modify only the staged content, and published content is modified only via the content deployment process.

The source site collection and the target site collection for the content may be in the same farm or in different farms. This functionality is managed by creating and using paths and jobs from the Central Administration site on the server farm. The content deployment path defines the relationship between the two site collections for deployment.

When paths from the source site collection and the target site collection have been designated, you then create a job to deploy the content.

Jobs determine the specific content to be deployed from the source to the target and the schedule upon which the deployment occurs.

Paths and jobs are created from the SharePoint 2010 Central Administration site.

1. From Central Administration, click on the General Application Settings from the Quick Launch bar.

2. In the Content Deployment section, click Configure content deployment.

3. Select Accept incoming deployment content jobs and select the Import and Export servers as shown in Figure 11.18. (In a stand-alone or testing environment these may be the same.) Click OK.

4. In the Content Deployment section again, click Content deployment paths and jobs.

5. On the Manage Content Deployment Paths and Jobs page, click New Path.

6. In the Name and Description section, enter a name and a meaningful description for the new path. This will aid users in employing the new path to create jobs.

7. In the Source Web Application and Site Collection section, select the Web application and site collection that contains the content you want to deploy.

8. Enter the URL to the Destination Central Administration server in the Destination Central Administration Web Application section.

9. You must supply Authentication Information in order to access the destination Central Administration Web site. Enter the means of authentication, the username, and the password in the required fields and click Connect.

FIGURE 11.18

Content deployment configuration

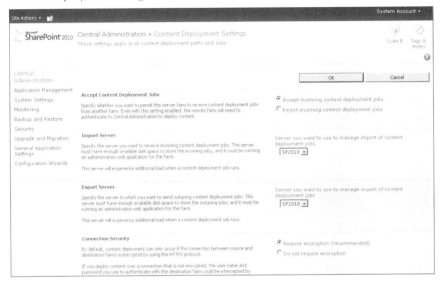

Note

Even though you select Use Integrated Windows Authentication, a username and password are still required to be entered. ∎

10. Upon successful connection, enter the destination Web application and site collection where you would like to deploy the content, as shown in Figure 11.19.

11. If you want the usernames associated with the content to be visible on the destination site collection, check the corresponding box in the User Names section.

12. Determine the security information to be associated with the content in the Security Information section. Select from the following:

- **None:** No security information associated with content is deployed with the content.

- **All:** All the security information associated with the content is deployed with the content.

- **Role Definitions Only:** Role definitions (collections of permissions) are deployed with the content. Users and groups, including those associated with the role definitions, are not deployed with the content.

13. Click OK.

FIGURE 11.19

Entering the destination site collection for your content deployment

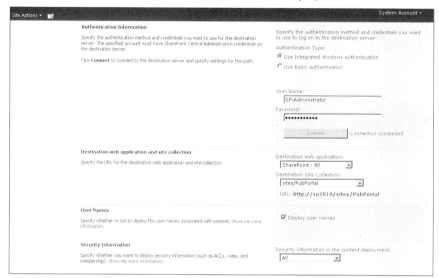

Now you will create a content deployment job using the new path.

1. On the Manage Content Deployment Paths and Jobs page, click New Job, as shown in Figure 11.20.

FIGURE 11.20

Create a new job for content deployment

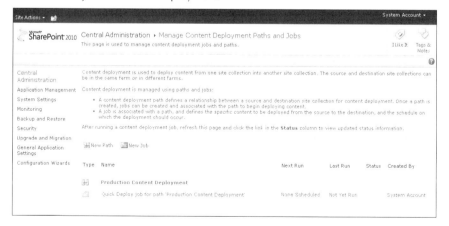

2. In the Name and Description section, give the content deployment job a meaningful name. (See Figure 11.21.)

3. In the Description box, enter a description for the content deployment job if desired.

4. In the Path section, select the content deployment path on the Select a content deployment path menu.

5. In the Scope section, select one of the following:

    - **Entire site collection:** Includes all sites in the site collection in the deployment.

    - **Specific sites within the site collection:** Specify sites within the site collection in the deployment. If you select this option, click Select sites to select the sites to include in the deployment.

FIGURE 11.21

Create Content Deployment Job page

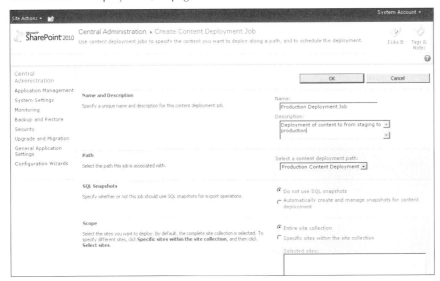

6. In the Frequency section, you may clear the Run this job on the following schedule check box if you want to run the job manually. Optionally, select the Run this job on the following schedule check box to specify a schedule.

7. Select the Send e-mail when the content deployment job succeeds check box in the Notification section if you want to receive e-mail upon successful completion of the content deployment job.

8. To receive e-mail notification when the content deployment job fails, check the Send e-mail if the content deployment job fails box.

9. If you select either of these options, enter an e-mail address in the Type e-mail addresses box.

10. Click OK. A new job appears in the Manage Content Deployment Paths and Jobs list. Using the drop-down menu on the item, you may run the job on demand, test the job, view its history, edit, or delete the job. Figure 11.22 displays the options.

FIGURE 11.22

Job item menu options

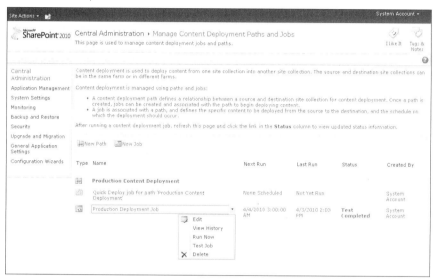

Tip

Test the job and run it manually before it starts kicking off on a scheduled basis. ∎

Using site variations and language translations

Your organization may require Web sites to provide content specific to different cultures, markets, or geographic locales. Implementing distinctive sites of this nature can prove challenging to deploy and maintain. To simplify the architecture and administrative processes, SharePoint Server 2010 provides site variations.

Site variations make content available to targeted audiences across different sites by copying and, if necessary, tailoring content from the source variation site to each target variation site.

By default, variation site redirection is based on the language setting of the browser from which the user is visiting the site. For example, if the user's default browser language is Spanish, the user is redirected to the corresponding Spanish variation site.

Using the Quick Deploy Job

After a path is created, a quick deploy job is automatically generated. A quick deploy job automatically detects and deploys updated content on a specified schedule. To enable the quick job:

1. Click on the quick deploy job in the jobs and paths list.
2. Check the box to allow quick deployment for the specified path.
3. Specify how many minutes between checks.
4. Specify the Quick Deploy Users (who can mark content to be quick deployed).
5. Enter the notification details.
6. Click OK.

The quick job is scheduled and runs the number of minutes you specified.

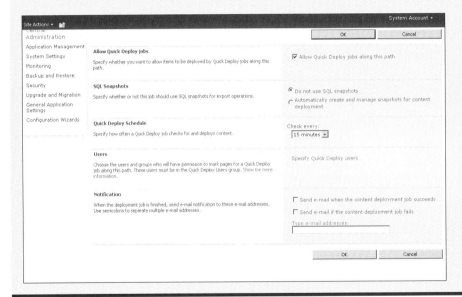

Site variations are defined through the creation of variation labels per each required variation. Variation labels are identifiers that name and configure a target variation site. You create a source variation label that denotes the site supplying the bulk of the site content. The complementary variation labels represent the destination site where the copied content is required.

Note

Up to 50 labels are supported in Microsoft Office SharePoint Server. ∎

The Create Hierarchy command creates the variation sites from these labels and is accessed from the Variation labels page from the SharePoint Server 2010 site administration pages.

Each site collection has a unique set of variation labels that may be defined. Variation sites may be initiated anywhere in the site hierarchy because the source variation and the target variation sites are always created as subsites of the variations home site. Upon arrival at the home site, users are redirected to the applicable variation site.

Note

An optional Variation Picker control applies a menu to the page, which enables users to select the desired variation site through a menu. This control is added to site master pages with SharePoint Designer 2010. ■

You must configure variation settings for your publishing sites or pages to enable the variation features. Variations for all sites in a site collection are configured at the top level site administration. Three elements are involved in configuring variation site support for your publishing sites or pages:

- **Variations:** These define the parameters of the site variations you want to apply to your site variation.

- **Variation Labels:** These determine the locale and create the site variation hierarchy.

- **Optional — Translatable Column Settings:** Defines any Site columns that may need to be translated for variations.

Note

Multiple source variations within a site collection are not supported in SharePoint Server 2010. ■

To configure site variations, follow these steps:

1. **From the top level site of a site collection, click Site Actions in the top-left corner.**

2. **Choose Site Settings.**

3. **Under the Site Collection Administration group, choose Variations.**

4. **In the Variation Home section, enter the location where the source and the target variations will be created, as shown in Figure 11.23.**

   Depending on the needs of your organization, you may not want to translate the entire site collection. Browse to the section of the site you want to set as the common location for both the source and target variations.

5. **In the Automatic Creation section, choose one of these options:**
   - Automatically create site and page variations to automatically create a copy of all variations.
   - Do not automatically create site and page variations to grant the owner of a site or page the means to decide when a site or page is created.

6. **In the Recreate Deleted Target Page section, select one of the following:**
   - Recreate a new target page when the source page is republished should you want a new target page to be created when the source page is republished.
   - Do not recreate a new target page when the source page is republished if you don't want a new target page to be created when the source page is republished.

FIGURE 11.23

Configuring variations for your site collection

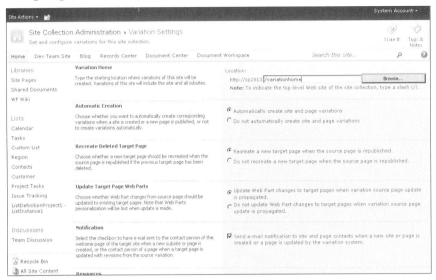

This field determines which actions will be taken when a variation page is deleted and its variation source is updated.

7. **Check the Send e-mail notification to owners when a new site or page is created or a page is updated by the variation system box from the Notification section.** This sends an e-mail notification that a new subsite or page of a target site is created, or when a target page is updated with revisions from the source variation to the site owner.

8. **In the Resources section, decide if it is necessary for a new page variation to use the same resources as the source page, or if the variation should use the resource copies which are created in the new page variation's location.** If this is the case, select one of the following tasks:

   • Reference existing resources to use existing resources.

   • Copy resources to copy the resources.

9. **Click OK.**

To configure site variation labels, follow these steps:

1. From the top level site of a site collection, click Site Actions in the top left corner.

2. Choose Site Settings.

3. On the Site Settings page, under the Site Collection Administration group, choose Variation labels.

4. On the Variation labels page, click New Label.

5. **From the Label and Description section, type a descriptive name in the Label Name field.** The name you enter becomes the URL string.

6. **Enter an optional description to help users understand the label's purpose.** (See Figure 11.24.)

7. **Choose a user-friendly name in the Display Name field.** These are typically localized versions of a label.

   The display name appears in the Site Management Tool hierarchy.

8. **Select the locale for the variation and enter it in the Locale field.** This denotes formatting for elements such as date, time, and currency.

9. **If Language Packs have been installed on the server, check the Language box to select a language to provision the variation label's site.**

10. **In the Hierarchy Creation section, select the portion of the source hierarchy that you would like to copy.** Select one of the following:

    - **Publishing Sites and All Pages:** This creates a hierarchy of publishing sites and all pages.

    - **Publishing Sites only:** This creates a hierarchy of publishing sites only.

    - **Root Site only:** Creates a hierarchy at the root.

FIGURE 11.24

Create Variation Label

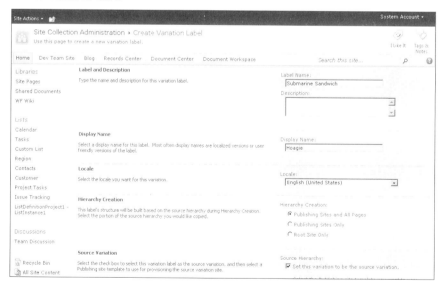

Note

This setting cannot be changed upon creation of a site variation hierarchy. In order to modify these settings the user must delete the variation label from the list and create a new label prior to creating a site variation hierarchy. ■

11. **You are returned to the Variation Labels page; click Create Hierarchies to create the site variation.**

     The creation of hierarchies is performed by SharePoint via timer jobs. Therefore, in order to see the results you may need to go to Central Admin and find the scheduled job under Monitoring. Click Run Now to run the job now instead of waiting for tomorrow to come.

     Variation sites and pages are created through this process, as shown in Figure 11.25. The Submarine Sandwich page now has a Hoagie variation.

Variation created

Using Document Conversion

The advent of new Web technologies has assisted many nontechnical end users in various organizations in the creation of rich, content-driven Web pages using nothing more than a Web browser. It used to be common to find pages on the portal that were created and copied directly from Microsoft Word. It was (and is) very easy to discern Web pages that have been fashioned in this manner through inconsistent formatting and style elements.

This gap has been bridged through the introduction of Smart Client Authoring. Smart Client Authoring uses Document Conversion, a feature in SharePoint Server 2010 built on the document converter infrastructure that empowers authors to convert documents directly into Web pages that may be published and revised from the original file. This is especially useful for these reasons:

- Ease of publishing for pre-existing content.
- Authors unfamiliar with Web publishing tools won't need to learn a new application.
- Complex documents may be converted readily to existing formatting and styles.

After a document is converted, all browser-based document management features become available on the converted Web page.

The document conversion feature is configured from the SharePoint Central Administration. Depending on the amount of content you anticipate using this process, the document converter service should be activated on specific application servers in your infrastructure. For example, if the servers in question are processing additional services such as Search or InfoPath Forms Services, it would be best to enable this feature on a different server or servers in your farm to accommodate load balancing.

In order to accommodate any strain of resources across the server farm, SharePoint Server 2010 utilizes two services, DocConversionLoadBalancerService and DocConversionLauncherService to manage the load balancing, prioritizing, and scheduling of the document conversion process.

Upon initiation of the document conversion process SharePoint Server 2010 passes the request to these two services. Content is first passed with an optional XML file containing specific converter settings to DocConversionLoadBalancerService, which shares all document conversion requests across the farm. Upon receipt of a request for conversion from SharePoint Server 2010, the DocConversionLoadBalancerService returns a URI to the appropriate DocConversionLauncher Service. The specified launcher is then connected and the request is passed. The DocConversion LauncherService is the service that calls the document converter to take the source file and create a converted copy. The converted copy is then readied for the Web with post-processing actions that include:

- Addition of the file's metadata

- Inclusion of identifier metadata for both the original file and the document converter employed for copy creation

- Notification of conversion to the creator of the source file

- Storing the converted document in the same locale as the source file

Note

Document conversions cannot be disabled for individual sites or document libraries. ■

Multiple converters that take original documents of the same file type extension may exist on a Web application and generate converted copies of the same file type extension. Each converter performs different conversion functions on the file, but the final file type extension is the same in every case.

The GUID rather than the file type extension is used to determine whether a specific converter has been used to create a converted copy.

Note

Documents that are secured with Information Rights Management produce converted copies that are also IRM protected. Documents protected in an IRM file format do not convert to non–IRM-protected file formats. ■

To enable document conversion on your server farm, follow these steps:

1. Open Central Administration.

2. Click the Application Management Quick Launch item.

3. Select Manage services on server from the Service Applications section.

4. Choose the server that you want to run the load balancer service on from the Server drop-down menu.

5. Click Start for the Document Conversions Load Balancer Service, as shown in Figure 11.26.

FIGURE 11.26

Starting the Document Conversions Load Balancer Service

6. Choose the server that you want to run the launcher service on from the Server drop-down.

7. Click Start for Document Conversions Launcher Service and choose the load balancer that you configured in Step 4, as shown in Figure 11.27. Click OK.

8. Click General Application Settings on the Quick Launch bar.

9. Select Configure document conversions from the External Service Connections section.

FIGURE 11.27

Configuring the Document Conversions Launcher Service

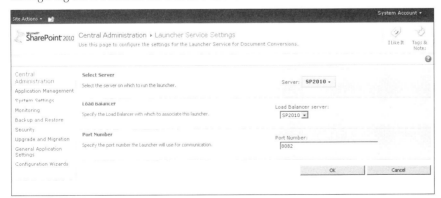

10. Choose the Web Application that you want to enable document conversions for.

11. Click Yes in the Enable document conversions for this site field.

12. Choose the Load Balancer server that you configured in Step 5.

13. Enter the Conversion Schedule that you want for processing of your documents, as shown in Figure 11.28.

14. Customize the Converter Settings as appropriate for your environment.

15. Click OK.

FIGURE 11.28

Configuring the document conversion processing settings

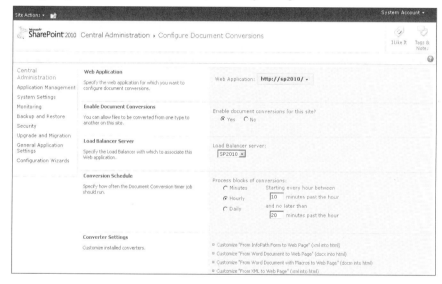

Managing Web Sites

It is important to manage your published Web content so that it stays fresh, and that you add, link to, and highlight popular content and delete stale content. SharePoint provides several methods for managing activity across your sites including auditing activity, site usage reports, setting and extending quotas, and deleting unused sites.

Auditing activity

There are many options to configure the auditing of activities in SharePoint Server 2010 site collections. You may enable the auditing of documents and items, or configure site searching and lists for auditing. These actions are performed from the Site Settings menu of the site collection you want to configure.

To configure audit settings, follow these steps:

1. Click the Site Actions menu in the top-left corner of the site collection that you want to audit.

2. Choose Site Settings on the site you want to configure.

3. In the Site Collection Administration section, click the Site collection audit settings link.

4. In the Audit Log Trimming specify whether or not you want to purge old log items after the specified amount of days. Optionally, enter a location to store the log items before they are trimmed.

5. On the Configure Audit Settings page, in the Documents and Items section, select the events you want to audit, as shown in Figure 11.29:

   - Opening or downloading documents, viewing items in lists, or viewing item properties
   - Editing items
   - Checking out or checking in items
   - Moving or copying items to another location in the site
   - Deleting or restoring items

FIGURE 11.29

Configuring the events that you want to audit

6. In the Lists, Libraries, and Sites section, select the events you want to audit:

    - Editing content types and columns

    - Searching site content

    - Editing users and permissions

7. Click OK.

Tip

Only audit on your production environment. Too many changes occur in development or staging. Use the search audits to further improve your portal content as well as defining best bets. ∎

To view the logs of the events you selected for auditing in an Excel Web page, perform the following steps:

1. Click the Site Actions menu in the top-left corner of the site collection that you want to audit.

2. Choose Site Settings.

3. In the Site Collection Administration section, click the Audit log reports link.

4. On the View Auditing Reports page (shown in Figure 11.30), select the report you want to view and select whether you want to open or save the file.

FIGURE 11.30

View Auditing Reports

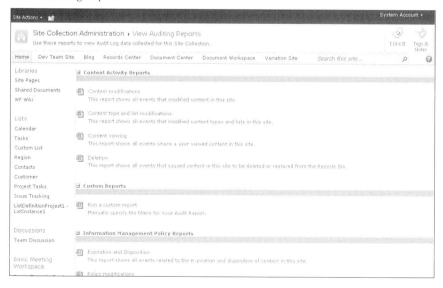

Configuring Web Analytics reporting

You can also configure SharePoint to process usage analysis reports so that you can view usage activity on a site-by-site basis. Site usage is now labeled as Web Analytics. Web Analytics provides reports for top pages, top referring sites, top users, and top referring pages for your sites.

Configuring usage processing

To enable usage analysis processing, follow these steps:

1. Open Central Administration for your SharePoint farm and click the Monitoring item on the Quick Launch bar.

2. Select Configure Usage and Health Data Collection from the Reporting section.

3. Select the Enable usage data collection check box, select the events to log, and confirm the correct location of your log files, as shown in Figure 11.31.

FIGURE 11.31

Enabling usage analysis processing for your Web farm

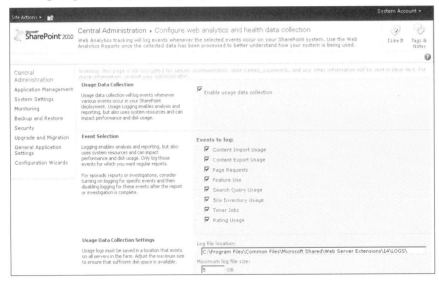

4. **Select the Enable Health Data Collection check box.** Optionally, click on the Health Logging Schedule link to modify the schedule of the health collection timer job. Optionally, click on the Log Collection Schedule link to modify the schedule of the usage logging timer job.

5. Click OK.

Viewing Web Analytics for your web application

To view the usage analysis reports for an entire Web application, follow these steps:

1. Open Central Administration for your SharePoint farm and click the Monitoring item on the Quick Launch bar.

2. Select View Web Analytics reports from the Reporting section.

3. Select the Web application you want to view from the Web Analytics Summary page, as shown in Figure 11.32.

FIGURE 11.32

Web Analytics Reports Summary page for web applications

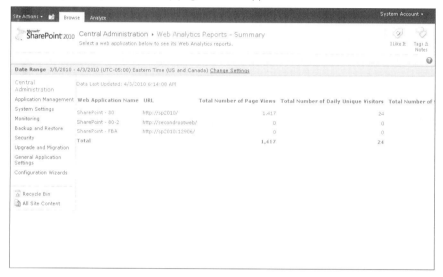

Viewing Web Analytics for a site collection

To view the usage analysis processing reports for a site collection, follow these steps:

1. Click the Site Actions menu in the top-left corner of the site collection for which you want to view usage analysis reports.

2. Select Site Settings.

3. Select Site Collection Web Analytics reports from the Site Actions section.

Viewing Web Analytics for a specific site

To view the usage analysis processing reports for specific site, follow these steps:

1. Click the Site Actions menu in the top-left corner of the site for which you want to view usage analysis reports.

2. Select Site Settings.

3. Select Site Web Analytics reports from the Site Actions section.

Analyzing the Web Analytics reports

Whether you are viewing Web Analytics reports for a Web application, site collection, or site, each page has an Analyze tab on the Ribbon, which you may use to modify the specifics of the reports, such as the date range.

The options available in the Analyze tab on the Ribbon change depending on what level or metric you are viewing. For example, when viewing Web Analytics at a site level, you may change the site scope to exclude subsites by selecting This Site Only, shown in Figure 11.33.

FIGURE 11.33

Web Analytics Reports — Analyze Ribbon Bar

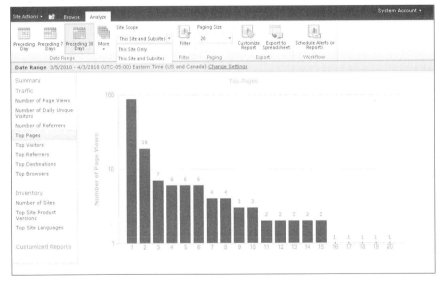

Extending quotas

Quotas and locks are two methods of controlling access to site collections. By employing the use of locks, site administrators can manually prevent user access.

Quotas are used to prevent users from adding content to a site collection or provide e-mail warning notification to the site collection administrator when specified limits on disk space are passed.

It is also possible to create and edit site quota templates that you can use during site creation. Site quotas are configured from the Application Management page of the Central Administration Web application.

Configuring site quotas

To configure site quotas, follow these steps:

1. From the Application Management page of the Central Administration site, click Configure quotas and locks under the Site Collections section.

2. Choose the site collection to configure from the drop-down list in the Site Collection section.

3. In the Site Lock Information section, choose the desired level of access to the chosen site collection, as shown in Figure 11.34.

FIGURE 11.34

Configuring site quotas

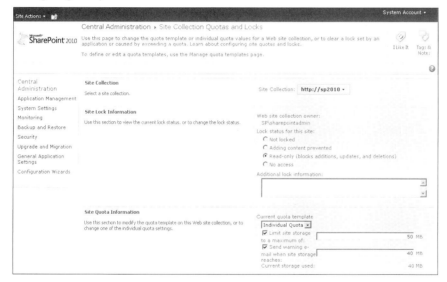

4. In the Site Quota Information section, choose the quota template you want to modify, and then select one or both of the following:

- Check the Limit site storage to a maximum of box, and then enter the amount of disk space in megabytes (MB).

- Check the Send warning e-mail when site storage reaches box, and then enter the amount of disk space in megabytes (MB).

- Enter the amount of usage points per day for sandboxed solutions.

Sandboxed solutions are SharePoint solutions that are installed at the site collection level and are isolated within that site collection such that other site collections, Web applications, or the entire farm are not affected. Points are accumulated based on certain events that occur from the sandboxed solution such as exceptions or extreme resource consumption. See the Microsoft Technet page (`http://technet.micro soft.com/en-us/library/ff603636(office.14).aspx#BKMK_srcPlan ResourceUsageQuotasSandboxed`) for more information on resource usage points.

- Check the Send warning e-mail when usage per day reaches box, and then enter the amount of points.

5. Click OK.

Configuring quota templates

Quota templates help you manage groups of sites so that when they are created or when you need to apply a template, the quota is already defined. To configure quota templates, from the Application Management page of the Central Administration site, click Specify quota templates from the Site Collections section and then perform one of the following two tasks:

- Select the Edit an existing template radio button.

    1. Choose the existing quota template you want to modify.

    2. Check the boxes next to the storage limit values you want to modify.

    3. Enter the new storage limit values and click OK.

        Or:

- Select the Create a new quota template radio button.

    1. Choose the template to start from, as shown in Figure 11.35.

    2. Give the new template a name.

    3. Check the boxes next to the storage limit values you want to modify.

    4. Enter the new storage limit values and click OK.

Deleting unused sites

There are two methods of managing unused sites in Microsoft Office SharePoint Server. You can either send notices to site collection owners requiring confirmation that the site collections are in use to keep the number of unused Web sites on your server in check; or you can configure sites to be automatically notified if site owners do not confirm that the site is not in use.

FIGURE 11.35

Creating a new site quota template

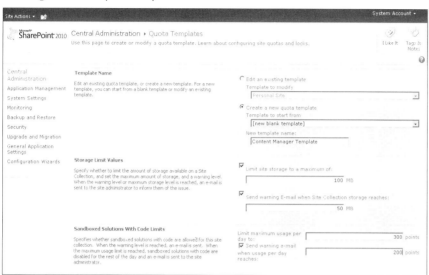

Upon creation of a site collection, the site is added to the database and logged as an active site. After a specified time, e-mail notification is sent to the site collection owner asking the owner to either reconfirm or delete the unused site collection. The e-mail notification contains links to alternately confirm that a site collection is active or to delete the inactive site collection. There are three scenarios in which to decide to keep or delete a site collection based on the configuration of unused site settings:

- **The site collection owner confirms that the site collection is active and the site collection is preserved.** When the owner clicks the confirmation link, the certification date of the site automatically renews.

- **The site owner may delete the site collection by following the instructions in the e-mail notification.** If no action is taken, the owner will continue to receive e-mail notifications according to the interval the server administrator specifies until the owner confirms that the site collection is in use or deletes the site collection.

- **If the automatic deletion feature has been enabled, e-mail notifications are sent to the site collection owner the number of times specified by the site administrator.** If the site collection owner does not confirm site collection use, the site collection is deleted automatically.

Tip

The following best practices are recommended to preclude inadvertent deletion of a site when this feature has been enabled.

Require a secondary contact when users create site collections. The site collection creator is listed as site collection owner by default. Depending on how site creation is configured, site creators must also specify a secondary contact for the site collection. Confirmation notifications are then sent automatically to the site collection owner and the secondary contact.

Stay abreast of vacations and leaves of absence within your organization. Ensure that there is a regular schedule to back up site collections so you can restore a recent copy if a site collection is deleted unintentionally. ■

Automatic deletion of unconfirmed site collections may be provisioned from the Central Administration site. This feature can be enabled and configured from the Application Management page of the Central Administration Web application.

To configure automatic site deletion, follow these steps:

1. From the Central Administration Web application, click Application Management on the Quick Launch bar.

2. Under the Site Collection section, click Confirm site use and deletion.

3. Select the Web application from the drop-down list of the Web Application section.

4. Specify whether or not you would like to send e-mail notification to site collection owners.

5. Determine when e-mail notification of unused sites should begin.

6. Specify the intervals to run checks for unused sites, and at what time they should occur.

7. Check the Automatically delete the site collection if use is not confirmed box to enable automatic site deletion, as shown in Figure 11.36.

8. Specify how many notifications should be sent prior to initiating automatic site deletion.

9. Click OK.

FIGURE 11.36

Configuring automatic site deletion

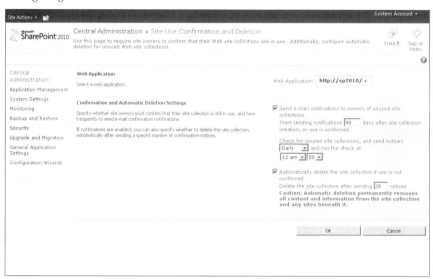

Configuring Mobile Access

Each site collection created in SharePoint Server 2010 can be accessed from a mobile device such as a PDA or SmartPhone.

Accessing the site from a mobile device displays site lists and document libraries in a simpler format than the rich site format typical of SharePoint Server. Any site list is available in this format, which takes the list to its most basic elements.

To access a SharePoint Server 2010 site from your mobile device, simply append /m to the URL you would ordinarily enter in the browser.

Summary

This chapter discussed the different methods available for creating, customizing, and publishing Web content, and covered the creation of master pages, layout pages, and content types, and a custom executive newsletter. The chapter discussed the approval process, walking you through how to create an approval workflow for content published to your site, and reviewed the means of deploying content between different sites and how to create site variations for different audiences in your organization. It also discussed best practices for managing your Web sites, how to configure locks and quotas, and best practices regarding the deletion of unused sites.

Implementing Records Management

Records management is an extremely important activity for companies and organizations and is often overlooked by management. Unfortunately, it is only after a legal dispute that includes discovery of damaging e-mails and documents that this discipline is taken seriously.

In addition to the day-to-day management of documents and e-mails, the compliance landscape is becoming more difficult to navigate and the risks associated with noncompliance are becoming more costly. With the mounting numbers of federal, state, and international laws and regulations being mandated, organizations are placing more focus on their compliance infrastructure and the risks of incorrectly managing the associated documentation.

This chapter discusses the planning and implementation of a records management solution using SharePoint Server 2010. It combines collaboration, document management, content management, and records management into one elegant and integrated package.

Planning for Records Management

Definitions abound, and in that spirit I submit yet another: *records management* is the systematic control of all organizational records during the various stages of their life cycle — from their creation or receipt, through their processing, distribution, maintenance, and use, to their ultimate disposition. The purpose of records management is to promote economic and efficient recordkeeping. This ensures that useless records are systematically destroyed, while valuable information is protected and maintained in a manner that facilitates its access and use as well as ensuring legal and regulatory compliance.

The basic element of a records management system is the record. A *record* is a document or other item in an organization that requires retention for a period of time. Records management is the process by which organizations:

- Identify the types of information that should be considered records
- Determine how live documents will be managed while in use, and how they should be collected once declared to be records
- Define disposition rules which determine in what manner and for how long each record type should be retained to meet legal, business, or regulatory requirements
- Perform tasks such as records disposition, or locating and holding records related to external events such as lawsuits
- Implement technological solutions and business processes to help ensure that the organization complies with its records management obligations in a cost-effective and productive way

Some of the properties common to a records management system are

- Documentation of the organization's information environment by describing and categorizing content that may become records, documenting source locations, and describing the content workflow into the records management application
- File plans describe where each type of record in the enterprise should be retained, as well as its policies, retention, disposition, and responsible managing party
- Compliance requirements document that defines the methods used to guarantee participation of the organization's employees as well as the rules that the organization's IT systems must follow to ensure compliance
- Methods for collecting records that are no longer active from collaboration document libraries, file servers, and e-mail systems
- Methods for capturing the metadata and audit histories of records
- Methods for auditing active records
- Processes for holding records for events like litigation and audits
- System reporting and monitoring of records to ensure that they are being filed properly

Planning overview

Planning for the records management process is extremely important and typically involves team members from across the organization. The steps are

1. **Identify roles.** The roles may include the following:
   - Records managers to own the categorization of the records in the organization and to manage the overall process

- Content managers to identify where information is kept and to ensure that their teams are following records management guidelines and practices

- IT personnel and systems that efficiently support records management

2. **Develop a file plan.** It is important to review and document file usage to determine which documents and other items may become records. After you have analyzed your organizational content and determined retention schedules, fill in the rest of the file plan. File plans differ from organization to organization, but in general they describe the kinds of items the enterprise acknowledges to be records, indicate where they are stored, describe their retention periods, and provide other information such as who is responsible for managing them and what broader category of records they belong to.

3. **Develop retention periods.** For each record type, determine when it will no longer be active, how long it should be retained past the active date, and how it should be disposed of.

4. **Determine the scope of your retention policy.** Policies can be applied at a site collection level or at an individual document library. If your policy will be widely used, implement it at the site collection and then apply it to your retention document libraries.

5. **Design the records management repository.** SharePoint Server 2010 includes a Records Repository site template, which is designed for records management. Using your file plan, design the site's content types, libraries, policies, and its record series.

6. **Develop workflows and methods to move content into the Records Repository.** In SharePoint Server 2010 you may optionally create custom workflows to move content into your Records Repositories. There are also APIs that allow you to integrate SharePoint Server 2010 Records Management functionality with other applications. Once again, these are optional as the built-in workflows handle most of your basic needs.

7. **Plan e-mail integration.** For organizations that are already planning to move to Exchange Server 2010 along with Office Outlook 2010, there are features designed to facilitate the flow of e-mail into the Records Repository, using specialized folders and commands. If you are using Exchange Server 2010 as your e-mail server, you can plan how to classify e-mail and move it to the Records Repository quite easily. Many third-party vendors are developing integration with SharePoint that will provide hooks for other e-mail systems. Additionally, it is possible to customize your own integration with SharePoint.

8. **Plan for compliance reporting and documentation.** If an organization becomes involved in a records-related legal dispute or is forced by a government agency to prove compliance, it is important to have the system and processes well documented.

Creating file plans and policies

A file plan lists the records in the organization and describes how they are organized and maintained; this is critical to a successful records management program. The file plan:

- Documents your activities
- Identifies records

- Helps to retrieve records quickly
- Provides retention and disposition instructions when records are no longer needed
- Documents responsibilities for managing the various types of records

Defining a record

The determination of which active documents may be declared as records often requires the collaboration of lawyers, records managers, content managers, and compliance officers. Records management is not only the domain of highly regulated industries. There are now broad accounting and tax laws, such as the Sarbanes-Oxley Act, which records managers need to be aware of.

Some suggestions to assist you with the identification of records are

1. **Identify the legal obligations and business needs of the enterprise.**
2. **Analyze active document usage across the organization.**
3. **Create a list of active document types that should become records.** For example:
   - Legal agreements
   - Employee benefits
   - Press releases

Next, categorize the records. See Table 12.1. Often, records in the same category will have the same retention periods.

TABLE 12.1

Sample Record Categorization Table

Record Type	Record Category	Description
401K, insurance, and stock option plans	Employee Benefit Description	Employee benefits
Subcontractor and employment agreements, statements of work	Legal Agreements	Legal agreements between the organization and individuals, companies, and government agencies
Press releases, articles	Press Releases	Statements released to the press

Documenting the file plan

After determining which documents to classify as records and creating a set of record categories, complete the file plan by defining retention periods for each record category, indicating how to dispose of records when their retention periods have expired, and supplying other information such as the primary records manager for each record type and media in which the record is stored.

Note

The example in Table 12.2 is provided only as a sample and is not intended to provide legal guidance. Please work with your extended team to document the proper file plan information and disposition durations. ∎

TABLE 12.2

Sample File Plan

Records	Description	Media	Record Category	Retention	Disposition	Contact
Insurance plan	Blue Cross/Blue Shield health care plan	Scanned PDF image	Employee Benefit Plans	(x) years	Archive	Roger Recordski
Sub-contractor agreements	Company agreements with subcontractors	Print	Legal Agreements	(x) years	Destroy	Linda Legale
Press releases	Public press announcements	Electronic documents	Press Releases	(x) years	Destroy	Paula Presston
Stock option plan	Employee stock option plan	Print	Employee Benefit Plans	(x) years	None	Stanley Stockton

Defining your policies

Policies determine the rules that apply to your records. They determine how long your content is retained and the labeling, auditing, expiration, and barcoding actions for your content. You can create policies at both the site collection level and the individual document library level. You will need to create a policy for each combination of retention and disposition in your file plan. You may also need to create additional policies if the options for the policy differ between file plans.

For each policy, you will need to define the following items:

- **Name and Description:** Define a distinct policy name and administrative description so that users can understand the size and scope of the policy.

- **Policy Statement:** The policy statement is presented to users when they open items that are managed by the policy. This allows you to inform users of the necessary record management circumstances for managed items.

- **Retention Period:** This is the period that the item will be managed by the records management site. You can calculate this period based on any date field that you define for the record, or the default date fields of create date or modified date. You should have already defined this period in your file management plan.

- **Disposition:** This defines the action that the records management site will perform when the retention period has elapsed. The options are to delete the record, delete the record and all the associated submission data, or submit the record to a workflow that you have defined. For example, you can create an archive workflow that moves the record to an archive location when the retention period elapses.

Cross-Reference
See Chapter 8 for information about implementing workflows. ∎

- **Labels:** If you enable labels for your policy, they are included when the document is printed. This feature allows you to ensure that important information is attached to your managed items. The label can be formatted as appropriate and include document properties that are calculated at the time of the printing, such as {Date}.

- **Auditing:** Auditing allows you to track when managed items are viewed, opened, edited, checked in/out, moved, or deleted.

- **Barcodes:** The records management process can assign barcodes so that you can track your physical records.

- **Scope:** Is this policy a local document library policy or should it be defined at the site collection level?

Determining how records are moved to the repository

There are three methods available for moving files to the records repository site. Based on your file plan, you will choose the appropriate method for moving your records. The methods for moving records are

- **User Action:** After you have a records repository site, the site collection administrator can configure the connection to the records repository. This enables a drop-down option on the edit menu for every item in the site collection so that users can choose to send it to the records repository. This action sends a copy to the records repository and leaves an active record in the original location that can continue to be used or deleted as appropriate for the purpose.

- **Managed E-mail Folders:** If you are using Exchange Server 2010, the e-mail administrator can configure a management policy for folders so that when messages are moved into those folders, a copy of the message is sent to the records repository site.

- **Custom method:** You can write a custom method that will move records to the records repository using the SharePoint object model. This method could be kicked off by a custom SharePoint workflow that walks a document through its entire life cycle. For example, if you have a contract, the workflow may flow through drafting the contract, finalizing the contract, obtaining control approval, and when complete, send the contract to the records repository.

Implementing a Records Repository Site and File Plan

Managing records in SharePoint Server 2010 is accomplished by planning and implementing a records repository site. This site, based on the out-of-the-box Records Repository Site template, provides the features for the implementation of your file plan and management of the records while they are being retained.

To design a records repository site, follow these steps:

1. **Plan the document libraries you will use for records retention.**

2. **Document the metadata for each record type.** The metadata will translate into document library columns.

3. **Document policies, such as retention periods and auditing requirements, for each type of record that reflects your enterprise's storage requirements.**

4. **Plan the record routing table.** The record routing table will map each type of record to the appropriate library in the records repository site. This table is used to determine how to classify and route the documents to the appropriate library based on the plan.

5. **Define your site columns.** Site columns are used to create the content types that are to be retained. For example, you may want to create columns like "Stock Options."

The records repository site template

The records repository site template combines many of the features of SharePoint Server 2010 with records management features, providing an integrated experience for users. Site features that are not suited to a records center, such as a picture library or discussions, are hidden by default. The records repository features are detailed in the following sections.

Record routing

When a document is moved to the repository, the record will be automatically moved to a document library based on its type. The mapping of document types to libraries is accomplished in the record routing list.

For each type of record in the list, you will specify the title and description of the record type, the location where you want to store those records, and the names of other record types (aliases) that you want to store in the same location. Any record type can be specified as a default, and any incoming record that doesn't match any of the types in the list will be stored in the default location.

When records are sent to the repository, additional information is sent along with the record, including the record's audit history (stored in an XML file) and its metadata.

Policy enforcement

SharePoint Server 2010 provides several features to facilitate policy enforcement:

- **Auditing:** The recording of actions on a record such as viewing and accessing the information.

- **Expiration:** This feature is essentially a clock that starts ticking when a record enters the repository and includes the logic that specifies what should happen to the record when the period documented for that type of record has expired. For example, moving the item to an offline storage repository or deleting the item.

- **Barcodes:** Each record is provided with a unique barcode graphic and associated numeric value. In the context of records management, barcodes are useful for retaining and tracking physical records. When the records in a library have hard copy versions, barcodes provide a way to correlate the hard copy versions with their electronic counterparts. Barcode values are stored and indexed along with the electronic versions of records.

Integration and extensibility

The site provides a programmable interface that allows the creation of additional record policies as well as the ability to programmatically import documents from other systems, including their associated metadata and audit history as part of a business workflow.

Holds

In the case of a litigation or regulatory audit or event, it may be necessary or required by law to prevent the removal, destruction, or editing of certain records as of a specified date. The hold feature in SharePoint Server 2010 allows the creation of named holds that will prevent records from expiring and/or being destroyed. Holds are described in more detail in the "Suspending Record Disposition with Holds" section of this chapter.

Tutorial: Records management deployment and configuration

After you've reviewed your enterprise content, created your file plan, and planned the metadata you would like to associate with both your documents and records, it is time to put this information to a practical application.

In this exercise, you create an initial document library that holds employee benefit documents, such as a stock option plan. Then you create a records repository site, configure it to receive and route records, and initiate the disposition of your record from the employee benefits library to the repository.

Provisioning a records repository site

Follow these steps to provision a records repository site:

1. Go to your portal home page and select New Site as in Figure 12.1.

FIGURE 12.1

Click New Site to add a new site.

2. Use these settings for the Create site dialog (see Figure 12.2):

    ● Template: Data ⇨ Records Center

    ● Title: Records Vault

    ● URL name: `http://(your portal name)/recordsvault`

FIGURE 12.2

Records center site settings

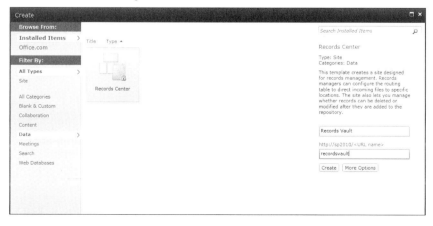

3. **Click the Create button.** The Operation in Progress screen appears. Your records repository site is created, and you are taken to the Home page (see Figure 12.3).

FIGURE 12.3

Records Center site home page

Note

You may want to create a separate Web application for the records repository to enhance records security and to provide for separate backup and restore options. This example skips that step for simplicity. ■

Creating the records storage location document libraries

Now implement a portion of the file plan you created during the planning process. For this example, just use the Stock Option portion as an example (see Table 12.3) and set the retention period for 7 years. Your first task is to create the document library:

TABLE 12.3

Stock Option File Plan

Records	Description	Media	Record Category	Retention	Disposition	Contact
Stock option plan	Employee stock option plan	Print	Employee Benefit Plans	7 years	None	Stanley Stockton

1. From the Site Actions menu, select New Document Library.

2. On the New Document Library page, enter Stock Options for Name and click Create, accepting the defaults for the rest of the fields as shown in Figure 12.4. The library is created as shown in Figure 12.5.

FIGURE 12.4

Creating the Stock Options document library

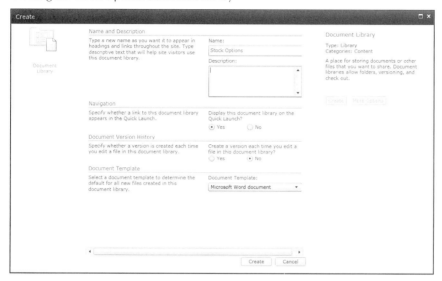

3. Click Create Column button on the Library tab on the Ribbon.

4. On the add Column page (See Figure 12.6) enter these values:

   - Column Name: Filing Date
   - Type: Date and Time
   - Require that this column contains information: Yes

5. Click OK.

6. Click Library Settings from the Library menu bar.

7. Under the Permissions and Management section, click Information management policy settings.

FIGURE 12.5

Records storage location for Stock Options

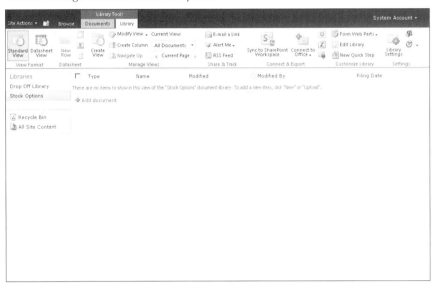

FIGURE 12.6

Creating Filing Date column

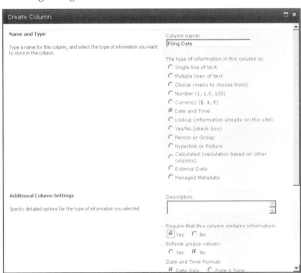

8. **On the Policy Settings page, click on the Document content type to create a policy for documents.** The Edit Policy page appears.

9. **On the Edit Policy page (See Figures 12.7 and 12.8) use the following values:**

   - Administrative Description: Stock Option documentation will be retained for 7 years after its filing date.

   - Policy Statement: Stock Option documentation will be retained for 7 years after its filing date.

   - Check Enable Retention. Click on the Add a retention stage link.

   - Under Event, select the Filing Data column and enter 7 in the amount box leaving the time element to Years.

   - Under Action select Permanently Delete from the drop-down.

FIGURE 12.7

Edit Policy page

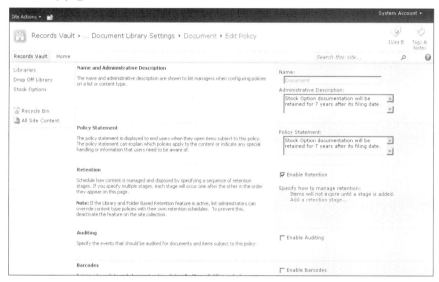

10. **Click OK.** The policy retention stage is created and shown in the Edit Policy page.

11. **Click OK.** The policy for this document library has now been configured.

FIGURE 12.8

Retention Stage dialog box

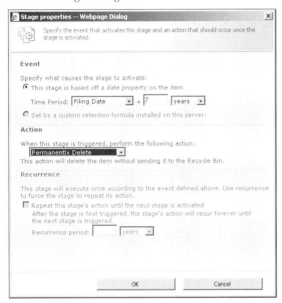

Defining the records routing behavior for the record type

Follow these steps to define records behavior for the record type:

1. Select Site Actions ⇨ Manage Record Center. Click on the Create content organizer rules link. (Alternate method is Site Actions ⇨ Site Settings ⇨ Content organizer rules.)

2. In the Content Organizer Rules page, click Add new item.

3. On the New Item page, enter the information for the Stock Option record routing, as shown in Figure 12.9:

   - Name: Stock Options
   - Content Type Group: Document Content Types
   - Content Type: Document
   - Destination: /recordsvault/Stock Options (use browse button for easy selection)

4. Click OK.

FIGURE 12.9

Content Organizer Rules: New Rule

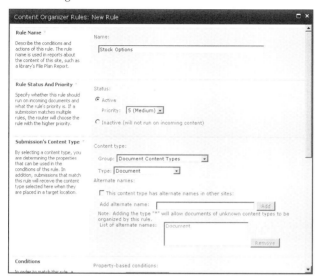

Tip

For this example, selecting a Document content type is sufficient. In a production environment, separate content types should be created for each type of record to insure proper routing. Relying on property-based conditions is not optimal as exceptions will always occur (when a user names a document wrong or selects a wrong value). ∎

Testing the records routing using the Drop-Off library

Now that the content organizer rule is in place, we can test it by uploading a document to the Drop-Off library within our Records Center site. To test the rule, follow these steps:

1. From the Records Center site, click on the Drop-Off library from the left Quick Launch bar.

2. Click **Add document.** Browse to a document and click Open. Click OK.

3. On document properties dialog, enter a title and click on Submit as shown in Figure 12.10.

FIGURE 12.10

Document properties dialog

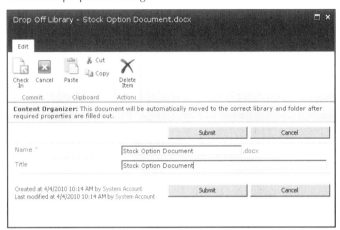

4. The content organizer rule kicks in and saves the document to the Stock Options library. A Saved to final location confirmation dialog box appears, as shown in Figure 12.11.

FIGURE 12.11

Saved to final location confirmation dialog box

5. Click OK.

Moving content from SharePoint Server 2010 sites to the Records Repository site

In the previous section you found out how records management can move records within a Records Center site. Now you explore how to move records between sites.

SharePoint Server 2010 has the ability to receive records via Web Services and e-mail. Additionally, SharePoint Server 2010 can be configured to send files to the Records Repository sites. This is accomplished by providing the URL to the Records Repository site on the Central Administration site, allowing both the UI and object model to use the Send To function when a document should be retained as a record.

This system allows users to simply send a document to the Records site while the site uses logic to route the record to the appropriate document library. This section of the exercise will:

- Configure the connection from a server running SharePoint Server 2010 to a Records Repository

- Configure a Document Libraries content type to match the record type described in the Records Repository file plan, configured earlier

- Submit a document from the document library to the Records Repository site

Configuring the connection to Records Repository settings

Follow these steps to configure the connection to the records repository settings.

1. **Access your SharePoint Server 2010 server console.**

2. **Go to Central Administration by choosing Start ⇨ All programs ⇨ Administrator Tools ⇨ SharePoint 2010 Central Administration.**

3. **Click General Application Settings on the quick launch.**

4. **Under the External Service Connections section, click Configure send to connections.**

5. **Set the values as follows (Figure 12.12):**
   - Display name: Records Vault
   - URL: `http://(your portal name)/recordsvault/_vti_bin/official file.asmx`
   - Send to Action: Move and Leave a Link

6. **Click Add Connection.** The Records Vault connection appears in the connection list.

7. **Click OK.** Your SharePoint applications are now able to send files to the Records Repository (if it refers to the template within SharePoint, it should be Records Center).

Caution

Make sure that you append the `_vti_bin/officialfile.asmx` portion of the URL to the path to your records repository site in Step 5. If you do not append this, your configuration will be saved without presenting an error but you will not be able to send to the records repository. ■

FIGURE 12.12

The Configure Connection to Records Center page

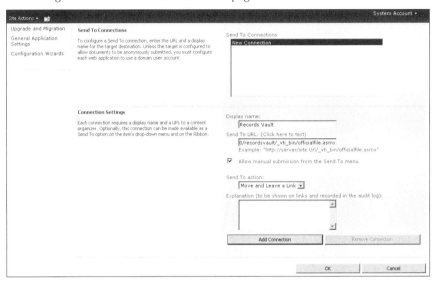

Sending content from a SharePoint site

The content type of a document is passed automatically as a routing parameter to the Records Repository site, directing the site to copy the file to the appropriate document library. In this part of the exercise, you will create a document library, change the name of that library's content type, and send a file to the Records Repository.

1. Go to the portal home page.

2. Choose Site Actions ➪ Site Settings from the menu on the upper-left side of the home page.

3. In the Galleries section, click Site content types.

4. Click Create.

5. Use the following entries (Figure 12.13):

   • Name: Stock Options

   • Select parent content type from: Document Content Types

   • Parent Content Type: Document

   • Existing Group: Document Content Types

FIGURE 12.13

Create content type

6. Click OK.

7. Return to your portal home page.

8. Select View All Site Content from the Site Actions menu.

9. Click Create.

10. On the Create page, in the Libraries section, click Document Library.

11. Create a document library named Employee Stock Options using the defaults for all other fields.

12. In the Stock Options document library, select Library Settings from the Library tab on the Ribbon.

13. In the General Settings section, click Advanced Settings.

14. On the Advanced Settings page, in the Content Types section, under Allow management of content types, choose Yes.

15. Leave the other default options and Click OK.

16. In the Content Types section, click Add from existing site content types.

17. Choose Document Content Types from the Select site content types from the drop-down.

18. Highlight Stock Options and click the Add button (see Figure 12.14).

FIGURE 12.14

Add Content Types: Employee Stock Options document library

19. Click OK.

20. Go to the Employee Stock Options document library.

21. Upload a sample document called Employee Stock Options.

22. Select Stock Options from the Content Type drop-down menu (See Figure 12.15).

23. Click Save.

FIGURE 12.15

Changing content type of uploaded document

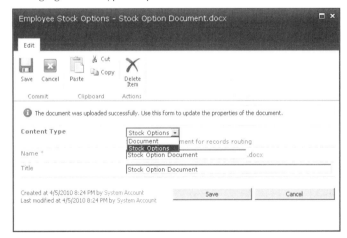

Tip

Instead of uploading, you could select New Document from the Document tab on the Ribbon and select the Stock Option document as shown in Figure 12.16. ∎

FIGURE 12.16

Creating a new document from a content type

24. Click the document select menu⇨Send To⇨ Records Vault to send the document to the Records Repository (see Figure 12.17).

FIGURE 12.17

Send the document to the records repository

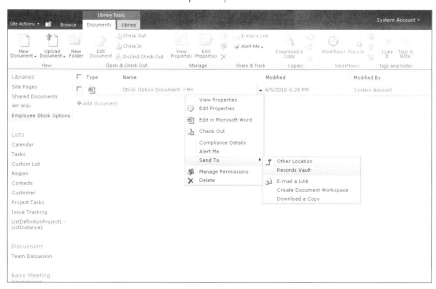

25. **Click OK on the confirmation message.**

26. **Submission pending.** The submission is pending in the drop-off library. Click on the new location document link in the Submission pending message (Figure 12.18).

FIGURE 12.18

Submission pending message

> Submission is pending
>
> The document is pending submission and requires attention from the submitter or a site administrator.
>
> Click the link below to access the document and finish the submission:
> http://sp2010/recordsvault/DropOffLibrary/Stock Option Document.docx
>
> OK

27. **Click Submit.** A Saved to Final Location message appears again.

28. **Verify that the record went to the Records Repository by opening the site and clicking the Stock Options document library.** You should see a screen similar to Figure 12.19.

FIGURE 12.19

Stock Options Record successfully copied

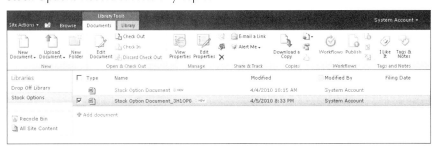

This completes the exercise. Note that the name of the document has some additional characters appended to it. These characters are added to ensure that all files sent to the Records Repository site have a unique name and will therefore never overwrite other files in the site.

The names and values for columns that have metadata associated with them are saved along with the record in a `(recordnumber).xml` file in a hidden _properties folder that is created in the destination library. The metadata values are copied to matching columns in the destination library.

In-Place Records Management

You no longer need a records center site to store records. You may now create record libraries in other locations within a site collection. Activating the In Place Records Management site collection feature enables the record library to appear as an option when creating a new library.

Once declared a record, a document is subject to a different set of policies, different permissions (such as who may edit/delete documents), and to the standard record hold functionality. Note also that a hybrid approach is also supported (that is, declare a record in-place, but after the expiration policy is reached move it to a records center). Guidance for selection of the employed method can be found at http://technet.microsoft.com/en-us/library/ee424394.aspx.

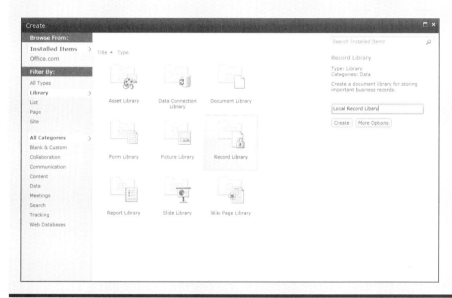

It is recommended that for each column of metadata for a type of record, a column should be defined in the destination document library that matches the incoming column's name and type. To have the column submitted along with the record and to require the column to have an associated data value, you should configure the column in the SharePoint Server 2010 user interface to require data. Required fields are configured by selecting the Require that this column contain information option when creating the columns.

Note

If required metadata is missing when the record is submitted, the submitter will be prompted for the missing metadata. If the metadata is not entered, the record will not be accepted by the repository for retention. If the document was sent to the repository by a programmatic interface, the file is placed in a temporary holding area, and the information is sent back to the calling program to be handled. ∎

Cross-Reference

For more information on creating required columns as well as columns that can be used in multiple document libraries, see Chapter 4. ■

Considerations for configuring permissions in the records repository site

Moving records between sites requires configuring the appropriate security model to allow this action while maintaining the integrity of the record and audit process. There are several security considerations that you should be aware of when creating a records repository site:

- **Create a separate Web application for the records repository site:** A separate Web application is a more secure option and can guarantee that the records won't be commingled with active documents in the database used by the site. Additionally, using a separate Web application can allow for the optimization of your backup and restoration schedule to meet your records management needs.

- **Don't configure the records repository Web application on which the records repository site is running to use Forms Authentication:** Requiring Forms Authentication requires enabling anonymous submissions to the records repository site to allow for the submission of records via the user interface or programmatically.

- **Configure rights on the files and repository site:** File submission to the records repository site requires users to have Edit Items rights to the files on the document management source library and Add Items rights on the records repository site. Microsoft advises the creation of a group on the records repository site with Create List rights, but not Edit Items rights. You should also add the accounts on other servers that will submit items to the repository to this group.

- **Assign "Edit Items" rights to records managers:** To manage records, a user of the records repository site must have Edit Items rights. Generally, it is advised to give only records managers and legal team members edit rights to content on the records repository site. SharePoint Server 2010 provides the ability to create granular security down to the item level for special cases. This ability was not available in the previous release of the product.

Suspending Record Disposition with Holds

Putting records "on hold" means suspending the process defined for that record type and ensuring that the records are not edited or deleted. To put a record type on hold you must define the parameters of the hold order. Typically this would include the identification of records types that are going to be relevant for the "hold order." From a SharePoint Server 2010 perspective, this process requires the creation of a new hold order in the system and the tagging of records associated with it. Often organizations don't have the luxury of having only one hold order in effect at a time, so it is also important to be able to know which records have relevance to which hold order.

The main steps in the holds process are

- Creating a new hold order
- Searching for and putting relevant records on hold
- Releasing the hold order

Creating a hold order

In the SharePoint Server 2010 Records Center, holds are managed in the Holds list that is included as part of the records center site template (see Figure 12.20). It can be accessed by Site Actions ➪ Site Settings ➪ Holds.

FIGURE 12.20

Manage holds using the holds list.

Entries in the list represent hold orders, and the hold orders are tagged with metadata such as the hold name, description, and the person responsible for tracking the hold order. Additional information is tracked automatically, such as:

- **Hold Status:** When a hold order is Active, the matter is still in process and the records tagged as relevant to the hold must be retained for as long as the status remains Active, although new records can be added to the hold. When the hold is no longer Active, the records will resume their defined disposition schedules.

- **List of items currently on that hold:** Each hold includes a listing of the items that are tagged as relevant to the hold.

The list also provides the three related actions for dealing with the hold orders as shown in Figure 12.21. These actions are

- **Search for items to add to this hold:** This method of search for items to hold is a good method for adding a lot of items to your hold at once. You can specify a search value and then apply the appropriate hold to all items that are returned by search.
- **Release hold:** This action removes the hold on all items.
- **View hold report:** This report allows you to view the items that this hold has been applied to.

FIGURE 12.21

Sample Active hold

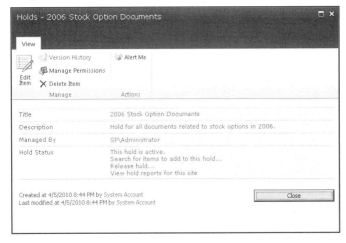

Files are put on hold in the Records Repository site by creating holds in a specialized Holds list. A hold is a list item, and to create a hold, a user must have the "Add Items" right to the Holds list. After a hold is created, a user must have Edit Items rights on the item being placed on hold and View Items rights to the Holds list. Because this list might contain very sensitive information, you should limit the set of users of the Holds list to team members who can create holds and team members who can put items on hold.

After you have created a hold order, it is available for you to apply it to the appropriate items. You can do this broadly by searching for items or you can apply it at the individual item.

Note

Holds are placed on records no matter where they are located if In-Place is active. ∎

Searching for and placing relevant records on hold

The concept of placing an item on hold is simple enough: find, then hold. Sounds simple enough until you are faced with a global company and millions of documents. Fortunately, the integration with SharePoint Server 2010 greatly facilitates this process by using search. The hold order has the ability to specify a search query to identify items of relevance and then put the matching items on hold as in Figure 12.22, which can be facilitated by the Discover and hold content link in Site Settings.

FIGURE 12.22

Search for items to hold

The search method for placing documents on hold is broad. You have the ability to apply a hold to all the items that were returned by your search query. So after the initial search and hold is completed, the records management team can add or remove individual items from the hold order to tune the appropriate record set. Each item in the Records Center can be tagged to multiple hold orders. Items on hold will not be disposed of if any of the holds are active.

Applying a hold to an individual record

You can also apply holds to an individual record by navigating to that record and editing the hold status directly. This can be cumbersome if you are trying to manage a large number of documents for a particular hold, and we'd recommend using the search and hold method if that is the case. But, for fine-tuning the hold settings for a particular record, the individual management option is available and useful.

To manage the holds on an individual record, follow these steps:

1. Navigate to the item for which you want to review the hold status.

2. From the drop-down menu on that item, select Compliance Details.

3. Click the Add/Remove from Hold link.

4. If you would like to add a hold for that document, select the Add to a hold radio button and select the appropriate hold name. If you have applied a hold to the item already, this list will only show the holds that have not been applied.

5. If you would like to remove a hold for the document, select the Remove from a hold radio button and select the appropriate hold name.

6. Enter comments if necessary to note why you have added or removed a hold (See Figure 12.23).

7. Click Save.

FIGURE 12.23

Adding hold to individual record

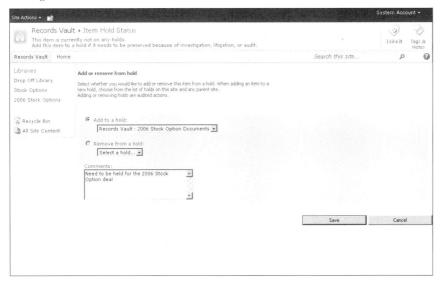

Releasing a hold order

After the reason that necessitated the hold has been resolved, hopefully in a positive fashion, you can proceed with removing the hold order and allowing the records to be managed by the policy you have chosen for them. To release a hold order, follow these steps:

1. Click the Holds list Site Settings in your records management site.

2. From the drop-down menu on the hold you want to release, select View Item.

3. Click the Release Hold link in the Hold Status section.

4. Enter any comments that you would like to record for why you have released the hold.

5. Click Release hold.

After you have released the hold, the hold item shows that it has a hold status of Pending Release in the hold order list. When all the items that were held have been released, the hold status is updated to inactive.

Managing a Records Management Program

Now that you have implemented a records management program that stores all contracts for seven years, you can now just walk away and ignore it for seven years, right? Wrong! A records management program needs regular care and feeding to ensure that it is operating properly and routing content appropriately.

Reviewing and resolving unclassified records

Unclassified records are records that were submitted to the records center but do not match a record routing entry. Documents that stay in the Drop Off library need to be reviewed regularly and moved to the appropriate location. In addition, the records center administrator needs to determine if another content type is necessary to manage regularly submitted documents that result in unclassified records.

To move records from the drop-off repository to the appropriate record library, follow these steps:

1. Select Drop Off Library from the left navigation of the records management site.

2. Review any documents existing in the library.

3. From the document item drop-down menu, select Send to and then Other location.

4. Enter the path to the appropriate records management library in the Destination document library or folder field.

5. Click OK.

6. After the file copy shows that it is finished, click Done to return to the Drop Off document library.

7. Select Delete from the drop-down of the document that you just copied to the correct records management folder.

Tip

The documents in the records management libraries will most likely appear to have been last modified by the System Account because of the method used when moving them to the records management site. If you want to view the properties for a particular document, navigate to the records management document library, select the Properties folder, and click the XML document for the document that you want. This XML document shows all the original author information for each record. ∎

Managing missing metadata

If your records management library requires particular columns of metadata and records are submitted without that metadata, the records will not be routed to the records library but will instead be placed in the drop-off document library until the records receive the appropriate metadata. If you are using the manual method of submitting records to the records management location, you do not need to be concerned about missing metadata because SharePoint will prompt the user submitting the content for the appropriate metadata. However, if you are using a programmatic method to push content to the records repository, it is possible for the content to be pushed without the right metadata.

To fill in the appropriate metadata for your documents, follow these steps:

1. Open the records management site and select the Drop Off library on the Quick Launch bar.
2. Review the documents still lingering in the library for possible missing metadata.
3. For each title presented in the list, select Edit Properties from the drop-down menu.
4. Fill in the missing metadata fields and click OK.

Reviewing hold reports

Holds are key to legal compliance. You should regularly review the hold orders for your records to make sure that they are sufficient for the compliance issues that are active in your organization. In addition to a hold, you should regularly review the hold reports for the holds that you have implemented to make sure that the necessary items have been added to the hold. Because holds suspend the disposition of your records, you should also regularly review whether all hold orders are still required.

On your records repository site, you can review the hold reports by following these steps:

1. Select Site Settings from the Site Actions menu on the records management site.
2. Under the Holds and eDiscovery section, click Hold Reports.

Summary

Records management is necessary for all sizes of organizations. To successfully implement a records management program, you need to identify the records in your organization and create the file plan, or action plan, for those records. You can then implement the SharePoint records management features to implement the submission, hold placement, and management of your organizational records. This chapter discussed planning your records management process, implementing records management, suspending the records management with holds, and managing your records management.

Integrating Office System with SharePoint

With the release of SharePoint Portal Server 2003, Microsoft made a big commitment to integrating SharePoint and Office. The deep integration provides a win-win situation for both users and Microsoft. Users have access to features that increase their productivity and reduce the learning curve, and Microsoft creates additional demand for their well-integrated products.

This chapter focuses on the integration provided between the new 2010 Office System applications and Microsoft Office SharePoint Server 2010. The 2010 Office System has significantly changed, providing a more intuitive interface that relies on the new Ribbon concept, which does away with the menu option approach of its predecessors. This chapter describes the enhanced properties integration with all applications as well as the improvements in publishing, exporting, offline access, and information synchronization between clients and servers.

While many of these improvements provide enhanced integration with Office 2010, you may take advantage of some of the SharePoint 2010 integration features with Office 2007 as well.

Integrating with Office Applications

Personal computer users still spend a great deal of time working with Microsoft Office applications. By integrating SharePoint into the menus and in the context of what users are doing, Microsoft has made it much easier for users to share their content with anyone that has access to a Web browser.

Integration points between Word, Excel, Access, PowerPoint, and SharePoint 2010 surface in the following locations, depending on the context of the activity:

- **Save and Save As:** Documents can be saved directly to SharePoint document libraries via Network Places.

- **Edit in Microsoft (Application name):** This option is available from a document saved to a SharePoint library and allows the user to edit the document directly on a SharePoint server. Any Save actions are saved on the server directly.

- **Publish:** Blogs (Word only), Document Locations, Excel Services (Excel only), Publish Slides (PowerPoint only), and Document Workspaces can be accessed from the publish action under the Office button menu.

- **Server:** The server option is available from the Office button when a document is opened from the server, providing access to server-based options.

- **Workflow and Metatagging:** From the Ribbon, you can enter SharePoint metadata and edit workflows.

Saving files to SharePoint

Since the first version of SharePoint, Microsoft has provided the ability to treat document libraries as Microsoft Windows folders using a technology called WebDAV. The abbreviation stands for Web-based Distributed Authoring and Versioning. Microsoft's implementation of this Web standard manifests itself in the ability to show an Explorer view of any document. Figure 13.1 is an example of a SharePoint Document Library with the standard All Documents view.

Changing to Explorer view, as in Figure 13.2, you see the WebDAV view of the same library, which allows you to copy folders and files directly into the library.

Both of these views enable you to upload or copy any document from any version of Office, and essentially any file that can be stored on a Windows machine, to a SharePoint library. Interestingly, when working for Microsoft on competitive portal engagements, this WebDAV capability was often what caused customers to choose SharePoint over other solutions. When training new users, it is very valuable to have a paradigm they are used to working with, such as Windows folders, available while they learn the new features. Over time, users will learn the benefits of working with rich document views in a SharePoint library, but adoption increases when done incrementally.

Another way to save Office files in SharePoint is to directly save them from the Office application itself. Office 2010 applications are now even more integrated with SharePoint.

FIGURE 13.1

All Documents view

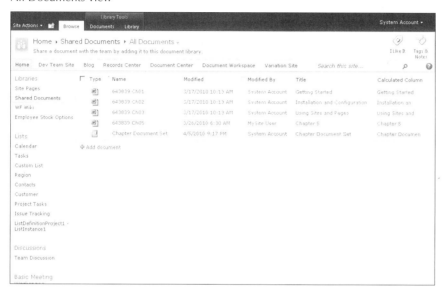

FIGURE 13.2

Explorer view

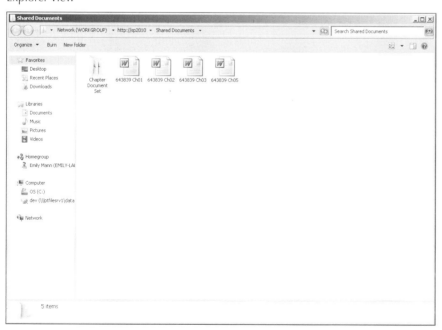

Saving Office Documents to SharePoint

1. From Word, Excel, or PowerPoint, choose File ⇨ Save & Send.

2. Click on **Save to SharePoint.** The Save to SharePoint information appears in the right-hand pane. See Figure 13.3.

FIGURE 13.3

Save to SharePoint

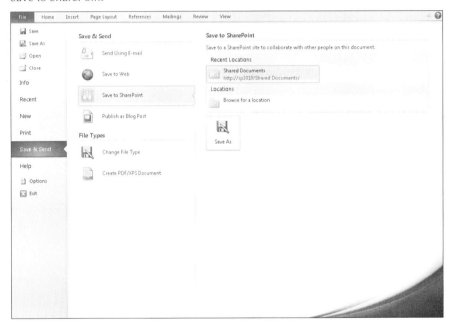

3. Choose a recent location (double-click on location button) or click Browse for a location. (**The next section explains how to add more locations.**) The document is saved.

Adding SharePoint locations to Office applications

When saving to SharePoint from Office, as in the previous example, the Save to SharePoint page showed recent locations (if any) as well as an option to browse for a location. Integrating SharePoint with Office also allows you to create locations and have Office list them such that saving documents to SharePoint is more streamlined.

Essentially, you are saving these locations as Quick Links in your personal site and you allow Office to interrogate that list. To add SharePoint locations to Office, follow these steps:

1. **Navigate to a frequently used document library (or any type of library).**

2. From the Library tab on the Ribbon, click Connect to Office and choose the Add to SharePoint sites (Figure 13.4). A dialog box appears.

3. Click Yes to allow Office to connect to your personal site (Figure 13.5).

FIGURE 13.4

Connect to Office

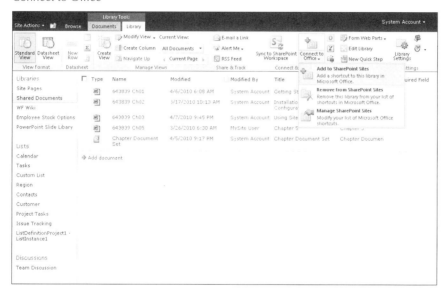

FIGURE 13.5

Allow Office to connect

4. Repeat Steps 1–3 for any other libraries.

5. Open any Office 2010 application (such as Word or Excel) and click File ➪ Save & Send. Click the Save to SharePoint button. The SharePoint locations added appear under the Locations section as shown in Figure 13.6. To manage your list of sites, click on the Manage SharePoint sites from the same menu you used to add the sites (shown in Figure 13.4).

FIGURE 13.6

SharePoint locations in Office

Check-in, check-out, and metadata capture

Capturing metadata and the ability to check documents in and out are core document management features that have been enhanced in the 2010 releases of SharePoint and Office. The integration with Office makes these tasks easier and more intuitive by including the options at the right time, place, and context. The example below uses Word but also applies to the other Office applications.

Check-in/check-out

To explore this functionality, open a SharePoint document library in your browser and upload a document to use in this example:

1. **Position your mouse pointer over a document name and click the down arrow to open the document actions menu.** Select Check Out.

2. **Open the drop-down menu again and choose the option to Edit in Microsoft Office Word.**

3. **Make some changes, save the document, and then click the X in the upper-right corner of Word to close the document.** Because you are in the context of editing a checked-out document in Word, a dialog box appears.

4. **Click Yes to check the document in.** The Version Comments dialog box appears, as in Figure 13.7.

FIGURE 13.7

The Version Comments dialog box

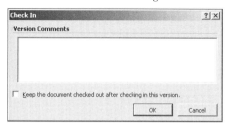

Your document has now been checked in and is available for other users to edit.

Metadata capture

As mentioned earlier, many of the integration behaviors are context-sensitive and will surface when needed. For example, if you have a document library with two custom columns and neither of the columns are required fields, it is possible to create a new document from Word 2010 and choose the URL as the save location without being prompted to enter metadata. Simply changing one of those fields to be required in the document library settings and repeating the same operation opens the dialog box shown in Figure 13.8.

FIGURE 13.8

The file cannot be saved dialog box

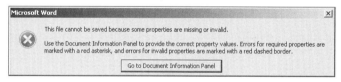

Click the Go to Document Information Panel button, and Word 2010 presents the fields below the Ribbon, as in Figure 13.9.

Integrating the capture of metadata into the application makes it easier and faster for users to complete the form. The biggest challenge of document management systems is often the user participation in the capture of business data. If it is too hard, users will find ways around the system or simply enter useless default data to get past an annoying dialog box. By adding the feature inside the application and providing developers the ability to customize the Ribbon using InfoPath, Microsoft has increased the likelihood of user participation in this process.

FIGURE 13.9

Document Information panel

Publishing documents to SharePoint 2010

Making the publishing of content from the Office applications easy was a design goal of the Office 2010 team. This section discusses the options available in Word, Excel, Access, and PowerPoint for getting around publishing content to SharePoint. Some of the options are available in all four applications and others are specific to augment custom application features — this section describes those also.

Word, Excel, Access, and PowerPoint, all have a Save to SharePoint option available from the File ⇨ Save & Send page for the publishing of files to SharePoint, allowing other users to access those files. The following examples illustrate the publishing integration.

Publishing — Saving Office document to SharePoint

1. From Word, Excel, or PowerPoint, click File ⇨ Save & Send.

2. Click on Save to SharePoint (Figure 13.3 in previous section).

3. Choose a recent location (double-click on location button) or click Browse for a location. The Office document is saved.

Note

In the Beta version of Office 2010, the Save & Send page was labeled Share. Share probably sounded like you were letting other people look at it but not sending it anywhere. ∎

Publishing blogs from Word

One of the publishing options unique to Word is the ability to publish a blog. The term *blog* comes from combining "Web log." Blogs typically provide commentary on a subject published on a schedule and sorted by most recent posting.

Cross-Reference

For more information on creating a blog in SharePoint see Chapter 3. ∎

Create your blog prior to walking through the example below.

1. Create a new document in Word 2010.
2. Click the Save & Send page from the File menu to display the Publish as Blog Post options as in Figure 13.10.

FIGURE 13.10

Publish as a blog post

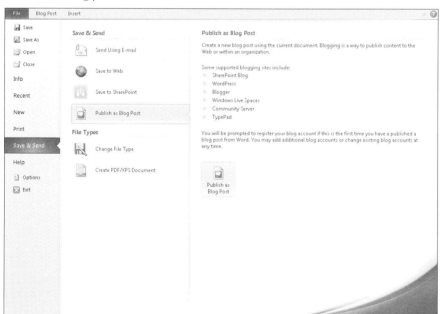

---

3. Click the Publish as Blog Post button on right-hand side.

4. If you have not registered a blog account, you will be prompted to register.

5. Click the Register Now button.

6. Select SharePoint Blog from the Blog Provider list and click Next.

7. Enter the URL to the SharePoint blog and click OK.

8. A warning may appear; click Yes to continue.

9. Enter your SharePoint login credentials if prompted.

10. **An Account registration successful message should appear (Figure 13.11); click OK.** Word opens with a Blog Post tab on the Ribbon on the top of your document.

11. **When you have finished creating your entries, click Publish.** Your screen should be similar to Figure 13.12, and your blog entry should have successfully posted to your SharePoint blog.

FIGURE 13.11

Blog registration successful

FIGURE 13.12

Word 2010 blog

SharePoint Server 2010 – Blog Posting

This is a blog posting on SharePoint Server 2010. It started as a Word document but one registered, that all changed. Now this will be published to the SharePoint blog site on the ....

Publishing — PowerPoint to slide library

One of the great, new collaborative features of PowerPoint 2010 is the integration with SharePoint slide libraries. Slide libraries allow you to share and reuse slide content by storing the individual slides in a centrally located server.

The slide library allows users to easily select and reuse just the slides they need for their presentations, as well as making sure that everyone has access to the most current versions of the core slides. When a change is made to one of the slides, SharePoint timestamps the slide and checks it out. The versioning capability of SharePoint is also used to track the history of changes to a slide. PowerPoint 2010 automatically stores the locations of multiple slide libraries, making it easy to locate them in the future.

Walk through steps in this example that uses this feature:

1. **Create a new slide library on a team site.** Go to any team site and click Site Actions ⇨ View All Site Content.

2. **Click Create, and then under Libraries click Slide Library.**

3. **Give your library a name and description and then click Create.**

4. **Open PowerPoint and create a sample slide deck or open a slide deck that you already have.**

5. **Click File ⇨ Save & Send ⇨ Publish Slides and click the Publish Slides button on the right (Figure 3.13).** You should see a dialog box similar to Figure 13.14.

FIGURE 13.13

The Publish Slides option in Save & Send

FIGURE 13.14

The Publish Slides dialog box

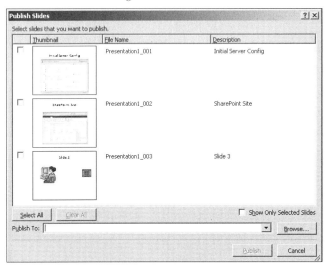

6. **Click the slides you would like to add to the library individually, or click Select All to pick all slides.**

7. **Paste the URL to your slide library into the Publish to field.** For example: `http://portal/SiteDirectory/office/PowerPoint%20Slide%20Library`.

8. **Click Publish; you should see the Publishing Slides indicator at the bottom right of the PowerPoint screen showing the status.** If you now go back to your SharePoint slide library, it should look similar to Figure 13.15.

Access integration

Access has always been a popular application in the Microsoft Office suite of products. Access allows a novice user to create useful database applications for tracking anything from sales opportunities to inventory. The limitation with Access has been allowing multiple users to share the data in various Access databases, providing enterprise scale and server-based backup and restore, as well as discovering which databases are available to them.

The integration with SharePoint allows Access users to create a copy of their data on a SharePoint site. The Access database has a live connection to that SharePoint data, and as information in the offline Access copy is updated, it can be updated on the SharePoint site in real time. Once the data is available on the site, anyone in the organization can interact with the data, and those changes are synchronized back down to the access database. Offline access is another strong point because the Access client can have a copy of SharePoint data, changes can be made, and the data can be synchronized on the server.

FIGURE 13.15

Your SharePoint slide library

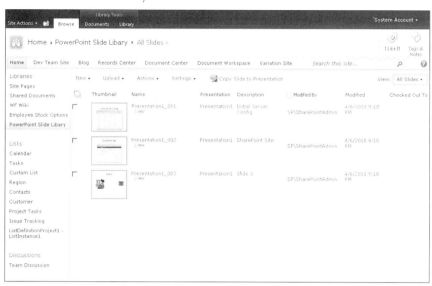

Think of Access as a rich client front end for data and SharePoint as the back end. This scenario can be reversed, too. An existing SharePoint list can be copied to Access and connected, allowing a user to create rich Access views and provide offline access to the data while still keeping the information in sync with a central SharePoint list.

Publishing an Access database to a SharePoint Web database site

In this short tutorial, you will create a new Contacts Web database application that can be published as a Web database site to SharePoint. Access Services needs to be provisioned on the SharePoint 2010 site for these steps to work properly.

1. **Open Access 2010.** Access defaults to the File ⇨ New page.
2. **Click Sample Templates and select Contacts Web Database. Click the Create button on the right-hand side to create a new database as shown in Figure 13.16.** Access opens to the Main Page.
3. **Open the Navigation Pane by clicking the >> on the left side.**
4. **Double-click the Contacts table.** Your screen should now look like Figure 13.17.

FIGURE 13.16

Create Contacts Web database

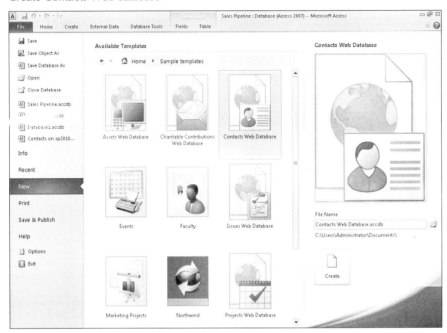

5. To prepare to publish this database to a SharePoint site, populate your Contacts and Comments tables with the sample data in the Northwind 2010 sample access database available on `http://office.microsoft.com`. This step is optional because you can simply add a couple of rows of date for testing.

6. From Access, click File ➪ Save & Publish and click the Publish to Access Services button.

7. Enter the SharePoint server URL and choose a new site name (Figure 13.15).

8. In the Export – SharePoint Site Wizard, enter the URL to your site, as shown in Figure 13.18.

FIGURE 13.17

All Access Objects sort

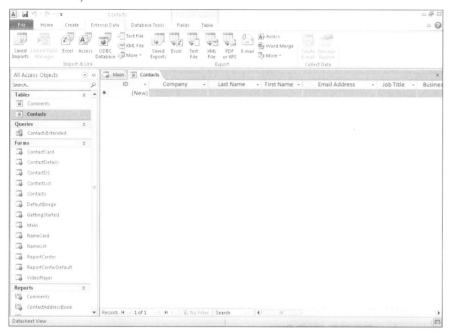

9. **Click Publish to Access Services.** The Web database is synchronized with SharePoint and a new site is created.

10. **Click the link on the Publish Succeeded message (Figure 13.19) to view the new Web database site.** See Figure 13.20.

FIGURE 13.18

Publish to Access Services

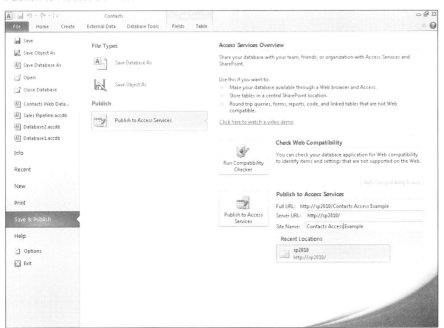

FIGURE 13.19

Publish succeeded message

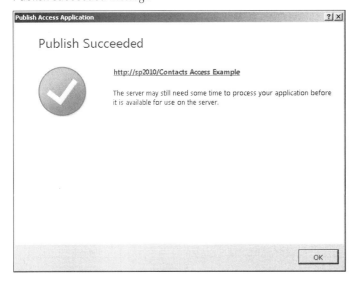

FIGURE 13.20

New Web database site

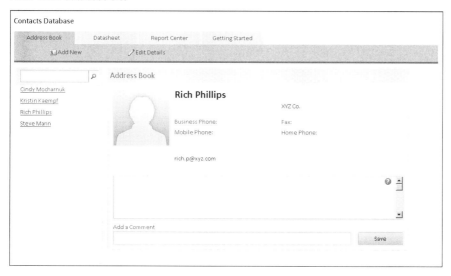

Cross-Reference

See Chapter 3 for more information on creating Web database sites. ∎

Integrating Outlook Features with SharePoint

There are several excellent integration points with Outlook in this new version of SharePoint. Probably the most useful integration is the ability to take tasks, lists, and documents offline and to synchronize changes seamlessly between Outlook and SharePoint. This offline integration will eliminate the need to purchase third-party products that provided this capability in the 2003 edition. Since this functionality is similar to the synchronization provided by SharePoint Workspace, organizations that already have the 2010 Office system should consider which products to purchase and roll out based on other factors such as full offline collaborative functionality.

The improved calendar functionality and integration make it much easier to coordinate individual and group events and activities. This section will describe and show examples that help to illustrate these new integration points.

Outlook integration with SharePoint tasks and contacts

Chapter 4 explored the various lists and libraries that are available in SharePoint. Lists are a very powerful feature of SharePoint that allow the tracking of sales, projects, small business inventory, and many other useful activities. In the 2010 release of Outlook, it is possible to synchronize task and project tasks lists with Outlook, making the offline access and maintenance of tasks as easy as working with e-mail.

Exploring Tasks list synchronization

To explore how this functionality works, create a few sample Tasks list entries, link the list to Outlook, and then make changes on both the server and the client.

1. **Open your Outlook client.**
2. **Access a SPS or SFS team site.** Create either a project Tasks list or use the default Tasks list that comes with most of the site templates for this walkthrough. Go to your list and create a few sample tasks as in Figure 13.21.

FIGURE 13.21

Tasks List sample

---

3. Click the List tab on the Ribbon and click Connect to Outlook.
4. Click Allow on security prompt (Figure 13.22).

FIGURE 13.22

Connect to Outlook security prompt

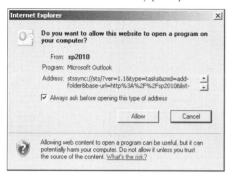

5. On the Connect this SharePoint Task List to Outlook? dialog box (shown in Figure 13.23) click Advanced to see the additional configuration options (shown in Figure 13.24). You can see the SharePoint List Options dialog box. This dialog box allows you to change the folder name that appears on the Outlook client as well as create a description of the list. Additionally, you can set this list to show up only on the computer you are currently using and adjust the Update Limit, which can change the update frequency of list synchronization. Leave the defaults and click OK.

FIGURE 13.23

Microsoft Outlook prompt

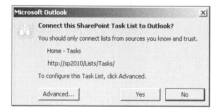

6. Answer Yes to the Connect this SharePoint Task List to Outlook? dialog box. Your Outlook client shows a view of the list. Click New in the Outlook client to create a new task entry.

7. Fill in the Assigned To field and give your task a subject like Task assigned from Outlook client to make it easy to see where it originated. Click Save & Close. The task list will look similar to Figure 13.25.

FIGURE 13.24

SharePoint List Options

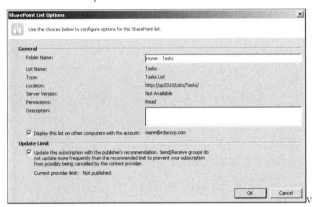

FIGURE 13.25

Tasks in Outlook

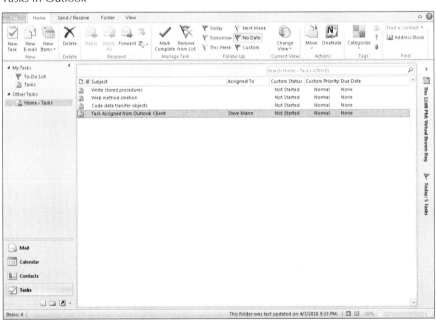

8. **Go back to your site and refresh.** You will see your new task entry as shown in Figure 13.26.

FIGURE 13.26

Site Tasks list updated via Outlook client

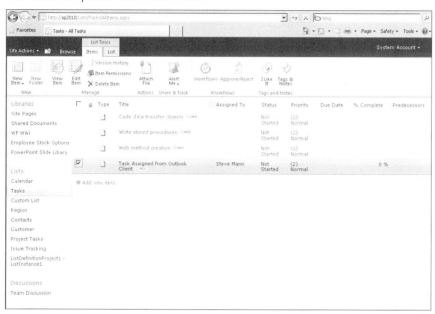

This powerful functionality allows users to take important Tasks lists with them when traveling, even in locations that don't provide network access. This capability also helps to increase productivity by putting task information in the Outlook client where many users spend most of their day.

Removing the Tasks list from Outlook

To remove the Tasks list, just go to Tasks in Outlook and look for your list under Other Tasks. Right-click the tasks and select Delete.

Add SharePoint contacts to your Outlook client

You can connect SharePoint contacts to Outlook, update them, and have those changes synchronized back to the SharePoint site.

1. In your browser, open a SharePoint contacts list.

2. Click Connect to Outlook from the List ribbon bar.

3. When prompted to connect the contacts, click OK.

The contacts are added under Other Contacts in Contacts in the left navigation. To remove the contact list, just right-click the name of this list and select Delete (name of list).

Access to SharePoint document libraries and discussions

In addition to Tasks list synchronization, SharePoint and Outlook are also integrated to provide offline access to SharePoint document libraries and discussions. Outlook can provide instant search capability by keeping an index of all Outlook data updated as new content and mail items are stored, which extends this capability to offline document libraries and discussions.

After you have connected a SharePoint library to Office Outlook 2010, your library will show up in a folder called SharePoint Lists. Once the file is in this folder, you can treat it as you would other Outlook files and mail messages, including the use of flags and categories. If you have folder structures in your SharePoint document library, those folder structures will also show up in Outlook. The files are stored in a PST file on your local disk, not on the e-mail server inbox.

While editing your documents, Outlook will prompt you for a location on the local drive to save the document for editing. This keeps you from having to save your file to the server over a slow link while working. When you are finished editing the document, you can simply update the server copy of the file.

Note

Documents that are synchronized to Outlook are not automatically checked out. To be sure that the document is locked for editing, it is important to go to the document on the site and select Check Out from the document drop-down menu. ■

To explore document library synchronization, follow these steps:

1. **Go back to your team site and go to a document library.** For this example, use the Shared Document library that is a default part of most templates.

2. **If you don't have any documents in your document library,** import two or three documents using the Upload control.

3. **Click the List tab on the Ribbon and then Connect to Outlook.** Again, you can use the advanced options to change the name and description as well as other options. Click Yes.

Note

If you would like to have all of the folders and files in your SharePoint document library copied down to Outlook, make sure that you have your browser pointed at the top level of your folders prior to selecting Connect to Outlook. ■

4. **Outlook then changes focus to the new (Team Site Name) Shared Documents under SharePoint Lists in your Outlook folders view, as in Figure 13.27.**

FIGURE 13.27

Outlook view of document library

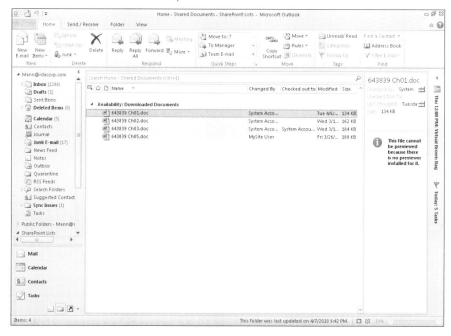

Note

If you add additional documents to your SharePoint Document library and they don't show up in your Outlook client immediately, simply click Send/Receive to force synchronization with the server and the document should appear. ■

5. Double-click one of the documents in your Outlook list to test out the server update.

6. **You may see an Opening File dialog box.** Click Open. The document opens in Word 2010, and you notice an Offline Server Document message in the Ribbon, as shown in Figure 13.28.

7. Click the Edit Offline button.

FIGURE 13.28

Word document edit

8. **The Edit Offline dialog box appears.** At this point you can change the Draft storage location on your hard drive as well as access the Word options settings by clicking Offline Editing Options. For this example, just click OK to put the document into offline editing mode.

9. **Notice that the Ribbon message goes away.** Make an edit to the document and then click Save.

10. **Close the document.** You will receive an update prompt message. Click Update to update the server copy. If you would like to keep working on the document and make sure that no one else edits the document, you can check it out on the server.

Note

If a file you are working on was not checked out, and that file is also edited from the server, a server conflict message will appear. Follow the instructions to complete the save. ∎

Working with discussions offline is almost identical to working with documents. Simply create a new discussion and then click Connect to Outlook on the List tab on the Ribbon and your discussion is copied to a folder under SharePoint Lists in the Outlook left navigation.

Calendaring integration

Calendars have been enhanced with richer calendar views, expanded support for recurring events, and all-day events.

To explore the calendaring integration, a good first step is to open your Outlook 2010 calendar and a SharePoint team site calendar up to a monthly view. As you can see in Figures 13.29 and 13.30, the two calendars look very similar.

FIGURE 13.29

SharePoint team site calendar — monthly view

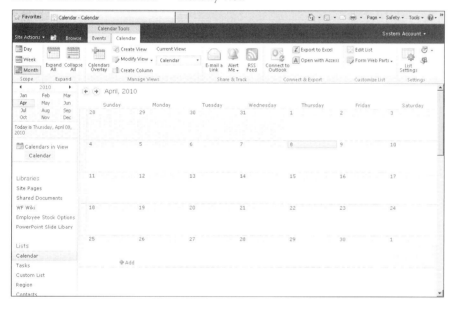

With both calendars still open, click to access the daily and weekly views on both calendars. Not bad, but what about the "integration," you may ask? In the 2010 releases, it is possible to both view and update both calendars. To explore this functionality, you must first connect a SharePoint calendar to your Outlook client.

FIGURE 13.30

Outlook calendar — monthly view

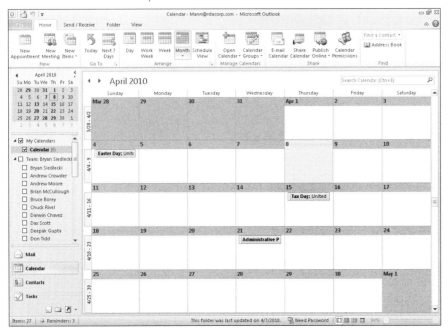

Connect a SharePoint calendar to the Outlook client

To connect a SharePoint calendar to the Outlook client, follow these steps:

1. **Go to your team site calendar in the browser.**

2. **Click Connect to Outlook from the Calendar tab on the Ribbon, as shown in Figure 13.31.** An Internet Explorer prompt appears, asking to allow the opening of Outlook.

3. **Click Allow.** A Microsoft Office Outlook dialog box prompts you to connect only to sources you can trust.

4. **Click Yes.**

5. **Open Outlook to your calendar view and notice a new calendar under Other Calendars in the left side task pane.** Also, notice the calendars show up side by side.

You can now do useful activities like copy calendar items from one calendar to another. For example, in my SharePoint calendar I have a recurring management meeting every Monday from 10 a.m. to 12 p.m. By simply clicking on the appointment and dragging it to the same day on my Outlook calendar, the appointment with its recurrence properties is copied over.

FIGURE 13.31

Connect to Outlook

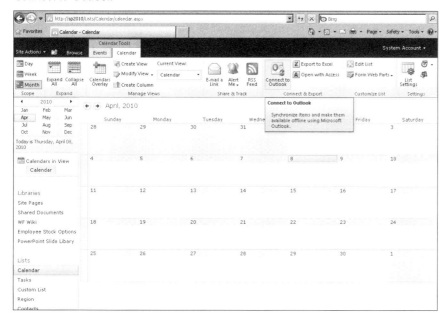

Note

Although the recurrence property of weekly, every 1 week from 10 to 12, copied over correctly, the end date that was set on the server did not transfer over. Be sure to check your copied items to be sure all properties are set the way you want. ∎

This copy capability works both ways: you can move appointments from your personal calendar to the shared calendar, too.

Overlaying the SharePoint calendar with your Outlook calendar

Overlaying the calendars allows you to see all of your events at one time, helping to avoid conflicts. Let's walk through how to do this with the two calendars you are working with now.

1. **Click the Arrow in the Calendar tab of the SharePoint calendar.** Now your overlay should look like Figure 13.32. Notice the entries match the colors of the calendar tabs to make it easy to see where each entry originated.

2. **To reverse/turn off the overlay, simply click either of the arrows on the tab.**

FIGURE 13.32

Calendar overlay

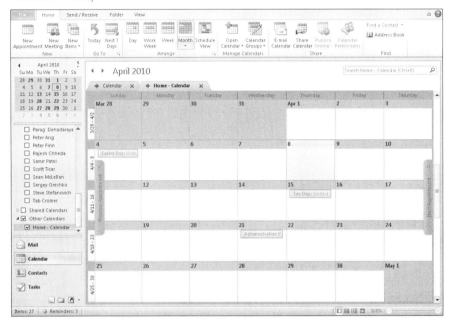

RSS subscription

Outlook integration with SharePoint via Really Simple Syndication (RSS) was designed to help you keep track of changing information in Tasks lists and to know when new documents have been added to a SharePoint library.

Similar to the Alerts capability in SharePoint, RSS enables you to subscribe to updates. This technology allows content publishers to distribute information in a standard format to RSS readers. Outlook is an RSS reader and can receive feeds of content from multiple sources.

The following steps show how to add a SharePoint list RSS subscription to Outlook:

1. Go to a SharePoint site or list in your browser and open your Outlook client.

2. In Outlook, open your RSS Feeds folder.

3. Go back to your SharePoint list and click RSS Feed from the List tab on the Ribbon. Click Subscribe to this feed on the page that appears, as shown in Figure 13.33.

FIGURE 13.33

Feed subscription page

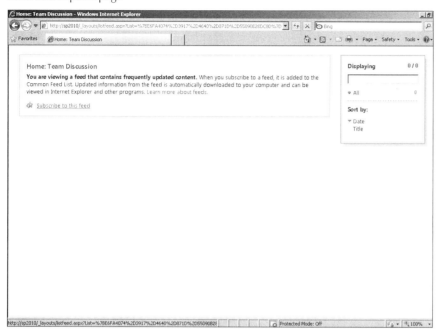

The Internet Explorer Subscribe to this Feed dialog box appears (Figure 13.34). Here you can change the name of your feed and select the folder you would like to create the feed in or create a new folder.

FIGURE 13.34

Subscribe to this Feed dialog box

4. Click the Subscribe button.

5. **The RSS Feeds page now shows any items that are in the list/library, and from this page you can view feed properties or sort and filter items.** If you click View feed properties, you can change your feed schedule to be as short as 60 minutes or as long as one week. You can also set it to Never if you would like to turn off a feed but keep it available to activate later.

6. **Go to your Outlook client and notice the new folder under your RSS Feeds folder.** Add items to your list and come back after the time you specified in the Feed Properties dialog box to see the new updates.

Using SharePoint Workspace with Office Server

The previous Office Document Workspace and Groove technologies have been replaced with SharePoint Workspace. SharePoint Workspace is a collaboration tool that allows team spaces to be created on a client machine, which then replicates the SharePoint Workspace space to invited users. As data and content are added to any space, the data automatically replicates to other machines using technology that was compared to the Napster peer-to-peer sharing model when SharePoint Workspace was first released. SharePoint Workspace has several advantages:

- Team members can exchange information within their SharePoint Workspace space inside or outside of a company firewall. SharePoint Workspace can be configured and managed without any assistance from IT because there is no need to configure firewalls, servers, security, or network access.

- SharePoint Workspace features include presence information, chat, application sharing, file sharing, contacts, messaging, project management, data sharing, and content synchronization.

- SharePoint Workspace can be fully customized by both technical and nontechnical users with simple form development tools as well as Visual Studio.

Determining when to use SharePoint Workspace with SharePoint

SharePoint has document libraries, contact lists, data sharing, and presence information. Why would you use SharePoint Workspace and SharePoint together? One of the main reasons would be to share information with users outside of your organization. Although some companies have extranets that allow collaboration with external suppliers and vendors, many still do not. If a company has an extranet, there are still issues around account creation, security, and Internet access that make a combined SharePoint Workspace/SharePoint solution attractive.

SharePoint Workspace/SharePoint Scenario

Here is a business scenario: Jim works as an attorney for a large pharmaceutical company. The company is planning to acquire a rival company and is working with an external law firm that specializes in mergers and acquisitions. The team has three weeks to prepare for a meeting in Boston. Jim's company is headquartered in Boston and the external firm contacts work in Washington, DC.

The internal legal team created a great SharePoint site to manage all of the content and then called on IT to create accounts for the external firm contacts that Jim is working with. The IT staff indicated they would need VP approval and then sent Jim to a Web site where he can make the request. After reviewing the business justification templates and the 15 steps to complete, including the creation of VPN accounts, network accounts, smart card activation, and so on, Jim worries that he will not be able to meet his deadline.

During lunch the next day, Jim talks with Bob in accounting about his challenges, and Bob points Jim to the SharePoint Workspace. Jim configures SharePoint Workspace from the internal portal server He synchronizes the sites which contain the key SharePoint document libraries that contain the merger project documents and then e-mails an invitation to the outside firm contact, Linda.

Linda receives Jim's e-mail, downloads a copy of the SharePoint Workspace client from the Web, and within minutes has a full copy of all the documents on Jim's SharePoint site. After reviewing several and making changes, Linda heads to lunch. Jim's machine began synchronizing the document changes within minutes of Linda making them, and Jim's laptop copied the changes to the SharePoint server where they are now available to everyone in the corporate legal department.

Other useful advantages of SharePoint Workspace are the ability to collaborate both without the intervention of the IT department as well as SharePoint Workspace's native ability to replicate collaborative spaces through firewalls. Many IT organizations block certain types of information and data packets from being sent and received. SharePoint Workspace has the ability to replicate through most firewalls unless an IT organization has taken steps specifically designed to block SharePoint Workspace.

SharePoint Workspace Account Configuration

In order to use SharePoint Workspace, your account must be created and configured. This can be easily facilitated via a step-by-step configuration wizard. To create a SharePoint Workspace account, follow these steps:

1. Navigate to a site in SharePoint.
2. Select Site Actions ⇨ Sync to SharePoint Workspace. The Account Configuration Wizard launches as shown in Figure 13.35. Click Next.

FIGURE 13.35

SharePoint Workspace configuration wizard

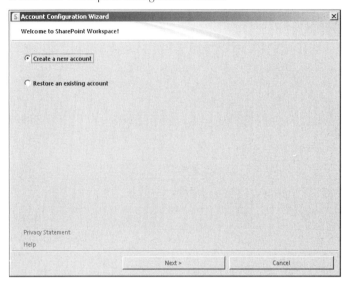

3. **Enter your name and e-mail and click Finish.** Your account is created, which may take a few seconds.

4. **Click Cancel on any sync message.** The next section will discuss synchronization.

Site synchronization

SharePoint Workspace synchronizes the libraries and lists within a specific SharePoint site. A workspace is generated for the site and uses the same name. Although this integration provides the benefit of offline SharePoint documents to the mobile worker as well as the ability to share them with colleagues across firewalls, there are a few limitations to be aware of:

- The tool maps to documents and lists stored in SharePoint Server 2010 or SharePoint Foundation Server 2010 only.
- Custom lists that use lookup columns are not supported.
- Calendars cannot be synchronized.
- Pages directories or Wiki Libraries are not synchronized but are available when online.
- The tool doesn't recognize custom SharePoint views, so users may notice more documents in the SharePoint Workspace folder because some documents may have been filtered out of the SharePoint view.

Note

I recommend having versioning enabled on SharePoint libraries that are synchronized with SharePoint Workspace to help reduce the risk of data loss that might occur because of synchronization errors or conflicts. ■

The following example walks you through how to set up site synchronization with SharePoint Workspace. Follow these steps:

1. In SharePoint, go to a site to synchronize.

2. Click Site Actions ⇨ Sync to SharePoint Workspace.

3. Click on OK on the synchronization prompt as shown in Figure 13.36. The synchronization process begins, as shown in Figure 13.37. Any errors or unsupported items will be displayed when finished.

4. Click the Errors tab to view the error details.

5. Click Open Workspace to view the workspace items, as shown in Figure 13.38.

FIGURE 13.36

Synchronization prompt

This example illustrates how easy it is to have an offline version of a site with documents and lists that can be shared with a team anywhere in the world, while keeping a central document library on SharePoint up to date.

This hub-and-spoke approach is what distinguishes this solution from saving a document library to Outlook. Outlook gives one user the ability to take a library offline — SharePoint Workspace adds the ability for that user to then invite whomever he or she wants from any other organization to share and collaborate on those same files.

FIGURE 13.37

Synchronization in progress

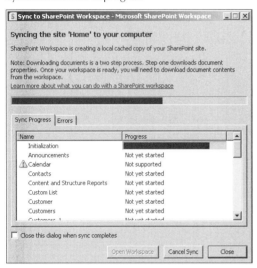

FIGURE 13.38

SharePoint site files in SharePoint Workspace

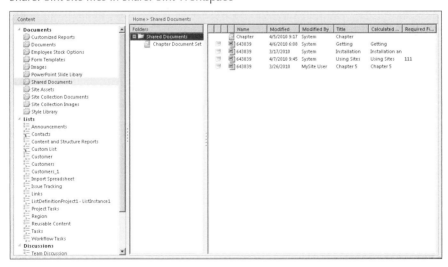

Check-in/check-out in SharePoint Workspace

When a file is checked out in the SharePoint Files tool in SharePoint Workspace, a lock is placed on the document in the SharePoint library. The lock prevents users on the server from editing your document while collaboration or editing takes place in one or many SharePoint Workspace spaces. A file does not need to be checked out for it to be updated in SharePoint Workspace; the feature just ensures exclusive editing rights.

To check out a file in SharePoint Workspace:

1. Select the file or files to be checked out.
2. **Click the Check Out button on the Home tab on the Ribbon.** An alternate method is to right-click the file and select Check Out.

To check in a file in SharePoint Workspace:

1. Select the file or files to be checked in.
2. **Click the Check In button from the Home tab on the Ribbon.**
3. **You are prompted to comment on the changes to the file.** For multiple files, the box lists the first file and then redisplays for each subsequent file after you click OK. Another option is to check in all files by clicking Edit ➪ Check In/Check Out ➪ Check in All My Checkouts.

Discarding a checkout removes the lock on the file on the SharePoint library and overwrites the document with the most current version in the library. To discard a checkout:

1. Select your file or files.
2. **Click the Discard Checkout button from the Home tab on the Ribbon.**

Tip

You may select multiple documents for Check Out or for Discard Checkout. Check In is only enabled when a single document is selected. ■

Summary

Office and SharePoint 2010 provide a rich collaborative experience for users. This chapter discussed integration in the core Office applications, Outlook mail client, and SharePoint Workspace.

It is now easier than ever to create rich Web sites and populate them with content created in the applications most of us are comfortable using.

Part IV

SharePoint Server and Business Intelligence

Using SharePoint as a Business Intelligence Platform

Business intelligence is a popular subject these days. The definitions of business intelligence vary based on the context and the solution that is for sale. This chapter defines it as the aggregation of data into information for users so that they can make smart and complete business decisions or actions. With SharePoint 2010, it is possible to host a wide variety of content and processes, from documents and reports to collaboration and workflow, and the challenge becomes how to present that content in a meaningful and actionable format for users.

This chapter introduces the topic of business intelligence and provides samples of how business intelligence can be used in an organization. We delve into how SharePoint delivers the toolset through components, connectors, and dashboards to enable business intelligence in your organization. We provide examples throughout the chapter of how those components can be connected to provide contextual information to users.

The SharePoint features that support BI are available in SharePoint Server only, not SharePoint Foundation Services. So, this chapter is targeted to the organizations that are deploying the enterprise version of SharePoint Server 2010 as their portal platform.

Defining Business Intelligence for Your Organization

What is business intelligence for your organization? Great question. We would all like to run our businesses (and our lives) intelligently, so how do we define, find, and create a system to make this easier? *Business intelligence,* also sometimes known as business performance management, is the presentation of information that is pertinent and meaningful to each user and role in an organization. According to Microsoft, their combination of software provides the business intelligence tools to transform data into information and information creates knowledge for users to take action on. That is a great concept, but sometimes it is easier to consume by considering the problems that BI is trying to solve:

- **Consolidation of data sources:** Most organizations, even small ones, have several different systems to support their business. Typically these systems include a customer relationship management (CRM) database, accounting and payroll system, employee time tracking system, an inventory and asset database, issue or bug tracking database, and human resource database. These systems vary based on the type and size of the organization, but regardless of the number, it is easy to create business efficiencies by consolidating the data. For example, the employee is a key piece of data for the payroll system, the employee time tracking system, and the human resource database. Instead of looking in three places for each portion of the employee information, we should be able to connect the three sources into one view. With a complete view of employee information, we can make better decisions.

- **Reporting key metrics:** Most organizations measure their progress based on key indicators. Are they profitable? Is their customer base growing? How many new hires did they have in the last 12 months? By knowing the answer to these questions, employees can make better informed decisions. However, after all the data is consolidated into a single view, reporting metrics becomes even more interesting. If the customer base is diminishing but the number of employees is growing, there usually is a problem. So, we use BI to first provide a consolidated view and then use BI reporting capabilities to easily display meaningful metrics.

- **Eliminating need for duplicate data:** Disparate systems usually mean that some data is being tracked in multiple places. Is there customer information in your CRM system that you want to show along with documents for that customer in SharePoint? By using BI integration, companies can eliminate or reduce the duplicated data.

If these issues occur in your organization, it is likely that business intelligence will help create efficiencies and a better informed workforce. Because this is a SharePoint book, let's now consider how SharePoint addresses business intelligence needs.

- **Consolidation of data sources:** SharePoint 2010 provides the ability to link to data sources through data connection libraries and through the Business Connectivity Services (BCS). Data connection libraries are libraries of links that can be analyzed by using SQL Server 2008 Analysis Services. All these sources can be combined on dashboard pages using the appropriate Web Parts and consolidated through filters that allow users to see exactly the information they need from all sources.

- **Reporting key metrics:** SharePoint allows you to display and report on key metrics through key performance indicator lists, Excel calculation services, and the SharePoint report center.

- **Eliminating need for duplicate data:** After data sources are defined in the Business Connectivity Services (BCS), the columns selected can be used as special lookup columns in SharePoint lists. Additionally, you can build dashboards using SharePoint Web Part pages and target each Web Part containing business data to the appropriate audience or role so that each user is receiving the most applicable information.

Cross-Reference

See Chapter 15 for more information on using Reporting Services and Chapter 16 for more information on defining KPIs and using Status List templates. The BCS is covered in Chapter 17.

Features of SQL Server 2008 provide two key components of BI. The first is the analysis capabilities provided by SQL Server 2008 Analysis Services (AS), which allows you to create online analytical processing (OLAP) cubes available for data mining. *Data mining* is the process of finding patterns, especially cause-and-effect relationships, in a large amount of data. For example, if you analyzed a database of call center transactions, you could determine the most effective times for reaching businesses in the Midwest to discuss upcoming training options.

The second SQL Server 2008 feature is Reporting Services (SSRS). This service allows you to build quick and easy reports and report controls, which you can then drop into a SharePoint Report Library for publication to SharePoint users.

To define the BI needs for your organization, it is helpful to identify your data sources, the connections between them, and the actions that users must take based on information in your organization. This exercise identifies the possible BI opportunities that you will analyze to determine if they provide efficiencies or improved process for the organization.

This chapter covers new BI features available within the SharePoint 2010 platform — PerformancePoint Services and PowerPivot.

Business Intelligence versus Business Data

Because the SharePoint features that support business intelligence also support business data, sometimes the line between these two scenarios becomes blurred. For the sake of clarity, we attempt to define these terms as we are using them in this section of the book dedicated to SharePoint and business intelligence.

Business intelligence is the processing of key business data to increase the understanding of the state of your business processes and the associated data. If BI is done correctly, your business data should be transformed into useful and actionable information that you can target to users in the organization. SharePoint enables you to display and target your BI results to portal users and roles.

Business data is data contained in a business application, usually in line-of-business (LOB) applications such as SAP Business Information Warehouse of mySAP ERP, Siebel eBusiness Applications, Attunity Legacy Data Access Solutions, or Microsoft BizTalk Server. Because this data is key to your organization and processes, it is often useful to make this business data available to other applications and users. SharePoint enables this bridge between business data and other applications through its Business Data Catalog feature. You can register your LOB applications in the BDC and then repurpose the necessary data in SharePoint lists and Web Parts. In addition, BDC application data becomes searchable.

Identifying your BI scenarios

BI scenarios vary based on the organization type and/or the business processes that support it. The following scenarios are some common BI scenarios that identify the key integration points:

- **Provide a complete view of an issue:** If you are presenting expense reports that need to be approved, you might also want to show users the trend of expenses in the organization and provide the ability to calculate the expense versus revenue ratio. By configuring a dashboard that shows in one place the following, SharePoint can aggregate all the data users need to make approval and budgeting decisions:
  - KPI for expense trends
  - Excel services access to the spreadsheet data for revenue and expenses in the organization
  - Document library that stores the expense reports

- **Cross-sell:** A dashboard created for an inside sales representative should provide the information needed for the sale, such as the customer and order information, but can also be configured to show other products that are in the same product category as the one the customer is interested in, or allow the representative to find orders for that customer by date.

- **Reduce overlap:** If you are running a call center that focuses on informing the partner community about upcoming events, you most likely want to call people and inform them about all the upcoming events in one call. However, if your data of who to call, what events are targeted to which people, and what events are imminent are in multiple databases specific to each event, it will be difficult to prompt the person making the call with the appropriate events for that particular target. By using BI tools, you can combine data that was historically siloed to create meaningful information for your organization.

Identifying actions

For each BI scenario, the goal is to drive action. Once you have identified the BI scenarios for your organization, you should define the actions for each scenario. The actions are the steps that users will take after they gain the knowledge created by the information that the BI tools provided by gathering data. Some sample actions are:

- **Reporting:** BI scenarios often result in reports. These reports need to be formulated so that the information is clear, concise, and actionable. In addition, these reports need to be targeted to the level of the consumer. For example, if my BI report is for store sales for a grocery store chain, I would like a district view for the district manager and store view for the store manager.

- **Updating:** If my business intelligence tool can spur users into action, I have created a close-the-loop circuit of continually improving process. For example, my BI tool combines all the unresolved product issues that customers have reported regardless of how or where they were reported. If I want to direct these issues to the appropriate feature owner to follow up on, I can resolve it with the customer and update that issue status to closed.

- **Providing consolidated views:** BI information often should be combined with other systems and data to provide users with a dashboard view of what they need to do. For example, for a customer service representative that has an order-taking system as the primary portion of his or her dashboard, including a BI component to that dashboard informing the customer service representative of the top hot items of the day, or what other things to offer with the items the customer has already selected, can improve the corporate sales and the customer experience.

Using PerformancePoint Services and Dashboard Designer

SharePoint 2010 contains a new site collection template for business intelligence named the Business Intelligence Center. This site collection activates the PerformancePoint services features so that you may take advantage of the business intelligence functionality of PerformancePoint. After you create a Business Intelligence Center site, you may use the Dashboard Designer product to create KPIs, Scorecards, and Dashboards for SharePoint. This section explores the use of PerformancePoint, Dashboard Designer, and the Business Intelligence Center.

Creating a Business Intelligence Center site collection

The first step to using SharePoint 2010 is to create a site collection for the business intelligence features. To create a Business Intelligence Center site collection, follow these steps:

1. **Open SharePoint Central Administration and select Application Management from the Quick Launch bar.**

2. **In the Site Collection section, click Create Site Collection.**

3. **Enter a title and description for your site.**

4. **In the Web site address section, click the Create site at this URL option and then choose sites in the URL path.**

5. **Enter a username for the site collection administrator in the Primary Site Collection Administrator section.**

6. **Select No Quota in the Quota Template section.** Alternatively, you can create a quota template to limit the size of the site collection by clicking the Manage Quota Templates link in that section and apply it to this site collection.

7. **Select the Business Intelligence Center template from the Enterprise Tab. (See Figure 14.1.)**

8. **Click OK.**

FIGURE 14.1

Creating the Business Intelligence Center site collection

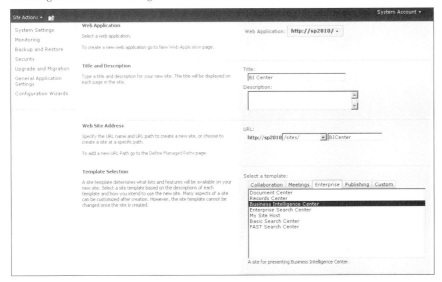

Configuring PerformancePoint services

Now that the Business Intelligence Center has been created, you need to configure
PerformancePoint services. To do this, perform the following steps:

1. **Open SharePoint Central Administration and select Application Management from the Quick Launch bar.**

2. **Select Manage service applications under the Service Applications section.**

3. **Scroll down and click on the PerformancePoint Service Application link.** The PerformancePoint Service Application administration page appears, as shown in Figure 14.2.

4. **Select the PerformancePoint Services Application settings.**

5. **Enter a domain account for the Unattended Service Account setting, as shown in Figure 14.3.** You may also modify the other settings here, but the default values are fine to start off with.

FIGURE 14.2

PerformancePoint Service Application administration page

FIGURE 14.3

PerformancePoint Service Application settings page

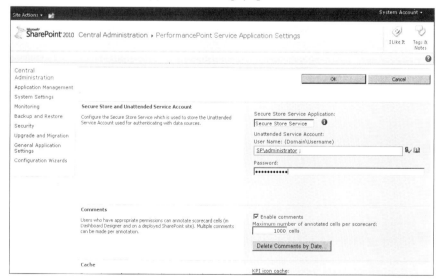

6. Click OK.

You have configured an account that you can use to access PerformancePoint data and allow for the rendering of the business intelligence objects generated in Dashboard Designer.

By default, all SharePoint locations are configured as trusted for both content and data sources. You may modify this by clicking on the Trusted Locations links and changing the settings. For this example, leave everything as default.

Defining data sources

Now that the Business Intelligence Center has been created and PerformancePoint Services has been configured, you need to generate content. The first step in generating BI content is defining the data sources for that content. You can do this by using the Dashboard Designer product. The Dashboard Designer is automatically downloaded and installed to your local machine when you begin to create PerformancePoint-based content in your Business Intelligence Center.

To define data sources, follow these steps:

1. **Navigate to your Business Intelligence Center.**

2. **Click PerformancePoint Content on the Quick Launch bar.**

3. **Click the Add New Item link.** Dashboard Designer is downloaded and installed. SharePoint redirects you to the Dashboard Designer product, as shown in Figure 14.4.

4. **Click on Data Connections.**

5. **Select the Create tab on the Ribbon and then click on Data Source.** The data source dialog appears as shown in Figure 14.5. There are several options:

   - **Analysis Services:** Use this template to create data source against an Analysis Services cube. You need this for creating analytical charts and grids.

   - **Excel Services:** Use this template to create data source against spreadsheets within Excel Services.

   - **Import from Excel Workbook:** Use this data source template to import fixed data values from an Excel workbook.

   - **SharePoint List:** Use this data source template to use data contained within a SharePoint list.

   - **SQL Server Table:** Use this data source template to utilize data from an SQL Server database table.

   For this example, I selected Analysis Services.

6. **Select the template you want to use and click OK.** The data source appears under Data Connections. Rename it to something useful. The settings page also appears in the main area.

7. **Enter the server name of the database server and select the database from the drop-down list. Select the Cube from the Cube drop-down list, as shown in Figure 14.6.**

FIGURE 14.4

Dashboard Designer

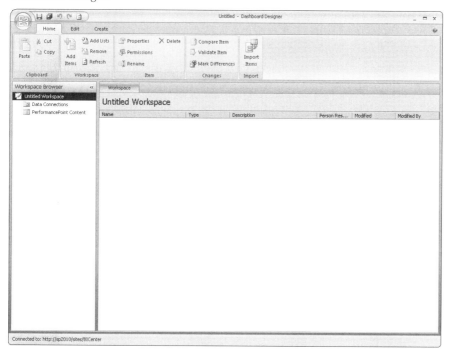

FIGURE 14.5

Data source template selection

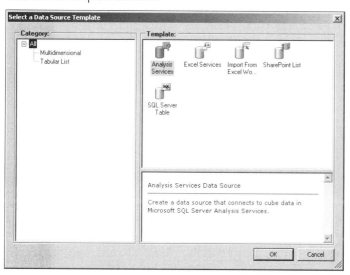

FIGURE 14.6

Data source connection settings

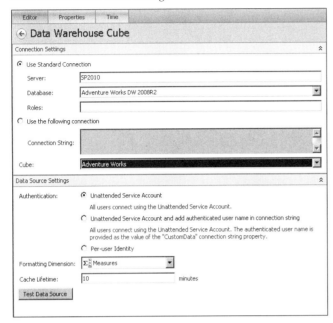

8. For Analysis Services cubes, select the Time tab in the main area and configure the time dimension, as shown in Figure 14.7.

9. Click Save using the floppy disc icon at the top of the Dashboard Designer application.

Defining KPIs

A main component of PerformancePoint is the ability to create scorecards that display key metrics of the business. Before a scorecard can be created, the necessary KPIs must be defined. Chapter 16 discusses in detail how to figure out what KPIs you should use. To define KPIs in Dashboard Designer, follow these steps:

1. From Dashboard Designer, with the PerformancePoint Content folder selected, click on the Create tab on the Ribbon and select KPI, as shown in Figure 14.8. The KPI template selection window appears.

FIGURE 14.7

Configuring the time dimension of an Analysis Services data source

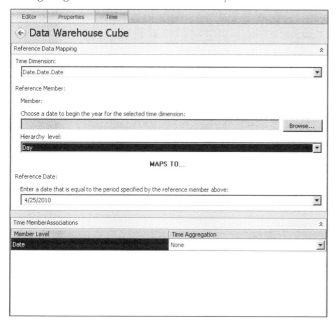

FIGURE 14.8

Creating a new KPI

> **2.** **Select Blank KPI and click OK.** The KPI Editor appears in the main area, as shown in
> Figure 14.9.

FIGURE 14.9

Configuring the KPI in the KPI Editor

3. **Click on the link in the Data Mappings column of the Actual row.** The Fixed Values Data Source Mapping dialog box appears.

4. **Click the Change Source button.** The Data Source dialog box appears.

5. **Click on the SharePoint Site tab and select the Analysis Services data source as shown in Figure 14.10.** Click OK.

6. **Click the Change Source button.** The Data Source dialog box appears.

7. **Click on the SharePoint Site tab and select the Analysis Services data source, as shown in Figure 14.10. Click OK.** The Dimensional Data Source Mapping dialog box appears.

8. **Select a measure from the Measure drop-down and optionally create a new dimension filter, as shown in Figure 14.11.** Click OK.

FIGURE 14.10

Changing the KPI data source

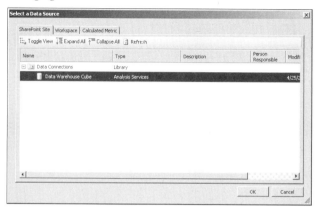

FIGURE 14.11

Configuring the dimensional data source mapping

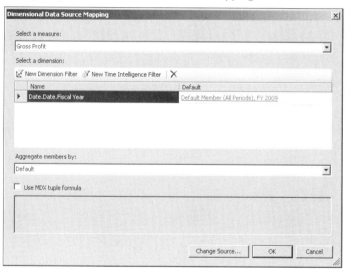

9. Repeat Steps 3–7 for the Target row.

10. **After configuring the Target row, you may change the thresholds,** as shown in Figure 14.12.

Target thresholds

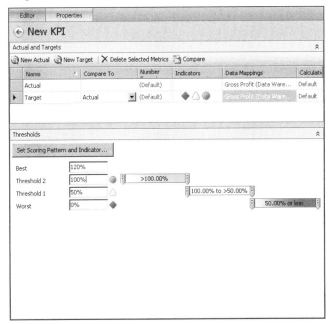

11. **Click on the New KPI in the workspace browser and enter rename the KPI.** Click the floppy disc icon to save.

12. **Repeat Steps 1–9 for each additional KPI.**

Creating a scorecard

A scorecard displays KPI values for actual and target along with an indicator to alert the user of potential issues. Now that KPIs have been defined, you may use them to create a scorecard. To create a scorecard in Dashboard Designer, follow these steps:

1. **From Dashboard Designer, with the PerformancePoint Content folder selected, click on the Create tab on the Ribbon and select Scorecard.** The Select a Scorecard template selection window appears. For this example, click OK for the default of Analysis Services. The scorecard wizard appears.

2. Click on the SharePoint Site tab and select the Analysis Services data source, as shown in Figure 14.13. Click Next.

3. Click Next on the Select a KPI source screen.

4. On the Select KPIs to Import screen, click on Select KPI, and then in the SharePoint Site tab, select the KPIs you created in the previous section, as shown in Figure 14.14. Click OK. Click Next.

FIGURE 14.13

Selecting the scorecard data source

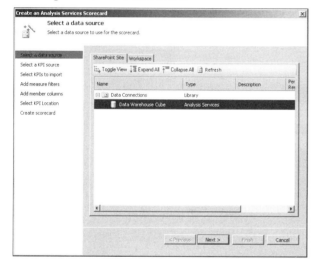

FIGURE 14.14

Selecting KPIs for the scorecard

5. Click Next on the Filter Measures screen.

6. Click Finish. Dashboard Designer generates the scorecard, which may take a few seconds. The New Scorecard is presented in the main area, as shown in Figure 14.15.

FIGURE 14.15

New scorecard in Dashboard Designer

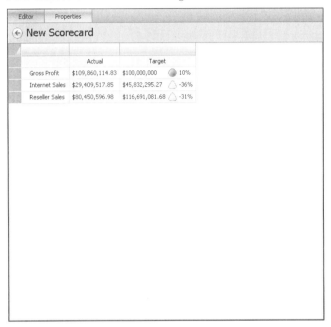

7. Click on the Properties tab and enter a new name for the scorecard, as shown in Figure 14.16. Save the changes.

FIGURE 14.16

Naming the scorecard

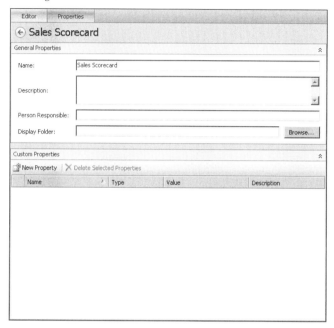

Creating an analytical chart

Analytical charts are interactive graphs that allow the user to investigate data from various angles. In order to use analytical charts, Analysis Services must be the data source. To create an analytical chart in Dashboard Designer, follow these steps:

1. From Dashboard Designer, with the PerformancePoint Content folder selected, click on the Create tab on the Ribbon and select Analytical Chart.

2. Select the Analysis Services data source from the SharePoint Site tab and click Finish. The new report appears in the main area, as shown in Figure 14.17.

FIGURE 14.17

New analytical chart

3. Drag measures and dimensions from the right pane to the Series and Bottom Axis boxes in the report, as shown in Figure 14.18.

4. Click on the Properties tab and rename the chart. Save the changes.

Creating a dashboard

A dashboard is a container for the PerformancePoint objects you created in the previous sections. The dashboard may contain scorecards, reports, charts, and/or filters. To create a dashboard in Dashboard Designer, follow these steps:

1. From Dashboard Designer, with the PerformancePoint Content folder selected, click on the Create tab on the Ribbon and select Dashboard. The dashboard page template appears.

2. Select the two-column template, as shown in Figure 14.19 and click OK. The dashboard object is created in your workspace.

FIGURE 14.18

Defining the analytical chart data

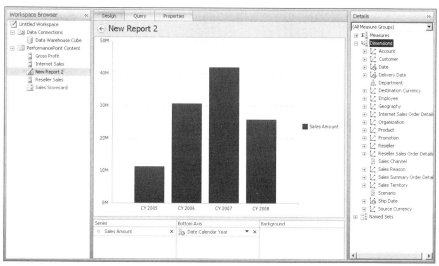

FIGURE 14.19

Selecting the dashboard template

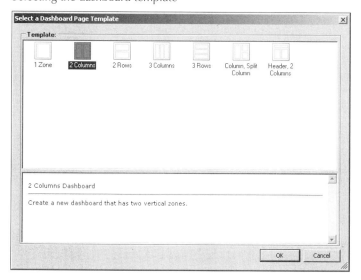

3. Drag the scorecard you created to the left column and drag the analytical chart you created to the right column, as shown in Figure 14.20.

Adding content to the dashboard

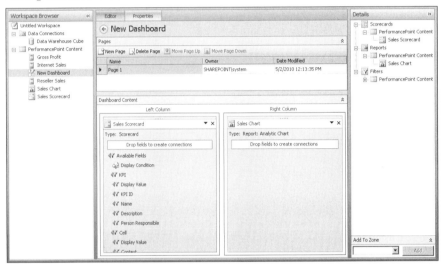

4. **In the Pages section, rename Page 1 to a more description page name.** Optionally, you may generate more pages with different BI content on them.

5. **Click on the Properties tab and rename the dashboard. Save the changes.**

6. **Right-click the dashboard in the workspace browser and select Deploy to SharePoint from the item menu, as shown in Figure 14.21.** The deployment dialog appears.

7. **Select a master page if you are using a custom master page for your portal as shown in Figure 14.22. Click OK.** The dashboard is deployed to your BI Center site within the Dashboards library. Dashboard Designer opens a new window to display the deployed dashboard page, as shown in Figure 14.23.

FIGURE 14.21

Deploying the dashboard to SharePoint

Using PerformancePoint Content in SharePoint

Even though deploying dashboards from Dashboard Designer automatically generates dashboard pages in SharePoint, you may create your own custom pages using the PerformancePoint Web Parts. The PerformancePoint Web Parts are available in your BI Center site or any site that has the PerformancePoint Services feature activated.

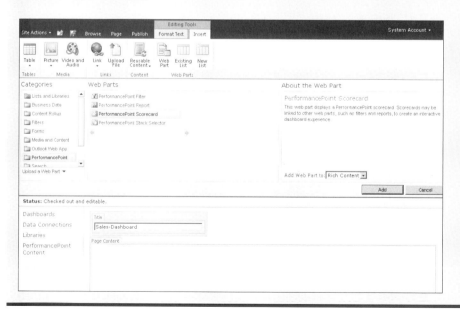

FIGURE 14.22

Dashboard deployment dialog box

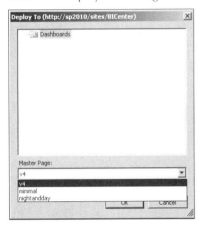

FIGURE 14.23

New dashboard page in SharePoint

Installing PowerPivot

PowerPivot is a new feature in SharePoint 2010 and SQL Server 2008 R2. PowerPivot allows users to generate BI-related Excel worksheets and deploy them to SharePoint for collaboration and reporting purposes.

PowerPivot is installed by using the SQL Server 2008 R2 installation for the SharePoint Server portion and the PowerPivot for Excel installation for the client portion (although the Excel version can operate on its own). This section steps through both installations.

PowerPivot for SharePoint Server installation

To install PowerPivot on your SharePoint Server farm, follow these steps:

1. **Insert the SQL Server 2008 R2 installation disc or .ISO into your server drive that is running SQL Server 2008 R2 for your SharePoint farm and launch setup.exe.** The SQL Server installation center appears.

2. **Select Installation and then click on New installation or add new features to an existing installation as shown in Figure 14.24.** SQL Server processes the current operation. Click OK on the setup support rules screen.

FIGURE 14.24

SQL Server Installation Center

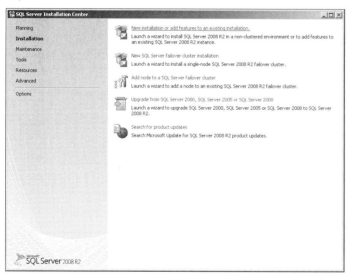

3. **Click Install to install the SQL Server Setup files.** The setup wizard appears.

4. Click Next.

5. Click Next on the Installation Type screen.

6. Enter your product key on the Product Key screen and click Next.

7. Accept the license terms on the License Terms screen and click Next.

8. Select SQL Server PowerPivot for SharePoint and select Existing Farm on the Setup Role screen as shown in Figure 14.25. Click Next.

FIGURE 14.25

SQL Server setup role

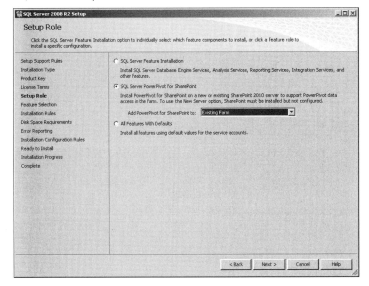

9. Click Next on the Feature Selection screen.

10. Click Next on the Installation Rules screen and click Next on the Instance Configuration screen.

11. On the SQL Server accounts screen, enter a service account for each service, as shown in Figure 14.26 and click Next.

12. On the Analysis Services Configuration screen, enter users that should have administrative privileges and click Next.

13. Click Next on the Error Reporting screen and on the Installation Configuration Rules screen.

14. **Click Install.** PowerPivot for SharePoint installs. The installation takes several minutes to complete.

15. Click OK on the completion screen.

FIGURE 14.26

SQL Server accounts

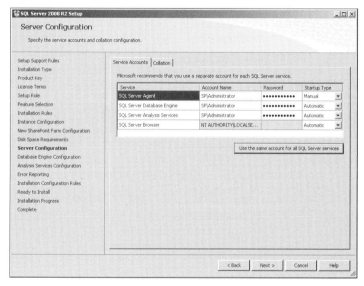

PowerPivot for Excel installation

After PowerPivot for SharePoint has been installed to your SharePoint farm, PowerPivot for Excel needs to be installed. The Excel portion of the PowerPivot installation requires the proper PowerPivot for Excel MSI file. A 32-bit and a 64-bit version are both available. The installation needs to be performed on each local machine that will use PowerPivot.

To install PowerPivot for Excel on a local machine, follow these steps;

1. **Launch the PowerPivot for Excel installation by double-clicking on the proper MSI file.** The PowerPivot for Excel installation wizard appears.

2. Click Next on the Welcome screen.

3. **Accept the license terms and click Next.**

4. **Enter the user information and click Next.**

5. **Click Install.** PowerPivot for Excel installs to the local machine.

6. **Click Finish on the completion screen.**

7. **Open Excel 2010 on the local machine.** An Office customization prompt appears as shown in Figure 14.27.

8. **Click Install.**

FIGURE 14.27

Microsoft Office customization installer

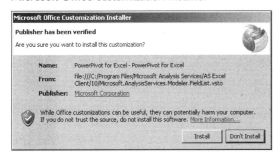

The PowerPivot tab on the Ribbon now appears in Excel. Users may now use Excel to generate PowerPivot worksheets and deploy them to SharePoint.

Summary

Business data is stored throughout your organization and, with the extended capabilities of SharePoint 2010, throughout your SharePoint sites. This chapter defined the data sources that need to be combined into dashboards so that they provide meaningful, contextual information, allowing users to derive knowledge and take action. You use the Business Intelligence Center to create your site collection that enables PerformancePoint services. PerformancePoint Services allow you to create KPIs, scorecards, and reports to generate and deploy dashboards to your BI Center. PowerPivot enables users to generate self-service BI solutions by using Excel and publish PowerPivot worksheets to SharePoint.

Using Reporting Services and Report Libraries

The Report Library template provided with SharePoint 2010 is a powerful tool for displaying reports and metrics for your organization. The Report Library combines the capabilities for providing status and trend information by using KPIs with the dashboard capability for combining Web Parts into a page so that related information from a variety of sources give users a full view.

In this chapter, we extend the Report Library functionality by installing and configuring the SQL Server 2008 R2 Reporting Services Add-in for SharePoint technologies so that SharePoint document libraries can store and manage reporting services reports, models, and data sources. This add-in also installs a Report Viewer Web Part that is designed to display reports in a dashboard or Web Part page.

Configuring the Reporting Environment

The Report Library template provided with SharePoint 2010 creates a library that supports Excel reports and Status List Web pages. To configure it for additional functionality, we install and configure the SQL Server Reporting Services Add-in for SharePoint technologies provided with SQL Server 2008 R2 and configure trusted locations for the Excel files that you will use as data sources for Excel Web Access.

Configuring Reporting Services integration

You can extend the functionality of your Report Library by installing the SQL Server 2008 R2 Add-in for SharePoint Technologies. This add-in will install the Report Viewer Web Part that is designed to display reports on your Web Part pages. In addition, the add-in extends the integration of SharePoint and SQL Server 2008 R2 Reporting Services by:

- Updating the Reporting Services Configuration tool so that you can configure your Reporting Services servers to create and manage SharePoint integrated databases

- Enabling report subscriptions to be delivered to SharePoint libraries

- Enabling synchronization from the SharePoint content database to the report server database so that the master reports live in SharePoint but the report server retains a copy

- Mapping SharePoint permission roles to report server operations so that users that have add items permissions in SharePoint can create reports and users that have manage Web site permissions in SharePoint can create a reporting services schedule

- Adding content types for reports, report data sources, and report models

The add-in is installed on your SharePoint servers but to support the integration, you must have the following configuration for your Reporting Services servers:

- SQL Server 2008 R2 Reporting Services.

- SharePoint on the Reporting Services server. This installation does not need to be configured but the software must be present to provide the WSS Object Model.

Installing the SQL Server Reporting Services add-in for SharePoint Technologies 2010

To install the Microsoft SQL Server Reporting Services Add-in for Microsoft SharePoint Technologies 2010 on your SharePoint servers, follow these steps:

1. **Double-click the rsSharePoint.msi installer package provided with SQL Server 2008 R2 (or downloaded from Microsoft Download Center).** The Welcome Screen appears.

2. **Click Next.**

3. **Accept the End User License Agreement (EULA) and click Next.**

4. **Type your name and company name in the Registration Information dialog box and click Next.**

5. **Click Install.** It may take a few minutes to remove the back-up files.

6. **When the installation has completed successfully, you will see the Finish screen. Click the Finish button.**

Creating a SharePoint integrated Reporting Services database

You must also configure a Reporting Services database that can store the subscription, schedule, and caching information associated with your reports. SharePoint will store reports, data sources, and models. To configure a Reporting Services database, follow these steps:

1. From your Microsoft SQL Server 2008 ⇨ Configuration Tools menu, select Reporting Services Configuration Manager.

2. Type the machine name and instance for your Reporting Services server and click Connect.

3. Click the Database Setup option in the left-hand navigation pane.

   You will need at least one database in SharePoint mode, and when you change the mode it will prompt you to create a new database. To change the mode and create a new Reporting Services database, click the Change Database in the database connection screen.

4. Select Create a New Report Server Database and click Next. Click Next again to accept the Report Server and Integrated Security settings.

5. Type the database name and select SharePoint Integrated mode, as shown in Figure 15.1. Click Next.

FIGURE 15.1

Entering database information for a new Reporting Services database

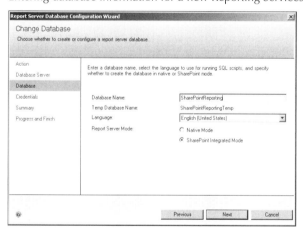

6. Enter the service credentials and click Next. Click Next again on the Summary screen.

7. **Click Finish.** The database setup runs. Click Finish when complete. Your database displays that it is in SharePoint integrated mode.

8. Close the Reporting Services Configuration tool.

Configuring the execution account

If you want to enable data sources to use stored credentials to access data or run subscription reports, you must configure the Reporting Services execution account. This account runs operations at a low security level. To configure a Reporting Services execution account, follow these steps:

1. From your Microsoft SQL Server 2008 ⇨ Configuration Tools menu, select Reporting Services Configuration Manager.

2. Type the machine name and instance for your Reporting Services server and instance and click Connect.

3. Click the Execution Account option in the left-hand navigation pane.

4. Select the Specify an Execution Account check box.

5. Type the username in domain\username format in the Account field.

6. Type the password and retype the password in the Password and Verify Password fields.

7. Click Apply.

Configuring the Reporting Services settings in SharePoint

To complete the Reporting Services integration, you need to configure the settings in SharePoint Central Administration. To configure SharePoint settings for Reporting Services integration, follow these steps:

1. Open SharePoint Central Administration for your farm and click General Application Settings from the Quick Launch bar.

2. Click Reporting Services Integration in the Reporting Services section.

3. Type the URL of the Report Server Web Service and choose the authentication mode, as shown in Figure 15.2. This URL will typically be `http://<servername>/reportserver` unless you've modified the virtual directory name during the Reporting Services installation. Select whether to activate in all site collections or specific site collections. Click OK.

4. Click Add a Report Server to the Integration in the Reporting Services section.

5. Specify the database server and instance for your Reporting Services server. The service account(s) for the report server Web service and report server windows service account will be granted rights to the SharePoint content databases.

6. Click OK and enter credentials that will allow access to the reporting server configuration in the username and password dialog.

FIGURE 15.2

Configuring the Reporting Services integration settings in SharePoint

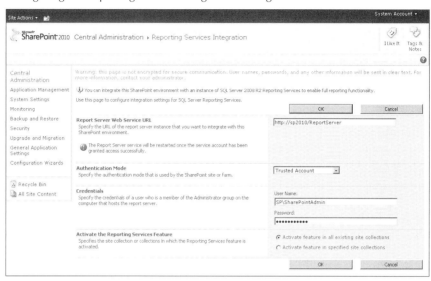

7. Click Set server defaults in the Reporting Services section.

    *   If you would like to limit the number of historical snapshots allowed for a report, select Limit number of snapshots to and enter the number of maximum snapshots.

    *   If you would like to limit the timeout for report processing, select Limit report processing (in seconds) and enter the maximum number of seconds.

    *   If you would like to enable logging for report processing and enable automatic removal of old logs, enter the number of days you would like logs to be retained.

    *   Select whether you would like to enable Windows integrated security for data sources or not.

    *   Select whether or not you would like to enable ad-hoc report processing. If you enable this option, users will be able to use Report Builder to create ad-hoc reports, and your reporting services will process those ad-hoc reports.

8. Click OK.

Adding reporting services content types

For each document library in which you want to store reports and enable users to create and store new reports, models, and data sources, you need to add the content types for those items to that library. To add the report builder report, report model, and report data source content types, follow these steps:

1. Navigate to the document library to which you want to add the content types.

2. Select Library Settings from the Document tab on the Ribbon.

3. In the content type section, click Add from existing site content types.

4. Select Report Library Content Types from the Select site content types from drop-down menu, as shown in Figure 15.3.

5. Select Report Builder Model and click Add.

6. Select Report Builder Report and click Add.

7. Select Report Data Source and click Add.

8. Click OK.

FIGURE 15.3

Adding the report server content type to a document library

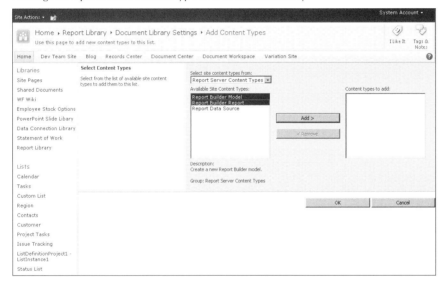

Tip

Add the Report Builder content types to a Report Library and add the Report Data Source to a Data Connection Library. ∎

Configuring the Report Library as a trusted location

If you plan to store Excel workbooks in your Report Library, which you will be using as sources for KPIs or dashboard components, you need to configure the Report Library as a trusted location. The trusted locations list is a security mechanism that is provided by SharePoint so that you can enable locations where you can ensure that the workbooks are trusted and without dangerous links or programming to outside data sources. The trusted file location is configured at the Shared Service Provider level. To configure SharePoint to trust the file location of your Excel workbooks, follow these steps:

1. Open the administration page for your Excel Services Application.

2. Select Trusted file locations.

3. Click Add Trusted File Location in the top navigation bar.

4. Enter the address for your Report Library in the Address field.

5. Select whether the location is a SharePoint site, file share, or Web site address by using the Location type radio buttons.

6. **Select whether you want to trust child libraries or directories by checking the Children trusted box.** This setting can be very helpful if you don't want to granularly manage libraries; however, you need to be confident that the users with the site creation permissions will not create subsites that should not be considered trusted locations.

7. **Enter the appropriate session management settings in the Session Management section:**

   - **Session Timeout:** Values between –1 and 2073600 seconds (no timeout — 24 days). This is the maximum time that an Excel Calculation session can stay active as measured from the end of the request. If you enter a value of 0, the session stays active only for that particular request.

   - **Short Session Timeout:** Values between –1 and 2073600 seconds (no timeout — 24 days). This is the maximum time that an Excel Web Access session can stay open but inactive as measured from the start of the open request. If you enter a value of 0, the session stays active only for that particular request.

   - **Maximum Request Duration:** Values are –1 (no limit) and between 1 and 2073600 seconds (1 second — 24 days). This defines the maximum duration of a single request in a session.

8. **Enter the appropriate workbook values in the Workbook Properties section:**

   - **Maximum Workbook Size:** Values are 1 to 2000MB. This is the maximum size of the workbook that Excel Calculation Services can open.

   - **Maximum Chart Size:** Any positive integer is a valid value. This is the maximum size of the chart that Excel Calculation Services can open.

9. **Enter the calculation behavior in the Calculation Behavior section.**

   - **Volatile Function Cache Lifetime:** Valid values are –1 (calculated once per session) and 0 (function is always calculated) and 1 to 2073600 seconds (1 second to 24 days). These values define the maximum time in seconds that a manual or automatic calculation will be cached.

   - **Workbook Calculation Mode:** File, manual, automatic, or automatic except data tables. This setting defines the calculation mode of Excel Calculation Services and overrides the workbook settings unless you select File.

10. **Enter the external data settings in the External Data section.** You want to configure these settings according to the needs and trust levels of workbook authors. External data allows Excel to process data from a variety of sources, such as databases and ODBC sources, and therefore surfaces sources that many users wouldn't otherwise see. By limiting the ability to use external data defined in trusted data connection libraries and limiting the publishing of DCLs to trusted authors, you can manage external data risk while still allowing a wide range of functionality.

    - **Allow External Data:** Select none, trusted data connection libraries only, and trusted data connection libraries and embedded. Because external data could potentially be harmful, you can select what external data sources are allowed. If you limit the external data to trusted data connection libraries, the spreadsheet must be calling a data connection from a trusted location. The trusted data connection libraries and embedded setting allows external data from DCLs and from custom connection strings that are embedded in the spreadsheet.

    - **Warn on Refresh:** Select this option if you want to display a warning before refreshing the data from external locations.

    - **Stop When Refresh on Open Fails:** Selecting this option stops the open operation on an external file if the file contains a Refresh On Open data connection, and the file cannot be refreshed when it is opening, and the user does not have open rights to the file.

    - **External Data Cache Lifetime:** Valid values are –1 (never refresh after first query) and 0 to 2073600 seconds (0 seconds to 24 days). These values define the maximum time in seconds that the system can use cached manual or automatic external data query results.

    - **Maximum Concurrent Queries Per Session:** Any positive integer is a valid value. This defines the maximum number of concurrent queries that can be executed during a single session.

11. **Select whether you would like to allow user-defined functions in the User-Defined Functions section.**

12. Click OK.

Managing Data Sources, Models, and Data Connections

The Report Library is designed to store data connections and data sources so that users can access those data sources without having to know all the details about server, database, and security settings. There are three types of data connections that are supported by the Report Library:

- **Office Data Connection files (ODC):** The ODC definitions enable Office applications to connect to your SQL Server, OLEDB, ODBC, or XML data sources.

- **Universal Data Connection files (UDC):** Connection file format for applications such as InfoPath to store their data connections. In an InfoPath scenario, the UDC allows browser forms to work across domain boundaries. UDC files are XML files with a particular namespace and schema.

- **Reporting Services Data Sources (RSDS):** The Reporting Services Data Sources is a new file format for data sources that are designed in SharePoint and are used to support models, reports, and report subscriptions.

Creating and uploading data connections

Data connections are stored in the data connection library for your Report Library site. We use Excel to create the (ODC) file and then upload that to a Data Connection library. You can configure whether you want to specify credentials for the connection or use Windows authentication so that the user's credentials are necessary for access to the data.

To create an ODC file, follow these steps:

1. Open Excel 2010 and select the Data tab.

2. Select whether you would like to connect to a SQL Server, Analysis Services, XML file, OLEDB, or ODBC source in the From Other Sources menu in the Get External Data section.

3. Enter the server name and connection credentials on the Connect to Database Server page of the Data Connection Wizard, as shown in Figure 15.4. Click Next.

FIGURE 15.4

Using the Data Connection Wizard to connect to your Analysis Services server

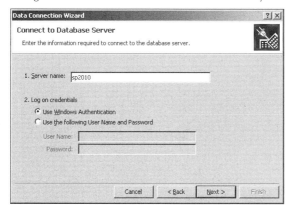

4. Select the database and cube that contain your KPIs in the Select Database and Table page of the Data Connection Wizard, as shown in Figure 15.5. Click Next.

FIGURE 15.5

Selecting your Analysis Services cube in the Data Connection Wizard

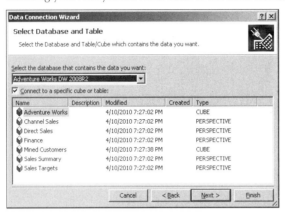

5. **Enter the filename and description for your ODC file.** The description should be used to let users know the details of the connection so that they can accurately pick the connection that meets their needs. If you do not select a filename location by using the Browse button, the file will be saved to your [My Data Sources] folder under [My Documents]. Click Finish.

6. **In the Import Data prompt that appears when you finish, select Only Create Connection, as shown in Figure 15.6.**

FIGURE 15.6

Creating a connection file using Excel 2010

7. **Using a browser, navigate to the Data Connection Library in which you want to store the ODC file.**

8. **Select Upload Document from the top navigation bar or select Add New Item. Browse to the location of your ODC file, and select OK. (By default the ODC file will be saved from Excel to My Documents\My Data Sources.)**

9. Provide a description for the ODC file so users know to what cube they will be connecting and select Check in. (Depending on your site settings, you may need to approve the new connection file.)

Note

Files that are uploaded to data connection libraries will need to be approved unless approvals have been disabled on the library. ■

You can create a UDC file by using Notepad to create and edit the XML according to the UDC file schema or by using InfoPath to create a data connection and converting to UDC file format. To create a UDC file using InfoPath, follow these steps:

1. **Open InfoPath 2010, design a blank form, and launch the Data Connection Wizard by selecting Data Connections from the Data tab on the Ribbon.**

2. **If you have an existing data connection that you want to convert, select that data connection.** There are many options for data sources, depending on the type of data you are connecting to and whether you will be reading and/or writing to the source. In the steps below, we create a data connection to receive data from a SQL Server database, and they will vary slightly if you are submitting data or have a different type of data source. Follow these steps:

   a. Select Add and select whether you would like to submit or receive data.

   b. Select the type of source that you will be receiving data from or submitting data to.

   c. Click Select Database.

   d. Click the New Source button.

   e. Select whether you would like to connect to SQL Server, SQL Server Analysis Services, ODBC, OLEDB, or other/advanced data source as shown in Figure 15.7. Click Next.

FIGURE 15.7

Configuring a new connection to a data source

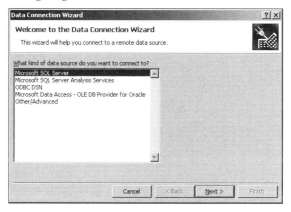

f. Type the server or filename and connection credentials on the Connect to Database Server screen of the Data Connection Wizard. Click Next.

g. Select the database and table or cube in the Select Database and Table screen of the Data Connection Wizard. Click Next.

h. Type the filename and description for your ODC file. The description should be used to let users know the details of the connection so that they can accurately pick the connection that meets their needs. If you do not select a filename location by using the browse button, the file will be saved to your My Data Sources folder under My Documents. Click Finish.

i. Add or remove tables that you need to be available in your data source in the Data Connection Wizard. Click Next.

j. Type a name for your data connection and select whether or not you would like to Enable submit for this connection. Click Finish.

3. **Select the data connection that you want to convert and click Convert, as shown in Figure 15.8.**

Converting a data connection to UDC file formatting

4. **Type the URL for your SharePoint data connection library including the filename but not the extension that you want your UDC named, as shown in Figure 15.9.**

   If you are writing to a data connection library that just supports your site, select Relative to site collection (recommended). If you are writing a data source that you will upload to the document library that supports InfoPath Forms services in SharePoint Central Administration, select Centrally managed data connection library (advanced). Click OK.

FIGURE 15.9

Publishing your converted data connection to your SharePoint data connection library

5. **If you are creating a centrally managed data connection, you will need to copy the file from the data connection library that you are publishing to the Central Administration Data Connection library.** To do this, follow these steps:

   a. Open Central Administration in your browser and select General Application Settings from the Quick Launch.

   b. Select Manage Data Connection Files from the InfoPath Forms Services section.

   c. Click Upload from the top navigation bar.

   d. Type the filename for the data connection that you just saved and the category, and select whether you would like the data connection to be able to access it via HTTP. Click Upload.

6. **To approve your data connection file, browse to your data connection library and left-click on the file you want to approve. Select Approve/reject from the menu, as shown in Figure 15.10.** Files that are uploaded to data connection libraries will need to be approved unless approvals have been disabled on the library.

FIGURE 15.10

Approving your data connection file

7. Select Approved and click OK.

Creating data sources and data models

Data sources support reporting services reports and models. If you are creating a new Report Builder report, you will need to have a data model that has been generated for your data source. You must first define your data source and then you can generate the data model. If you are uploading a different type of reporting services report (.rdl), such as one that has been generated by report designer, you do not need to have a data source or data model configured.

To create a data source in your report library or data connection library, follow these steps:

1. Use a Web browser to navigate to your reports library or data connection library (depending on where you added the Report Data Source content type).

2. From the New Document button in the Documents tab on the Ribbon, select Report Data Source. If this option is not available, you must add the report data source content type. For information on how to add this content type, see the "Adding Reporting Services content types" section earlier in this chapter.

3. **Type a descriptive name for your data source in the Name field.** This name helps users to identify if this is the appropriate data source for their needs.

4. **Select whether you want to connect to SQL Server, SQL Server Analysis Services, Oracle, ODBC, OLE DB, XML, SAP Netweaver BI, or Hyperion data source in the Data Source Type drop-down menu.**

5. **Type the connection string for your data source in the Connection string area, as shown in Figure 15.11.**

FIGURE 15.11

Defining a connection string for a data source

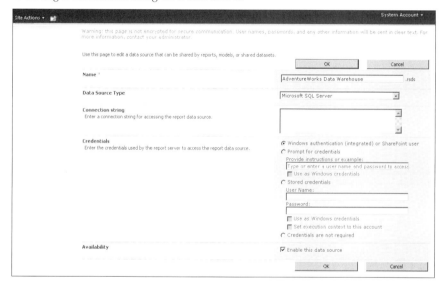

6. **Select whether you want to use Windows authentication or stored credentials, or prompt for authentication in the Credentials section.** Alternatively, you can select to use the Unattended report processing account, which uses the account credentials configured in the Reporting Services Configuration Manager. This authentication option is required if you want to add subscriptions for the reports that will be using this data source. See the Configuring the Execution Account procedure below for more information on how to set this account.

7. **Confirm that the Enable this data source option is selected.**

8. **Edit the properties of the data connection item and provide a title. Also, you may need to approve the connection by selecting Approve/Reject from the item drop-down menu.**

9. **Click OK.**

To generate a report builder model for your data source, follow these steps:

1. **Use a Web browser, to navigate to your reports library.**

2. **From the New menu, select Report Builder Model. If this option is not available, you must add the report data source content type.** For information on how to add this content type, see the "Adding Reporting Services content types" section earlier in this chapter.

3. **Type a descriptive name for your data source in the Name field.** This name will help users to identify if this is the appropriate data source for their needs.

4. **Type the path or browse to the data source on which this report builder model will be based.**

5. **Click OK.**

Managing Reports and Models

The SharePoint integration with Reporting Services and the content types associated with the report objects extend the capabilities for managing report objects in your SharePoint library. Once a report has been uploaded or published to your library, you can perform the following management actions in addition to the standard document library options such as viewing and editing the items:

- **Manage Subscriptions:** Subscriptions trigger report processing and the resulting report can be published to file shares or SharePoint libraries in several different formats. SharePoint allows you to view and add subscriptions for your reports.

- **Manage Data Sources:** From within SharePoint, you can modify which data source is used for your report. This capability applies even if your report was uploaded with a custom data source.

- **Manage Parameters:** If your report contains parameters, you can manage the order in which they are displayed, default values for those parameters, and the behavior for displaying the parameters from the SharePoint interface.

- **Create Historical Snapshots:** SharePoint allows you to create and view historical snapshots of your reports.

- **Manage Processing Options:** Each report has its own processing options so that you can manage how often the data is refreshed, the processing time, and the behavior of the snapshot capabilities.

The extended management options apply to models as well so you can perform the following management tasks for models in your document libraries:

- **View Dependent Items:** This capability allows you to see what reports use the data model.

- **Manage Data Sources:** From within SharePoint, you can modify which data source is used for your model. This capability applies even if your model was uploaded with a custom data source.

- **Manage Clickthrough Reports:** Each entity within a data model can have two reports associated with it — one for a single instance and one for multiple instances.

- **Manage Model Item Security:** Each entity within a data model can have permissions that are unique from the parent.

- **Regenerate Model:** You can regenerate your model from the item menu in SharePoint to update it for recent data structure changes.

Managing reports

SharePoint provides options for managing reports once they are uploaded or published to the reports library. You can set subscriptions, processing, data sources, parameters, and historical snapshot settings for each report in your library.

Uploading reports

Report files can be uploaded or published to your report library. If you are using Report Designer, Model Designer, or Report Builder, you can set the target URL for your report to be your report library and then publish directly after you've built the report. For reports that you have already built and deployed, you can upload the RDL files directly to the report library by following these steps:

1. Using a browser, navigate to your reports library.
2. Click Upload Document from the Documents tab on the Ribbon or click Add new item on the page.
3. Type the path to your RDL file or click the Browse button to navigate to the file.
4. Click OK.

Note

If you are uploading or publishing a report that contains subreports, the link to the subreport must be configured in the report as a fully qualified URL. Linked reports are not supported by the SharePoint Reporting Services document library. ■

Managing subscriptions

Subscriptions can be used to publish reports to a SharePoint library, file share, or to the Reporting Services server based on a schedule or when a snapshot of the report is taken. If you choose null delivery provider, the report will be written to the report database. The option to save to the report database is usually used if you want to cache a report that has multiple parameters. Reports stored in SharePoint do not support data-driven subscriptions.

Subscriptions create a snapshot of the report at the time of the subscription event, but these snapshots are static files and will not include any interactive features that might be included in the report itself.

If you are delivering a report to a SharePoint library, the library must be on the same site as the report library and you must be using stored credentials on your data source. The credentials used in the stored credentials must have add items permissions on the target document library to successfully write the report subscription.

Adding a report subscription

To add a report subscription that will save to a SharePoint library, follow these steps:

1. Use a Web browser to navigate to your reports library.

2. Left-click on the report that you want to view or manage subscriptions and select Manage Subscriptions.

3. Click Add Subscription from the top navigation bar.

4. Select SharePoint Document library in the Delivery Type field.

5. Type the URL for the document library for the report to be saved in the Document Library section.

6. Type the filename and title for your report and select whether or not you would like to append a file extension to the name.

7. Select the output format in the Output Format drop-down. The MHTML (Web archive) format is recommended when you are saving to a SharePoint document library because it creates a MHTML format file that is self-contained. You can also opt for PDF, Excel, TIFF, HTML, comma-delimited, or XML based on your user preferences.

8. In the Overwrite Options section, select whether you want to overwrite any previous files with the same name or create a new file. If you choose to overwrite the file and have versioning turned on in the library, it will create a new version for that file. If you choose to create a new file, SharePoint will append a number to the file to create a unique name.

9. In the delivery event section, choose whether you want the subscription to be delivered when a snapshot is created or based on a shared or custom schedule, as shown in Figure 15.12.

FIGURE 15.12

Selecting the delivery event for a report subscription

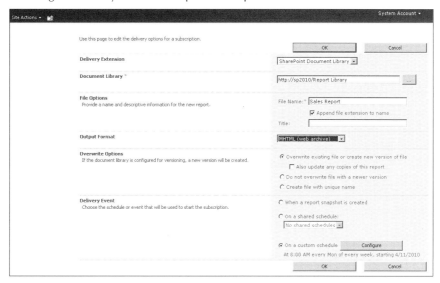

To create a custom schedule, follow these steps:

a. Click the Configure button.

b. Select the frequency of your schedule in the Frequency section. Reports can run hourly, daily, weekly, monthly, or just once.

c. In the Schedule section, choose how often the schedule will be repeated and pick the day and time. For example, if you want a report to run bi-weekly on Saturdays, you will choose a weekly frequency and have it repeat every two weeks as shown in Figure 15.13.

FIGURE 15.13

Configuring custom schedule options for a report subscription

d. Type the start and stop dates for which you want the subscription to be active in the Start and End Dates section.

e. Click OK.

To create a shared schedule, follow these steps:

a. Select Site Settings from the Site Actions menu in the top-left corner.

b. Click Manage Shared Schedules from the Reporting Services section at the bottom of the second column.

c. Click Add Schedule from the top navigation bar.

d. Type the name in the Schedule name field.

e. Select the frequency of your schedule in the Frequency section. Reports can run hourly, daily, weekly, monthly, or just once.

f. In the Schedule section, choose how often the schedule will be repeated and pick the day and time.

g. Type the start and stop dates for which you want the subscription to be active in the Start and End Dates section.

h. Click OK and click Close.

10. Type the parameter values that you want to use or configure to use the default values in the Parameter section.

11. Click OK.

Adding a report subscription for a file shared

To add a report subscription that will save to a file share, follow these steps:

1. Using a browser, navigate to your reports library.

2. Left-click on the report that you want to view or manage subscriptions and select Manage Subscriptions.

3. Click Add Subscription from the top navigation bar.

4. Select Windows file share in the Delivery Type field.

5. Type the filename for your report file.

6. Type the path to the file share, as shown in Figure 15.14.

FIGURE 15.14

Entering the path for a report writing to the Windows file share

7. **Select the report format in the Render Format drop-down menu.** The default format for a file share report is HTML 4.0 but you can also opt for Excel, PDF, Atom Data Feed, RPL Renderer, TIFF, MHTML, comma-delimited, or XML based on your user preferences.

8. **In the Write mode section, select None, Autoincrement, or Overwrite.** The None option will not write the report if a report with the same name is present; the Autoincrement option will append a number to the filename to create a unique name, and the Overwrite option will overwrite any files with the same name.

9. **Select True in the File Extension field to have the report subscription file include the file extension.**

10. **Type a username and password that has permissions for the file share in the User name and Password fields.**

11. **In the delivery event section, choose whether you want the subscription to be delivered when a snapshot is created or based on a shared or custom.**

    To create a custom schedule, follow these steps:

    a. Click the Configure button.

    b. Select the frequency of your schedule in the Frequency section. Reports can run hourly, daily, weekly, monthly, or just once.

    c. In the Schedule section, choose how often the schedule will be repeated and pick the day and time.

    d. Type the start and stop dates for which you want to subscription to be active in the Start and End Dates section.

    e. Click OK.

    To create a shared schedule, follow these steps:

    a. Select Site Settings from the Site Actions menu in the top-left corner.

    b. Click Manage Shared Schedules from the Reporting Services section at the bottom of the second column.

    c. Click Add Schedule from the top navigation bar.

    d. Type the name in the Schedule name field.

    e. Select the frequency of your schedule in the Frequency section. Reports can run hourly, daily, weekly, monthly, or just once.

    f. In the Schedule section, choose how often the schedule will be repeated and pick the day and time.

    g. Type the start and stop dates for which you want the subscription to be active in the Start and End Dates section.

    h. Click OK.

    i. Click Close.

12. **Type the parameter values that you want to use or configure to use the default values in the Parameter section.**

13. **Click OK.**

Creating a report subscription for caching

To add a report subscription that will save to the reporting server to be used for a cache, follow these steps:

1. Use a Web browser to navigate to your reports library.

2. Left-click on the report that you want to view or manage subscriptions and select Manage Subscriptions.

3. Click Add Subscription from the top navigation bar.

4. Select Null Delivery Provider in the Delivery Type field.

5. In the delivery event section, choose whether you want the subscription to be delivered when a snapshot is created or based on a shared or custom schedule.

    To create a custom schedule, follow these steps:

    a. Click the Configure button.

    b. Select the frequency of your schedule in the Frequency section. Reports can run hourly, daily, weekly, monthly, or just once.

    c. In the Schedule section, choose how often the schedule will be repeated and pick the day and time.

    d. Type the start and stop dates for which you want the subscription to be active in the Start and End Dates section.

    e. Click OK.

    To create a shared schedule, follow these steps:

    a. Select Site Settings from the Site Actions menu in the top-left corner.

    b. Click Manage Shared Schedules from the Reporting Services section at the bottom of the second column.

    c. Click Add Schedule from the top navigation bar.

    d. Type the name in the Schedule name field.

    e. Select the frequency of your schedule in the Frequency section. Reports can run hourly, daily, weekly, monthly, or just once.

    f. In the Schedule section, choose how often the schedule will be repeated and pick the day and time.

    g. Type the start and stop dates for which you want the subscription to be active in the Start and End Dates section.

    h. Click OK.

    i. Click Close

6. Type the parameter values that you want to use or configure to use the default values in the Parameter section.

7. Click OK.

Managing data sources

You can use the option to manage data sources to update the data source that is used for your report. To manage a data source, follow these steps:

1. Use a Web browser to navigate to your reports library.

2. Left-click on the report that you want to manage and select Manage Data Sources.

3. Click the name of the data source.

4. Select whether you want to use a custom or shared data source. If you choose a custom data source, type the data source connection information. If you choose shared data source, type or browse to your shared data source file.

5. Click OK and then click Close.

Managing parameters

You can manage any parameters that are available for a report to set default values and whether they are presented to your users or not. To manage your report parameters, follow these steps:

1. Use a Web browser to navigate to your reports library.

2. Left-click on the report that you want to manage and select Manage Parameters.

3. Click the parameter that you want to manage.

4. Type the default value in the Use this value field or select Do not use a default value.

5. In the Display field, select whether you would like to prompt the user for a default value and enter the Prompt field name, as shown in Figure 15.15. Do either of the following:

   • Select Hidden if you want to use the default value configured in the report and do not want the parameter to be displayed to the user.

   • Select Internal if you want to use the default value configured in the report and do not want the parameter to be displayed to the user or to anyone configuring a subscription.

6. Click OK and then click Close.

FIGURE 15.15

Configuring the prompt field for a report parameter

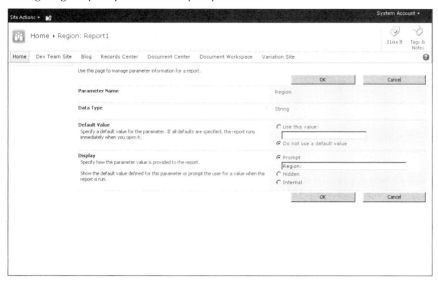

Managing processing options

You can manage the processing options for each report to tune the performance and ability to save historical snapshots. To manage the processing options for a report, follow these steps:

1. Use a Web browser to navigate to your reports library.

2. Left-click on the report that you want to manage and select Manage Processing Options.

3. In the Data Refresh Options, choose from the following options:

   - Live data: The report will be processed every time it is opened.
   - Snapshot data: This option will prevent the report from being run at an arbitrary time.
   - Cached data: The report will use the data cached according to the cache options based on an expiration time, or a shared or custom schedule, as shown in Figure 15.16.

FIGURE 15.16

Configuring a report to be processed using cached data

4. If you are using cache processing, type the elapsed time you want to use for cached data or select a shared schedule or configure a custom schedule in the Cache Options section.

5. Enter whether you want to use the site processing time out, configure your report processing limit in the Limit report processing (in seconds) field, or configure your report to not limit processing time in the Processing time-out section.

6. In the History Snapshot Options section, configure whether or not you want to enable manual snapshots and whether or not you want to store those snapshots in the report history. You can also configure the report to take snapshots based on a custom or shared schedule.

7. In the History Snapshot Limits section, configure whether you want to use the site settings for a history snapshot limits, configure your own snapshot limit, or not use a snapshot limit for that report.

8. Click OK.

Viewing and creating snapshots

Snapshots allow you to store report layout and data that were current when the snapshot was taken. You can use snapshots to retain a historical view of the data over time or to store a report that will be used when users click on it as per the processing options. Snapshots are similar to subscriptions, except they are only saved within the same library as the report and they are rendered when clicked upon. You must be using a data source that has stored credentials to support report snapshots. To view and create a report snapshot, follow these steps:

1. Use a Web browser to navigate to your reports library.

2. Left-click on the report for which you want to view history and select View history.

3. Click New Snapshot.

4. Click Close.

Managing models

After you have generated or published your data models, you can use the SharePoint management options to see how the models are used and to customize the clickthrough behavior and security for model entities.

Viewing dependent items

The ability to view dependent items lets you quickly see what items will be affected if you modify your model. To view the dependent items for a model, follow these steps:

1. Use a Web browser to navigate to your reports library.

2. Left-click on the model that you want to view and select View dependent items.

3. Click Close.

Managing clickthrough reports

You can configure the reports that will be available for each entity in your data model as a clickthrough item. This extends the information available to report users so that they can return either a report that shows information on the single instance of the entity or a report that shows multiple instances for the entity.

1. Use a Web browser to navigate to your reports library.

2. Left-click on the model that you want to manage and select Manage Clickthrough Reports.

3. Select the Entity that you want to configure reports for, as shown in Figure 15.17.

4. Type or browse the path of a report to show a single instance of the entity.

5. Type or browse the path of a report to show multiple instances of the entity.

6. Click OK.

FIGURE 15.17

Selecting an entity that you want to configure clickthrough reports for

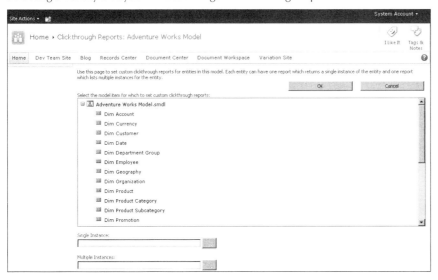

Managing model item security

SharePoint allows you to set security for each entity within the model so that you can limit access to specific portions of a model. By default, all entities within a model inherit permissions from the parent, which is the document library in which they are stored. To modify the model item permissions, you must have permission to edit items on the model. Follow these steps to modify the model permissions:

1. Use a Web browser to navigate to your reports library.

2. Left-click on the model that you want to manage and select Manage Model Item Security.

3. Select Secure individual model items independently for this model.

4. Select the entity that you would like to secure.

5. Select Assign permissions to the following users and groups, as shown in Figure 15.18, and enter the usernames in the box.

6. Click OK.

FIGURE 15.18

Assigning individual permissions for model item entities

Regenerating a data model

You will need to regenerate your data model when the data structure changes. To regenerate your data model, follow these steps:

1. Use a Web browser to navigate to your reports library.

2. Left-click on the model that you want to regenerate and select Regenerate model.

Implementing the Report Viewer Web Part

When you installed the SharePoint Add-in for reporting services in the configuration section of this chapter, the Report Viewer Web Part was added to your Web Part gallery. You can use this Web Part to insert reports on your Web Part pages and also to connect reports to filter controls on the page. This Web Part can only be used with reports that are stored/published to a SharePoint library and cannot be used with reports stored on your native reporting services server.

Adding and configuring the Report Viewer Web Part

To insert the Report Viewer Web Part on your Web Part page, follow these steps:

1. Open the page on which you want to add the Report Viewer Web Part and select Edit Page from the Site Actions menu in the top-left corner.

2. Click Add a Web Part in the zone that you want to add the Report Viewer Web Part.

3. Scroll to the Miscellaneous section and select SQL Server Reporting Services Report Viewer and click Add, as shown in Figure 15.19.

FIGURE 15.19

Adding the Report Viewer Web Part to a page

4. From the Edit menu in the Report Viewer Web Part, select Modify Shared Web Part.

5. In the Report field, type the URL of your report or browse to select your report.

6. Click Apply.

7. Click on the right side of the view section to expand.

8. Select whether you would like a full, navigation, or no toolbar in the Toolbar field. The full toolbar presents the users with the Actions menu so that they can Open, Print, or Export the report, the refresh control, the control to go forward/backward between pages,

the ability to zoom in/out and search within the report, as shown in Figure 15.20. The navigation toolbar presents only the control to go forward/backward between pages.

FIGURE 15.20

The Report Viewer Web Part with the full toolbar option

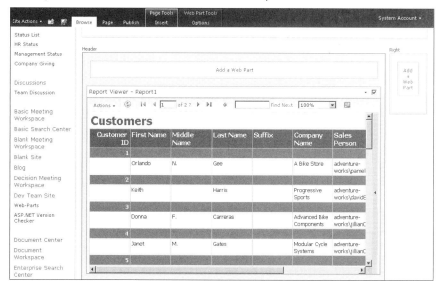

9. **If you have parameters configured for your report, select whether you want the prompt area to be displayed, collapsed, or hidden in the Prompt Area field.** The prompt area is where users can enter the parameters and if displayed by default, they can click on it to hide it, and if collapsed by default, they can click to expand it. If the prompt area is hidden, the user cannot enter the parameters.

10. **If you have a document map configured for your report, select whether you want the document map to be displayed, collapsed, or hidden in the Document Map field.** The document map is a control that allows users to navigate directly to a section or sub-report. If the document area map is hidden, it will not be available for users.

    If you want to display the document area map, enter the width for it in the Document Area Map Width field.

11. **If your report has parameters, click on the right side of the parameter section and click Load Parameters if they have not been loaded since the report was configured.**

12. **Select whether you want to use the default setting for the parameter or override the parameter setting with your own value for each parameter, as shown in Figure 15.21.**

13. **Click OK and then click Exit Edit Mode.**

FIGURE 15.21

Configuring the report parameters

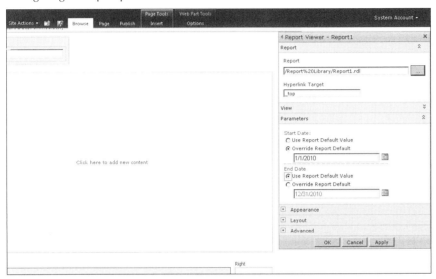

Connecting the Report Viewer Web Part to a filter Web Part

Instead of using the report parameter prompts, you may choose to use the filter Web Parts provided with SharePoint to provide report parameters. This configuration is useful if you want to configure filter parameters to drive more than one Web Part when selected or eliminate the user having to select View Report after entering parameters.

To configure this functionality, we will first add the Web Parts to the page and then connect them to the report Web Part. In the example we use, we will the date filter Web Parts since the parameters of our report are date driven, but this procedure will work for any of the filter Web Parts that match your parameters. To add the filter Web Parts to your page, follow these steps:

1. **Open the page on which you want to add the Report Viewer Web Part and select Edit Page from the Site Actions menu in the top-left corner.**

2. **Select Add a Web Part within a zone on the page.**

3. **Select the Date filter and click Add.** Since we have both a start date and end date for our example, we added this filter twice.

4. From the Edit menu on the first Date Filter Web Part, select Modify Shared Web Part.

5. Type the name of the filter field in the Filter Name field and the default value in the Default Value section as shown in Figure 15.22. The default value can be set to no default value, a specific date, or an offset date calculated based on the current date.

FIGURE 15.22

Configuring the Date Filter Web Part

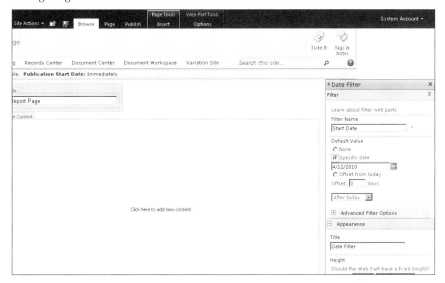

6. Click OK.

The Web Part(s) will now appear in the left column and will show a warning that the filter is not connected. To connect the filter Web Part(s) to your report, follow these steps:

1. Open the page on which you want to add the connect the filter Web Part and Report Viewer Web Part and select Edit Page from the Site Actions menu in the top-left corner.

2. Choose Connections ⇨ Send Filter Values To ⇨ [Your Report Web Part] from the edit menu of the filter Web Part, as shown in Figure 15.23.

FIGURE 15.23

Configuring the filter Web Part connections

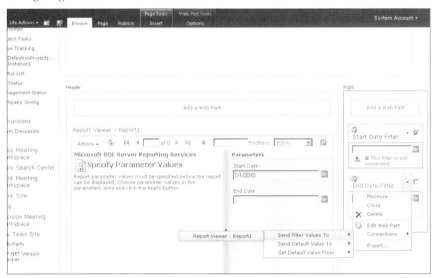

3. Select the filter parameter that you want to connect to from the Configure Connection dialog, as shown in Figure 15.24.

FIGURE 15.24

Select the report parameter to which the filter is connected.

4. Click Finish and exit Edit Mode.

Note

You can configure your Report Viewer Web Part to hide the prompt area so that users are not confused whether they should use the report parameters or the filter Web Parts. ■

You can now see the filter Web Parts on the report page, and if you change the filter values, the report will refresh based on your inputted values, as shown in Figure 15.25.

FIGURE 15.25

Date Filter Web Parts that are connected to a Report Viewer Web Part

Summary

In this chapter, we extend the Report Library functionality provided by SharePoint 2010 by installing and configuring the SQL Server Reporting Services add-in for SharePoint technologies. Once this add-in was installed and configured, we added the reporting content types so that we could upload and manage reporting services reports, models, and data source and configure snapshots, subscriptions, and report parameters. Finally, we combined the reporting services features with other Report Library features in report pages and configured the filter Web Parts and report Web Parts to work together.

Using Status Lists to Implement KPIs

Status Lists help display key performance information for your organization in a manner that drives actions. Key Performance Indicators (KPIs) are configured to represent the progress of the organization or team in a meaningful way so that it focuses the team on the right actions and goals. To do this, KPIs aggregate data that resides in locations throughout the company, providing a view of trend information from that data source. Multiple indicators are combined in a single list so that users see at a glance the high-level information that they need.

Defining the appropriate indicators for your organization can be a big job to get your head around. This chapter goes through the steps to define your KPIs and combine them for your audiences. Then we delve into the specifics of creating KPIs for each possible data source, SharePoint lists, Excel worksheets, SQL Server Analysis Services, and manual KPIs. Throughout these steps, we provide a lot of examples to help you envision how to turn the data in your organization into knowledge that drives action.

Defining Your Key Performance Indicators

Your Key Performance Indicators follow the goals of your organization. Because KPIs are very popular for managing business objectives, they can definitely be overused so that you see a myriad of green, yellow, and red lights on every site you traverse. The planning process will help you identify the appropriate indicators for your goals and define an action for each of those indicators. Finally, you can determine where and how these indicators will appear on your sites.

Defining indicators

Each indicator that you define for your portal should reflect the scope and goals of your organization. If your organization has a detailed planning process that results in yearly and quarterly goals for each department, the exercise of discovering the indicators for your portal should be a cakewalk. If your organization has a five-year business plan where the only goal is to make profit, defining indicators will be a more time-consuming process.

Here's how we recommend defining the indicators for your organization or division:

1. **Work with business unit managers to discover their yearly and quarterly goals.** If you are supporting a centralized organization, you may want to start with the top organizational goals and then work through each of the departments that support those goals. As you discover each goal, document the group that it applies to and the timeframe in which the organization will work to achieve the goal.

2. **Translate each goal into a sentence that describes the formula that will measure success.** This description is easier to write for some goals than for others, but it will help you determine whether the goal is appropriate for measurement and, therefore, a good candidate for a KPI. It is important to share these translations with the business managers to make sure that you have described the goal and measurement accurately.

3. **Determine the systems that support measurement of each goal.** For each variable in your formula, there should be a source of the data that provides that variable, even if it's just a notepad.

4. **Identify the audience(s) for each goal.** The audience may simply follow the business unit that you worked with to identify the goals, but they also may cut across the organization by role. For example, an administrator in the sales division may want to see the same indicator as an administrator in the customer service division.

Once you have gathered your goals and therefore your potential indicators, narrow down the indicators that you will implement. There are a few rules of thumb that you can use while determining the appropriate goals to map to key indicators:

- **Do not inundate your users with indicators:** If users start seeing every item in their work life as red, yellow, or green, they will start to tune them out. Keep the indicators appropriate for each user set, and generally keep the Status List to five or fewer items that they can affect or that affect them.

- **Make sure the indicators change:** If you have an indicator that tracks a ten-point change over five years, you probably don't need a pretty icon to track its slow progress. The indicators should drive change and to do so need to track a measurement that does change. If necessary, divide the goal into smaller time segments or measurement factors so that the indicator reflects something pertinent today.

- **Keep it simple:** If you can't explain how to measure the success of a goal in a sentence or two, or if any part of the formula involves an actuarial table, it is probably too complicated to drive action. The message behind the indicators should read like exclamations — Sales are down! Our customers hate us! This component of our product sucks! All employees are happy!

- **Go for quick wins:** When initially deploying KPIs on SharePoint, make sure the first few are fairly straightforward to implement and integrate to demonstrate the capability. If any requires a six-month development plan to integrate five systems, shelve it until you have validated that indicators are valuable to and appreciated by your organization.

Table 16.1 shows some sample business goals and their associated planning factors.

TABLE 16.1

Sample Business Goals to Indicator Mapping

Business Goal and Timeframe	How to Measure	Systems Involved	Targeted Audience(s)
Grow profit by 150 percent over last year by meeting quarterly targets	Compare revenue less expenses for each quarter to target	Order processing	Management, sales division
Keep expenses at reasonable level	Manage expense to revenue ratio to be 25 percent	Accounting software	Management, HR
Improve customer satisfaction by reducing bugs in software (yearly goal)	Compare number of bugs reported for each product against previous quarter	Issues tracking list	Software development
Improve customer satisfaction by reducing resolution time on issues	Measure elapsed time between open date and closed date for issues	Issues tracking list	Customer service
Deliver projects on time	Measure percentage of tasks that are delivered after the due date	Tasks list	Management
Reduce employee attrition by improving employee satisfaction	Measure average employee satisfaction rating provided by training	Employee survey	HR, management
Improve customer and employee experience through employee training	Measure attendance of training sessions and rating of training sessions	Attendance worksheet, session feedback survey	HR, customer service
Improve process for expense reimbursement	Measure number of expense reports waiting for approval	Expense report library	HR, management, accounting
Improve sales reach	Measure expansion of customer list	Customer Relationship Management database	Sales
Q3 Sales	Sum of sales from all regions for Q3	Excel workbook	Sales, management

Based on this compilation of business rules, a couple of Status Lists look viable — one for customer service and one for management. The details of the HR KPI list are shown in Table 16.2.

TABLE 16.2

HR KPI List Detail

Indicator Name	Indicator Formula	Type of Indicator
Expense to Revenue Ratio	Amount of expenses divided by amount of revenue	Indicator using data from Analysis Services
Expense Reports Awaiting Approval	Percentage of expense reports with status waiting for approval	Indicator using data from a SharePoint list
Training Attendance	Count of attendees at latest training session	Indicator using data from Excel
Employee Satisfaction	Average of survey responses to question about employee satisfaction	Indicator using data from a SharePoint list
Softball Games Wins	Number of games the HR softball team has won	Manual indicator

After these indicators are implemented, the Status List looks as shown in Figure 16.1.

FIGURE 16.1

The HR Status List

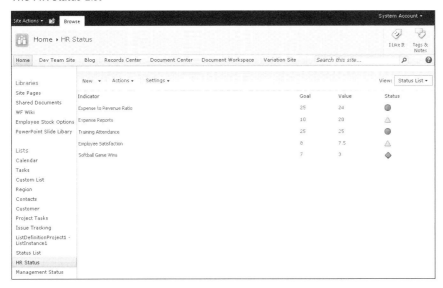

The details of the Management KPI list are shown in Table 16.3.

TABLE 16.3

Management KPI List Detail

Indicator Name	Indicator Formula	Type of Indicator
Operating Profit	Amount of revenue less amount of expenses	Indicator using data from Analysis Services
Expense to Revenue Ratio	Amount of expenses divided by amount of revenue	Indicator using data from Analysis Services
On-time project delivery	Percentage of active tasks that are not complete and are past due	Indicator using data from a SharePoint list
Employee Satisfaction	Average of survey responses to question about employee satisfaction	Indicator using data from a SharePoint list
Q3 Actual Sales	Sum of Q3 sales for all regions	Indicator using data from Excel

After these indicators are implemented, the Status List looks as shown in Figure 16.2.

FIGURE 16.2

The Management Status List

Driving users to action

Each KPI that you have defined for your organization should have an associated action so that users can affect the value that is being reported. Actions are easier to define for some indicators than others, and members of your front-line team may more directly affect the indicators whereas management might be charged with motivating others to affect the indicators; but, regardless, it is important to take advantage of the focus of your users.

Each SharePoint indicator allows you to configure the details link for that indicator. This is the link that users are directed to if they click the indicator. Configuring the details link to direct the user to the appropriate action makes it easy for users to affect the indicator. Some suggested actions are shown in Table 16.4.

TABLE 16.4

Example KPI Actions

Indicator List	Indicator Name	Details Link to
HR, Management	Expense to Revenue Ratio	Link to report that shows sales and expenses by division
HR	Expense Reports Awaiting Approval	View of expense report library that shows items that are waiting for approval
HR	Training Attendance	Excel workbook that shows all the employees that signed up and which ones attended
HR	Employee Satisfaction	View of summary of all responses to questions in survey
HR	Softball Game Wins	Web site that discusses softball strategy
Management	Operating Profit	Child indicators that show revenue and expenses
Management	On-time Project Delivery	SharePoint view of active, past-due tasks grouped by owner for project
Management	Q3 Actual Sales	Excel workbook where sales numbers are tracked for each region

Designing KPI Web Parts for your sites

After you have gone through the effort to find the appropriate indicators for your organization, you need to design an effective way to display them. You should display them in a prominent location on your sites, like the top right, and keep the KPI location fairly consistent between sites so that users start to expect them.

SharePoint provides two Web Parts that you can add to your site pages; they display KPIs from anywhere on your site collection. The first is the Status List Web Part that shows values from your indicator list. You can configure the icons that are shown to vary the KPIs throughout your sites.

The second is the Indicator Details Web Part, which allows you to display all the information for that KPI on site. This Web Part is effective for driving attention to a particular KPI and maybe changing the focus for your site or team on a regular basis.

Note

Both Web Parts can be configured for target audiences so only the members of the audience that you select for the Web Part see the KPI information. This allows you to tune the user experience for KPIs to only the appropriate users. ■

Showing data using the Status Indicator Web Part

The Status List Web Part displays the Status List to which it is pointed, and that Status List can be located anywhere on the site collection. You can then tune the Web Part to optimize the viewing experience for your users.

One of the most noticed configuration options is the ability to change the KPI icons. The following icons are available:

- **Default:** Green circle, yellow triangle, red diamond.
- **Check marks:** Green circle with a check mark, yellow circle with an exclamation point, and red circle with an X.
- **Flat:** Green, yellow, and red circles.
- **Traffic lights:** Green, yellow, and red circles encased in a square traffic light box.
- **Smileys:** Yellow circles with happy, neutral, and sad faces. Because the visual cues in the smileys are so subtle, it is difficult to see the difference.

In addition, you can configure the Web Part to show only icons. This is helpful when you do not want to display the values or if the values are not meaningful in and of themselves. You can also configure whether the Web Part will show only problems (indicators that are red and yellow) or show all indicators. Because some of the value of indicators is to encourage and motivate users and to advertise accomplishments, showing only the problems seems like short-circuiting that value, but you can select that option if the full list takes up too much vertical space. To minimize the vertical and horizontal real estate, the Web Part allows you to hide the toolbar or to display the edit toolbar in View mode.

The option to display multiple indicator columns is interesting because it adds another column for the KPI to consider and show status for. You can pick a KPI that has this column, and then select from the available columns to create the additional column that you want to display, as shown in Figure 16.3. However, this column appears at the top of the list and so appears relevant to all of the indicators, even though it's likely that the same column is not applicable to the other indicators.

After you have configured the Web Part as appropriate for your organization, it should display your indicators as shown in Figure 16.4. Each indicator is clickable and links to its link detail action, if configured, or to a detail view of the KPI if the link detail is not configured.

FIGURE 16.3

Configuring the Status List Web Part to display multiple indicator columns

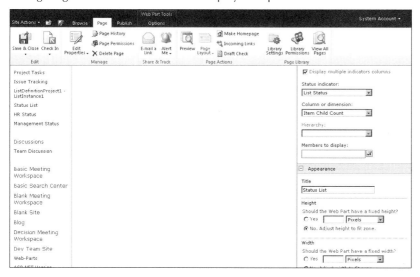

FIGURE 16.4

Using the Status List Web Part to display indicators

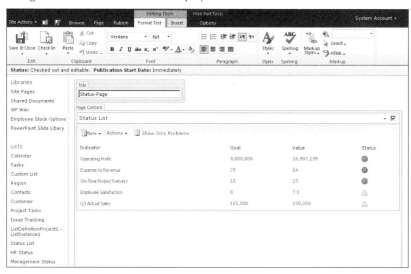

Showing data using the Indicator Details Web Part

The KPI Details Web Part is used for showing the values and status of just one indicator. You configure this Web Part to point at the appropriate Status List, and it lets you select the KPI that you want to detail and the icon style that you would like, as shown in Figure 16.5.

Once configured, the KPI Details Web Part displays an indicator as shown in Figure 16.6. In this view, you can see the importance of a good description and good comments to help users really understand what the KPI is and how it is measured. In addition, this Web Part shows the source of the KPI data and links to that source.

Configuration options for the Indicator Details Web Part

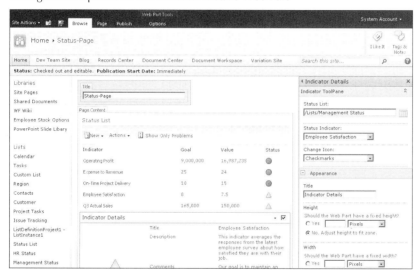

Showing a KPI using the Indicator Detail Web Part

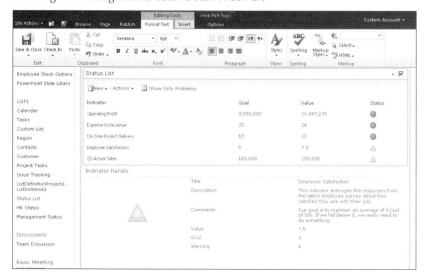

Implementing Status List KPIs from SharePoint Lists

Creating KPIs from data in SharePoint lists is an easy way to summarize the status collected in the wealth of valuable data around your organization, and to drive people to update the status of their items. However, the fact that there is a wealth of information in SharePoint can make the indicator hard to define.

When you create a KPI from a SharePoint list, you combine a view of the list with calculations performed on a column or columns. This combines the SharePoint flexibility of creating a view for all the pertinent items with the KPI ability to calculate and compare a value against a goal and display that result to drive action.

Cross-Reference

See Chapter 4 for details on how to create metadata, custom lists, and views that can then be used in a KPI based on SharePoint data. ∎

For example, you can create a KPI that turns red if 10 percent or more of active tasks in a Tasks list are past due and not complete. To do this, you create a view for tasks where status does not equal complete. Next, define a KPI based on that list that calculates the percentage of items where the value of the due date column is less than the current date, and the value of the % Complete column is not equal to 100. Then proceed to set the success level to be 5 percent or below and the warning level to be when this percentage is between 6 percent and 10 percent. The stop sign would then appear for anything above 10 percent.

The process for planning a KPI from a SharePoint list has three steps:

1. **Identify the source list and view for your KPI and confirm that it has the right metadata to calculate your value.** For example, if you will be counting the number of items in a document library that are classified as "customer reference" type items, you will want a column for content types that have a choice value of "customer reference." You will then need to create a view that shows only content where content type is equal to customer reference.

2. **Determine how you will calculate the value for your item.** This can be either a formula that calculates a percentage of items that meet a criteria or a calculation of average, sum, minimum, or maximum for a selected column.

3. **Determine the values for success, warning, and failure.**

Identifying the SharePoint source and view

The SharePoint lists and libraries within your organization contain a wealth of information. Identifying the lists and libraries that you want to use as a source for KPIs involves discovering the ones that can be analyzed to indicate action, inaction, or bottlenecks in your organization. Lists that are the most effective sources for indicators will have enough data so that the analysis provides meaningful results and/or represents a key decision point or bottleneck that needs to be highlighted to drive action.

To help with the visualization of KPIs based on your SharePoint lists, some possible KPIs for the core SharePoint list types are suggested in Table 16.5.

KPIs Based on SharePoint Lists

List Type	Columns Used	Resulting KPI
Document Library	Status	What percentage of documents are waiting for approval?
Tasks	Due date, % complete	What percentage of tasks are not complete and are due today or before?
Issue Tracking	Priority, Due Date	What high-priority issues need to be resolved today?
Issue Tracking	Category, Issue Status	How many active and unresolved issues are in my category?
Announcements	Expires	What announcement lists need to be refreshed?
Events	Amount of funding request (custom), Funding approval status (custom), Start date	What events are within the next month that have not been approved?
Discussion Lists	Replies	What percentage of discussion topics have no replies?
Survey	Question about customer satisfaction	What percentage of responses are above your target rating?

After the list has been identified, choose or create the view that represents the core entries that you want to evaluate and that represent future activity. For example, a KPI on a Tasks list should most likely be focused on all active tasks because closed tasks are not relevant to the goal of driving action. Or, you can use a view to narrow down a particular type of document in a library, such as expense reports or documents whose audience is external customers, if those are the ones that need attention.

Determining the KPI calculation

The KPI calculation for a SharePoint list can be either a value calculation of the number or percentage of items that meet the selected criteria or a calculation of sum, average, minimum, or maximum of a selected column. The value calculation lets you use text fields and calculations to define your criteria and then calculates the number or percentage based on those fields. For example, if we wanted to know what percentage of active tasks are due but are not complete, we would create a percentage calculation for the active view of a Task lists where the % Complete field is equal to 100 and the Due Date field is equal to or less than today, as shown in Figure 16.7.

The KPI entry can also calculate the value based on the sum, average, minimum, or maximum of a particular field on your SharePoint list for all items included in the view. If you define a view of all active tasks, you can then average the % Complete field to calculate a KPI value, as shown in Figure 16.8. This calculation can only be done on number fields.

FIGURE 16.7

Calculating a KPI percentage value calculation on a SharePoint list

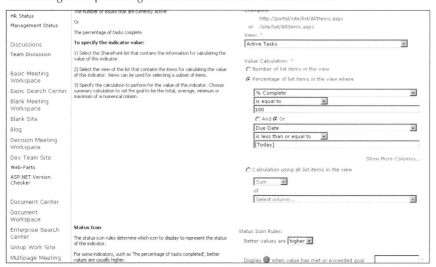

FIGURE 16.8

Calculating an average of a field on a SharePoint list

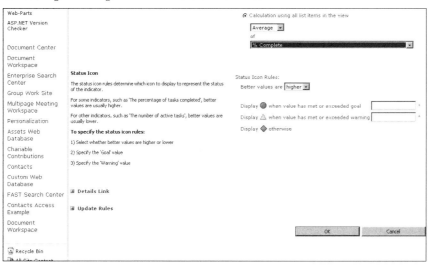

Tip

The calculation of a value will fail if any of the items do not have a value. To prevent this, you can require that the column contain data and set an appropriate default value for items so that the calculation of the KPI will succeed even if the task owner has not updated that field. ■

Determining values for goals and warnings

After you have calculated your KPI value, you must determine what values it will be compared against to determine the KPI status of red, yellow, or green. You need to determine whether higher or lower values are better, and the goal levels you set must be consistent with this determination. That is to say if higher values are better, the value will be green if the KPI calculation is higher than the goal and yellow if lower than the goal but higher than the warning.

Determining the goal and warning values for a percentage or average calculation is the most straightforward because the values are fairly predictable — between 0 and 100 for percentages and the average of expected values for the average calculation. The goal is the value for which you want the indicator to show green, the warning is the value for which you want the indicator to show yellow, and red will show for the values that are over/under the yellow value depending on whether better values are higher or lower. For the example of average of the Percent Complete field for a Tasks list, higher values would be better, and we could set the goal value at 85 percent (green shows when the average percent complete for all active tasks is 85 percent or higher) and the warning value at 50 percent (yellow shows when the average percent complete for all active tasks is 50 percent–84 percent) as shown in Figure 16.9.

FIGURE 16.9

Setting the goal and warning values for an indicator

Note

If you are calculating a percentage field, make sure you enter the goal and warning values as numbers less than 1. For example, an 85 percent goal would be entered as .85 and a 100 percent goal would be entered as 1. Although SharePoint allows you to fill in the goal field as 85 percent, it strips off the percentage and then tries to match the calculated field against 85 instead of .85. ∎

Setting values for sum, minimum, and maximum values can be a little more difficult because the numbers can presumably vary widely depending on the allowed values. Setting a goal for a field that will be summed is useful for measuring progress to date on a company initiative or goal. For example, maybe your company has a yearly giving campaign where everyone donates items for an auction and provides an estimated value for that item. The items are tracked in a SharePoint list as shown in Figure 16.10, and the company goal could be to gather $100,000 of donated items. You could create a KPI for the giving campaign, create the value to be a sum of the estimated value column, and set a goal of $100,000 and a warning at $75,000. Anything below will show red so that campaign organizers know that they need to continue to drum up effort.

The minimum and maximum fields help to identify KPI values that are outside the range of expectations. Do you want a KPI that identifies if someone has submitted a customer approval feedback form that has an overall satisfaction rating of 3 or below? In this case, you would create an Indicator that calculates the minimum value for the overall satisfaction rating and set a goal of 4 and a warning level at 3.

FIGURE 16.10

Giving Campaign list that will drive a summed KPI value

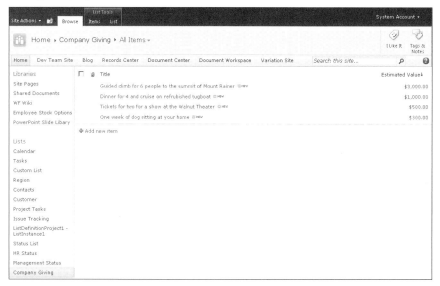

To create your KPI based on a SharePoint list, follow these steps:

1. **Navigate to the Status List to which you would like to add the manual indicator.** If you do not already have a Status List, follow these steps:

   a. Open the site that you want to host your Status List and select View All Site Content from the Site Actions menu.

   b. Select Create in the top navigation bar.

   c. Select Status List from the List section.

   d. Enter the Title and Description for your Status List and select Create.

2. **Select Indicator using data in SharePoint list from the New menu.**

3. **Enter the name of the indicator in the Name field.**

4. **Enter the location of the SharePoint List and View to support the indicator in the SharePoint List and View section.** Views can be used to select a subset of the items.

5. **Select the fields necessary to create the value calculation.** The value calculation will be either a number of items that match your criteria, a percentage of items that match your criteria, or a calculation of average, sum, minimum, and maximum for a column.

   - **Number of list items in the view:** Add the columns that you want to use to determine which items should be counted, the method of comparison, and the value for that column. The columns can be text or numeric as long as they can be compared to the value, which can be a number, text entry, or calculation such as [today]. As an example, you can ask SharePoint to calculate the number of documents in the library where the type column equals "expense report" and the status column equals "waiting for approval."

   - **Percentage of list items in the view where:** Add the columns that you want to use to determine which items should be used to calculate the percentage, the appropriate method of comparison such as greater than, less than, equal to, and the value for the comparison. The columns can be text or numeric as long as they can be compared to the value, which can be a number, text entry, or calculation, such as [today]. As an example, you can calculate the percentage of items in an issue list where the priority column equals "high" and the resolution fields do not equal "closed."

   - **Calculation using all the list items in the view:** Add whether you want the indicator to sum, average, or provide the minimum or maximum for the selected column.

6. **Set the status icon rules.** Choose whether better values are higher/lower. If you choose lower, your goal value will be lower than your warning value. Enter the goal (green) and warning (yellow) values.

7. **Enter the details page in the Details Link section for drilling down on the indicator.** If no page is entered, a default details page showing all the properties, including description and comments, appears when the user clicks the item. Ideally, the details link should direct users to the location where they can take action to update the information driving the KPI, such as the list view.

8. Enter whether you want the indicator to be recalculated every time it is viewed or when the update value link is clicked in the Update Rules section.

9. Select OK.

Implementing Status List KPIs from Excel

Indicators can also be created for data that is stored in an Excel workbook. In this scenario, Excel is doing all the calculation work, and the indicator is simply getting the value of the indicator from a particular cell that you enter. You can enter the goal and warning values as fixed values in the indicator definition or to be driven by values in the Excel spreadsheet.

Identifying your Excel KPI source

Out of all the data stored in Excel workbooks throughout your organization, you will identify the source of a KPI as a cell in a workbook that has meaning and whose location will not change regardless of the growth of the data in the spreadsheet or any possible updates to the spreadsheet from an outside data source. If that seems like a daunting task, think of it this way: The cell is most likely going to be part of a total or summary row and should be the cell that brings all the data in the rows and columns together, such as a sum of Q3 sales for all regions, as shown in Figure 16.11.

Tip

If your spreadsheet will be growing so that the location of the summary cell will change, you can create a summary worksheet that grabs the value of the cell calculated on another page. This way when the details page is updated with more rows, Excel manages the relationship between the details and the summary worksheets, and you can grab your cell value from the summary worksheet, as shown in Figure 16.12. ■

FIGURE 16.11

Sales summary data

	A	B	C	D
1	Region	Q3 Goal	Q3 Actual	% of goal
2	Northeast	$ 20,000,000.00	$ 18,423,897.00	92%
3	Northwest	$ 15,000,000.00	$ 14,867,627.00	99%
4	Southwest	$ 2,800,000.00	$ 653,412.00	23%
5	Southeast	$ 1,800,000.00	$ 1,125,256.00	63%
6	Midwest	$ 10,000,000.00	$ 12,525,313.00	125%
7				
8	All Regions	$ 49,600,000.00	$ 47,595,505.00	96%

FIGURE 16.12

Using a Summary Worksheet to define a static cell location

Configuring a trusted source for your Excel storage location

You must designate your Excel storage location as a trusted file location so that the Status List can access the data provided in the spreadsheet. This is a security mechanism SharePoint provides so that you can enable locations for trusted workbooks without dangerous links or programming to outside data sources. The trusted file location is configured at the Shared Service Provider level. To configure SharePoint to trust the file location of your Excel workbooks, follow these steps:

1. Open the administration page for your Excel Services Application.

2. Select Trusted file locations.

3. Click Add Trusted File Location in the top navigation bar.

4. Enter the address for your document library, file share, or Web site address in the Address field, as shown in Figure 16.13.

FIGURE 16.13

Entering the address for your trusted file location

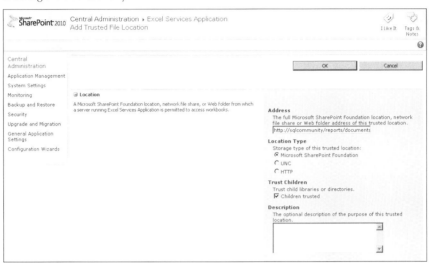

5. **Select whether the location is a SharePoint site, file share, or Web site address by using the Location type radio buttons.**

6. **Select whether you want to trust child libraries or directories by checking the Children trusted box.** This setting can be very helpful if you don't want to granularly manage libraries; however, you need to be confident that the users with the site creation permissions will not create subsites that should not be considered trusted locations.

7. **Enter the appropriate session management settings in the Session Management section:**

   - **Session Timeout:** Values between −1 and 2073600 seconds (no timeout — 24 days). This is the maximum time that an Excel Calculation session can stay active as measured from the end of the request. If you enter a value of 0, the session stays active only for that particular request.

   - **Short Session Timeout:** Values between −−1 and 2073600 seconds (no timeout — 24 days). This is the maximum time that an Excel Web Access session can stay open but inactive as measured from the start of the open request. If you enter a value of 0, the session stays active only for that particular request.

   - **Maximum Request Duration:** Values are −1 (no limit) and between 1 and 2073600 seconds (1 second – 24 days). This defines the maximum duration of a single request in a session.

8. Enter the appropriate workbook values in the Workbook Properties section:

   - **Maximum Workbook Size:** Values are 1 to 2000MB. This is the maximum size of the workbook that Excel Calculation Services can open.

   - **Maximum Chart Size:** Any positive integer is a valid value. This is the maximum size of the chart that Excel Calculation Services can open.

9. Enter the calculation behavior in the Calculation Behavior section.

   - **Volatile Function Cache Lifetime:** Valid values are –1 (calculated once per session) and 0 (function is always calculated) and 1 to 2073600 seconds (1 second to 24 days). These values define the maximum time in seconds that a manual or automatic calculation will be cached.

   - **Workbook Calculation Mode:** File, manual, automatic, or automatic except data tables. This setting defines the calculation mode of Excel Calculation Services and overrides the workbook settings unless you select File.

10. Enter the external data settings in the External Data section as shown in Figure 16.14. You want to configure these settings according to the needs and trust levels of workbook authors. External data allows Excel to process data from a variety of sources, such as databases and ODBC sources, and therefore surfaces sources that many users wouldn't otherwise see. By limiting the ability to use external data defined in trusted data connection libraries and limiting the publishing of DCLs to trusted authors, you can manage external data risk while still allowing a wide range of functionality.

    - **Allow External Data:** Select none, trusted data connection libraries only, and trusted data connection libraries and embedded. Because external data could potentially be harmful, you can select what external data sources are allowed. If you limit the external data to trusted data connection libraries, the spreadsheet must be calling a data connection from a trusted location. The trusted data connection libraries and embedded setting allows external data from DCLs and from custom connection strings that are embedded in the spreadsheet.

    - **Warn on Refresh:** Select this option if you want to display a warning before refreshing the data from external locations.

    - **Stop When Refresh on Open Fails:** Selecting this option stops the open operation on an external file if the file contains a Refresh On Open data connection and the file cannot be refreshed when it is opening, and the user does not have open rights to the file.

    - **External Data Cache Lifetime:** Valid values are –1 (never refresh after first query) and 0 to 2073600 seconds (0 seconds to 24 days). These values define the maximum time in seconds that the system can use cached manual or automatic external data query results.

    - **Maximum Concurrent Queries Per Session:** Any positive integer is a valid value. This defines the maximum number of concurrent queries that can be executed during a single session.

FIGURE 16.14

Configuring the external data settings for your trusted data location

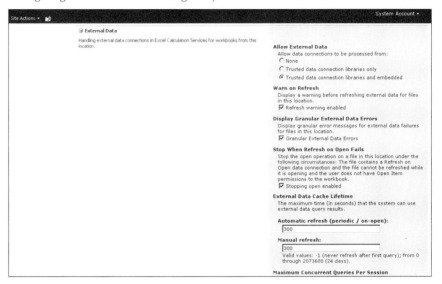

11. Select whether you would like to allow user-defined functions in the User-Defined Functions section.

12. Click OK.

Creating your KPI from an Excel worksheet

You can create a KPI from an Excel worksheet. To do so, follow these steps:

1. **Navigate to the Status List to which you would like to add the manual indicator.** If you do not already have a Status List, follow these steps:

   a. Open the site that you want to host your Status List and click View All Site Content from the Site Actions menu.

   b. Click Create in the top navigation bar.

   c. Click Status List from the Custom Lists section.

   d. Enter the Title and Description for your Status List and click Create.

2. Select Indicator using data in Excel workbook from the New menu.

3. Enter the name of the indicator in the Name field.

4. Enter the location of the workbook in the workbook URL field.

5. Enter the cell location of the indicator value in the Cell Address for Indicator Value field.

6. Set the status icon rules.

   Choose whether better values are higher/lower. If you choose lower, your goal value will be lower than your warning value.

   Enter the goal (green) and warning (yellow) values.

7. Enter the details page in the Details Link section for drilling down on the indicator. If no page is entered, a default details page is displayed when the user clicks. If no page is entered, a default details page showing all the properties, including description and comments, appears when the user clicks the item. Ideally, the details link should direct users to the location where they can take action to update the information driving the KPI, such as the spreadsheet.

8. Enter whether you want the indicator to be recalculated every time it is viewed or when the update value link is clicked in the Update Rules section.

9. Click OK.

Implementing Status List KPIs from Analysis Services

KPIs can also be created from data in SQL Server Analysis Services. In this scenario, Analysis Services has done all the work to analyze the data and create the KPI within its own framework, and SharePoint creates an indicator from the data as it is presented. The values of the goal, the warning, and the indicator itself are all defined in Analysis Services, as shown in Figure 16.15, so there are not many options that you need to configure at the SharePoint level other than selecting which indicators to display on your Status List. Indicators created from Analysis Services are the only ones that can show trends because this information is processed by Analysis Services.

Creating an Office data connection to your Analysis Services cube

The first step in creating an indicator from SQL Server Analysis Services is to configure the connection to the cube for the KPI to use. You do this by using Excel 2010 to create the Office Data Connection (ODC) file and then uploading that to a data connection library. By storing your ODC files in a data connection library, you enable user access to those data sources without having to know all the details about server, database, and security settings. You can, however, use Windows security for the connection so that the user's credentials are necessary for access to the data.

FIGURE 16.15

A KPI defined by SQL Server 2008 Analysis Services

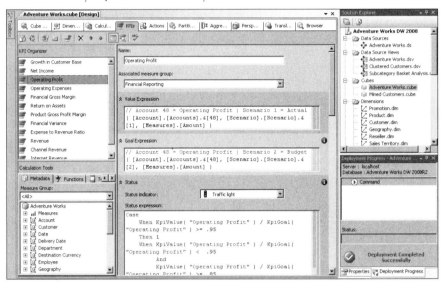

To create an ODC to your Analysis Services cube, follow these steps:

1. Open Excel 2010 and select the Data tab.

2. Select From Analysis Services in the From Other Sources menu in the Get External Data section.

3. Enter the server name and connection credentials on the Connect to Database Server page of the Data Connection Wizard, as shown in Figure 16.16. Click Next.

FIGURE 16.16

Using the Data Connection Wizard to connect to your Analysis Services server

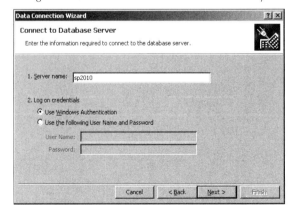

4. Select the database and cube that contains your KPIs in the Select Database and Table page of the Data Connection Wizard, as shown in Figure 16.17. Click Next.

Selecting your Analysis Services cube in the Data Connection Wizard

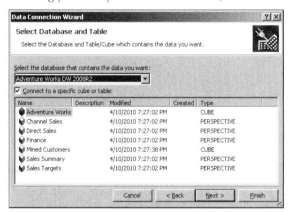

5. Enter the filename and description for your ODC file as shown in Figure 16.18. The description should be used to let users know the details of the connection so that they can accurately pick the connection that meets their needs. If you do not select a filename location by using the browse button, the file will be saved to your [My Data Sources] folder under [My Documents]. Click Finish.

Entering the filename and description for your ODC file

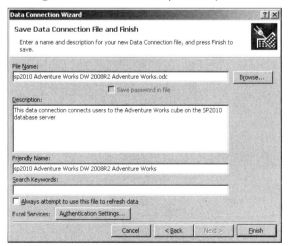

6. In the Import Data prompt that appears when you finish, select Only Create Connection, as shown in Figure 16.19.

Creating a connection file using Excel 2010

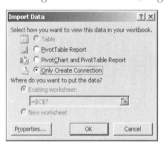

7. Using a browser, navigate to the data connection library in which you want to store the ODC file.

8. Select Upload Document from the top navigation bar or select Add New Item as shown in Figure 16.20. Browse to the location of your ODC file, and select OK. (By default the ODC file will be saved from Excel to My Documents\My Data Sources.)

Uploading the ODC file to the SharePoint Data Connection Library

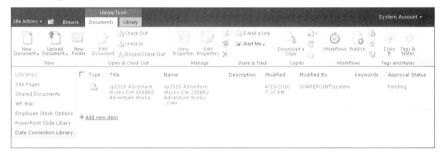

9. Provide a description for the ODC file so users know to what cube they will be connecting and select Check in. (Depending on your site settings, you may need to approve the new connection file.)

Creating an indicator from data in SQL Server 2008 Analysis Services

You can create an indicator from data in SQL Server 2008 Analysis Services. Follow these steps:

1. **Navigate to the Status List to which you would like to add the manual indicator.** If you do not already have a Status List, follow these steps:

   a. Open the site that you want to host your Status List and click View All Site Content from the Site Actions menu.

   b. Click Create in the top navigation bar.

   c. Click Status List from the Custom List section.

   d. Enter the title and description for your Status List and click Create.

2. **Select Indicator using data in SQL Server Analysis Services from the New menu.**

3. **Select the ODC in a data connection library in the Data Connection field as shown in Figure 16.21 and click OK.**

FIGURE 16.21

Selecting your ODC from the data connection library

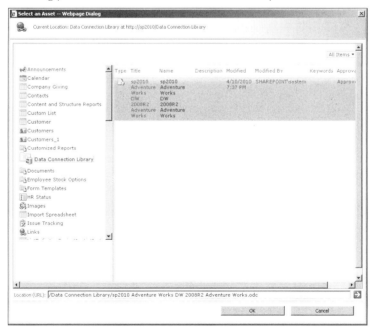

4. **Filter by KPI folder and select the appropriate Status List in the SQL Server Analysis Services KPI section.** Select whether you would like any defined child indicators included in the KPI, as shown in Figure 16.22.

Note

If you add a parent indicator and select that you would like to include the child indicators, it would be redundant to add the child indicators as their own KPI entries. ■

FIGURE 16.22

Selecting your KPIs from the Analysis Services cube

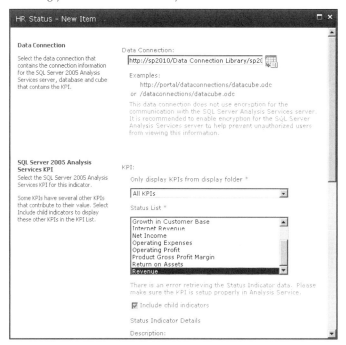

5. **Enter the name of the indicator in the Name field and the comments to help explain the value or status.**

6. **Enter the details page in the Details Link section for drilling down on the indicator.** If no page is entered, a default details page appears when the user clicks. If no page is entered, a default details page showing all the properties including description and comments appears when the user clicks the item. Ideally, the details link should direct users to the location where they can take action to update the information driving the KPI, such as the application that pushes the data to the Analysis Services cube.

7. Click in the Update Rules section whether you want the indicator to be recalculated every time it is viewed or when the update value link is clicked, as shown in Figure 16.23.

FIGURE 16.23

Entering the update rules for a KPI

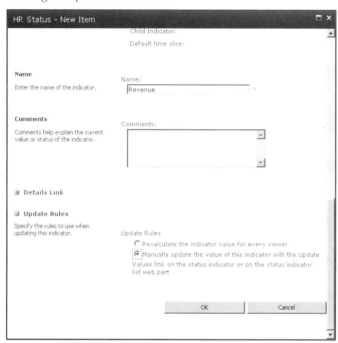

8. Click OK.

Implementing Status List KPIs Manually

KPIs entered manually are not very useful. These indicators are simply items for which you enter the value, goal, and warning; they are not connected to any other source of data. Updating manual KPIs means editing the KPI itself, and because they do not represent any body of data, the action that they drive is not clear. However, these KPIs can be useful for quickly prototyping the KPI concept so that you can enlist support for a full KPI project. Also, they can be used in conjunction with other KPIs such as SharePoint list KPIs to capture an item that isn't data driven or is external to your organization. An example of this might be the number of people who participated in the last blood drive or the number of games the softball team won.

Ideally, manual KPIs would be items that do not change frequently so that you do not have to hire a whole crew of KPI-updaters to gather the data and enter the changes every day or every week. To create a manual KPI, follow these steps:

1. **Navigate to the Status List to which you would like to add the manual indicator.** If you do not already have a Status List, follow these steps:

   a. Open the site that you want to host your Status List and click View All Site Content from the Site Actions menu.

   b. Click Create in the top navigation bar.

   c. Select Status List from the List section.

   d. Enter the title and description for your Status List and click Create.

2. **Select Indicator using manually entered information from the New menu.**

3. **Enter the name of the indicator in the Name field and the comments to help explain the value or status.**

4. **Enter the KPI value of the indicator in the Value field.** This field is manually updated when the value changes.

5. **Set the status icon rules.**

   Choose whether better values are higher/lower. If you choose lower, your goal value will be lower than your warning value.

   Enter the goal (green) and warning (yellow) values as shown in Figure 16.24.

6. **Enter the details page in the Details Link section for drilling down on the indicator.** If no page is entered, a default details page appears when the user clicks.

7. **Select OK.**

A manual indicator appears just like the others that are created from SharePoint, Analysis Services, and Excel. Figure 16.25 shows the manual KPI, softball wins, in the list with our indicators from dynamic sources. Values, goals, and warnings that are configured in the indicator itself are shown in this view, whereas dynamic values are not retrieved.

FIGURE 16.24

Configuring an indicator from manually entered data

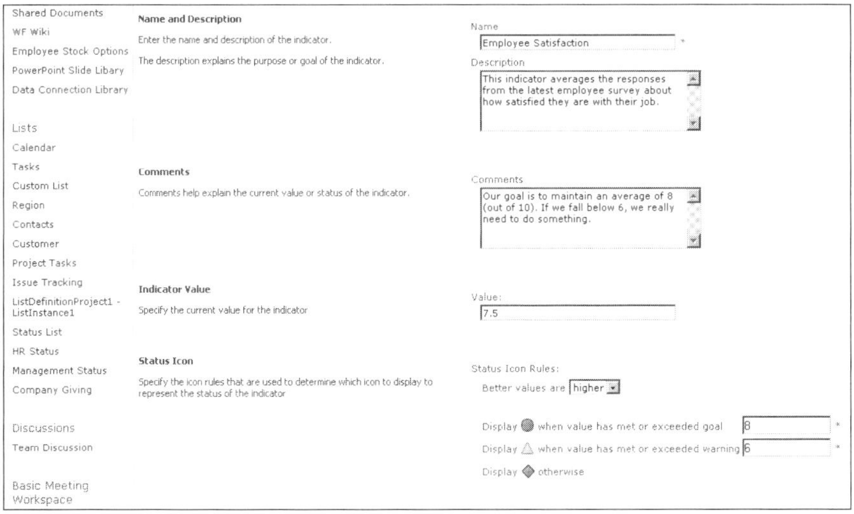

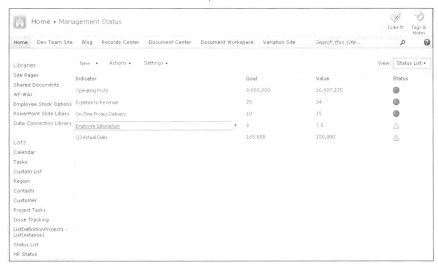

FIGURE 16.25

A KPI that is created from a manual entry

Summary

When correctly defined and implemented, KPIs grab the attention of your portal users and drive them to action. This chapter walked through how to define the right indicators for your business, assign appropriate actions for them, and then display them in a prominent yet efficient way. We also covered the implementation details for indicators based on each type of data source available — SharePoint lists, Excel workbooks, Analysis Services, and manual information. By following the steps shown in this chapter, you should have a portal that is full of clear signs of where you need more or less effort to achieve goals in your organization.

Implementing Business Data Connectivity Services

The Business Data Connectivity Services (BCS) is a service that allows you to reuse other sources of data in your organization by centrally surfacing business data from other applications and making that data available to SharePoint lists, Web Parts, search, and user profiles.

You can use the BCS to display data from Siebel, SAP, or other applications through Web services or database access. The most common sources for BCS data are line-of-business applications so that you can reuse that information throughout the organization without giving all users access and/or training on that line-of-business application.

This chapter discusses the scenarios that may require use of the BCS, defines applications and entities to make business data available, and implements the Secure Store Service which can be leveraged by the BDC for ease of application access. Finally, we will use the integrated data in SharePoint components throughout your site.

Identifying Your Business Data

The first step to successfully implementing a business data application is to define what the data is and in what scenario it can be leveraged in SharePoint. This allows you to define the success criteria and goals for your business application that can be used to guide your application definition and implementation.

Identifying data sources

The BCS functionality is primarily designed to integrate the line-of-business (LOB) applications in your organization. *LOB applications* are the critical applications at the heart of running an enterprise. At the line-of-business application level, there are several common types of data sources, including:

- **Accounting:** An LOB application that contains all of your invoicing, accounts receivable, accounts payable, payroll, and expense information.

- **Supply chain management:** An application that tracks the data through all the phases from design to distribution of a manufacturing process. This includes inventory management and order fulfillment processes.

- **Customer relationship management (CRM):** A CRM application that tracks all of your customers and interactions with customers. This can be a very complex set of data if your business is centered on customer interactions like a call center, or simple data if the CRM is just tracking the actions for a couple of salespeople.

- **Human resource:** A human resource application that focuses on tracking all the information on current and previous employees. This data is typically very sensitive because it includes data like social security numbers, home addresses, phone numbers, and hiring status.

- **Issue tracking:** An application that stores the active and closed issues or bugs for your organization.

Identifying scenarios and goals

Each organization has unique scenarios and goals that define the success of the BCS implementation. However, there are broadly used categories of scenarios and goals that might be helpful to scenario and goal planning, including:

- **Integrating columns of business data with SharePoint lists:** For data consistency, ease of maintenance, and faster data entry, you should leverage information already contained in an LOB application as a column in a SharePoint list or library. This allows the BCS object to be selected in a list entry; SharePoint will then show the selected business data in the SharePoint entry. An example would be associating customer contact information stored in a CRM application with an issue tracking list so that the user's name, e-mail address, and phone would be selected from the entries in the CRM business data.

- **Searching business data:** In this scenario, business data that would not have been previously searchable, or whose search application was not integrated with SharePoint search, can now be searched by SharePoint and integrated with SharePoint search results of other types of information.

- **Integrating business data into SharePoint Web pages:** By using the BCS application definition, business data becomes accessible to end users and Web designers who want to integrate that information on their sites and pages.

- **Simplifying user access management:** By combining a business data application definition with the secure store service provided with SharePoint, you can eliminate the pain of multiple passwords to disparate systems and still secure your password information.

SharePoint provides easy connectivity to SAP Business Information Warehouse or mySAP, Siebel eBusiness Applications, Attunity Legacy Data Access Solutions, Microsoft BizTalk server, and SQL Server.

Defining your entities

Entities are logical groupings of data from your application that you make available via the BCS. Examples of entities include customers (for which you pull several fields such as first name, last name, e-mail, and so on) or orders (including order date, customer name, and total price). Using the metadata attributes for the entity object, you describe what fields are returned, which are used to filter the data in SharePoint, how the object is returned, what actions are possible, and if there are associated entities. The following components make up an entity:

- **Identifier:** The key or keys used to uniquely identify an instance of the entity.
- **Method:** The method used to get data from the source. This component is the equivalent of a `select` statement in SQL.
    - **FilterDescriptor:** The filter descriptors define the fields available for users to filter the data in the BCS.
    - **Parameter:** The parameters work with the filter descriptor to describe what parameters will be passed to the BCS to find data and what fields are returned for the data. Each parameter has a type descriptor to describe the expected data.
    - **MethodInstance:** This parameter describes how to call the method by defining the input parameter that the method takes and default values. A method may have more than one MethodInstance so that it can be called using different default values.
- **Action:** Available actions are presented to the user for the data. An action can be anything that is URL-addressable (Web link, mailto tag, and so on) and is visible anywhere the entity is referenced, whether in a list field or in a business data Web Part. Actions should be used to help drive the user to interact with the data.
    - **ActionParameter:** This parameter defines the parameters that the action URL can accept.

Defining associations

Associations are used to link relationships between entities in a parent-child type relationship. The business data-related link Web Part uses the association definition to select the related child objects given the parent entity object. For example, a parent entity is a customer, a child entity is the orders, and the relationship defines how to find the orders, given the identity of the customer.

Another optional component for your BCS model is to define associations. Associations are related entities within your source application, and if you think of the entity as the parent, the associations are the children of that parent. For example, a customer is your entity and the contacts for that customer are the associations. By defining associations, you can create models that show related details for an entity.

Defining Business Data Models

BCS is the replacement of the MOSS 2007 Business Data Catalog (BDC). The underlying paradigm in SharePoint Server 2010 is the creation of external content types. This is what the BCS provides to the overall farm and sites. External content types are similar to regular content types because they define a specific structure of data, but instead of providing internal data, they provide external business data.

External content types are generated by the BCS by using business data models. While BCS is the new acronym, BDC is still engrained from MOSS 2007. Therefore, these models may be referenced as BCS models or BDC models.

BCS models may be created in three different ways:

- **BDC Application Definition:** This model is an XML-based file that defines the external content types. The sole method in MOSS 2007 still exists as a backward-compatibility option. You need a third-party tool or the Microsoft Business Data Catalog Definition Editor tool to generate this file. Creating one by hand is not ideal, although possible.
- **SharePoint Designer 2010:** The new version of SharePoint Designer has the ability to create external content types. This method is straightforward and allows you to easily generate external content types by using SQL Server or a WCF Service. You may also leverage custom .NET assembly data sources which have been implemented using Visual Studio 2010.
- **Visual Studio 2010:** With Visual Studio 2010 you may generate BSC models using real .NET classes and methods. This is the most extensible method as additional services and assemblies may be coded or referenced.

Because the XML-based file method is being phased out, I focus on the two new ways to generate external content types in this section.

The underlying principle of a BCS model or external content type is that BCS and therefore SharePoint need to understand how a single entity is defined as well as a way to get a single instance of an entity and the entire set. Therefore, two methods (or types of methods) are required in your BCS model:

- **Read List:** This method will return all entities available from your data source (unless constricted by a filter)
- **Read Item:** This method accepts an identifying key of one the entities and returns a single instance of the entity.

These are similar to the Finder and Specific Finder methods that were used in MOSS 2007. Previously you also needed an ID Enumerator method to allow searching. Although it is still possible to use this method and make the entity crawlable, there is an easier way to allow searching by marking the Read List method as a RootFinder. This is explained in the "Creating BSC Models using Visual Studio 2010" section.

Creating external content types using SharePoint Designer

SharePoint Designer 2010 provides the ability to generate and manage external content types on your sites. Although it is limited mainly to SQL Server or WCF Service data sources, using SharePoint Designer 2010 is the easiest way to use BCS and provide external content types to SharePoint.

To create a new external content type by using SharePoint Designer 2010, follow these steps:

1. Navigate to your root site collection and select Site Actions ⇨ Edit in SharePoint Designer or launch SharePoint Designer 2010 and open your root site collection from there.

2. Select External Content Types from the Site Objects navigation pane, as shown in Figure 17.1.

FIGURE 17.1

Selecting External Content Types in SharePoint Designer

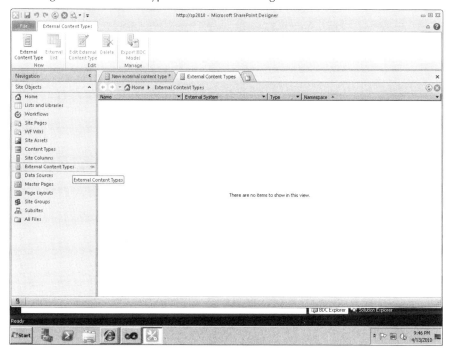

3. **Click External Content Type from the New section on the Ribbon.** A New External Content Type tabbed page appears in the main area as shown in Figure 17.2.

4. **Click the links for Name and Display Name and enter a value.** For this example, I use Customers.

5. **Click the link on the External System prompt to open the Operation Designer page as shown in Figure 17.3.**

6. **Click Add Connection and select the data source type.** For this example, I will select SQL Server.

7. **Fill out the appropriate connection properties for the data source selected. The SQL Server example connection entries are shown in Figure 17.4.** Use the user's identity for Windows authentication or Impersonate by using the Secure Store Service and providing a Secure Store Application ID (see the "Implementing Single Sign-On Using the Secure Store Service" section of this chapter for generating an application ID).

Note

Using the user's identity implies Windows authentication and therefore the service or database must be part of the SharePoint farm or Kerberos must be implemented as the SharePoint authentication protocol. ■

FIGURE 17.2

New External Content Type Page

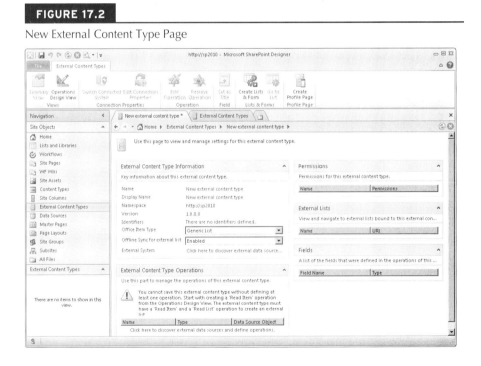

FIGURE 17.3

Operation Designer

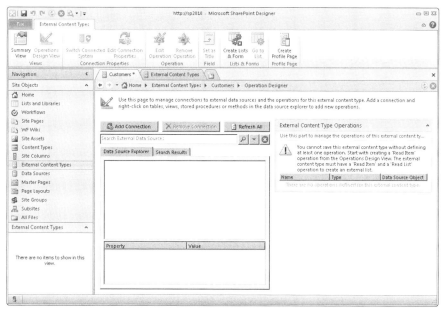

FIGURE 17.4

Data connection properties

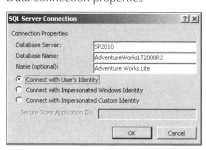

8. **Click OK.** The Data Source Explorer populates with the data source items.

9. **Define Operations.** The next step is to define operations. An external content type must at least have a Read List and Read Item operation. Right-click a data source entity to define the appropriate operations as shown in Figure 17.5.

FIGURE 17.5

Operation menu

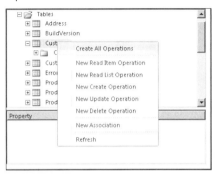

10. **Create Read Item Operation.** Select New Read Item Operation from the Operations menu. The Read Item operation wizard appears as shown in Figure 17.6. Enter an Operation Name and an Operation Display Name (or keep the defaults). Click Next.

FIGURE 17.6

Read Item wizard

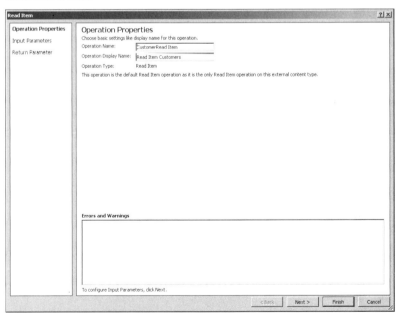

11. Select the identifier of the data source entity and enter a display name. Click Next.

12. Select the attributes or columns to return. You may optionally change the display name of the fields here as shown in Figure 17.7. Notice you may not be able to generate an update operation if all columns are not returned.

FIGURE 17.7

Return parameter configuration

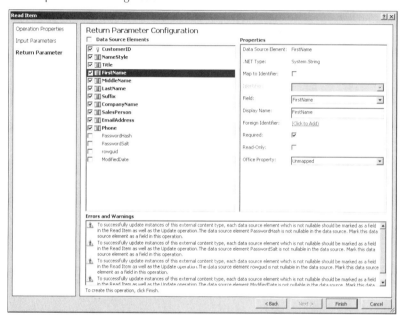

13. **Click Finish.** The Read Item operation appears in the Operation list.

14. **Create Read List Operation.** Select New Read List Operation from the Operations menu. The Read List operation wizard appears. Enter an Operation Name and an Operation Display Name (or keep the defaults). Click Next.

    The filter parameters page appears, and you are warned about having a limiting filter. The filter that is being recommended will indeed reduce the amount of records or list items that are returned, but this may restrict users from seeing all available data. A more useful filter is one that an end user can use to find specific sets of data.

15. **Create Filter Parameters.** Click Add Filter Parameter and then click the Click to Add link as shown in Figure 17.8. The filter configuration dialog appears.

FIGURE 17.8

Create Filter Parameters page

16. Enter the following values as shown in Figure 17.9:

Name:	Last Name
Filter Type:	Wildcard
Filter Field:	Last Name
Ignore Filter:	Check
Custom value:	*
Is default value:	Check
Use to create match list:	Check

17. **Click OK.** There are warning messages. Change the Data Source Element to Last Name and enter a * in the Default Value as shown in Figure 17.10 (even though it is a drop-down, you may enter your own values as well). Click Next.

FIGURE 17.9

Filter configuration dialog

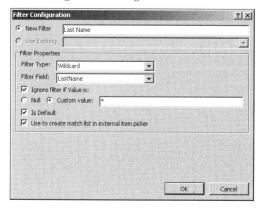

FIGURE 17.10

Correcting the properties

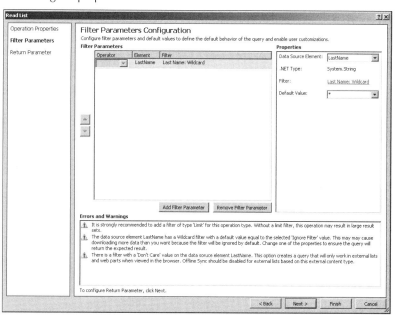

18. **Return Parameter Configuration.** Select the Last Name column and check the Show In Picker check box as shown in Figure 17.11. Click Finish.

FIGURE 17.11

Return Parameter Configuration

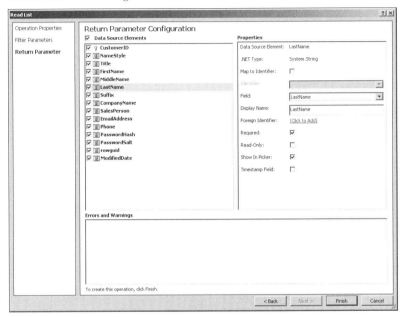

19. **Save the External Content Type.** Click File ➪ Save to save the external content type back to SharePoint. Click on the External Content Types breadcrumb tab to confirm the new entry exists.

You now have a BCS model that can be used within your SharePoint site collection. See the "Setting permissions on BCS external content types" section before moving forward.

Creating BSC Models using Visual Studio 2010

The more advanced option for generating external content types in SharePoint 2010 is constructing BDC Models within the Visual Studio 2010 development environment. While this is a more advanced method, it provides great flexibility in connecting to external data sources as well as the ability to incorporate any business logic necessary. This section will outline the steps and processes involved in creating a BDC Model with Visual 2010, although the actual implementation will depend on your own customization needs.

Follow these steps to generate a BDC Model with Visual Studio 2010:

1. **Launch Visual Studio 2010 and click New Project.**

2. **Under Visual C# select SharePoint and click on the 2010 folder. Select the Business Data Connectivity Model template and provide a name, as shown in Figure 17.12. Click OK.**

FIGURE 17.12

New Business Data Connectivity Model Project in Visual Studio 2010

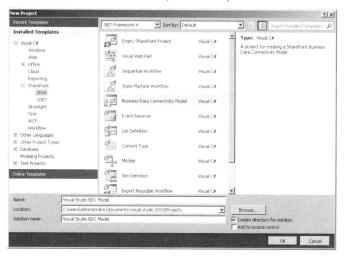

3. **Enter your main site collection in the SharePoint Customization Wizard screen that appears (Figure 17.13) and click Finish.** Your new project is generated and the solution appears within the Solution Explorer pane. The BDC Model elements appear in the BDC Explorer pane.

FIGURE 17.13

SharePoint Customization Wizard

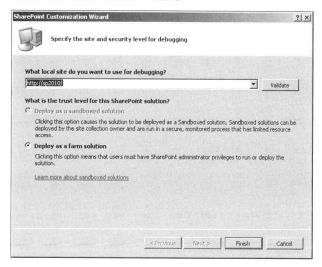

4. Expand the elements within the BDC Explorer pane to examine the contents (Figure 17.14). This is the resultant model interface that BCS will use to provide the external content source, but what makes up the model is found in the solution code.

FIGURE 17.14

BDC Model contents

5. Switch to the Solution Explorer pane by clicking the bottom Solution Explorer tab. Expand BDCModel1 to expose its elements.

Tip

You may (and probably should) rename any elements in the solution by right-clicking the element and selecting properties. Enter a new name in the Name property. ∎

6. Entity1.cs is the class representation of the external entity you wish to exploit. This class defines the object that will be returned. The sample code as shown in Figure 17.15 should be replaced with the appropriate properties that relate to the columns or fields from your external data source.

7. EntityService1.cs defines the methods that are part of the BDC model (Figure 17.16). The two required methods, ReadItem and ReadList, are generated as part of the project template. The code in these classes should be replaced with data access calls which return a single item and the entire data set, respectively. Notice they return the object type defined as the entity class.

FIGURE 17.15

Entity class

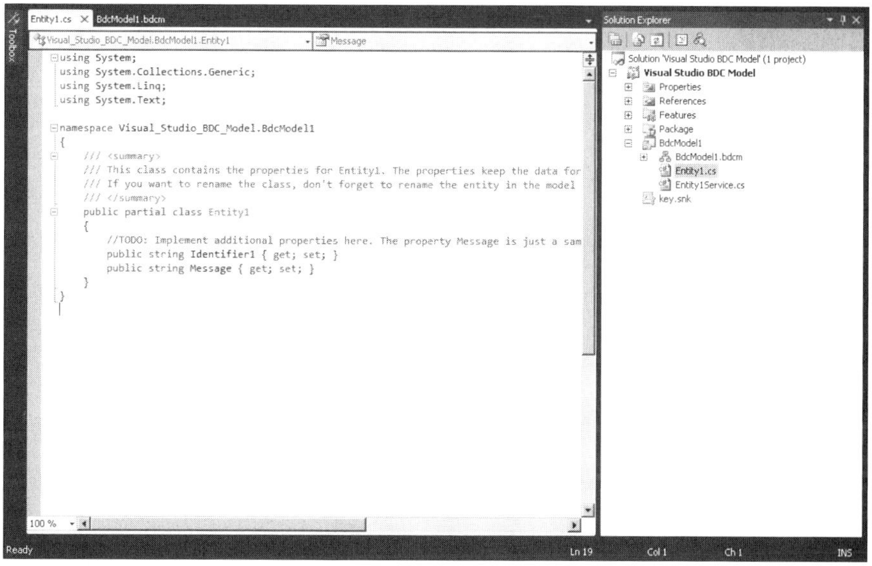

FIGURE 17.16

Entity service class

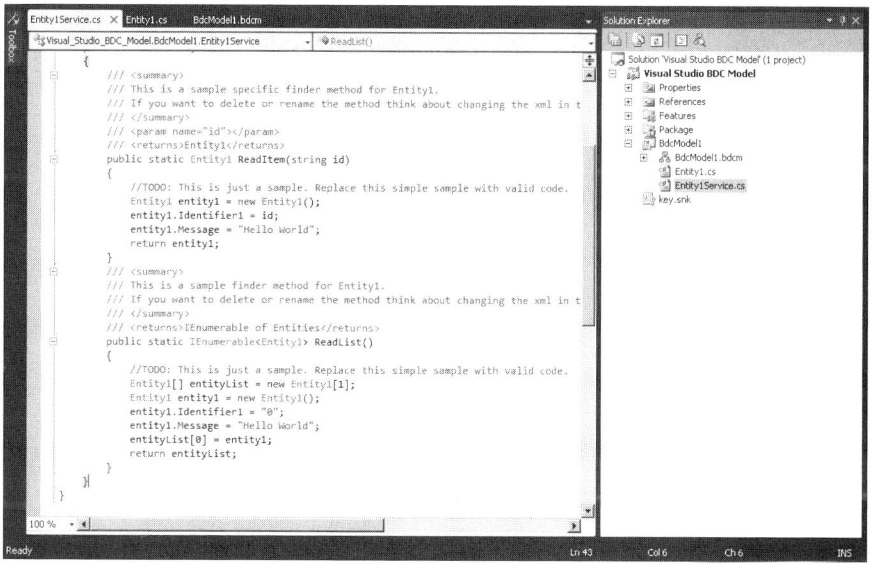

Note

Because this is .NET, you can easily add references or additional classes to the project that produce a data access layer. Your entity service methods only need to produce the populated objects. ∎

8. **Making the BDC Model searchable.** You no longer need to go through the trouble of creating an ID Enumerator method. This removes at least six additional steps and possibilities of error. The new easier way to make your business data entity searchable is to simply add a RootFinder property to the ReadList method. Start off by right-clicking the ReadList method in the BDC Explorer pane and select properties (Figure 17.17).

Selecting the ReadLIst properties

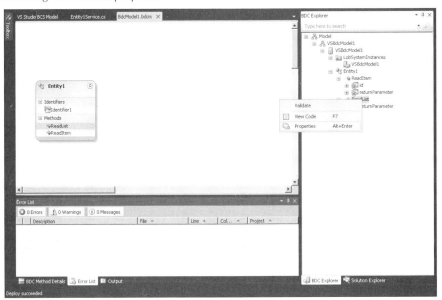

9. **Click the ellipsis in the Custom Properties item.** The custom properties dialog appears.

10. **Enter RootFinder in the name box and enter an "x" as the value as shown in Figure 17.18.**

11. **Click back into the Name box and press Enter to accept the entry. Click OK.**

12. **Visibility in search administration.** There is another property that needs to be set in order for the BDC Model to be selectable in the search settings. Under LobSystemInstances within the BDC Explorer pane, right-click the BDCModel LobSystemInstance item and select Properties.

FIGURE 17.18

Entering the RootFinder property

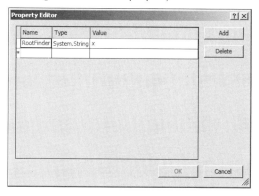

13. Click the ellipsis in the Custom Properties item. The custom properties dialog appears.

14. Enter ShowInSearchUI in the name box and enter "true" as the value.

15. Build the project to ensure it compiles properly by selecting Build Solution from the Build top menu.

16. Right-click the project in the Solution Explorer pane and select Deploy to deploy the solution to SharePoint as shown in Figure 17.19. Visual Studio adds the solution to your farm and deploys it appropriately.

Note

In a production environment deployment may not be that easy. You probably need to take the resultant WSP file and deploy it as a solution to the farm using PowerShell. ∎

You now have an external content type that can be used within your SharePoint farm. See the "Setting permissions on BCS external content types" section before moving forward.

Note

When viewing the BDC Model entity within the Business Data Connectivity Services application, the Crawlable property may state "No." Don't be alarmed. It states that it is not crawlable because we didn't create an ID Enumerator method; however, as long as you set the RootFinder property, you will be able to crawl this external content type. See the Configuring Business Data Search section for more information on searching the external content type. ∎

FIGURE 17.19

Deploying the BDC Model

Setting permissions on BCS external content types

Whether you created an external content type using SharePoint 2010 or Visual Studio 2010, you need to allow users to access the actual BCS external content type regardless of the data source authentication or credentials. To do this, follow these steps:

1. Navigate to Central Administration and select Application Management from the Quick Launch.

2. Click on the Manage Service Applications link under the Service Applications section.

3. Click on the Business Data Connectivity Service proxy link as shown in Figure 17.20.

4. Click on Set Permissions from the external content type drop-down menu as shown in Figure 17.21.

FIGURE 17.20

Business Data Connectivity Service proxy selection

FIGURE 17.21

External content type drop-down menu

5. Use the Set Object Permissions dialog box to find users or groups and give them appropriate permissions. You will need at least one user or group to have the Set Permissions permission. After finding users in the top box, click Add to add them and then select the appropriate check boxes to grant the corresponding permissions (Figure 17.22).

FIGURE 17.22

Set Object Permissions dialog box

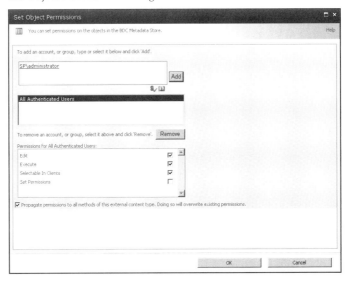

6. Click OK.

Creating profile pages on BCS external content types

When using an external content type for search, you need to create a profile page so the results have a way of presenting the data returned by a search of the entities. To do this, follow these steps:

1. Navigate to Central Administration and select Application Management from the Quick Launch bar.

2. Click on the Manage Service Applications link under the Service Applications section.

3. Click on the Business Data Connectivity Service link.

4. Click the Configure button on the Ribbon. Enter your SharePoint site to host the profile pages. Click OK.

5. Create/Update Profile Page from the external content type item menu.

6. Click OK on the informational dialog. The profile page creation process starts.

7. Click OK on the profile page creation confirmation.

Importing MOSS 2007 Application Definitions

The XML-based application definition files used for the MOSS 2007 Business Data Catalog may still be used in SharePoint 2010. You may import your BDC model using an application definition file by clicking the Import button within the Business Data Connectivity Services application page. An import page appears similar to MOSS 2007. Browse to your application definition XML file and click the Import button. You may now use your imported BDC Model as an external content type in SharePoint 2010.

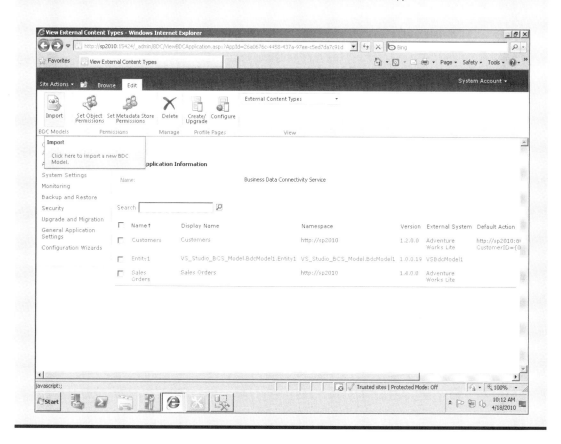

Implementing Single Sign-On Using the Secure Store Service

The Single Sign-On (SSO) capabilities provided with SPS allow you to configure stored application passwords for individuals and groups. In SharePoint 2010, this is handled by the Secure Store Service (SSS). The SSS offers smooth, integrated access between applications without continual password prompts to irritate users. Additionally, SSS gives you the capability to provide application access to groups of users that you would not normally give individual access to without having to distribute the username and password information. You can embed application integration within SharePoint and provide seamless information access.

The following components of SPS can leverage SSO capabilities:

- Excel Services
- InfoPath Services
- Business Data Catalog
- Status Lists
- SharePoint Designer DataForm Web Part
- Custom Web Parts

To configure SSO using the Secure Store Service, follow these steps:

1. Launch SharePoint 2010 Central Administration from Start ⇨ Administrative Tools ⇨ SharePoint 2010 Central Administration.

2. Click the Application Management Quick Launch and select Manage service applications under the Service Applications section.

3. Scroll down and click on the Secure Store Service link to open the SSS Administration page.

4. You need to generate a key before proceeding. Click on the Generate Key button on the Ribbon.

5. Enter a pass phrase in the Generate New Key dialog.

6. Click New on the Ribbon to create a new target application.

7. Enter your target application details. An example is shown in Figure 17.23. Click Next.

Tip

Select Group if you would like to allow all users to connect with the credentials stored in SSS for the target application. If you would like individual users to have individual credential mappings to the target application, select Individual. ■

8. Enter the target application fields and field types as show in Figure 17.24. Click Next.

FIGURE 17.23

Target application settings

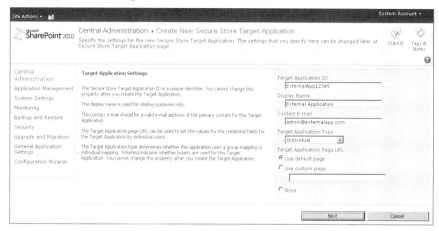

FIGURE 17.24

Target application fields

9. Enter accounts or users that are allowed to administer the target application settings. This is not to be confused with administrators of the target application. This action is giving rights to people to change the settings that you are entering now. Click OK.

10. The new target application appears in the main page list. Select the entry by checking the check box to the left of the name.

11. With the target application checked, click on the Set button in the Credentials section on the Ribbon.

12. Enter the account name and the credentials to use in the Set Credentials page as shown in Figure 17.25.

FIGURE 17.25

Target application credential mapping

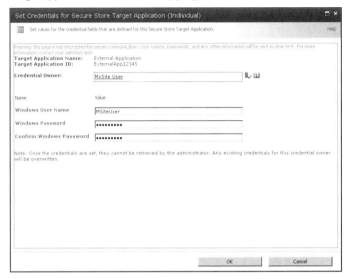

13. Click OK. These credentials fade into thin air. There is no way to manage them once they are set. Entering another mapping for a given account will overwrite any existing credentials for that account for the same target application.

14. You may now use the Secure Application ID when creating external content types.

Configuring Business Data Search

Configuring SharePoint so that it indexes and returns search results for your business data is a multistep process. You need to add a content source for your business data, manage the profile metadata for your objects, add a search scope for business data, and then create search pages for searching and returning business data search results. SharePoint does not return business data in the all sites search scope.

Adding a content source

You need to create a content source so that SharePoint will index your business data. The external content type provides the connection to and information about the business data, but the search and indexing processes will not include the data until it is defined as a content source.

To add a content source for your BCS application, follow these steps:

1. From Central Administration, select Application Management from the Quick Launch and then click on the Manage service applications under the Service Applications section.

2. Open the Search Service Application administration page by clicking the Search Service Application link in the list of applications.

3. Select Content sources from the Quick Launch menu.

4. Click New Content Source from the top navigation bar.

5. Type a name for your content source in the Name field and select Line of Business Data as the type of content to be crawled.

6. Select whether you would like to crawl the all external data sources or just the application(s) that you select, as shown in Figure 17.26.

FIGURE 17.26

Configuring a search content source for your business data

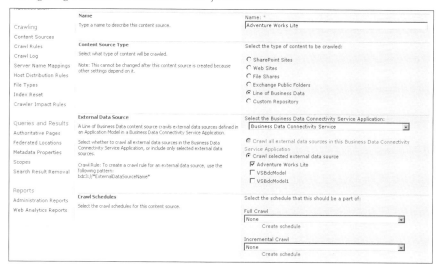

7. Select an existing schedule for full and incremental crawls or enter a new schedule.

8. Select the Start a full crawl of this content source check box.

9. Click OK.

Mapping metadata properties

Mapping the properties of your BCS application allows search to return results in a profile context that makes sense for users. To map the properties of your BCS, follow these steps:

1. Open the Search Service Application administration page.

2. Select Metadata Properties from the Queries and Results section of the Quick Launch bar.

3. Click Crawled Properties from the top page menu bar.

4. Click the Categories link at the top of the page.

5. **Click Business Data.** The list of business data crawled properties appears (Figure 17.27).

Business Data crawled properties

6. Click the business data entity identifier that you want to include in your index.

7. Select the Include Values for this Property in the Search Index check box. Notice you may add mappings here, but we will step through the mappings next.

8. Click OK.

After you have configured the business data entity to be included in search results, you can configure how search returns each field. To do this mapping, follow these steps for each field that you want to manage:

1. Open the Search Service Application administration page.

2. Select Metadata Properties from the Queries and Results section of the Quick Launch bar.

3. Click New Managed Property in the top navigation bar.

4. Enter the name of your property in the Property name field (spaces are not allowed) and select text from the type of information in this property selection.

5. Select the Include properties from a single crawled property based on the order specified option and check the Allow this property to be used in scopes (Figure 17.28).

FIGURE 17.28

New Managed Property page

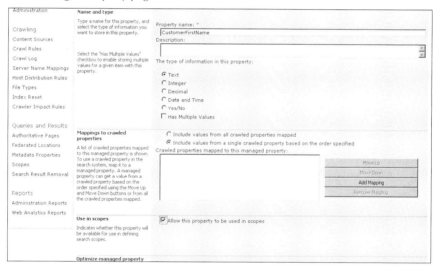

6. Click Add Mapping in the Mappings to crawled properties section.

7. Select Business Data from the list of categories and select the field from your entity that you want to map to that property from the list as shown in Figure 17.29.

8. **Click OK and click OK on the managed property page.** You may optionally check the optimization options to reduce storage and query sets sizes.

FIGURE 17.29

Crawled property selection

Creating a search scope

Business data is not included in the all content scope, so you need to create a new search scope for searching business data. This search scope must be a shared search scope that is created within the Search Service Application.

1. Open the Search Service Application administration page.

2. Select Scopes from the Queries and Results section of the Quick Launch bar.

3. Click New Scope from the top navigation bar.

4. Type a name for your search scope in the Title field and select the Specify a different page for searching this scope radio button. Click OK.

   Enter the new page name for the search results in the Target results page field. Use the same URL as your existing Enterprise Search Center pages and type a new name as shown in Figure 17.30. We create the page in the "Adding a custom search page" section of this chapter.

FIGURE 17.30

Configuring a search scope for your business data

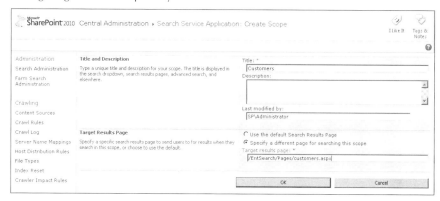

5. In the View Scopes page, select Edit Properties and Rules from the drop-down menu for your search scope (or click the Add Rules link in the Update Status column).

6. Select New rule from the Rules section (if you didn't select Add Rules link).

7. Select Content Source in the Scope Rule Type section, and select your business data content source in the Content Source section (Figure 17.31).

FIGURE 17.31

Add scope rule

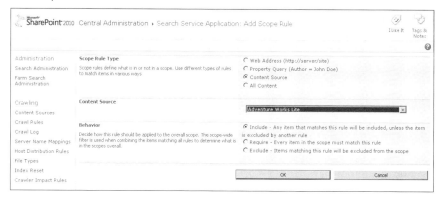

8. Confirm that the Include option is selected in the Behavior section.

9. Click OK. The scope is ready after the next update.

Adding a custom search page

Once business data results are available via search, create a page to search business data and a page to return the search results and add tabs in the Enterprise Search Center to navigate between the search pages. To create a custom search page to search your business data, follow these steps:

1. Open your site and navigate to your Enterprise Search Center site.

2. From the Site Actions menu in the top-left corner, select New Page.

3. Enter the title for your business data search page, which should be same as you entered for the scope target page, and click Create.

4. Click Add New Tab at the top of the new page that is created.

5. Enter the name for your tab in the Tab Name field and the URL for the page you just created in the Page field. Optionally, enter a tip that you would like to appear when the user hovers over the tab in the Tooltip field, as shown in Figure 17.32, and click Save.

6. Click Edit Web Part on the Edit Web Part menu for the Search Box Web Part.

7. Expand the Miscellaneous section, and in the Scope display group text box enter your business data scope as shown in Figure 17.33.

8. Click OK.

9. Click the Save & Close button on the Ribbon.

10. Test the search by clicking the Customers tab and entering a search term in the search box. Click the magnifying glass to search. The search results appear as shown in Figure 17.34.

FIGURE 17.32

Creating a new search tab

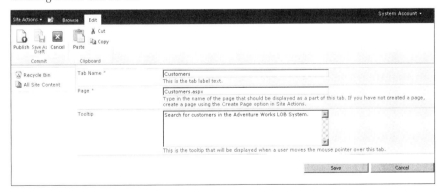

FIGURE 17.33

Configuring the search box to use the business data search scope

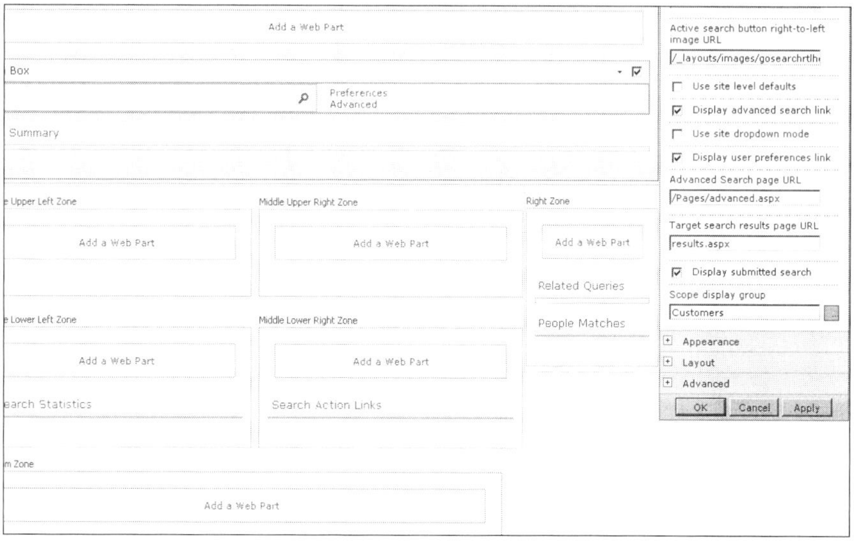

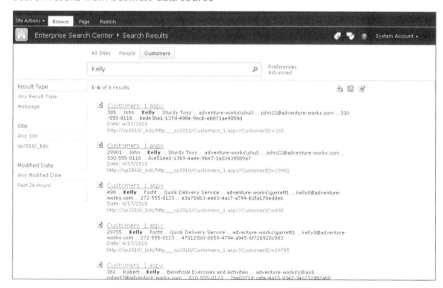

FIGURE 17.34

Search results from business data source

Tip

If you do not see any search results, make sure that you performed a full crawl on the search content source. ■

11. Click on a result to open the business data item within the profile page, as shown in Figure 17.35.

Tip

If you cannot navigate to the business data item page, ensure that a profile page was created. See the "Creating profile pages on BCS entity content types" section of this chapter. ■

FIGURE 17.35

Business data item in profile page from search results

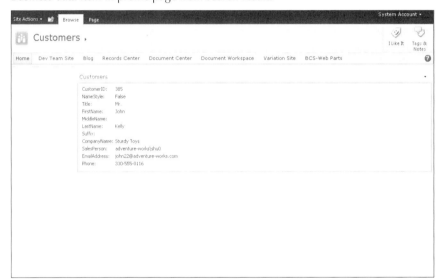

Integrating Business Data with Lists and Sites

There are several ways to make use of your business data within SharePoint sites. You can create business data columns for your SharePoint lists so that you have a drop-down selection of your business data in your list. Additionally, you can use the business data Web Parts SharePoint provides to display and connect business data within the context of your site.

Adding business data to lists

SharePoint 2010 provides a new column type for your lists so that you can associate business data with the content stored in lists and libraries. There are several reasons for doing this:

- **Centrally stored information:** If you want to be able to reuse the customer list from your CRM tool throughout your organization, it should be added to your BCS.

- **Consistent use of data and fields:** By reusing a business data field, you can consistently refer to the same customer list every time you tag a document or list item. This consistent use should make finding all SharePoint related items for that customer easier.

- **Exposing business data actions:** BCS columns added to a list will also expose the associated action for that business data, enabling users to execute the actions.

Note

When you add a BCS column, you can select other attributes of the BCS entity that you would like to show along with the primary value for the Business Data. For example, if your BCS contains a customer list, you may want to add Contact as a business data column, but also show the e-mail address and phone number for that contact. ■

To add a business data column to your list, follow these steps:

1. Open the list to which you would like to add a business data catalog column and select List Settings from the List tab on the Ribbon.

2. Select Create Column in the Columns section.

3. Enter your column name in the Column name field and select External Data as the type of information in your column.

4. Click the external data icon (the one without the check mark) next to the Type field to open a list of all your business data types and select the business type that you would like to display, as shown in Figure 17.36.

5. Select the field that you would like to display as the column value in the Display this field of the selected type field.

6. Select what additional fields you would like to display in the list. Click OK.

After you have added this business data column, you will see it as an available column for views and as an entry field on your new item form, as shown by the Customer field in Figure 17.37.

You can either enter the last name of the contact into the business data field or search for the last name by using the external data icon next to the business data field.

Note

The column(s) that appear in the search dialog box are the filter parameters we specified during the external content type creation. For our example in the previous section, we only specified Last Name. This may not be practical for production systems and additional filters may be warranted. ■

FIGURE 17.36

Selecting the business data type for your business data column

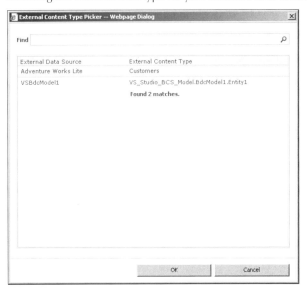

FIGURE 17.37

A business data column in a new item form

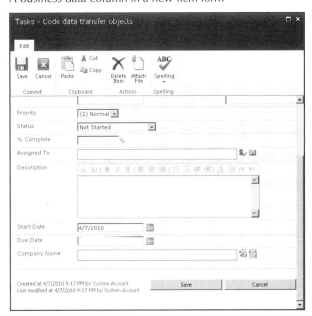

After you have selected the business data value in the new list item and saved the list item, you can see the associated fields of business data that you selected for your business data column, as shown in Figure 17.38.

FIGURE 17.38

Showing associated data for a business data column

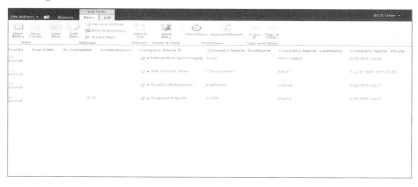

Integrating business data on your site

You can add business data to your sites through five different Web Parts that are designed to show the business data types you have defined in your application definition. These Web Parts work together to expose the items, actions, and related information for business data.

Cross-Reference

The business data Web Parts are customized implementations of the Data View Web Part. For more information on the Data View Web Part, see Chapter 20. ■

Business Data List Web Part

The Business Data List Web Part displays a list of rows from an application registered in the BCS. To configure the Business Data List Web Part, follow these steps:

1. From the Site Actions menu on your Web Part page, select Edit Page.

2. Select Add a Web Part in the zone in which you want the Business Data List Web Part to appear, select the Business Data List Web Part in the Web Part list, and click Add.

3. To configure the Web Part, select the Open the tool pane link in the Business Data List Web Part, or select Edit Web Part in the Edit menu of the Web Part.

4. Click the external data icon (the one without the check mark) next to the Type field to open a list of all of your business data types, and select the business type that you would like to display.

5. Click OK.

6. In the Web Part on your page, select the filter criteria that you want and select Add if you want to filter by more than one dimension. After the filter criterion has been entered, click the green arrow as shown in Figure 17.39 to retrieve the data.

FIGURE 17.39

Entering filter criteria into the Business Data Web Part

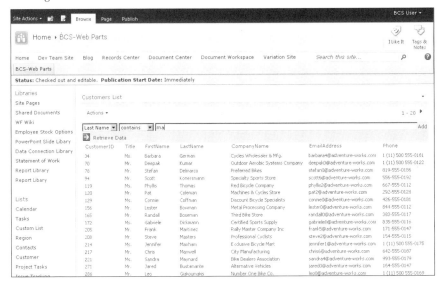

Business Data Item Web Part

The Business Data Item Web Part displays the details of a row from the BCS application. To configure and add the Business Data Item Web Part to your page, follow these steps:

1. From the Site Actions menu on your Web Part page, select Edit Page.

2. Select Add a Web Part in the zone in which you want the Business Data Item Web Part to appear, select the Business Data Item Web Part in the Web Part list, and click Add.

3. To configure the Web Part, select the Open the tool pane link in the Business Data Item Web Part or select Edit Web Part in the Edit menu of the Web Part.

4. Click the external data icon next to the Type field to open a list of all of your business data types and select the business type that you would like to display.

5. In the Item field, enter the item that you want to display or use the external data button to search for your item. If you would like the item view to show the details of the item selected in the Business Data List Web Part, you can skip this field and follow the steps below to connect the Web Parts. (See Figure 17.40.)

FIGURE 17.40

Configuring the Business Data Item Web Part to display a single item

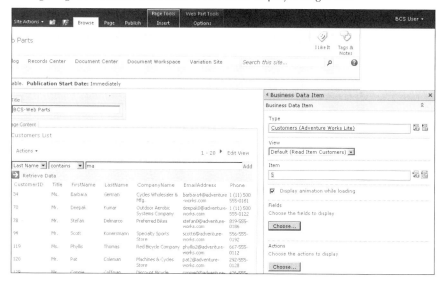

6. Select Choose in the Fields section of the tool pane to select what columns you would like to show.

7. Click OK.

If you would like to configure the Business Data Item Web Part to show the item detail for the selected row in the Business Data List Web Part instead of a specific, preselected item, you can connect the Business Data List Web Part and the Business Data Item Web Part using these steps:

1. From the Site Actions menu on your Web Part page, select Edit Page.

2. In the Edit menu on the Business Data List Web Part (which is now titled the name of your business data type), scroll down to Connections, select Send Selected Item To, and select the name of your Business Data Item Web Part as shown in Figure 17.41.

   Once this is configured, you will notice that radio buttons appear to the left of the rows in your Business Data List Web Part, and when those items are selected, the detail appears in the Business Data Item Web Part as shown in Figure 17.42.

FIGURE 17.41

Connecting the Business Data List Web Part to the Business Data Item Web Part

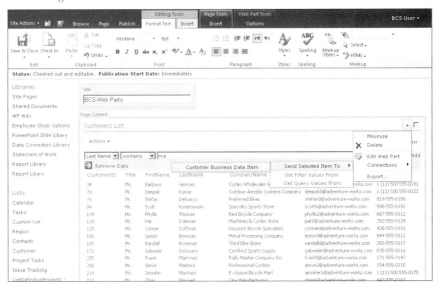

FIGURE 17.42

Displaying item detail in the Business Data Item Web Part

Business Data Related List Web Part

The Business Data Related List Web Part displays a list of related rows from a BCS application. For example, if the business data list shows a particular customer and the business data item shows the details of an order, the business data related list might display the order history for that customer.

To configure and add the Business Data Related List Web Part to your page, follow these steps:

1. From the Site Actions menu on your Web Part page, select Edit Page.

2. Select Add a Web Part in the zone in which you want the Business Data Related List Web Part to appear, select the Business Data Related List Web Part in the Web Part list, and click Add.

3. To configure the Web Part, select the Open the tool pane link in the Business Data Related List Web Part or select Edit Web Part in the Edit menu of the Web Part.

4. Click the external data icon next to the Type field to open a list of all of your associated business data types and select the business type that you would like to display. Only types that have been defined with an association are available.

5. Select the association from the Relationship drop-down.

6. Click OK.

After this Web Part has been added to the page, you will need to connect it to a Web Part that provides the parent item. The Web Part will display default text to indicate which relationship item is required based on the business type you selected and the associations you configured in the BCS application. To connect your Business Data Related List Web Part, follow these steps:

1. From the Site Actions menu on your Web Part page, select Edit Page.

2. In the Edit menu on the Business Data Related List Web Part (which is now titled the name of your business data type), scroll down to Connections, select Get Related Item From, and select the name of your parent Web Part as shown in Figure 17.43.

When this is configured, you will see the three Web Parts working together with the Business Data Web Part, allowing the user to select a product, the Business Data Item Detail Web Part showing the detail of the product category, and the Business Data Related Web Part showing the product subcategories, as shown in Figure 17.44.

FIGURE 17.43

Connecting the Business Data Related List Web Part to the Web Part providing the parent item

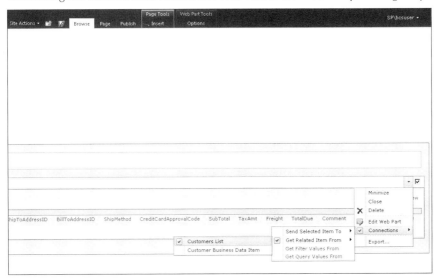

FIGURE 17.44

The Business Data List Web Part, the Business Data Item Web Part, and the Business Data Related List Web Part working together

Business Data Actions Web Part

The Business Data Actions Web Part makes the actions available for an item in a business data list. To add and configure the Business Data Action Web Part to your page, follow these steps:

1. From the Site Actions menu on your Web Part page, select Edit Page.

2. Select Add a Web Part in the zone in which you want the Business Data Action Web Part to appear, select the Business Data Action Web Part in the Web Part list, and click Add.

3. To configure the Web Part, select the Open the tool pane link in the Business Data Action Web Part or select Edit Web Part in the Edit menu of the Web Part.

4. Click the external data icon next to the Type field to open a list of all your business data types, and select the business type that you would like to display

5. **Enter the item that you want to display the actions for in the Item field or use the address book to search for your item.** If you would like the item view to show the details of the item that is selected in the Business Data List Web Part, you can skip this field and follow the steps below to connect the Web Parts.

6. Select Choose in the Actions section of the tool pane to select what actions you would like to show.

7. Click OK.

If you would like to configure the Business Data Action Web Part to show the item detail for the selected row in the Business Data List Web Part instead of a specific, preselected item, you can connect the Business Data List Web Part and the Business Data Action Web Part using these steps:

1. From the Site Actions menu on your Web Part page, select Edit Page.

2. In the Edit menu of the Business Data Action (which is now titled the name of your business data type), scroll down to Connections, select Get Item From, and select the name of your Business Data Item Web Part.

Tip

Any subsequent Business Data Web Part that is configured for the same external content type can accept the same business data item. For example, since the Business Data Item is accepting an item from the Business Data List, we are connecting the Business Data Action Web Part to the item; however, you can also connect it directly to the list itself. You may want to connect everything to the list, but the example is showing how you may string these connections. ∎

After this is configured, the selected item in the list is passed to the Business Data Item Web Part, which then passes the item to the Business Data Action Web Part. The action(s) of the external content type appears in the Business Data Action Web Part as shown in Figure 17.45.

FIGURE 17.45

Displaying actions for a selected item in the Business Data Action Web Part

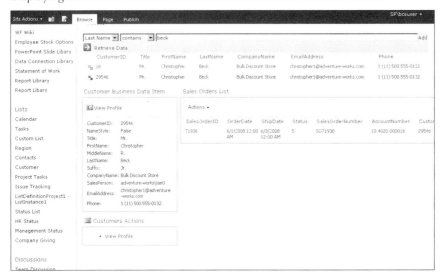

Business Data Item Builder Web Part

This Web Part is used only on business data profile pages and is only visible when the page is in edit mode. The Business Data Item Builder Web Part builds the business data item based on the parameters of the URL and sends the item to other Web Parts on the page.

Summary

This chapter discussed the scenarios in which you would want to integrate your line of business application business data with SharePoint. This chapter also covered how to define an application definition using the BCS XML model, how to implement search of your business data, and the steps necessary to configure Single Sign-On for SharePoint and within your application definition. Finally, we covered using business data within your SharePoint lists and sites.

Part V

Customizing SharePoint

Implementing Content Types

Document management really hit the scene in the early 1990s and began to have a big impact in the legal industry and other heavily regulated environments. As more and more digital content was created, organizations strained to manage the growing volume of content; therefore, document management systems and other electronic content management applications have gained popularity.

The best document and content management systems have evolved to map templates and other system behaviors to types of content. The cores of most systems have the ability to tag content with metadata so that management "actions" can take place on or in relation to the content. In some cases it is a workflow that requires approval; in other cases the content needs to be moved into long-term storage.

This chapter explores how content types and site columns in SharePoint Server 2010 provide a centralized structure for managing content and the related metadata. We answer the question, "What are content types?" and review the types of workflows and content types that are available out of the box. We also explore the ability to create custom Content Types to help you solve the unique business problems you have in your organization.

Defining Content Types

Content types are a way to manage the metadata and behaviors of a document, list item, or folder in a centralized, reusable way. At their core, content types contain a set of properties, a document template, a set of policies, and any applicable workflows. Site content types created on the site can be reused in multiple lists, and they are visible in that site and all child sites.

Content types can store custom XML data, allowing for the implementation of custom solutions. SharePoint 2010 doesn't care what file format or type of media you are working with. In other words, Office files, PDFs, TIFFs, e-mail, videos, and physical records can all be classified using content types.

Site columns work nicely with content types as a way to standardize the metadata that is captured when a particular content type is selected. Both site columns and content types are created at the site level and then copied locally as customizable instances or list content types and list columns when you add them to a list. When a site column is added to a content type, the content type actually references that site column definition.

Content types can include the following:

- **Document type:** Word, PowerPoint, Excel, InfoPath, TIFF, PDF, and so on
- **Metadata:** Project Type, Project Status, Date Created
- **Workflow assigned to it:** If project amount > $5,000 send on to Workflow1
- **File Plan:** Delete after five years
- **Event handlers:** Convert a document to PDF
- **XML information:** Use in a custom solution

You can create content types using three different methods:

- Through the Windows SharePoint Services user interface
- Through the Windows SharePoint Services object model
- By deploying a feature that installs the content type based on an XML definition file

Cross-Reference
For more information about using Features, see Chapter 9. ∎

A content type can be associated with a list or library. When configured, the content types show up under the New command in that list or library so that users can create new items with those properties.

Lists and document libraries often contain more than one content type. When they do contain more than one, the New command allows them to create new items of all associated content types. Additionally, the columns associated with those content types all appear.

Content types are not tied to a particular list or library, which means that they can be used on multiple sites. Administrators are able to manage the templates, properties, and workflows of a content type from one location, while that information is updated in the sites downstream.

Features Overview

Features are a powerful tool for developers in SharePoint. With Features, you can deploy application functionality anywhere that a content type is deployed. Features can reduce the complexity involved in making site customizations, and hold up nicely when upgrades are applied to a server. Features now eliminate the need to copy large blocks of code when changing simple functionality. They also reduce versioning and inconsistency issues that can be present on front-end Web servers. Features provide these capabilities:

- Scoping semantics for determining where custom code will run
- Pluggable behavior for installing or uninstalling Features in a deployment
- Pluggable behavior that can activate or deactivate Features at a given scope
- Scoped property bag that stores data required by a Feature within its scope
- The basis of a unified framework for distributed deployment of WSS solutions

Implementing Features

You implement a Feature by adding a subfolder that contains a Feature definition inside the Features setup directory (`Drive:\Program Files\Common Files\Microsoft Shared\web server extensions\14\TEMPLATE\FEATURES\`). The subfolder includes a Feature.xml file defining the base properties of the Feature and lists elements bound to it, such as XML files that contain element manifests and other supporting files.

Developers who want additional information on Features can reference the MSDN Web site and search for "Working with Features."

Content type hierarchy

Content types are organized in a parent/child hierarchical relationship. There are site content types and list content types. It is useful to think of site content types as templates and list content types as instances of those templates. An advantage of site content types is that they are not bound to a particular list. The site level where the site content type is created determines the scope of that content type.

When a site content type is assigned to a list, a copy of that content type is copied locally onto the list. Once copied locally, it can be modified so that it is different from its site content type parent. A content type can be created directly on a list, but it would not be available to other sites or lists.

Site content types can be based on other site content types. Take the out-of-the-box content types that come with SharePoint such as Folder, Document, and Task as an example. You can create site or list content types based on any of these types. All content types derive from the top of the hierarchy type, which is System. Changes made to a site content type can be pushed down to the child types, both site and list. This is a one-way push from parent to child.

Note

When multiple content types are allowed on a list/document library, you will be forced to select a content type every time you place a new document in the library and to configure policies explicitly for each content type, rather than on the list/library. ■

Creating content types from other content types

Content types can be created based on other content types. Your existing library of content types is like a set of templates for you to choose from. You can save time by building your custom types hierarchically. In other words, build base types that can be the foundation for other types by incorporating core company fields and other properties.

Site content types are available for their child sites and also for sites lower in the hierarchy. The content type hierarchy included in SharePoint 2010 maps to the available types of lists that can be created. Examples of base content types are Issue, Contact, Announcement, Document, and so on. Each time a list is created, SharePoint creates a list content type based on the base site Type. In other words, if you create an Event list, the Event content type is copied locally to the list.

Property integration with Office 2010

Office 2010 applications all have a new feature called the document information panel. The panel displays an InfoPath-editable form that is used to enter and display properties that are on the server. When configuring a content type, you can use InfoPath 2010 to generate a default property form that is based on the properties of your content type. Your form will include the controls and layout and you can then customize it as you would any other InfoPath form, in addition to using it in the document information panel.

Data collection in Office overall has been enhanced through this integration with InfoPath. Electronic forms can be presented in the InfoPath client or in a Web browser as well as embedded in Outlook 2010 e-mail messages. These options provide new ways to collect data in more intuitive ways that are in the context of what the end user is doing.

Using site columns

Site columns are a huge productivity gain for SharePoint site administrators and designers. In SharePoint 2003, adding custom columns to a list and library was a very useful feature. It allowed the quick creation of useful metatags, and then views were created to show just the content that matched a particular context, page, or site. You would quickly find that you were creating the same type of metadata and columns over and over again — for example, a column called Document status that showed the following:

- Draft
- In Review
- Approved
- Archive

Not only would you find yourself creating the same columns over and over again, but you would also have to try to remember every place that used the column to make changes and updates. This repetitive work is history with site columns in SharePoint 2010.

Site columns are similar to content types in that they keep metadata in sites and lists consistent, and they can be used in multiple lists and sites. Site columns are SharePoint list fields and are defined at the site level. Again, similar to content types, you will want to pay attention to your site hierarchy. Sites columns that you would like to have available to all lists and sites should be created at the topmost site in your portal.

One example of a useful site column would be a Company Name lookup column. There are many sites and documents where you may want to track the company name associated with the documents and activities. Creating a Company Name list and then a site column that does a lookup on the list will provide access to it on all child sites.

Site columns are defined by properties such as name and data type. The name of your site column must be unique within the site structure or scope where it is defined. When added to a list or content type, you can specify site column properties such as required, read only, and hidden.

Cross-Reference
Site Columns can also be deployed as Features. For more information about Features see Chapter 9. ■

Creating Custom Content Types and Site Columns

Consultants work on projects, and each project has a Statement of Work, or SOW, that defines what the goals, scope, duration, and cost of the project are. In this exercise you will create a Project Management team site. This site could be the location for all of your organization's project templates and project management best practices, and where all new Statements of Work are created and stored. You will then create a document library in which to store your SOWs, columns to track information about the projects, and a template to create new SOWs from, and all of this will be associated to a content type called Statement of Work.

Cross-Reference
For detailed steps on how to create a new site, refer to Chapter 3. ■

Step 1: Create site columns
Organize your site columns and content types at the top of the Portal hierarchy so that they have the ability to be associated with any team site or document library. When you create a top-level SOW content type and design your site columns at the top level, you ensure that required information such as project number will be available to all downstream child sites.

You can begin this step at your portal home page.

1. **Choose Site Actions ⇨ Site Settings.**

2. **Under the Galleries section, click Site columns.** The Site Columns Gallery (Figure 18.1) lists all of the site columns available on the portal, the type of column, and their source site.

FIGURE 18.1

Site Columns Gallery

3. **Click Create (See Figure 18.2).**

4. **Enter these values:**

   - Column name: Project Status

   - The type of information in this column is: Choice

   - Put the site column into: Click New group: and enter **Project Management**

   - Description: Current status of active project

   - Require that this column contains information: No

   - Type each choice on a separate line

5. **Leave the default values for the remaining items and click OK.**

FIGURE 18.2

Creating new column

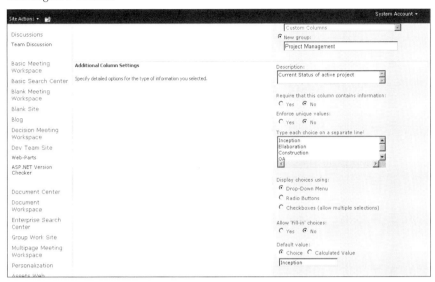

In a production scenario you would probably create additional project management–related columns such as Project Name, Customer Name, and so on. For this example you will move on to creating your content type and associate your new column with it.

Step 2: Create site content type

1. Click Site Settings in the breadcrumb at the top of the page to return to the Site Settings page.

2. Under Galleries click Site content types.

3. Click Create.

4. Enter these values:

   - Name: Statement of Work

   - Parent Content Type: Document from the Document Content Types

   - Put this site content type into: Click New group: and enter **Project Management** for the new group name. Your screen should look like Figure 18.3.

5. Click OK.

6. At the bottom of the Site Content Type: Statement of Work page, click Add from existing site columns to add the columns you created earlier in Step 1.

7. From the Select columns from drop-down menu, choose Project Management.

8. Click the Add button to add the Project Status column. Your screen should look like Figure 18.4.

FIGURE 18.3

Setting up a new site content type

FIGURE 18.4

Adding columns to site content type: Statement of Work

9. Click OK.

Step 3: Configure template to use for column type

1. On the Site Content Type: Statement of Work page, under Settings, click Advanced settings.

2. **If you have a sample document to use as the SOW template, you can just browse to it at this time.** If you don't have a sample document, open Word and create a document to use as your sample SOW. Click the radio button next to Upload a new document template and then click Browse. Your screen should be similar to Figure 18.5.

3. Click OK to make this document an associated template for your new content type.

FIGURE 18.5

Site content type advanced settings: Statement of Work

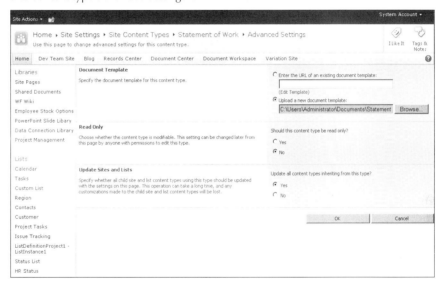

Step 4: Create a new team site and document library

1. Click Site Actions in the upper right-hand corner of the screen.

2. Choose Create Site.

3. Enter the following values:

    *   Title: **Project Management**

    *   URL name: **http://(your server)/project management**

4. Leave the other default values and click Create.

5. Click Site Actions in the upper right-hand corner of the new team site.

6. Click Create from the drop-down menu.

7. Under Libraries click Document Library.

8. Enter Statement of Work **for the name and click Create.**

617

Step 5: Associate the content type with a document library

1. From the Library tab on the Ribbon, click Library Settings.

   Notice that there are no options available for working with content types under the current options. You must first enable content types.

2. Under General Settings, click Advanced settings.

3. Select Yes under Allow the management of content types.

4. Leave the default options for remaining items and click OK.

5. To remove the default content type, Document, and add your new one, under Content Types click the default content type Document.

6. Under Settings, click Delete this content type and click OK to confirm.

7. Under Content Types, click Add from existing site content types.

8. In the Select site content types from drop-down, choose Project Management.

9. Click Add to add the SOW content type and click OK (Figure 18.6).

10. Click Statement of Work in the breadcrumb link at the top to return to the document library.

FIGURE 18.6

Adding existing content type

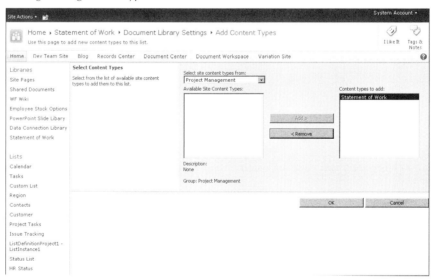

11. On the Documents tab on the Ribbon, click the arrow next to New. You can see the Statement of Work template in the New drop-down, as shown in Figure 18.7.

12. Choose the Statement of Work template to open a new document.

13. Click Save to save your new SOW.

14. Click OK to save it with a new document name.

15. Choose Project Status from the drop-down menu as shown in Figure 18.8.

FIGURE 18.7

The New drop-down menu

FIGURE 18.8

Document properties dialog box

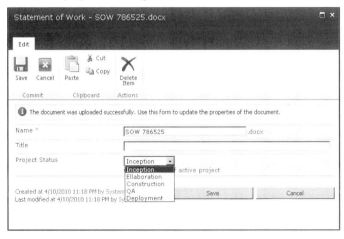

Using the object model to update content types

Depending on your application of content types, it may be more useful to you to update content types using the object model. The object model allows you greater granularity in "pushing down" the child content type changes. Changes you make to a site content type in code are applied to the memory representation of that content type. Calling the Update method applies those changes to the database.

This code snippet updates a content type description, adds a field, then updates the content type and its children:

```
// open your site and get the SPWeb
SPSite site = new SPSite("http://mysite.com");
SPWeb web = site.OpenWeb();
// get the solution content type
SPContentType type = web.ContentTypes["Solution"];
// set the updated description
type.Description = "Updated description";
// add the new field names contact which is a user and not
    required.
type.Fields.Add("Contact", SPFieldType.User, false);
// update the content type.
// adding true in the arguments updates the children as well.
type.Update(true);
```

Extending content types

SharePoint content types are extensible. You can add custom information in content type definitions using the XmlDocuments property of the SPContentType object. These XmlElements can be accessed programmatically through the object model, and you can add as many XmlDocument objects to the content type as you require. The only rule with the XmlDocument object is that it must be valid XML.

As an example, you'll add an RSS item definition to a SPContentType object.

```
// open your site and get the SPWeb
SPSite site = new SPSite("http://mysite.com");
SPWeb web = site.OpenWeb();
// get the solution content type
SPContentType type = web.ContentTypes["Solution"];

// create an xml document based on a simple rss schema
string ItemXml = @"<item><title /><link /><subject
/><description /><pubDate /></item>";
XmlDocument RssItem = new XmlDocument();
RssItem.LoadXml(ItemXml);
// add that XmlDocument to the XmlDocuments collection
type.XmlDocuments.Add(RssItem);
//adding true in the arguments updates the children as well.
type.Update(true);
```

Document Set Content Type

A new content type is available in SharePoint 2010 named Document Set. The Document Set content type becomes available after you activate the Document Set feature at the site collection level. A document set groups multiple documents together. It is similar to a folder structure, however. Because it is a content type, you may create workflows and act upon a group of documents as if they were a whole.

Note

By performing a "push down" operation (updating the children of the content type) the XmlDocument object of the child is completely overwritten. It is important to take note of this because changes made to the child and not to the parent, by you or someone else, could be lost. It is also important to note that if a push down change fails on a certain content type — if that content type is sealed, for example — the operation will continue and those changes will be attempted on any child content types. Any errors encountered will be returned. ■

Content Types and Workflows

Chapter 8 discussed in detail how SharePoint provides the ability to represent custom business processes to document and list items. For the enterprise, the ability to associate workflows with content types provides even more power and centralized control for the business process architect.

Workflows that are associated with a content type — think about that for a moment. Instead of a workflow being triggered by an event to one document library, you now have the ability to have a workflow kick off every time someone tags an item as a type of content. Another way to think about this concept is that the content type now brings along the workflow that is applicable to it.

To add on to the previous Statement of Work exercise by adding workflow to your content type, follow these steps:

1. **Begin at the top level of your site hierarchy and click Site Actions ⇨ Site Settings2.**

2. **Under Galleries, click Site content types.**

3. **Filter the Show Group box by Project Management.**

4. **Click Statement of Work.**

5. **Click Workflow settings.**

6. **Click Add a workflow.**

7. **The approval template is selected by default.** Enter SOW Approval as the unique name for the workflow.

8. **Check the Start this workflow when a new item is created box.** Your screen should be similar to Figure 18.9. Click Next.

FIGURE 18.9

Add a Workflow page

9. On the Customize Workflow page, place the cursor next to the Approvers button. Enter at least your login as an approver, and click the button to confirm the name is correct.

10. Add a message to include with the request Please review and approve this SOW.

11. Check the Post-completion Workflow Activity box to update the approval status.

12. Click OK.

13. **Return to your Statement of Work document library and create a new SOW.** Save it. If you have configured your e-mail settings properly on your SharePoint server, you should receive an e-mail letting you know that the approval workflow has started for your new document, followed by another letting you know that you have an approval.

This exercise demonstrates the power of content types and workflows together. Imagine a deployment that has hundreds of team sites that refer back to the SOW content type. From a central location you can require a workflow to kick off each time this type of content is saved.

Summary

Content types and site columns provide the central administration that is needed for true enterprise content management. This chapter defined content types and site columns, as well as introduced you to some of the ways they can be extended and the properties and workflows that can be associated with content types. Content types are useful for records management, associating workflows, events, and adding templates to types of content.

Using SharePoint Designer

SharePoint Designer 2010 can help you enhance your productivity by creating powerful solution applications on the SharePoint platform. SharePoint Designer delivers a complete set of instruments and tools for application building and Web authoring. Although SharePoint Designer is a powerful workflow and business process automation tool, this chapter focuses specifically on how to customize SharePoint Web sites with SharePoint Designer.

Most organization plan for and consider presenting information to people in their organization in a way that feels familiar to them. This can be achieved using SharePoint Designer by manipulating the graphical or branding of the site as well as the layout of the information that is presented to each user. The more familiar people feel when they access your SharePoint sites, the more comfortable they will be as they perform the tasks they have accessed the site to complete.

Exploring SharePoint Designer

Microsoft SharePoint Designer 2010 is a powerful Web development and management software program for the creation, customization, and extension of SharePoint 2010 sites.

With the new SharePoint Designer, you can customize SharePoint sites for individuals and teams. SharePoint Designer 2010 includes an intuitive interface that enables rapid creation and customization of SharePoint-based sites. You can take advantage of industry standards such as XHTML (Extensible Hypertext Markup Language) code and CSS (cascading style sheets) and the

IN THIS CHAPTER

Finding out about SharePoint Designer

Customizing SharePoint sites

power of ASP.NET to build SharePoint sites that meet your business needs, all based on industry standards for browser compatibility and accessibility.

The interface allows you to see what the end result will look like as you view and modify pages as it pulls in CSS and ASP.NET controls and technologies into the environment as you author your applications.

Microsoft IntelliSense technologies help eliminate errors caused by writing code by hand or not knowing precise syntax when working with CSS, ASP.NET, and XHTML tags. As you get familiar with working in code view, IntelliSense can also suggest in-context commands based on the work you are currently doing. These suggestions can help you develop pages and tie in and customize the rendering of data sources more quickly and efficiently.

Similar to Visual Studio, SharePoint Designer's multiple dockable task panes mean that you can pull in and arrange the tools, information, and views you need in the way that works best for you.

As a site administrator or IT manager, you have control over exactly how SharePoint Designer users interact with your SharePoint sites and applications. This helps ensure that designers and developers interact in ways that comply with your policies and procedures. By defining SharePoint Designer 2010 contributor settings, you can modify existing SharePoint roles to limit what types of content users can edit, add, or delete; whether they can access and modify content in code view and how users access data; and on which site locations these changes can be made and whether users can change the underlying master pages and style sheets.

Examining Key Features

In this section, we dive into the tools and features of SharePoint Designer that enable you to customize the look and feel of your SharePoint sites. You may want to apply your company branding and other customizations to different areas of your sites to make it easy for employees to differentiate one department area from another. After you become familiar with these features, you can do the basic customizations detailed later in the chapter.

Automatic CSS style generation

As you customize pages in SharePoint designer, styles are automatically created to reflect your changes to content. After you have customized a specific item, such as a table or area, you can easily apply that same customization to other areas without redoing all of your work. This is accomplished using the following tools:

- Apply Styles task pane
- CSS Properties Grid
- New Style Dialog
- Code View Improvements (code hyperlinks while you are in code view)

No code Read/Write Data View Web Part and forms

Although the Data View Web Part is not new to SharePoint, there are some notable improvements that make adding data from dynamic data sources even easier and more powerful.

- Write support
- Related/linked data sources
- Visual Web Developer ASP.NET Style UI
- XPath tools
- Create Data View
- Insert a formula column
- Add conditional formatting
- Turn on editing mode
- Bonus: Insert Data View as a form

SharePoint Designer 2010 no-code features means that solution creators need not be solution developers. You can build collaborative no-code tracking, reporting, and data management applications quickly and easily. The application provides a professional-grade design environment for rapid solution development, and powerful tools for testing compatibility and helping to ensure a professional presentation of the information and applications on your site.

You can even access external data by using the ASP.NET Data Source Control architecture. You can create custom Data Views and data forms that leverage Microsoft ASP.NET technology, allowing you to integrate external data into your Web site, including views that display data from multiple sources.

For example, suppose that your enterprise has a product database and a customer database, and you want to display product information on your SharePoint site. You can do this quickly and easily by creating a view on that data. Suppose that you also want a Web page that displays which customers have ordered which products. You can do this by linking your data sources — in this case, your two databases — so that you can view this information in a single joined Data View. What's more, you can use this Data View as a form so you can write data back to your data sources.

Tools such as calculated fields, conditional formatting, sorting, grouping, and filtering capabilities help you create high-impact reports in the form of Data Views. For example, you can apply conditional formatting to a Data View so that items in your inventory are highlighted when they drop below a specific number and need to be reordered.

Access a wide variety of data from SharePoint Designer in the Data Source Library. The following list includes the types of supported data sources you'll find:

- Add RSS feeds to the Data Source Library, and create Data Views by using the RSS feeds as a data source.
- Add XML files to the Data Source Library, and create Data Views that display XML data.

- Create Data Views from 2010 Microsoft system documents. For example, create a view on data in Microsoft Word 2010 documents by using their new XML-based file format as a data source.

Cross-Reference

The Data View Web Part is described in detail in Chapter 20. ■

No-code workflow creation

With Microsoft SharePoint Designer 2010, you can design workflows that add application logic to your site or application without having to write custom code. SharePoint Designer makes it easy to create and modify rules-based workflow applications. With the Workflow Designer tool in SharePoint Designer 2010, you can use drop-down lists and check boxes to identify the events that trigger a workflow. You can then specify the actions and responses that follow, and even identify the conditions under which other workflow events will occur.

For example, you can design workflows to automate business processes in your organization, such as document review, approval, and archiving, among others. Or you can quickly create workflows just to take care of routine processes on your team site, such as sending notifications or creating tasks.

Cross-Reference

Workflow is covered in detail in Chapter 8. ■

Working with enhanced management capabilities

Site administrators and IT managers can use SharePoint Designer's enhanced management capabilities to control the levels of access and ensure a consistent user experience across the site.

By determining the levels of control for team members according to their roles, you can control which SharePoint Designer 2010 commands users can access and what kinds of modifications users can make to your SharePoint site. With Contributor mode, you can:

- Create user groups and assign them specific permissions
- Create user groups that have access only to specified editable regions and content types
- Limit who can create and edit master pages, change cascading style sheets, and edit or delete the home page
- Control which master pages and style sheets can be used to create pages, and in which folders the site contributors can save their files

You can access tools and reports for a wide variety of site maintenance tasks including hyperlink checking, CSS usage, and more.

You can easily track customized pages by using the Site Template Pages report. With this report you can see a list of pages that have been customized, including the filename and file type, as well as the folder in which the file is located. You can also use the Revert to Template Page command and the Site Template Pages report to restore previous versions of the page. Making changes to the live site is no longer a problem. If unwanted changes have been saved, you can now restore previous versions of the same page with the click of a button.

Defining Contributor Settings and SharePoint roles

After you have built, tested, and refined your SharePoint site to the point where it is ready for public access, you can upload it to a SharePoint Server. But how can you help ensure that site visitors and contributors will not inadvertently break it? SharePoint Designer 2010 provides powerful tools for managing the risk of users inadvertently breaking a page or site such as Contributor Mode.

A SharePoint site administrator or an organization's IT department can use established SharePoint role definitions to define the broad actions that specific groups of users can perform. With SharePoint Designer 2010, however, the administrator or IT team can also use SharePoint contributor settings to refine the permissions enabled by the standard SharePoint roles, making it possible to specify exactly what, where, and how individuals can interact with the SharePoint site.

SharePoint Designer 2010 Contributor Settings provide increased control over what individuals can do within each defined SharePoint role. SharePoint Designer 2010 extends and refines the default SharePoint roles. For example, you could allow one group of contributors to add text, another to add text and images, and still another to add text and images but also make layout changes. SharePoint Designer 2010 contributor settings make it easy for a SharePoint administrator or an IT department to lock or unlock features, define specific areas where contributors can read and save information, or identify which master pages and CSS files specific users can use to create new pages.

Finally, there is the Revert to Template feature that provides protection within the site development realm as well. It enables site designers to test refinements to a SharePoint site and then, if the refinements do not work as expected or, worse, if they break the site, return the site to its previous state by clicking the Revert to Template icon.

Customizing SharePoint Sites

SharePoint sites by default have a consistent look and feel and are created from templates that are included with the out-of-the-box installation of Microsoft SharePoint Server 2010 and SharePoint Foundation. SharePoint Designer provides the tools you need to customize your sites to meet your branding and visualization needs. Utilizing the master page capabilities of ASP.NET 2.0 you can build and change entire SharePoint sites quickly and easily.

As you create team sites, department-level sites, blog sites, and various other SharePoint-based sites from the wide variety of included site templates, you may find that they function and look adequate for your immediate needs. In some scenarios, however, you might find it useful or important to customize the look and feel of a page, site, or entire site collection. For example, if you want to create a site to publish materials to get your organization's field sales team trained and excited about new services your company is offering, you can create the site from a SharePoint Team Site template. Then you can use SharePoint Designer to add graphics, change colors and fonts, rearrange the layout, and apply changes to the navigation across the site or on individual pages. The next section will walk you through the steps to accomplish these tasks.

Opening a SharePoint site from SharePoint Designer 2010

You can open your SharePoint site directly from within SharePoint Designer. After you have launched SharePoint Designer, execute the following steps to get started.

Note

To open a SharePoint site, you must have at least the View permission for that site. This permission is included by default in the Full Control, Design, Contribute, and Read SharePoint Groups. ■

1. On the File ⇨ Sites page, click the Open Site button as shown in Figure 19.1.

FIGURE 19.1

Sites page from File menu

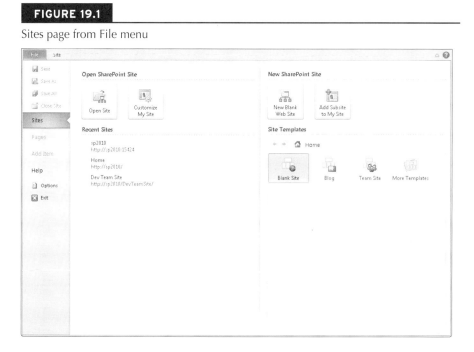

2. **The Open Site dialog box appears.** By default, the Open Site dialog box opens with Web Sites visible from the Web Sites system folder and displays all sites that have been opened using SharePoint Designer 2010.

3. **In the Open Site dialog box, shown in Figure 19.2, do one of the following:**

    - In the large list box, click the folder entry of the site that you want to open, and then click Open.

    - In the Site name box, type the URL of the site that you want to open, and then click Open. For example, you might type http://my-sharepoint-server/site.

FIGURE 19.2

Open Site dialog box

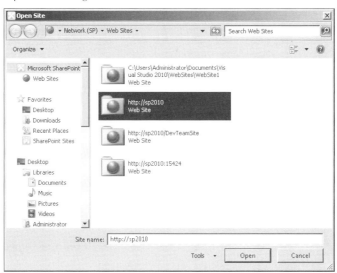

Tip

You may configure SharePoint Designer 2010 to open the last site that you were working on automatically when the application launches. To modify this setting, click Options from the File menu and under the General section, click on Application Options. Select or deselect the Open last Web Site automatically when SharePoint Designer starts. ∎

To remove a site from the list in the Open Site dialog box, right-click the site, click Remove on the shortcut menu, and then click Yes to confirm. This action does not delete the site itself, only the link to that site presented here.

Once you have selected the site you would like to open, click the Open button to see all of the lists, libraries, and sites you have access to represented in the Site Objects navigation pane, as shown in Figure 19.3.

FIGURE 19.3

SharePoint site opened in SharePoint Designer 2010

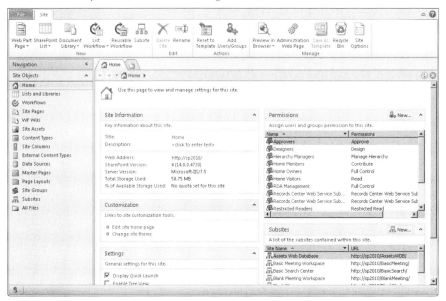

Editing a site in SharePoint Designer

Another way to begin customizing a SharePoint site is to navigate to any page in that site and select Edit in SharePoint Designer from the Site Actions menu, as shown in Figure 19.4.

Note

To open a SharePoint site, you must have at least the View permission for that site. This permission is included by default in the Full Control, Design, Contribute, and Read SharePoint groups. ■

Editing and publishing master pages

SharePoint 2010 is built on the ASP.NET platform, which opens up a brilliant way for you to manage the layout and look and feel of an entire site collection from a central gallery of master pages. All site master pages are accessible to you via SharePoint Designer. The role of master pages is to provide the design and layout of a page that you want to repeat across multiple pages in your sites. This allows you to give your sites a more consistent appearance and helps keep common elements in their expected locations on every page. If you decide later that you want to move an element or functional area to a different location on the page, your change can immediately be seen across all pages that have been assigned your master page. For example, after receiving feedback that it would be nice to have an issue tracking report on every page as people navigate through your site, you could add that element to your master page and every site will instantly have that element in every page. In an enterprise deployment, this could mean saving countless hours of manually adding the new feature to every page if a change needs to be deployed across hundreds of pages.

FIGURE 19.4

Editing a SharePoint site in SharePoint Designer

By default, every site has one master page assigned to it, which is stored in the Master Page Gallery. You can store as many master pages in the Master Page Gallery as you want, but you can select only one master page as the Site Master and one as the System Master.

To see which master page is currently assigned to your site:

1. Navigate to the home page of your site.

2. On the Site Actions menu, click Site Settings.

3. In the Look and Feel section, click Master Page.

In the drop-down list you can see which master page is assigned to your site and system as well as others that are available, and apply any one of them to your site.

A good way to get familiar with using SharePoint Designer 2010 to customize the look of your site is to start by editing a copy of an out-of-the-box master page. By default, your site will be assigned the default.master. Start by creating a working copy of default.master and assign it to the site as the master page.

Note

By default the Master Page Gallery has versioning and approval workflow turned on. ■

When you open a master page for editing, you must check it out before you can make any changes. (See Figure 19.5.) Users won't be able to see the changes you have made and saved until you check the page back in and publish a major version.

To check out a master page, you can simply right-click the page to be edited and select Check Out. If the file you want to work on is not checked out, you will be prompted to check it out if you attempt to open it for editing.

To check in master pages, you can right-click the file and select Check In. The process is similar to publish your work. After the page has published a major version, users will be able to see changes that have been made.

After following the instructions in the "Opening a SharePoint site from SharePoint Designer 2010" section of this chapter, try these steps:

1. **In the Site Objects navigation pane, click on Master Pages.**

FIGURE 19.5

Master pages in SharePoint Designer

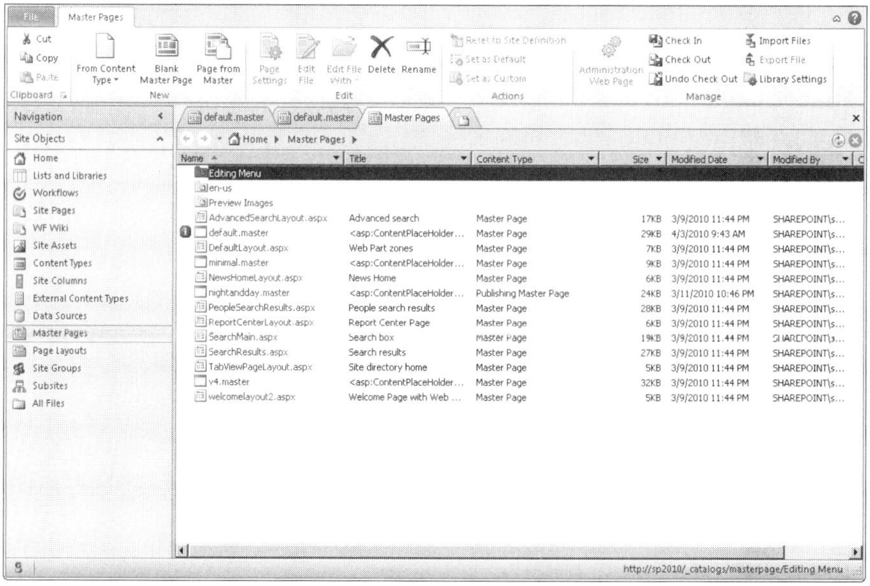

2. **Click the default.master.** The details page appears in the main area and a Master Pages pane appears in the left navigation.

3. **Right-click default.master in the Master Pages navigation pane and choose Copy (Figure 19.6).**

4. **Click on the Master Pages in the Site Objects pane again. Right-click in the main area and choose Paste (Figure 19.7).** You will find that a copy of the default.master master page has been created with the name of default_copy(1).master in your Master Page Gallery.

5. **Right-click the new file, choose Rename, and type** SharePointBible.master.

FIGURE 19.6

Copying the default.master

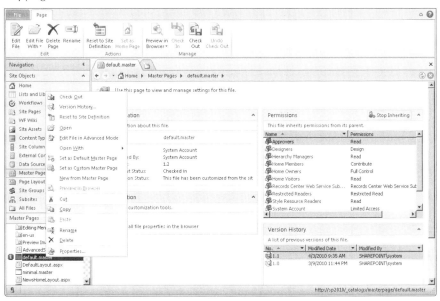

FIGURE 19.7

Pasting a copy of the default.master

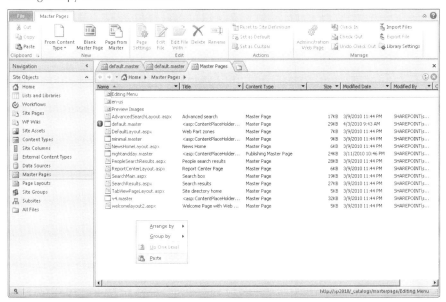

You have now successfully created a good working copy of the `default.master` that your site is using. Now you can navigate to the Site Settings pages of your site and assign the `SharePointBible.master` page to your site. You can choose to reset all subsites to inherit from this site's master page settings to push the change to all sites in your site collection. Without any changes made to this master page at this point, you shouldn't see changes in the way your sites appear. With the site open to the home page in your browser, you can click Refresh to quickly see how the customizations you do in the next section affect the look and feel of your site.

Common SharePoint customizations

This section provides step-by-step instructions for personalizing the look and feel of your SharePoint sites.

Publishing your company logo and brand to your SharePoint sites

Organizations commonly want to brand all of their SharePoint sites with their company logo. The image you use for this needs to be universally accessible to all site users. It is a good idea to upload your logo to a picture library within the same site collection in which you are working. For this example, we have our company logo stored in the out-of-the-box PublishingImages picture library at the root of the site.

1. In the Site Objects navigation pane, click Master Pages and select SharePointBible. master. In the details page, click Edit File under the Customizations section to open it in SharePoint Designer (see Figure 19.8).

2. Click Yes in the dialog box asking you if want to check the file out.

FIGURE 19.8

SharePointBible.master open in Split view for editing in SharePoint Designer

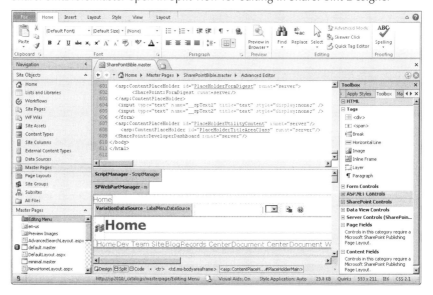

3. Click the SharePoint people icon (the blue, yellow, green, and red-colored people icons).

4. Press Delete to remove the default image.

5. On the Ribbon, click Insert.

6. Click the Picture button.

7. In the Picture dialog box, find and double-click the PublishingImages or Site Assets folder, depending if your root site collection is a publishing site or team site.

8. Locate your image file and double-click it. (See Figure 19.9.)

9. From the File menu, click Save. Click Yes on the Site Definition warning.

10. Right-click SharePointBible.master in the Master Page List and choose Check In.

11. In the Check In dialog box, check in a minor version and select the Keep files checked out check box.

12. Click OK.

To see the change to your site, refresh the home page of your site in your browser.

FIGURE 19.9

Updated logo in the SharePointBible.master page

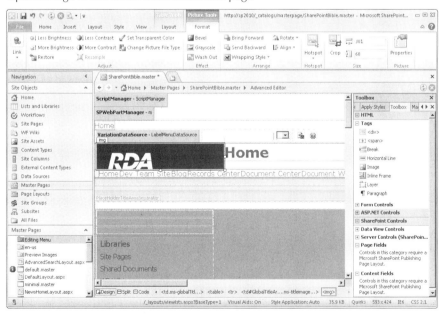

Add a global footer to your site

The following steps add a global footer to your site pages highlighting how to contact the help desk for support and how users can submit feedback about their experience on the sites. You may want to include copyright information or privacy policies as other examples.

1. In the Site Objects navigation pane, click Master Pages and select SharePointBible. master. In the details page, click Edit File under the Customizations section to open it in SharePoint Designer.

2. Click Yes in the dialog box asking if you want to check the file out. (If you are continuing from the previous section you can skip this step.)

3. Switch to Code view and select `<TABLE.ms-main>` in the menu above the code window.

4. Scroll to the bottom of the highlighted code and place your cursor at the end of the last highlighted `</TABLE>` HTML tag.

5. Press Enter and add the following code:

```
<table class="ms-globallinks"style="width: 100%" cellspacing="0"
    cellpadding="3">
<tr>
        <td><a href="mailto:feedback@example.com">Submit Feedback</
            a></td>
        <td class="ms-alignright">   <a href="mailto:helpdesk@
            example.com">Contact Helpdesk</a></td>
    </tr>
 </table>
```

6. You can preview in Design or Split view by clicking the appropriate view button (see Figure 19.10).

7. From the File menu, click Save.

Now you can go to the home page of your site and see the new custom footer. For this custom footer we used existing styles included in the default `corev4.css` style sheet. You may want to create your own custom style sheet to control the way your footer looks throughout your site (see Figure 19.11). Navigate around your site and see how the pages in your site are affected by the changes to your custom master page.

FIGURE 19.10

Custom footer added to SharePointBible.master in Code view

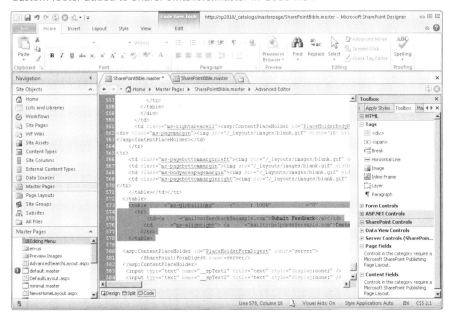

FIGURE 19.11

Custom footer shown on the site, driven from strictly SharePointBible.master customization

Cascading style sheets

With Microsoft SharePoint Designer 2010, you can customize the look and feel of a single SharePoint site by making changes to the default styles that are applied to that site. You can also apply your customized styles to other sites or choose at any time to remove all customized styles and revert to the default style sheet that resides on the server for that site collection. You can make any of these changes for SharePoint Foundation sites and SharePoint Server 2010 sites.

By default, the styles for all SharePoint sites in a single site collection are defined in a single style sheet that resides on the server. In SharePoint Foundation, the name of this file is `Corev4.css`. In SharePoint Server 2010, this file may have any of several names. For example, the styles for the custom master page named `BlackBand.master` are defined in a style sheet named `Band.css`.

SharePoint Server 2010 comes with several sample style sheets for you to work from. The default style sheet is called `corev4.css`. It resides and is protected on the file system of each Web front-end server. It is applied to all pages and elements in your site and site collection. With SharePoint Designer it is easy to begin changing the way pages look to end users to match your organization's branding requirements.

SharePoint Designer 2010 automatically generates style references as you customize elements in pages. This makes it easier to manage the graphical look and feel of the visual elements in your site from a central location, affecting pages across your site instead of having to edit each page individually.

Customize the default style sheet

This example helps you get familiar with editing the default styles by changing the look of the top navigation in your SharePoint site. To get started, edit the `corev4.css` file that comes with SharePoint. Start by opening your site in SharePoint Designer and then the master page assigned to your site. For this exercise, use `SharePointBible.master` from the previous section of this chapter.

1. **In the Site Objects navigation pane, click Master Pages and select SharePointBible. master.** In the details page, click Edit File under the Customizations section to open it in SharePoint Designer.

2. **Click Yes in the dialog box asking if you want to check the file out.** (If you are continuing from the previous section you can skip this step.)

3. **Make sure to switch your view to Split after you have successfully opened the master page as shown in Figure 19.12.**

4. **Click the TopNavigation menu control in the Design view.**

5. **Inside the control tags, find** `class=ms-topnav` **in the Code view.**

Note

SharePoint Designer underlines styles in Code view as if they are hyperlinks. By pressing and holding the Ctrl key and clicking the link, you are taken to the class in the style sheet that is applied to that page. ■

FIGURE 19.12

<SharePoint:Aspmenu#TopNavigation...> shown selected in Split view

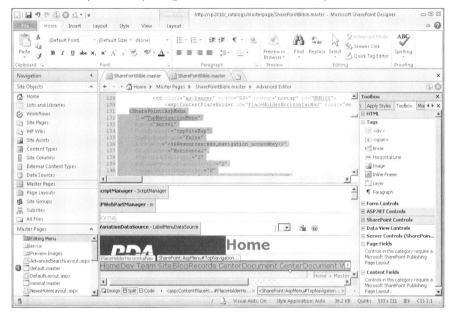

6. Press and hold the Ctrl key and click `ms-topnav`. SharePoint Designer opens a copy of `corev4.css` for you to edit as shown in Figure 19.13.

7. From the File menu, click Save. The `corev4.css` file is saved under `http://<root site>/_layouts/1033/Styles/Themeable/`

Note

The first time you modify and save any style on a page in any site, SharePoint Designer 2010 automatically opens a new local copy of the default style sheet and updates it with your changes. When you save or close the page or the copy of the default style sheet, you are prompted to confirm your customizations. ■

8. Click Yes in the Stylesheet Customization Warning dialog box.

9. On the Edit menu, click Find (Ctrl+F).

10. Type ms-nav a in the Find what text box.

11. Click the Find Next button until you find the class entry in the style sheet. SharePoint Designer highlights the style in Code view and also highlights it in the Manage Styles tool pane. If you are not familiar with CSS syntax, you can use the wizard to help you.

12. In the Manage Styles task pane, right-click the highlighted `.ms-nav` links style and select Modify Style (Figure 19.14).

FIGURE 19.13

Editing `Corev4.css` in SharePoint Designer

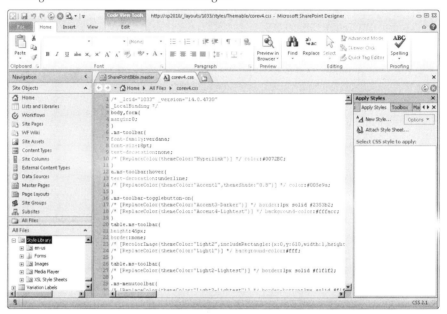

FIGURE 19.14

Modifying the selected style

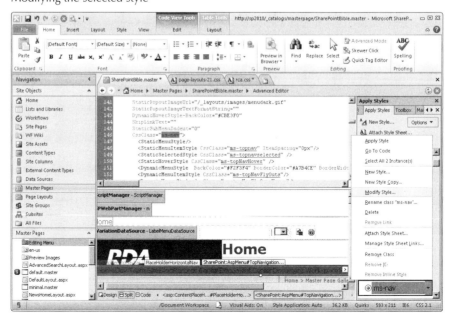

13. Click the blue color box to the right of color in the Modify Style dialog box (see Figure 19.15).

FIGURE 19.15

The Modify Style dialog box with the More Colors dialog box

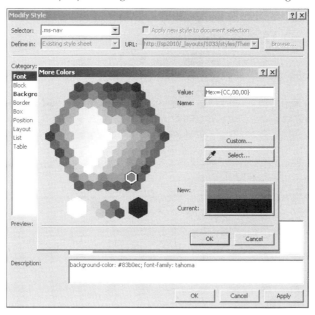

14. Select a maroon font color and click OK.

15. Click OK in the New Style dialog box.

16. From the File menu, click Save.

You can preview your changes by clicking the SharePointBible.master tab in SharePoint Designer or by refreshing the home page of your site in your browser.

Reverting back to the default SharePoint styles

After you customize the default style sheet (Corev4.css) so that a new copy appears in the _styles folder of your Site Objects navigation pane, the customized style sheet will be used on all of the pages in your site. If you decide you would like to return to the default look, you can revert to using the default style sheet at any time by either renaming or deleting Corev4.css in the _styles folder.

Warning

After you've customized a style sheet, do not move the customized file or the _styles folder. If you accidentally do move or delete the file or the folder, each page in your site will appear with a broken link to the style sheet. No styles will be applied on any page at that point. ■

To recover your customized look you can either:

- Reapply your customized style sheet, locate it, and move it back into the _styles folder at the top level of the site directory in your Site Objects navigation pane

- Restore the site to the out-of-the-box default look, move the customized style sheet back into the _styles folder at the top level of the site directory in the Site Objects navigation pane, and then either delete the style sheet or rename it

If you cannot recover the style sheet you customized (if it is permanently deleted), create a new blank file that has the same name (for example, Corev4.css) in the _styles folder of the site, and then either delete the empty file or rename it. This initiates the process of reverting back to the default style sheet of the site.

After you have customized a style sheet to your requirements, you can apply it to other sites. By default, a customized local style sheet is applied to only the site or subsite in which it is customized.

If you want to apply a single customized local style sheet both to the site you are working on and to more or all of that site's subsites, you may find it easiest to create the customized style sheet in the site you are working on and then to use one of the following methods to apply it to other sites.

Attaching a style sheet to another single site

In SharePoint Foundation or SharePoint Server 2010 site deployment, you can manually attach a customized style sheet that is located in one site to another site.

1. In SharePoint Designer 2010, open the site to which you want to apply an existing customized style sheet.

2. In the site, locate and double-click the default master page.

3. On the Format menu, hover over CSS Styles, and then click Attach Style Sheet.

4. In the Attach Style Sheet dialog box, click Browse to locate and select the customized style sheet that you want to apply.

5. In the Attach to section, click Current page.

6. In the Attach as section, click Link, and then click OK.

The specified customized style sheet is applied to the default master page and to all content pages attached to that master page.

Note
Make sure that you have the proper permissions in each style library of both sites to properly attach the customized style sheet. ■

Tip
In SharePoint Designer, to see the updated styles in Design view, you may have to press F5 to update the view. ■

To save the master page with the new style sheet link, on the File menu, click Save. (Alternatively, you can press Ctrl+S.)

To apply the same style sheet to other sites, repeat this procedure for each site, one site at a time. If you are working in a SharePoint Server 2010 environment and you want to apply a single customized style sheet to a site and all of its subsites, see the following section.

Apply a style sheet to a site and all of its subsites

In a SharePoint Server 2010 site collection, you can use your browser to apply a customized style sheet to multiple or all of your sites in a single operation.

Note

You are able to do this only in SharePoint Server 2010, not in SharePoint Foundation. ∎

In SharePoint Server 2010, sites can inherit style sheet and master page settings. This functionality is appropriately named *inheritance*. A site can be set to inherit the styles it uses from its parent site, which is the site directly above it in the site structure or hierarchy.

If you have customized the style of one site and would like to propagate the customization to all of that site's children or subsites:

1. From your browser, navigate to the home page of the SharePoint Server 2010 site whose styles you have customized.

2. Click Site Actions select Site Settings.

3. In the Look and Feel section of the Site Settings page, click Master page.

4. On the Site Master Page Settings page, in the Alternate CSS URL section, click Specify a CSS file to be used by this publishing site and all sites that inherit from it, and then type the full path for the customized style sheet, including the filename, in the box (for example, `http://servername / _layouts/1033/Styles/ Themable/corev4.css`).

Tip

Because the `_layouts` folder is a hidden folder that cannot be viewed in the browser; you cannot use the Browse button to locate it. ∎

5. Select the Reset all subsites to inherit this alternate CSS URL check box, and then click OK as shown in Figure 19.16.

FIGURE 19.16

Alternate CSS URL configuration

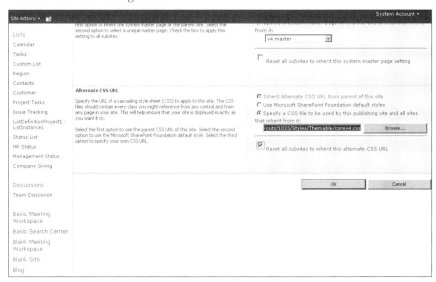

You have forced all subsites, or children of this site, to inherit from your current site.

Tip

You may have to refresh your browser to see the updated style in your sites. ■

Configure a subsite to inherit styles from its parent site

In a SharePoint Server 2010 site collection, you can use your browser to configure a single site to inherit its style from the parent site directly above it.

Note

You are only able to do this in SharePoint Server 2010, not in SharePoint Foundation. ■

To configure a single subsite to inherit the styles used by the site immediately above it:

1. From your browser, navigate to the home page of the SharePoint Server 2010 site that you want to inherit from its parent.

2. Click Site Actions and select Site Settings.

3. In the Look and Feel section of the Site Settings page, click Master page.

4. On the Site Master Page Settings page, in the Alternate CSS URL section, click Inherit Alternate CSS URL from parent of this site (see Figure 19.17).

FIGURE 19.17

Alternate CSS URL settings for subsite

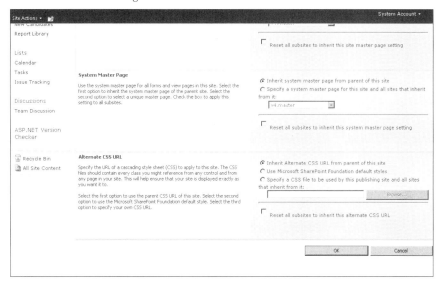

5. Make sure the Reset all subsites to inherit this alternate CSS URL check box is deselected.

6. Click OK.

Tip
You may have to refresh your browser to see the updated style in your sites. ■

Content pages

In Microsoft SharePoint Products and Technologies, content pages consist of ASP.NET pages, which have the .aspx file extension. Each page contains an @page directive, which identifies the master page assigned to it. The following is an example of an @page directive:

```
<%@ Page MasterPageFile="~masterurl/default.master" %>
```

A content page is not a valid stand-alone page; a master page must be referenced in order to be rendered. Although there can be ContentPlaceHolder controls in your master page, you can override them on the content page.

By default, a SharePoint site includes several available content pages. Examples of these content pages are the Web Part, List View, and List Form pages. Each of these pages contains the content to be displayed in the body of the page. As a user accesses a page from the browser, the content page is merged with the assigned master page to produce the rendered page. Each content page uses the same page structure and common features defined by the master page to which the content page is attached.

In Microsoft Windows SharePoint Services 4.0, `Default.master` is applied to all of the default content pages, including:

- Default.aspx (the home page for each site)
- Default content pages which contain list views and list forms including:
  - AllItems.aspx
  - DispForm.aspx
  - NewForm.aspx
  - EditForm.aspx
- Default content pages that contain views and forms for document libraries including:
  - Upload.aspx
  - WebFldr.aspx

Creating a content page from a master page and adding Web Part zones

When you create new custom content pages, you can easily start from an existing master page. That way, the new page has the same look and feel as the rest of the pages in your site that are derived from the same master page.

The content regions on the content page cannot be edited by default when you create a content page from a master page. To add custom content to the content page, you must first locate the region to which you want to add content — this includes the main content region that will likely contain the bulk of your content — and then make it editable.

Note
If you want to use a Web Part zone, you must insert it on a content page. Web Part zones cannot be inserted on a master page. ∎

1. On the File menu, click Add New and then click Create from Master Page, as shown in Figure 19.18.

Tip
You can also right-click the master page in the Site Objects navigation pane, and then click New from Master Page on the shortcut menu. ∎

2. In the Create Page from Existing Master Page dialog section either double-click the existing master page you want to use or select the icon and click on the Create button located on the right-hand pane.

3. In the New Web Part Page dialog box enter a name and select a location to save the new page, as shown in Figure 19.19.

FIGURE 19.18

New page from a master page

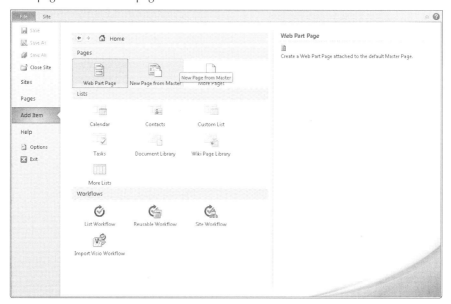

FIGURE 19.19

New page from a master page

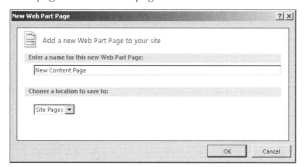

4. Click OK.

5. Click Yes if prompted to open the page in advanced mode.

Note

All content pages link off the `default.master` page. The `_layouts` directory isn't site specific and isn't affected by the `default.master` page. The `_layouts` directory relies on a different master page. ■

By default, the new content page that has been created contains the code below:

```
<%@ Page Language="C#" masterpagefile="../_catalogs/masterpage/v4.
    master" title="New Content Page" inherits="Microsoft.SharePoint.
    WebPartPages.WebPartPage, Microsoft.SharePoint, Version=14.0.0.0,
    Culture=neutral, PublicKeyToken=71e9bce111e9429c"
    meta:progid="SharePoint.WebPartPage.Document" meta:webpartpageexp
    ansion="full" %>
```

The code is referencing the master page from a content page. You now have a content page that has the same look and feel as the rest of the site. To add content, you can customize an existing content placeholder exposed by the master page. For this example use the PlaceHolderMain content placeholder.

1. In Design view, click PlaceHolderMain(Master).

2. After you have it highlighted, click the arrow to the right of the placeholder and select Create Custom Content, as shown in Figure 19.20.

The title of the placeholder control has been changed to PlaceHolderMain(Custom).

FIGURE 19.20

Enable the custom content placeholder

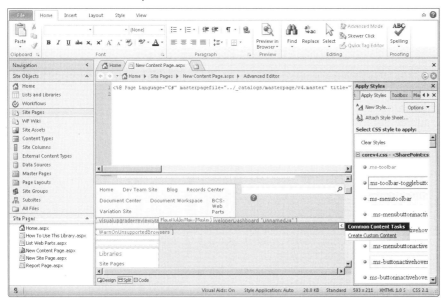

From Code view you will see these additions to the code:

```
<asp:Content id="Content1" runat="server" contentplaceholderid="Place
    HolderMain">
</asp:Content>
```

With the PlaceHolderMain content placeholder now ready for customization, you can add any content you want to that area. Keep in mind that anything you add in becomes static within that content placeholder and appears on the page. To add an area where you can add Web Parts and manage from the browser interface, start by adding a Web Part zone.

1. **Click in between the added code and select Web Part Zone from the Insert tab on the Ribbon. (See Figure 19.21.)**

2. **From the File menu, click Save.** The file is saved with the name you entered when creating the page along with a .aspx extension.

FIGURE 19.21

Adding a Web Part zone within the content

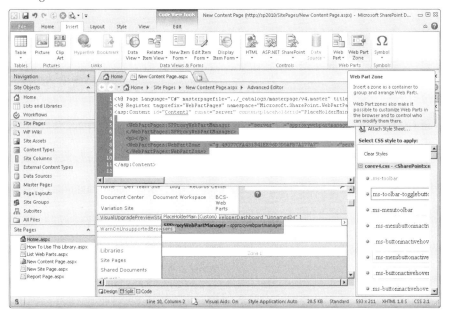

If you navigate to the new content page in your browser, you will see the new custom content page. Notice that now you can click Site Actions Edit Page, and here you can see your newly added Web Part zone. Users can now start adding Web Parts into that zone, as shown on Figure 19.22.

FIGURE 19.22

New custom content page in Edit mode

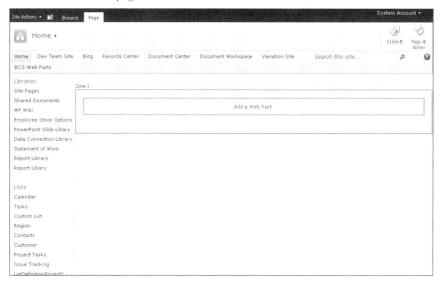

You can also easily expand this concept to generate a custom page with multiple Web Part zones to fit your Web Part page needs. For example, you may want to create a content page with an area for a top Web Part zone, four columns for Web Part zones just below, and a Web Part zone at the bottom of the page. The next steps explain how to accomplish this:

1. Switch to Design view.

2. Place your cursor in the custom PlaceHolderMain(Custom) placeholder.

3. From the top Insert tab on the Ribbon, click Table and choose Insert Table.

4. In the Insert Table dialog box, set the following (as shown in Figure 19.23):

   - Rows: 1
   - Columns: 1
   - Width: 100%
   - Cell padding: 5
   - Cell spacing: 2

5. Click OK.

FIGURE 19.23

Insert Table dialog box settings

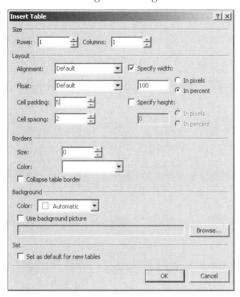

The table is created in your content placeholder. Next, add the four-column table underneath.

1. Press the right arrow key on your keyboard or place the cursor just outside the right side of your new table. To ensure the right location, you may switch to Split View and make sure the cursor is after the `</table>` tag but before the `</asp:content>` tag.

2. From the top menu, click Table and choose Insert Table.

3. In the Insert Table dialog box, set the following:

   - Rows: 1
   - Columns: 4
   - Width: 100%
   - Cell padding: 5
   - Cell spacing: 2

4. Click OK.

A new table is created with four columns. Next, create a place to put the bottom Web Part zone.

1. Press the right arrow key on your keyboard four times or place the cursor just outside the right side of your new table.

2. From the top menu, click Table and choose Insert Table.

3. In the Insert Table dialog box, set the following:
   - Rows: 1
   - Columns: 1
   - Width: 100%
   - Cell padding: 5
   - Cell spacing: 2

4. Click OK.

The table coding within the page should look similar to Figure 19.24.

You have just created a custom structure that allows you to place content in the page in a specified custom layout. Following the next steps will create Web Part zones in which end users can display Web Parts.

Tip

Right-click in each of the four columns (`<td>` tags) in the code view and select Tag Properties to change the Vertical Alignment from Default to Top. If you leave the Vertical Alignment as Default, Web Parts that are taller than others in the four columns will end up looking like they are floating and out of place. ■

FIGURE 19.24

Inserted table code

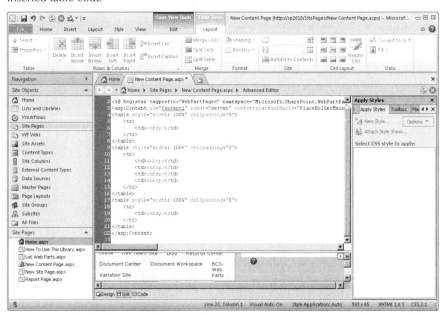

1. Place your cursor in the top table cell you created.
2. On the Insert tab on the Ribbon, click the Web Part Zone button.
3. Repeat Step 2 in the remaining five cells in the tables you created.
4. From the File menu, click File and choose Save.

Now each of the cells has its own Web Part zone, as shown in Figure 19.25.

Navigate to your custom content page from the browser to see what the rest of your organization will see. You can view the page in edit mode to see how the Web Part zones render on the page. See Figure 19.26 for an example.

Page layout and design

SharePoint Server 2010 with publishing turned on allows you to create sites using a publishing template. Publishing sites enable users to edit and publish Web pages using only their browser. Page layouts are page templates that define how a page should look, what page fields and content fields are available, and exactly which elements should be present on the page (such as lists and libraries). For example, you can set up one page layout for trip reports, another page layout for newsletter articles, and a third page layout for plan updates. Authorized users can then create new publishing pages that are based on these page layouts, and their new pages for each specific type of content will follow a consistent format.

FIGURE 19.25

Web Part Zones residing in the custom content page

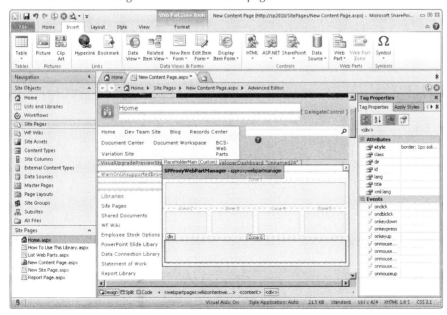

FIGURE 19.26

Custom content page as seen in edit mode in the browser

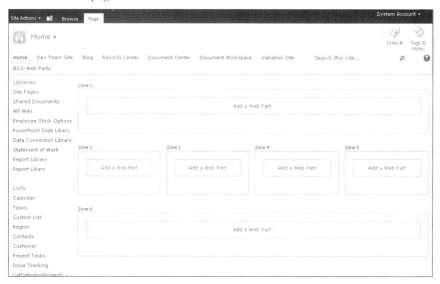

After getting familiar with the features available in Microsoft SharePoint 2010, you may decide that you want to create a set of custom layouts to apply to pages in your site for different types of content. For example, you may want to publish a monthly executive newsletter to your site based on a specific layout. After you create your executive newsletter page layout, you can fully customize it using \SharePoint Designer 2010.

Open a page layout for editing

All publishing pages in a publishing site are stored in the provided Pages document library, where you can identify which page layout was used to create each page. To see all of the publishing pages for your site from your browser, follow these steps:

1. On the Site Actions menu, click View All Site Content.

2. Click the Pages document library heading.

The Pages document library is created automatically by the publishing feature and contains all of the pages in a site that are created from page layouts. You can see which page layout is applied to your pages by looking in the Page Layout column, as shown in Figure 19.27. To view the page in the browser, you can click the page title.

FIGURE 19.27

Pages displayed in list format in the Pages document library

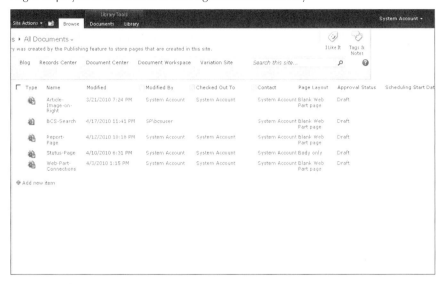

To open and customize a page layout with SharePoint Designer 2010, do the following:

1. Select Page Layouts from the Site Objects navigation pane. (See Figure 19.28.)
2. Click on the page layout file you wish to modify. On the details screen that appears, click the Edit File from the Customizations section.
3. You are prompted to choose whether or not to check the file out; click Yes.
4. You may be prompted to choose whether or not to open in advanced mode; click Yes.

SharePoint Designer opens the layout page you selected to edit.

Add custom content to a page layout

After you have successfully opened the page layout for editing in SharePoint Designer 2010, you can edit it as you would a content page that is attached to a master page. Adding custom content to a page layout causes the customized content to appear on all publishing pages that have that page layout assigned to them.

Warning

If you remove a component from a layout page, any page that has that layout assigned to it and content residing in that component causes the content to disappear. ∎

FIGURE 19.28

Page Layouts in SharePoint Designer

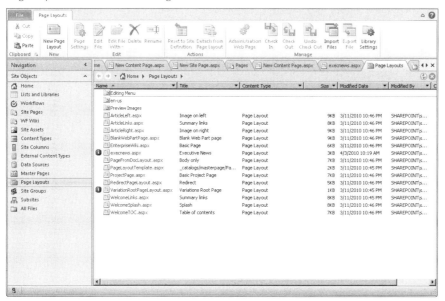

With the page layout open in SharePoint Designer in Design view, click to highlight the place-holder in which you want to customize content, click the arrow that appears to the right, and then click Create Custom Content to unlock the placeholder for editing.

With the placeholder unlocked and ready for customization, you can edit this section of the page by using the features that you commonly use to edit content or master pages, such as:

- **Tables:** Click the Insert Table option on the Table menu to create tables to help align content.

- **Graphics:** Click and drag images from the images folder into this section of the page.

- **Text:** Click and then type where you want text to appear.

- **Web Part Zone:** Insert a Web Part zone to give visitors to the page the option to add or remove Web Parts, such as views of document libraries and lists.

- **Web Parts:** Insert views of document libraries, lists, and more into the page.

After you have customized the layout page, save the page by clicking Save on the File menu.

Insert a page field

In some cases, you may want the page layout to display information about the Web page itself on that Web page. For example, on an articles page you might want to display not just the article content, but also a contact name, or the filename, or the date that the article is scheduled to be published or pulled from the site. These examples can be accomplished by inserting page fields into your page layout.

Page fields can also be used to enable content managers to enter information in these fields from the browser. For example, with publishing you can set a Scheduling Start Date so that you can specify when the page should be automatically published. You can also set a Scheduling End Date so that when the expiration date is reached, the page will no longer appear on your site. Because the Scheduling Start Date and the Scheduling End Date are page fields that you can add to your layout page, a content manager can change these dates via a browser for an immediate update to the scheduling engine in the publishing system.

To insert page fields into editable regions of a page layout that is open in SharePoint Designer, click the placeholder in which you want to add content, click the arrow that appears, and then click Create Custom Content to unlock the placeholder for editing.

Tip

When you are creating a table that you want to add to an existing layout page, it is sometimes easier to first create the table on a blank page. That way, you can get the formatting and structure for the information set up just how you want it, copy the table, and then paste it into the placeholder on the page where you want to publish it. Then you can follow the rest of these steps to insert the page fields into the allocated spaces in the table. ■

1. If the Toolbox task pane is not visible, on the Task Panes menu from the View tab on the Ribbon, click Toolbox.

2. Select the Toolbox tab in the Toolbox pane. Expand the SharePoint Controls section and scroll down to the Page Fields section and drag Scheduling End Date to the editable region, as shown in Figure 19.29.

Note

If the items in the Page Fields section of the Toolbox are not visible, it is probably because you are not editing a page layout. Page Fields and Content Fields are available only for page layouts. ■

Insert a content field

You can add content fields for displaying information about the page content that you have inserted into a page layout. For example, you may want to add a byline to an article on each page that uses your custom layout page. If your page includes a field for publishing the body of an article, you could add another field to display the author's name. This is done by adding a content field to a page layout. Follow these steps to add the Byline Content Field:

FIGURE 19.29

Scheduling End Date page field added to the Article Links page layout

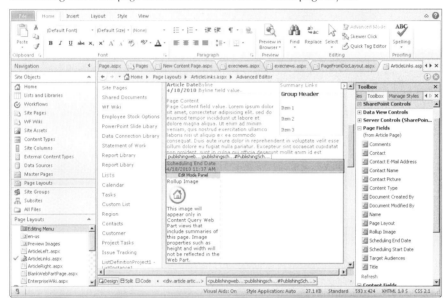

1. With the page layout open in SharePoint Designer 2010, click the placeholder in which you want to add content, click the arrow that appears, and then click Create Custom Content to unlock the placeholder for editing.

2. If the Toolbox task pane is not visible, on the Task Panes menu from the View tab on the Ribbon, click Toolbox.

3. From the Content Fields section, drag the content field that you want to insert into the editable region, as shown in Figure 19.30.

Note

If the items in the Content Fields section of the Toolbox are not visible, it is probably because you are not editing a page layout. Page fields and content fields are available only for page layouts. ∎

Web Part zones and Web Part customization

On Web Part pages, Web Part zones are Web Part containers that can be configured to control the organization and format of the assigned Web Parts. Web Part zones enable you to group, arrange, and customize Web Parts in the browser. They also allow you to control who can modify them. Web Parts, though controlled by the Web Part settings when assigned, can also live on a page outside a Web Part zone.

FIGURE 19.30

Byline content field added to the Article Links page layout

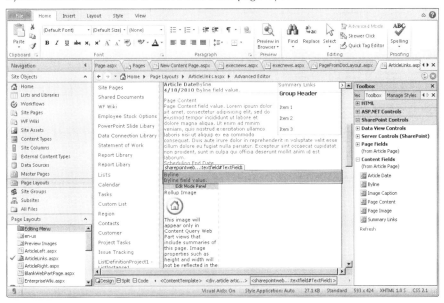

Web Parts located in Web Part zones

Inside a Web Part zone, Web Part settings are stored in the content database in SharePoint, not in the ASPX code in the page. Inserting a Web Part inside a Web Part zone makes it possible for users to interact with or modify Web Parts through the browser.

Web Parts not located in a Web Part zone

When a Web Part is not located inside a Web Part zone, users can still view the Web Part contents. This can be useful if you do not want users to be able to make any changes, and eliminates the ability to interact with or modify the Web Part properties or the way it is displayed. In this scenario, the Web Part configuration settings are stored in the ASPX page code and not in the content database.

Web Part pages, Web Part zones, and Web Parts are nested containers. The Web Parts themselves contain the data that you want to present on a page, and perhaps modify or interact with. Web Part zones are optional subcontainers to Web Part pages, each of which can house one or more Web Parts. This enables you to group and arrange Web Parts on the page, modify them from the browser interface, and manage what users have permissions to view and modify. Web Part pages house both Web Parts and Web Part zones.

Note

Within a given Web Part zone, you can control whether Web Parts can be arranged horizontally or vertically. ∎

Insert and customize a Web Part zone

The following steps will guide you through adding a Web Part zone to an existing page and configuring it to control the arrangement and user access of Web Parts that will ultimately live there.

1. In SharePoint Designer 2010, open the page in which you want to insert the Web Part zone.

2. In Design view, click the location on the page where you want to insert the Web Part zone.

3. Click the Web Part Zone button from the Insert tab on the Ribbon. Click Zoom to Contents from the View tab on the Ribbon to zoom in to the new Web Part Zone for easier management and configuration.

The new Web Part zone is inserted on the page, as shown in Figure 19.31.

FIGURE 19.31

New Web Part zone inserted into a Web Part page

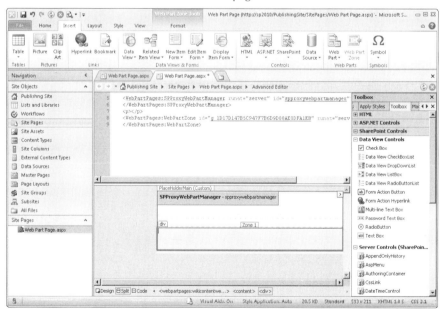

One of the properties that you can control for all Web Parts in a single Web Part zone is whether the Web Part displays a title bar only, both a title bar and a border, or neither.

Web Part zones also allow you to control whether users are allowed to:

- Add, delete, resize, and move Web Parts
- Manage their own personal Web Part settings
- Change Web Part settings for all users

The following steps will guide you through the process of accessing and modifying your Web Part Zone properties:

1. **Double-click the Zone 1 in Design View to open the Web Part Zone Properties.**

2. **In the Web Part Zone Properties dialog box, do any of the following (see Figure 19.32 for reference):**

   - **Give the zone a title:** Under General settings section, in the Zone title box, type a name for the new zone.

   - **Choose a frame style:** Under General settings section, in the Frame style list, select the style that you want.

   - **Choose a layout for the zone:** Under Layout of Web Parts contained in the zone, click either Top-to-bottom (vertical layout) or Side-by-side (horizontal layout).

   - **Control changes made in the browser:** Under Browser settings for Web Parts contained in the zone section, select check boxes to allow users to make the indicated changes while they view the page in a browser, or clear check boxes to prevent users from making those changes.

3. **When you finish, click OK.**

FIGURE 19.32

Web Part Zone Properties dialog box

Warning

If you change the Zone Title property in the General settings section of the Web Part Zone Properties dialog box and users have already assigned Web Parts to that Zone, the Web Part will be deleted. ■

Deleting a Web Part zone

Although you can delete a Web Part zone from a page, you must realize that you are also deleting any Web Parts assigned to that zone in that Web Part page.

When selecting a Web Part zone that you would like to delete, make sure that you select only the zone and not any other elements. The Quick Tag Selector makes this easier to do by identifying the precise object that you have selected. The Quick Tag Selector is located at the bottom of the document window and is updated every time you select an object anywhere in the page, as shown in Figure 19.33.

Tip

The arrow keys on your keyboard may be more useful than the mouse for changing your selection, especially when elements overlap other objects. Each time that you press an arrow key, check the Quick Tag Selector to see which element is selected. ■

FIGURE 19.33

Web Part zone selected and highlighted in the Quick Tag Selector

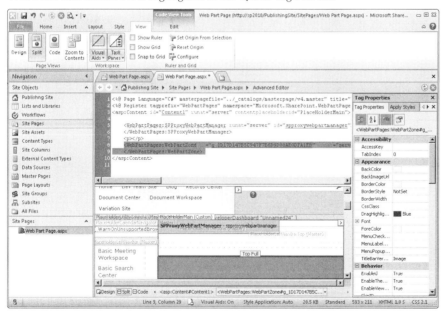

1. In SharePoint Designer 2010, open the page from which you want to delete a Web Part zone.

2. In Design view, click the Web Part zone that you want to delete.

3. Check the Quick Tag Selector to make sure that you have selected only the Web Part zone.

4. Press Delete.

5. From the File menu, select Save.

Add and configure a Web Part

In this section, you will add a Web Part to the Web Part page outside any existing Web Part zones to display content that cannot be edited by users accessing your site through the browser.

In this example, follow these steps to add copyright information to the bottom of the home page of your site:

1. In SharePoint Designer 2010, open the page in Design view to which you want to add a Web Part.

2. Click within the page where you would like the Web Part to be inserted.

3. From the Insert tab on the Ribbon, select the Web Part button and select More Web Parts, as shown in Figure 19.34.

FIGURE 19.34

Web Part Button menu

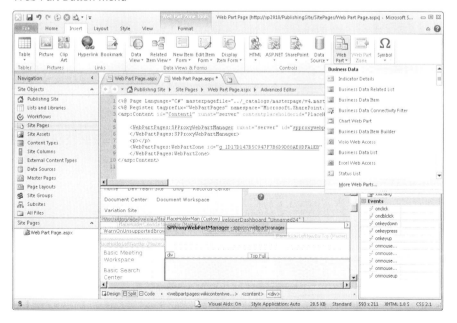

4. Scroll through or search the Web Part list in the Web Parts Picker dialog box to find the Content Editor Web Part, as shown in Figure 19.35.

FIGURE 19.35

Web Part Picker dialog box

5. Select the Content Editor Web Part and click OK.

The Content Editor Web Part is now inserted onto the page. By default, you see the Web Part header (Content Editor Web Part) and text that notifies you "to add content, select this text and replace it by typing or inserting your own content." You can see an example of this in Figure 19.36.

6. **Delete the editable text in the Web Part and type** Copyright 2010, all rights reserved.

7. **Double-click on the Content Editor Web Part in Design view to open the properties.**

8. **Click the plus sign next to the Appearance section.**

9. Click on the Chrome Type drop-down and select None, as shown in Figure 19.37.

10. Scroll down to the Layout section and select Right to Left from the Direction drop-down list (Figure 19.38).

11. Click OK.

12. From the File menu, click Save.

FIGURE 19.36

Content Editor Web Part added to page

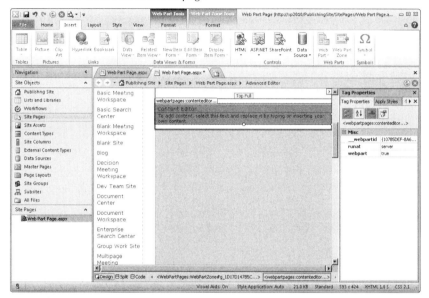

FIGURE 19.37

Content Editor Web part Appearance properties

FIGURE 19.38

Content Editor Web part Layout properties

You can see your changes persist in the Design view of SharePoint 2010. To review and test, navigate to the home page of your site in the browser. You should see the changes reflected.

Summary

This chapter discussed the new SharePoint Designer 2010 key features and how you can use the included tools to create, customize, manage, and control the visual and content presentation aspects of SharePoint sites. It also demonstrated the steps to create and customize master pages, style sheets, content pages, layout pages, content placeholders, Web Part zones, and Web Parts using SharePoint Designer 2010.

CHAPTER

20

Using the Data View Web Part

The Data View Web Part is a very flexible tool for accessing, connecting, styling, and displaying data in your Web Part pages. By allowing you to present data from a variety of data sources including SharePoint lists and libraries, databases, REST Web Services, XML data, and SOAP Web services, the Data View Web Part creates many opportunities to include data sources on your SharePoint sites without needing to create and install custom Web Parts. The data view capabilities also enable you to create writable views of data if allowed by the data source so that users can create new or update existing data.

This chapter covers the functionality of the Data View Web Part and describes in detail how you can use it to connect to the data sources it supports and present that data in the Data View Web Part using SharePoint Designer. In addition, we customize the presentation of data in your portal by sorting, grouping, filtering, linking to data sources, connecting to other Web Parts, and applying conditional formatting so that you can transform your data into information for your users in this Web Part. Finally, we cover the ability to use XPath expressions to calculate fields and sorting, filtering, and formatting criteria.

IN THIS CHAPTER

Importing and displaying data

Customizing the Data View presentation

Using XPath expressions

Importing and Displaying Data

The Data View Web Part allows you to flexibly display data from several data sources on your SharePoint site. Using SharePoint Designer, you can connect to, select fields from, or display and format data from these sources:

- **SharePoint Lists and Libraries:** Lists and libraries on the site on which you are using the Data View Web Part are automatically populated in the SharePoint Designer Data Source Library. You can define connections to SharePoint Lists and Libraries from other sites in the site collection.

- **Databases:** The Data View Web Part can consume a database connection to any SQL Server database, through the SQL Server database connection provider or another database through its corresponding OLE DB data provider. Additionally, you can use a custom connection string to configure a connection to any Oracle, ODBC, OLE DB, or SQL Server.

  You can configure the database connections with a specific account or use SSO authentication. If you configure the connection with a specific account, the password is stored in clear text, so this method is not recommended if the password needs to be secured.

- **XML files:** Any XML files can be added to the Data Source Library for use in the Data View Web Part.

- **REST Web Services:** You can define server-side scripts or RSS feeds as data sources for the Data View Web Part.

- **SOAP Web Services:** SOAP Web services allow you to define connections to Web services to get data. This includes, of course, connecting to SharePoint Web services to get data — for example, list data from another site collection.

- **Linked sources:** Linked sources are combinations of other data sources that can be sorted together or joined. For example, if you have multiple sources that have similar fields (like two contact lists or a contact list and a contact database), you can create a linked source that identifies each source and defines a sorted relationship. If you have multiple sources that have related data like a customer list and contacts for those customers, you can create a linked source that identifies each source and defines a joined relationship.

Defining data sources

The Data Source Library in SharePoint designer stores all of your defined data sources that are available to be used in a Data View Web Part. While some sources are populated automatically, like the lists and libraries on the current site, you will need to define the other connections, like database connections, before using the sources in the Data View Web Part.

Adding SharePoint lists and libraries data sources

SharePoint lists and libraries that have already been created are listed automatically as sources in the Data Source Library, as shown in Figure 20.1. You can also create new lists and libraries in the current site from SharePoint Designer and connect to list and libraries on other sites.

FIGURE 20.1

SharePoint lists and libraries in the SharePoint Designer Data Source Library

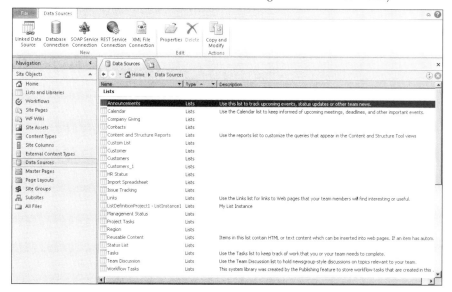

To create a new list or library in the current site from SharePoint Designer, follow these steps:

1. Open SharePoint Designer and choose Open Site from the File ⇨ Site page.

2. Enter the URL in the Site Name field and click Open.

3. Click Lists and Libraries from the Site Objects navigation pane.

4. To create a new list, click the SharePoint list button from the Ribbon and select a list type.

5. Enter a name and description for the list in the Create list or document library dialog box and click OK.

Defining database connection data sources

To define a database connection, you need to know the server name, type of connection provider (SQL Server or OLE DB), and authentication information, or be able to define a custom connection string to your database source.

To define a database connection, follow these steps:

1. Open SharePoint Designer and choose Open Site from the File ⇨ Site page.

2. Enter the URL in the Site Name field and click Open.

3. Click Data Sources from the Site Objects navigation pane.

4. Click Database Connection from the New tab on the Ribbon.

5. Click Configure Database Connection.

6. **Enter the server name in the Server Name field, select the connection provider and enter the username and password or select User Single Sign-On authentication in the Authentication section, as shown in Figure 20.2.** If you choose to store a username and password in the data connection, other authors can see this information in clear text. If you choose to use SSO, you need to provide the application name, the field to use for the username, and the field to use for the password.

Alternatively, you can choose to enter a custom connection string. You will need to provide that string as well as select whether you want to use an ODBC, OLE DB, SQL Server, or Oracle provider type.

FIGURE 20.2

Entering the database connection information

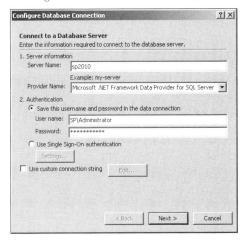

7. Click Next.

8. **Choose your database from the Database drop-down menu and select the table or view.** Alternatively, you can select that you will use custom SQL commands or stored procedures in the data view.

9. Click Finish.

10. **Once the source table is selected, you can enter filter and sort criteria for the data in the Source tab of the database connection, as shown in Figure 20.3.**

FIGURE 20.3

Using the sort and filter options for the database connection

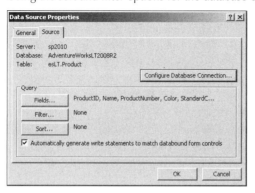

11.   Click the General tab.

12.   **Enter the name for your database connection in the Name field and the description in the Description field.** Make sure that you provide enough information about the connection (database, table, and authentication method, as appropriate) so that anyone designing a data view can make use of the data source.

13.   Click OK.

Adding XML files

You can upload XML files with data that you want to use in a Data View Web Part. This allows you to add data that is structured exactly to your specifications.

To add an XML file to the Data Source Library, follow these steps:

1.   Open SharePoint Designer and choose Open Site from the File ⇨ Site page.

2.   Enter the URL in the Site Name field and click Open.

3.   Click Data Sources from the Site Objects navigation pane.

4.   Click XML File Connection from the New tab on the Ribbon.

5.   Enter the location in the Location field or browse to your XML source file.

6.   **Click the Login tab and enter appropriate authentication info as necessary for your XML file.** If you choose to store a username and password in the data connection, other authors can see this information in clear text. If you use SSO, you must provide the application name, the field to use for the username, and the field to use for the password.

7.   **Click the General tab and enter the name for your XML data in the Name field and the description in the Description field.** Make sure that you provide enough information about the connection data so that anyone designing a data view can make use of the data source.

Connecting to REST Web Services (server-side scripts or RSS feeds)

Server-side scripts allow you to connect to data that is selected by the script and processed on the server on which it lives. The capability to connect to RSS feeds allows you to present the data made available via RSS in your Data View Web Part. To create a connection to a server-side script or RSS feed, follow these steps:

1. Open SharePoint Designer and choose Open Site from the File ➪ Site page.

2. Enter the URL in the Site Name field and click Open.

3. Click Data Sources from the Site Objects navigation pane.

4. Click REST Service Connection from the New tab on the Ribbon.

5. Choose whether you will use HTTP Get or HTTP Post in the HTTP Method field.

6. **Select which command you are configuring in this dialog box.** The default value is Select (as it appears in the drop-down) which is the most common method of returning data. However, you have the option of configuring the Insert, Update, and Delete commands as well in the server-side script configuration.

7. **Enter the URL to the script or RSS feed in the Enter the URL to a server-side script field, as shown in Figure 20.4.**

FIGURE 20.4

Configuring the URL for a server-side script or RSS feed connection

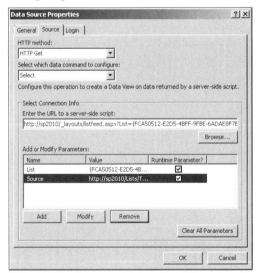

8. **Enter the parameters that you would like to pass to the script.** In the example shown in Figure 20.4, the URL is to an RSS feed for a list, and the list parameter is automatically populated as a parameter for the connection.

9. **Click the Login tab and enter the appropriate authentication information or select Don't attempt to authenticate if authentication is not necessary.** If you provide username and password credentials, they are stored in clear text. If you use SSO, you must provide the application name, the field to use for the username, and the field to use for the password.

10. **Click the General tab and enter the name for your server-side script or RSS feed in the Name field and the description in the Description field.** Make sure that you provide enough information about the connection data so that anyone designing a data view can make use of the data source.

11. **Click OK.**

Connecting to a SOAP Web service data source

Connecting to data via a Web service is a very flexible option that can leverage the full power of the Web service. For example, using the SharePoint Web service to connect to (or update) SharePoint information (list data and so on) allows you to configure the data source to perform operations and authenticate exactly per your specification, even if the list is not on your local site collection or server.

1. **Open SharePoint Designer and choose Open Site from the File ⇨ Site page.**

2. **Enter the URL in the Site Name field and click Open.**

3. **Click Data Sources from the Site Objects navigation pane.**

4. **Click SOAP Service Connection from the New tab on the Ribbon.**

5. **Enter the Web service address in the Service description location field.** If you are connecting to a Web service for a SharePoint site, the address will be `http://<servername>/<sitename>/_vti_bin/lists.asmx`.

6. **Click Connect Now.**

7. **Select which command you are configuring in this dialog box.** The default value is Select, which is the most common method of returning data. However, you have the option of configuring the Insert, Update, and Delete (as it appears in SharePoint Designer command dropdown) commands as well in the Web services configuration.

8. **Configure the port and operation for your Web service.** If you are using a SharePoint 2010 Web service, choose ListsSoap12 as the port as shown in Figure 20.5. If you want to return list items for a SharePoint list, choose GetListItems as the operation.

FIGURE 20.5

Connecting to a SharePoint Web service

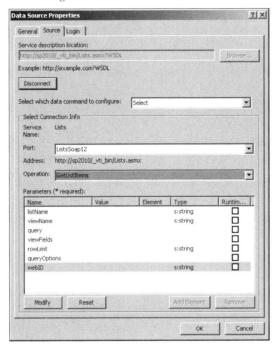

9. **Enter the parameters that you would like to pass to the service.** In the example shown in Figure 20.6, the Web service is provided by SharePoint to get items, and the appropriate parameters are automatically populated as a parameter for the connection. If you are using the data view to get items as shown in the Figure 20.6 example, double-click the `listName` parameter and enter the name of the list for which you want to return, as shown in Figure 20.6.

10. **Click the Login tab and enter the appropriate authentication information, or select Don't attempt to authenticate if authentication is not necessary.** If you provide user-name and password credentials, they will be stored in clear text. If you use SSO, you must provide the application name, the field to use for the username, and the field to use for the password.

11. **Click the General tab and enter the name for your Web services connection in the Name field and the description in the Description field.** Make sure that you provide enough information about the connection data so that anyone designing a data view can make use of the data source.

12. **Click OK.**

FIGURE 20.6

Configuring the list name parameter for which you want the Web service to return items

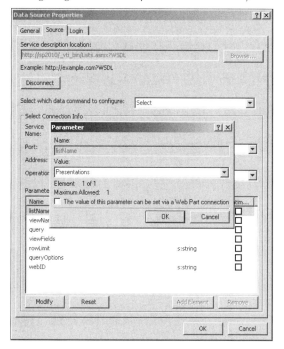

Note

Although using the Web service to access SharePoint data is very flexible, it loses some of the automatic formatting of the list or library provided by inserting SharePoint list Web Parts. You will need to format the columns to make the document title link to the document and the document creator link to the user profile, both of which are provided by a native document library Web Part. ■

Cross-Reference

For more information on formatting and styling data view information, see the "Customizing the Data View Presentation" section in this chapter. ■

Creating linked sources

Linked sources are sources in your data catalog that you want to link together so that the data can be either joined based on a common field or combined so that it is sorted together. You want to create your linked sources in your Data Source Library before inserting the data in a Data View Web Part because you want to show and select the fields for insertion from the linked data source instead of the individual data sources.

1. Open SharePoint Designer and choose Open Site from the File ⇨ Site page.

2. Enter the URL in the Site Name field and click Open.

3. Click Data Sources from the Site Objects navigation pane.

4. Click Linked Data Source from the Data Sources tab of the Ribbon.

5. Click Configure Linked Source and add two or more data sources from your Data Source Library.

6. Click Next.

7. **Select whether you want to merge or join the data sources as shown in Figure 20.7.** If the sources are two RSS feeds that you want to show in one feed, merge the sources. For the case where you will join the data so that you can show all orders for a particular customer and those are two data sources, choose to join the data.

FIGURE 20.7

Choosing the method for linking data sources

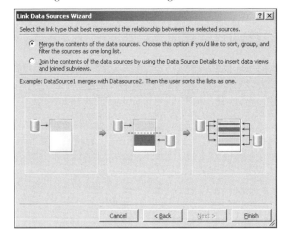

8. **Click Finish.** You will enter the criteria for the join when you insert the subview, so that is not managed when you create the linked sources.

9. **Click the General tab and enter the name for your linked source in the Name field and the description in the Description field.** Make sure that you provide enough information about the connection data so that anyone designing a data view can make use of the data source.

10. Click OK.

Implementing the Data View Web Part

After your Data Source Library has been populated with the data sources that you need for your site, you implement the Data View Web Part on Web Part pages to display that data. You will want to configure your linked data sources before implementing the Web Part. This allows you to insert the data from the linked data source instead of from the separate data sources.

There are two ways that you can display data in your Data View Web Part: as a view (read-only) or as a form (read-write). The data source must allow updates for you to insert data as a form, so you cannot insert a form of RSS feeds, for example.

Whether you are inserting a view or a form, SharePoint also lets you choose whether to insert the data as a single item or multiple items. For form items, you can also create a view with a new form that presents your selected fields so that users can add new items. These options allow you to design the page so that the data is presented to the user in a readable format and optimized for your page width.

The single item view provides a control so that users can scroll through the record, as shown in Figure 20.8.

FIGURE 20.8

A multiple item and single item with scroll control data view

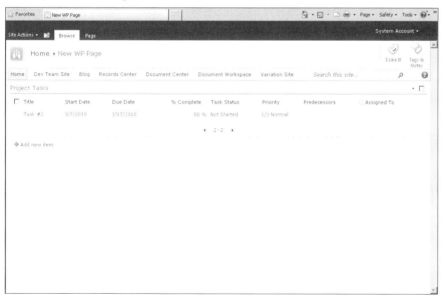

If you have a form view, inserting a multiple item form can make the page long very quickly, and therefore hard to use, because the save or cancel control is at the bottom of all the values.

Tip

To make a multiple item form more usable on a page, you can connect it to another Web Part that filters the values so that only a few are shown at a time. For example, you can connect a multiple item form for a contact list to a Company list so that multiple item form only shows contacts for the selected company. ∎

Cross-Reference

For more information on connecting Web Parts, see the "Customizing the Data View Presentation" section of this chapter. ∎

For linked sources that are joined, you have the option to insert a joined subview for the joined data. In this scenario, you insert the fields from the linked source that are the primary fields and then insert the joined subview for your related list fields. For example, in Figure 20.9 the primary data view fields are the customer fields, and a joined subview for issues has been inserted that shows all the contacts for each customer.

FIGURE 20.9

A joined linked data source that is inserted as a data view and a joined subview

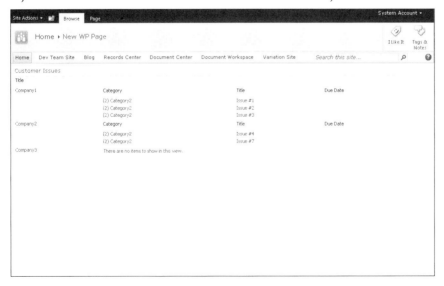

Inserting a data view

To insert a data view on a Web Part page, follow these steps:

1. Open the page on which you want to add the Data View Web Part using SharePoint Designer.

2. Click the zone in which you want to insert the data view.

3. Choose Data View from the Insert tab on the Ribbon and select the data source from the drop-down menu or chose Blank Data View.

4. **If you insert a Blank Data View, click on the link to select the data source. Select the fields that you want to insert in the data view from the Data Source Details pane.** If you are selecting more than one field, you can hold down the Ctrl key while selecting the fields you want with your mouse.

5. **Click Insert Selected Fields as.**

   Select Single Item View if you want to show just one item from the list.

   Select Multiple Item View if you want to show multiple items from the list.

   If your data source allows updates, you have three options for inserting data in a form view that will present the fields for adding records or updating records. If you want to insert forms for writing data, select one of these options:

   - Select Single Item Form if you want to have the data view insert your fields to a single item in a format that can be updated.

   - Select Multiple Item Form if you want to have the data view insert the selected fields to show multiple items that can be updated.

   - Select New Item Form if you want the data view to present the fields so that users can fill them in and save them.

6. **Choose Save from the File menu to save your Web Part page.**

Inserting a linked source joined data view

To insert a data view on a Web Part page, follow these steps:

1. Open the page on which you want to add the Data View Web Part using SharePoint Designer.

2. Click the zone in which you want to insert the data view.

3. Choose Data View from the Insert tab on the Ribbon and select Blank Data View.

4. Click the link in the Data View part and select the Linked Data Source.

5. **Select the fields from your primary list fields that you want to insert in the data view from the Data Source Details pane.** If you are selecting more than one field, you can hold down the Ctrl key while selecting the fields you want with your mouse.

6. **Click Insert Selected Fields as.**

   Select Single Item View if you want to show just one item from the list.

   Select Multiple Item View if you want to show multiple items from the list.

7. Click the column to the left of where you want to insert the joined menu and right-click Select Column to the Right from the Insert submenu.

8. Place the cursor in the first row that contains a value (not the header row).

9. Select the fields from your secondary list fields that you want to insert in the data view.

10. Click Insert Selected Fields as and select Join Subview.

11. From the Join Subview dialog box, select the field from your primary list on the left and the field from your secondary list on the right that should be joined, as shown in Figure 20.10. If you don't see your field, click More Fields at the bottom of the dialog box.

FIGURE 20.10

Selecting a joined field for your join subview

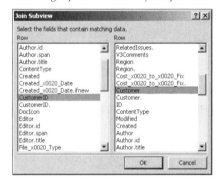

12. Click OK.

13. Choose Save from the File menu to save your Web Part page.

Customizing the Data View Presentation

Once you have inserted a data view on your page, you can modify the selection and presentation of data by setting filters and group-by options, and configuring conditional formatting and columns as links. These options provide additional flexibility and almost endless opportunities for customizing and presenting data. You can customize your data views using the following methods:

- **Filtering:** By filtering the data returned in your data view, you can present the data that users need.

- **Grouping and sorting:** Grouping allows you to create distinct, expandable/collapsible containers for the data in your data view and to sort based on these grouping criteria.

- **Conditional formatting:** You can format the data in your data views according to conditions so that data that needs particular attention because it's met a threshold stands out, or you can downplay information or records that are not critical.

- **Creating hyperlinks:** Linking back to source data or actions is important when you are presenting data so that users can research further or take action, especially if you are combining multiple data sources.

- **Connecting Web Parts:** By connecting Web Parts, you can enable users to drill down on a particular item and see details or connected information. Connected Web Parts also allow you to use Web page space wisely because you can filter the range of information that needs to be displayed based on user interaction.

- **Modifying data view columns:** If your data changes and columns are added or become relevant to the current task, you can add, delete, or modify the columns that appear.

- **Styling:** The styling options available with SharePoint Designer and the Data View Web Part provide flexibility for the layout and presentation of your data.

Filtering your data

To configure a filter for your data, follow these steps:

1. **Open the page with the Data View Web Part using SharePoint Designer.**

2. **To display the Data View Tools contextual Ribbon tabs, select the Data View Web Part. The Options tab on the Ribbon is selected as shown in Figure 20.11. Click the Filter button.**

FIGURE 20.11

The Data View Tools — Options tab on the Ribbon

3. **Select the field that you want to filter from the Field Name field, the comparison type, and the value, as shown in Figure 20.12.**

You can add more than one filter criterion. If you have more than one, you must select whether the filters are AND so that they are cumulative and items have to meet all filters, or OR so that items have to meet only one of the filter criterion. You can mix AND and OR criteria so that the filter pulls all items that match the AND filters and all items that match the OR filter.

The Data View Web Part provides comparison types and possible calculated values that are appropriate for the field. For example, if you choose a date field, SharePoint Designer suggests [Current Date] as a value option, or if your field is a text field, it includes begins-with and contains-as comparison types.

FIGURE 20.12

Modifying the filter options for the Data View Web Part

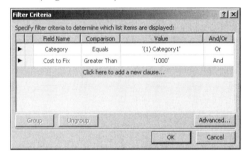

4. **Click OK.**

5. **Choose Save from the File menu to save your Web Part page.**

Sorting and grouping your data

Grouping items allows you to present them in broad categories, and if you collapse your groups, to fit more items onto one page. For example, you can group your bug tracking items by region and by priority so that users can find the high-priority items in their region easily.

To configure sorting and grouping for your data, follow these steps:

1. **Open the page with the Data View Web Part using SharePoint Designer.**

2. **To display the Data View Tools contextual Ribbon tabs, select the Data View Web Part.** The Options ribbon bar is selected as shown in Figure 20.11.

3. **Click the Sort & Group button.**

4. **Add the field or fields that you want to sort and/or group by from the column on the left, as shown in Figure 20.13.** You can add multiple fields and order them because the top field will be sorted first. Each field can be sorted in ascending or descending order.

Configuring the sort and group options for a data view

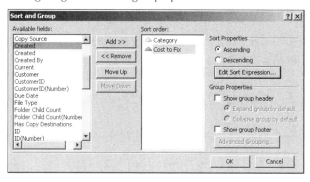

4. **Configure the Group Properties if you want to group by your sort fields.** Selecting the Show group header check box enables grouping, and you can select whether you want to expand or collapse your groupings. If you select to Show Group Footer, the data view includes the count at the bottom of each grouping (for the first level of grouping).

5. **Click OK.** If you want to show more than the ten items that the data view configures by default because you are grouping the items, you must configure the paging options. Select the Paging button from the Insert tab on the Ribbon and then select an option from the drop-down menu as shown in Figure 20.14.

Paging button menu

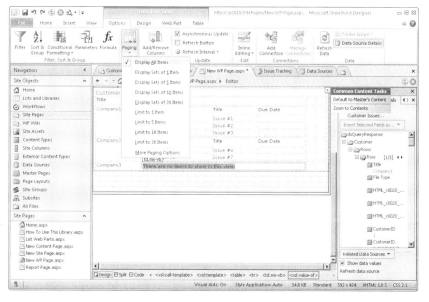

6. **You can choose to show all items, to display items in sets of a certain size (this is the number of items shown at any time) or to limit the total number of items returned to a specific number.** If you limit the total number of items, it will show only the number of items that you configure and there will not be a control for users to see the remaining items.

7. **Choose Save from the File menu to save your Web Part page.**

Applying conditional formatting

Conditional formatting enables you to apply a particular format based on the value or combination of values for a field. There are so many scenarios in which this capability can be used, so we'll just suggest a couple of examples to get the juices going.

In an issue tracking list, you can use conditional formatting to turn the rows in a view red if the priority of the issue is high and if the due date has passed. You can turn the rows yellow in the view if the priority of the issue is high and if the due date is in the next 48 hours.

Conditional formatting can also be used to show or hide columns. In this application, we can choose to hide the due date value if the issue is closed. If you are using the hide content capability, you will want the columns that you are hiding to be at the right side of your list because the cells will slide left if the column for that item is hidden.

1. **Open the page with the Data View Web Part using SharePoint Designer.**

2. **Select the Data View Web Part on the page and then click the column (or row) to which you want to apply the conditional formatting and click Create in the right-hand task pane.**

3. **Click the Conditional Formatting button on the Ribbon.**

4. **Select whether you want to show content, hide content, or apply formatting to the row, column, or just the selection.**

5. **Enter the condition criteria for the fields that will select the fields for which formatting should be applied, as shown in Figure 20.15.**

FIGURE 20.15

Entering the condition criteria for conditional formatting

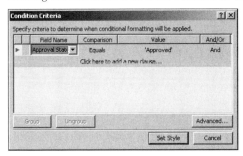

6. If you are applying formatting, click the Set Style button and select the formatting options that you want in the Modify Style dialog box.

7. Click OK.

8. Choose Save from the File menu to save your Web Part page.

Connecting Data View Web Parts

Connecting your Data View Web Parts allows you to design Web Part pages where the data drives intelligent changes in other, related Web Parts. This allows you to filter values shown in the slave Web Parts based on the value selected in the master Web Part, so that users easily see the information they need for their choice and the page space is used wisely. For example, you can connect a customer list and writable view of a contact list so that users can view and update the contacts for a particular customer that they choose, as shown in Figure 20.16. You can connect a Data View Web Part to any other Data View Web Part(s) or any other connectable Web Part(s). However, the fields that you want to use to connect the data must be present on all connected parts.

FIGURE 20.16

Connected Web Parts that allow users to view and update the contacts for a particular customer

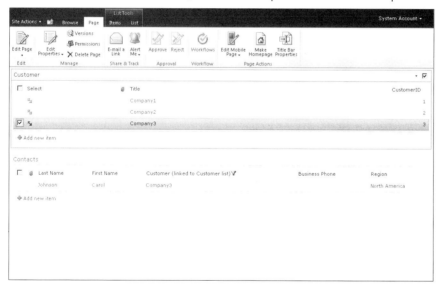

1. Open the page with the Data View Web Parts that you want to connect using SharePoint Designer.

2. Select the parent Web Part and then click Add Connection from the Options tab on the Ribbon. The Web Part Connections Wizard displays.

3. **Select whether you want to Send Row of Data To, Get Filter Values From, or Get Parameters From.** The Send Row of Data To option is typically used because it is logically more straightforward than clicking the target Web Part and selecting the Get Filter Values From option.

4. **Click Next.**

5. **Choose the location where the connected Web Part resides by selecting Connect to a Web Part on this page if the Web Part is on the current page or Connect to a Web Part on another page in this Web and entering the page URL if the Web Part is on another page.**

6. **Click Next.**

7. **Select the Web Part that you want as your target Web Part and select Get Filter Values From if you want to filter the list based on the value provided by the source Web Part.** If you want to use the value in a parameter field, select the Get Parameters From option.

8. **Click Next.**

9. **Find the field in the target list (right-hand column) that matches the filter value you will send and pick the related column in the left column, as shown in Figure 20.17.**

FIGURE 20.17

Selecting the column in the source Web Part that matches the column in the target Web Part

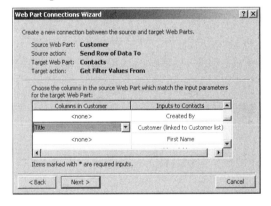

10. **Click Next.**

11. **Review the values and click Finish.**

12. **Choose Save from the File menu to save your Web Part page.**

Cross-Reference

For more information on connecting Web Parts, see Chapter 5. ∎

Modifying columns

Because data views pull data from one or more sources, one of the most important aspects of customizing your data view is to link the data back to the source or to an action so that the user has the ability to find more detail. You should plan how to link columns so that they are most usable, especially with connected Web Parts or linked data sources. With connected Web Parts, the link in the source column controls the action in the target Web Parts. In the case of linked columns that are merged, it is important to link your items to the source URL to direct the user to the correct source. With linked columns that are joined, you may want to configure more than one column to link to the data sources that are combined to create that view.

To make columns linkable, follow these steps:

1. Open the page with the Data View Web Part using SharePoint Designer.

2. Select the column that you want to link and right-click to display the item menu. Select Format Item As ⇨ Hyperlink to ⇨ Display Form, as shown in Figure 20.18.

3. Confirm that your data source is safe to trust for a hyperlink.

4. Click OK.

5. Choose Save from the File menu to save your Web Part page.

FIGURE 20.18

Format a column as a hyperlink.

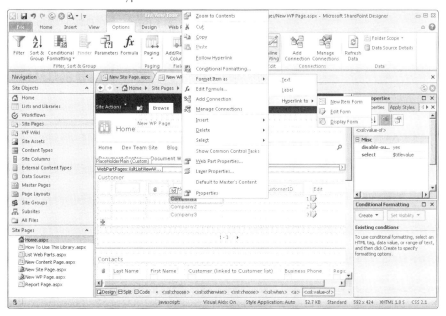

You may want to modify the columns for your data view to add, delete, or reorder your columns, especially after you see how the Web Part is used. The ability to easily modify columns for the Data View Web Part is included in the SharePoint Designer data view controls. To add, delete, or reorder columns, follow these steps:

1. **Open the page with the Data View Web Part using SharePoint Designer.**

2. **Select the Date View Web Part and click on the Add/Remove Columns button on the Ribbon.**

3. **Use the Displayed Fields dialog box, as shown in Figure 20.19, to add, remove, or reorder columns.**

FIGURE 20.19

Using the displayed fields control to add, delete, or reorder columns

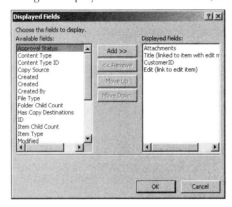

4. Click OK.

5. **Select Save from the File menu to save your Web Part page.**

Styling data views

SharePoint Designer provides six layouts to choose from your data view. Each option provides different advantages for presenting the data and utilizing page space, as described below.

- **Basic Table:** This is the default layout when you insert data in your Data View Web Part. The basic table presents each selected column as a column in a table and each item as a single row.

- **Boxed:** The boxed layout presents items on the page in a business card fashion.

- **Boxed, no labels:** This layout is the same as the boxed layout but the column labels do not appear in the boxes. (See Figure 20.20.)

FIGURE 20.20

The boxed, no labels table layout

- **Newsletter:** This layout presents several columns across and the content of multiline text boxes underneath.

- **Newsletter, no lines:** This layout is a newsletter layout but without lines to separate the items.

- **Shaded:** The shaded layout presents the data in a report-type format and presents each row of data in an alternating background pattern.

- **Preview Pane:** A simple layout that displays each column of data in a vertical list.

To select the layout for your Data View Web Part, follow these steps:

1. **Open the page with the Data View Web Part using SharePoint Designer.**

2. **Select the Design tab on the Ribbon and expand the View Style section, as shown in Figure 20.21.**

3. **Select the desired layout from the options.**

4. Choose Save from the File menu to save your Web Part page.

FIGURE 20.21

View styles from the Design tab

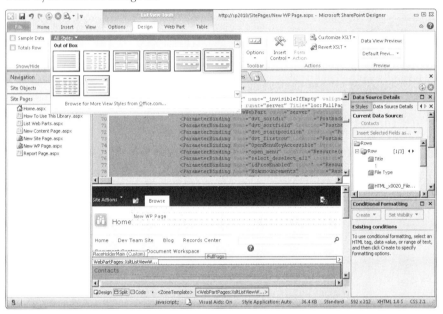

Using XPath Expressions

SharePoint Designer provides an XPath Express Builder for creating XPath expression. XPath is a language that can locate and process XML information. It can be used in the data view to create expressions to provide advanced sorts and calculated fields for data sources, whether they are XML sources or other sources like SQL databases or SharePoint lists. If you use XPath expressions on non-XML sources, the data is rendered first as XML and then the XPath expression is applied, so you may see a performance impact.

Working with the XPath Expression Builder is similar to working with functions in Excel. You can create formulas of the following types:

- **Math/Number:** These functions perform mathematical operations such as returning the average, finding the minimum or maximum value, rounding a value up or down to the next integer, or formatting the number.

- **Text/String:** These functions perform operations such as concatenating two values, calculating the length of a string, normalizing the spaces in a string of text, evaluating whether a string starts with or contains the value provided, or translating characters if present in a string with a new character.

- **Field/Node:** These functions return values particular to the structure of the XML such as the namespace URI or all the comments or processing instructions present in the document.

- **Date/Time:** These functions allow you to format the date or the date and time, return today's date, and evaluate whether items have been created in the last two days.

- **Boolean:** The Boolean operations evaluate whether conditions are met or not. You can provide a condition, determine whether the current user has rights, evaluate whether a value is null, or set automatically to true or false.

- **Parameters:** The `parameters` function returns the values of the selected parameter such as `firstrow` or `nextpagedata`.

- **XPath Axes:** These functions return related nodes to the context node such as child, descendant, parent, and ancestor.

- **Operators:** The operator category allows you to select operators commonly used in equations such as not equal to, minus, plus, greater than, and less than.

- **XSLT:** The XSLT functions allow you to determine whether elements or functions are available for the string provided, generate unique IDs for the context node, or return nodes that match a key name and value.

You can use XPath expressions to define additional columns of your data, create advanced sort or filter arguments, or calculate conditional formatting rules. Your XPath expressions are performed on the rows of your data, not the aggregation of the rows. For example, if you have data that contains orders and values for each order, sales tax, and shipping, XPath can be used to calculate the total cost (order + sales tax + shipping) but it cannot be used to add the sales tax value for all rows.

Tip

Because XPath is a language, users that are familiar with it can edit the XPath expressions themselves instead of using the XPath Expression Builder in SharePoint. For others, the Expression Builder makes creating functions for rows of your data straightforward. ∎

To insert a column based on an XPath expression in your data view using the SharePoint Designer XPath Expression Builder, follow these steps:

1. Open the page with the Data View Web Part using SharePoint Designer.
2. Select a field in the Data View.
3. Click on the Formula button in the Options tab on the Ribbon.
4. Enter your XPath expression in the Edit the XPath expression field, as shown in Figure 20.22. You can double-click fields or functions you want to insert into the expressions. The preview field allows you to preview the results.
5. Click OK to save the expression.
6. Click OK to exit the Edit Columns dialog box.
7. Choose Save from File menu to save your Web Part page.

FIGURE 20.22

Entering an XPath expression

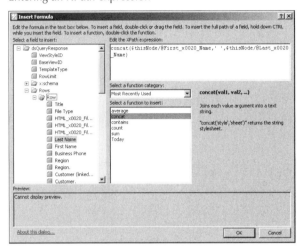

You can customize the table heading for your XPath formula column by editing the XSL for the Data View Web Part within the Web Part page. To edit the formula table heading, follow these steps:

1. Open the page with the Data View Web Part using Internet Explorer.

2. Left-click the down arrow for the Web Part and choose Edit Web Part.

3. Click XSL Editor.

4. Select the text that is currently being used in the table header row (HTML value of `<th>`) and replace with your new text.

5. Click Save to exit XSL Editor.

6. Click OK to save the Web Part changes.

Summary

This chapter discussed how you can connect to various data sources and present read views and/or write forms using the Data View Web Part functionality. In addition, it covered the options for customizing the presentation of that data by filtering what data is shown, sorting and grouping the data, connecting to other Web Parts, linking to source data, and formatting the data based on conditional criteria. Finally, we discussed the advanced capabilities for creating formulas to calculate rows and provide advanced sorting, filtering, or formatting criteria provided by XPath expressions included in your data view.

Part VI

SharePoint Solution Scenarios

Intranet Portal Solution Scenario

This chapter combines the concepts presented in the other parts of the book to create an intranet portal for a sample company. We walk through the requirements presented for a typical intranet portal and then propose a SharePoint architecture to meet each requirement.

Our solution creates a portal on which users can collaborate within a structure that provides templates, consistent data usage, access to business data, and search so that corporate consistency is maintained. We walk through using self-service site creation, lists and libraries, custom list fields, content types, and site templates to create this collaboration infrastructure with fields and content types that will be used throughout the organization. In this chapter, we also implement a business data application, use SQL Server Reporting Services, report Web Parts and design data views to access, and connect and present business data throughout the portal.

Scenario Background

This scenario implements an intranet portal for a medium-sized IT consulting firm with 500 employees. This firm has the following organizational units:

- **Consultants:** The consultants are organized by competency grouping for developers, system integrators, and networking experts. They work with different team members of every project depending on project size and scope.

- **Sales Staff:** The sales organization has both internal and external sales people who are responsible for the sales process from cold calling through proposal delivery and acceptance.

- **Project Managers:** The project managers are responsible for making sure that projects are delivered on time and on budget. They are distributed throughout the company in the different competency areas.

- **Recruiting Team:** The recruiters are responsible for providing candidates in all competency groups.

- **Accounting Personnel:** The accounting team is responsible for invoicing and tracking profitability on project, group, and company profits.

- **Executive Leadership:** The executive leadership team drives the direction of the company by deciding what investments and areas need focus.

Because they work in the high-tech sector, the company users are fairly sophisticated users of technology; however, they have primarily been using e-mail and file shares for collaboration. This has resulted in a culture where new employees discover the templates and tools that they use for their jobs by asking existing employees, and there are duplicated and differing versions of those tools and templates throughout the company.

Solution Requirements

This consulting company wants to implement a portal that allows them to collaborate in teams, gathers information from their various data sources, and helps them to make informed decisions. In addition, it is really important that this solution help them to reduce the variations on their core document templates so that customer deliverables are prepared consistently.

Table 21.1 outlines the specific requirements that the solution must satisfy for the portal to be considered a successful implementation.

TABLE 21.1

Intranet Portal Requirements

Requirement	Goal	Audience
Collaborative spaces must be easily instantiated for projects and corporate initiatives.	Enhanced team communication	All
Place for community and unstructured collaboration.	Enabling free-thinking communities and communication	All
Consultants need to be able to find collaborative spaces for their specialty.	Reuse of corporate assets	Consultants, Executives
Sales team must be able to share leads and track sales progress of items in the pipeline.	More efficient sales process	Sales, Executives
Project documentation needs to have specific format and latest template applied. Template must be in a location that can be easily updated.	Consistent deliverables	Consultants and PMs

Requirement	Goal	Audience
Project managers need to have a central view of all active projects and their status.	Ability to see and track active projects	PMs
Executives must be able to see sales pipeline and project status overall for each consulting group.	Ability to drive project resource decisions	Executives
Project managers must be able to see invoice status on projects.	Accurate communication with clients	PMs
Accounting department needs to have invoices and hours billed in one interface.	Integration of data sources so that profitability can be measured	Accounting, Executives
Resource managers need to be able to view the workload for job descriptions throughout the company.	Resource management forecasting	Resource Managers
Existing file shares need to be indexed so that posted materials are available.	Reuse of corporate assets	All
Portal content needs to be available when employees are not on the corporate network.	Availability of data when consultants are working at customer site	All

Solution Overview

Because this is a SharePoint book, it should be no surprise that SharePoint has an answer for each of these requirements. Table 21.2 outlines the SharePoint solutions that will be implemented to meet each requirement.

TABLE 21.2

SharePoint Requirement Mapping

Requirement	Solution
Collaborative spaces must be easily instantiated for projects and corporate initiatives.	Enable self-service site creation for all portal contributors.
Consultants need to be able to find collaborative spaces for their specialty.	Modify the site directory so that the categories for sites are customized.
Place for community and unstructured collaboration.	Create a site collection dedicated to Wikis and blogs that can be provisioned by anyone in the company.
Sales team must be able to share leads and track sales progress of items in the pipeline.	Create custom sales pipeline list that stores opportunities, leads, and opportunity ownership.

TABLE 21.2 *(continued)*

Requirement	Solution
Project documentation needs to have specific format and latest template applied. Template must be in a location that can be easily updated.	Define a content type for the project documentation that you need and add it to a site that will be used as a project template site.
	Create a project site template from your project site and add that site template to the templates available in self-service site creation.
Project managers need to have a central view of all active projects and their status.	Project list that contains status fields that is filtered by project manager.
Executives must be able to see project status overall for each consulting group.	Indicators for project status.
Project managers must be able to see invoice status on projects.	Accounting dashboard that allows PMs to enter a project number and start/end date.
Accounting department needs to have invoices and hours billed in one interface.	Accounting dashboard that shows invoices and report for submitted time filtered by project number and start/end date.
Resource managers need to be able to view the workload for job descriptions throughout the company.	Excel services access to central workbook that is updated by PMs on a weekly basis to track employee time.
Existing file shares need to be indexed so that posted materials are available.	Configure a content source and search scope for the file share location.
Portal content needs to be available when employees are not on the corporate network.	Configure portal as extranet portal.

In this solution, you are going to create a SharePoint portal with the following structure:

- **Home Site Collection:** The home page of the portal will provide a central point for news and navigation with the following structure:

  - **Accounting:** A reporting site for storing the accounting lists, dashboards, reports, and resources.

  - **Consulting Resources:** This site presents the consulting information for the rest of the company to consume.

  - **Management:** Site for executive dashboards.

  - **News:** This area contains the organizational news sorted for each area of the company.

  - **Project Central:** This subsite centrally stores information about projects for the organization.

  - **Recruiting:** The recruiting site is a location where the recruiting organization can present information for the rest of the organization, such as active job postings and who has received the latest referral bonus.

- **Sales:** The sales node of the portal stores the opportunities and metrics for the sales organization.

- **Search:** The search center provides the search capability for the portal.

- **Sites:** The site directory is the jump-off point for creating new collaboration sties and finding existing collaboration sites.

- **Enterprise Wiki Site Collection:** This site collection stores the unstructured Wiki and blog sites for ad-hoc collaboration.

You are going to implement the portal in a small farm configuration with a single SharePoint server front end executing all services with the databases stored on a separate SQL 2008 database configuration with SAN storage. This configuration takes advantage of the existing SQL configuration in the company, while providing an easy method to grow the infrastructure by adding Web front ends or separating the application server role out in the future if necessary. For 500 users, we could have also installed in a single-server configuration.

Once you install SharePoint, you create a Web application for the root site and use the Team Site template provided in the Collaboration tab of Site Templates. From the newly created root site, you will perform the following actions to build out your designed site structure:

- Create a team collaboration subsite for Accounting
- Create a team collaboration subsite for Consulting Resources
- Create a team collaboration subsite for Management
- Create a team collaboration subsite for Sales
- Create a team collaboration subsite for Recruiting
- Create a team collaboration subsite for Project Central

Implementing the Solution

This section walks through each requirement and implements each element outlined in the solution overview.

Enabling self-service site creation

We want to encourage team and project collaboration for employees by allowing employees to create their own WSS sites. Configuring this setting involves two steps:

1. **Turn on self-service site creation in Central Administration.**
2. **Configure the permissions for the portal so that all users with contributor rights can also create sites.**

To turn on self-service site creation in Central Administration, follow these steps:

1. Open SharePoint Central Administration and select Application Management.

2. Click Configure self-service site creation in the Site Collection section. (You may also reach the same settings from the Security Page under the General Security section.)

3. Select the Web application that you want to enable self-service site creation from the Web application drop-down menu.

4. Select On (or Off).

5. Select the Require secondary contact box if you want to force users to enter at least two contacts when creating a site. Having a secondary contact often prevents sites from becoming orphaned when the primary contact leaves the organization or changes roles.

6. Click OK.

To configure the permissions of the portal so that users with rights to contribute can also create sites, follow these steps:

1. Click Site Actions in the top-left corner of any page of the top level site.

2. Choose Site Permissions from the Site Settings menu.

3. Choose Permissions Levels from the Ribbon.

4. Click Contribute.

5. In the Site Permissions section, select the Use Self-Service Site Creation permission box as shown in Figure 21.1.

FIGURE 21.1

Configure the right to use self-service site creation for contributor role

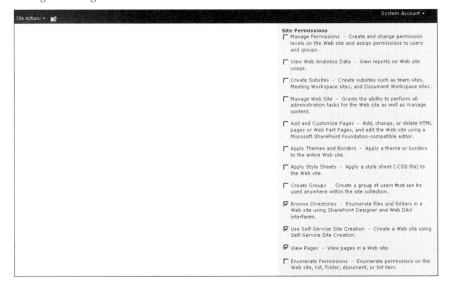

6. Click Submit.

Creating an Enterprise Wiki site collection

To support the unstructured collaboration and communication, you should create an Enterprise Wiki site collection for users to provision Wiki sites and blogs. Implementing this objective involves three high-level tasks:

1. Creating a new managed path for the Wikis namespace so that the new site collection will have the following namespace: `http://<servername>wikis/team/<sitename>`.

2. Creating a new site collection using the site directory template in the new managed path.

3. Limit the site templates available for the sites created in this site collection to only the Wiki and blog site templates.

This section breaks each of these high-level tasks into detailed steps.

To create a new managed path for your Wikis namespace, follow these steps:

1. Open the central administration site for the portal and click Application Management from the Quick Launch bar.

2. Click Manage web applications under the Web Applications section.

3. Select your port 80 Web Application in the Web Application list.

4. Click on the Manage Paths button on the Ribbon.

5. Enter wikis in the Path field and select Wildcard inclusion in the type section, as shown in Figure 21.2.

6. Click Add Path to add the managed path.

7. Click OK to close the dialog box.

To create a new site collection and site directory in your new managed path, follow these steps:

1. Open the central administration site for the portal and click Application Management from the Quick Launch bar.

2. Click Create site collections under the Site Collections section.

3. Select the port 80 Web application in the Web Application section.

4. Enter a title in the Title field.

5. Select wikis in the URL drop-down and enter team for the URL, as shown in Figure 21.3.

FIGURE 21.2

Defining a new managed path

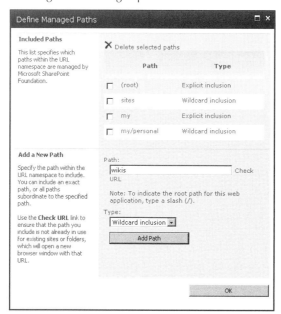

FIGURE 21.3

Creating a new site collection for your unstructured collaboration in the Wikis namespace

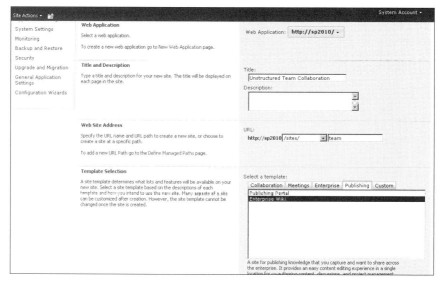

6. Click the Publishing tab and select the Enterprise Wiki template for the site.

7. Enter primary and secondary site administrators, making sure to include yourself as one or the other so that you have access to the site.

8. Click OK.

To modify the site templates available for subsite creation from the site directory, follow these steps:

1. From the home page of the new site directory in the Wikis namespace, click Site Actions.

2. Choose Site Settings from the Site Settings menu.

3. Select Page layouts and site templates from the Look and Feel section.

4. Select the Subsites can only use the following site templates radio button.

5. Add Wiki Site and Blog, as shown in Figure 21.4.

FIGURE 21.4

Restricting the subsites to only the Wiki site and blog templates

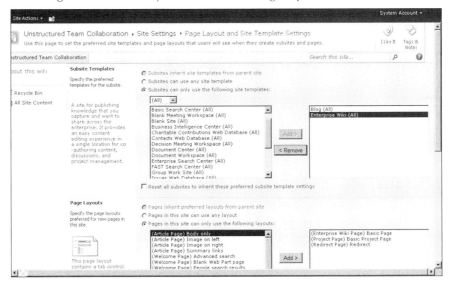

6. Click OK.

Creating a custom sales pipeline list

To track sales opportunities, you are going to create a custom SharePoint list for the inside and outside sales people to use. The customer contacts are stored in an SQL Server database used by the CRM application, so that you have three high-level steps for implementing the custom sales pipeline list:

1. Creating an External Content Type for the customer contacts so that they can be used in the sales pipeline list.

2. Creating and customizing the sales pipeline list.

3. Creating the default view for the sales home page.

Creating an External Content Type for customer contacts

The External Content Type enables you to refer to the customer contacts in your sales pipeline list. To enable this functionality, you need to create and configure the External Content Type in SharePoint Designer 2010.

1. Navigate to your root site collection and select Site Actions ⇨ Edit in SharePoint Designer or launch SharePoint Designer 2010 and open your root site collection from there.

2. Select External Content Types from the Site Objects navigation pane.

3. Click External Content Type from the New section on the Ribbon. A New External Content Type tabbed page appears in the main area.

4. Click the links for Name and Display Name and enter Customers.

5. Click the link on the External System prompt to open the Operation Designer page.

6. Click Add Connection and select the SQL Server data source type.

7. Fill out the appropriate connection properties for the data source selected.

8. Click OK. The Data Source Explorer populates with the data source items.

9. Define Operations. The next step is to define operations. An external content type must at least have a Read List and Read Item operation. Right click a data source entity to define the appropriate operations.

10. Create Read Item Operation. Select New Read Item Operation from the Operations menu. The Read Item operation wizard appears. Enter an Operation Name and an Operation Display Name (or keep the defaults). Click Next.

11. Select the identifier of the data source entity and enter a display name. Click Next.

12. Select the attributes or columns to return. You may optionally change the display name of the fields here. Notice you may not be able to generate an update operation if all columns are not returned.

13. Click Finish. The Read Item operation appears in the Operation list.

14. **Create Read List Operation.** Select New Read List Operation from the Operations menu. The Read List operation wizard appears. Enter an Operation Name and an Operation Display Name (or keep the defaults). Click Next.

    The filter parameters page appears and you are warned about having a limiting filter. The filter that is being recommended will indeed reduce the amount of records or list items that are returned, but this may restrict users from seeing all available data. A more useful filter is one that an end user can use to find specific sets of data.

15. **Create Filter Parameters.** Click Add Filter Parameter and then click the Click to Add link. The filter configuration dialog appears.

16. **Enter the following values as shown in Figure 21.9:**

Name:	Last Name
Filter Type:	Wildcard
Filter Field:	Last Name
Ignore Filter:	Check
Custom value:	*
Is default value:	Check
Use to create match list:	Check

17. **Click OK.** There are warning messages. Change the Data Source Element to Last Name and enter a * in the Default Value (even though it is a drop-down you may enter your own values as well). Click Next.

18. **Return Parameter Configuration.** Select the Last Name column and check the Show In Picker check box as shown. Click Finish.

19. **Save the External Content Type.** Click File ⇨ Save to save the external content type back to SharePoint. Click on the External Content Types breadcrumb tab to confirm the new entry exists.

Creating sales pipeline list

After you have added the BCS application definition, you are going to create the sales pipeline list to track opportunities with these fields:

- Opportunity Name
- Contact Name, phone number, e-mail, company name (from BDC)
- Consulting Area (AppDev, Networking, or SI)
- Chance of Closing (10, 30, 60, 90, 100)
- Sales Status (in progress, proposal preparation, proposal delivered, won, lost)
- Estimated Revenue
- Account Manager (person)

To create the sales pipeline list, follow these steps:

1. Click More Options from the Site Actions menu in the top-left corner of the sales site home page.

2. Select Custom List from the Custom Lists section.

3. Enter the Name as Sales Pipeline and select that you would like the list to appear on the QuickLaunch (under More Options).

4. Click Create.

To add your columns to the sales pipeline custom list, follow these steps:

1. Open the sales opportunity list and choose List Settings from the List tab on the Ribbon.

2. Select the Title column. Change the Column name to **Opportunity Name**.

3. Click OK.

4. Click Create column in the Columns section.

5. Enter Contact Name as the column name and select External Data as the column type.

6. Select the contacts External Content Type using the external content type button next to the Type field.

7. Select Last Name as the display field.

8. Select that you want to include company name, e-mail, first name, and phone in the additional fields section, as shown in Figure 21.5.

FIGURE 21.5

Configuring the External Data columns for the sales pipeline list

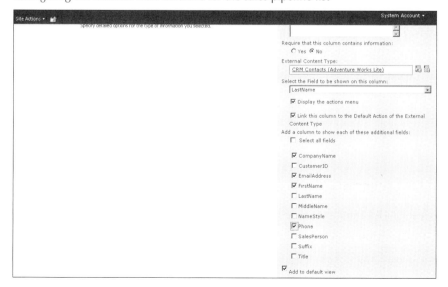

9. Click OK.

10. To create the consulting area as a site column so that it is usable throughout the portal, navigate to the home page of the portal and choose Site Settings from the Site Settings menu in the Site Actions control.

11. Click Site columns in the Galleries section.

12. Click Create from the top navigation bar.

13. Enter Consulting Area as the column name and select Choice as the column type.

14. Enter App Dev, Networking, and SI as the choice values on separate lines.

15. Click OK.

16. Navigate back to your sales opportunity list settings and click Add from existing site columns in the Columns section.

17. Select Consulting Area from the Available Site columns and click Add.

18. Click OK.

19. Click Create column in the Columns section.

20. Enter Chance of Closing as the column name and select Choice as the column type.

21. Enter 10, 30, 60, 90, 100 as the choice values on separate lines.

22. Click OK.

23. Click Create column in the Columns section.

24. Enter Sales Status as the column name and select Choice as the column type.

25. Enter in progress, proposal preparation, proposal delivered, won, and lost as the choice values on separate lines.

26. Click OK.

27. Click Create column in the Columns section.

28. Enter Estimated Revenue as the column name and select Currency as the column type.

29. Click OK.

30. Click Create column in the Columns section.

31. Enter Account Manager as the column name and select Person or Group as the column type.

32. Click OK.

Creating sales pipeline list views

You are going to create two views for the sales pipeline list. The first groups and totals all active opportunities (not won or lost) by consulting area and chance of closing and will be used on the sales home page. The second view shows each sales person which opportunities are in his or her pipeline.

To create the Active Opportunities view, follow these steps:

1. From the List tab on the Ribbon, choose Create View.

2. Choose Standard View.

3. Enter Active Opportunities as the view name and select Make this the default view.

4. Deselect Attachments, Contact:email, Contact:workphone, Consulting area, and Chance of Closing fields in the Columns section.

5. Select Estimated Revenue in the Sorting column and select Show items in descending order.

6. In the Filter section, select "show items when the following is true" and select Sales Status is not equal to lost and Sales Status is not equal to won, as shown in Figure 21.6.

7. Expand the Group By section and select Chance of Closing in descending order as the first group-by field, and Consulting Area in ascending order as the second group by field as shown in Figure 21.7.

8. Select Expanded in the By default, show groupings field.

9. Expand the Totals section and choose Sum for the Estimated Revenue field.

10. Click OK.

11. Review your new default view, as shown in Figure 21.8.

FIGURE 21.6

Configuring the filter values for the Active Opportunities view

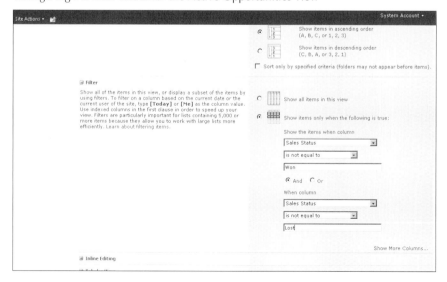

FIGURE 21.7

Configuring the Group By settings for the Active Opportunities view

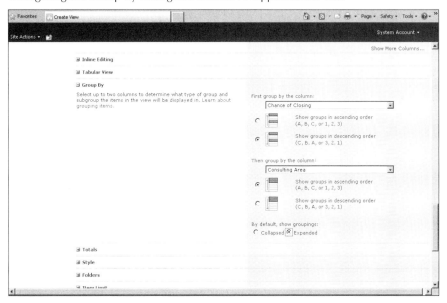

FIGURE 21.8

The Active Opportunities view of the sales pipeline list

To create the My Opportunities view, follow these steps:

1. From the List tab on the Ribbon, choose Create View.

2. Choose Standard View.

3. Enter My Opportunities as the view name and do not select that it is a default view.

4. Deselect Account Rep, and Chance of Closing in the Columns section.

5. In the Filter section, select show items when the following is true, and select Account Rep is equal to [Me].

6. Expand the group by section and select Chance of Closing in descending order as the first group by field.

7. Select Expanded in the By default, show groupings field.

8. Click OK.

9. Review your new default view.

Standardizing project documentation

To ensure that documentation is tagged consistently across projects, and that project templates are standardized across the organization and easily updated from a central location, you are going to create a content type for project documentation (the statement of work, in this case) and a template site for projects. This process involves several steps:

1. Create Site Columns for project documentation.

2. Create content type for Statement of Work (SOW) project documentation.

3. Associate SOW template with content type.

4. Create sample project site and associate SOW content type and other default lists for projects.

5. Create project site template from sample project site and add to site gallery.

Creating site columns

To create the site columns that will provide the metadata for the statement of work project documentation, follow these steps:

1. From the home page of the top level site of the portal, click Site Actions.

2. Choose Site Settings from the Site Settings menu.

3. Under the Galleries section, select Site columns.

4. Click Create.

5. Enter these values:

   - Column name: Project Status
   - The type of information in this column is: Choice

- Put the site column into: New group: Project Management
- Description: Current status of active project
- Require that this column contains information: No
- Type each choice on a separate line

6. **Leave the default values for the remaining items and click OK.**

You can create additional site columns for your other project documentation if desired.

Creating a site content type

In this section, you create a site content type using the site column(s) you created in the previous section.

1. **From the home page of the top level site of the portal, click Site Actions.**
2. **Under Galleries click Site content types.**
3. **Click Create.**
4. **Enter these values:**
   - Name: Statement of Work
   - Parent Content Type: Document from the Document Content Types
   - Put this site content type into: Click New group: and enter **Project Management** for the new group name
5. **Click OK.**
6. **At the bottom of the Site Content Type: Statement of Work page, click Add from existing site columns to add the columns you created earlier in Step 1.**
7. **From the Select columns from drop-down menu, choose Project Management.**
8. **Click the Add button to add the Project Status column.** Your screen should look like Figure 21.9.
9. **Click OK.**

Adding a template to the content type

Adding a template to a site content type allows you to associate a document with the content type. If you update the document template, you can update it at the content type, and all new content types will then use the updated template.

1. **From the home page of the top level site of the portal, click Site Actions.**
2. **Choose Site Settings from the Site Settings menu.**
3. **Under Galleries, click Site content types.**
4. **Click the Statement of Work content type.**
5. **In the Settings section, click Advanced settings.**
6. **Select Upload a new document template and browse to your SOW template.**

7. Select Yes in the "Should this content type be read-only?" field so that only administrators can modify the statement of work content type, as shown in Figure 21.10.

8. Click OK.

Adding columns to site content type: Statement of Work

Associating a template with the content type

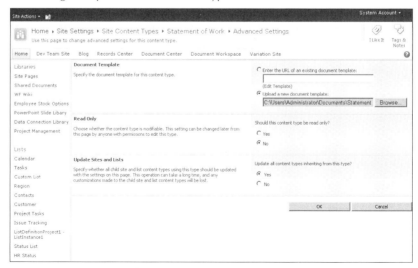

Creating a Project Team site

You must add the statement of work content type in a project site so that site can be used as a project site template. To create and customize this site, follow these steps:

1. Click Site Actions in the upper right-hand corner of the screen.

2. Choose Create Site.

3. Enter the following values:

   - Title: **Project Management**

   - URL name: **http://(your server)/project management**

4. Leave the other default values and click Create.

5. Click Site Actions in the upper right-hand corner of the new team site.

6. Click Create from the drop-down menu.

7. Under Libraries click Document Library.

8. Enter Statement of Work for the name and click Create.

9. From the Ribbon under the Library tab, click Library Settings.

   Notice that there are no options available for working with content types under the current options. You must first enable content types.

10. Under General Settings, click Advanced settings.

11. Select Yes under Allow the management of content types.

12. Leave the default options for remaining items and click OK.

13. To remove the default content type, Document, and add your new one, under Content Types click the default content type Document.

14. Under Settings click Delete this content type and click OK to confirm.

15. Under Content Types click Add from existing site content types.

16. In the Select site content types from drop-down choose Project Management.

17. Click Add to add the Statement of Work content type and click OK (Figure 18.6).

18. Click Statement of Work in the breadcrumb link at the top to return to the document library.

19. In the Documents Ribbon click the arrow next to New and you will see the Statement of Work template in the New drop-down, as shown in Figure 21.11.

20. Choose the Statement of Work template to open a new document.

21. Click Save to save your new SOW.

22. Click OK to save it with a new document name.

23. Choose Project Status from the drop-down menu. Click OK.

FIGURE 21.11

The New drop-down menu

Creating a custom site template for projects

Now that you have created a project site and added the Statement of Work content type, create a site template from that site so that all new project sites can be provisioned with that content type already added. To do this, follow these steps:

1. From any page in the project site, click Site Actions from the upper-left corner.

2. Choose Site Settings.

3. Click Save site as template in the Look and Feel section.

4. Enter Projects in the File name field.

5. Enter Projects in the Template name field and a description, as shown in Figure 21.12.

6. Click OK.

7. To confirm that your template has been added to the site template gallery for the site directory, browse to the site directory home page.

8. Click Create Site. You should see a new tab for Custom that contains the Projects template, as shown in Figure 21.13.

FIGURE 21.12

Creating a new site template

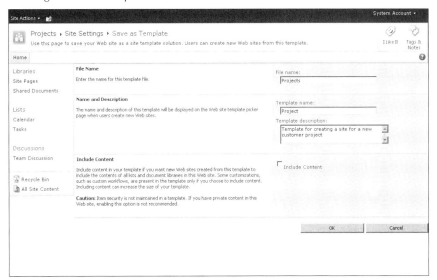

FIGURE 21.13

Viewing the new project template

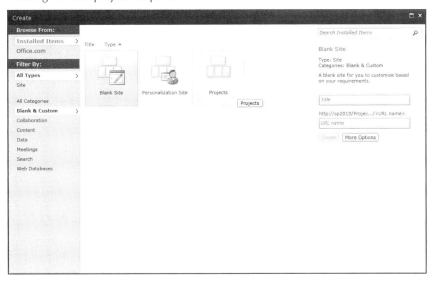

Create project status tracking for PMs

You can now build out the lists that will be used for project managers and executives to track project activity and status. There are three components to this process:

1. Create Project Status List for overall project tracking
2. Create Milestone Tracking list for tracking project milestones
3. Create PM view of lists for Project Central home page

Creating a project status list

To track active projects, you must create a project list that provides all the key information for projects that you are delivering on. This list tracks:

- **Project name:** Name of project.
- **Contact:** The customer contact stored in the CRM database and accessible to the project list by use of the external content type that you created and added in the sales pipeline section of this chapter.
- **Project code:** Unique code for each project that will be used in this project list and in the accounting and time tracking systems to identify projects.
- **Consulting Area:** Selection of primary group that is responsible for the project from the values provided by the site column you created in the sales pipeline section of this chapter.
- **Project Status:** Choice of Active, Closed, and Waiting for Signoff.
- **PO Number:** Reference to the PO number provided by the customer.
- **PO Amount:** Amount of project.
- **Project Manager:** Choice of project manager alias.

To create this list, follow these steps:

1. Choose Create from the Site Actions menu in the top-left corner of the project central site home page.
2. Select Custom List from the Custom Lists section.
3. Enter the Name as Project Status and select that you would like the list displayed on the QuickLaunch.
4. Click Create.

To add your columns to project status custom list, follow these steps:

1. Open the sales opportunity list and choose List Settings from the Settings menu.
2. Select the Title column. Change the Column name to **Project Name**.
3. Click OK.
4. Click Create Column in the Columns section.

5. Enter Contact as the column name and select External Data as the column type.

6. Select the contacts external content type using the external content type button next to the Type field.

7. Select Last Name as the display field.

8. Select that you want to include company name, first name, e-mail, and phone in the additional fields section.

9. Click OK.

10. Click Create column in the columns section to create a calculated column that will return a unique four-digit number for each project code.

11. Enter Project Code as the column name.

12. Select Calculated as the column type.

13. In the Formula field, enter [ID]+1000.

14. Select Single line of text as the type of data returned by this formula.

15. Click OK.

16. To add the Consulting Area column, select Add from existing site columns in the columns section.

17. Select Consulting Area from the Available site columns and click Add.

18. Click OK.

19. Click Create column in the Columns section.

20. Enter Project Status as the column name and select Choice as the column type.

21. Enter Active, Closed, and Waiting for Signoff as the choice values on separate lines.

22. Click OK.

23. Click Create column in the Columns section.

24. Enter PO Number as the column name and select Single Line of Text as the column type.

25. Click OK.

26. Click Create column in the Columns section.

27. Enter PO Amount as the column name and select Currency as the column type.

28. Click OK.

29. Create column in the Columns section.

30. Enter Project Manager as the column name and select Person or Group as the column type.

31. Click OK.

Creating the milestone tracking list

The milestone tracking list provides a place where project managers can enter and track milestones for their projects, and the overall organization can get an idea of upcoming milestones. To create this list, use the Task List template and modify the fields for your purposes.

To create the milestone tracking list, follow these steps:

1. Select Create from the Site Actions menu in the top-left corner of the project central site home page.

2. Select Tasks from the Tracking section.

3. Enter the Name as Milestone Tracking and select that you would like the list displayed on the QuickLaunch.

4. Click Create.

To customize the columns for your milestone tracking list, follow these steps:

1. Open the milestone tracking list and choose List Settings from the Settings menu.

2. Select the Title column. Change the Column name to Milestone Name.

3. Click OK.

4. Click the Assigned To field and rename to Project Manager.

5. Click OK.

6. Click the Task Group field and select Delete.

7. Click OK to confirm deletion.

8. Click Create column.

9. Enter Project Code as the Column name and select Lookup as the column type.

10. Select Project status as the Get information from field and Project code as the In this column field, as shown in Figure 21.14.

11. To add the Consulting Area column, select Add from existing site columns in the Columns section.

12. Select Consulting Area from the Available site columns and click Add.

13. Click OK.

Creating the project central list view

We need to create a view for each of the consulting areas that shows active and upcoming milestones. To create these views, follow these steps:

1. From the View menu in the upper-right corner of the list, choose Create View.

2. Select Active Tasks in the Starting from an existing view section.

3. Enter Active AppDev Milestones as the view name and do not select that it is a default view.

4. Select Project code in the Columns section.

5. In the Filter section, add an additional filter for when Consulting Area is equal to App Dev, and make sure that the criteria is set to And between the two filter sections, as shown in Figure 21.15.

FIGURE 21.14

Creating a lookup field for project code

FIGURE 21.15

Adding an additional view filter for the Consulting Area

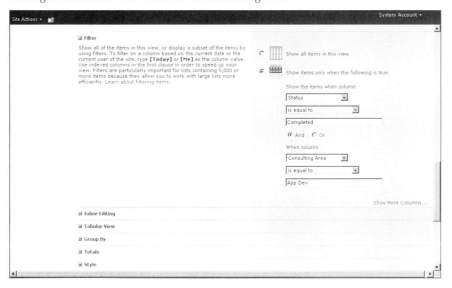

6. Click OK.

7. Repeat Steps 1 to 5 for the Infrastructure and networking active tasks view, replacing the filter criteria with the appropriate area.

Executive Indicators

The executives want to see a status overview of the sales pipeline and project status to identify areas that might need help and focus. To achieve this objective, you are going to create sales and project Indicators for the Executive site main page by following three high-level steps:

1. Create the views for the sales pipeline to support the Indicators for all pipelines for all opportunities that have 60 percent or better chance of closing and opportunities that have 60 percent or better chance of closing for each consulting area.

2. Create sales Indicators.

3. Create project Indicators.

4. Add the Status List Web Part to the executive home page.

Creating the sales views to support Indicators

You need to create four views of the sales lists to support the Indicators you want to configure:

- 60 percent or higher of closing for all opportunities

- 60 percent or higher of closing for App Dev opportunities

- 60 percent or higher of closing for Networking opportunities

- 60 percent or higher of closing for Infrastructure opportunities

To create these views, follow these steps:

1. From the List tab on the Ribbon of the sales pipeline list, choose Create View.

2. Choose Standard View.

3. Enter 60% Opportunities as the view name.

4. Scroll to the Filter section and select Show items only when the following is true, and select Chance of closing is not equal to 10 *or* Chance of closing is not equal to 30.

5. Click OK.

To create the view for each consulting area, follow these steps:

1. From the List tab on the Ribbon of the sales pipeline list, choose Create View.

2. Select 60% Opportunities in the Starting from an existing view section.

3. Enter 60% AppDev Opportunities as the view name.

4. Scroll down to the Filter section and click Show More Columns.

5. Select "And" between the existing filters and the new one and set the new filter to be Consulting Area equals App Dev.

6. Click OK.

Repeat Steps 1 to 6 for the Infrastructure and Networking active tasks view, replacing the filter criteria with the appropriate area.

Creating sales Indicators

You can now add an Indicator for each view that you created in the previous section.

1. Navigate to the Management site.

2. Select More Options from the Site Actions menu.

3. Select List in the Filter By section.

4. Select Status List from the Tracking List category section.

5. Enter the name of the Status list as Organizational Indicators **and click Create.**

6. Choose Indicator using data in SharePoint list from the New menu.

7. Enter All Sales Opportunities **in the Name field.**

8. Enter the location of the sales pipeline list and select the 60% opportunity view in the SharePoint List and View section, as shown in Figure 21.16.

FIGURE 21.16

Entering the list and view for an Indicator

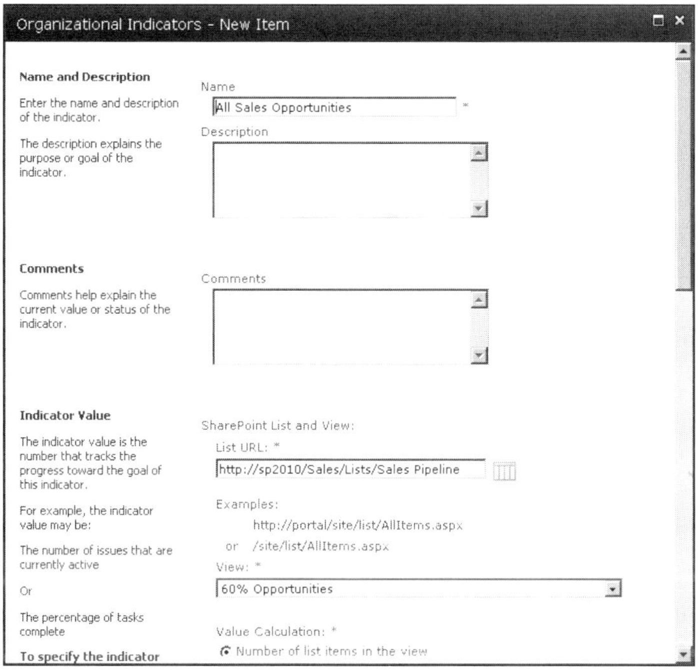

721

9. Select "Calculation using all the list items in the view" and select that you would like to sum the estimated revenue field.

10. Enter the goal (green) and warning (yellow) values for the organization. This example used 4,000,000 for the green value and 3,500,000 for the yellow value.

11. Enter the link to the sales pipeline view in the Details Link section for drilling down on the Indicator.

12. **Click OK.** Repeat Steps 6 to 12 for the AppDev, Networking, and Infrastructure views/indicators using 1,000,000 for the green value and 500,000 for the yellow value.

Creating projects Indicators

You will now add Indicators for your project milestones. To do this, follow these steps:

1. Choose Indicator using data in SharePoint list from the New menu.

2. Enter AppDev Project Status in the Name field.

3. Enter the location of the milestone tracking list and select the Active AppDev Milestones view in the SharePoint List and View section.

4. Select Percentage of the list items in the view where and enter % complete is less than 100 *and* Due Date is less than [Today], as shown in Figure 21.17.

Calculating percentage of not completed items that are past due

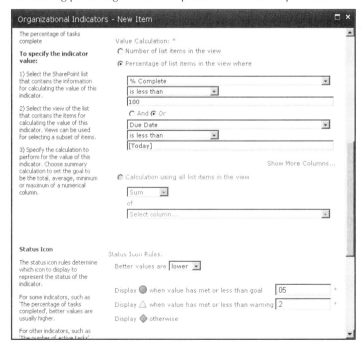

5. **Change the better values to be lower and enter the goal (green) and warning (yellow) values for the organization.** This example used 5 (5%) for the green value and 30 (30%) for the yellow value.

6. **Enter the link to the milestone tracking list in the Details Link section for drilling down on the Indicator.**

7. **Click OK.** Repeat Steps 1 to 7 for the Networking and Infrastructure views/indicators.

Adding the Status List Web Part to the Management home page

To highlight the importance of the Indicator list items, add them to the home page of the management site so that executives can easily see them every time they visit the site. To do this, follow these steps:

1. Navigate to the home page of the Management collaboration site.

2. Choose the Site Actions menu, select Edit Page.

3. Click in the content area where you want to add the Indicators and select Web Part from the Insert tab on the Ribbon.

4. Select Status List from the Business Data section.

5. Click Add.

6. From the Edit menu of the Status List Web Part, select Edit Web Part.

7. Browse or enter the path to the Organizational Indicators in the Indicator List field.

8. Select Traffic Lights in the Change Icon field as shown in Figure 21.18

FIGURE 21.18

Configuring the Status List Web Part

9. Click OK.

10. Click Save & Close from the Ribbon.

11. Confirm that the Status list has been added to the page and looks similar to Figure 21.19.

FIGURE 21.19

Status List Web Part on the Management home page

Creating an accounting dashboard

To create a central location so that the accounting department and project managers can see the invoices and time submitted for a project and date range, create an accounting dashboard. This dashboard will use a Datasheet Web Part to display the invoicing data from a SharePoint list and a Report Viewer Web Part to display the time tracking data from an SQL Server database.

You will complete the following high-level tasks to create this dashboard:

1. Create an invoice list in SharePoint by importing an invoicing spreadsheet.

2. Publish a reporting services report for the time tracking information.

3. Create a dashboard page that hosts the Report Viewer and Datasheet Web Parts and filters.

4. Implement the data view of the invoicing list.

5. Add the Report Viewer Web Part to the dashboard page and connect the filters.

Note

If you have an Enterprise license and are using Performance Point Services, you may also create scorecards, dashboards, and reports using PPS to include within your Accounting dashboard page. ■

Create an invoicing list by importing a spreadsheet

You have an Excel spreadsheet for invoicing data that you will use to create the invoicing list and import the existing data. To do this, follow these steps:

1. Select View All Site Content from the Site Actions menu of the Accounting site.

2. Select Create in the top navigation bar.

3. Select Import Spreadsheet from the Blank & Custom Lists section.

4. Enter Invoices as the name for your list and enter or browse to the location of the spreadsheet.

5. Click Import.

6. Select Range of Cells in the Range Type Field and then click the – symbol to the right of the Select Range field.

7. Drag the selector circle around the data that you want to include in your spreadsheet import, and click the icon with the red down arrow to the right of your named range, as shown in Figure 21.20.

FIGURE 21.20

Using the Range Selector to define your spreadsheet import

8. Click Import.

Publishing a reporting services report to the report library

In this section, you publish the time tracking report with defined parameters for start date, end date, and project code to your report library.

Cross-Reference

To publish a reporting services report to SharePoint and use the Report Viewer Web Part, you must have a SharePoint server in which SQL Server 2008 R2 has been installed and the Reporting Services add-in for SharePoint 2008 R2 has been installed. See Chapter 15 for more information about configuring these components. ■

To publish a report to a SharePoint report library, follow these steps:

1. Open your report project in SQL Server Business Intelligence Development Studio.

2. Right-click your report project and select Properties. Set the path to the report library, as shown in Figure 21.21.

3. From the Build menu, choose Deploy <project name>.

FIGURE 21.21

Setting the publishing URLs

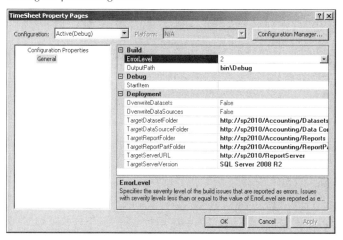

Note

You need to create the Reports library and Data Connections libraries on the Accounting team site. ■

Creating a dashboard page

To create the dashboard page that will host your connected Web Parts, follow these steps:

1. Browse to your Accounting site.

2. From the Site Actions menu select New Page.

3. Select Enter Accounting Dashboard.

4. Click Create.

Implementing the Data View Web Part for the invoicing list

In this section, you use the Data View Web Part to add the invoicing list data to the accounting dashboard. You use the Data View Web Part because a SharePoint list can connect to only one filter and you want to connect to three.

1. Open the accounting dashboard page on which you want to add the Data View Web Part using SharePoint Designer.

2. Click the middle-right zone.

3. Choose Insert Data View from the Data View menu.

4. Select the invoices list from the Data Source Library tool pane in the right-hand column and select Show Data.

5. Select the QB invoice, Date, Amount, and Project No. fields by holding down the Ctrl key while selecting the fields you want with your mouse.

6. Click the Insert Selected Fields as multiple item view.

7. Right-click the Data View Web Part and choose Show Common Control Tasks. Click the Filter link.

8. Select the Date in the field name field, the comparison type as greater than or equal to, and Create a new parameter as the value. In the dialog box that appears, enter **StartDate** as the parameter name as shown in Figure 21.22. Click OK.

FIGURE 21.22

Entering the parameter name

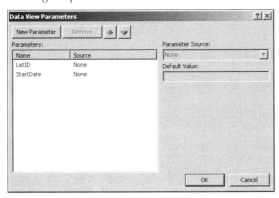

9. Click the Click here to create new clause link.

10. Select the Date in the field name field, the comparison type as less than or equal to, and Create a new parameter as the value. In the dialog box that appears, enter **EndDate** and click OK.

11. Click the Click here to create new clause link.

12. **Select Project No. in the field name field, the comparison type as equals, and Create a new parameter as the value.** In the dialog box that appears, enter **ProjNo** and click OK. The filters should appear as they do in Figure 21.23.

13. Choose Save from File menu to save the page.

FIGURE 21.23

Reviewing the three filter parameters for the data view

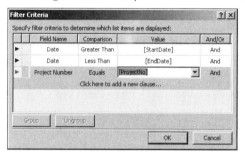

Adding the Report view Web Part and connecting the filters

In this section, you add the Report view Web Part to display your timesheet report and connect the report to the Filter Web Parts so that the Filter Web Parts provide the report parameters. To do this, follow these steps:

1. **Open the accounting dashboard page and choose Edit Page from the Site Actions menu in the top-left corner.**

2. **Click Add a Web Part in the zone that you want to add the Report Viewer Web Part.**

3. **Scroll to the Miscellaneous section and select SQL Server Reporting Services Report Viewer and click Add as shown in Figure 21.24.**

4. **From the Edit menu in the Report Viewer Web Part, select Modify Shared Web Part.**

5. **In the Report field, type the URL of your report or browse to select your report.**

6. **Click Apply.**

7. **Click on the right side of the view section to expand.**

8. **Select whether you would like a full, navigation, or no toolbar in the Toolbar field.** The full toolbar presents the users with the Actions menu so that they can Open, Print, or Export the report, the refresh control, the control to go forward/backward between pages, the ability to zoom in/out and search within the report, as shown in Figure 21.25. The navigation toolbar presents only the control to go forward/backward between pages.

FIGURE 21.24

Adding the Report Viewer Web Part to the page

FIGURE 21.25

The Report Viewer Web Part with the full toolbar option

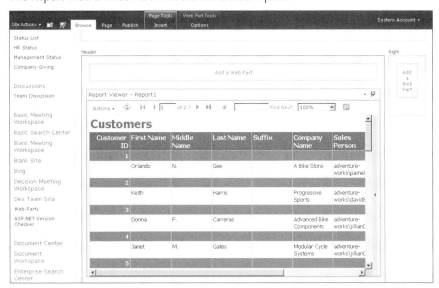

9. **If you have parameters configured for your report, select whether you want the prompt area to be displayed, collapsed, or hidden in the Prompt Area field.** The prompt area is where users can enter the parameters, and if displayed by default, they can click on it to hide it, and if collapsed by default, they can click to expand it. If the prompt area is hidden, the user cannot enter the parameters.

10. **If you have a document map configured for your report, select whether you want the document map to be displayed, collapsed, or hidden in the Document Map field.** The document map is a control that allows users to navigate directly to a section or sub-report. If the document area map is hidden, it will not be available for users.

    If you want to display the document area map, enter the width for it in the Document Area Map Width field.

11. **If your report has parameters, click on the right side of the parameter section and click Load Parameters if they have not been loaded since the report was configured.**

12. **Select whether you want to use the default setting for the parameter or override the parameter setting with your own value for each parameter, as shown in Figure 21.26.**

13. **Click OK and then click Save & Close from the Ribbon.**

FIGURE 21.26

Configuring the report parameters

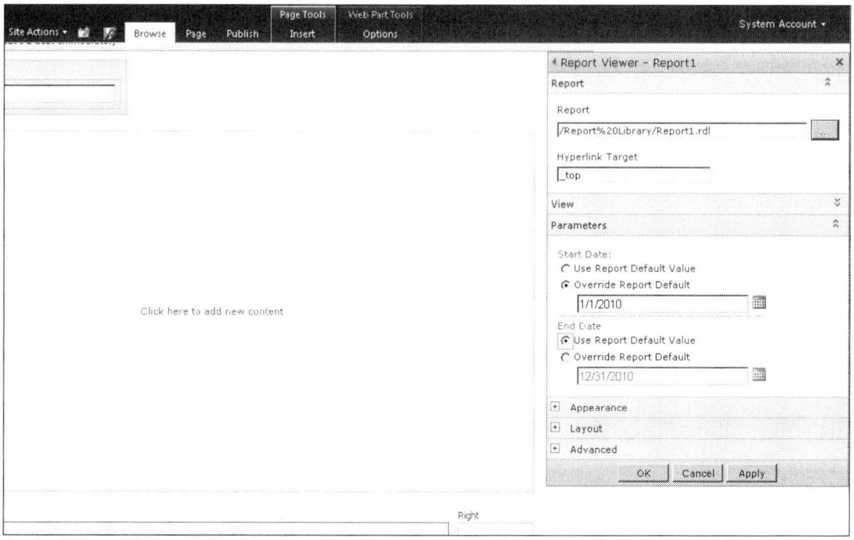

Now you are going to add two date filters and a text filter to the dashboard page by following these steps:

1. Open the accounting dashboard page and choose Edit Page from the Site Actions menu in the top-left corner.

2. Select Add a Web Part within a zone on the page.

3. **Select the Date filter and click Add.** Because you have both a start date and end date for our example, you add this filter twice.

4. From the Edit menu on the first Date Filter Web Part, select Edit Web Part.

5. **Type the name of the filter field in the Filter Name field and the default value in the Default Value section, as shown in Figure 21.27.** The default value can be set to no default value, a specific date, or an offset date calculated based on the current date.

6. Click OK.

FIGURE 21.27

Configuring the Date Filter Web Part

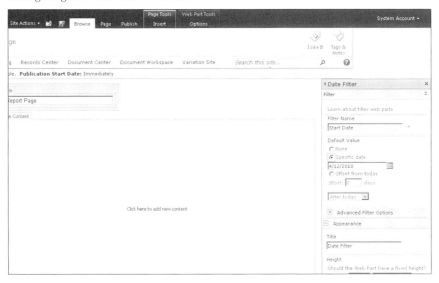

The Web Part now appears in the left column and shows a warning that the filter is not connected. To connect the filter Web Part to your report, follow these steps:

1. **Open the page on which you want to add the Connect the filter Web Part and Report Viewer Web Part and select Edit Page from the Site Actions menu in the top-left corner.**

2. **Select Connections ➪ Send Filter Values To ➪ [Your Report Web Part] from the Edit menu of the filter Web Part, as shown in Figure 21.28.**

FIGURE 21.28

Configuring the filter Web Part connections

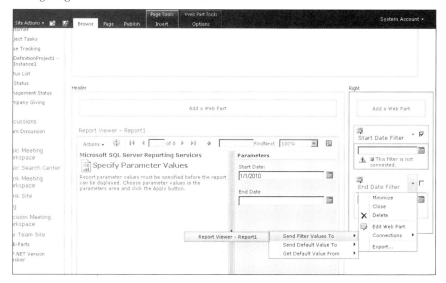

3. Select the filter parameter that you want to connect to from the Configure Connection dialog box, as shown in Figure 21.29.

FIGURE 21.29

Select the report parameter to which the filter is connected.

4. Click Finish and exit Edit Mode.

You can now see the filter Web Parts on the report page, and if you change the filter values, the report will refresh based on your inputted values, as shown in Figure 21.30.

FIGURE 21.30

Date Filter Web Parts that are connected to a Report Viewer Web Part

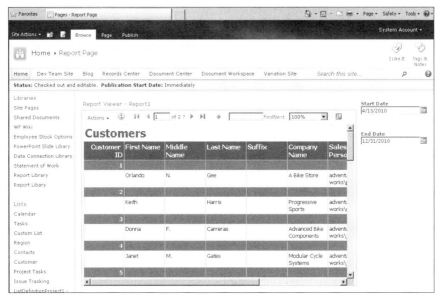

Excel Services

This scenario uses Excel Services to expose spreadsheets that are used to track what resource positions have the most bench time. This provides a communication path between the project managers and the recruiting team so that the recruiting team knows what positions to focus on. While you are configuring Excel Services, you are going to add a trusted path for the Accounting library as well because you know that they will be distributing ad-hoc financial reports.

To accomplish your architecture to meet this requirement, you have two high-level steps:

1. Add the library that the project managers use to store the resource mapping spreadsheet and the accounting document library as trusted Excel Services file locations.

2. Publish the resource spreadsheet to the project management library and add the Excel Services Web Part to the recruiting home page.

Adding trusted file locations

You are going to add two trusted file locations to the Excel Services configuration — one for the resource management spreadsheet and one for the accounting reports. To add a trusted file location for the resource spreadsheets, follow these steps:

1. Open the administration page for your Excel Services Application.

2. Select Trusted file locations.

3. Select Add Trusted File Location in the top navigation bar.

4. Enter the address for the project management document in the Address field.

5. Select that the location is a SharePoint site.

6. Leave the option to trust child libraries or directories cleared by unchecking the Children trusted box.

7. Enter volatile function cache lifetime value of 86,400 (24 hours) because this data is not updated frequently.

8   Set the Allow External Data field to none.

9. Deselect that you want to allow user-defined functions in the Allow User Defined Functions section.

10. Click OK.

For the accounting spreadsheets, you know that you have a sophisticated group of spreadsheet users that will be accessing data from many different sources. Because of those factors, you are going to add a trusted file location for the accounting site with more external data capability than the settings you used for the resource management spreadsheet. To add a trusted file location for the accounting spreadsheets, follow these steps:

1. Open the administration page for your Excel Services Application.

2. Select Trusted file locations.

3. Select Add Trusted File Location in the top navigation bar.

4. Enter the address for the accounting subsite in the Address field.

5. Select that the location is a SharePoint site.

6. Enable the option to trust child libraries or directories by checking the Children trusted box.

7. Enter a volatile function cache lifetime value of 300 (5 minutes).

8. Set the Allow External Data option to Trusted data connection libraries and embedded sources.

9. Select to allow user-defined functions in the Allow User Defined Functions section.

10. Click OK.

Publishing resource Excel file

Now that you have trusted the document library on the project management site that will store the resource management spreadsheet, you can publish your resource file to the site. However, the spreadsheet has four worksheets that you want to expose, so you will first name those ranges so that the users can flip between them. To do this, follow these steps:

1. Open the Excel spreadsheet, select the cells that you want to name on the first worksheet, right-click your selection, and choose Define name from the menu.

2. Enter a name (no spaces or special characters allowed). Click OK.

    Repeat Step 2 for the AppDev, Networking, and Infrastructure tabs and ranges.

3. From the main Excel File menu, choose Save & Send and then click on Save to SharePoint.

4. Click Publish Options located on the top right of the Save & Send page.

5. In the Show tab, select Items in the Workbook from the drop-down menu and select All Named Ranges, as shown in Figure 21.31.

FIGURE 21.31

Configuring the Excel Services options

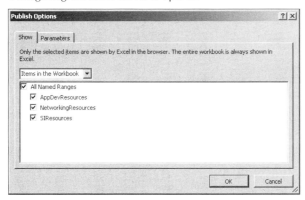

6. Click OK to exit the Excel Services Options dialog box.

7. Click a location to save the file. Click OK.

To add the Excel Web Access Web Part to the recruiting page, follow these steps:

1. Browse to the home page of the recruiting site and choose Edit Page from the Site Actions menu in the top-left corner.

2. Click Add a Web Part in the left zone and select Excel Web Access from the Business Data Web Part list.

3. Click Add.

4. From the edit menu in the top-right corner of your Excel Web Access Web Part, choose Modify Shared Web Part.

5. In the Workbook field, enter or browse to the URL of the published resource management file.

6. Enter the default tab that you want to show in the Named Item field, as shown in Figure 21.32.

FIGURE 21.32

Configuring the Excel Web Access Web Part for your named range

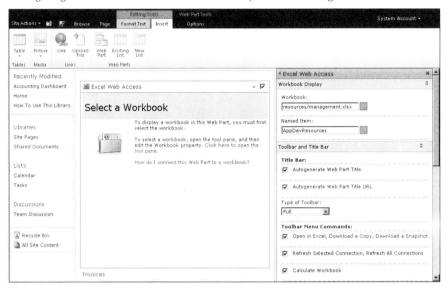

7. Click OK.

Configuring file share content source

To make the archive content on the file share available, add a content source for that file share and create a search scope for the site collection to expose that content.

To implement the content source for the file share, follow these steps:

1. Navigate to the administration page for Search Service.

2. Select Content sources and crawl schedules.

3. Click New Content Source in the top navigation bar.

4. Enter Fileshare in the Name field.

5. Enter the address of the file share as \\server\share in the start address box.

6. Set the schedule for the full crawl and incremental crawls in the crawl schedules section. For the file share crawl, stagger the schedule to start at 4 a.m. to give SharePoint enough time to crawl the SharePoint sites (starting at midnight), and only perform incremental crawls every 6 hours (360 minutes) because the content should not be changing frequently.

7. Select to start a full crawl immediately.

8. Click OK.

To define a scope for your site collection, follow these steps:

1. Go to the top level site of the portal and select Site Settings from the Site Actions menu in the top-left corner.

2. Select Search scopes from the Site Collection Administration section.

3. Select New Scope from the top navigation bar.

4. Enter file share scope in the Title field and provide your contact information in the Contact field.

5. Select whether to use the default Search results page and click OK.

6. From the View Scopes page, choose View Properties and Rules from the drop-down menu on the scope title that you just added.

7. Select New Rule.

8. Select hostname and enter the hostname of the file share.

9. Select to include content based on the rule.

10. Select OK.

You are going to enter keywords because you know that SOWs have also been named Statements of Work in the past and so to ensure that historical SOWs are returned with our newly published SOWs, we add the keywords as detailed in the following steps:

1. Go to the top level of the portal and choose Site Settings from the Site Actions menu in the top-left corner.

2. Choose Search keywords from the Site Collection Administration menu.

3. Select Add Keyword from the top navigation bar.

4. Enter SOWs as the keyword phrase.

5. Enter SOW, Statements of Work, Statement of Work in the synonyms field.

6. Click Add Best Bet to create a link to the best bet content on the project central site. Enter the URL, Title, and Description for the project central best bet.

7. Enter the definition for the keyword in the Keyword Definition section.

8. Enter your contact information as the contact for the keyword.

9. Enter the start date and no end date.

10. Click OK.

Configure the portal as an extranet portal

To enable consultants to reach the portal content when they are working from home or from a client site, configure your portal as an extranet portal. The server front end will still sit on the corporate network, and the ISA server that provides a network firewall will reverse proxy requests to the SharePoint server.

To configure the portal to enable extranet access, complete the following high-level tasks:

1. Configure SSL.

2. Create an alternate access mapping for the extranet URL.

Configuring SSL

To configure SSL, follow these steps:

1. Open IIS and select the server from the left hand tree-view.

2. Double-click on the Server Certificates in the main area.

3. **Click Create Certificate Request... from the right-side Action pane.** The Request Certificate Request wizard opens.

4. **Enter the Distinguished Name Properties.** Enter a common name for your site (this is the name with which users will access the site, and so it needs to be valid). Enter your Organization name and Organizational unit. Enter the geographical information and click Next.

5. Select the Cryptographic Provider and Bit Length on the next screen and click Next.

6. Select an output location and filename for your certificate and click Finish.

7. Use the contents of the outputted certificate request file to process a certificate request either with a local certificate authority (if you are accessing this site only on the local network), or with a third-party certificate issuer that processes certificates for Web servers (if you are going to access this site via the Internet).

8. **Once you have processed your certificate request you can complete the request process.** (If this is a third-party certificate, follow the instructions provided by the issuer because you may need to install root certificates.)

9. Open IIS and select the server from the left hand tree-view. Double-click on the Server Certificates in the main area.

10. Select Complete Certificate Request... from the right-side Action pane.

11. Browse to the file location of your processed certificate request, as shown in Figure 21.33, select the file, provide a friendly name, and click OK.

Creating alternate access mapping

Once you have an SSL enabled on the IIS site, add an alternate access mapping so that the site can be accessed via https. To do this, follow these steps:

1. Go to Applications Management in Central Administration and click Alternate access mappings under the Web Applications section.

2. Choose the site to which you need to add the new alternate access mapping from the drop-down menu.

3. After the proper collection is selected, click Edit Public URLs.

4. Enter the new URL in the Extranet zone.

5. Click Save to complete the process.

FIGURE 21.33

Complete a Certificate Request

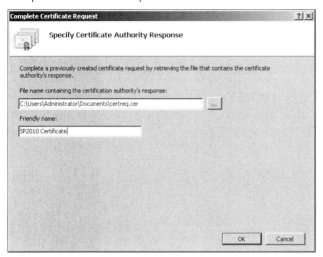

Summary

In this scenario, you designed and implemented an intranet portal that was available via the extranet as well for a medium size consulting company. This scenario showed how SharePoint features such as self-service site creation, list, libraries, custom list fields, content types, site templates, data views, site columns, Excel Web Access, the Reporting Services reports add-in, search content sources, and search scopes all work together to meet corporate intranet requirements.

Internet Portal Solution Scenario

T his chapter discusses using the SharePoint features to create an Internet presence. In this chapter, we gather the requirements and goals for a company's Internet portal and then design the SharePoint implementation to meet each requirement.

In this solution scenario, we use many of the features that were incorporated from previous releases of Content Management server, including content deployment, site variations, and use of page layouts, master pages, site columns, and content types. These features allow us to deploy an Internet portal where all the content has a consistent look and feel and a centrally managed page layout. In addition, our solution creates a structure where all content is published to a staging server so that the published portal content is only modified programmatically and the site structure is replicated to support other language content.

Scenario Background

This scenario shows you how to use SharePoint to support the Internet platform for a medium-sized software product company. This firm has the following roles that will be publishing or consuming information from the Internet presence:

- **Marketing:** The product marketing team is responsible for creating marketing materials such as datasheets, product overviews, and whitepapers that are posted on the Internet site.

- **Public Relations:** The public relations group is responsible for issuing and archiving press releases.

- **Web Managers:** The Web managers run the Internet services and are responsible for the content, maintenance, and design of the Internet site.
- **Support Engineers:** The support engineers provide assistance with customer problems and author technical articles that provide workarounds and information on bugs.
- **Management:** The management team provides product direction and executive decision-making.
- **Customers:** The Internet presence is intended to provide information on products and support to current and potential customers.

Table 22.1 outlines the specific requirements that the solution must satisfy for the portal to be considered a successful implementation.

TABLE 22.1

Requirements for a Successful Implementation

Requirement	Goal
No publishing is allowed to Internet-facing server	Reliable service enhanced by not allowing connections directly to public service
Public must be able to anonymously access content	Internet audience should not be required to provide information
Internet presence must be professional, clean, and consistent	Consistent look and feel
Easy navigation	Consistent navigation throughout site
PR group needs to publish occasional press releases easily	Ease of publishing for group that is not expert Web publishers
PR press releases must be archived to records management center	Archive of company history
Support engineer management and product developers want to see flow and feature area of active bugs	Understand trends of areas that need help
Support engineers will be publishing technical articles based on bug information that needs to be reviewed by technical editors before release	Fast bug fix information posting that is edited before release
Site content needs to be in English and Latin	Ability to appeal to two-language audience
Web managers require site auditing information to make key publishing decisions	Informed site management

Solution Overview

The new content management features provided in SharePoint 2007 and the flexible platform provided by SharePoint can provide an answer to each of the Internet portal requirements.

Table 22.2 maps each specific requirement to the solution architecture that SharePoint will provide.

TABLE 22.2	
SharePoint Requirement Mapping	
Requirement	**Solution**
No publishing is allowed to Internet-facing server	Use SharePoint content deployment features to push content from internal staging server to Internet-facing server
Public must be able to anonymously access content	Internet-facing server must be configured for anonymous access
Internet presence must be professional, clean, and consistent	Use SharePoint master pages and page layout to provide consistent framework
	Master page will be customized with company logo to emphasize professional Internet presence
	Use global navigation to provide consistent and easy-to-use navigation of the site
Easy navigation	Use SharePoint Global Navigation control
PR group needs to publish occasional press releases easily	Create a site content type that provides the structure and fields for the press releases so that even occasional publishers have a straightforward publishing process
PR press releases must be archived to records management center	Configure records management features to allow users to archive press release
Support engineer management and product developers want to see flow and feature area of active bugs	KPIs for bug tracking
Support engineers will be publishing technical articles based on bug information that needs to be reviewed by technical editors before release	Create site content type for technical articles that has an approval workflow that routes the articles to technical editors before being published
Site content needs to be in English and Latin	Use site variations to replicate English site structure to the Latin site structure
Web managers require site auditing information to make key publishing decisions	Enable SharePoint auditing

In this solution, you will create the following site structure:

- **External Server:** The external presence will link to all site resources using the global navigation bar.
  - **Product Information:** A subsite that provides product information and resources for company products.
  - **Press Releases:** The press release page provides summary information for all current press release articles.
  - **Support articles:** A subsite for publishing support articles.
  - **About Us:** This page provides contact information for the organization.
- **Internal Server:** The internal server mirrors the external site structure but in addition has a site collection that hosts the bug tracking list and KPIs for bugs.

You are going to implement these servers using single-server implementations for each server. The external server will be configured behind a firewall to protect against network eavesdropping and unauthorized access, and a firewall will be configured between the internal and external server as shown in Figure 22.1.

FIGURE 22.1

Server-to-server configuration diagram

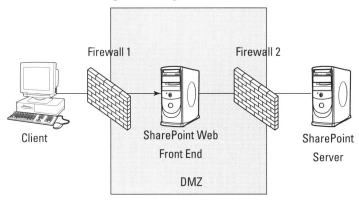

Firewall 1   Firewall 2

Client   SharePoint Web Front End   SharePoint Server

DMZ

In addition, you can configure the following items to protect your environment and information:

- Use NTLM secure authentication so that the authentication process does not send packets over the network.
- Encrypt SQL Server authentication credentials by installing a server certificate on the database server.

- Use SSL to encrypt browser-to-server communications and IPSec to encrypt all IP traffic that flows between the two servers.

- Create firewall policies that will block traffic from any port with exceptions for those used by SharePoint communications to the client for Firewall1 and server-to-server communications for Firewall2.

- Configure IP filtering and IPSec policies that will prevent unauthorized hosts from establishing connections.

- Disable any services that are not being used, which reduces that threat surface for attacks.

Cross-Reference
For more information about the threats posed for server-to-server communications, see Chapter 10. ■

Implementing the Solution

By mapping each goal to a specific requirement and solution, you create an easy to follow architecture for your portal. Each requirement is implemented by one of more features, and you can create an installation and configuration checklist that maps directly to your requirements.

This section walks though the SharePoint implementation for each requirement and solution outlined in Table 22.2.

Publishing allowed only to staging server

You will configure the ability to deploy content across multiple servers, from one site collection to another so that staged content is modified on the internal server and published content is modified only via the content deployment process.

You must first define the content deployment path and then configure a job to deploy content for the content path. The content deployment path defines the relationship between the two site collections for deployment. Jobs determine the specific content to be deployed from the source to the target and the schedule upon which the deployment occurs.

Creating content deployment path
Paths and jobs are created from the SharePoint 2010 Central Administration site.

Cross-Reference
For more information on content deployment jobs, please see Chapter 11. ■

1. From Central Administration, click on the General Application Settings from the Quick Launch bar.
2. In the Content Deployment section, click Configure content deployment.

3. Select Accept incoming deployment content jobs and select the Import and Export servers. (In a standalone or testing environment these may be the same.) Click OK.

4. In the Content Deployment section again, click Content deployment paths and jobs.

5. On the Manage Content Deployment Paths and Jobs page, click New Path.

6. In the Name and Description section, enter a name and a meaningful description for the new path. This helps users in employing the new path to create jobs.

7. In the Source Web Application and Site Collection section, select the Web application and site collection that contains the content you want to deploy.

8. Enter the URL to the Destination Central Administration server in the Destination Central Administration Web Application section.

9. You must supply Authentication Information in order to access the destination Central Administration Web site. Enter the means of authentication, the username, and the password in the required fields and click Connect.

Note

Even though you select Use Integrated Windows Authentication, a username and password are still required to be entered. ∎

10. Upon successful connection, enter the destination Web application and site collection where you would like to deploy the content, as shown in Figure 22.2.

FIGURE 22.2

Entering the destination site collection for your content deployment

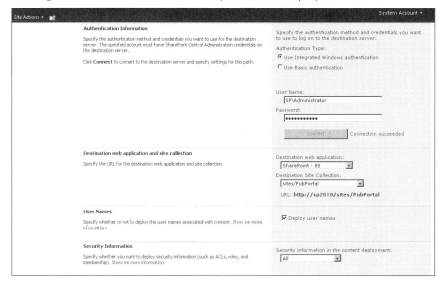

11. If you want the usernames associated with the content to be visible on the destination site collection, check the corresponding box in the User Names section.

12. Determine the security information to be associated with the content in the Security Information section. Select from the following:

   - **None:** No security information associated with content is deployed with the content.

   - **All:** All the security information associated with the content is deployed with the content.

   - **Role Definitions Only:** Role definitions (collections of permissions) are deployed with the content. Users and groups, including those associated with the role definitions, are not deployed with the content.

13. Click OK.

Creating a content deployment job

To create a content deployment job using the new path, follow these steps:

1. On the Manage Content Deployment Paths and Jobs page, click New Job, as shown in Figure 22.3.

2. In the Name and Description section, give the content deployment job a meaningful name.

FIGURE 22.3

Create a new job for content deployment

3. In the Description box, enter a description for the content deployment job if desired. (See Figure 22.4).

4. In the Path section, select the content deployment path on the Select a content deployment path menu.

5. In the Scope section, select one of the following:

    • **Entire site collection:** Includes all sites in the site collection in the deployment.

    • **Specific sites within the site collection:** Specify sites within the site collection in the deployment. If you select this option, click Select sites to select the sites to include in the deployment.

6. **In the Frequency section, you may clear the Run this job on the following schedule check box if you want to run the job manually.** Optionally, select the Run this job on the following schedule check box to specify a schedule.

7. **Select the Send e-mail when the content deployment job succeeds check box in the Notification section if you want to receive e-mail upon successful completion of the content deployment job.**

8. **To receive e-mail notification when the content deployment job fails, check the Send e-mail if the content deployment job fails box.**

9. **If you select either of these options, enter an e-mail address in the Type e-mail addresses box.**

10. **Click OK.** A new job appears in the Manage Content Deployment Paths and Jobs list. Using the drop-down menu on the item, you may run the job on demand, test the job, view its history, edit or delete the job. Figure 22.5 displays the options.

FIGURE 22.4

Create Content Deployment Job page

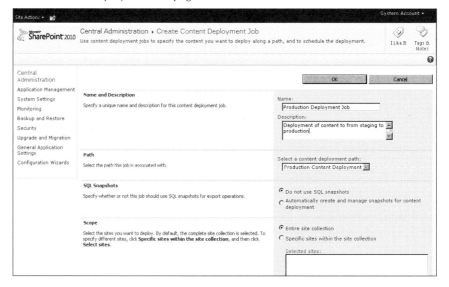

FIGURE 22.5

Job item menu options

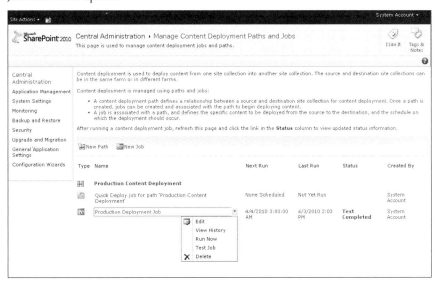

Tip

Test the job and run it manually before it starts kicking off on a scheduled basis. ∎

Enabling anonymous access

You will enable anonymous access on the Internet-facing server only. Because security information is not preserved in your content deployment job, the permissions that are configured on your internal server are not applied to the external server. There are two places that anonymous access must be enabled — in central administration and in the site.

Enable anonymous access using central administration

To configure anonymous access for the Internet-facing server, follow these steps:

1. From the server desktop click Start ⇨ Programs ⇨ Administrative Tools ⇨ SharePoint 2010 Central Administration.

2. In Central Administration click Security in the Quick Launch bar.

3. Under General Security, click Authentication providers.

4. Click the zone for which you would like to enable anonymous access.

Note

If you don't see the site/zone you are looking for, you may need to click the Web Application selector and choose the appropriate Web application. ∎

5. From the Edit Authentication page, as shown in Figure 22.6, click the box to enable Anonymous Access and then click Save.

FIGURE 22.6

Edit Authentication page

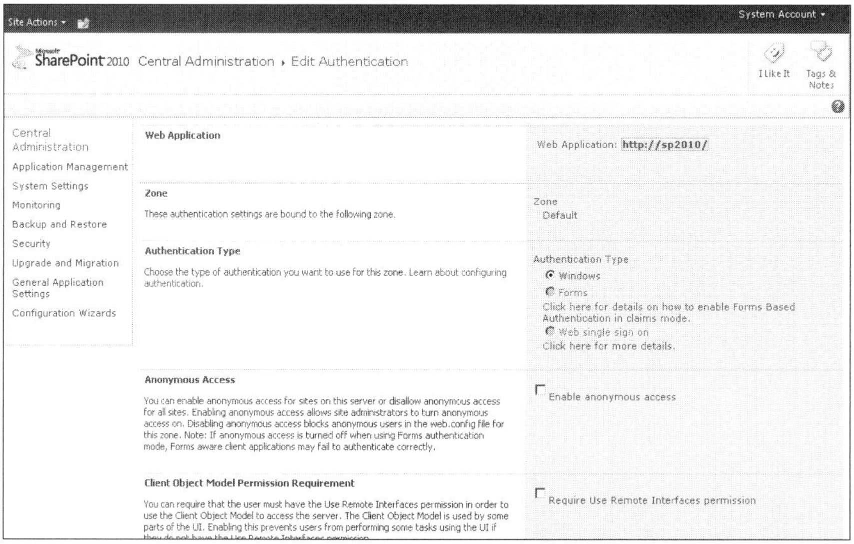

Enabling anonymous access in the site

After anonymous access has been enabled in central administration, it needs to also be enabled on the site collection. To do that for the Internet-facing root site collection, follow these steps:

1. From the home page of the SharePoint 2010 site to grant the anonymous access, click Site Actions ⇨ Site Permissions.

2. Click on the Anonymous Access button on the Ribbon. The Anonymous Access Settings dialog box appears as shown in Figure 22.7.

The Anonymous Access Settings dialog box enables you to specify what parts of your Web site (if any) anonymous users can access. If you select Entire Web site, anonymous users can view all pages in your Web site and view all lists and items which inherit permissions from the Web site. If you select Lists and libraries, anonymous users can view and change items only for those lists and libraries that have enabled permissions for anonymous users.

FIGURE 22.7

Anonymous Access Settings dialog box

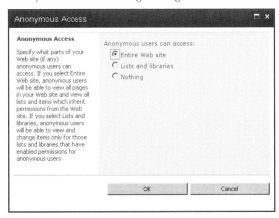

Creating a professional Internet presence

You have provisioned a site collection using the Publishing Portal template in the Publishing template tab. This site has a clean, centered look and feel, as shown in Figure 22.8. However, you should modify this look and feel with your company logo and help link in the footer.

FIGURE 22.8

The Publishing Portal template

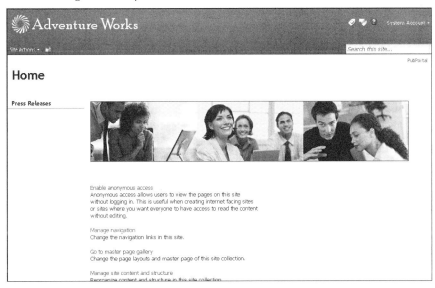

Customizing the master page with a company logo

Before modifying the master page to include the logo, you must upload your corporate logo to the Site Collection Images library. To do this, follow these steps:

1. From the home page of the site, click Site Actions and choose View All Site Content.
2. Click Site Collection Images.
3. Click Upload on the top navigation bar.
4. Enter or browse to your company logo file and click OK.
5. Click Check In to complete the upload.

After uploading the image, proceed with modifying the master page to incorporate the logo. To do this, follow these steps:

1. From the home page of the site, click Site Actions.
2. Choose Site Settings in the Site Settings menu.
3. In the Galleries section, select Master pages and page layouts.
4. Click the item menu on the `nightandday.master` file and choose Edit in Microsoft Office SharePoint Designer.
5. Click Yes in the dialog box asking you if want to check the file out and the security warning dialog box.
6. Switch to Design view. Click the Adventure Works logo in top-left corner of the master page and press Delete on your keyboard to remove the default image.
7. In the top menu, choose Picture from the Insert menu.
8. Select From File.
9. Browse to or enter the path to the company logo graphic in the Site Collection Images library and click Insert.
10. Click OK in the Accessibility Properties dialog box.
11. From the File menu in SharePoint Designer, click Save.
12. Click Yes in the Site Definition Page Warning dialog box.
13. Right-click `nightandday.master` in the Master Pages file list navigation pane and choose Check In.
14. In the Check In dialog box, select Publish a major version.
15. Click OK.
16. When prompted, approve the new master page.

Add a global footer to your site

You can add a global footer to the site pages so that users have a link to provide feedback and ask for help. To do this, follow these steps:

1. From the home page of the site, click Site Actions.

2. Choose Site Settings.

3. In the Galleries section, select Master pages and page layouts.

4. Click the item menu on the `nightandday.master` file and choose Edit in Microsoft Office SharePoint Designer.

5. Click Yes in the dialog box asking you if want to check the file out and the security warning dialog box.

6. Switch to Code view and scroll to the bottom locating the `</body>` tag.

7. Place your cursor right before the `</body>` tag.

8. Press Enter and add the following code, replacing "address" with an e-mail.

```
<table class="ms-globallinks" style="width: 100%"
  cellspacing="0" cellpadding="3">
   <tr>
        <td><a href="mailto:address">Submit Feedback</a></td>
   </tr>
</table>
```

9. From the File menu in SharePoint Designer, click Save.

10. Right-click `nightandday.master` in the Master Pages file list navigation pane and choose Check In.

11. In the Check In dialog box, select Publish a major version.

12. Click OK.

13. When prompted, approve the new master page.

14. Refresh the home page in your browser and review the changes, as shown in Figure 22.9.

FIGURE 22.9

Reviewing the design changes

Creating global navigation

To create the global navigation, first build out your site structure and modify the navigation to suit your purposes. Then you can use the global navigation controls to configure and order your navigation.

Building the site structure

You will create the following site structure:

- **Product Information:** A subsite that provides product information and resources for company products.
- **New Releases:** The new release page provides summary information for all newly released products.
- **Support Articles:** A subsite for publishing support articles.
- **About Us:** This page provides high-level information about the company.

To build out this structure, follow these steps:

1. From the Site Actions menu on the Internet portal home page, choose New Site.
2. Keep the Publishing Site with Workflow as the site template and enter Product Information as the site title and URL and then click Create.
3. From the Site Actions menu on the Internet portal home page, choose New Page.
4. Enter New Releases for the title.
5. Click Create. On the new page that appears Click Save & Close.
6. Repeat Steps 1 to 2 to create the Support Articles site.
7. Repeat Steps 3 to 5 to create the About Us page.

After you have created your sites and pages, you must publish the pages so that they are visible to your users. To do this, follow these steps:

1. From the Site Actions menu on the Product Information home page, choose View All Site Content.
2. Select the Pages library.
3. On the item menu on the New Releases page and choose Check In.
4. Select the option to publish a major version. Click OK.
5. Cancel the new workflow.
6. Navigate to the Pages library. You may need to refresh the page to see the version changes.
7. On the item menu of the New Releases page and click Approve/reject.
8. Select the Approved. This Item Will Become Visible to All Users option and click OK. Confirm OK when prompted that this will cancel the workflow.
9. Repeat using the Support Articles site for publishing and approving the About Us page.

Modifying the global navigation

Your site structure now supports your goals, but you should reorder the global navigation. To do this, follow these steps:

1. Click the Site Actions menu on the Internet portal home page and select Site Settings.

2. Click Navigation from the Look and Feel section.

3. Select Support Articles and click Move Up so it is in the third position, as shown in Figure 22.10.

FIGURE 22.10

Modifying the global navigation order

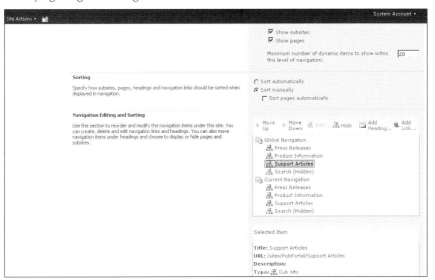

4. Select Search and click the Show option if you want to provide search capabilities to your Internet site.

5. Click OK.

Creating a press release publishing process

The press release publishing process will be governed by using a site content type and a page layout so that public relations staff can easily create a new press release, even if they do not do it frequently. To create the press release process, complete the following high-level steps:

1. Create a site column for product versions.

2. Create a Press Release content type.

3. Create a Press Release page layout.

4. Associate the Page Layout with a site.

5. Enable page scheduling.

6. Create a new Press Release page.

Creating a site column for press releases

You need a new site column to support the press releases so that the content type can specify a product name. To create this site column, follow these steps:

1. Click Site Actions on your portal home page.

2. Choose Site Settings.

3. In the Galleries section, click Site columns.

4. Click Create.

5. Enter these values:

   - Column name: Product Version

   - The type of information in this column is: Choice

   - Put the site column into: Existing Group: Custom Columns

   - Require that this column contains information: No

   - Type each choice on a separate line: Beta, RTM, Final

6. Click OK.

Creating a Press Release custom content type

Once the site column has been created, you can create the content type for a press release using that site column. Follow these steps to create a content type:

1. Select Site Actions from the top-left corner on the portal home page.

2. Choose Site Settings.

3. Select Site content type in the Galleries section.

4. Click Create from the Site Content Type Gallery toolbar.

5. Name the new content type Press Release.

6. Select Publishing Content Types in the Select parent content type from drop-down menu of the Parent Content Type section.

7. Select Page from the Parent Content Type drop-down menu of the Parent Content Type field.

8. Select the New Group radio button and enter Press Release as a name for the new group as shown in Figure 22.11. Click OK. Now add columns to the new content type from the Site Columns gallery.

9. Click Add from existing site columns from the bottom of the Columns section.

10. Add Article Date, Byline, Page Content, and Product Version from the Available columns list, as shown in Figure 22.12. Click OK when warned that the Page Content control must be updated by using a Web browser.

FIGURE 22.11

Creating the Press Release content type

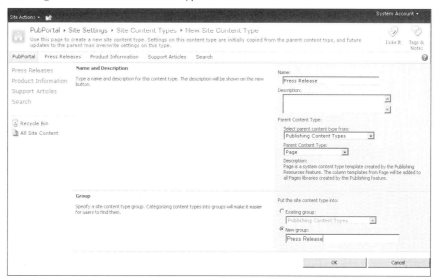

FIGURE 22.12

Selecting the site columns for the Press Release content type

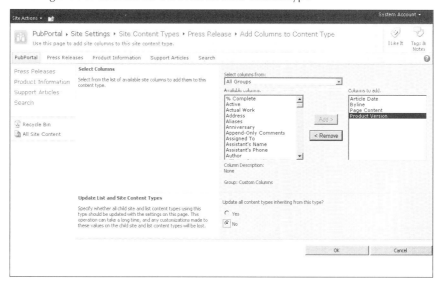

11. Select No from the Update List and Site Content Types section and click OK.

Creating page layouts in SharePoint Designer

To create the page layout template that will be used to author new press releases, follow these steps:

1. Open your portal site in Office SharePoint Designer.

2. Select Page Layouts from the Site Objects left navigation pane.

3. Click on the New Page Layout button from the Page Layouts on the Ribbon.

4. Choose Press Release from the Content Type Group and Content Type Name drop-down menus, as shown in Figure 22.13.

FIGURE 22.13

New page layout dialog box

5. Enter a URL and Title for the new page layout.

6. Click OK.

7. In the Toolbox pane in the top right, expand the SharePoint Controls node.

8. Expand the Content Fields node.

9. Drag the Article Date, Byline, Product Version, and the Page Content fields into the PlaceHolderMain content placeholder.

10. **Save and check in the new page layout.** Go back to the Page Layouts section and select Check In from the item menu. Publish as a Major Version. You are prompted to approve the item. In the new browser window that appears, select Approve/Reject from the layout item menu and select Approve from the dialog. Click OK. Close the new browser window.

Associating page layouts with libraries

Now that you have a page layout, associate the page layout with the pages library by following these steps:

1. Click Site Actions in the top-right corner of the portal home page.

2. Choose Site Settings.

3. Select Page layouts and site templates from the Look and Feel category.

4. Select "Pages in this site can use only the following layouts" and add the Press Release and (Welcome Page) Blank Web Part Page page layouts.

5. Click OK.

Enabling page scheduling

Page scheduling allows you to set the start date and end date for each press release. To enable page scheduling, follow these steps:

1. On the portal home page, choose View All Site Content from Site Actions menu.

2. Select the Pages library.

3. From the Library tab on the Ribbon, choose Library Settings.

4. **Select Versioning settings and enable content approval; verify as well that both major and draft versions are allowed.** These settings must be activated in order to enable item scheduling.

5. Click OK.

6. Select Manage item scheduling.

7. Select Enable scheduling of items in this list.

8. Click OK.

You are now able to schedule the publication of pages in this document library. To do this, follow these steps:

1. On the site that stores your page library, click View All Site Content from the Site Actions menu.

2. Select the Pages library.

3. On the item for which you want to edit the scheduling, select Edit Properties.

4. Enter the scheduling start date (or choose "immediately") and the scheduling end date.

5. Click OK.

Creating pages

Now that you have created a new page layout using a custom content type, create a new press release ready for use on the site by following these steps:

1. On the site on which you want to publish your new page, select New Page from the Site Actions menu.

2. Enter today's date as the Title of the new page. Click Create.

3. From the Page tab on the Ribbon, click the Page Layout button and select the Press Release page layout you created.

4. Fill out the content fields and click Publish.

Using the Content Query Web Part

Use the Content Query Web Part to display the titles and descriptions of your technical articles, grouped by Product Version on the Support Articles site home page. To do this, follow these steps:

1. Navigate to the press release page.

2. Choose Edit Page from the Site Actions menu.

3. Click the Page Content area and select Web Part from the Insert tab on the Ribbon.

4. Select Content Query from the Content Rollup category and click Add.

5. Select Edit Web Part from the edit menu of the Content Query Web Part.

6. Expand the Query section and select Press Release as the content type.

7. In the Additional Filters section, configure to show items when Scheduling End Date is less than or equal to [Today].

8. Expand the Appearance section and enter Press Releases in the Title field.

9. Click OK.

Configuring press release archive

Use the Records Repository feature to store press releases in our archive. To enable this functionality, complete these high-level steps:

1. Provision a Records Repository site.

2. Create a Records Repository storage document library.

3. Define the routing behavior.

4. Configure the connection settings for the records repository.

Provisioning a Records Repository site

The records repository site is the site that will contain the archived content. To create your records repository site, follow these steps:

1. Go to your *intranet* site collection home page and choose New Site from the Site Actions menu.

2. Use these settings for the New SharePoint Site page:

   - Title: Records Vault

   - Description: Location for press release storage

- URL name: `http://intranet/records`
- Template: Data Category ⇨ Records Center

3. Click Create. The Operation in Progress screen appears.

Create the records storage location document libraries

Now implement a file plan for press releases, as shown in Table 22.3.

TABLE 22.3

Press Release File Plan

Item	Value
Records	Press Release
Description	Press Releases that were published to the Internet
Media	Internet
Record Category	Publicity
Retention	3 years
Disposition	None
Contact	Admin

Your first task is to create the document library:

1. From the Site Actions menu, select New Document Library.
2. On the New Document Library page, enter Press Releases for Name and click Create, accepting the defaults for the rest of the fields.
3. Click Create Column button on the Library tab on the Ribbon.
4. On the add Column page enter these values:
   - Column Name: Filing Date
   - Type: Date and Time
   - Require that this column contains information: Yes
5. Click OK.
6. Click Library Settings from the Library menu bar.
7. Under the Permissions and Management section, click Information management policy settings.
8. On the Policy Settings page, click on the Document content type to create a policy for documents. The Edit Policy page appears.
9. On the Edit Policy page use the following values:

- Administrative Description: Press releases will be stored for 3 years after their filing date.
- Policy Statement: Press releases will be stored for 3 years after their filing date.
- Check Enable Expiration.
- Under The retention period is, click A time period based on the item's properties.
- Select Filing Date + 3 years.
- Select Perform this action and Delete from the drop-down.
- Click OK.

10. Click OK. The policy retention stage is created and shown in the Edit Policy page.

11. Click OK. The policy for this document library has now been configured.

12. Return to the Records Vault home page by clicking Records Vault in the breadcrumb at the top of the page.

Define the records routing behavior for the record type

By setting the records routing, you define how documents are mapped to the appropriate document libraries. To define records routing for your press releases, follow these steps:

1. Select Site Actions⇨Manage Record Center. Click on the Create content organizer rules link. (Alternate method is Site Actions⇨Site Settings⇨Content organizer rules.)

2. In the Content Organizer Rules page, click Add new item.

3. On the New Item page, enter the information for the Press Release record routing:

- Title: Press Releases
- Description: Public Relations press releases
- Location: Press Release Archive
- Aliases: PR

4. Click OK.

Configure the connection to Records Center settings

Now provide the URL to the Records Center site on the Central Administration site, allowing both the UI and object model to use the Send To function when a press release should be retained as a Record.

1. Open SharePoint Central Administration.

2. Click General Application Settings on the Quick Launch bar.

3. Under the External Service Connections section, click Configure send to connections.

4. Set the values as follows (Figure 22.14):

   - Display name: Records Vault
   - URL: http://(your portal name)/recordsvault/_vti_bin/official-file.asmx
   - Send to Action: Move and Leave a Link

5. **Click Add Connection.** The Records Vault connection appears in the connection list.

6. **Click OK.** Your SharePoint applications can send files to the Records Repository (if it refers to the template within SharePoint, it should be Records Center).

The Configure Connection to Records Center page

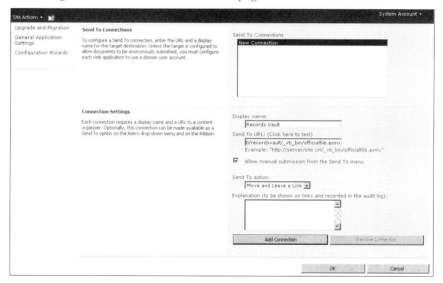

Configuring bug tracking indicators

Product bugs are stored in an Issue Tracking list on the intranet. The product tracking list has been customized with the following columns:

- **Product Version:** Choice of product to which the bug applies
- **Product Build:** Build number (if applicable)
- **Product Feature (to be consistent with the rest of the exercise):** Choice of feature to which the bug applies
- **Bug Type:** Choice of setup, typical usage, documentation, or update

The executives and product managers want to see the status of active bugs. To achieve this objective, we are going to create indicators by product version, product feature, and bug type for the Executive Dashboard.

To satisfy this requirement, you have four high-level steps:

1. Create the views for the bug tracking list.
2. Create product version indicators.
3. Create product feature indicators.
4. Create bug type indicators.

Creating the sales views to support Indicators

You need to create views of the bug list to support the Indicators that you want to configure:

- All Open Bugs with High Priority
- Active bugs for each product
- Active bugs for each feature
- Active bugs for each bug type

To create the high-priority view, follow these steps:

1. **From the List tab on the Ribbon of the bug tracking list, choose Create View.**
2. **Select Standard View.**
3. **Enter** High-Priority Active Bugs **as the view name.**
4. **Scroll to the Filter section and select Show items only when the following is true.** Select Issue Status is equal to Active, and radio button, and Priority is equal to (1) High, as shown in Figure 22.15.
5. **Click OK.**

To create the view for each product view, follow these steps:

1. **From the List tab on the Ribbon of the bug tracking list, choose Create View.**
2. **Select Active Issues in the Starting from an existing view section.**
3. **Enter** Active ProductA Bugs **as the view name.**
4. **Scroll down to the Filter section and select "And" between the existing filter and the new one and set the new filter to be Product Version equals ProductA.**
5. **Click OK.**
6. **Repeat Steps 1 to 5 for any other product versions that you want to include as Indicators.**

FIGURE 22.15

Setting the filter criteria for your High-Priority Active Bugs view

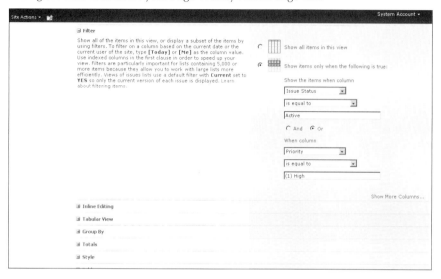

To create the view for each feature, follow these steps:

1. From the List tab on the Ribbon of the bug tracking list, choose Create View.

2. Select Active Issues in the Starting from an existing view section.

3. Enter Active Feature1 Bugs as the view name.

4. Scroll down to the Filter section and select "And" between the existing filter and the new one and set the new filter to be Product Feature equals Feature1.

5. Click OK.

6. Repeat Steps 1 to 5 for any other product features that you want to include as Indicators.

To create the view for each bug type, follow these steps:

1. From the List of the bug tracking list, choose Create View.

2. Select Active Issues in the Starting from an existing view section.

3. Enter Active Setup Bugs as the view name.

4. Scroll down to the Filter section and select "And" between the existing filter and the new one and set the new filter to be Bug Type equals setup.

5. Click OK.

6. Repeat Steps 1 to 5 for any other bug types that you want to include as Indicators.

Creating bug Indicators

Now add an Indicator for each view that you created in the previous section.

1. Navigate to the Management site on the intranet.

2. Select View All Site Content from the Site Actions menu.

3. Select Create in the top navigation bar.

4. Select List as the Filter and select Status List from the Tracking section.

5. Enter the name of the Status List as Bug Status Indicators **and click Create.**

6. Select Indicator using data in SharePoint list from the New menu.

7. Enter High-Priority Bugs in the Name field.

8. Enter the location of the bug tracking list and select the High-Priority Active Bugs view in the SharePoint List and View section, as shown in Figure 22.16.

9. Select Number of list items in the view.

10. Select that lower values is better and enter the goal (green) and warning (yellow) values for the organization. For this example, use 0 for the green value and 1 for the yellow value.

FIGURE 22.16

Entering the list and view for an Indicator

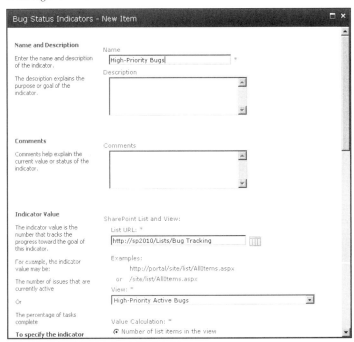

11. Enter the link to the bug tracking list in the Details Link section for drilling down on the Indicator.

12. Click OK.

Now add Indicators for your product views by following these steps:

1. Choose Indicator using data in SharePoint list from the New menu.

2. Enter Product A Bugs in the Name field.

3. Enter the location of the bug tracking list and select the Active ProductA Bugs view in the SharePoint List and View section.

4. Select Percentage of the list items in the view where and due date is less than [Today], as shown in Figure 22.17.

5. Change the better values to be lower and enter the goal (green) and warning (yellow) values for the organization. For this example use 5 (5%) for the green value and 30 (30%) for the yellow value.

FIGURE 22.17

Calculating percentage past-due bugs

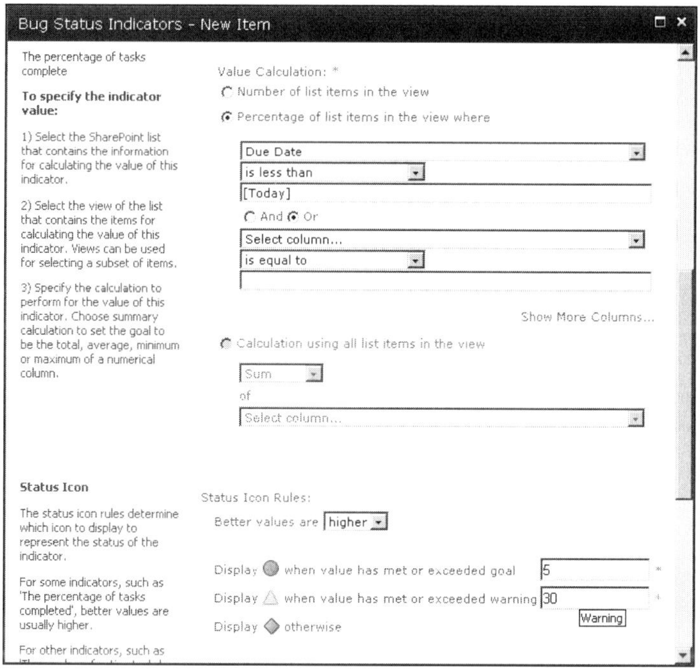

6. Enter the link to the bug tracking list in the Details Link section for drilling down on the Indicator.

7. Select OK.

8. Repeat Steps 1 to 7 for the product feature and bug type views/indicators.

Adding the Status List Web Part to the Management home page

To highlight the importance of the Status List items, add them to the home page of the management site so that executives can easily see them every time they visit the site. To do this, follow these steps:

1. Navigate to the home page of the Management collaboration site.

2. From the Site Actions menu, choose Edit Page.

3. Select Web Part from the Insert tab on the Ribbon.

4. Select Status List from the Business Data section.

5. Click Add.

6. From the Edit menu of the Status List Web Part, select Edit Web Part.

7. Browse or enter the path to the Bug Status Indicators in the Indicator List field.

8. Select Traffic Lights in the Change Icon field.

9. Click OK.

10. Click Save & Close from the Page tab of the Ribbon.

11. Confirm that the Status List has been added to the page.

Configuring the technical article workflow process

The technical article workflow process requires that you create a content type for the technical article and associate a workflow with the content type. After you have done that, you create a page layout for your technical article and associate that with the support subsite you created.

Create a site content type for the technical article

To support the technical article publishing process, you will create a content type that will contain the site columns for the technical article fields. To create this content type, follow these steps:

1. Choose Site Actions on the Internet portal home page.

2. Choose Site Settings.

3. Under Galleries, click Site content types.

4. Click Create.

5. Enter these values:

   - Name: Technical Article
   - Parent Content Type: Article Page (from the Page Layout Content Types type group)
   - Put this site content type into: Click New group: and enter **Technical Article** for the new group name as shown in Figure 22.18.

FIGURE 22.18

New Site content type

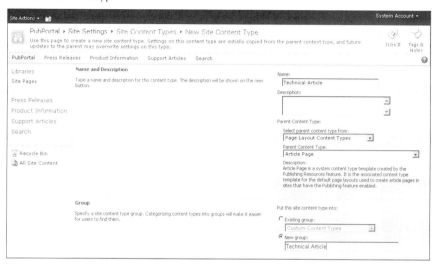

6. Click OK.

7. At the bottom of the Site Content Type: Technical Article page, click Add from existing site columns to add the Product Version column that you created for your press release process.

8. From the Select columns from: drop-down, pick Custom Columns.

9. Click the Add button to add the Product Version column, and your screen should look like Figure 22.19.

10. Click OK.

Adding workflow to your Technical Article content type

To add a workflow to your technical article, follow these steps:

1. Begin at the Internet portal home page and click Site Settings from the Site Actions menu.

2. Under Galleries click Site content types.

3. Filter the Show Group: box by Technical Article.

4. Click Technical Article.

5. Click Workflow settings.

6. Click Add a workflow.

7. Enter **Article Approval** as the unique name for the workflow.

8. Check the **Start this workflow when a new item is created** box. Your screen should be similar to Figure 22.20. Click Next.

FIGURE 22.19

Adding site columns

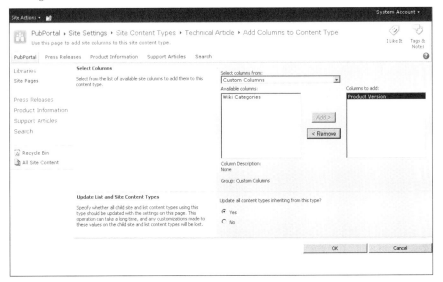

FIGURE 22.20

Add a workflow page

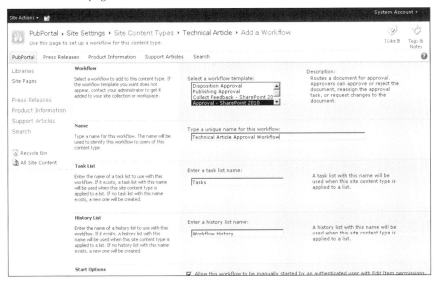

9. On the Customize Workflow page, place the cursor next to the Approvers button, enter the technical editor as an approver, and click the Check names button to confirm the name is correct.

10. Add a message to include with the request Please approve this article.

11. Check the Post-completion Workflow Activity box to update the approval status.

12. Click OK.

Creating page layouts in SharePoint Designer

Now create the page layout template that will be used to author technical articles by following these steps:

1. Open your portal site in Office SharePoint Designer.

2. Select Page Layouts from the Site Objects left navigation pane.

3. Click on the New Page Layout button from the Page Layouts tab of the Ribbon.

4. Choose Technical Article from the Content Type Group and Content Type Name drop-down menus as shown in Figure 22.21.

FIGURE 22.21

New page layout dialog for the Technical Article

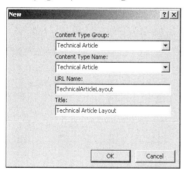

5. Enter a URL and Title for the new page layout.

6. Click OK.

7. In the Toolbox pane in the top right, expand the SharePoint Controls node.

8. Expand the Content Fields node.

9. Drag the Title and Contact Name from the Page Content fields and the Product Version field from the Content fields section into the PlaceholderMain (Custom) content placeholder.

10. **Save and check in the new page layout.** Go back to the Page Layouts section and select Check In from the item menu. Publish as a Major Version. You are prompted to approve the item. In the new browser window that appears, select Approve/Reject from the layout item menu and select Approve from the dialog. Click OK. Close the new browser window.

Associating page layouts with libraries

Now that you have a page layout, associate the page layout with the technical article subsite by following these steps:

1. Click Site Actions in the top left corner of the Support Articles home page.

2. Choose Site Settings.

3. Select Page layouts and site templates from the Look and Feel category.

4. Select Pages in this site can use only the following layouts and add the Technical article page layout, as shown in Figure 22.22. You may need to remove all of the selected layouts first.

5. Under the New Page Default settings select the Select the default page layout option and make sure Technical Article is selected in the list box.

6. Click OK.

FIGURE 22.22

Adding the Technical Article page layout

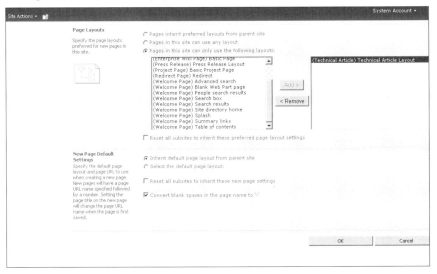

Using the Content Query Web Part

Use the Content Query Web Part to display the titles and descriptions of your technical articles, grouped by Product Version on the Support Articles site home page. To do this, follow these steps:

1. Navigate to the home page of the Support Articles site.

2. Choose Edit Page from the Site Actions menu.

3. Click Add Web Part from the Left Column zone on the page. You may need to scroll down to see the zones.

4. Select Content Query from the Content Rollup Web Part category and click Add.

5. Select Edit Web Part from the Edit menu of the Content Query Web Part.

6. Expand the Query section and select Technical Article as the content type, as shown in Figure 22.23.

7. Scroll to the Additional Filters section and select Product Version is equal to Beta, as shown in Figure 22.24.

8. Expand the Appearance section and enter Beta Product Articles in the Title field.

9. Click OK.

10. Repeat Steps 3 to 10 to create Content Query Web Parts for RTM and Final product versions.

11. Click Submit for Approval to publish and approve page.

FIGURE 22.23

Configuring the Content Query Web Part to use the Technical Article content type

12. **Add article pages and view the page to see the published articles appear in the Content Query Web Part, as shown in Figure 22.25.** To modify the product version of the article page use the Edit Properties button from the Ribbon when editing the page.

FIGURE 22.24

Applying additional filters to the Content Query Web Part

FIGURE 22.25

Reviewing the Content Query Web Part results

Configuring site variations

You are going to use site variations to publish the Internet content for your company to Latin. You must complete two high-level steps to configure site variations.

1. Define Variations parameters.

2. Configure Variation Labels to determine the locale and create the site variation hierarchy.

Configuring variation support

To configure site variations, follow these steps:

1. From the top-level site the Internet portal site collection, click Site Actions in the top-right corner.

2. Choose Site Settings from the Site Settings menu.

3. Under the Site Collection Administration category, select Variations.

4. In the Variation Home section, enter the / as the location for the target variations to indicate that the root site will be used.

5. In the Automatic Creation section choose Automatically create site and page variations to automatically create a copy of all variations.

6. In the Recreate Deleted Target Page section, select Recreate a new target page when the source page is republished so that a new target page is created when the source page is republished.

7. Click the Send e-mail notification to owners when a new site or page is created or a page is updated by the variation system check box. This sends e-mail notification that a new subsite or page of a target site is created, or when a target page is updated with revisions from the source variation by the site owner.

8. In the Resources section, select Reference existing resources to use existing resources.

9. Click OK.

Configure site variation labels

To configure site variation labels, follow these steps:

1. From the home page of the Internet portal, click Site Actions in the top-left corner.

2. Select Site Settings.

3. On the Site Settings page, under the Site Collection Administration section, select Variation labels.

4. On the Variation Labels page, click New Label.

5. From the Label and Description section, type a descriptive name in the Label Name field as shown in Figure 22.26. The name you enter will become the URL string.

FIGURE 22.26

Configuring variation labels

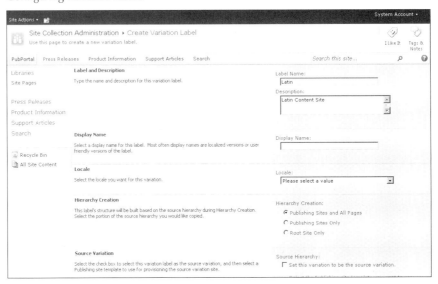

6. **Choose a user-friendly name in the Display Name field.** These are typically localized versions of a label.

   The display name appears in the Site Management Tool hierarchy.

7. **Select the locale for the variation and enter it in the Locale field.** This denotes formatting for elements such as date, time, and currency.

8. **In the Hierarchy Creation section, select Publishing Sites and All Pages.** This creates a hierarchy of publishing sites and all pages.

9. **Click OK.**

10. **Click Create Hierarchies to create the site variation.**

A link now appears in the Global Navigation bar for the source site defining the different language variations available for users requiring native language support.

Enabling auditing

Enable the auditing settings for the Internet site so that Web managers can view the activity for the site and make appropriate decisions for future growth and usage.

To configure audit settings

The audit settings tell SharePoint which events you want to track. To configure audit settings, follow these steps:

1. Click the Site Actions menu in the top-left corner of the Internet Portal home page.

2. Choose Site Settings.

3. In the Site Collection Administration section, click the Site collection audit settings link.

4. On the Configure Audit Settings page, in the Documents and Items section, select the events you want to audit:

   - Opening or downloading documents, viewing items in lists, or viewing item properties

   - Editing items

   - Checking out or checking in items

   - Moving or copying items to another location in the site

   - Deleting or restoring items

5. In the Lists, Libraries, and Sites section, select the events you want to audit:

   - Editing content types and columns

   - Searching site content

   - Editing users and permissions

6. Click OK.

Summary

In this chapter, you used SharePoint to create the Internet presence for a fictional company. This allowed you to walk through the implementation of content deployment between staging and production server. In addition, you used master pages and page layouts to create a consistent and clean look and feel, and content types, site columns, and workflows to create a straightforward process for publishing content such as press releases and technical articles for users who are not advanced Web authors. And finally, you used Indicators to provide high-level indicators for executives and product managers about the status of active bugs.

Index

Index

Index

Index

K

Kerberos, 24, 25, 31, 334
key performance indicators (KPIs)
    actions, 540
    from Analysis Service, 555–561
    defining, 482–486, 536
    from Excel, 550–555
    goals in mapping, 536–537
    HR list detail, 538
    icons, 541
    implementing manually, 561–563
    Indicator Details Web Part, 542–543
    Management list detail, 539
    from SharePoint lists, 544–550
    Status List, 561–563
    Status List Web Part, 541–542
keywords, 229–230
knowledge, 4
KPIs. *See* key performance indicators (KPIs)
.ksh file, 330

L

labels, 410
libraries
    advanced settings, 92–93
    associating page layouts with, 373
    audience targeting settings, 94
    checked-out files, managing, 95
    communication settings, 97
    creating, 87
    custom columns, 99–103
    data sources, 668–669
    deleting, 94
    folders, 98–99
    general settings, 91
    permissions, 95, 106–107
    permissions, configuring, 95
    RSS settings, 97
    saving as template, 94–95
    security, 357–358
    versioning settings, 91–92
    viewing RSS feed for, 97
    views, 107–113
    workflow settings, 96
library Web Parts, 114–116
line-of-business (LOB) applications, 566
link column, 72
linked sources, 668

links, 45, 84
Links list, 49
list data entry form, 119–122
List Instance element, 301–302
List Template element, 302–304
List View Web Part, 145–146
list Web Parts, 114–119
Listen, 239
lists
    adding additional columns to, 89
    adding business data column to, 596–599
    adding business data to, 596–599
    adding columns to, 88
    adding ratings to, 94
    advanced settings, 93
    audience targeting settings, 94
    communication settings, 97
    creating, 86–90
    custom columns, 99–103
    deleting, 94
    folders, 98–99
    general settings, 91
    information management policies, 96–97
    lookup, 104–106
    permissions, 95, 106–107
    RSS settings, 97
    saving as template, 94–95
    security, 357–358
    versioning settings, 91–92
    viewing RSS feed for, 97–98
    views, 107–113
    workflow settings, 96
.lnk file, 330
LOB (line-of-business) applications, 566
logical calculation, 102–103
lookup column, 101
lookup lists
    creating, 104–105
    linking to, 104
    as reference in lists or libraries, 105
Lotus Notes Index Setup Wizard, 214
Lotus Notes servers, 214

M

.mad file, 330
.maf file, 330
.mag file, 330
major versioning, 377
.mam file, 330

786

Index

Index

Q

Query String (URL) Filter, 153
quick deploy job, 386
Quick Deploy users, 352
quotas
    defined, 398
    site, 399–400
    templates, 400

R

Read Item method, 568
Read Item Operation, 572
Read Item wizard, 572
Read List method, 568
Read List Operation, 573
Receiver element, 309
Recent Activities, 161
Recent Blog Posts, 161
record, 406
Record Center site template, 46–47
Record Library, 47
records management
    defined, 406
    deployment and configuration, 412–420
    description, 5
    functions, 406
    holds, 429–434
    in-place, 427
    managing missing metadata, 434
    planning, 406–410
    properties, 406
    purpose of, 405–406
    repository site, 411–412, 428
    reviewing and resolving unclassified records, 433
Records Repository, 407
records repository site
    designing, 411
    extensibility, 412
    holds, 412
    integration, 412
    moving content from SharePoint Server sites, 420–426
    permissions, 428
    policy enforcement, 412
    provisioning, 412–414
    record routing, 411
    template, 411–412
recruiting team, 696

Refinement Panel, 157
Region property, 200
Related Queries, 157, 231
Relevant Documents Web Part, 143
Remove User Permissions button, 357–358
Replicate Changes permission, 187
report libraries, 87
Report Library
    configuring as trusted location, 504–506
    data connections, 506–512
    data models, 514
    data sources, 512–513
    managing models, 525–527
    managing reports, 514–524
    template, 500
report subscription
    adding, 516–518
    adding for file shared, 519–520
    for caching, 521
Report Viewer Web Part
    adding, 528–529, 728–730
    configuring, 528–530
    connecting to filter Web Part, 530–533, 731–733
    overview, 528
Reporting Services
    adding reporting services to content types, 503–504
    configuring, 500
    configuring database, 501–502
    configuring execution account, 502
    configuring settings in SharePoint, 502–503
    installing SQL Reporting services add-in, 500
Reporting Services Data Sources (RSDS), 506
reports, uploading, 515
Require Secondary Contact box, 29
Resources list, 49
REST Web Services, 668, 672–673
restricted readers, 352
retention period, 407, 409
Return Parameter Configuration, 576
rich-text editor, 140
roles, identifying, 406
root sites
    creating, 64–66
    multiple, 67
RSA encryption, 328
RSDS (Reporting Services Data Sources), 506
RSS feed, 97–98, 672–673
RSS subscription, 462–464
RSS Viewer, 152

Index

Index